AL-HIND

THE MAKING OF THE INDO-ISLAMIC WORLD

VOLUME II

AL-HIND
THE MAKING OF THE INDO-ISLAMIC WORLD

VOLUME II

AL-HIND
THE MAKING OF THE
INDO-ISLAMIC WORLD

ANDRÉ WINK

VOLUME II

THE SLAVE KINGS
AND THE ISLAMIC CONQUEST
11th–13th CENTURIES

OXFORD
UNIVERSITY PRESS

OXFORD
UNIVERSITY PRESS

YMCA Library Building, Jai Singh Road, New Delhi 110001

Oxford University Press is a department of the University of Oxford. It furthers the
University's objective of excellence in research, scholarship, and education
by publishing worldwide in

Oxford New York
Athens Auckland Bangkok Bogota Buenos Aires Cape Town
Chennai Dar es Salaam Delhi Florence Hong Kong Istanbul
Karachi Kolkata Kuala Lumpur Madrid Melbourne Mexico City Mumbai
Nairobi Paris Sao Paolo Singapore Taipei Tokyo Toronto Warsaw

with associated companies in

Berlin Ibadan

Oxford is a registered trade mark of Oxford University Press
in the UK and in certain other countries

Published in India
By Oxford University Press, New Delhi

© 1997 by Koningklijke Brill, Leiden, The Netherlands
By arrangement with Koningklijke Brill, Leiden, The Netherlands

The moral rights of the author have been asserted
Database right Oxford University Press (maker)
First published 1997
Oxford India Paperbacks 1999
Second impression 2001

ISBN 0 19 565176 6

For sale in India, Pakistan, Bangladesh, Bhutan,
Myanmar, Nepal and Sri Lanka only

Printed in India at Rashtriya Printers, Delhi 110 032
and published by Manzar Khan, Oxford University Press
YMCA Library Building, Jai Singh Road, New Delhi 110 001

CONTENTS

MAPS

These maps supplement the ones provided in *Al-Hind, I.* Some geographical references which remain uncertain or controversial have been left out. A few could not be located at all.

ABBREVIATIONS

AH   A. Zajaczkowski (ed.), *Le Traité Iranien de l'Art Militaire: Ādāb al-Harb wa-sh-Shaghā'a du XIIIe Siècle* (Warszawa, 1969).

FS   A. M. Husain (ed.), *Futūḥ as-Salāṭin of 'Iṣāmī* (Agra, 1938).

KT   C. J. Tornberg (ed.), *Ibn al-'Athīr, Al-Kāmil fi'l-Tārīkh*, 12 vols (Leiden, 1853-1869).

MD   Al-Mas'ūdī, *Murūj adh-Dhahab*, 2 vols (Cairo, 1948).

TB   W. H. Morley (ed.), *Ta'rīkh-i-Baihaqī* (Calcutta, 1862).

TF   *Ta'rīkh-i-Firishta* (Lucknow, 1864).

TFM   E. Denison Ross (ed.), *Ta'rīkh-i-Fakhr ad-Dīn Mubārakshāh* (London, 1927).

TFS   S. Ahmad Khan (ed.), *Ta'rīkh-i-Fīroz Shāhī of Ẓiā' ad-Dīn Baranī* (Calcutta, 1862).

TM   *Tāj al-Ma'āthir: BM: Add. 7623.*

TMS   M. Hidayat Hosaini (ed.), *Ta'rīkh-i-Mubārakshāhī of Yahya bin Ahmad bin 'Abdullāh as-Sirhindī* (Calcutta, 1931).

TN   N. Lees et al (eds), *Ṭabaqāt-i-Nāṣirī of Ābū 'Umar al-Jūzjānī* (Calcutta, 1894).

TNL   *Ṭabaqāt-i-Nāṣirī of Ābū 'Umar al-Jūzjānī* (Lahore, 1954).

TNM   *Ṭabaqāt-i-Nāṣirī of Ābū 'Umar al-Jūzjānī: IOL: MSS no. 2553.*

TNR   H. G. Raverty (transl.), *Ṭabakāt-i-Nāṣirī: a General History of the Muhammadan Dynasties of Asia*, 2 vols (London, 1872-81).

TYA   Al-'Utbī, *Tārīkh al-Yamīnī* (Delhi, 1847).

TYP   Al-'Utbī, *Ta'rīkh-i-Yamīnī: Persian translation by Jurbādqānī (1206 AD)* (Teheran, 1334 H.).

ZA   M. Nazim (ed.), *Zayn al-Akhbār of Gardīzī* (Berlin, 1928).

PREFACE

This book has been long in the making. Inevitably I incurred numerous debts with individuals and institutions across the world. I began my research on the thirteenth century in the Netherlands, as a Huygens fellow of the Nederlandse Stichting voor Wetenschappelijk Onderzoek (N.W.O.) in 1984-1989, and, in 1985, as a Visiting Scholar at the University of Cambridge. Most of the book however was 'made in the U.S.A.', in Madison, after I joined the History Department of the University of Wisconsin. To my colleagues and students at the UW I cannot but express my deepest gratitude for the constant interest they have expressed in my work. In addition, I owe a special debt to the Research Committee of the Graduate School for providing research money, travelgrants, summer support over a number of years, as well as a semester's leave of absence. Most helpful was also the award of a Vilas Associateship for the years 1992 and 1993, and a residency fellowship at the Institute for Research in the Humanities at Madison in the Fall Semester of 1993. Other institutions where I spent time include the Center of Middle Eastern Studies at Harvard University, where I am indebted to its director William Graham for an affiliation in the Fall of 1991; the Ecole des Hautes Etudes en Sciences Sociales, Paris, where I was able to conduct seminars in Dec. 1992- Jan.1993 at the invitation of Marc Gaborieau, Claude Markovits and Alexander Popovic; the Rockefeller Foundation which provided a residency scholarship at the Villa Serbelloni in August 1993; and the Woodrow Wilson Center in Washington D.C., where the book was completed during a residential fellowship in 1995-96.

Most of the chapters of this book were presented in earlier forms at meetings, lectures or conferences: in Paris at the EHESS, at the annual South Asia conferences in Madison, at the history departments of the University of California at Berkeley and Harvard University, at ARIT in Istanbul, at the Southern Asia Institute at Columbia University, and at meetings of the Association for Asian Studies in Chicago and the World History Association in Honolulu, at the University of Pennsylvania in Philadelphia, as well as at meetings in Washington. To all these audiences I must express my gratitude for their generous comments.

The list of individual scholars to whom I am indebted for ideas, intellectual and moral encouragement, correspondence on selected topics, and various forms of aid is even longer. I would like to thank in particular Chris Bayly, Burton Stein, Robert Frykenberg, A. K. Narain, Dick Eaton, Tosun Aricanli, Gavin Hambly, Katherine Bowie, Kingsley de Silva, Sumit Guha, Steve Album, Max Nihom, Mark Kenoyer, Richard Davis, Jan Vansina, George Brooks, Patricia Crone, John Newman, Marie Martin, Uli Schamiloglu, Christopher Beckwith, James Hoover, Mesfin Kebede, Heinz Bechert, Muzaffar Alam, Tom Allsen, Bill Spengler, Jos Gommans, Ticia Rueb, Douglas Mudd, and Victor Lieberman. My thanks are also due to Dick Eaton, Anatoly Khazanov and Jan Heesterman for reading the entire manuscript before it went to the press. For research assistance I am indebted to S. Y. Saikia and E. Palm. Over the past five years, above all, I derived a great deal of *fā'ida* from discussions with Michael Chamberlain and Anatoly Khazanov, who, like myself, were recent arrivals at Wisconsin and did their best to educate me in the intricacies of Middle Eastern and Central Asian history respectively. Lastly, I cannot fail to mention, once again, my general intellectual debt to Jan Heesterman. It has been a matter of no small satisfaction for me that we could continue to meet regularly, both in the Netherlands and the U.S.A., and that I could continue to benefit from his unrivaled erudition.

Washington, D. C.
May, 1996

INTRODUCTION

In the preceding volume the argument has been put forward that in the period up to the early eleventh century the impact of the expansion of Islam on the area which the Muslims called *al-Hind*, 'India' and the 'Indianized' world of the Southeast-Asian mainland and Indonesian Archipelago, was largely of a commercial nature. Sind, the passage of overland and maritime traffic to and from the Middle East, politically and culturally an unsettled 'frontier of al-Hind' which generated brigandage and piratical activity as far off as Sri Lanka, was conquered by the Arabs in order to safeguard the Persian Gulf and the feeder routes of the India trade which was to become a great source of wealth in the newly evolving Muslim economy. But the early conquests did not extend beyond Sind. In effect, the commercial ascendancy of the Islamic world in the early medieval period derived from its intermediate position as a conduit of exchange between the Mediterranean and the Indian Ocean; in other words, from being at the crossroads of world trade, at the junction of Christendom, Africa, Central Asia and China, and India. In monetary terms this resulted in the transition to a unified bi-metallic currency based on the gold *dīnār* and the silver *dirham* which had a stable exchange rate and was made possible by the systematic exploitation of all known sources of precious metals. The political frontiers of early Islam were, thus, more or less stationary from the early eighth until the early eleventh century, but its commercial hegemony continued to increase far beyond.

Secondly, it was also suggested in the same volume that the often complex and protracted political, social and economic developments in those areas of *al-Hind* which remained beyond the frontier of Islamic conquest were determined or significantly influenced by interaction with the outside world—that of Islam above all, but also Tibetan power and Tang and Sung China. Political power in India did not arise in isolation from the great pan-Asian movements of conquest and trade of this age. To the contrary, by tapping into the world of nomadism and commerce outside the settled parts of the subcontinent such power could be all the more effectively asserted. Here the peculiar dynamic of

early medieval India became manifest in two complementary
forces which seemingly pulled in different directions. In the subcontinent generally we noted an increase in town-building and
the multiplication of small and middle-sized market-centres, i.e. a
densification of regional exchange patterns, and, with it, an overall increase of sedentary agriculture and the formation of new,
more vertically organized states—epitomized by monumental
stone temple building— and widespread brahmanization in many
areas, including the periphery, which resulted in a more structured social system. In the 'Middle Country', the Indian heartland
of *madhyadesha*, the city of Kanauj remained the pre-eminent and
'exemplary' sacred centre throughout the early medieval period.
Here the agricultural state had the longest pedigree, the social
hierarchy of caste was relatively rigid, and here too the ritual standard of brahmanical orthodoxy was preserved. Spreading out
from this epicentre, the brahmans of Kanauj would reconstitute
its ritual infrastructure in the periphery of the Indian subcontinent which sought to overcome its semi-barbarian or *mleccha* status by endowing such brahmans with land and other wealth and
by replicating the sacred geography of the Ganges-Yamuna region.

Kanauj, however, was also a 'dead centre'. Political and military
power and mobile wealth (trade goods and precious metals), in
general, continued to be found on the frontier of settled society.
Hence *madhyadesha*, the agricultural heartland of the North-Indian plains, during this period continued to be dominated by political formations which arose and maintained themselves in the
periphery of the subcontinent, and whose hegemony, in effect,
was based on a compromise with 'barbarian' power across the
Islamic-Sino-Tibetan frontier: Greater Kashmir, extending into
Turkestan, and allied to the Tang Chinese in a scramble for the
proceeds along the silk route; Bengal, the ruling dynasty of which
was propped up by Tibetan military power; the Rashtrakuta
dynasty in the Western Deccan, which was part of the Persian Gulf
trading system of the Muslims; and Maʿbar or Southeast India,
extending itself (through the famous Cola expeditions) in the late
tenth and eleventh century into the burgeoning Southeast-Asian
maritime economy which became dominated by the Chinese
under the early Sung. It is in these peripheral states of the Indian subcontinent that we can locate the fluid resources, intensive
raiding and trading activity, as well as the social and political flu-

idity and openness which produced a dynamic impetus that was absent in the densely settled agricultural (and civilizational) heartland. This second argument, then, sought to show that shifts of power occurred, in combination with massive transfers of wealth, across multiple centres along the periphery of *al-Hind* in the seventh to eleventh centuries. It was an attempt to show, in short, how these multiple centres mediated between the world of mobile wealth on the Islamic-Sino-Tibetan frontier (which extended into Southeast Asia) and the world of sedentary agriculture, epitomized by brahmanical temple Hinduism in and around Kanauj. In a diachronic perspective, this was the familiar dialectic between civilization ('ritual purity') and 'barbarian' power.

What happened now, in the subsequent period, the eleventh to thirteenth centuries, can be summarized as the successful fusion of the organizational mode of the frontier (with its patterns of long-distance trade and mobile wealth as well as its raiding capacity) with that of the settled society of the agricultural plains, inland, from the Panjab to the Ganges-Yamuna Doab and to Bihar and Bengal, but also in the coastal areas of Gujarat, Malabar, the Coromandel, and Sumatra. The rhetorical demonization on both sides notwithstanding, it was this fusion that would make India the hub of world trade, while in the Middle East re-nomadization occurred (the fusion of frontier and settled society, in other words, was unsuccessful here) under Mongol rule. The Mongols hardly penetrated into India—for a variety of reasons, most important of which was probably the lack of sufficient good pasture land. Instead of being devastated by the Mongols during one or several major invasions, the agricultural plains of North India were brought under Turko-Islamic rule in a gradual manner. This conquest, which continued throughout the eleventh to thirteenth centuries, was effected by professional armies, built around a core of Turkish slave soldiers, which were relatively small in size and were not accompanied by any large-scale invasions of nomadic elements (complete with flocks and herds), as happened in the Middle East. Unlike the Mongols, too, these Turkish groups had already converted to Islam before they came to India. The military differential between the Turkish invaders on the one hand and the opposing Indian armies on the other was both technical and social in its origin, revolving as it did around the co-ordinated deployment of mounted archers. In India, of course, the horse and horsemanship had a long history. But it seems that archery was largely left to infantry and a relatively small number of elephant-riders. Like in the case of the Byzantines, it was the failure of the Indians to develop mounted archery that was exposed by the Turks from the steppes of Central Asia. And it was, paradoxically, this military differential that made possible the fusion of nomadic and agricultural society in the eleventh to thirteenth centuries.

Another essential part of the process which is dealt with in this volume was that, as soon as the conquest of *al-Hind* was under way, a migration corridor was opened up between the eastern Islamic world, including Central Asia, and the subcontinent. The gradual establishment of a new Muslim ruling elite in India was further enhanced by the immigration of fugitives from the lands which had been overrun by the pagan Mongols. The total number of Muslim immigrants could at no time have been very high, and it was dwarfed by the number of India's native population (which was probably already then over 70 million, while Iran and Central Asia each contained no more than a few million people at most). No massive demographic shifts occurred in India, unlike in Iran. There was no re-nomadization but the imposition of purposeful Islamic rule by invading horse warriors who recruited perhaps tens of thousands of supporters as military retinue. The Turkish conquest uprooted the sacred geography of Indian peasant society, during innumerable campaigns, but it did not result in any significant loss of population. In the Indo-Islamic world, long-distance trade, elite slavery, and monetization (the result of the de-hoarding of Indian temple treasure) went hand in hand with imperial expansion. The result of the conquest was, in short, the revitalization of the economy of settled agriculture through the dynamic impetus of forced monetization and the expansion of political dominion.

The argument of this volume, focusing on long-distance trade, agricultural expansion, migration, and nomadic penetration, culminates in the negative conclusion that conversion to Islam among the native population is insignificant in most parts of al-Hind except the coasts almost throughout the eleventh-thirteenth centuries. More specifically, the conversion of some key groups in Sind and the Panjab, as well as among the coastal communities of Malabar and Northeast Sumatra, does not appear to have gained momentum before the second half of the thirteenth century. Recent work by R. M. Eaton shows that in the Panjab and Sind, and in Bengal, Muslim converts were drawn from indigenous groups which had hardly been integrated in the Hindu social order or caste system (however defined) at all, such as forest tribes and pastoral groups who were in the process of settling down as tax-paying agriculturists.[1] Elsewhere too, conversion, rather than providing 'liberation' from the allegedly intolerable rigidities of the Hindu caste system, seems to have largely affected previously marginal groups living in frontier areas. Such groups, if they were not forest tribes or pastoralists in the process of becoming peasants, could also be, as in Malabar or Indonesia, part of the newly rising trading communities on the coasts. In Indian terms, the seaside was always a place of extraordinary license.

Much of the conversion to Islam that occurred in these frontier areas of *al-Hind* did not, it must be emphasized, begin to affect large numbers of people until the early modern era. Until then, Islam, in any part of our area, was primarily the culture of an immigrant military and political elite which was usually urban-based and at one remove from peasant society. It represented a link between the world of mobile wealth (money, trade) and of mobile—we could even say monetized—elites, including slaves, of Iran and Central Asia, on the one hand, and the sedentary world of primordial kinship ties of the Indian peasantry and fixed field cultivation on the other. But, strikingly, even when Islam became a peasant religion, as in Sind and Bengal, it still mediated between the realm of settled agriculture and the frontier of pastoralists and shifting cultivators.

It is in this direction, probably, that we have to look for an answer to the question why Buddhism disappeared, in the eleventh to thirteenth centuries, from its homeland in the South-Asian subcontinent, while being successfully disseminated to the peasant societies of mainland Southeast Asia. When one turns to the secondary literature on Buddhism one finds mere hints of an explanation of this issue. If it is addressed somewhat more sys-

---

[1] R. M. Eaton, 'The Political and Religious Authority of the Shrine of Bābā Farīd', in: Metcalf, B. D. (ed.), *Moral Conduct and Authority: The Place of Adab in South Asian Islam* (Berkeley, Los Angeles and London, 1984), pp. 333-56; idem, *The Rise of Islam and the Bengal Frontier, 1204-1760* (Berkeley, Los Angeles and London, 1993).

tematically, it usually amounts to one or another version of the theory that since Buddhism at one time prevailed only in those areas which later converted to Islam, and since there are no Buddhists left in these areas, we must deduce that the Buddhists converted to Islam. Thus it is most often observed that Buddhism disappeared from those parts of South and Southeast Asia which were overrun by Muslim armies in the medieval period and henceforward became subject to Islamic rule. Mass conversion of Buddhists to Islam in Sind and Bengal, it is then alleged, occurred due to political pressure or because Buddhists saw in Islam a means to escape from the Hindu caste system and brahmanical oppression. This, we are told, is also the reason why Buddhism survived in areas which did not suffer the largely 'destructive' Islamic impact: the Himalayas and beyond, Sri Lanka, mainland Southeast Asia (but not Indonesia, which was conquered by indigenous Islamic rulers).

An alternative explanation will be offered here—one that is in line with the previously presented arguments. We have to begin by recognizing that there was a vast difference between ancient Indian Buddhism and all surviving later forms in Sri Lanka, Southeast Asia, and Tibet and the Himalayas. Buddhism in ancient India to a large extent remained embedded in the cosmopolitan context of long-distance trade and itinerant monkhood, but never became a peasant religion with broad, socially inclusive, underpinnings. In this sense, it can be argued, Buddhism remained a phenomenon of the frontier of settled society, to some extent similar to the Islam of the Arab or Turkish immigrant groups of later times. But this type of Buddhism belonged to a time when the Indian subcontinent was still mostly a forested realm with a but scattered and small population in comparison with medieval times. On a purely abstract level again, it can perhaps be said that Buddhism, like Islam, mediated between settled society and the frontier of mobile wealth (the world of money, trade goods, nomads, cities), but at an earlier stage in the evolution of the Indian economy. For the same reason, we should probably abandon the idea that there ever was a 'Buddhist India'. By the time that the Turko-Islamic conquerors arrived in North India, in the eleventh to thirteenth centuries, Buddhism was no longer a religion of a floating population of itinerant monks but had become institutionalized in monasteries, which, supported by royal endowments of land as well as by donations from the mercantile communities, tended to become large academically oriented centres with permanent residents, vulnerable to outside attack, but still aloof from the rural masses (which only adopted random cultic elements from the religion). What happened, then, during the Islamic conquest, is that the academic (and soteriological / philosophical) tradition of Buddhism was uprooted in India itself, but replaced, outside the orbit of Muslim rule, by a variety of regional forms of Buddhism. These regional forms of Buddhism, in Sri Lanka, Tibet and the Himalayas, and in mainland Southeast Asia, still developed in conjunction with kingship (especially in the early modern period), but took on the aspect of a communal religion as well. In other words, they were, apart from perpetuating the high tradition, above all peasant religions—trade and money matters being left in these areas to foreign communities of Muslims and expatriate Chinese. As a peasant religion, Buddhism took root in areas of *al-Hind* with relatively little previous exposure to organized scriptural religion and with relatively little social and economic differentiation of their own. Like Islam at a later stage in the peripheral parts of our area which were not yet brought under cultivation (Sind, the Panjab, Bengal, parts of Indonesia), Buddhism developed in the context of the formation of settled states on the frontier of agriculture.

In broad terms, then, the religious transformation of *al-Hind* can be analysed as the result of the same dynamic interaction between frontier and settled society, or parallels to it, that the earlier parts of this volume discuss. The making of the Indo-Islamic world is synonymous with the successful integration, from the seventh century on, of relatively densely settled and still expanding agricultural societies into the patterns of long-distance trade and the mobilization of wealth, as well as raiding and conquest activity, which were characteristic of the frontier peoples of Central Asia, China and the Middle East, and later of Europe. This, in the final analysis, also implies an essential continuity between the ancient and medieval periods of Indian history, at least on the level of social and economic development, rather than the discontinuity which was perceived by earlier writers on the subject who focused on culture and religion, or by even earlier writers who focused on race.

CHAPTER I

NOMADS, CITIES AND TRADE

In this first chapter, we will begin by looking at the changing global context of the eleventh to thirteenth centuries and briefly analyse the different ways in which this affected the economy and commerce of India and the Indian Ocean. If in the previous centuries the Islamic Middle East maintained its position as a connecting link between Africa, Europe, Byzantium and the Mediterranean, and India, Central Asia and China, in the period from the eleventh century onwards the situation in the Middle East and the relative importance of the other areas changed considerably. A large part of the Middle East came to be occupied by nomads from Central Asia, and, with its agricultural economy and some of its urban centres severely damaged, acquired the characteristics of a frontier zone. At the same time, through the Mongols, the Middle East became more closely linked to Central Asia. Europe and China ('Cathay'), with large settled populations, rose in relative importance at both ends of the Turko-Mongol world. And India, also with a large settled population, now partly under Muslim rule, assumed an ever more central position in the trading economy of Islam and the world at large. Put differently, India's expanding agricultural economy was integrated, in the eleventh to thirteenth centuries, in a widening global market through the new Turko-Mongol nomadic intermediary which projected itself across the Eurasian landmass.

THE MIDDLE EAST AND THE INDIAN OCEAN

Before the arrival of the Seljuqs, in the tenth and early eleventh century, the most important dynasty in the Middle East had been the Būyids. These came from Dailam, in the Alborz mountains, to the southwest of the Caspian Sea. Of Iranian origin, establishing their power in Shiraz, Ray and Baghdad—first on the Iranian plateau, then in Iraq—, the Būyids presided over the most sustained attempt to link Islamic kingship with the Sasanid tradition.

The Iranian empire of the Būyids however had crumbled fast after the succession struggles which ensued at the death of ʿAdud ad-Daula in 983 A.D., and it was not much later that they had to yield to the Seljuqs, who took control of Baghdad in 1055 and of Shiraz in 1062.

The arrival of the Seljuqs in the Middle East in the eleventh century marks the beginning of Turkish rule, i.e. of formerly nomadic chiefs with origins in Central Asia, which in one way or another was to continue in the area until the early sixteenth century, and, in a more restricted sense, until the twentieth. The Seljuqs were able to downplay Iranian notions of monarchical legitimacy and, unlike the Būyids, did not present themselves primarily as *Shāhanshāhs* (although this title is sometimes found on their coins) by introducing a new claim to authority through the institution of the Sultanate, a form of Islamic dominion derived from the caliphate and supported by the Sunni-Islamic establishment. The Seljuqs were a tribe of Ghuzz or Oghuz Turks (later also styled Turkomans), who had long been living on the pastures to the north of the Caspian and Aral Seas, on the periphery of the Islamic world. They were named after their leader Seljuq, under whom, in about 950 AD, they withdrew from the Ghuzz confederacy and settled in and around Jand, along the lower Syr Darya (Jaxartes) river, where they soon converted to Islam. The Seljuqs then rose to prominence and power while the Ghaznavid rulers Mahmūd and his son Masʿūd were preoccupied with their campaigns in India and had their backs turned to the Turkish nomads in Transoxania. They were able to take Khurasan in 1035, five years after the death of Mahmūd of Ghazna, and made Nishapur the first of their capitals in 1037. Warfare with the Ghaznavids culminated in the battle of Dandanqan in 1040, where the Ghaznavid forces, under Masʿūd, were routed and forced to withdraw, first to Ghazna and ultimately to the Panjab. In 1059, four years after Baghdad was taken, and the capital restored to Sunni rule, the Seljuq Sultanate was established throughout Iran and Iraq, and up to Syria and the Byzantine empire in Anatolia. Under Alp Arslan (1063-72) and his son Malik Shah (1072-92), Seljuq power reached its zenith, and both the Ghaznavids and the Qarakhanids (992-1211) of Transoxania and eastern Turkestān were forced to accept the Seljuqs as overlords. From Ajarbayjan nomadic raids continued to be made into Byzantine territory, and

while Alp Arslan's reign did not see much further expansion of
Seljuq control, in 1071 the Byzantines suffered a major defeat at
Manzikert. In due course, a new Turkish state, the Seljuq Sultanate
of Rum ('Rome') was created in Anatolia, a distant precursor of
the Ottoman Sultanate.

It is thus striking that the Seljuqs established their dominion
in an area which more or less overlapped with that of the Sasanid
empire in Iran and Iraq, and in what are now parts of Turkey, the
Central-Asian post-Soviet republics, and Afghanistan, but, as
nomadic conquerors, kept their distance from the Iranian tradition. The Seljuq wazir Nizām al-Mulk (1047-92), in his *Siyāsatnāma*, nowhere refers to 'Iran' as the name of the Seljuq ruler's
domain. By the eleventh century, the term 'Iran' had long lost all
the political connotations which it had had under the Sasanids.
And these were not resuscitated until the rule of the Mongol
Ilkhans in the thirteenth century, when the founder of the
Ilkhanate, Hülegü (who, like Kublai in China, was a grandson and
not a son of Chingiz Khan), needed a proper denomination for
his dominion in distinction to the other Mongol dominions of
the Ulus Chaghatay ('Chaghatay's Patrimony') of Transoxania and
its eastern hinterland, and the Ulus Juchi ('Juchi's Patrimony'),
the so-called Golden Horde of the southern Russian steppes.[1] The
internal organization of the Seljuqs in Iran was not modelled
upon that of the Sasanids but remained a kind of 'family confederation' or 'appanage state', in which the leading member of
the paramount family assigned portions of the domain as
autonomous appanages to other members of his house.[2] This was
not unique to the Seljuqs, but rather an implicit code of tribal
organization which the nomads brought with them to the Islamic world. The Seljuqs did not make this code part of their public
claims to authority among their Muslim subjects in the Middle

---

[1] D. Krawulsky, *Iran-Das Reich der Īkhāne. Eine topographisch-historische Studie*
(Wiesbaden, 1978), pp. 11-17; G. Gnoli, 'Ēr-mazdēsn—zum Begriff 'Iran' und seiner Entstehung im dritten Jahrhundert', in: *Transition Periods in Iranian History.
Actes du symposium de Fribourg-en-Brisgau*, 22-24 May 1985 (=Studia Iranica, Cahier
5) (Paris, 1987), pp.83-100; idem, *The Idea of Iran: An Essay on its Origin* (Rome,
1989).
[2] Cf. R. S. Humphreys, *Islamic History: A Framework for Inquiry* (Princeton, 1991),
p.166; idem, *From Saladin to the Mongols: The Ayyubids of Damascus, 1193-1260*
(Albany, 1970); J. E. Woods, *The Aqquyunlu: Clan, Confederation, Empire* (Minneapolis, 1976).

East. Again, in this they were unlike their Mongol successors, who arrived in the Middle East as pagans and did systematically promote Turko-Mongol concepts and symbols in their public image among the Muslim population. The Seljuqs, after all, had already converted to the faith before their arrival. It was their business to fight the Shi'ite heretics. Even so, the Seljuqs, while essentially keeping up itinerant courts (next to a series of fixed capitals on the Iranian plateau and as far as Anatolia) and disowning the Iranian heritage in general, did not fail to adopt an Iranian bureaucracy, with many of the leading officials (like Nizām al-Mulk) weaned away from the Ghaznavids. They also adopted the *iqtā'* system, next to a standing army of slave troops, of Turkish origin, about 10,000 to 15,000 strong, who, unlike the nomadic Ghuzz tribesmen which continued to migrate into the eastern parts of the empire, were the personal property of the Sultan.

Since the Seljuqs had already converted and had been exposed to Islamic civilization, and because, moreover, the numbers involved in their migration were not large—probably in the tens of thousands—there was little destructive violence which resulted from their conquest.[3] The most important effect of the Seljuq conquest of Iran, apart from the beginnings of Turkicization, was a shift away from the settled to the nomadic and semi-settled sector of the population, but this too appears to have been localized, and it did not necessarily mean a reduction of the cultivated area as the nomads occupied land that had previously been largely unexploited. Many parts of the Seljuq empire were too hot and dry for the Ghuzz or Turkoman pastoralists and their flocks. The major concentrations were found in Anatolia, Ajarbayjan, parts of Diyarbakr, northern Kurdistan, and in Gurgan, Dihistan, and Marv. There were also isolated groups which migrated to Fars and Khuzistan.

Seljuq rule lasted for a century after the death of Malik Shah and his minister Nizām al-Mulk, and for much longer still in Rum, even though it was always prone to succession struggles. Gradually, in the twelfth century, the Seljuqs lost control of outlying

---

[3] A. K. S. Lambton, *Continuity and Change in Medieval Persia: Aspects of Administrative, Economic and Social History, 11th-14th Century* (New York, 1988), pp.5-6; idem, 'Aspects of Seljūq-Ghuzz settlement in Persia', in: *Theory and Practice in Medieval Persian Government* (London, 1980); D. Morgan, *Medieval Persia, 1040-1747* (London and New York, 1988).

areas to their kinsmen, the Seljuqs of Rum, the Zangids of Mosul and Aleppo, the Dānishmendids of Sivas, and the Ortuqids of Armenia. They suffered their most serious setback from the newly arriving Qara Khitay or 'Black Cathay', a branch of the Khitan or Liao dynasty which had been expelled from its realm in northern China by Jürchen Manchurian tribesmen and then moved west to set up a new empire in Turkestan, forced the Qarakhanids to accept their hegemony in 1137, and in 1141 defeated the Seljuqs on the Qatwan steppe near Samarqand. In the 1150s, groups of Turkoman tribesmen sacked a number of cities in Khurasan and Transoxania, including Bukhara. Soon afterwards, most of northern Iran came under the control of the Khwārazm Shah, who ruled the region until the coming of the Mongols in 1219-23. The Khwārazm Shahs occupied Transoxania in 1210, and in 1215 conquered a large part of what is now Afghanistan from the Ghurids, who retreated further to the east.

The Mongols were different from the Seljuqs in essential respects: they arrived as pagans and did not become Muslims until they had been in Iran for many years; they did not prop up the caliphate but extinguished it; among the Mongols too, until the reign of Ghazan (1295-1304), an attitude of contempt towards the townsmen and peasants of Iran continued to prevail.[4] What distinguished them also was the number and military organization of their forces, although the majority of the rank and file were Turks.

In origin, the Mongols, like the Turks, were nomads, with flocks and herds of sheep and horses. They had become identifiable as a group during the rule of the Khitan Liao (10th-12th centuries) in Mongolia and North China, whose collapse before the Chin of Manchuria brought direct Chinese control in Mongolia to an end, creating a power vacuum which the Mongols filled. It is difficult to obtain a definite figure for the size of the Mongol armies. We know that since each Mongol soldier took along several horses, and the army was accompanied by flocks and herds, there would be a limit imposed on their number anywhere in Iran. Nonetheless, it is clear that the Mongol armies which invaded Iran were very large, and certainly much larger than those of the Seljuqs of

---

[4] Morgan, *Medieval Persia*, p. 53.

two centuries earlier.[5] Moreover, while the Seljuqs destroyed little, this is not true of the Mongols.

There were numerous Mongol incursions into Iran, and two major invasions, the first by Chingiz Khan in the years after 1219, and the second by his grandson Hülegü in the 1250s. From the latter date until the 1330s, Iran was ruled as a Mongol kingdom, the Ilkhanate, which did not convert to Islam during the first forty years of its existence. The first Mongol invasion of Iran, in pursuit of the Khwārazm Shah, already caused considerable destruction in *Mā warā' an-nahr*, but much more so in the eastern provinces of Khurasan, where entire cities, such as Balkh, Herat and Nishapur, which refused to surrender at the first summon, were razed to the ground, their population virtually exterminated. Persian chroniclers, contemporaries of Chingiz Khan, speak of millions of dead—figures that need not be taken literally to understand that this was a calamity on an unparalleled scale; and it is, in effect, one about which our sources are unanimous.[6] Ibn al-Athir wrote that the irruption of Chingiz Khan's armies was 'a tremendous disaster such as had never happened before, and which struck all the world, though the Muslims above all ..'.[7] Having comprehensively wrecked Khurasan and other parts of Iran, Chingiz Khan withdrew in 1223 to Mongolia, leaving Iran, or rather the northern grasslands, under Mongol viceroys for three decades. Iran, then, was not yet fully incorporated into the Mongol empire, and there were still continuous campaigns being conducted, including one in 1243 to subject the Seljuq Sultanate of Rum.[8] In 1251 the Great Khan Möngke despatched, at last, his brother Hülegü to deal the final blow to the Ismā'īlī Assassins at Alamut and the Abbasid caliphate at Baghdad. Effectively, Ismā'īlī power was put to an end in both Kohistan and the Alborz mountains in 1256, while Baghdad was taken and sacked in 1258, the caliph executed, and, according to variant sources, another 200,000 to 800,000 people massacred.[9] Aleppo and Damascus were also taken, but, after the establishment of the Mamluk regime,

---

[5] Cf. Lambton, *Continuity and Change*, pp. 15, 20-21, 24.
[6] Lambton, *Continuity and Change*, pp. 14, 19-20; Morgan, *Medieval Persia*, p. 57.
[7] Quoted in Lambton, *Continuity and Change*, p. 14.
[8] Morgan, *Medieval Persia*, p. 58.
[9] *Ibid.*, pp. 59-60.

Syria was attached to Egypt again in 1260. Iran (including Iraq, and much of Anatolia), however, was now definitely brought under Mongol control; the Ilkhanate was established and was to be ruled for seventy years by Hülegü and his descendants.

It does not appear that this improved matters a great deal.[10] At the beginning of the Ilkhanate, Juwaynī wrote: 'Every town and every village has been several times subjected to pillage and massacre and has suffered this confusion for years, so that even though there be generation and increase until the resurrection the population will not attain a tenth part of what it was before'.[11] And at the end of the Ilkhanate period, another Mongol official, Qazwīnī, could still maintain that 'there is no doubt that the destruction which happened on the emergence of the Mongol state and the general massacre that occurred at that time will not be repaired in a thousand years, even if no other calamity happens; and the world will not return to the condition in which it was before that event'.[12] It can thus hardly be doubted that the Mongol invasions were unprecedented disasters with long-term effects. All that can be said to mitigate the picture is that the destruction was not universal but patchy, with some areas less affected than others—the southern parts of Iran, or Fārs, in particular, never faced a full-scale assault—and that Hülegü's invasion was less disastrous than his grandfather's. On the other hand, there was not only the destruction of cities and their inhabitants, but also of agriculture, due, especially, to the flight of peasants, as in many parts of Iran cultivation was dependent on the qanāt system of underground water channels which required constant maintenance and could not be abandoned for long. After the invasions were over, the conditions in the rural areas of Iran did not improve much, as Ilkhanid taxation remained erratic and exceedingly harsh up to the accession of Ghazan, and possibly until even later. With the peasantry in ruin, many members of the Turko-Iranian ruling elite dispossessed, and the old urban network severely damaged, the religio-academic institutions that traditionally supported the bureaucratic and scholarly elites suffered a drastic decline in income. When these sources of revenue were depleted, an exodus of 'ulamā' appears to have occurred, the

---

[10] *Ibid.*, pp. 5-6, 79-82.
[11] Quoted *ibid.*, p. 79.
[12] Quoted *ibid.*

NOMADS, CITIES AND TRADE

majority going to India, and a minority moving westward, e.g. to Cairo.[13]

But by far the most important consequence of the Mongol invasions in Iran was that the equilibrium between the nomadic and the settled population was upset due to the large influx of new nomads which now occurred and the concomitant decline of the settled population in rural areas as well as towns.[14] The newly arriving nomads did not just occupy marginal land, but, unlike the Seljuqs, turned much agricultural land over to pasture. It is especially from the Mongol conquests on that we can trace the increasing importance of Turkish tribes in Iran, even though their infiltration had begun much earlier. The Iranian plateau now became overcrowded with Turkish tribes of horse-riding and stock-breeding nomads. As a result, even as late as the nineteenth century, in Qajar Iran, these constituted 30-50% of the total population of Iran. The militant Turkish tribes, which were mobile over long distances, achieved almost a monopoly of military and political power, and the politics in Iran, from then on, continued to be based on instable tribal coalitions. Centralized power was the exception rather than the rule, and was typical only of the Safawids for a brief period in the sixteenth and seventeenth centuries, and, even then, entirely dependent on the creation of a slave corps which was loyal to the Shah personally.

We do not know whether Ghazan's attempt to put things right in Iran, after he became Ilkhan in 1295 and he and the other Mongols in Iran converted to Islam, was successful even in a minimal degree. Administrative reforms were instituted, to repair some of the damage, but it is not clear whether these reforms were actually implemented.[15] There was probably some temporary relief, and a change of attitude which led to a closer identification with the subject population. It is perhaps significant that, although the Ilkhanate collapsed, the Mongols were not driven

---

[13] See Chapter VI.

[14] Cf. Lambton, *Continuity and Change*, pp. 26-27; Morgan, *Medieval Persia*, p. 81; J. Masson Smith, 'Turanian Nomadism and Iranian Politics', *Iranian Studies*, 11 (1978), pp. 57-81; idem, 'Mongol Manpower and Persian Population', *The Journal of the Economic and Social History of the Orient*, 18 (1975), pp. 271-99; B. G. Fragner, 'State Structures in the Safavid Empire: Towards a Comparative Investigation' (Paper presented at the workshop on The Political Economies of the Ottoman, Safavid and Mughal Empires, Harvard University, March 1991).

[15] Cf. Morgan, *Medieval Persia*, pp. 72-77.

out of Iran, as they were out of China, but instead were absorbed into the Turkish Muslim population of Iran.[16]

Other elements of a positive legacy which can be attributed to the Ilkhanids include a broadening of the intellectual horizons, and the final establishment of New Persian as the dominant medium for historical writing, a process which had already begun under the Seljuqs, when the centre of Arabic-language culture shifted from Baghdad to Cairo. More generally, as we have seen (p. 10), the Ilkhanids re-introduced a political conception of Iran which had a remarkable longevity. In the context of this new Iran, Turko-Mongol concepts, symbols, and practices, as well as Mongol genealogy, remained of great importance among the Ilkhans and their successors. And with the new political conception of Iran came the idea—which was to survive to the end of the sixteenth century—of Tabriz as its new capital. When the fifteenth-century Turkomans, the Qaraquyunlu and the Aqquyunlu from eastern Anatolia, succeeded in capturing Tabriz—on the northwestern fringe of Iran—, they immediately proclaimed themselves *pādshāh-i-Irān* or *kesrā-yi-Irān*, irrespective of the real extent of 'Iranian' territory actually under their control.[17] It appears, therefore, that Iran survived as a political concept, although it was profoundly transformed in substance and effectively had become part of Central Asia.

The renomadization of Iran and the 'return of the frontier' brought about an increased mobility of people, goods and precious metals in the whole area. While the size of the internal Iranian market may have shrunk, the Turko-Mongol conquest of much of the Middle East appears to have had positive effects on the trade with India and, although this varied over time and space, on the position of much of the Middle East as a conduit for long-distance trade. But it took until the thirteenth century before these effects became manifest, and it was doubtlessly preceded by a steep decline in the importance of the Persian Gulf route and a shift of the trade towards the Red Sea.

We have seen, in the previous volume, that the route through the Persian Gulf had been the most important commercial link between the Middle East and *al-Hind* and *aṣ-Ṣīn* in the Arab peri-

---

[16] Cf. Morgan, *Medieval Persia*, p. 81.
[17] Fragner, 'State Structures in the Safavid Empire', pp. 6-7.

od.[18] A great expansion of the India trade had followed upon the Arab conquest of Sind and the foundation of Baghdad, in the late eighth and ninth centuries. The Abbasid capital, receiving the traffic from Egypt, and, via the Tigris and Euphrates, from Armenia and the Levant, and 'without an obstacle' between itself and China, became the world's largest harbour and 'the most prosperous town in the world'.[19] This upsurge of trade in the Persian Gulf and along India's westcoast provided the underpinnings to the rise to hegemony of the *Ballaharā* kings in Western India—a hegemony which lasted as long as the Persian Gulf trading system and its extension remained intact, i.e. until the late tenth and eleventh century.

As al-Muqaddasī shows, by 986 A.D., when the Būyids had reduced the caliph to a figurehead, Baghdad was falling to ruin and decay, its population dwindling, 'the city daily going from bad to worse',[20] Basra, the financial emporium of the caliphate, mediating the trade between India and Baghdad, reached the height of its prosperity in the ninth century, but was sacked by the Zanj in 871, and again in 923 by the Carmathians, after which it lost some of its importance to Sīrāf, and was half-ruined by 1052, deteriorating further down to the Mongol age, together with the entire Gulf zone.[21] Like Basra, Kūfa and Wāsit, Al-Ubulla became a Gulf port of outstanding importance in the eighth and ninth centuries, when it was considered virtually 'part of al-Hind' on account of its large share in the India trade, but it suffered similar setbacks from the Zanj and the Carmathians, after which it, too, lost in importance in the late tenth century.[22] Sīrāf, further down the Persian coast, surpassed Basra in importance during the Būyid period, when it was an entrepot for the trade with India, Malaya, China, and with the Red Sea and the East-African coast.[23] Its merchants spread their activity to Suhār, in Oman. The latter place

[18] *Al-Hind*, I, pp. 53-59, 63, 308.
[19] V. Minorsky (transl.), *Hudūd al-ʿālam* (London, 1937), p. 138.
[20] G. Wiet, *Baghdad: Metropolis of the Abbasid Caliphate* (Norman, 1971), p. 83 ff; J. L. Abu-Lughod, *Before European Hegemony: The World System A. D. 1250-1350* (Oxford, 1989), p. 191.
[21] *Al-Hind*, I, pp. 53-54, 58; R. M. Savory, 'The History of the Persian Gulf, A. D. 600-1800', in: A. J. Cottrell (ed.), *The Persian Gulf States: A General Survey* (Baltimore and London, 1980), p. 16; Abu-Lughod, *Before European Supremacy*, p. 196.
[22] *Al-Hind*, I, p. 54.
[23] *Al-Hind*, I, pp. 54-55, 58; Savory, 'Persian Gulf', p. 17.

(as well as the Red Sea and Qays) is where many of them retired to after Sīrāf began to decline, after an earthquake in 977 and after the decline of Būyid power unleashed piratical activity at the island of Qays, 200 km to the southeast of the city and about 20 km offshore. Although the Seljuqs tried to revive Sīrāf, a century later it was a port of but local significance, and, by the end of the twelfth century, Sīrāf was in ruins. In Oman, next to Suhār, other ports which rose to importance before the eleventh century, were Julfār, Dabā, and Masqat, focal points of the *Azdī* trading diaspora which extended throughout the Indian Ocean. These picked up some of the slack, but by no means all.

Changing conditions in the Gulf first led to a general decline of the commercial networks in the eleventh century. Fārs was eclipsed in the eleventh and twelfth centuries, especially in the eighty years or so after the Seljuq take-over, when the province was devastated by the local Shabānkāra tribes, whose tribal rackets were unhinged by the re-alignment of trade towards Central Asia and eastern Iran which was occurring at that time.[24] It did not recover before the first half of the thirteenth century. The Seljuq occupation of Baghdad in 1055 did not put an end to the intercontinental trade route from the Mediterranean, Antioch and Asia Minor, via Baghdad, to the Persian Gulf and onwards, to India, but the importance of this route from then on diminished further, in favour of the Red Sea and Egypt, where the Fatimids had established themselves in 969 AD. While Baghdad lost its status of a capital under the Seljuqs, from 1057 well into the twelfth century the city went through a series of catastrophic famines, fires, floods, and earthquakes, as well as religious conflicts, which accelerated its decline.[25] Sīrāf was, in the second half of the eleventh century, superseded as the chief emporium in the Persian Gulf by Qays, an island which is described by Qazwīnī as 'hotter than the hottest room in a bathhouse', with a predominantly Arab population ruled by Arab amirs of the Banu Qaisar tribe.[26] A large walled city was built on Qays, and cultivation was carried on by means of *qanāts*. By the early twelfth century, the inhabitants of the island were still notorious as pirates, but there-

[24] *Al-Hind, I*, pp. 55, 57-58.
[25] Wiet, *Baghdad*, p. 106 ff, 122-7.
[26] Savory, 'Persian Gulf', p. 18.

after they attracted whatever was left of the Persian Gulf trade with India and China when the Seljuq ruler Turan Shah turned Qays into the harbour of Kirman, the province adjacent to Fārs, where the transition from the Būyids to the Seljuqs had been smooth.[27] Commerce in Kirman had been uninterrupted, and even boosted, by intensified contact with eastern Iran, and the Seljuqs succeeded without much effort in keeping down the Baluchi tribes, while retaining a hold on the Oman coast until 1140 as well.[28] In the first half of the twelfth century, in fact, Qays and (Old) Hormuz—the latter since the tenth century the seaport for the provinces of Kirman, Sistan and Khurasan—and the entire Kirman hinterland increased in prosperity, when again the trade of India, China, Ethiopia, and East Africa passed along this coast from Makran.[29] Thus the east-west route of the Būyid period had been replaced by a south-north route in the Seljuq period.

There was intense rivalry between Qays and Old Hormuz for hegemony in the Persian Gulf. Qays maintained its pre-eminence until the early thirteenth century, when the ruler of Old Hormuz, with the help of troops sent by his overlord, the atabeg of Kirman, captured the island in 1229.[30] During Mongol rule in Fārs, Old Hormuz and Qays were exposed to a variety of contenders for the control of their proceeds. European trade with Old Hormuz went via Little Armenia and the Ilkhanid capital of Tabriz. Direct voyages between the Gulf and China resumed in the thirteenth century. Qays, in Mongol times, while Baghdad was in full decline and Antioch captured by the Mamluks of Egypt, remained of some importance as an entrepot of Asian trade and operated a large fleet.[31] But in 1302 the whole population of Qays was moved to the island of Qishm, then in 1315 to the island of Jarūn, about 6 km off the mainland, where 'New Hormuz' was constructed.

The decline of Sīrāf, thus, in the long run, did not entail the cessation of maritime traffic between the Persian Gulf and India.

---

[27] Al-Hind, I, p. 58.
[28] Al-Hind, I, p. 59.
[29] Ibid.
[30] Savory, 'Persian Gulf', p. 18.
[31] J. Aubin, 'Y a-t-il eu interruption du commerce par mer entre le Golf Persique et l'Inde du XIe au XIVe siècle?', in: M. Mollat (ed.), Océan Indien et Méditerranée (Paris, 1964), pp. 170-1; E. Ashtor, A Social and Economic History of the Near East in the Middle Ages (Berkeley, Los Angeles and London, 1976), pp. 264-5.

The decline of Baghdad was also not absolute, and there are references to its continued role in the India trade in both European and Arabic sources.[32] Marco Polo, travelling in 1272 from Trebizond to the Persian Gulf, refers to Baghdad as a trading town, about which he had been told that it traded with Qays and that the Indian goods arriving there from the Persian Gulf were sent to Tabriz. Significantly, however, he travelled to the Persian Gulf by the new route from Tabriz to Kashan, to Yazd, through Kirman, and then to Hormuz.[33] Connecting with Tīz, on the Makran coast, New Hormuz retained its unchallenged position as the chief emporium in the Persian Gulf, even after the Ilkhans had been Islamicized, until the advent of the Portuguese in the early sixteenth century.[34] The island of Hormuz in its heyday is said to have supported 40,000 people, although, as Ralph Fitch described it, 'it is the dryest island in the world, for there is nothing growing in it but only salt'.[35] An island of about 19 km in circumference, its hills covered with a thick saline incrustation (of which ornamental vases were manufactured locally, as well as pillars to hold lamps), there was no water on the island, and all drinking water (except a minimal amount of rain) had to be imported from Qishm.[36] In 1331, Ibn Battuta described it as 'a beautiful large city, with magnificent markets (aswāq), as it is the port of India and Sind (marsaṇ al-hind wa-l-sind), from which the wares of India are exported to the two 'Irāqs, Fārs and Khurāsān'.[37]

The Ilkhans, then, like their Mongol predecessors in Iran, as much as they neglected and directly or indirectly helped to destroy agriculture in Iran, appear to have spared no effort to encourage the trade with India, and Tabriz attracted increasing numbers of Italian merchants, especially after the loss of Acre, the last Crusader port in the Levant, in 1291— an event which also appears to have coincided with an early attempt to reach India by circumnavigating Africa, of the Vivaldi brothers of Venice

---

[32] Cf. Ashtor, Social and Economic History, p. 265.
[33] Ibid.
[34] Savory, 'Persian Gulf', p. 18; Aubin, 'Y a-t-il eu interruption du commerce?', pp. 165-71.
[35] Quoted in Savory, 'Persian Gulf', p. 20.
[36] C. Defrémery & B. R. Sanguinetti (eds and transl.), Voyages d'Ibn Batoutah, 4 vols (Paris, 1853-58), II, p. 231.
[37] Ibid., pp. 230-1.

(whose praise was sung by Dante).[38] In contrast to the Mamluk Sultans of Cairo, the Ilkhans allowed European merchants free travel everywhere, and even let them continue to India.[39] In 1320 Venice concluded a commercial treaty with the Ilkhan, but the Genoese, Florentines and Sienese had a share in the trade in Iran as well.[40] It was a wholesale trade, in which however the lighter and more delicate spices, as well as pearls from the Gulf itself, and various silk fabrics appear to have predominated. The Genoese in particular became heavily involved in the northeast route to Central Asia and Cathay as well, via the Black Sea ports, from Kublai's time onwards. Sustained attempts were made to eliminate the Venetians from this northern route, and the latter, deprived of the Levant, instead concentrated more and more on Mamluk Egypt, which they reached via the Mediterranean islands and Alexandria. Some Genoese even attempted schemes to disrupt the India trade of Egypt altogether, in order to divert it to Hormuz and Tabriz, and accordingly, under Ilkhanid supervision, they built warships to be sent to Aden.[41] These schemes failed, but Hormuz, at the beginning of the fourteenth century, had become the great emporium of the Persian Gulf and the destination of Indian ships, by then eclipsing Baghdad and Basra entirely. The Florentine Pegolotti, in effect, in his *Manual of Trade*, of the fourth decade of the fourteenth century, does not mention Baghdad at all.[42]

At the same time, while the commercial links with the Persian Gulf declined from the late tenth and eleventh century and were then re-established in the thirteenth century, the Red Sea route via Aden continuously gained in relative as well as absolute importance under the Fatimids (969-1171) and Ayyubids (1171-1250), through the Mamluk period (1250-1390; 1390-1517), until the Portuguese led the India trade around the cape, and the Mamluks lost their independence to the Ottomans. With its coral reefs on both sides, shoals in unknown places, and irregular currents,

---

[38] R. S. Lopez, 'European Merchants in the Medieval Indies: The Evidence of Commercial Documents', *The Journal of Economic History*, 3 (1943), pp. 164-84; Ashtor, *Social and Economic History*, p. 264.

[39] Ashtor, *Social and Economic History*, p. 265.

[40] *Ibid.*, pp. 265-6.

[41] *Ibid.*, p. 266.

[42] *Ibid.*, pp. 266-7.

this route was the more perilous one, and had in the past lagged far behind, although it did not fail to attract trade from all sides. By the beginning of the Crusades, in 1096, Fatimid Egypt and Syria were already quite important distribution centres of the Indian spice trade for Europe. Via Aden, then Mocha and Jiddah, through the Red Sea, it passed to Fustāt (Old Cairo) and Alexandria, and then to the Italian merchants, who at the same time became involved in the Crusading enterprise in the Levant.[43] After the Venetians captured Constantinople in 1204, Egypt emerged as the new centre where the bulk of the Indian transit trade arrived—pepper, 'the black gold of India', and spices largely, but these have to be understood in their medieval sense, including drugs of an almost infinite variety, perfumes, and so on, with particularly pepper becoming increasingly popular in Europe as a preservative. Throughout its rise to prominence, the Red Sea links with Malabar and the Coromandel were increasingly given emphasis, although Western India, Gujarat and Sind soon regained an important share.[44] Especially important for Mamluk Egypt became the new Arab trading centre of Calicut, in Malabar, 'the pepper country'. There was also a very important trade in textiles, especially large quantities of 'cotton stuffs of every colour', which were exported to the Middle East from Gujarat, Bengal, the Panjab and Multan, Malwa, Kalinga, many parts of South India, and Sri Lanka, as is abundantly documented by Indian and Chinese authors, as also by Marco Polo.[45]

The Sultans of Egypt, unlike the Ilkhanid rulers of Iran, reserved for their own subjects direct trade with India and China, while prohibiting foreign merchants bound for India to cross their state. European merchants, if they wanted to reach the Indian Ocean, had to take long detours overland, through Asia Minor or Syria. The profits of the extremely lucrative and ever-expanding India trade fell to the Mamluk Sultans themselves and to the trading consortium of the *Kārimīs*, upon whom the Italians were completely dependent. While this arrangement brought great prosperity to Egypt, as can be seen in the architectural remains in

[43] Cf. *Al-Hind*, I, pp. 53, 56.
[44] Cf. *Al-Hind*, I, p. 308.
[45] L. Gopal, 'The Textile Industry in Early Medieval India, c. A. D. 700-1200', *Journal of the Bombay Branch of the Royal Asiatic Society*, n. s. 39-40 (1964-65), pp. 95-103.

Cairo but is also recorded in a vast literature, it made Egypt more dependent on her role as an intermediary between Europe and the Indian Ocean trading world, and this was the real reason that the Portuguese circumnavigation of Africa led to such a drastic decline of revenue for the Egyptian state.

The *Kārimī* merchants appear on the scene in the late twelfth century as a somewhat enigmatic corporation which was about to monopolize the commerce of the southern seas.[46] The very etymology of the name is obscure. In an early stage they appear to have been traders in spices which were imported from Yemen to Egypt. We hear of the *'tujjār al-kārim'*, the 'merchants of kārim', or the *'bahar al-kārim'*, the 'spices of kārim'. Fairly soon the name was applied to Muslim merchants of a variety of origins who practiced trade between India and Egypt via the harbours of Arabia. Spices were their most profitable and important business. These merchants had a wide geographical range, some travelling as far as Cathay. Many had operations in India, above all in Calicut, but also in Cambay, in Gujarat. Almost all had a basis in Aden, Yemen, already in the twelfth century, but especially after 1229, when the Rasūlids restored this port.[47] This was some years after the Mongols of Iran had attempted, by the blockage of Aden, to interrupt the commerce between Egypt and India—in an early attempt to divert it to their own dominion. In 1279 the Rasūlid Sultan took possession of Zafar, a focus of corsair activity, on the Hadramaut coast. The historian of the dynasty confirms that this procured him the esteem of the princes of India and China, as well as the land of Oman, and that the commerce of these regions began to thrive as never before.

EUROPE, BYZANTIUM AND THE MEDITERRANEAN

In the eleventh century the concept of Europe barely existed. Having no emotional or political appeal, it was used merely to distinguish the European subcontinent from the Byzantine empire and Islam, geographically an area bounded by the Atlantic Ocean

---

[46] *Al-Hind, I*, pp. 57, 92, 102; G. Wiet, 'Les marchands d'épices sous les sultans mamlouks', *Cahiers d'histoire Egyptienne*, Séries VII, Fasc. 2 (May 1955), pp. 81-147; Abu-Lughod, *Before European Hegemony*, chapter 7 (pp. 212-47).

[47] Cf. *Al-Hind, I*, p. 102; Wiet, 'Marchands d'épices', p. 88.

and the River Don or Volga or the mountains beyond Macedonia inhabited by the descendants of Gog and Magog. For the inhabitants of early medieval Europe, the Mediterranean and the Baltic had been hostile seas—one inhabited by Muslims, the other by Northmen—, while on the Dnieper route and the Danubian plain there lurked the hostile power of the Hungarian Magyars. Hemmed in on every side, the population of Europe was isolated, essentially confined to its local environment and to subsistence agriculture, with trade limited and erratic, and little or no consciousness of the wider world except as a source of life-threatening danger.

Now, however, the relationship of Latin Christendom with its neighbours was beginning to turn around. Internally, within Europe, a set of institutions was created from which arose a new stability, while, for the first time since the collapse of the Roman Empire, it was freed from outside attack. By about 1100 AD, Muslim power in Europe and the Western Mediterranean was either held in check or definitely waning. The raids of the Hungarian nomads had been brought to a stop in 955 by Otto the Great. And the Scandinavian raids, too, had ceased by the eleventh century, with the Danish and Normans settling down in Northern France, England and Ireland. It was, clearly, the end of an era in European history.

The emergence of cities was a first sign of the new sedentarization of society which was made possible and enhanced by the cessation of the invasions. In Europe, unlike the Middle East, India or China, in the eleventh to thirteenth centuries there were no Turkish conquests nor a 'Mongol storm' to alter or upset the gradually unfolding pattern, except on its eastern fringes—but even here the Mongol incursions of the thirteenth century were the last. Thus, with the migrations having come to an end, and lacking a nomadic pastoralist population of its own, Europe, from the beginning of the second millennium, enjoyed an extraordinary immunity from internal as well as external disruption. This was perhaps the most significant factor in its history, as it allowed for a linear and regular evolution of its institutions—unaffected by great and sudden physical movements of nomadic or conquering peoples.

With the gradual stabilization of Europe at the end of a long
period of invasion and migration, the state had to be created
almost from scratch. More than half a millennium after the fall
of Rome, imperial unification was not even a remote possibility,
although the memory of Rome was kept alive, first by the 'revival'
of the empire by Charlemagne, and then by the attempted revival
of Charlemagne's empire by Otto the Great in 962 AD, which however doomed Germany to a conflict between pope, emperor and
princes. The Investiture Conflict weakened the Empire, and the
victory of the Church which allowed it to assert its unique character and separateness also sharpened the concepts of secular
power. This, too, contributed to the emergence of the European
state and the foundation of a multi-state system.[48] It was due to
the spread of Christianity to unorthodox or heathen Germanic
peoples, especially in the late tenth century, that Western Europe
became a religious unit. But it never became a political unit and,
instead, was moved forward by competition among its constituent
parts.

In the eleventh to thirteenth centuries some of the essential
elements of the modern state were beginning to appear.[49] More
successful than the Empire were the kingdoms of England,
France, Sicily, and the new kingdoms of Castile and Aragon which
emerged out of reconquered Spain, and in Central Europe, those
of Poland, Hungary and Bohemia. In these incipient national
monarchies, especially England and France, the range of effective
government became greater, permanent financial and judicial
institutions were established and in the late thirteenth and early
fourteenth centuries the concept of the sovereignty of the state
appeared which dovetailed with the fundamental idea that the
state was based on law and existed to enforce law. 'By 1300', as
Strayer says, 'it was evident that the dominant political form in
Western Europe was going to be the sovereign state ... [But] it
took four to five centuries for European states to overcome their
weaknesses, to remedy their administrative deficiencies, and to
bring lukewarm loyalty up to the white heat of nationalism'.[50] The
development of a strong sense of political community, the devo-

---

[48] Cf. J. R. Strayer, *On the Medieval Origins of the Modern State* (Princeton, 1970),
pp. 15, 22-23.
[49] *Ibid.*, pp. 34 ff.
[50] *Ibid.*, p. 57.

lution of political power to corporate bodies of powerful subjects and the general spread of corporate thinking, rendered empire infeasible in Europe. In due course, the European state was to be characterized by a well-defined, continuous territory, a relatively centralized government, differentiation from other organizations, a monopoly of physical coercion within its territory, standing armies, regular taxation, mercantilist trading policies, and Roman sovereignty.

Whatever empires emerged in Europe, therefore, generally fell in the category of 'trading empires', and typically these had large overseas components. For such trading empires, as for the modern state in general, war, or raiding, remained an organic need. Warrior-merchants of Venice and Genoa, of Lübeck and Hamburg, pioneered the 'raiding-and-trading empires' of Portugal and Spain, Holland, and England.[51] The European state's growth as a military enterprise, in other words, also shaped the rise of the merchant empires, and, conversely, the expansion of long-distance trade in the European context required a highly centralized and militarized state.

The medieval expansion of European states, beginning in the eleventh century, was, at the same time, intimately linked to a general rise in the level of population—an estimated doubling in the period 1000-1250—which led not only to urbanization but also to the internal colonization of forest and waste or otherwise empty lands within Europe itself as well as substantial population transfers into newly conquered lands, heathen or infidel (like in Central and Eastern Europe, the regions beyond the Elbe and the Oder, or the Iberian plateau), and Christian (like the Normans of England, Brittany and Flanders moving into Wales, Scotland and Ireland).[52] In the German lands, some 200,000 peasants migrated during the twelfth century. Migration could be set off by overpopulation, famine, increasing seignorial exploitation, or the restrictive inheritance code which developed in Western Europe around 1000 AD. But in general, in these demographic

---

[51] Cf. T. A. Brady, Jr., 'The Rise of Merchant Empires, 1400-1700: A European Counterpoint', in: J. D. Tracy, The Political Economy of Merchant Empires: State Power and World Trade, 1350-1750 (Cambridge, 1991), pp. 117-60.

[52] Cf. J. R. S. Phillips, The Medieval Expansion of Europe (Oxford, 1988), pp. 21-22, 51; R. Bartlett, The Making of Europe: Conquest, Colonization and Cultural Change, 950-1350 (Princeton, 1993); Al-Hind, I, p. 37.

shifts, leading to migration, colonization and repopulation, can be seen the effects of greater physical security—including the absence of major outbreaks of plague—and vast agricultural and technological progress. The latter produced an increase in Europe's productivity in every branch of economic activity between the tenth and thirteenth centuries—even though some of the improvements, such as the heavy plough, field rotation, watermill and windmill, as well as others, had already been achieved by the ninth century or earlier.[53] By about 1200 AD, Islam transmitted the Indian concept of perpetual motion (first found in Bhaskara's *Siddhānta Shiromani* of about 1150) to Europe, together with Indian numerals and positional reckoning. These were significant elements that went into Europe's scientific thinking, but even more significant was that perpetual motion in thirteenth-century Europe, in contrast to India and Islam, aroused a widespread interest and led to attempts to diversify its motors and efforts to do something useful with it.[54]

If the increased population was at first siphoned off in the development of new lands, it did not take long before it was drawn into trade and commerce. By the twelfth century an urban society, the product of this commercial revival, was emerging. As mercantile centres, organized in autonomous communes and developing their own commercial and town law, the newly emerging towns and cities were disruptive of the feudal-agrarian order. Although Europe was still overwhelmingly a peasant society, for the inhabitants of the towns money not land constituted wealth. In the 'long thirteenth century', stretching from the 1160s to the 1330s, fundamental changes took place in the European economy, as money acquired a central role in its transactions. The quickening tempo of commerce transformed business practices and the attitudes to credit and usury. Commercial capitalism took off. The old feudal and manorial systems, in which labour rent had been

---

[53] L. White, Jr., 'What accelerated technological progress in the Western Middle Ages', in: A. C. Crombie (ed.), *Scientific Change* (New York, 1963); M. Mann, 'European Development: Approaching a Historical Explanation', in: J. Baechler, J. A. Hall & M. Mann (eds), *Europe and the Rise of Capitalism* (Oxford and Cambridge, Mass., 1989), pp. 6-19.

[54] L. White, Jr., 'Tibet, India, and Malaya as Sources of Western Medieval Technology', *American Historical Review*, LXV, 3 (1960), pp. 515-26; idem, 'Cultural Climates and Technological Advance in the Middle Ages', *Viator*, II (1971), pp. 171-201.

predominant, weakened under the impact of a widespread attenuation of services. And the problem of financing post-feudal war
began to be resolved.[55]

Europe proved to have a great potential for internal commerce
on account of its extraordinary ecological variety as well. Surplus
foodgrains and wines became commodities of exchange within
Europe, and the major product of the northern trade was Flanders wool. Overland commerce to the north from the Lombard
cities began to flourish in the late eleventh century, and on the
North and Baltic seas the antecedents became visible of what later was to be known as the Hanseatic League. By the thirteenth
century, the distribution of goods throughout Europe was facilitated by the growth of the great fairs.

But even more dramatic was the increase, in the eleventh to
thirteenth centuries, of Europe's trade with the East. It was the
Italian city-states which connected the internal commerce of
Europe with the long-distance trade of Byzantium, the Levant,
Egypt, Trebizond and Tabriz, Hormuz, Astrakhan and Tana, and
hence with China and the lands of the Indian Ocean. Facilitated
by the Mongol conquests, these expanding trade links and activities of the Italian merchants in the East were a direct result of
the expansion of the European economy and the increasing
demand in Europe for high-value eastern products. From the
eleventh century, and increasingly so in the twelfth, Western
Europe became an important export area, of wool and cloth above
all, but also of timber and arms among many other things, for its
eastern Mediterranean neighbours.[56] As a consequence of the
increased European productivity and its radically changed position in the world at large, the sharp distinction between the 'silver bloc' of Latin Christendom and the 'gold bloc' of its Muslim
and Byzantine neighbours was attenuated.[57] Until then, this distinction of currency domains had been a reflection of the more
basic distinction between the area of active commerce along the

---

[55] Cf. P. Spufford, *Money and its use in medieval Europe* (Cambridge, 1989), esp.
pp. 240-9.

[56] Cf. *Al-Hind, I*, p. 37.

[57] M. Lombard, 'L'or musulman du VII au XI siècle', *Annales*, II (1947), pp.
143-60; M. Bloch, 'Le problème de l'or au Moyen Age', *Annales d'histoire économique
et sociale*, V (1933), pp. 1-33; R. W. Southern, *The Making of the Middle Ages* (New
Haven and London, 1953), pp. 46-49.

caravan routes to China and the sea routes from the Indian Ocean to the Mediterranean on the one hand and the area of primitive commerce and backward communications of Western Europe on the other. In the latter area the domestic supply of gold was very small, but the supply of silver could be made good, to an extent, from indigenous sources. The scarcity of gold in Europe could only be met by a reversal of the terms of trade; in other words, by an expansion of the productivity of Europe to meet the needs of the area which had access to the gold supplies. Much of the gold that went into the new gold coinages which appeared in Genoa, Florence, Venice, and subsequently elsewhere in Europe, was, then, obtained through trade with the Byzantine empire and Egypt.[58]

The new gold coinages were a mark of European economic success. But they were of practical use only in the trade in the Mediterranean and in Western Europe. In the Muslim Middle East and the Mongol territories, and in general in Asia, silver was needed. In the Muslim Middle East, the stocks of silver had shrunk rapidly at the end of the tenth century and a 'silver famine' is in evidence down to the end of the Seljuq period.[59] This situation was suddenly transformed when vast amounts of European silver— of Freiberg and Montieri—became available, in Egypt and Syria under Saladin (1169-93) and his successors, in Iraq under An-Nasir (1180-1225) during the revived caliphate in Baghdad. By the end of the twelfth century there were at least nine mints striking silver dirhams in large quantities again in the Middle East, and over the course of the thirteenth century the continued influx of silver from Europe is reflected in the appearance of dirhams at more and more mints further into Asia. In the trade with Mongol Iraq and Iran considerable quantities of European silver continued to find their way through Christian Armenia, where it merged with a silver stock which was apparently supplied from reopened silver mines in Central Asia. The European silver, from the late twelfth to the early fourteenth century paid for an increasing volume of Middle-Eastern exports and re-exports by Italians to Europe (Syrian cotton for manufacture in Lombardy, for

---

[58] *Al-Hind, I,* pp. 36-37; Phillips, *Medieval Expansion of Europe,* p. 103.

[59] Ashtor, *Social and Economic History,* pp. 175, 216, 234, 239-48; A. M. Watson, 'Back to gold—and silver', *The Economic History Review,* 2nd series, XX (1967), pp. 1-34; Spufford, *Money,* pp. 148-152.

instance) and, in particular, the spices of India that passed through Egypt and the Levant, or Tabriz. From the Middle East, the silver, in effect, largely went on eastwards to India, or travelled overland to China.[60]

These changes in the terms of European trade coincided with the restoration of the Mediterranean in European politics or, viewed from a Muslim perspective, a shift in the political equilibrium across the Mediterranean in favour of the Franks. For the Muslims, the power of the Franks first became apparent when in the year 1085-6 the latter invaded the territories of Islam and took Toledo and other parts of the *Jazirat al-Andalus*; when, in 1091, they conquered the island of Sicily and turned their attention to the African coast; and, in 1097, when they attacked Syria. Sicily was wealthy and commanded the trade routes across the Mediterranean. Together with Southern Italy, it was Frederick II's most cherished kingdom and had a highly centralized administration which was built on Arab and Byzantine foundations, and for long maintained the most splendid court in Europe. Sicily probably never ceased to supply Africa with grain, nor did the extraction of sub-Saharan gold dust to mint the gold coinage of the Norman kingdom come to a stop. But the political frontier of Islam was pushed back here, and Sicily gradually withdrew from the cultural world of Islam. As in Sicily, in Spain, too, conquest progressed steadily, albeit in a more chequered way, and new kingdoms began to emerge among the Christian population. Toledo remained in Christian hands, and by 1095 the peninsula was roughly divided between the Spanish Christian kingdoms and the North-African Muslims. By 1204, two-thirds of Spain was reconquered. Sardinia, Corsica, Crete, Cyprus, and Malta were all within the orbit of European politics, and the Balearics were soon to fall to the King of Aragon. The repeated Crusades against the Muslims, the result of the revitalization of the Western Church and the development of the idea of Christendom—rather than 'Europe'—as a potent source of loyalty, combined with dynastic ambitions, had led to the foundation of Latin states in Greece, in Macedonia, in Antioch, Jerusalem, and even in Constantinople itself.[61] Jerusalem was retaken in 1187, but a Christian revival took place within a few

---

[60] Cf. Spufford, *Money*, p. 156.
[61] Cf. *Al-Hind*, I, p. 37.

years after the battle of Hattin. and allowed the perpetuation of the Latin states in the Levant for another century. Following Baldwin I and Amalric I in the twelfth century, and again attracted by the prospect of great wealth which would result from the control of the routes of the India trade, unsuccessful attacks were made on two occasions, in 1218-21 and 1248-50, against the Egyptian state, which since Saladin had become the most formidable adversary of the Crusaders in Syria and Palestine. The Crusades themselves proved to be a dead end. Between the accession of the Mamluk Sultan Baybars in 1260 and 1291, the Crusading ports and fortresses fell one by one. But it has been argued that the growth of long-distance trade, wherever it occurred, was of far greater importance to the economy of Western Europe than the Crusading movement, which, after all, involved relatively small numbers of people.[62] And, to the extent that it was being subjected to a new economic order, the Mediterranean was no longer an Islamic possession.[63] Instead, we see the beginning of a growing split between the two parts of the Mediterranean which were, respectively, under Christian and Muslim rule.[64]

The upsurge in Eurasian trade brought into existence commercial powers that rivalled in wealth and importance the power of kings, nobles and Church. The Western leaders aspired both to unite the Church by the submission of Constantinople to Rome and to remove the Byzantine barrier to the extension of their commercial interests in the Middle East and along the Black Sea. The Latin occupation in 1204, in effect, broke the continuity of Byzantine history. But in the thirteenth century the Italian city-states became strong enough to emancipate from the dinars of Islam and not only benefited from the fall of Byzantium but also of Chingiz Khan's unification of the Central-Asian steppes which, after an initially quite destructive impact, from about 1240 to 1340 opened a new and secure trade route from the Black Sea to China and India.

---

[62] Cf. Phillips, *Medieval Expansion of Europe*, p. 54.

[63] Cf. *Al-Hind, I*, pp. 37, 56.

[64] P. M. Holt, *The Age of the Crusades: The Near East from the Eleventh Century to 1517* (London and New York, 1986), p. 95; Southern, *Making of the Middle Ages*, pp. 11, 59, 66-67; A. C. Hess, *The Forgotten Frontier: A History of the Sixteenth-century Ibiro-African Frontier* (Chicago and London, 1978), esp. pp. 1-2, 4, 6, 9, 207.

Foremost among the Italian city-states dominating the eastern trade after 1000 AD—fusing the interests of merchants and the state— were Venice, Genoa and Pisa. In the tenth century it had been Amalfi that was regarded, by Muslim merchants as far away as Baghdad, as the pre-eminent city in Italy. Merchants from Amalfi continued to be found all over the eastern and western Mediterranean until 1073, when the city was captured by the Norman Robert Guiscard and its independence and privileged position at Constantinople came to an abrupt end. Venice, by contrast, played a relatively passive role, and its history remains obscure, before 1000 AD.[65] Up to at least the early thirteenth century, the city remained under nominal Byzantine suzerainty. In practice, from the late eleventh century onwards, when Byzantine power began to decline and its commercial hegemony in the Christian world faded, the Venetians increasingly came to take over much of the commerce of the Byzantine empire.[66] Political successes in the Adriatic and then the Crusades expanded Venetian opportunities. By the late twelfth century the Venetians had commercial bases in all strategic areas of the Byzantine East. With the extension of commercial power to the Black Sea area and to the markets of Syria and North Africa came the drive for conquest and colonization, resulting in the capture of Constantinople in 1204 during the fourth Crusade, which was conducted with Venetian naval support. In contrast to Venice, the rise of Genoa and Pisa had from the beginning been more closely connected to the Christian struggle to drive the Muslims out of the western Mediterranean. The Crusades in the Holy Land established Genoa and Pisa as serious commercial rivals of Venice in the East. As with Venice, trade followed closely on naval operations, and in the eleventh century Genoese and Pisan commercial colonies were established in Constantinople, Antioch (which was then under Byzantine rule), and Jerusalem, while Genoese trade with Alexandria was actively encouraged by the rulers of Egypt. With the diversion of much of the Muslim trade with India from the Persian Gulf to the Red Sea and Egypt, Italian involvement in the eastern Mediterranean increased. In 1215-16 Alexandria was said to

---

[65] F. C. Lane, *Venice: A Maritime Republic* (Baltimore and London, 1973), pp. 2-5.
[66] Cf. *Al-Hind, I*, p. 38.

have had three thousand Italian merchants. The Crusades were a mixed blessing for the Italians as they were prone to upset the delicate trading relationship with the Egyptian *Soldan*. The Crusader states in Syria and Palestine were involved in the Italian-led growth of trade in the twelfth and thirteenth centuries, but none of them was of vital interest to the European economy. The two great termini of the trade with the East continued to be Alexandria and Constantinople, as had been the case before the Crusades.[67] Here the spices and luxury goods of India and China could be obtained much more easily than in Beirut or Tyre. And these were also the most important overseas markets for European exports. Until well into the twelfth century, trade in Palestine and Syria was conducted with the aid of the Byzantine hyperperon and the Egyptian dinar—both gold currencies.[68] The trade with India, although small in volume, consisted of the goods which were of the highest value and most in demand in Europe, pepper and spices above all. With the new wealth available in Europe, these assumed an importance out of all proportion to their quantity.

The problem was that they originated in areas to which the Europeans did not have access. The possibility of penetrating to the Indian Ocean from the Crusader states, which in any case had always seemed limited, ceased to exist altogether with the elimination of those states in 1291. The route through Egypt was closed to Europeans at all times, and attempts to penetrate to the Red Sea via the Gulf of Aqaba were foiled, while the Genoese who sailed down the Tigris in 1290 were part of a contingent enlisted by the Ilkhanid ruler to be employed on the Indian Ocean against Egyptian trade—a scheme of which nothing came. Later attempts to blockade Egyptian trade similarly failed, and no European naval power arose in the Indian Ocean until the arrival of the Portuguese. Other routes to India and China, like that of Egypt, were closed to European merchants until the Mongols' arrival. A common starting point then became Trebizond on the southern Black Sea coast, and from there the route went to Tabriz, south to Hormuz, or to Bukhara, Samarqand, Kashgar and to China; or, via a more northerly route, from the Crimea through Central Asia.

---

[67] Cf. Phillips, *Medieval Expansion of Europe*, p. 49.
[68] *Ibid.*, p. 50.

Tabriz could also be reached from a number of points on the Mediterranean. Europeans became active on these routes even before the 1260s, when the Venetians Niccolo and Maffeo Polo undertook the journey all the way to China. Black Sea trading posts remained of vital importance, as did Tabriz, into the fourteenth century, until about half a century after Marco Polo's return to Europe, although the number of Italians that actually penetrated to India remained small.

Still, commercial expansion advanced jointly with religious propaganda. From the late twelfth century onwards, with the prospect of the Crusades becoming uncertain, attention shifted to the more distant horizon, for long a world of legend and mystery, beyond Islam.[69] The idea arose that long-forgotten groups of Christians existed between the Black Sea and China. The existence of Christians in India was already known in Europe through the legend of St. Thomas. And Western interest was stimulated by the prospect that a Christian king, Prester John, ruled over a kingdom of great wealth somewhere in the Three Indias and that his aid might bring about the final triumph of Christendom over Islam.[70] The long series of ventures into Asia in the thirteenth century aimed to discover his whereabouts and was also motivated by the possibility of evangelization, especially among the Mongols—to secure them too as allies against the Infidels. Within a few years after the return of Carpini and Rubruck, Rome was ordaining missionaries, bishops and even an archbishop for the conversion of the Partes Indiae, 'the Indies', as India, China and Malaya were collectively known.[71]

'CATHAY'

Through the Mongol connection, people in Europe also began to familiarize themselves with China. Chingiz Khan had first attacked the Chin empire of North China, taking its capital Peking in 1215, but he had returned to Central and Western Asia in the subsequent years. In 1218 he destroyed the empire of the Qara

---

[69] Cf. Southern, *Making of the Middle Ages*, pp. 71, 73.

[70] Phillips, *Medieval Expansion of Europe*, pp. 59-61, 79; see also L. N. Gumilev, *Searches for an Imaginary Kingdom* (Cambridge, 1987).

[71] Lopez, 'European Merchants in the Medieval Indies', pp. 164-5.

Khitay, in the vicinity of Lake Balkash. And it is the name of the Khitay which lived on as 'Cathay' in European medieval writings which concern themselves with China (as it is still used in the Russian language today).

Even so, the Chin territories did not come fully under Mongol control until 1234, after Chingiz Khan's death, under his first successor Ogedai. And we have to wait until the reign of the Great Khan Möngke (1251-59) before Kublai, the emperor's brother who had been granted authority over North China, was directed to undertak a campaign in Southwest China to establish a base of operations in Szechwan and Yunnan from which further assaults could be launched against the Sung dynasty of South China and against the rulers of the Southeast-Asian mainland. With the intention to implement to the full the Chingisid mandate to 'conquer every country in the world', Möngke conducted these operations while simultaneously placing Khurasan and the Transcaucasus under the jurisdiction of his brother Hülegü and ordering the latter to extend Mongol rule over Iraq and Syria, while smaller campaigns were started in 1252 into Korea and Kashmir.[72] It was left to Möngke and his successor as Great Khan, Kublai (who promptly abandoned the old Mongol capital of Karakorum for Khanbalik (Peking)), to add the Sung empire to the south of the Yangtse to the Mongol dominions. The conquest of the Southern Sung was completed in 1276 with the fall of its capital of Hangchou, and in 1279 Kublai Khan became the first emperor of the new dynasty of the Yüan, which was to rule all of China for almost a century.[73] Significantly, no previous steppe conqueror had succeeded in taking hold of all of China. The subsequent campaigns in Southeast Asia and the attempt to incorporate Japan in the empire, by contrast, were expensive failures. The Mongol army remained in essence a force of mounted archers, ill-equipped to operate in dense jungle or at sea. In the 1280s, the Burman kingdom of Pagan was disrupted. Vietnam and Champa were also invaded. But the principal beneficiaries of these interventions appear to have been the Tai, who from then on began to organ-

---

[72] For the reign of Möngke, see especially T. T. Allsen, 'Guard and Government in the Reign of the Grand Qan Möngke, 1251-59', *Harvard Journal of Asiatic Studies*, 46, 2 (1986), pp. 495-521.

[73] M. Rossabi, *Khubilai Khan: His Life and Times* (Berkeley, Los Angeles and London, 1987).

ise a series of small states which gradually filled the space formerly taken by Pagan, Angkor and Shrivijaya.

We have already seen in the preceding volume that China's
trade with many parts of South and Southeast Asia had increased
dramatically during the Sung period, from the late tenth to the
thirteenth century.[74] This tráding boom of the Sung era had led
to the first Chinese commercial settlements in Southeast Asia, fur-
thered the decline of Shrivijayan hegemony in the Archipelago,
the expansion of Cola power in South India and its projection
eastwards, the rise of numerous rival ports in Sumatra and Java,
and a general galvanization of commerce which was also felt in
the states of mainland Southeast Asia. Innumeráble, often quite
valuable, commodities had entered this eastern trade: manufactured textile fabrics (mostly of cotton, which was not manufactured in China on a large scale until the fifteenth century) from
Malabar, Gujarat, Malwa and the Coromandel, as well as Bengal;
aromatic products, perfumes, pepper, spices and drugs, the flow
of which soon became much larger than that which went to the
West, in spite of the fact that many spices, including cinnamon
and ginger, were grown in China itself; and, most valuable, jewels and semi-precious substances such as ivory, rhinoceros horn,
ebony, amber, coral, and the like.

In the earlier part of the Sung period, the government greatly encouraged the coming of foreign, largely Muslim, traffic, to
the ports of Canton and Ch'uan-chou—in which the sea-trade was
concentrated—, while the sale of many of the more expensive
trade items in the empire became a governmental monopoly. In
return, China exported silk and other textiles, porcelain, lac-
querware, iron and steel, but especially precious metals and copper cash. A large smuggling trade had developed by the middle
of the twelfth century, evading the government monopoly, which
was paid for nearly exclusively in gold, silver, iron, as well as copper cash, and the resulting drain of these metals was of such magnitude that it caused the government very serious concern, as for
years the production of precious metals had been decreasing
rapidly, while copper currency threatened to disappear entirely.[75]

---

[74] Cf. Al-Hind, I, pp. 323-34.
[75] W. W. Rockhill, 'Notes on the relations and trade of China with the Eastern Archipelago and the coast of the Indian Ocean during the fourteenth century, Part I', T'oung Pao, XV (1914), pp. 418-21.

Sung officials, from the eleventh century onwards, generally attributed the drain of metallic coinage to the sea-trade. They spoke alarmingly of the sea-going junks which were leaving Chinese ports full of cash, and warned that the currency was drained off like the waters of the sea into the *wei-lu* (the 'rear gate', a hole somewhere in the Pacific into which the waters were supposed to empty).[76] In the twelfth and thirteenth centuries they continued to call attention to the many ships which arrived 'laden with useless goods', and to point at the great amount of money which was wasted in the Muslim trade in precious stones and other 'useless things', blaming the people for their extravagance in purchasing such luxuries as perfumes, ivory, and rhinoceros horn.[77] Attempts to stem the outflow of cash, first by the issue of treasury bonds and later by paper money, appear to have been of little or no avail, and the drain of money out of the country continued, while the restrictions put on foreign seaborne trade only served to drive it more and more into irregular channels.

When in 1277 Kublai Khan established his power over the coastal provinces of southeastern and southern China he maintained the Sung organization of merchant shipping offices but in addition opened some ports to foreign trade which appear to have been closed in the later years of the Sung. Thus, the main centre of the trade remained at Ch'uan-chou, but, in an effort to boost the maritime trade further, additional merchant shipping offices were established at K'ing-yuan (Ning-po), Shanghai, Kan-fu (near Hangchou, Polo's Ganfu), while, again in continuity with Sung practice, the empire was flooded with a rapidly depreciating paper currency.[78] This meant that under the Yüan the drain of China's metallic currency was only accelerated. Prohibitions of gold and silver export were once again issued in 1296, and further attempts were made to limit private trade with South India (Malabar and the Coromandel), but again to no avail.[79] At the same time, the Superintendents of Maritime Trade, in the interest of increasing the revenue of the empire, encouraged by all available means the coming to Chinese ports of foreign traders from India and the Archipelago, 'the savage people of the south',

---

[76] *Ibid.*, p. 422.
[77] *Ibid.*, pp. 422-3.
[78] *Ibid.*, pp. 423-4.
[79] *Ibid.*, pp. 425-6.

all of whom were invariably depicted as utterly loyal in their devotion to the Great Khan, the emperor of China.[80] In 1279 and
1280, in effect, missions arrived at the Mongol court from Annam
and Maʿbar, which presented the emperor with a live elephant
and a rhinoceros, and bearing memorials from their rulers in
which the emperor was recognized as their overlord. In the case
of Maʿbar, the protection of the Mongols was sought against a
domestic rival. It was suggested by the ruler of Maʿbar that 'all
the gold, pearls and precious things of the Muslim countries come
from here, and all the Muslims come here to trade. All the kingdoms (of Southern India) will show their submissiveness if Maʿbar
has once done so ..'.[81]

Missions from South India and the Archipelago to the Mongol
court became more numerous in the 1280s, while, reversely,
envoys from Yüan China started to arrive in Kulam (Quilon) and
Seng kia-yeh (Sri Lanka) and adjacent places, and for some time
these became quite frequent too. Official relations between China and the rulers of South India, Sri Lanka and Sumatra came
to an end in 1344; but even after that date the commercial relations between these areas were continued uninterruptedly, as they
were still of considerable importance, although of much less volume and value than during the earlier days of the Yüan dynasty.[82]
Java represents a somewhat special case in terms of its relations
with Yüan China. Missions, aiming to establish friendship, went
back and forth between 1279 and 1282.[83] Then, a decade later,
in 1292, the Yüan emperor sent a large expedition to eastern Java,
allegedly consisting of a force of 20,000 soldiers and a thousand
Chinese vessels. In 1293 this Chinese-Mongol force advanced on
Majapa(h)it, the capital of the Lord of Java, who submitted in
order to secure Mongol aid against the neighbouring state of Ko-
lang (Singhosari), but turned against them as soon as Ko-lang was
defeated, forcing the troops to return to China with heavy losses.[84] Here too, commercial relations were too important for a dis-
rupture to last for long. So that, after 1322 again, at regular intervals until the downfall of the Yüan dynasty, frequent official

---

[80] *Ibid.*, pp. 429-30.
[81] *Ibid.*, p. 433.
[82] *Ibid.*, pp. 439, 443-4.
[83] *Ibid.*, p. 444.
[84] *Ibid.*, pp. 445-6.

missions were sent from Java (Majapahit). But such military intervention was unprecedented in the Archipelago, and it appears to
have had important consequences which were not just political.
A Javanese epic poem shows evidence that a type of junk 'such as
was made in the land of the Tartars' was first beginning to be
copied in Java in the 1290s.[85] Chinese copper coins, or *picis* as
they were known in Java and the Java Sea area, a currency first
found in Chinese-governed Vietnam in the Tang period and in
the Straits region from the tenth century on, now, from about
1300, appear to have driven out Javanese weights or coins entirely, while they also spread to the Philippines at about the same
time.[86]

Marco Polo, arriving in either 1274 or 1275 at Shangtu
(Xanadu), the summer palace of the Great Khan, 320 km north
of Peking, and spending the next sixteen or seventeen years in
and about China, gives a good idea of the magnitude of the Yüan
trade with India. '... The very great and noble city of Zayton
[Ch'uan-chou] ... At this city you must know is the Haven of Zayton, frequented by all the ships of India, which bring thither
spicery and all other kinds of costly wares. It is the port also that
is frequented by all the merchants of Manzi [South China], for
hither is imported the most astonishing quantity of goods and of
precious stones and pearls, and from this they are distributed all
over Manzi. And I assure you that for one shipload of pepper that
goes to Alexandria or elsewhere, destined for Christendom, there
come a hundred such, aye and more too, to this haven of Zayton; for it is one of the two greatest havens in the world for
commerce'.[87] Chinese ships sailing to India, according to Polo,
carried a much bigger cargo than Venetian ships in the Mediterranean and needed a crew of 150 to 300, while taking as much

---

[85] P.-Y. Manguin, 'Relationship and Cross-Influences between Southeast Asian
and Chinese Shipbuilding Traditions', in: *Final Report, SPAFA Consultative Workshop on Maritime Shipping and Trade Networks in Southeast Asia* (Bangkok, 1984), p.
210; A. Reid, *Southeast Asia in the Age of Commerce, 1450-1680, Volume II: Expansion
and Crisis* (New Haven and London, 1993), p. 38.

[86] Cf. Reid, *Southeast Asia*, II, pp. 95-96; idem, 'The Rise and Fall of Sino-
Javanese Shipping', in: V. J. H. Houben, H. M. J. Maier & W. Van der Molen
(eds), *Looking in Odd Mirrors: The Java Sea* (Leiden, 1992), pp. 177-211; R. S.
Wicks, *Money, Markets, and Trade in Early Southeast Asia: The Development of Indigenous Monetary Systems to AD 1400* (Ithaca, 1992).

[87] Yule, *Marco Polo*, II, pp. 234-5.

as five or six thousand baskets of pepper.[88] The revenue derived
from Zaiton's port by the Great Khan was 'very large', as the ships
coming from India paid 10% duty on all their goods.[89] The importance of Zaiton is substantiated by Chinese evidence, textual and
archaeological, which shows the city to have been in existence
from the sixth century AD and reaching its apogee under the Sung
and Yüan, when it took the form of a mercantile city-state of a
type that was to become common in the Indian Ocean in the
future.[90] Ibn Battuta, in the fourteenth century, calls it 'the largest
port in the world'. There was a number of foreign communities
living in Zaiton, by far the most important of which appears to
have been that of the Muslims, largely with Persian antecedents.
Funerary inscriptions, some of which are bi-lingual, from as early as 1171 AD, refer to the Yemen, Hamdan, al-Malaq (Turkestan),
Khalat (in Armenia), Siraf, Shiraz, Bukhara, Khwarazm, Khurasan,
Isfahan, Tabriz, and Gilan, as the places of origin of the Muslim
traders of the city.

Like spices in general, pepper was much in demand in China.
And it becomes clear from Chau Ju-kua's and other accounts that
the main source was still Malabar, although pepper by this time
was beginning to be cultivated in Sri Lanka and some parts of the
Indonesian Archipelago—this was apparently a fairly recent development, as it was not yet among the products of Shrivijaya and
was not yet mentioned by the Arab authors of the ninth and tenth
centuries. Friar Odoric (1318-30) writes that 'pepper ... grows in
a certain kingdom where I myself arrived, being called Malabar,
and it is not so plentiful in any other part of the world as it is
there'.[91] Marco Polo says that the 'kingdom of Coilum [Quilon]'
produced pepper 'in great abundance' everywhere, in addition to
other spices, and he points at merchants from China and Arabia
and the Levant who came there to trade.[92] But Quilon, in the second half of the thirteenth century, was beginning to be eclipsed
by Calicut, the focus of the Karimi traders from Cairo and Aden,

---

[88] *Ibid.*, p. 250.
[89] *Ibid.*, p. 235.
[90] Chen Dasheng and D. Lombard, 'Le role des étrangers dans le commerce de Quanzhou ("Zaitun") aux 13e et 14e siècles', in: D. Lombard and J. Aubin (eds), *Marchands et hommes d'affaires asiatiques dans l'Océan Indien et la Mer de Chine, 13e-20e siècles* (Paris, 1988), pp. 21-29.
[91] M. Komroff (ed.), *Contemporaries of Marco Polo* (New York, 1937), p. 218.
[92] Yule, *Marco Polo*, II, pp. 375-6.

who, joining forces with the Samudri Raja or 'Zamorin' and the Arab-Indian or Mappilla element on the coast, would soon triumph over their Chinese rivals.[93] And, possibly as a result of this, the focus of the Chinese pepper and spice trade seems to shift more and more to the Indonesian Archipelago. Chau Ju-kua writes of pepper growing on the hills in Sunda (West Java) and of 'a great abundance of pepper' in other parts of Java (which may, however, as an editorial note by the Chinese editor of his work explains, have been imported from Malabar).[94] Polo writes of Java as 'a very rich island, producing pepper, nutmegs, spike-nard, galingale, cubebs, and cloves, and all the precious spices that can be found in the world. It is visited by a great number of ships and merchants who buy a great range of merchandise, reaping handsome profits and rich returns. The quantity of treasure in the island is beyond all computation. And I assure you that the Great Khan has never been able to conquer it. ... It is from this island that the merchants of Zaiton and of Manzi in general have derived and continue to derive a great part of their wealth, and this is the source of most of the spice that comes into the world's markets'.[95] Although Polo does not mention it, it may well be that Banten, or 'Banten Girang', 'Banten-up-the-River', was already an important pepper port as early as the eleventh and twelfth centuries, long before the arrival of a Muslim dynasty at the beginning of the sixteenth century. Research carried out on the Banten Girang site in 1988 has shed new light on this period, indicating that Banten must already have been an important urban area, encircled by ramparts and supporting many different craftsmen, and that coins were used here, while relations were maintained with China, the Indochinese Peninsula, and, in all probability, the South-Asian subcontinent.[96]

Marco Polo, again, does not mention Sumatra as a source of pepper, but his account (which does not suggest that he had ever been there) shows that it was, at the time that the first Islamicization was occurring on the north-east coast, entirely within the

---

[93] Cf. Al-Hind, I, pp. 75-77.

[94] F. Hirth and W. W. Rockhill (transl. and annot.), Chau Ju-kua: His Work on the Chinese and Arab trade in the twelfth and thirteenth Centuries, entitled Chu-fan-chi (New York, 1966), pp. 70, 78, 83, 223 note 2.

[95] R. Latham (transl.), The Travels of Marco Polo (New York, 1987), p. 252.

[96] L. Guillot, The Sultanate of Banten (Jakarta, 1990), p. 12.

Chinese-Mongol orbit of trade relationships, although it was 'savage' by comparison with Java. He calls it 'Lesser Java', but warns his readers that this is a misleading name for the island, as it was more than 3200 km in circumference, while being ruled over by no less than eight crowned kings.[97] 'The island abounds in treasure and in costly products, including aloe wood, brazil, ebony, spikenard, and many sorts of spice that never reach our country because of the length and perils of the way but are exported to Manzi and Cathay'.[98] Polo affirms that all the people of the island professed allegiance to the Great Khan, although they did not render him tribute, 'because they are so remote that the Khan's men cannot go to them', and just passed on objects of beauty or curiosity by way of gifts.[99] Ferlec, on the northeast coast, is mentioned as one of Sumatra's eight kingdoms, which converted to Islam 'owing to contact with Saracen merchants, who continually resort here in their ships'.[100] Nearby Ferlec there was the kingdom of Basman, 'without a law, except such as prevails among brute beasts', but still professing allegiance to the Khan.[101] Polo describes Samudra-Pasai ('Sumatra'), where he claims to have spent five months, as 'wealthy' and with a 'savage population', but also professing allegiance to the Great Khan.[102] And he mentions Dagroian, the people of which were 'out-and-out savages', Lambri and Fansur, whose people were all 'idolaters' but loyal to the Khan.[103]

All of this serves to demonstrate, again, the expanded involvement of Yüan China in the southern seas. And, to conclude this chapter, it can thus be observed that the Mongol conquests—extending from the Mediterranean and Black Sea areas to the South China Sea—integrated *al-Hind* in new patterns of economic interdependence and flows of precious metals which far exceeded in volume those of the early medieval period.

---

[97] Latham, *Travels of Marco Polo*, p. 252.
[98] *Ibid.*
[99] *Ibid.*, p. 253.
[100] *Ibid.*
[101] *Ibid.*
[102] *Ibid.*, p. 254.
[103] *Ibid.*, pp. 255-6.

CHAPTER II

THE COMING OF THE TURKS

What the foregoing chapter should have shown as well is that the developments occurring in the nomadic world of Central Asia in the period under consideration are complementary to those we observe in the maritime trading world of the Indian Ocean, and not, as has been assumed so often for all periods of Indian history, mutually antagonistic. In our terms, Central Asia and the Indian Ocean are comparable in that they represent the frontier of mobile wealth, as defined in terms of people, trade goods and precious metals. The contrast that we have to draw is not one between steppe nomadism and maritime enterprise but one between this frontier of mobile wealth—extending over sea and land—and the realm of settled agriculture in India, and we have concluded that these two modes of organization organically fused in the eleventh to thirteenth centuries. This, as we have analysed, became manifest in the expanding volume of the India trade in this period, and the proliferation of trade relations between India on the one hand and the Middle East, Eurasia and China—most of which was politically controlled by the Mongols by the thirteenth century—on the other.

In India itself, the fusion of frontier and settled society occurred, principally, through the successful establishment and consolidation of political dominion by formerly nomadic people in the same period. Internally, the stereotype of immobility notwithstanding, India has always been characterized (until the present day) by a high degree of horizontal mobility and, within more restricted parameters, nomadic movement has thus been a relatively 'natural' phenomenon within the subcontinent too. Possibly this provides one of the major reasons why the merger of the organizational mode of the frontier which the Turks brought along and the rural society of the Indian plains was possible in the first place. Put differently, in India the nomadic frontier world inserted itself—not without using force—in the interstices of the world of expanding agricultural settlement, thereby connecting it more closely with the world outside. This was achieved through conquest and, while complementary to trade, we will analyse it separately in the following six chapters. On the interface of frontier and settled society, at the very point where people, goods and precious metals were cut loose, in order to be mobilized, violence was endemic, and the transition between trading and raiding became fluid. This was a pattern of state formation which can be observed, perhaps, thoughout much of Indian history. But, in order to understand better in what way the developments of the late tenth to thirteenth centuries brought about a new situation (at least in its scope), we will first, in the present chapter, review the earlier history of nomadic intervention in the Indian subcontinent. This is what the present chapter proposes to do. Then, in the five chapters that follow, we will analyse the actual conquest, its phases, its itinerary, and, finally, the ways in which conquest was turned into dominion.

Al-Bīrūnī, in his *Kitāb al-Hind*, dates the beginning of 'the days of the Turks' (*'ayyām at-turk*) from 'the time when they seized power in Ghazna under the Sāmānī dynasty, and sovereignty fell to Nāsir ad-Daula Sabuktigīn'.[1] To all appearances this was an age when linkages between the nomadic steppe populations of Central Asia and the sedentary civilizations of the Middle East, China and India crossed a critical threshold whereby a series of conquests was set off which climaxed with the 'Mongol storm' in the thirteenth century. We do not know much about the causal factors at work here. But it is evident that, on one level, these conquests were the result of an enhanced effectiveness of the social and military organization of the Central-Asian nomads which allowed them to transcend earlier tribal limitations. We also find, at this time, increasing numbers of detribalized Turks being imported into the Islamic world as military slaves. In either way, a situation arose which saw people of Turko-Mongol origin— rather than Arabs or Iranians—becoming the most important ruling elites of the Islamic Middle East and India henceforward. In the West, it was the Turks who took parts of Anatolia and Asia Minor from Byzantium, defying Latin Christianity (which responded with the Crusades), and ultimately opening the way for the establishment of Ottoman power in parts of Europe. In the East,

---

[1] Al-Bīrūnī, *Kitāb fī Taḥqīqī mā li-l-Hind* (Hyderabad, India, 1958), p. 16.

in *al-Hind*, the Turks added the Panjab and subsequently most of the Gangetic plain or *Hindūstān* to the conquests of Islam, establishing the Sultanate of Delhi in the thirteenth century.

Originally, by definition almost, the Turks (including those that conquered India) came from Central Asia. The early Arabic texts often refer to all inhabitants of the Central-Asian steppes as Turks indiscriminately. But this is an area of which the boundaries are nowhere given. The expression 'Central Asia' is vaguely understood to refer to the landlocked region between the Ukraine or Rumania and Hungary and the Chinese Wall which is completely isolated from oceanic influences and hence is largely an arid and in part cold zone.[2] In Arabic ethnological theory it was the climate which was always of overriding importance, and the Arab geographers related the Turks, as a thinly-spread people, to their homeland in the deterministic manner in which eighteenth-century European authors still wrote about the American climate as the cause of the 'impotence', the deficient physical and moral faculties, and the resulting lack of numbers of the inhabitants of the New World.[3] Like the American Indians, the Turks had a 'weak desire for intercourse' and few children because, like the climate of their habitat, their temperament was cold and moisture was prevalent in them.[4] Similar ideas about the Scythians prevailed among the ancient Greeks, although Herodotus, 'lover of barbarians', is silent about their physical characteristics. An unknown

---

[2] Definitions of Central Asia vary a great deal with different scholars, as do those of Inner Asia. A. M. Khazanov, for instance, refers to Central Asia merely as 'the area which is flanked in the north by the Aral Sea and the Kazakh steppes, in the south by the Kopet-Dagh and Hindu Kush, in the west by the Caspian Sea, and in the east by the Pamirs' ('Nomads and oases in Central Asia', in: J. A. Hall and I. C. Jarvie (eds), *Transition to Modernity: Essays on Power, Wealth and Belief* (Cambridge, 1992), p. 69). In D. Sinor (ed.), *The Cambridge History of Early Inner Asia* (Cambridge, 1990), on the other hand, there is the concept of Inner Asia, which is equated with Central Eurasia, and both of these are defined as cultural rather than geographical concepts; thus, the boundaries of this area fluctuated because the essential historical feature of Central Eurasia/Inner Asia, as Sinor sees it, is that its societies were usually characterized predominantly by pastoral nomadism rather than sedentary agriculture. In this conception, Seljuq-Turkish Anatolia in the eleventh century, for example, becomes part of Inner Asia in so far as nomads displace a Byzantine agricultural peasantry. *Mutatis mutandis*, this should apply to Iran in the thirteenth century as well.

[3] Cf. H. S. Commager and E. Giordanetti, *Was America a Mistake? An Eighteenth-Century Controversy* (New York, Evanston and London, 1967).

[4] Al-Mas'ūdī, *Murūj adh-Dhahab*, 4 vols (Paris, 1964), IV, p. 32 ff.; J. Schacht & E. Meyerhof, *The Theologus Autodidactus of Ibn-an-Nafis* (Oxford, 1968), p. 80.

writer of the fifth century BC, commonly referred to as the Pseu-
do-Hippocrates, expressed his concern about the health of the
Scythian inhabitants of the north-Pontic steppes as follows:
plagued with arthritis, their women were practically sterile, and
because of the constant cold their skin was reddish, while the life
on horseback rendered the men impotent; together with the obe-
sity of women, the constant life on horseback was the reason for
their low birth rate and this placed the Scythian nobility at an
extreme disadvantage.

Thinly populated and predominantly steppe and desert, Central Asia can be divided in two zones with the Jaxartes or Syr Darya
river and the Tien Shan mountain range as boundary: a northern one which receives sufficient rainfall to permit extensive grazing, the pastoral nomadism of the Turkish and Mongol tribes
which until recently dominated the area; and a southern, arid one
which counts many deserts (of which the Gobi and the Takla
Makan are the most formidable) and which saw the growth of an
urban oasis society and underwent more or less strong Persian
and Islamic influences along the trade routes but which did not
permit grazing and which confined agriculture to the riverain
tracts to which the nomads would only come down to raid or
trade.[5] As the southern boundary of Central Asia can be regarded the chain of mountain ranges which run from China to the
Black Sea: the Nan Shan, the Altin Tagh, the Kun Lun, the Karakorum, the Hindu-Kush, the Paropamisus, the Alborz, and the Caucasus. At the point where the Himalayas, the Karakorum and the
Hindu-Kush intersect, another diagonal chain of mountains
begins which runs from the Pamirs (the highest mountains of the
chain) to the Tien Shan (which separate the valley of the Ili and
Jungaria to the north from the Tarim basin or Kashgaria to the
south), to the Altai (the traditional *Urheimat* of the Turks), and
on to the eastern and western Sayan ranges, the mountains of
Outer Mongolia, extending up to Lake Baikal.[6] This diagonal
chain again divides Central Asia in two halves, with its central
reach lying between the Tarim basin and Transoxania, the basins
of the Oxus (Amu Darya) and Jaxartes (Syr Darya). Persian and

---

[5] Cf. G. Hambly, *Central Asia* (New York and London, 1969), pp. 2-3.
[6] *Ibid.*, pp. 2-4; K. de B. Codrington, 'A geographical introduction to the history of Central Asia', *The Geographical Journal*, CIV (1944), pp. 30-31.

Islamic influence tended to be predominant to the western side of this chain, while the eastern side was more strongly influenced by Chinese and Tibetan civilization. But nowhere in Central Asia did mountain chains prevent the movement of people, as they are rarely impassable. In fact, the history of the two plateaux to the south of the southern mountain range, those of Tibet and Iran, has always been inextricably linked to that of Central Asia. Similarly, the Indian subcontinent was closely linked to Central Asia with lines of communication running through the complex of parallel ridges and valleys between the Pamirs and Herat. The most important of these were the valleys of the Ghorband and the Upper Kunduz. The Ghorband, with its tributary the Panjshir, is part of the Indus system, while the Kunduz flows into the Oxus.

Ethnically and linguistically the steppe went through major transformations, but its characteristic way of life remained that of an extensive pastoral nomadism, to which severe constraints were set by the prevailing arid climate and which allowed only a low population density but produced a greater surplus than the nomadism of the Middle-Eastern deserts.[7] As a result, the Central-Asian nomads—which by the tenth century belonged mostly to the Altaic linguistic family—were divided in social groupings of greater structural complexity, which were more highly stratified, and disposed of greater resources, than their Middle-Eastern counterparts.[8] Supplemented by agriculture, nomadic life in Central Asia invariably alternated with a sedentary period. The steppe's staple product was the horse, which dominated all aspects of the nomads' life, and assumed the role of the dromedary in the Middle East. Camels were rare, and were even more rarely ridden, but used as beasts of burden. 'The Turk is groom and horseman', wrote Al-Jāhiz, 'and trainer and seller of horses and veterinary surgeon and rider .... [if] at the end of a Turk's life one were to number his days, it would be found that he had spent longer time sitting upon his beast than he had spent sitting upon

[7] Cf. A. M. Khazanov, 'Ecological limitations of nomadism in the Eurasian steppes and their social and cultural implications', Asian and African Studies, 24 (1990), pp. 1-15.

[8] L. Krader, 'Principles and Structures in the Organization of the Asiatic Steppe-pastoralists', Southwestern Journal of Anthropology, 11, 2 (1955), pp. 67-92; R. Patai, 'Nomadism: Middle Eastern and Central Asian', Southwestern Journal of Anthropology, 7 (1951), pp. 401-14.

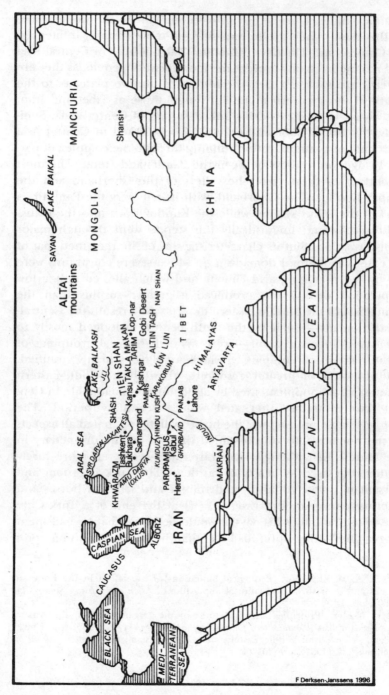

Map 1. Central Asia

F Derksen-Janssens 1996

the earth'.[9] The horse was ridden, its fermented milk (*kymish*) drunk, its meat eaten, its fat salted and smoked. Large herds of sheep, goats and cattle were also kept, while the produce from this livestock was bartered with the sedentary neighbours for grain and metal ware. This was combined with a way of life which allowed for the greatest mobility. The nomads' skill in horsemanship and archery, combined with unique battle tactics, until the sixteenth-century development of gunpowder warfare, and long after, gave them decisive superiority over peasant armies. The greatest virtue of nomadism was its capacity to produce cavalry, while sedentary societies could produce cavalry armies only at a high social, political and economic price, as they had to produce a professional soldiery which had to be maintained by landed wealth or state salaries.[10] Indeed, thanks to those factors, a structured nomadic power would be a constant menace for the sedentary states of Eurasia until early modern times.

It is important however to understand the Turkish-Mongol penetration of the Islamic world and India and China as the result of multiple interactions occurring at a specific historical conjuncture rather than as a random series of outbursts. Here we come up against an ancient but misleading tradition, running from Greek writings on the Scythians (which had early Chinese counterparts) to the medieval Central-Asian missionaries like Giovanni di Piano Carpini and William of Rubruck, which dramatizes Central Asia as a seething cauldron filled with 'barbarians'. The result has been a rather abstract and unhistorical definition of nomadism and a doctrinaire equation of Central Asia with Nomadic Man. A positive evaluation of Nomadic Man was not impossible, but more frequently he was portrayed as a beast of hell, in the monotheistic traditions often destined to act as the punishment of God.[11] Since historical interest has been focused upon an abstract idea of nomadism and a constant threat of invasion from the north, the barbarian status of the invading hordes tended to be taken for granted. Firdausi's *Shāhnāma*, for instance,

---

[9] C. T. Harley Walker, 'Jahiz of Basra to Al-Fath ibn Khaqan on the "Exploits of the Turks and the army of the Khalifate in general"', *Journal of the Royal Asiatic Society* (1915), pp. 667-8.

[10] Cf. Masson Smith, 'Turanian Nomadism', p. 60.

[11] Cf. A. M. Khazanov, 'Myths and Paradoxes of Nomadism', *Archives Européennes de Sociologie*, XXII, 1 (1981), pp. 141-53.

with its strong mythological element, assumed the Oxus to have been the dividing line between 'Īrān' and 'Tūrān'. Īrān represented urban administration; Tūrān the tribal cauldron. In fact, the ensuing frontier conflict was a creation of Iranian imperialism under Darius. In the sixth century BC the northern Scythians were still in close contact with the cities of Iran, through the Caucasus as well as the Greek ports of the southern Black Sea coast. Scythian art of the Black Sea hinterland, in its early stages, evidences strong Mesopotamian and Iranian influences. The Greek cities, with their fashions and wealth, were part of Scythian life. Scythians were an everyday sight in Athens, and, speaking broken Greek, were an object of ridicule in Aristophanes' plays. Iran's imperial history however was passed on mainly through oral tradition. And if we know little of ancient Iran, we know even less of the Iranian periphery. It can be made out, however, that it was confused with the Scythian menace only by a much later tradition.[12]

Geopolitically, it is true, Central Asia kept apart the major civilizations along its peripheries. But it also connected these by its caravan routes and, from ancient times onwards, there was co-existence with mercantile cities and constant cultural exchange: pure nomadism cannot exist.[13] In terms of intercontinental commerce and cultural sophistication the most important parts of Central Asia were *Mā warā' an-nahr* or Transoxania, between the Oxus and the Jaxartes (with its capitals at Bukhara and Samarqand in the Muslim period), Khwārazm, south of the Aral Sea, and Shāsh, beyond the Jaxartes, the country around Tashkent. It has been suggested that the increased urbanization of Khurasan and the Oxus basin in the Islamic period reduced the power of its gentry to such a degree that it almost necessitated the entrance of the Turks in the eleventh century. On the side of the nomads, the potential for state formation was greatest in Mongolia, the area along the Chinese Wall, where powerful polities of tribes could be created under united leadership by using material

---

[12] Cf. Codrington, 'Geographical Introduction'; M. A. Dandamaev and U. G. Lukonin, *The Culture and Social Institutions of Ancient Iran* (Cambridge, 1988); A. M. Khazanov, 'Les Scythes et la Civilisation Antique: Problèmes des Contacts', *Dialogues d'histoire ancienne*, 8 (Paris, 1982), pp. 8-51; R. Rolle, *The World of the Scythians* (Berkeley, Los Angeles and London, 1989).

[13] A. M. Khazanov, *Nomads and the Outside World* (Cambridge, 1984).

resources from their more civilized neighbours. These would then snowball by gathering up local forces (Turkish or otherwise) over large areas, with the result that the steppe went through a long tradition of tribal conquest and unification, which was always quickly undone in the steppe itself but which could lead to more permanent formations among settled nations.[14]

Thus, on the one hand, nomads were condemned to tribalism because of the ecological limitations of their habitat; and, although nomadic leaders could make ample use of kinship ties, to a large degree a tribe was whatever following a chief could collect.[15] On the other hand, the key to the nomads' strength was their mobility and (relative) tribal lack of differentiation: in comparison with a settled state, the nomadic tribe had little in terms of a coercive apparatus—and did not need it, as it was not bogged down by proliferating private interests.[16] The translation of policy into action was a question of individual leadership mobilizing the tribe for a common purpose, and, when this happened, it would happen fast. Typically, the steppe empire was very closely tied to the ruler's person, so that when the latter died it stood in danger of immediate collapse.[17] If the steppe ruler could make optimum use of human resources, the resulting strength was, more often than not, ephemeral. Unity would easily be lost in the steppe itself; or, when settled lands were conquered, the nomadic polity would be quickly transformed into a settled state of one type or another. Nonetheless, the aggressiveness which has often been taken as characteristic of nomads in general develops only when a combination of internal and external stimuli and opportunities is present.[18] And the character of the nomadic conquests—which were made possible by intensified commercial and cultural exchange between Central Asia and the surrounding

[14] Cf. M. G. S. Hodgson, *The Venture of Islam: Conscience and History in a World Civilization*, 3 vols (Chicago, 1974), II, pp. 396-7, 400-3; P. Crone, *Slaves on Horses: The Evolution of the Islamic Polity* (Cambridge, 1981), p. 19; Codrington,'Geographical Introduction', pp. 28-30.
[15] P. B. Golden, *An Introduction to the History of the Turkic Peoples: Ethnogenesis and State-Formation in Medieval and Early Modern Eurasia and the Middle East* (Wiesbaden, 1992), p. 4.
[16] P. Crone, 'The tribe and the State', in: J. A. Hall (ed.), *States in History* (Oxford and Cambridge, Mass., 1986), pp. 48-77.
[17] Cf. J. Fletcher, 'The Mongols: Ecological and Social Perspectives', *Harvard Journal of Asiatic Studies*, 46, 1 (1986), pp. 10-50.
[18] Khazanov, 'Myths and Paradoxes', p. 151.

sedentary civilizations, not seldom in the form of subsidies from China—changed considerably over time, from the Hiung-nu in the centuries BC to the Mongols in the thirteenth century, when nomad power reached the full capacity of its organizational potential and striking force and could be extended over both the steppe and the sedentary parts of Eurasia simultaneously.

The southward movements across the Hindu-Kush included the Bactrian Greeks, the Shākas or 'Scythians', and the Kushānas, in close succession; then followed the Hephthalites, the Turks and, finally, the Mongols and their later descendants the Mughals.[19]

In the Bactrian Greeks the nomad idea is not implicated, the origin of their settlements—between the Hindu-Kush and the Oxus—going back to the Achaemenid period. When Alexander encountered some of these first settlers, 'they had not ceased to follow the customs of their native land'; at that time, a new wave of settlers is believed to have founded a number of cities in the east, *poleis* in the political sense, or possibly just *katoikiai*, military foundations.[20] The Greek rulers of Bactria and the Iranian rulers of Parthia (Khurasan) broke away from Seleucid control in the mid-third century BC. One of them, Demetrius I, conquered Arachosia (Afghanistan) and Gedrosia (eastern Makran). Another, Demetrius II, crossed into the Panjab and the Indus valley and Cutch. Menander extended Indo-Greek power in 155-130 BC to

---

[19] Current archaeological data do not support the occurrence of any large-scale invasion(s) of Indo-Aryan (speaking) nomadic tribes into South Asia at any time in the pre- or proto-historic periods. What can be documented archaeologically is an indigenous cultural development from the pre-historic to the historic period, while the late Vedic literature, rather than pointing at a nomadic invasion into the area, probably reflects a fundamental restructuring of North-Indian society and the rise of an hereditary social elite which referred to itself as 'Aryan'.(Cf. J. G. Shaffer, 'The Indo-Aryan Invasions: Cultural Myth and Archaeological Reality', in: J. R. Lukacs (ed.), *The People of South Asia* (New York and London, 1984), pp. 77-90; G. Erdosy, 'Ethnicity in the Rigveda and its Bearing on the Question of Indo-European Origins', *South Asian Studies*, 5 (1989), pp. 35-47; C. Renfrew, 'The Origin of Indo-European Languages', *Scientific American*, (October 1989), pp. 106-14; A. Parpola, 'The coming of the Aryans to Iran and India and the cultural and ethnic identity of the Dāsas', *Studia Orientalia*, 64 (1988), pp. 195-302; C. Renfrew's review of the latter in the *Journal of the Royal Asiatic Society* (April 1991), pp. 106-9; E. Leach,'Aryan Invasions over Four Millennia', in: E. Ohnuki-Tierney, *Culture through Time: Anthropological Approaches* (Stanford, 1990), pp. 227-45.)

[20] Cf. A. K. Narain, 'The Greeks of Bactria and India', in: *The Cambridge Ancient History* , Vol. VIII (Cambridge, 1978), pp. 388-9.

the area of the Swat valley and Hazara, holding on to the Panjab as far as the Ravi river.

It was the *Shākas* who overran the Yavana kingdom of Bactria, an event which is recorded to have taken place prior to their invasion of India. *Shākas* is the Sanskrit ethnonym for the Central-Asian people who were called *Sakas* in Iran, where, as recent scholarship has proposed, the name was perhaps derived from the Iranian *sak-*, 'to go, flow, run', and hence *saka*,'running, swift, vagrant, nomadic'.[21] As in Herodotus, the Scythians are often referred to as a western branch of the Sakas, and, if not equated, the two are included in a single term, the 'Scytho-Sakas', a category of tribes which spoke either Iranian or other Indo-European dialects and which were nomads, 'horse-archers', with arrows hooked and poisonous, 'promising double death' (in Ovid's description), offering sacrifice to their gods, but not usually erecting images, altars (although they may have had portable ones, like those found in women's tombs of the Sarmatians), or temples. Archaeology revealed veritable 'pyramids of the steppes' which were royal burial-mounds, showing the horse as the supreme icon of Scythian culture and confirming Herodotus' account of royal Scythian funerary rites. From the sixth century BC there was at least a core of heavily-armoured riders in a Scythian army. Only in the easternmost ranges of their habitat did they intermarry with local Mongoloid populations. The importance of the Eurasian hinterland lay in the gold supply (*altai*; cf. Turkish *altin*, 'gold') which aroused the interest of the Greeks in the Black Sea area.

The Scythian hordes had been moving from the Central-Asian steppe to the west at an early stage, but neither India nor China nor Persia had been much affected by their movements before the third century BC. The Shāka invaders of India, however, do not appear to have come from Central Asia directly but, after an interval, from Iran, and, again, the Iranian periphery. The Puranic and Jain literature is misleading here, as it wants us to believe that the Shāka conquerors preceded the Greeks in India; it is even suggested, on this basis, that the Shākas entered India before Alexander. This is an unsubstantiated claim. The earliest reference to the Shākas is found in the *Mahābhāshya* of about 150 BC, where the commentator Patañjali mentions them as 'pure Sūdras

---

[21] Golden, *History of the Turkic Peoples*, pp. 46-49.

... who need not be excluded from the dish'.[22] This seems to indicate that by that time they had settled in India, albeit possibly in the periphery of *Āryāvarta*. Most likely, as horse-keepers they kept to the surrounding semi-arid zones less fit for cultivation. Buddhist authors and the Epics show an early awareness of the people of the area beyond the northern and northwestern frontier which they call 'Shākadvīpa'. But it seems futile to try and sift out the basic ethnic units here. If the Indians referred to the tribal confederations of this area as 'Shākas' it is sometimes because this was the oldest name which was applied to them. They are in fact often mentioned together with the 'Pahlavas' (i.e. Persians) or 'Yavanas' (i.e. Greeks). The names 'Tushāras' and 'Tukhāras' occur as well.[23] The latter were sometimes identified as the 'Yueh-chih' in Chinese and came to be known as the 'Kushānas' somewhat later, but there seems to be very little difference between them and they appear to have intermingled before they invaded India.

The movements of these tribes further to the west and south began with Chinese attempts in the third century BC to check the Hiung-nu, Wusun and Yueh-chih (all of which are sometimes identified with the Huns). The ousting of the Hiung-nu from Inner Mongolia set in motion all the other tribes in the west, while causing the dispersal of some of the sedentary people of Central Asia as well. During the Han dynasty (206 BC-220 AD), the Hiung-nu extended their power from Lake Baikal to Jehol and southward to the cities of Kansu and Shamsi, pushing out the Wusun in Lop-nar and the Yueh-chih in western Kansu. The latter then pressed hard upon the Shākas in the south who moved into Bactria and Parthia, destroying the Greek kingdom. But shortly afterwards a Wusun-Hiung-nu confederation forced the Yueh-chih to move still further south, while the Shākas are then seen moving across the Bolan Pass into the lower Indus valley, western India, Kathiawar and Ujjaynī, and as far as Mathura. The bulk of the Yueh-chih remained in the Oxus valley. But the Periplus speaks about the port of Barbarikon at the mouth of the Indus as being

---

[22] *Patañjali Vyākaraṇa Mahābhāshya*, 3 vols (Bombay, 1892), II, 4. 10.

[23] J. E. van Lohuizen-De Leeuw, *The "Scythian" Period: An Approach to the History, Art, Epigraphy and Palaeography of Northern India from the 1st Century bc to the 3d Century* AD (Leiden, 1949), pp. 44, 327, 329.

in 'Skythia', while Ptolemy speaks of Sind as 'Indoskythia'.[24]

The Shāka invasion of India, apparently, resulted from the Parthian conflict with the tribes of outer Iran. Like the Parthians themselves, the Shākas who came to India belonged to the Iranian frontier rather than 'Tūrān'. The Parthians, founding the Arsacid dynasty in 247 BC, remained under the bondage of their nomadic background but were *Philhellenic*, with Greek remaining for long one of the official languages of the state, while later they were instrumental in the revival of Iranian religion. The Shākas had helped in the foundation of the Arsacid dynasty and underwent a powerful Parthian influence, adopting an eastern Iranian dialect. Possibly a Parthian invasion of the Panjab by the King of Kings Mithradates (173-138 BC) brought the earliest Shākas across the Kabul valley, to the Panjab. Mithradates II (137-23 BC) settled large numbers of Shākas in Sistan. And he was not the first to do so. Already the inscriptions of Darius mention Sistan as 'Sakastāna'.[25] From here, as the Sanskrit-Prakrit *Kālakācārya-Kathānaka* confirms, they eventually passed on to India, via the Bolan Pass, together with some Parthian detachments.[26] Now the Indo-Greek kingdoms to the south of the Hindu-Kush were also overrun. But this final move was due to the further southward migration of the Yueh-chih and their subordinates, the later Kushānas.

Having come to India, the Shākas gradually vanished after the fourth century AD, becoming an indistinguishable element in Indian society, and leaving but traces of their Central-Asiatic background. 'Scythian' costumes, and the pointed cap or helmet, are found in the Ajanta frescoes, and many such elements survive among the peoples of western India. The royal fillet and the cylindrical crown which may have been the prototype of the later Indian *kirīṭamukuṭa*, and other pieces of jewelry (such as the torque-shaped necklace which is still found today among tribes in

---

[24] L. Casson (ed. and transl.), *The Periplus Maris Erythraei* (Princeton, 1989), pp. 74-75, 86.

[25] F. W. Thomas, 'Sakastana. Where dwelt the Sakas named by Darius and Herodotus?', *Journal of the Royal Asiatic Society* (1906), pp. 181-200, 460-4.

[26] H. Jacobi, 'Das Kālakācārya-Kathānakan', *Zeitschrift D. M. G.*, 36 (1880), pp. 247-318; Bhau Daji, 'The inroads of the Scythians into India, and the story of the Kālakāchārya', *Journal of the Bombay Branch of the Royal Asiatic Society*, IX (1873), pp. 139-46.

Rajasthan), thrones in the shape of high arm-chairs, are also due to Central-Asian nomadic influence.[27] But mostly the Shākas played the role of cultural middlemen, passing on Iranian and Roman-Hellenistic elements to the Indian subcontinent, or they were promoters of particular aspects of Indian culture which appealed to them. Certain elements from among the Shākas may have merged with clans that were later constituted as 'Rajputs'; but this should not induce us to postulate a Central-Asian origin for India's medieval Hindu rulers.[28] The Mahabharata still mentions the Shākas, like the Yavanas, as *mlecchas* who have a ruinous effect on law, religion and society. The Puranas refer to their 'strange customs'. Soon however they were suitably accommodated in brahman mythology, and the Shākas, Pahlavas and Yavanas were said to have been created by Vasishtha's cow, Kāmadhenu. Patañjali, as we have seen, mentions them as Sūdras, but not as outcasts; and Manu includes all these groups among the *kshatriya* tribes that are said to have sunk to Sūdra status due to their non-observance of the sacred rites and their indifference to brahmans (X,43-44). The Shākas were also in a peculiar way idealized; we read, in the Mahabharata again, that the *varnāshramadharma* is fully observed in *Shākadvipa*.[29] The latter view, presumably, could only develop after the Shākas had been completely assimilated within brahmanical society. It is quite possible that this happened because they took to brahmanism. 'The Shāka brahmanas who are called Magas', says the Govindpur inscription of the Shāka year 1059, 'were from Shākadvīpa and originated from the Sun-god'.[30]

The remnants of the Shāka-Parthian satrapies and the Indo-Greek kingdoms were destroyed by the Kushāna royal horde, an offshoot of the Yueh-chih of Kansu, who, in a semi-nomadic pastoral oasis context, headed a heterogeneous assortment of tribes, reported by the Chinese to have counted some one or two hundred thousand archer warriors. This happened in the first century AD, when the Kushānas set up an empire which for the first

---

[27] Cf. J. E. Van Lohuizen-De Leeuw, 'The Contribution of Foreign Nomads to the Culture of the Indian Subcontinent', in: L. S. Leshnik & G.-D. Sontheimer (eds), *Pastoralists and Nomads in South Asia* (Wiesbaden, 1975), pp. 16-29.

[28] Cf. *Al-Hind, I*, p. 200 ff.

[29] *Mhb.* VI, 21, 28.

[30] *Epigraphia Indica* (Delhi/Calcutta, 1892-), III, pp. 333-47.

time crossed the mountainous divide between Central Asia and India—extending from the Oxus to the Ganges, and to Kashmir in the north—and which lasted for about five generations. Indian sources, the Puranas, Epics and Buddhist texts, do not mention the name 'Kushanas' but speak of the same people as 'Tushāras' or 'Tukhāras'. In effect, all sources, whether Sanskrit, Chinese, Greek, or Latin, from about the second century BC to about the middle of the seventh century, identify a people called the 'Tukhāras' in the country which was later to become known as *Tukhāristān* and embraced both banks of the Oxus and was dependent on Balkh. An earlier seat of the Tukhāras had been the Upper Oxus valley, in the region of Badakhshan. Tukhāristān was the first country of Central Asia where, on the threshold of India, various nomadic groups coming from the north underwent their first sedentarization. The basis of the 'thousand cities' of this area—the ancient Bactria was not only surplus agriculture but also trade. In Tukhāristān, Buddhism was the prevalent religion from the second century BC up to the early eighth century AD, when the area was conquered by the Arabs. The Kushānas first established their power here in the old cities of the Shākas. And what happened is that in India the regional name simply occluded the dynastic. But the Tukhāras or Kushānas are also bracketed with the Shākas and Pahlavas in numerous texts. Kushāna administrative models appear to have been derived from the Achaemenids and their successors. The names of the Kushāna kings also evidence prolonged Iranian contacts. In the later Sanskrit literature the names 'Tukhāra' and 'Turushka' or 'Turk' are often confused; this is probably due to the fact that Tukhāristān passed into the hands of the western Turks in the seventh century. Kalhana's *Rājatarangini*, for instance, tells us that some of the Kushāna kings—amongst which Kanishka—had a 'Turushka' origin.[31] Nowadays, no historian considers them to be Turkish-Mongoloid or 'Hun', although there is no doubt about their Central-Asian origin. The Kushāna kings became known in particular for their promotion of Buddhism and of Buddhist and Jain iconography. Demonstrating their preference for a non-brahmanic ideology, the first Kushana king, Kujula Kadphises, had already adopted the epithet of *sacadharmathida*, 'steadfast in the

[31] M. A. Stein (ed.), *Kalhana's Rājatarangini* (Delhi, 1960), VIII, 3612.

true dharma', which was more in line with Buddhist and Ashokan conceptions than with brahmanic ones. In addition to the Buddha, they used the names and images of various other gods and goddesses, of Indian, Iranian and Greco-Roman origin, on their coins. Buddhism prospered more than any other religion under the Kushanas and, with the extension of trading contacts, it was transmitted by them farther into Central Asia. Their capital was at Purushapura, near modern Peshawar, but Mathura achieved an almost equally important status. When, after 226 AD, Ardashir established the Sasanid dynasty in Iran, Purushapura was conquered in the mid-third century and the Kushanas became subordinate to the Sasanids and their power dwindled rapidly, while in India the Guptas established their dominion.

Various petty Kushāna dynasties held on to a portion of the Indus basin and the Kabul valley or maintained themselves in Sistan under the Sasanids for some time, but generally the Central-Asian Buddhist impulse receded behind the Gupta attempt to restore a more brahmanically oriented Hindu orthodoxy. By the fifth century however the Guptas in turn were challenged by the (Chionite-) Hephthalites, i.e. the *Shveta Hūnas* or 'White Huns', another people from Central Asia which eventually destroyed the Guptas' power.[32] The Hephthalites were, possibly, an offshoot of the later Kushānas and they were allied with the Huns who conquered most of Kashgaria, Turkestan and Bactria in the fourth century. It was only the Hephthalites who broke into Northern India in the later fifth century (probably around 465), after occupying the countries south of the Hindū-Kush, including Gandhara and Zabulistan as far as the Indus. By the end of the fifth century the Panjab was subjected, together with areas of Rajasthan and Kashmir, where considerable dislocations were caused. For a time they became a great power in Northern India, and extended themselves at the same time over Soghdiana, the Oxus basin and to the north and south of the Hindū-Kush, this giving them control over the major trade routes. They continued to rule as viceroys of the Huns, at least in the fifth century, even in the areas across the Hindū-Kush. Toramāna, a White Hun leader, assumed the title of *mahārāja* while ruling from Bamiyan. After bringing Gupta rule to an end, Toramāna became the paramount ruler of

---

[32] Cf. *Al-Hind, I*, pp. 110-1, 114-5, 240.

all of Northern and Central India. His successor Mihirakula is depicted as a great destroyer, especially hostile to Buddhism, and responsible for the destruction of Bamiyan, and with Shaivite leanings. A contemporary author, Procopius, writes that 'the Hephthalites are of Hunnish stock (ounnikon men ethnos) and bear the Hunnish name; however they do not mingle with any of the Huns known to us .... They are the only ones among the Huns who have white bodies and countenances which are not ugly'.[33] And, in fact, their leadership appears to have been speaking an Indo-European language, while they may have absorbed certain Turkish elements in the sixth century. The Chinese carefully distinguished the two, but not so the Arabs, who misleadingly referred to the Hephthalites (Ar. *Hayātila*) as 'Turks'.[34] By the time they came to India they had clearly been exposed to powerful religious stimuli from Iran.

Mihirakula was finally driven from the plains into Kashmir by an Indian ruler named Yashodharma. There he died in 542 AD. Hephthalite power, and that of the Huns backing them in Bactria, was subverted in 563-8 AD by the Sasanids in alliance with the rising power of the Western Turks. The northern Hephthalite dominions were then divided up between the two of these. But the Turks encroached further, to incorporate all Hephthalite lands to the north of the Hindū-Kush. The result was that the Hephthalites retained power only in the south of Tukhāristan, in north-west Afghanistan, and in Zamīndāwar, Zābulistān and Kābul. In the latter regions they were not dislodged by the Muslims until as late as the ninth century.

India, it is now evident, has since the centuries BC been characteristically open to Central Asia and the world of the nomadic frontier. The Turks, however, were relative newcomers on the scene. The very word 'Turk' or 'Türk' appears as the name of a Central-Asian nomad people only from the sixth century AD onwards, when in 552 the 'Türk' Qaghanate was founded on the Orkhon river in Mongolia.[35] The Chinese name for the Turks was

---

[33] Procopius, *History of the Wars, Books I and II* (London and New York, 1914), I-iii, 2, 4.

[34] *Al-Hind, I*, pp. 43, 114.

[35] H. Ecsedy, 'Tribe and Tribal Society in the 6th Century Empire', *Acta Orientalia Hungarica*, 25 (1972); P. B. Golden, 'Imperial Ideology and the Sources of

Tu-kueh, which was apparently derived from *Türküt*, the Mongol plural of *Türk*. The Greeks called them *Tourkoi*, the Arabs *Atrāk* (sg. *Turk*), while in New Persian they became known as *Turkān* (sg. *Turk*). In Sanskrit they were called *Turushkāh*, while the Tibetans identified all Turks with the Qarlugh tribe, and hence referred to the Turks usually as *Gar-log*.[36] Originally, *Türk* was an ethnonym which was associated with a small tribe headed by the Ashina clan; it meant 'the strong one' and fell within the semantic range of a whole series of tribal names which connoted 'force', 'violence', 'ferociousness', and so on. These original Turks or Türkü had, in the first half of the fifth century, become vassals of another nomadic empire, that of the Juan-Juan. In the middle of the sixth century, however, the Turks destroyed the Juan-juan empire while founding their own nomad state. This state reached at its greatest extent from the Great Wall to the Oxus and even beyond, covering therefore not only the whole of Inner and Outer Mongolia but also settled areas far to the West. Intermittently it lasted up to the middle of the eighth century.

The origins of the Turks, as of other Central-Asian peoples, are obscure since the earliest tribal nomenclature is full of unresolved complexities, the evidence is scanty and fragmented and shrouded in legend.[37] Byzantine and Chinese records of the early stages of Turkish development are also exceedingly complicated and do not always supplement the earliest Turkish records in a sufficiently informative way. Just as the Greek and Roman sources used the name 'Scythian' for a variety of 'barbarian' tribes, and Byzantine sources used the name 'Turk' in the same loose way, so the Chinese used a word like *hu*, 'barbarian', or a 'tribal' name like *Hiung-nu*, for various ethnic groups (which were moreover in constant flux). The idea prevailed in the Chinese accounts that the Turkish-speaking tribes of the seventh century were all descended from the Hiung-nu, which in practice meant little more than that they were neither Chinese nor Iranian.[38] They were definitely non-

---

Political Unity amongst the Pre-Činggisid Nomads of Western Eurasia', *Archivum Eurasiae Medii Aevi*, II (1982), pp. 39-62; idem, *History of the Turkic Peoples*, pp. 115-53.

[36] Cf. H. Hoffmann, 'Die Qarluq in der Tibetaischen Literatur', *Oriens*, III, 2 (1950), pp. 190-208.

[37] G. Clauson, *Turkish and Mongolian Studies* (London, 1962), pp. 1-3, 6, 11, 14.

[38] *Ibid.*, pp. 8-9, 11.

Mongol, non-Tibetan, and unlike the Indo-European speaking tribes, while, in a more positive vein, they have been equated with the 'Huns' of the first five centuries AD. It is probable that the Hiung-nu spoke an earlier form of Turkic, although it would be anachronistic to call them 'Turks' at that early date.[39] Even in the case that the Hiung-nu were not 'Turks' or 'Turkic-speaking' (evidence to which effect exists) in the third century BC, they were evidently in close contact with Turkic-speaking people from very early on and certainly by the fourth century AD the Huns included various 'Turkish' elements.[40] The earliest Hiung-nu or Huns are described by the Chinese as a tribe 'wandering about in search of pastures and water' in the steppes running between the Manchurian forests through Inner and Outer Mongolia, to Zungaria.[41] According to the 'Discourses on Salt and Iron' (*Yen-t'ieh lun*), the Hiung-nu possessed no permanent houses, did not distinguish between men and women, dressed in animal skins, and 'eat meat raw and drink blood; they wander to meet in order to exchange goods and stay (for a while) in order to herd cattle'.[42] They may have had some contact with the Shākas in south-west Sinkiang in the early centuries AD.

It was to resist people like these that the Great Wall was built. But contact between China and the West already proceeded via the steppes and nomadic middlemen. At some stage the Indo-European speaking nomadic population of the steppes must have made room for the Huns and their allies, or, as in Sinkiang, became subordinate to the Huns.[43] Still, as late as Hellenistic and Seleucid times, the Eurasian steppes were peopled by largely Indo-European speaking tribes like the Scythians, Sarmatians, Massagetae, and possibly the Issedones. These were Firdausi's *Tūrān* of heroic times, separated by the Oxus from the civilization of Īrān. Obviously, the *Tūrān* of the *Shāhnāma* are not the historic Turks with which Firdausi anachronistically equates them.[44] In the

[39] *Ibid.*, pp. 9-11, 15-16.

[40] Cf. C. E. Bosworth and G. Clauson, 'Al-Xwārazmī on the peoples of Central Asia', in: C. E. Bosworth, *The Medieval History of Iran, Afghanistan and Central Asia* (London, 1977), XX, p. 3.

[41] Clauson, *Turkish and Mongolian Studies*, pp. 26, 28.

[42] Golden, *History of the Turkic Peoples*, p. 60.

[43] Clauson, *Turkish and Mongolian Studies*, p. 21.

[44] T. Kowalski, 'Les Turcs dans le Šāh-nāme', *Rocznik Orientalistyczny* (Cracow, 1939-49), XV, pp. 84-99.

first century of Islam the Chionite-Hephthalites were the only Indo-European speaking group still in power, offering resistance to the Arabs in northern and eastern Afghanistan. At that time most of the lands beyond Khwārazm, Transoxania and Farghana were occupied by Turkish nomads, and most of this milieu was Turkish-speaking.

Not surprisingly, the ethnonym 'Turk' soon became politicized and began to comprise tribes who were under the political and military dominance of the Qaghanate as well, while the name 'Turk' and the 'Turkish' language spread through conquest and gradual assimilation. The Qarlughs, the Oghuz, and others over a wide area all claim historic and genetic ties with the peoples of the Turk Qaghanate. Other peoples, who may not have had or even claimed such ties to the 'original' Turk tribe, could still use the name to make a political statement. All this means, in fact, is that the word had an independent tradition in the Turkic world which was not necessarily associated with Islamic usage. But the Muslims greatly aided the spread of the term 'Turk' to the non-Turkic world.

The people from whom the Turks asserted their independence, the Juan-juan, had themselves risen in the second half of the fourth century and it had been their ruler who proclaimed himself *Qaghan* in 402 AD—apparently the first use of the title which the Turks took over.[45] The Juan-juan empire covered the territory between the watersheds of the Orkhon and Selenga rivers, the northern edge of the Tien Shan mountains, and the Ordos steppe.[46] Soon they were fighting the Wei for the control of Sinkiang. Their ethnic and linguistic affiliation is doubtful. The Turks, by contrast, living primarily in the Altai mountain range, in the fifth and early sixth century are known to have been tributary to the Juan-juan and to have served as their 'blacksmith slaves' and ironworkers.[47] Chinese as well as Greek records emphasize the importance of the early Turks' metallurgical industry.

---

[45] Clauson, *Turkish and Mongolian Studies*, pp. 26, 28.

[46] L. Kwanten, *Imperial Nomads: A History of Central Asia, 500-1500* (Philadelphia, 1979), p. 18.

[47] *Ibid.*, pp. 20, 32; C. I. Beckwith, 'Aspects of the Early History of the Central Asian Guard Corps in Islam', *Archivum Eurasiae Medii Aevi*, IV (1984), p. 32; Golden, 'Imperial Ideology', pp. 42-43; Codrington, 'Geographical Introduction', p. 86.

'Iron gates' were to mark the borders of the Turkish empire, and swords passed as currency. Connected with the belief in the magical power of fire, the association with smithing clearly had 'shamanic' connotations, with the smith ranking immediately below the shaman himself.

From the year 545 AD the Turks began to rid themselves of Juan-juan overlordship. A year later their leader was in a position to demand a Juan-juan princess in marriage. Ten years later the Turks had defeated the Juan-juan decisively. Recognition by the Western Wei was acquired soon. Bumin became the Turks' first emperor, ruling from the Great Wall to the borders of Iran, as well as in the far north. A victory over the Hephthalites followed, and control over the entire steppe can now be said, for the first time, to have been in the hands of a single ethnic group—in the sense of 'a named human population with shared ancestry myths, histories and cultures, having an association with a specific territory and a sense of solidarity'.[48] The Turks were, apart from blacksmiths, pastoral nomads, with each household having definite grazing rights, armed with bows, singing arrows, coats of chainmail, and the long sword. With their victory over the Juan-juan, the Turks obtained control over the Central-Asian trade as well, including the silk trade between China and Byzantium. Due to the Turkish unification of the steppe, Central-Asian trade received a great impulse as the region became again more closely attached to the peripheral civilizations.[49] But as far as can be made out, the Turks had already been traders in silk fabrics and floss-silk for wadding at an earlier stage; Turkish society apparently has never been purely nomadic and included an urban element —not the first in the history of the steppe.[50] Turkish relations with the Chinese on one side and with the Byzantines on the other had always been determined by their commercial interests. While it is not clear yet how the Turks operated the silk trade, it has been con-

---

[48] This definition of an ethnic community is proposed by A.D. Smith, *The Ethnic Origins of Nations* (Oxford, 1986), p. 32, and adopted for the Turks by Golden, *History of the Turkic Peoples*, pp. 1-2. Such a community does not need to be able to refer to a common biological descent; in fact, they are always 'polyethnic' and political in character, with members who were born into it as well as others who joined it, a community of 'descent through tradition' and through recognition of the political leadership of a charismatic clan.

[49] Cf. *Al-Hind, I*, p. 43.

[50] Kwanten, *Imperial Nomads*, pp. 32, 39-40; Codrington, 'Geographical Introduction', p. 86.

cluded that their empire was the outcome of the cooperation between the charismatic nomadic clans and capital-providing international merchants.[51] Beyond doubt the early Turks at times were clothed in silk, unlike the skin- and wool-wearing barbarians which the Chinese annals point out.

Furthermore, if Turkish society was nomadic and mercantile, it was not held together by territory but rather by kinship relations and religio-shamanic cult elements. The political and social structure, generated by common residence in a winter quarter, was that of a precarious tribal union headed by the charismatic Ashina clan. The tribes, composed of clans, were organized into *boduns*; political power over the *bodun* was expressed by the term *el/il*, a 'polity' mandated by heaven. At the top of the tribal union stood the Qaghan, the leader who established the *törü*, the tribal law. Of the greatest importance was the biological association of the charismatic ruling clan with the tribal totem.[52] The ruling clan's charisma was heavenly ordained and as such would override election. The belief in the celestial origin of authority linked up with an ideal of world domination that acquired a prominent and historical form among the sixth-century Turks but existed before as part of the shamanic creed.[53] The related idea that domination was an exclusive right of the Turks was later passed on to the Uyghurs and Mongols, and it seemed to receive confirmation by Islam.[54] Much of this political and cultural apparatus the Turks inherited from their predecessors in Mongolia rather than from China. In fact, the Chinese cult may have Altaic origins, rather than the reverse.[55] But the cult of heavenly ordained rule was not peculiar to the Altaic world; even less were the principle of legitimation by descent and of charisma residing in royal blood which allowed individual members of the clan to be elevated to the Qaghanate. What is peculiar about the Turkish ceremony of qaghanal investiture is that, like blacksmithing, it had a specific shamanic context.[56] The first Chinese account of the origins of

---

[51] Cf. O. Pritsak, *The Origin of Rus'*, I (Cambridge, Mass., 1981), pp. 15-16.

[52] Golden, 'Imperial Ideology', pp. 44, 49-52.

[53] *Ibid.*, pp. 42-45; Ecsedy, 'Tribe and Tribal Society'.

[54] O. Turan, 'The Ideal of World Domination among the medieval Turks', *Studia Islamica*, IV (1957), pp. 76-90.

[55] Cf. Golden, 'Imperial Ideology', p. 48.

[56] *Ibid.*, pp. 46-47.

the Turks (itself derived from Turkish materials) is already full of shamanic symbolism, relating to the totem ancestor and the wolf ethnogenetic legend. The wolf re-appeared in the military standards of the Turks. Ancestor worship was practiced too, and the principal deities—the objects of cults presided over by the Qaghan—were heaven and sun.[57] Being shamanic, however, did not preclude the Turks from being literate. With the creation of the Turkish empire, in effect, the steppe people began to document their own history. Early eighth-century stone inscriptions survived, in 'Runic Turkic', from the Orkhon region, the seat of Turkish imperial power; these became known as the 'Orkhon inscriptions'. The Turks were also susceptible to Buddhist propaganda.[58] Initially this meant Buddhism in its Chinese form; later, when the Turks expanded into the Tarim basin, Buddhism in a form closer to the Indian variety was assimilated.

The main difference between the Turkish empire and earlier nomadic empires undoubtedly lay in its more structured and complex political system. While the ultimate leadership was in the hands of the *Qaghan* founder of the empire (residing near the Otuken mountain in the Altai chain, the place of ancestor-worship), there was a plethora of administrative-military posts with titles of diverse origins associated with the Qaghanate.[59] Another feature of Turkish administration, elements of which were taken over by most later nomadic states, was the bipartite principle of rule or a form of dual kingship. There was a secondary leader, the *Yabghu*, who can be traced to ancient times among the Hiungnu. The *Yabghu*'s domains were always the western parts of the empire, and in theory he was always the brother of the *Qaghan*. But the spheres of action between the *qaghan* and the *yabghu* were not clearly demarcated. Both positions were in principle hereditary but needed confirmation by the tribal aristocracy. There was, also, no clearly defined command structure, even though the arrangement of Turkish military forces in multiples of ten is already in evidence in these earliest phases of recorded Turkish history.[60]

---

[57] Ecsedy, 'Tribe and Tribal Society'.
[58] H.-J. Klimkeit, 'Buddhism in Turkish Central Asia', *Numen*, XXXVII, 1 (1990), pp. 53-69.
[59] Golden, 'Imperial Ideology', p. 52.
[60] The decimal system is not a unique feature of the Turks; it was, for instance,

Following the conquests in central and western Eurasia and as a result of the bipartite principle of rule, the First Turkish Empire broke in two parts in the year 583 AD, the Western and Eastern (or Northern) Turks. Of these the former dominated politically and militarily under the Yabghu Qaghan, while the latter formally held the higher position under the supreme Qaghan. For the next half century the Chinese exploited their rivalry as much as possible, until in 629-30 AD the Eastern Turks suffered a major defeat from the Tang, and the Qaghan, together with some of the most prominent members of the Ashina clan, was taken to the imperial capital. The Chinese now became the supreme sovereigns of the Turks, of whom a great number became officers in the Imperial Guards. Rising to the top of the military institution, Turks were instrumental in conquering East Turkestan for the Tang.[61] The Ashina clan is found among the Chinese military and governing bodies until as late as the second half of the eighth century. But the eastern dynasty was again set free from direct Chinese control in 682 until its final collapse in 742, the latter being the period which produced the Orkhon inscriptions. The Western Qaghanate lingered on until 766, after suffering several setbacks resulting in the establishment of Chinese control in eastern Turkestan and the Oxus valley to the south of the Hindū-Kush.[62] The control of these areas was then also beginning to be challenged by the Arabs and the Tibetans. Hiuen Tsang passed through the domains of the Khan, the 'Sheh-hu Khan' (probably a relative of the Yabghu), of the Western Turks in 630 AD; making little mention of Turkish Buddhism, he calls the Turks 'fire-worshippers' and remarks on the fine bearing of the Khan 'although he was a frontier ruler'.[63] The Second Turkish Empire, in effect, was deeply rooted in urban civilization, the joint enterprise of the Ashina clan and the Soghdians, with large numbers of Chinese bureaucrats being involved as well.[64] The Western Turks, ruling through scions of the royal clan or older

---

found under the Sasanids (cf. H. Temporini (ed.), *Aufstieg und Niedergang der römischen Welt* (Berlin and New York, 1872), p. 281 ff).

[61] Beckwith, 'Central Asian Guard Corps', pp. 32-33.

[62] Cf. *Al-Hind*, I, p. 115.

[63] T. Watters, *On Yuan Chwang's Travels in India, 629-645 AD*, 2 vols (London, 1904-5), I, p. 74 ff.

[64] Pritsak, *Origin of Rus'*, p. 16.

Hephthalite, Kushana and Iranian subregimes, controlled the territory between the Syr and the Amu with the entrepots of the Chinese trade, Samarqand, Bukhara, and others.[65]

This symbiosis with Soghdian and other trading communities along the silk route was perpetuated by another Turkic tribe, the Uyghurs, those 'professors of culture' (as Grousset called them) at the crossroads of the Chinese and Iranian worlds, who crushed the Türkü in 742 AD.[66] Uyghur hegemony over the eastern steppe was then recognized by the Chinese in 745; an Uyghur state under a Qaghan lasted until 840 (with some offshoots surviving into the thirteenth century). The claim to dominion over large parts or the whole of the Turko-nomadic world continued to rest on descent from or connection with the Ashina clan. The Uyghur state too, to some extent, had a mixed nomadic-sedentary structure, and in course of time became increasingly more sedentarized while adopting Manichaeism and, later, Buddhism. They were the first Central-Asian people to erect walled cities. Otherwise, up to 840, they maintained the structural forms of the Turk Qaghanate (including the system of decimal military-administrative divisions).

Iran and Transoxania had thus been familiar with the Turks— and even more with other peoples of Central-Asian origin—long before the appearance of the Ghaznavids and Seljuqs. In the Iranian-speaking parts of Central Asia, in Transoxania, Farghāna and Khwārazm, and across the Dihistān steppe towards the Caspian coastlands, the penetration by the Turks had begun earlier than in the Indianized parts of Afghanistan. The Iranian rulers of Soghdiana who opposed the Arabs in the seventh and early eighth century were aided by Turks—who were probably mercenaries and guards from the steppes rather than indigenized settlers.[67] The

---

[65] Al-Hind, I, p. 43.

[66] Enzyklopaedia des Islams, IV (Leiden and Leipzig, 1934), p. 971; Kwanten, Imperial Nomads, pp. 49-56; Golden, 'Imperial Ideology', pp. 53-56; idem, History of the Turkic Peoples, pp. 155-76.

[67] Cf. Al-Hind, I, pp. 110-11, 115; R. N. Frye and A. M. Sayili, 'Turks in the Middle East before the Saljuqs', Journal of the American Oriental Society, LXIII (1943), p. 196; C. E. Bosworth, 'Barbarian Incursions: The Coming of the Turks into the Islamic World', in: The Medieval History of Iran, Afghanistan and Central Asia, XXIII, p. 3.

most crucial date in the Turkish encounter with Islam is perhaps 751 AD, the year of the battle of the Talas river, when an alliance of Arabs, Tibetans and Qarluq Turks achieved a victory over the Tang Chinese. From that date onwards Turkish peoples began to assimilate within the sedentary Muslim world in considerable numbers. The Qarlugh Turks or 'Qarakhanids' (who may still have been claiming Ashina descent) were the first to undergo almost complete sedentarization, after moving into Farghāna, an area which in the ninth century was gradually becoming Islamicized. The Qarluqs established capitals at Kashgar in Sinkiang and Balasaghun in the valley of the Chu river. Their rulers converted to Islam after the middle of the tenth century, and in 961 AD this was followed by the conversion of some 100,000 Turkish 'tents' in the area.

The extent of Turkish infiltration into the Muslim world in the first three centuries is however disputed, partly due to a peculiarity of the source material in Arabic. We have references in Arabic to the 'land of the Turks' from the late Jāhilīya, where it signifies the end of the known world. More precise and reliable knowledge emerged among the Muslims by the ninth century, when the Samanids extended the frontier along the Syr Darya and Turks began to enter the caliphate as military slaves. But the use of the word 'Turk' still remained vague. For instance, the Hephthalite rulers of Kabul, Bādghīs, Tukhāristān, and Bactria were referred to as 'Turks' even though they in fact spoke an Indo-European language and merely accommodated some Turkish elements.[68] The Arabs, at times, applied the term to all their opponents on the eastern frontier. By the second half of the ninth and the tenth century, Muslim authors began to mention specific groups among the Turks: the Türgish, Kīmāk, Qarluq, Qipchaq, Toghuzghuzz, Ghuzz, Pecheneg, Khīrkhīz, Khallukh, and others, with the 'Uyghurkhān' holding a supreme position among them.[69] Turks who maintained a nomadic existence solely, outside the borders of Islam, prominent among which were the Oghuz and later the Qipchaq, were also often described in Persian as Turk-mān, 'Turk-like'. Even then, the term 'Turk' was still applied in a loose sense, and we find for instance the Magyars (Majgharī) or the Rūs

---

[68] Cf. Al-Hind, I, p. 115.
[69] Ibid., p. 226; Minorsky, Hudūd al-'ālam, esp. pp. 34, 94-101.

described as Turks by the same Muslim writers.[70] And this is a fact which cannot be explained by assuming that these were people who were under the rule of the Turks, or, in other words, by assuming that the word is always used as a political-territorial ethnonym.[71] Tibetans are also frequently confused with Turks, for instance by Al-Bīrūnī, who speaks of 'Turks from Tibet' and 'Turks of Tibetan origin';[72] or by Al-Masʿūdī who speaks of settled and nomad 'Tubbat Turks' near Badakhshan, south of Farghāna, and north of Kabul;[73] or, again, by Juzjani, in the mid-thirteenth century, when he refers to the people of 'the open country of Tibet (Tibbat)' and of the mountains between Tibet and Bengal as 'Turks' and 'people with Turkish features' respectively.[74]

Poorly documented as it is, such loose application of the term makes the early infiltration of the Turks into the Gurgān-Dihistān area, Khurasan, Khwārazm, Transoxania, and the frontier areas of al-Hind, difficult to analyse. Generally the Turkicization of these areas was not yet profound. Some Turkish settlers in Khurasan, as Al-Jāhiz points out, may have become very much 'like' the original inhabitants.[75] There already were non-nomadic Turks in Khurasan and Transoxania at the time of the Arab conquest. A variety of sources points at groups of Turks on both sides of the Oxus before the seventh century. There were 'Turkish towns' in Soghd and there were, by the tenth century, Turks in the valleys of Tukhāristān, Badakhshan, in and to the south of Farghāna, to the north of Kabul, and in Shash and vicinity; 'Khalaj' but also Ghuzz Turks were found in the regions of Balkh, Sistan, Bust, and Bistam. It can be made out, then, that Turks were an important but not predominant element, often as town- and village-dwellers, between the mountains of Khurasan, the Jaxartes river and al-Hind, in pre-Seljuq and pre-Ghaznavid times. But the adoption of the term 'Turkestān' for Mā warāʾ an-nahr as a whole, and the term 'Tājīk' for the whole of the sedentary, largely Iranian-speak-

---

[70] Minorsky, Hudūd al-ʿālam, p. 456, note 2.
[71] As does Beckwith, 'Central Asian Guard Corps', pp. 31-32.
[72] Kitāb al-Hind, pp. 165, 348; Al-Hind, I, p. 234.
[73] Cf. Frye and Sayili, 'Turks in the Middle East', p. 199.
[74] TN, pp. 151-2.
[75] Cf. Bosworth, 'Coming of the Turks', p. 3; Frye and Sayili, 'Turks in the Middle East', pp. 194-207.

ing, Muslim population of Iran and Central Asia, by the Turks, dates from the eleventh century.[76]

We have already seen that the Islamic geographical literature of the tenth century also points to the pastoral nomads of the Indianized areas of what is now eastern Afghanistan, the plateaux of Kabul and Bust, as 'Khalaj Turks'.[77] Najīb Bakrān, in a geographical treatise of the early thirteenth century, attributed their relatively dark complexion to the heat of the area around Ghazna, and calls them Turks too.[78] But here, again, it is by no means sure that we are dealing with Turks. More likely, they are the remains of earlier Shāka, Kushāna and Hephthalite invasions, as can probably be said about the 2000 'Ghuzz Turk' slaves that the Arab governors of Khurasan stipulated as annual tribute from the Kābul Shāh. These 'Khalaj Turks' from Ghazna were to be found in the Ghaznavid armies, and later also served the Ghurids, as well as the Slave Kings, finally producing a ruling dynasty of their own around 1290 AD, the Khalajī dynasty of Delhi. Their name derives from *Khalaj*, which is the land on both sides of the river Helmand in Afghanistan. A variety of nomadic tribes had occupied *Khalaj* from very remote times. While the Arab geographers and later authors call them 'Turks' or say that their 'customs and dress' are like those of the Turks,[79] a fourteenth-century author, Barani, again distinguishes them from Turks.[80] Later they were assimilated within the tribal category of Ghilzai. And, under such circumstances, it is perhaps best to leave the question of their ethnogenesis open.

A second, better documented, process through which Turks entered Islam, as already indicated in the preceding volume, was the recruitment of military slaves.[81] It has been suggested by David Ayalon that the early recruitment of *mamlūks* from Central Asia in a substantial measure prepared the way for the later Turkish non-mamlūk tribesmen which followed them, the Seljuqs in par-

---

[76] L. Krader, *Peoples of Central Asia* (Bloomington, 1966), p. 54; V. V. Barthold, *Zwölf Vorlesungen über die Geschichte der Turken Mittelasiens* (Berlin, 1935), p. 42.
[77] *Al-Hind*, I, pp. 115-6.
[78] Minorsky, *Hudūd al-'ālam*, p. 348; idem, 'The Turkish dialect of the Khalaj', *Bulletin of the School of African and Oriental Studies*, X, 2 (1940), pp. 426-34; A. Ahmad, 'The Early Turkish Nucleus in India', *Turcica*, IX (1977), pp. 103-6.
[79] See, for instance, *TFM*, p. 47.
[80] *TFS*, pp. 175-6.
[81] Cf. *Al-Hind*, I, pp. 13-16.

ticular, but also the Mongols.[82] Since the *mamlūks* penetrated deep into the societies of the Middle East several centuries before the Seljuqs and the nomadic tribes, the latter found, as the sources stress again and again, people 'of the same stock' (*min jins wāḥid*) with whom key positions of power were to be shared. The Mongols were also regarded in numerous Muslim texts as 'Turks' (*Atrāk*), or as belonging to the same stock or ethnicity (*jins*) or having very close relations with the Turks, and these bonds were regarded as generating strong feelings of ethnic affinity, solidarity or sympathy. All Turks moreover—whether mamlūks, Seljuqs, Turkmāns or, soon enough, Mongols—could easily be Islamicized; as it turned out, more easily in general than people from the other areas beyond the Islamic frontier (Africa, Christendom, India). In this way the arrival of the mamlūks, the Seljuq Turks and the Mongols may be studied as three separate stages or aspects of a single process, even without denying that the nomad invasions could be accompanied with great devastation. Meanwhile, we should again stress the uniquely Islamic/Middle-Eastern background of the *mamlūk* institution and the complex set of socio-political, economic, and military factors of early Islam which led to its rise in the Middle East rather than being imported from Central Asia ready-made.[83] If the institution became fully-fledged in the ninth century, the trade in Turkish *mamlūks* (building on raiding but more commonly on peaceful exchange with tribes engaging in internecine warfare themselves) reached a peak under the Samanids in the tenth century and then assumed its central position across the length and breadth of Islamdom in the eleventh century. The migration of Turkish people southward thus became a constant and disproportionately important factor, even though the numbers of mamlūks may have been relatively small.

Not before the eleventh century, however, with the establishment of the Qarakhanids in Transoxania and the Seljuqs in Iran, Anatolia and the Fertile Crescent, do the movements of nomadic Turks into the Islamic Middle East become truly significant. It was the collapse of the Samanids under pressure of the Qarakhanids

---

[82] 'The European-Asiatic Steppe: A Major Reservoir of Power for the Islamic World', in: *The Mamlūk Military Society* (London, 1979), VIII, pp. 48-51; 'Aspects of the Mamlūk Phenomenon', *ibid.*, Xa, pp. 204-12; 'Preliminary Remarks on the Mamlūk Military Institution in Islam', *ibid.*, IX, p. 57.

[83] Cf. *Al-Hind, I*, p. 14; and see Chapter VI.

and the Ghaznavids which ultimately opened the gates to pastoral Turkish penetration. By origin the Ghaznavids were a slave dynasty which began as governors of the Samanid territories in the eastern and southern parts of Afghanistan in the last quarter of the tenth century.[84] The establishment and expansion of the Ghaznavid Sultanate in Afghanistan, eastern Iran and parts of northwestern India from the end of the same century onwards signified the first major breakthrough of Turkish power in Islam, and it helped, again, to prepare the way for the Seljuqs. Under the latter dynasty, Turkish horsemen, fully exploiting the advantage of mobility, extended their hegemony with great ease. But even now, as we have seen, the incoming groups of pastoralists could not have been very large.[85] Rather, it must have been the cumulative effect of several centuries of Turkish immigration, as military slaves, settlers and pastoralists, which began to change the ethnic composition of the Middle East, or the northern parts of it, while the major part of the process did not occur until the Mongols arrived .[86] Very few of the Seljuqs appear to have made it into India, although there are such isolated cases as that of, for example, the rajas and wazirs of Baltistan—possessing a different cast of physical features from their Balti subjects (light complexion and light eyes, and a hooked nose, among others)—, who claim descent from Seljuq Turks that settled in Baltistan just before their more ambitious fellow tribesmen pushed west into Iran and Anatolia.[87] There do not appear to have been any Turkish invasions on the North-Western Frontier or elsewhere, and we do not hear at all of Muslim Turks in *al-Hind*, before the late tenth and eleventh century. If we could identify (in the preceding sections of this chapter) various groups from Central Asia which migrated into the subcontinent in earlier times, these were not Turkish. In addition, from the seventh century on there had been Tibetan and other Mongoloid invaders coming from the north, threatening Kanauj, but not establishing permanent dominion.[88] In the early eighth century the Kashmir king Lalitāditya

---

[84] *Al-Hind, I*, p. 21.
[85] Cf. Chapter I.
[86] Cf. Bosworth, 'Barbarian Incursions', pp. 10-11.
[87] Dervla Murphy, *Where the Indus is Young. A Winter in Baltistan* (London, 1977), p. 185.
[88] *Al-Hind, I*, pp. 234, 241, 258-9.

Muktāpidā was repeatedly confronted with Tibetan military intru-
sion. Between the eighth and eleventh centuries the Tibetans successfully encroached upon the countries to the north of Kashmir,
reducing the Indo-Iranian zone of cultural and political dominion, while incorporating Baltistan, Ladakh and parts of Gilgit into
the Tibetan-speaking area. The Tibetans also obtained hegemony
over Nepal from the early seventh to almost the end of the ninth
century. Mongoloid people that we cannot clearly identify had
been present in Assam (*Kāmarūpa, Prāgjyotisha*), and two dynasties of Mongoloid origin had successively ruled here from the
fourth to the ninth century, while Mongoloid incursions occurred
even later than that. None of these were Turks either, even though
Al-Bīrūnī, as indicated, repeatedly refers to Tibetans on the northern frontier of *al-Hind* by that name.[89] And then there are clans
among the Sinhar and Bandiji tribes of Las Bela in Baluchistan
which are known as *Tūrānīs* and display some of the Turkish organizational heritage in their tribal structure, with Turkish terms
(e.g. *tūmān, bolak, el*, and *ulus*) and Turkish names (e.g. *Sanjar*)
occurring as well; while some ethnographers speculated that these
groups date back to pre-Islamic immigration in the area, others
have denied that there is any evidence for this.[90]

The first real evidence of Turks in *al-Hind* comes from Kashmir
during Lālitāditya Muktāpidā's reign. This king, while extending
his power into Central Asia, is recorded to have recruited soldiers
from the western Central-Asian highlands and Tukhāristān.[91]
Again, in 747 AD a Tibetan invasion of Kashmir caused Lalitāditya
to return to the Himalayas and then enter the Tarim basin, cross
the Takla Makan, and conquer Kuchā and Turfān. Tukhāristān,
including Badakhshan and the Upper Oxus tracts which were
inhabited by Turkish tribes, were also invaded again.[92] Al-Bīrūnī
has recorded that the people of Kashmir celebrated an annual
festival to commemorate the victory of their king Muttai
[Muktāpidā] over the Turks.[93] The Rājataranginī seems to locate
these Turks between the Tukhāras and Bhauttas.[94] Lalitāditya

[89] Cf. p. 94.
[90] *Baluchistan District Gazetteer, VIII, Las Bela* (Allahabad, 1907), p. 44; M. Longworth-Dames, *The Baloch Race* (London, 1904), p. 13.
[91] Stein, *Rājataranginī*, IV, 131-64; *Al-Hind, I*, pp. 239, 243.
[92] *Al-Hind, I*, p. 244.
[93] Al-Bīrūnī, *Kitāb al-Hind*, p. 486.
[94] IV, 167.

made the conquered rulers—to indicate their defeat—adopt various characteristic marks, and the Turushkas, by his command, had to carry their arms at their back and shave half their head.[95]

The *Rājatarangini* also mentions the *Tuhkhārāh* (sic) as a people of the northern region defeated by Lalitāditya.[96] These are the *Tukhārās* of other Sanskrit authors, the *Tocharoi* or *Tochari* of the Greeks and Romans, considered to be a branch of the Yuehchih which gave its name to the Upper Oxus valley, including Balkh and Badakhshan. Lalitāditya's minister Cankuna (probably Chinese *Tsiang-kiun*, 'general') came from the Tukhāra country—the Tukhāristān of the early Muslim authors—and this establishes the likelihood that he was Turkish, as by this time the region was inhabited by Turks. A stūpa is attributed to Cankuna, at Parihāsapura,[97] and the foundation of two vihāras with gold statues and a caitya, one of which was observed by the Chinese Buddhist pilgrim Wu-k'ung in the period 759-63 AD.[98] In payment for his services, Cankuna merely asked for a Buddha statue to be carried from Magadha on the back of an elephant, to be placed on one of his vihāras—where Kalhana could still observe it four centuries later.

Wu-k'ung noted numerous other Turkish pious endowments in Kashmir (Kia-che-mi-lo) which point at an entire Turkish dominion in the bordering regions: *vihāras* (wei-houo-lo) or 'monasteries' founded by the son of the king of the *Tu-kueh* or the wife of the Turkish Khan. The same situation prevailed in Gandhara (K'ien-t'o-lo), where the pilgrim also points at monasteries founded by Kanishka or his descendants.[99] Probably the Turkish dynasty which endowed the monasteries in Kashmir and Gandhara ruled in Tukhāristān and the valleys leading up to the Kabul valley and the Upper Indus. The endowments appear to have been of recent date—most likely of Lalitāditya's period—and the titles and names of the *Tu-kueh* family correspond with those of the Chinese annals and the Orkhon inscriptions. In Kashmir we do not hear of Turks or Turushkas again until the period of the Ghaznavids, the

---

[95] *Rājatarangini*, IV, 178-9.
[96] IV, 166, 211.
[97] *Al-Hind*, I, p. 250.
[98] S. Lévi and E. Chavannes, 'L'Itineraire d'Ou-k'ong (751-790)', *Journal Asiatique*, 9e séries, VI (1895), p. 352.
[99] *Ibid.*, pp. 354-7.

eleventh-twelfth centuries. The kings of Kashmir opposed the Ghaznavids but also employed Turks in their service, as soldiers (horsemen) and artists.[100] By that time the Turks however were Muslims, and Kalhana comments on certain *mleccha* customs that the kings of Kashmir supposedly adopted from the Turks: the iconoclasm of 'Harsharājaturushka' (1089-1101) (who however continued to eat 'domesticated pigs'),[101] and the keeping of excessively large seraglios of women, Turushka and otherwise, bought or kidnapped, and the concomitant daily use of fishbroth and other aphrodisiacs by Harsha's predecessor.[102]

Wu-k'ung, finally, introduces us to the dynasty which ruled over *Kipin*, i.e. Gandhara and neighbouring countries, as 'descendants of Kanishka' bearing names and titles which were Turkish and sometimes can be identified in the Tang annals.[103] Wu-k'ung makes them out to be Buddhists, while Al-Bīrūnī refers to them as kings of the Hindus who were themselves 'Turks ,..., of Tibetan origin—who wore Turkish dress, a short tunic open in front, boots (*khaff*) and arms and bore the title of Kābulshāhs'.[104] These Kābulshāhs—subordinates of the Kashmir kings for part of the first half of the eighth century—are the dynasty which became known as the 'Turk-Shāhi' kings of *al-Hind* and were identified as 'Turks' in the Arab conquest literature as well, but, as already mentioned, like the Zunbīls of Zābul they were not Turks but descendants of a branch of the Chionite-Hephthalites or 'White Huns', successors of the Kushānas which absorbed some Turkish groups but maintained a predominantly non-Turkish leadership.[105] Their employment of Turkish soldiers was also quite limited, although 'local Turks' are said to have contributed their personal guard corps. This 'Turkish' Shāhi dynasty continued up to the late ninth century, when it was replaced by a brahman dynasty of the same title. Names of apparent Turkish origin, e.g. Toramāna, survived even among these Hindu 'Shāhi' kings.[106] The fact remains—here Al-Bīrūnī was right—that 'the days of the Turks'

---

[100] Stein, *Rājataranginī*, VII, 544, 1149, 1158; VII, 919, 885-7, 2843.
[101] *Ibid.*, VII, 1095, 1149; *Al-Hind, I*, p. 249.
[102] Stein, *Rājataranginī*, VII, 519-22.
[103] Lévi and Chavannes, 'Ou-k'ong', pp. 377-8.
[104] *Kitāb al-Hind*, p. 348.
[105] *Al-Hind, I*, p. 114.
[106] Stein, *Rājataranginī*, III, 103; V, 233.

did not begin before the arrival of the Ghaznavids in this area in the late tenth and the eleventh century.

Countless Muslim authors have left us graphic descriptions of what they considered the essential attributes of the Turks as an ethnic group and the reasons for the latter's pre-eminence in the Islamic world from the eleventh century onwards. These accounts are counterbalanced, often, by descriptions of what these same authors considered the all too obvious limitations of the same people. All authors of *adab* works, manuals of war, and mirrors for princes, agree on the military superiority of the Turks, their hardiness, their skill with horses and the bow and arrow, as well as their 'lion-like' qualities and pride.[107] Ibn Khaldun considered the Turkish mamlūks to be—thanks to these virile virtues—the saviours of Islam.[108] Nizām al-Mulk recalls that Al-Mu'tasim, the caliph who first introduced a *mamlūk* army, 'always said that there was none for service (*khidmatkār*) like the Turk'.[109] 'I can tell that Al-Mu'tasim knew very well what he was about when he made them into a corps and took them into his service', writes also Al-Jāhiz, for '... nothing can withstand [the Turks], and none desires to oppose them'.[110] Mobile as they were, they were never pursued for 'the Turk does not need to escape'.[111] Turkish prowess in arms not only buttressed the caliphs' power in the *dār al-Islām*, but was also especially effective against the infidel kings of Hind.[112] 'Arrow-shooting Turks' are a favorite topos of Persian poetry, where they are compared with the bubbles in a glass of wine.[113] No other army could charge as well, and Turkish horsemen were taught to carry two or three bows and strings to match them.[114] From ethnological parallels it is known that a skilled archer can shoot at least six aimed arrows a minute.

---

[107] Cf. E. Mainz, 'Die Türken in der klassischen arabischen Literatur', *Der Islam*, XXI (1933), pp. 278-85; C. E. Bosworth, 'Ghaznevid Military Organisation', *Der Islam* (1960), pp. 37-77; Ayalon, 'Aspects of the Mamlūk Phenomenon', p. 206, note 18.

[108] *Kitāb al-'Ibar* (Cairo, 1284 H.), v. 37.

[109] *Siyāsatnāma* (Teheran, 1334 H.), p. 52.

[110] Harley Walker, 'Jahiz of Basra', pp. 677, 672.

[111] *Ibid.*, p. 669.

[112] *TFM*, p. 48.

[113] A. Schimmel, 'Turk and Hindu: A Poetical Image and its Application to Historical Fact', in: S. Vryonis Jr (ed.), *Islam and Cultural Change in the Middle Ages* (Wiesbaden, 1973), p. 110, note 17.

[114] Harley Walker, 'Jahiz of Basra', pp. 666-7.

The image of the Turk in Persian poetry soon developed into an ideal of manliness, the ideal beloved, white and beautiful, albeit cruel. 'Turk' came to relate to 'Hindu' like 'ruler' to 'slave', 'angel' to 'devil', while for Rūmī, for instance, Turkestan became the heavenly world of light (from which the beloved appeared) and Hind the dark world of matter.[115] Often enough the word 'Turk' was turned into the equivalent of 'Muslim', at least in India, where at times it also became a synonym for soldier. Ultimately the 'lion-like' Turk, with his disdain for menial household tasks, was linked to the climate of his country of origin which predisposed him to a certain robustness and military valour. The nomadic Turks had a strongly developed 'love of homeland' (mahabbat al-waṭan) or 'longing for homeland' (al-ḥanin 'ilā-l-waṭan). 'They are more strongly attached to their country than the camels'.[116] This attachment reinforced the mutual similarity and homogeneity of the Turks which expressed itself in an absolutely single-minded desire to achieve military command. The Turks' very single-mindedness was praised by Muslim writers as 'the only way to achieve anything'. Solely the Dailamites were at times regarded as more warlike. But the dark side of the Turkish character—regarded as equally universal—was an insatiable love of plunder and violence. In their own country, 'the Turks do not fight for religion nor for interpretation of Scripture nor for sovereignty nor for taxes nor for patriotism nor for jealousy—unless their women are concerned—nor for defense of their home, nor for wealth, but only for plunder'.[117] Given to violent appropriation, they were however free from unnatural vice, they treated prisoners well, kept their promises, and were not given to hypocrisy or intrigue, while being impervious to flattery, and not addicted to 'rivalry in poetic display'.[118] 'The Turks know not how to flatter or coax, they know not how to practise hypocrisy or backbiting, pretence or slander, dishonesty or haughtiness on their acquaintance, or mischief on those that associate with them. They are strangers to heresy and not spoiled by caprice; and they do not make property lawful by quibbles. Their fault which makes

---

[115] Schimmel, 'Turk and Hindu'.
[116] Harley Walker, 'Jahiz of Basra', p. 679.
[117] Ibid., p. 670.
[118] Ibid., p. 672.

them most unpopular is their love of land and love of moving freely up and down the country and propensity for raiding and preoccupation with plunder ...'[119] Such, in short, were the characteristics of a people which had mastered 'the art of war' to the same degree of perfection as 'the Chinese have attained in art, and the Greeks in philosophy and literature and the Sasanids in empire'.[120] By the time that the Turks had become sedentary Muslims in the Middle East, inhabiting towns, they often came to be seen as rivals of the Arabs and Persians and their relative lack of cultural sophistication began to receive more emphasis due to a developing anti-Turkish undercurrent.[121] Popular detestation was expressed in poetry, and an hadith of as early as the ninth century speaks of 'the small-eyed, redfaced, flat-nosed Turks'. Their alleged slow-wittedness is expressed in the frequently occurring phrase *Turk-i-ablah*. By the thirteenth century we find that descriptions divide the Turks, as a people, in two sections: the civilized town-dwellers and the backward migrating tribes. Turkish converts to Islam, moreover, went through a change of heart which made them zealous in their faith and oblivious of their Central-Asian pagan past.[122] And, unlike other ethnic groups, the Turks were bound to obscurity if they did not leave Turkestān; they achieved fame and fortune only if they left their homeland. 'Since the creation of the world until today no slave (*banda*) bought for money achieved the position of king (*pādshāh*) except the Turk'.[123] A former, legendary, king of the Turks is supposed to have said: 'The Turk is like a pearl (*durr*) in its shell at the bottom of the sea, when it is worth nothing; but when it comes out of its shell, and out of the sea, it becomes valuable and adorns the crown of kings and the neck and ears of brides'.[124]

---

[119] *Ibid.*, p. 678.

[120] *Ibid.*, pp. 682-5.

[121] Mainz, 'Die Türken', pp. 278-83; I. Goldziher, *Muhammedanische Studien*, 2 vols (Halle, 1897), I, pp. 270-1; Bosworth, 'Ghaznevid Military Organization', p. 52.

[122] *TFM*, pp. 35-36.

[123] *Ibid.*, p. 36.

[124] *Ibid.*, p. 37.

CHAPTER III

KINGS, SLAVES AND ELEPHANTS

In order to be able to identify the factors which made the conquest possible, and the foundations of Muslim rule in India, we will first have to explore further the question of the military differential between the Turkish invaders and the Indian armies in general, and the extent to which this differential was technical or social in its origin.

We have already pointed at the advantages of nomadic warfare and to the fact that, in the medieval world, those accustomed to the nomadic life normally, if there were no special adverse circumstances, possessed a degree of military superiority over sedentary states. What, however, do we find in India? This is a question to which the answer is by no means obvious.

To begin with, the horse has a long history in India.[1] The horse (*ashva, haya*) is first met with in Vedic and post-Vedic times in conjunction with the war-chariot, and subsequently, in a strictly subordinate role, as an appurtenance of the chariot and as a flank-guard of elephants. The horse was admired for its great speed: 'swift as thought' (*manojava*) is 'a regularly recurring epithet for horses in the epics. And individual horses—like elephants—had petnames. The epics however do not appear to have had a word for 'cavalry' but only for 'horse-riders' or 'those mounted on a horse' (*ashvāroha, hayāroha*). Hence, while the Vedic age knew no cavalry at all, the epics show merely an unorganized body (*kula*) of mounted soldiers who did not act together but guarded the chariot or elephant to which they were formally assigned, while they were clearly not part of the main strength of the army. As such, the horse was quite common, and appears to have been well-trained. The epic horseriders, without saddle or stirrup, are however conspicuous for falling off their horses.

---

[1] G. Oppert, *On the Weapons, Army Organisation & Political Maxims of the Ancient Hindus* (London, 1880); E. W. Hopkins, 'The Social and Military Positions of the Ruling Caste in Ancient India', *Journal of the American Oriental Society*, VII (1888); P. C. Chakravarti, *The Art of War in Ancient India* (Dacca, 1941); S. D. Singh, *Ancient Indian Warfare* (Leiden, 1965).

Still later, the cavalry gradually came into its own as a tactically important constituent of the armies of ancient India—on account of its mobility it was rated above the infantry—, while the chariot gradually lost terrain and, in North India, already seems of no consequence under the Guptas, while it is not even mentioned in Harsha's kingdom or in eighth-century Sind. The richly decorated two-wheeled or four-wheeled vehicles, drawn by horses, in which gods and heroes are seen using the bow, and which we find depicted in Hoysala bas-reliefs of the twelfth and thirteenth centuries, were not war-chariots but models used in processions or in temples that were meant to represent the war-chariot described in the epics.[2] Large cavalry forces, running into tens of thousands or, according to some contemporary writers, even a hundred thousand (which is probably an exaggeration), came to be maintained by the rulers of early medieval India.[3] The Gurjara-Pratihara, at Kanauj, enjoyed a special reputation among contemporaries as 'lord of the horses' (*hayapati*). The importance of the horse in India on the eve of the Islamic conquest is also iconographically attested, and it is reflected for instance in the 'bull-and-horseman' coinage of North-Indian rulers. Indian theorists began to assign an ever more important role to the cavalry in the tenth to twelfth centuries, and a 'science of horses' (*ashvashāstra*) arose which classified horses according to breed, age, physical appearance, psychology, anatomy, skin, colour, and so on, putting special emphasis on the auspicious and inauspicious marks of horses as expressed in smell or twists of the hair (of the latter, especially those on the forehead).[4] The number of important works on horses escalates in the twelfth century, but the genre was perpetuated into the fourteenth century by Hemasūri, a Jain author of Ashvashāstra, and translations were made into Persian and Arabic (which indicate that the early Muslim rulers of India also attached great importance to the auspicious and inauspicious marks of horses).[5] Nakula, the controller of the horses of the

---

[2] J. Deloche, *Military Technology in Hoysala Sculpture (Twelfth and Thirteenth Century)* (New Delhi, 1989), pp. 13, 46.
[3] *TYP*, p. 38.
[4] Cf. C. M. Ridding (transl.), *The Kādambarī of Bāna* (London, 1896), p.63; Kalhana, *Rājatarangini, passim*.
[5] Cf. *Mānasollāsa*, 2 vols (Baroda, 1925-39); *Harihara-caturanga of Godavara Mishra* (Madras, 1950); *Ashvashāstra of Nakula* (Tanjore, 1952); S. S. Misra, *Fine Arts and Technical Sciences in Ancient India with Special Reference to Someshvara's Mānasollāsa* (Varanasi, 1982).

Pāndavas in the great Mahābhārata war, is said to be the original author of the 'science of horses', which he composed with the help of the works attributed to the sage Shālihotra. According to Nakula, horses were the means of obtaining *dharma*, 'merit', and *artha*, 'wealth'. The twelfth-century Caulukya king Someshvara III agreed with Nakula that even distant enemies could be kept off with good horses.

Much attention, in effect, was given to the training of good horses for war, and the cavalry acquired an important and multifarious role, becoming, as some texts say, 'the queen of battles'. Even so, it never achieved a high standard of performance, and, as we will see below, elephants not horses became pre-eminent. There were two problems with the Indian cavalry: one, a deficiency in equipment and weaponry; the other, a problem of supply of the actual horses themselves.

Let us begin with the first problem. We have evidence, from texts, bas-reliefs and coinages, that Indian horses and horsemen were armoured with coats of mail or leather cuirasses; that they were equipped with long lances, swords and sabres, spears, darts, and shields, and that saddles, in various modified forms, became increasingly widely used in the eleventh to thirteenth centuries; moreover, that horse-shoeing became more current in the thirteenth century; and that by the eleventh century the real foot-stirrup (as opposed to the surcingle or toe-stirrup which is found from the beginning of the Christian era) was already diffused throughout the Indian subcontinent and mainland Southeast Asia.[6] It appears that the lance became the principal weapon of the cavalry.[7] But, while the stirrup gave lateral support to the riders and made possible a more effective mode of attack, the lances used were almost always of the light one-handed variety. Thus, in India, the diffusion of the foot-stirrup did not lead to the development of mounted shock combat and a new preponderance of cavalry like in Europe, where, from the eighth century onwards, it contributed to the consolidation of feudalism, superseding the infantry of antiquity.[8] Instead, elephants were used to break the enemy lines.

---

[6] Deloche, *Hoysala Sculpture*, pp. 30-31, 48; S. Digby, *War-horse and Elephant in the Delhi Sultanate* (Oxford, 1971), p. 14.

[7] Deloche, *Hoysala Sculpture*, pp. 34, 48.

[8] Cf. L. White, Jr., *Medieval Technology and Social Change* (Oxford, 1963), pp. 1-38.

At the same time, archery was largely left to infantry and a relatively small number of elephant-riders. As in the case of the Byzantines, it was the failure of the Indians to develop horse-mounted archery that was exposed by the Turkish steppe nomads.[9] It was not that archery as such was unknown in India. Even before bows and arrows became the pre-eminent weapons of the infantry and elephant-riders, they had been used by the Vedic charioteers. In the Veda, bowmen were often synonymous with charioteers, and *āyudha* was both a word for weapon and for the bow, synonymous with *dhanus*.[10] The bow was made of *kṛmuka* wood or horn or cane, painted in many colours, ornamented with gold figures, and set with gems, while the cane or reed arrows were iron-tipped (and sometimes poisonous—which was however considered dishonourable), and the string made of *mūrva* grass. The force of the shot was described as terrific. Yet it appears to have been unable to do much damage. The Epic heroes of the bow were famous for their 'quickness and lightness', the uninterrupted discharge or *hastavāpa*, the 'hand-throw' resulting in a 'rain of arrows' or 'flood of arrows', but not sureness.

The later *Dhanurveda* or 'science of archery' mentions a variety of bows, including composite bows. And the Indian bow that Persian authors refer to as the *kaman-i-hindavī*—and which was probably the bow with which the Rajput armies mainly confronted the Turkish armies—was made from cane, its strings from the bark of the cane, and had a somewhat shorter range than the bows which were used in the late Ghaznavid and Ghurid armies, but was not decisively inferior to the latter.[11] Of horse-mounted archery, however, there is little trace, although, as the coins show, the Shākas introduced it to India, as did the Parthian satraps. A few Gupta coins, as well as sculpture of the Palas, also show horse-riders with bows, but the practice cannot be demonstrated to have become widespread. The Hoysalas appear to have employed mounted archers only in exceptional circumstances.[12] The *Shivadhanurve-*

---

[9] For the Byzantine case, see W. E. Kaegi, Jr., 'The Contribution of Archery to the Turkish Conquest of Anatolia', *Speculum*, XXXIX, 1 (1964), pp. 96-108.

[10] Hopkins, 'Ruling Caste in Ancient India', pp. 262, 269-81.

[11] Digby, *War-horse and Elephant*, p.17; E. McEwen, 'Persian Archery Texts: Chapter Eleven of Fakhr-i-Mudabbir's *Ādāb Al-Harb* (Early Thirteenth Century)', *The Islamic Quarterly*, XVIII, 3 & 4 (1974), pp. 77-99.

[12] Deloche, *Hoysala Sculpture*, pp. 34, 46.

da, a treatise on archery of the fifth or sixth century AD, does not mention mounted archers at all.

The second problem was that of the supply of horses. Given the importance of cavalry in the army, vast numbers of horses were needed in India. Horses were much in demand both for the cavalry on the battlefield and as a means of personal transport. Relatively few were used as beasts of burden, since the climate was too hot and humid for the effective use of horses as draught animals, although Marco Polo mentions the export from Aden to India of 'a very large number of Arab chargers, and palfreys, and stout nags adapted for all work (*de bons destriers Arrabins et chevaux et grans roncins à ij selles*)'.[13] There is abundant testimony not only that the few horses which were bred in India were mostly of poor quality but also that imported horses did not do well there. As Duarte Barbosa writes: 'Horses do not thrive well in this country, and live therein but a short time'.[14] And according to Marco Polo again, '... the number of horses exported ... to India is something astonishing. One reason is that no horses are bred there, and another that they die as soon as they get there, through ignorant handling; for the people there do not know how to take care of them, and they feed their horses with cooked victuals and all sorts of trash ... and besides they have no farriers'.[15] Elsewhere we read that 'in India the climate is so hot that horses cannot be bred and are not born, or, if they are, they are monstrosities, blemished and misshapen in their limbs and quite worthless'.[16] There were, to be sure, areas in India where horses could be and were bred because the ecological conditions were suitable or because they were favourably situated for regular regeneration by foreign breeds.[17] These areas remained more or less the same throughout the historical period and were situated in the arid zone which stretched from the Bhima river behind the Western Ghats, via Cutch, Kathiawar and Sind into Rajasthan, and then extending

---

[13] Yule, *Marco Polo*, II, pp. 438, 440 n. 2.

[14] M. Longworth-Dames (transl.), *The Book of Duarte Barbosa*, vol.I (Nendeln/Liechtenstein, 1967), p. 211.

[15] Yule, *Marco Polo*, II, p. 450.

[16] This passage is not found in Yule's edition but in R. Latham (transl.), *The Travels of Marco Polo* (New York, 1987), p. 61.

[17] J. J. L. Gommans, *The Rise of the Indo-Afghan Empire, c. 1710-1780* (Leiden, 1995), p. 71 ff.

northwards along the Luni and Indus rivers to the Panjab and eastwards into the Himalayas. Throughout this zone there were indigenous breeding grounds which were linked to the Central-Asian centres north of the Hindu-Kush and in the foothills of the Alborz mountains in Khurasan. An especially important horse-breeding area were, thus, the Sulaymān mountains, to the west of the Indus, where the Afghans lived,[18] the Kamboja of the epics, and the habitat of the ancient Ashvaka or 'horse people'. Among the indigenous breeds of India, however, the military qualities decline sharply when we move to the south and east of the sub-continent.[19] Horses breed with great difficulty in the south of the Indian peninsula. Here, in places, cross-breeding could still be resorted to in order to keep up the indigenous breeds. In the sculptures of the Hoysala kingdom, for instance, it appears that local breeds were crossed with imported mares: the represented steeds, with their broad head, dished face, thin ears, and huge open nostrils, have the features of Arab horses, but their thick legs indicate that they are not thoroughbreds.[20] In general how-ever the conditions for horse-breeding in these parts of the sub-continent were relatively poor. Like in Southeast Asia and South-east China, there was little room for the horse since the best soil was reserved for the cultivation of grains and vegetables to sup-ply a dense population.[21] There was, hence, a scarcity of grazing ground and a lack of appropriate fodder grasses. Ecologically it was Central Asia, with its temperate climate and high proportion of rich feather grasses and fescue, that provided the optimal con-ditions for breeding, and parts of Iran and Arabia. In India, the breeding of horses was circumscribed by the shortage of exten-sive pastures and the competitive relation of nomadic pastoralism with sedentary agriculture. Only in those parts of India which were an extension of the arid zone, in the north-west, nutritious fod-der grasses could be found. But even there horse-breeding, though viable, stood in tension with arable farming.

Taking these circumstances in consideration, as well as the fact that wars could result in great losses of horses, the 'astonishing' magnitude of the Indian import trade in horses becomes under-

---

[18] Cf. Al-Hind, I, pp. 167-9.
[19] Digby, War-horse and Elephant, p. 43.
[20] Deloche, Hoysala Sculpture, p. 36.
[21] Gommans, Indo-Afghan Empire, pp. 71-74.

standable. It seems safe to say that the Indian demand for horses shows a definite increase from the early medieval period
onwards, as literary sources (especially foreign accounts) then
begin to refer more frequently to the trade.[22] In the long run,
like the indigenous breeding grounds, the main external breeding areas which provided India with most of its war-horses, and
with all of its best ones, remained the same and were located in
Central Asia as well as Iran and Arabia. The first category, trans-
ported relatively cheaply overland from Central Asia, Afghanistan
and, to a lesser extent—an inferior quality—from the north-east,
i.e. from areas across the mountains into Bengal,[23] came to be
known as *Turkī* or *Tatarī* horses. The second category, from Iran
and Arabia, was referred to as *Bahrī* or 'sea-borne' horses as they
were imported by sea—by far the most valuable breeds but with
a higher casualty rate during and immediately after the journey,
when they had to adapt to an entirely different treatment and
diet while they were trained locally in special schools.[24] Marco
Polo writes that no ship goes to India from the Persian Gulf and
Aden 'without horses in addition to other cargo'.[25] The ships
'have no mast, one sail, and one rudder, and have no deck, but
only a cover spread over the cargo when loaded. This cover con-
sists of hides, and on the top of these hides they put the horses
which they take to India for sale'.[26]

We know that Iran, already in the seventh century, produced
the 'noblest' horses, known as *Pārasika*, 'possessed of all the favourable marks'.[27] By the late thirteenth century, according to Marco Polo, 'in this country of Persia there is a great supply of fine
horses; and people take them to India for sale, for they are horses of great price ... .Dealers carry their horses to Kisi [Qays] and
Curmosa [Hormuz], two cities on the shores of the Sea of India,
and there they meet with merchants who take the horses on to
India for sale'.[28]

---

[22] Cf. R. Chakravarti, 'Horse Trade and Piracy at Tana (Thana, Maharashtra,
India): Gleanings from Marco Polo', *Journal of the Economic and Social History of
the Orient*, XXXIV (1991), p. 168.
[23] For the latter, see Yule, *Marco Polo*, p. 119.
[24] Deloche, *Hoysala Sculpture*, p. 36.
[25] Yule, *Marco Polo*, II, p. 395.
[26] *Ibid.*, I, p. 108.
[27] Ridding, *Kādambarī of Bāna*, pp. 62-63.
[28] Yule, *Marco Polo*, I, pp. 83-84.

Even greater numbers of Arabian horses were exported from or via Aden, the ruler of which received a large amount of money in duties from the ships that traded between India and his country and who was 'one of the richest princes in the world'; from Shihr, at 640 km from the port of Aden and subject to it; Zafār, at 800 km to the north-west of Shihr, also subject to Aden; and Kalhat, at 960 km from Zafār to the north-west.[29] When, after the eleventh century, Aden and the Red Sea began to eclipse the Persian Gulf in importance in the trade with India, ships sailing from there would find it much easier, safer and faster to reach the Malabar coast than the more northern ports on the westcoast of the subcontinent.[30] This resulted in a shortage in the supply of *Bahrī* horses in the Konkani port of Tana (Thana), creating problems for the rulers of the Western Deccan, just as the general shift in trade to the Red Sea had meant the end of Rashtrakuta hegemony at the beginning of the same period.[31] While increasing preference was given to Malabar ports in the far south, the ruler of Tana, plagued by a short and uncertain supply of Arabian and Iranian horses, took recourse to piracy in order to procure them. This state of affairs was also noted by Marco Polo: 'With the King's connivance many corsairs launch from this port to plunder merchants. These corsairs have a covenant with the King that he shall get all the horses they capture, and all other plunder shall remain with them. The King does this because he has no horses of his own, whilst many are shipped from abroad towards India ...'[32] Chau Ju-Kua speaks of the availability of Bahrī horses at Ku-lin (Quilon) and other Malabar ports, as well as in Gujarat.[33] Hoysala inscriptions point at horses being imported from Arabia and from the 'Turushkas' of the westcoast, who in all likelihood were Arabs.[34] Perhaps the largest numbers of horses were shipped to the southeast of India. As Marco Polo says of Ma'bar: '... here there are no horses bred; and thus a great part of the wealth of the country is wasted in purchasing horses ... the merchants of Kis [Qays] and Hormes [Hormuz], Dofar [Zafār]

---

[29] *Ibid.*, II, pp. 438, 442, 444, 449.
[30] Chakravarti, 'Horse Trade', p. 177.
[31] *Ibid.*, p. 181.
[32] Yule, *Marco Polo*, II, p. 395; Chakravarti, 'Horse Trade', pp. 181-2.
[33] Chakravarti, 'Horse Trade', p. 177.
[34] Deloche, *Hoysala Sculpture*, p. 36.

and Shihr and Aden collect great numbers of destriers [battle chargers] and other horses, and these they bring to the territories of this king and of his four brothers, who are kings likewise ... vast numbers are sold there each year. Indeed this king wants to buy more than 2000 horses every year, and so do his four brothers who are kings likewise. The reason why they want so many horses every year is that by the end of the year there shall not be one hundred of them remaining, for they all die off. And this arises from mismanagement, for those people do not know in the least how to treat a horse; and besides they have no farriers. The horse-merchants not only never bring any farriers with them, but also prevent any farrier from going thither, lest that should in any degree baulk the sale of horses, which brings them in every year such vast gains. They bring these horses by sea aboard ship'.[35] All or most of these ships from the west, laden with horses, came to Kāyal, 'a great and noble city', which was situated along a famous port on the coast of what is now the Tirunelveli district at the southern tip of Tamil Nadu.[36]

Given these problems on the supply side, the question why the Indians failed to develop great skills in horsemanship and, more specifically, mounted archery, loses some of its pungency. The Arabs also did not introduce it to India in the seventh and eighth centuries, and they appear not to have had it themselves. It was a mode of warfare that was confined to the Turks and other nomadic peoples of the Central-Asian steppes. As Al-Jāhiz wrote of the Turks: 'if a thousand of their horse join battle and let off a single shower of arrows, they can mow down a thousand [Arab] horse. No army can withstand this kind of assault. The Khārijites and the Beduin have no skill worth mentioning in shooting from horseback, but the Turk can shoot at beasts, birds, hoops, men, sitting quarry, dummies and birds on the wing, and do so at full gallop to fore or to rear, to left or to right, upwards or downwards, loosing ten arrows before the Khārijite can nock one'.[37] In early Islamic times, the battles of the Arabs were mostly fought by infantry, and, while the Meccans succeeded in raising a cavalry

---

[35] Yule, *Marco Polo*, II, p. 340.
[36] *Ibid.*, II, pp. 370-3.
[37] Quoted by J. D. Latham, 'The Archers of the Middle East: The Turco-Iranian Background', *Iran*, VIII (1970), p. 97.

force, it was smaller and technically inferior (in body armour, horse accoutrements and especially stirrups) to those of their Byzantine and Iranian opponents.[38] It appears that the Arabs, in pitched battles, did not effectively deploy heavy cavalry but chose positions which favoured infantry, supported by archers. It was the infantry which—at Badr, Uhud, the Yarmūk, and at Qādisiyya— broke the power of the Byzantines and Iranians, and it was not made up of nomads but of the sedentary population of the towns and oases. The nomadic element in the Arab armies was certainly not negligable, but, while making maximum use of mobility, it was largely put to tactical use as light cavalry, specializing in surprise attacks, *ghazw* warfare and raiding expeditions. Superior mobility also played a decisive role in the strategic conduct of campaigns in the desert. Here it was essential that the Arabs could concentrate their forces and cover great distances rapidly by making use of the dromedary. Without the dromedary, the Arab conquests could not have been undertaken at all. It played a crucial role in the Arab conquest of Sind as well, and we find that as late as the early eleventh century, during the Ghaznavid expeditions to Somnath, in Kathiawar, 20,000 dromedaries were used to carry supplies.[39]

It was the people of the Eurasian steppes who first began, long before the invention of the stirrup, practising bowshooting on horseback and then established a quasi-monopoly over it, acquiring thereby a qualified military superiority over their sedentary neighbours in Iran, Byzantium, China, and India.[40] Among the steppe peoples, the evolution of military technique was determined by experiments with the range of the bow in reaction to various applications of defensive armoury, among themselves as well as among their sedentary opponents, over three millennia.[41]

---

[38] D. R. Hill, 'The role of the camel and the horse in the Early Arab Conquests', in: V. J. Parry and M. E. Yapp (eds), *War, Technology and Society in the Middle East* (London, 1975), pp. 36-42.

[39] *Al-Hind, I*, p. 203; *TF*, p. 32.

[40] C. Cahen, 'Les changements techniques militaires dans le Proche Orient médiéval et leur importance historique', in : V. J. Parry and M. E. Yapp (eds), *War, Technology and Society in the Middle East* (London, 1975), pp. 115-6. It was not an absolute superiority; the 'barbarian' cavalry was powerless against the phalanx (Strabo, VII, 3, 7).

[41] C. Uray-Kūhalmi, 'La Périodisation de l'Histoire des Armements des Nomades des Steppes', *Etudes Mongoles*, 5 (1974), pp. 145-55.

In the wake of improvements in defensive metal armoury among the Scythians in the sixth century BC, heavy cavalry or *cataphractarii* of the Sarmatian type, carrying bows, but also equipped for close battle, with two-handed lances and double-edged swords, began to prevail as well.[42] The earliest stirrups are found in Korean tombs of the first centuries AD. In due course, it allowed the bowshot to be effected in full gallop—a development of the greatest importance, which however never drove out the use of heavy cavalry among the nomads.

It has to be concluded that the Turkish armies of Islam which penetrated into India from the late tenth and early eleventh century onwards were not only made up of light cavalry, with superior archery abilities as described, but also, simultaneously, of heavily armoured sections of fairly large numbers—frequently if not usually *mamlūks*—which were trained as much in the *cataphractarii* tradition as in that of the 'typical' Western-Turkish steppe warriors.[43] In India we already became familiar with such armies in the early medieval period. Central-Asian or Turkish soldiery employed in Kashmir by Lalitāditya Muktāpīdā in the eighth century seems to have been entirely of the heavy Sasanid-Chinese cavalry type.[44] Lalitāditya's Buddhist-Tukharian minister Cankuna, while re-organizing the Kashmir army, introduced highly perfected Chinese armoury, of mixed scale and plate type. And, similarly, the methods of warfare of the early Tibetans, penetrating into India in the seventh to ninth century, were those of warriors who wore full suits of heavy iron and chain mail—but these dismounted for battle.[45] The Turkish archers of the Ghaznavid and

---

[42] A. M. Khazanov, 'Cataphractarii and their role in the history of military arts' (Katafraktarii i ikh rol' v istorii voennogo iskusstva), *Vestnik drevnei istorii* (Moscow, 1968), p. 191; idem, 'Characteristic features of the Sarmatian military art' (Kharakternye cherty sarmatskogo voennogo iskusstva), *Sovetskaia Arkheologiia*, 2 (1970), p. 63; idem, *Otscherki wojennogo dela sarmatow (Grundriss des Sarmatischen Kriegswesens)* (Moscow, 1971); White, *Medieval Technology*, pp. 8-20; E. V. Chernenko, *Skifskii dospekh* (Kiev, 1968), p. 155 ff; Lynn White Jr,'The Crusades and the technological thrust of the West', in: V. J Parry and M. E. Yapp (eds), *War, Technology and Society in the Middle East* (London, 1975), p. 98.

[43] This was also the case with the Turks in the Middle East: cf. Y. Bregel, 'Turko-Mongol influences in Central Asia', in: R. L. Canfield (ed.), *Turko-Persia in Historical Perspective* (Cambridge, 1991), p. 67.

[44] *Al-Hind, I*, pp. 239, 243; D. R. Sahni, 'Pre-Muhammadan Monuments of Kashmir', *Archaeological Survey of India: Annual Report 1915-16.*

[45] *Al-Hind, I*, pp. 241, 266; C. I. Beckwith, *The Tibetan Empire in Central Asia: A History of the Struggle for Great Power among Tibetans, Turks, Arabs, and Chinese during the Early Middle Ages* (Princeton, 1987), p. 11.

Ghurid armies in India, standing on their stirrup, possessed the power of quick penetration, but many of them wore coats of mail and various other types of defensive armoury which were so heavy that they could make their wearers drown, and they carried leather-covered or metal shields.[46] The sources also contain scattered but substantial evidence that the Ghaznavid and Ghurid cavalry wielded, in addition to bows and arrows, weapons such as battle-axes, maces, lances, spears, sabres, and long, curved swords (qalāchūrs), while whatever (non-Turkish) infantry there was carried bows, maces, short swords and spears, and that there was an array of missiles, 'fire-eyed rockets', slinging and stoning machines which were used in siege operations.[47]

However, the general situation remained that, in contrast to the pre-Islamic Iranian and Indian rulers, who routinely used peasant infantry in their armies, the Ghaznavids relied heavily on professional and slave soldiers on horseback, especially in their early operations in India.[48] And although in India by the thirteenth century locally recruited peasant infantrymen were making their entrée in the Muslim armies once again, it is quite clear that the coming of the Turks resulted in a shift away from a popular to a professional army and—as had happened in the Middle East somewhat earlier—a widening gap between the class capable of carrying arms and the rest of the people which supported it.[49] This gap did not come about in the same way as in Western feudalism, although technical evolution played a role in it, but it was in some respects more pronounced because of the superimposition of an ethnic factor and the fact that the new military rulers were invaders from Central Asia.[50] The main military advantage always remained that mounted archers were more mobile than any infantry and, in addition to being able to use the bow from horseback, were still capable of making decisive charges with spears and swords or operated in conjunction with heavy caval-

---

[46] TN, pp. 119, 237; TF, pp. 57-58; FS, vs 1465-74; C. E. Bosworth, The Ghaznavids: Their Empire in Afghanistan and Eastern Iran, 994-1040 (Edinburgh, 1963), p. 283.
[47] Bosworth, Ghaznavids, pp. 120, 283; TYA, pp. 332-4; TYP, pp. 206-9; AH, ff. 107a-b, 109b, 184b, 185a; TF, p. 32; ZA, p. 72.
[48] Cf. Bosworth, Ghaznavids, p. 141.
[49] Cf. Cahen, 'Changements Techniques Militaires', p. 122.
[50] Ibid.

ry.[51] On the steppe, every male individual could be recruited as a soldier and had been trained in mounted archery from as young as three or four years old.[52] The skills of the horse-archer are not easily taught, and the short recurved bow of the Turks made unusual demands of strength and application.[53] In effect, the difficulty of training an army of mounted archers was its one great disadvantage. In the Islamic world of the eleventh to thirteenth centuries, these specialized skills were often taught within the framework of *mamlūk* slavery. Here elites could be trained within the army to perform at the highest level and forced into a degree of discipline which earlier Islamic rulers could not impose on their general levies.[54]

The growing reliance on horse-archers, in combination with heavy cavalry, thus changed the mode of warfare entirely. And this was the case even though the invading armies included large components of 'irregulars' or 'volunteers', i.e. 'non-professionals'. The *mamlūks* were a small elite corps within the 'regular' army which provided leadership or was reserved for special occasions at which their superior skills—acquired at such great expense—would be decisive. The 'irregulars' were not necessarily infantry—the Ghaznavids in fact had a permanent force of infantry—but could be horsemen (*sawār*) as well as infantry.[55] The Indian expeditions of the early Ghaznavids in particular attracted many 'volunteers of the holy war' (*ghāzīs, mutaṭawwiʿ, mutauwiʿ*). These, whether horsemen or infantry, normally went in 'without being registered and salaried' (*be-musauwam-o-mawājib*).[56] Only sometimes they were given a sum of money for equipment and provisions. Otherwise they lived on plunder only.[57] The volunteers were never in the vanguard, as from a military standpoint they were grossly inferior to

---

[51] For the importance of this change, see also D. E. Streusand, *The Formation of the Mughal Empire* (Delhi, 1989), p. 54.

[52] See, for instance, A. Waley (transl.), *The Travels of an Alchemist* (London, 1931), p. 118: '... we Mongols are brought up from childhood to shoot arrows and ride'.

[53] Cf. R. Irwin, *The Middle East in the Middle Ages: The Early Mamluk Sultanate, 1250-1382* (Carbondale and Edwardsville, 1986), p. 4.

[54] *Ibid.*

[55] *TF*, p. 32.

[56] *Ibid.*

[57] Alptigin started out with a force of 200 ghulāms or 'slaves' and 800 ghāzīs, but soon expanded this to 15,000 cavalry and 5000 infantry, many of whom were

the regular army, and they were inadequate by themselves.[58] It was the regular army that represented the real strength of the Turks. And the sources emphasize again and again that in the Ghaznavid and Ghurid campaigns in India, within the regular armies, the military slaves (*bandagān, mamālīk, ghulāmān*) were of pivotal importance, above all the Sultan's 'personal slaves', that is the 'royal slaves' (*ghulāmān-i-khāṣṣ, ghulāmān-i-salṭānī, ghulāmān-i-sarāy*, a few of which were eunuchs), and operated under their own special officers with their own flag 'with a lion and spears' and wore 'golden belts', as well as other 'special' bodies of slaves which belonged to high commanders or governors.[59] Here the numbers would get smaller and smaller: the total number of military slaves—the vast majority of which were Turks—was probably never more than a figure in the thousands, while the special corps or *kaukaba* of 'royal slaves' could be as small as 60 to 200. The latter would produce the commanding officers, and often, as in the case of the Ghaznavids—who began their career in the slave guard of the Samanids—, the rulers.

The comparison with the opposing Hindu armies is always unfavourable for the latter, at least in the Muslim sources. This concerns not so much the number of troops on their side as, to the contrary, the effectiveness of the usually much smaller numbers of Muslim forces. The slave king Balban (1266-86) held, according to Barani, that six to seven thousand Delhi horsemen could overthrow a 100,000 strong army of infantry and archers of

---

volunteers, collected from Khurasan. In Lahore, the concentration of ghāzīs caused frequent disruption and a special *sālār-i-ghāziyān* or 'commander of the ghāzīs' had to be appointed. Again, in the battle of Multan in 1005 AD, next to the regularly mustered cavalry, Muslim 'volunteers' were added (*TYA*, p. 275). In the expedition to Kanauj, in 1017 AD, Mahmud employed 100,000 'selected horsemen' (*sawār-i-khāṣṣa*), but to this number were added 20,000 'volunteers of Islam' (*muṭauwiʿaʾ islām*) from Turkestan, Mā warāʾ an-nahr, 'and thereabout' (*TYA*, p. 396; *TYP*, p. 242; *TF*, p. 29). In 1025-26 AD, in the campaign to Somnath, 30,000 'volunteer horsemen' (*sawār-i-muṭauwiʿa*) participated, 'from Turkestan and elsewhere', next to the 'regular army' (*lashkar-i-khāṣṣa*) (*TF*, p. 32; *KT*, IX, p. 343 has: 'fī thalāthīn ʾalf fāris min ʾasākir siwan al-mutaṭawwiʿ...'. There are numerous other examples of ghāzīs being added to the 'regular army', often in thousands or even tens of thousands, but generally in smaller numbers than the regular army itself.

[58] E.g. *AH*, ff. 148a-149a.

[59] *TB*, pp. 263, 274, 327-9; *AH*, f. 43a; *TF*, pp. 31, 46; *TYA*, pp. 278, 332-4 ; *TYP*, pp. 187, 199; *TN*, pp. 15, 17.

Hindu rais and ranas.[60] The superior military strength and effectiveness of the early Ghaznavids in India is the object of considerable hyperbole, even though the conquest of Hind was considered an extremely hazardous undertaking.[61] In Timur's time, at the very end of the fourteenth century, these hazards were well known, and by then it had also become clear that it was difficult to maintain any military superiority in India for long.[62]

In actual fact, Turkish mounted archery, from the late tenth and eleventh century onwards, does appear to have played a decisive role in the establishment and, ultimately, the consolidation of Muslim power in India.[63] While the Perso-Arabic annals of the conquest of India are not nearly as numerous and detailed as those of the anti-Crusades of Muslim dynasties like the Zangids, Mamluks and others, the superiority of Turkish modes of warfare is documented on numerous occasions throughout the eleventh to thirteenth centuries,[64] and above all in the fatal Second Battle of Tarā'in of 1192 AD, where 10,000 mounted archers under Muhammad Ghuri decided the outcome and ensured the success of Muslim arms in Hind.[65] Sanskrit sources, for all their deficiencies, do not fail to confirm that the relatively small but well-armed mobile cavalry of the archers of the *mlecchas*, fighting under a single undivided command, could play havoc with and rout the

---

[60] See I. Habib, 'Barani's Theory of the History of the Delhi Sultanate', *The Indian Historical Review*, VII, 1-2 (July 1980-January 1981), pp. 99-116.

[61] Cf. *TF*, p. 19; *TYP*, p. 246; *TYA*, pp. 404-6: '... wa qaus al-hallaj (*sic*) ghayr qaus al-nāshib (*sic*) ... mahmūd an laisa min jins akābir al-hunūd wa umarā' rijālhum as-sūdān ....', et cetera. For the perceived difficulty of the conquest of Hind see also *Al-Hind, I*, p. 192.

[62] Cf. W. Davy (transl.), *Political and Military Institutes of Tamerlane* (Delhi, 1972), p. 48: 'Although we may subdue Hind, yet if we tarry in that land, our posterity will be lost; and our children, and our grandchildren, will degenerate from the vigour of their forefathers, and become speakers of the languages of Hind'.

[63] As already mentioned, parallels exist elsewhere. For evidence of the paralysing effects of archers 'fighting in the Turkish way' (the backbone of Saladin's army) from Frankish sources, see D. Ayalon, 'Aspects of the Mamluk Phenomenon', pp. 196-225; for Byzantine historians who, similarly, contributed numerous Turkish victories to the dexterity of the Seljuqs with the bow on horseback and the Byzantine weakness at mounted archery, see Kaegi, 'The Contribution of Archery'.

[64] See, for instance, Barani's description of the role of the '5000 archers' (*panj-hazār mard-i-tīr*) in Katahr under Balban in *TFS*, p. 59; and other encounters, at Somnath and elsewhere, described in *TF*, pp. 33, 35 and *ZA*, pp. 72, 88-89.

[65] *TN*, p. 120.

cumbrous Indian hosts which were supplied by innumerable rajas. One twelfth-century text, the *Prabandhacintāmani*, for instance, takes us back to 'the Middle Country' of the Yamuna-Ganges Doab, while describing the last of the Rathors of Kanauj as follows:

'Then, in the town of Varanasi, a king, of the name of Jayachandra, cherishing the fortune of a mighty kingdom, bore the title of "the cripple", because he was so embarrassed with the multitude of his forces, that he could not march anywhere without resting on the two staves of the Yamuna and the Ganges ... after some time, he heard that the mlecchas [i.e. Turks] were drawing near ... [and that] Varanasi was surrounded by the army of the mlecchas, for the twanging of their bows drowned the sound of fourteen hundred pairs of kettle-drums, and as his mind was bewildered by the mighty army of the mlecchas, he placed that son of queen Suhava on his own elephant, and plunged, elephant and all, into the waters of the Ganges'.[66]

Finally, it has to be stressed that in the contest with Indian rulers, the Ghaznavids, Ghurids and their slave-king successors at Delhi had the distinct advantage of having better access to good war-horses. Not merely the Indian but some of the most famous breeding grounds for horses in the eastern Islamic world fell within the Ghaznavid dominions: the Sulaymān mountains, west of the Indus, but also, on the Upper Oxus, the valleys and upland pastures of Gūzgān, Gharchistān, Tukhāristān, Khuttal, Chaghāniyān, and other areas beyond the Oxus which were held by tributaries.[67] Later, it became an object of the policy of the Delhi Sultans to deprive Hindu rulers of access to war-horses both overland and by sea, and in this they were often successful, thereby creating a further advantage over their opponents.[68]

In the fourteenth century, an Egyptian author, Al-Qalqashandī,

---

[66] C. H. Tawney (ed. and transl.), *The Prabandhacintāmani of Merutunga Ācārya* (Calcutta, 1901), pp. 183-6, 292-5.

[67] Bosworth, *Ghaznavids*, pp. 58-59.

[68] This point is stressed by Digby, *War-horse and Elephant*, esp. pp. 48-49. Digby, however, unlike many earlier writers on the subject, denied—in our view erroneously—that there was a 'practical military superiority' on the part of the Muslim invaders. Thus, while Digby is right in stressing that 'the view that *mounted combat* was unfamiliar to their [i.e. the Muslims'] Hindu opponents cannot be maintained' (*op. cit.*, p. 12; my italics), the crucial point that *mounted archery* was decisive is missed.

in his *Ṣubḥ al-Aʿshā fī Sināʿat al-Inshāʾ*, an encyclopaedia, succinctly summarizes what was known of 'al-Hind and its environs' (*mamlakat al-hind wa muẓāfāthā*) in his time:

'... very important country, incomparable with others on account of its size, the abundance of its wealth and armies, the greatness of its Sultan ... there is gold, aloeswood and camphor ... its inhabitants have wisdom and are very intelligent ... they are the ones with the greatest mastery over their passions and are devoted to religion ... Most of the horses there are not of high quality and they are therefore brought there from the neighbouring areas in the country of the Turks (*bilād at-Turk*). The thoroughbred Arabian horses are brought from Bahrayn, Yaman and ʿIraq. And if there are in the interior of al-Hind (*dākhil al-Hind*) Arabian horses they are very expensive and there are not many of them. When these horses stay in al-Hind for a long time their legs become weak. They also have mules (*bighāl*) and donkeys (*hamīr*) ... but even jurists and scholars do not like to ride them, ... regarding it as a great insult and disgrace. ... There are few dromedaries (*jimāl*). ... The animals in the country are the elephant (*al-fīl*) and the rhinoceros (*al-karkaddan*) ...'[69]

It is on the elephant that we must now focus our attention, and on the uniquely important role it played in India (unlike the rhinoceros, which was not domesticated). For what has been said about the horse can almost be reversed for the elephant: it does not do well anywhere except in *al-Hind*, and the Indians put it to military use against horses—which added not a little to their fame in the Arab and Turkish lands. In addition, what will be argued in the remainder of this chapter is that from the eleventh-thirteenth centuries onwards the horse gradually drove the elephant from its pre-eminent military position—at least in those parts of *al-Hind* which were conquered by the Turks.

The first known appearance of elephants in battle was the squadron of 200 in the army of the Indian king Porus against Alexander in 326 BC, although the *Nikāyas* and the Epics point to the use of elephants in war as well, and Arrian, in his *Anabasis* (3-8), has recorded the presence of an Indian contingent with 15 elephants at Gaugamela in 331 BC. By that time the elephant appears to have been in general use in India, having been domesticated many centuries earlier. According to another Egyptian

---

[69] Al-Qalqashandī, *op. cit.*, 14 vols (Cairo, 1964), V, pp. 61-62, 82.

author, Ibn Zāfir (b. 1171), the Indians held to the belief that it was the founder of the fort of Kālanjar who became the first raja to capture and ride elephants and whose example was followed by the others.[70] The earliest archaeological evidence includes Harappan seals and amulets which sometimes have a figure of an elephant engraved on them, with trappings and rugs indicating that the elephant was domesticated already then. The term used for elephant in the Vedas is *hastinmṛga*, 'animal with a limb functioning as a hand [i.e. trunk]', and under this name it makes its debut as a royal mount.

At this very early date, the elephant was known and domesticated not in India alone.[71] Egyptian monuments, especially those of the eighteenth dynasty, as well as Assyrian records, indicate that elephants were used in regions to the west of India, and were possibly being imported from there. If it was ever native to any of those regions, the elephant disappeared from Western Asia in later times. And this is also what must have happened in China. The *Yu-Kung*, in the early part of the first millennium BC, refers to present South Hunan as 'the country of the docile elephants', pointing beyond doubt at the domestication of elephants in Central China.[72] Here they may have been used in battle too; but they did not find a permanent place in Chinese warfare and, in fact, became extinct in the Yangtse valley—their last resort in China—before the end of the fourth century BC.

Somewhat later, the Iranians learned to use elephants in war from the Indians. Under the Seleucids, Indian elephants became a not uncommon sight in Syria. There is a terracotta figurine of an Indian elephant, with *haudaj*, of Antiochus I of Syria. And Antiochus III, in 217 BC, had 102 Indian elephants in his army. The Romans were first introduced to them in battle in Italy in 280 BC; a painted dish from Capena, in Campania, of Etruscan style, of the third century BC, shows an Indian elephant, with its driver and *haudaj*, and two Macedonian warriors. Elephants from India remained in regular use in Iran and Iraq among 'the kings who

---

[70] Ibn Zāfir, *Kitāb al-Duwal al-Munqaṭiʿa*, BM: Or. MSS 3685, f. 149b.

[71] S. D. Singh, 'The Elephant and the Aryans', *Journal of the Royal Asiatic Society* (1963), Pts 1 & 2, pp. 1-6.

[72] C. W. Bishop, 'The Elephant and its Ivory in Ancient China', *Journal of the American Oriental Society*, 41 (1921), p. 291.

preceded Islam' and they are known to have been used, for instance, by the Sasanids at Al-Qādisiyya.

Hannibal's elephants, as the coins show, were mostly African, of the forest variety (which is not much bigger than the horse), with perhaps one Indian elephant accompanying them, obtained from Egypt. These small African elephants were pressed into service by the Egyptians and Carthaginians, both of whom employed 'indoi' as drivers and trainers. But they were used by the Carthaginians merely to strike terror in the tribes of Italy, while in Egypt they shirked the fight against Indian elephants; whose smell and trumpeting they could not bear. The problem was that the great bush elephants of central and southern Africa, 'of the Zanj country and other areas of Abyssinia', where they were abundant, could not be domesticated and always continued to live in a wild state.[73] The Zanjis could not use them for war or any other purpose, and instead used bullocks, which they dressed up like horses and often equipped with armour.[74] The elephants were merely hunted down for the ivory,[75] which was traded in large quantities to Oman, and hence to India and China.[76] Many medieval writers came forward with false information on the use of elephants in Abyssinia, and there is no trustworthy authority since the Portuguese discoveries which confirms this.[77]

---

[73] Cf. *Al-Hind, I,* p. 27; *MD,* II, p.6.

[74] The use of bullocks in warfare, with litters on their backs, was not unknown in India; see, for instance, Tawney, *Prabandhacintāmani,* p. 187.

[75] As Indian elephants sometimes were. Marco Polo includes elephants' tusks in the list of items brought by ship from India to Hormuz (Latham transl, p. 66). Whether many elephants were killed specifically for their ivory in India we do not know, but the Arab geographers show that it happened (while Kautilya seems to indicate the same (*Arthashāstra,* 2. 2. 6)). In early modern times, ivory—of which seven different grades were distinguished—, as well as other body parts of the elephant (bone, skin) were also exported from Thailand (Siam) to South Asia and China, or sent as tribute as far as Burma (K. A. Bowie, 'Ethnicity and Elephants: A Consideration of Society and the State in the Nineteenth Century Lannathai Kingdoms'(Mimeo, 1993), p. 20). It is not clear to what extent the Thai situation was unlike that in Africa, but some authors suggest that elephants were not routinely killed for their ivory here, and largely gathered from those which died naturally (*ibid.,* p. 21). Whether this differs, again, from the situation which prevailed in our period can only be a matter of speculation.

[76] Marco Polo says about Madagascar and Zanzibar: '... [in these islands] there are more elephants than in any country in the world. The amount of traffic in elephants' teeth in these two Islands is something astonishing. ... the staple trade of the Island is in elephants' teeth, which are very abundant ...'(Yule, *Marco Polo,* II, pp. 411, 422-3; and see II, pp. 424-5, 429, 431, 433-4).

[77] Yule, *Marco Polo,* II, p. 434.

The use of elephants in war was thus not entirely unknown out-side of *al-Hind*, but nowhere else did it attain more than marginal importance. As all Arabic authors confirm, in India the elephant (*al-fīl*) was much more in use than anywhere else, and only here did it reproduce, while it did not live, as in Africa, in a wild state. For the Arabs 'the king of kings of al-Hind' was 'the king of the elephants' (*malik al-fīla*).[78] And the Chinese Buddhist pilgrim Hiuen Tsang also observed that India was ruled by 'the Elephant-Lord'.[79]

The characteristic advantage of Indian elephants was not mere-ly that they could be domesticated and tamed but also that the size of these 'mountainous beasts'[80] made it possible to install a *haudaj* (Skt *varaṇḍaka, etc.*) on their backs. Thai and Khmer war-elephants were equipped in the same way. African forest elephants were too small for this and never seem to have carried a *haudaj* but were ridden bareback. The *haudaj* (an Arabic word which orig-inally denoted merely the litter on a camel) was a kind of tower or castle, a structure made of wood, attached to a platform, and usually covered, but with apertures through which arrows, Greek fire, pots of oil, daggers, and other missiles could be hurled at the enemy beneath. A typical *haudaj*, according to various sources, contained four to ten or even twelve to sixteen men equipped with bows and arrows and all of the above, next to a driver with a goad and rod.[81] Classical sources quote smaller numbers of archers in the *haudaj*, and the sculptures at Sanchi and Mathura, as well as the Ajanta frescoes, depict merely three. Also, in the Epics, as distinct from later times, the elephant is still rarely ascended by kings or princes and the elephant warriors appear to have been common soldiers—although there are a few instances of *yavana* princes riding the elephant in war.[82] The *gajarahāḥ* or *hastisādināḥ* could crawl down on the tusks of their elephant to hit at the horses or men sent against them, or reach down and seize their opponents by the hair and behead them. According to

[78] *Al-Hind, I,* pp. 5, 226.
[79] Watters, *Yuan Chwang,* I, pp. 35-36.
[80] *Mhb.,* VIII, 85, 4 ff.
[81] S. Maqbul Ahmad, *India and the Neighbouring Territories in the Kitāb Nuzhat al-Mushtāq fī 'khtirāq al-'Āfāq of al-Sharīf al-Idrīsī* (Leiden, 1960), p. 71; Yule, *Marco Polo,* II, pp. 99-100.
[82] Hopkins, 'Ruling Caste in Ancient India', pp. 265-7.

all descriptions, the elephants were protected by mail armour (*var-ma*) on the head (which could be struck to produce frightening noise), joints and other vital parts, as well as by spikes.[83] They also carried flags, neckchains, nets, umbrellas, and 'sharpsounding' bells, while the trunk of the elephants could also be equipped with a kind of sabre (*qartal*).[84] Each elephant, thus armed, would be protected by a large number—at least several hundreds—of footsoldiers and horsemen who defended it from behind.

Countless authors testify that, from ancient times onwards, properly trained and equipped elephants were considered crucial to a king's military undertaking. Elephants were 'destroyers of men',[85] 'the best division of the king's army which always brings victory to the owner'.[86] Barani maintained 'that elephants and horses were the strength of Hindustan, and that one elephant was worth five hundred [Indian] horsemen'.[87] Or a good elephant, defended from behind by 500 men, was said to be able to fight 6000 horsemen.[88] An inscription relating the battle between the Hoysala king against a subordinate of the Cola, to the south of the Kaveri river, in 1006 AD, states that 'the invincible elephant corps was as vast as an ocean'.[89]

In the Hindu armies, elephants were employed as a moving wall, in the front rank and centre, i.e. preceding the infantry, in order to attack at the outset of the battle; or they were used as a standing wall in defense. Especially celebrated was their ability to break enemy lines and trample to death large masses of footsoldiers, to toss standardbearers in the air, and to force open the gates of fortresses as a living battering ram. Apart from such feats, they could perform a great many services in war operations generally: clearing roads, helping to build bridges, serving as rallying points for dispersed troops, or as pack animals, carrying siege machinery, and so on. If not used in warfare, elephants rendered similar services as the bullock and dromedary. More specifically,

---

[83] Cf. *Arthashāstra*, II, ch. 32; Stein, *Rājatarangini*, VII, 1552-6; Maqbul Ahmad, *Al-Idrīsī*, p. 71; *MD*, II, p. 7.

[84] *MD*, I, p. 167.

[85] Davy, *Political and Military Institutes of Tamerlane*, p. 47.

[86] *Hastyāyurveda of Pālakāpyamuni* (Pune, 1894), 1.5. 1-2.

[87] '*kah ārāstagī' mulk-i-hindustān az pīl-o-asp ast wa har pīl-e dar mulk-i-hindustān muwāzana' pānṣad sawār ast*' (*TFS*, p.53).

[88] *MD*, I, p. 167.

[89] Deloche, *Hoysala Sculpture*, p. 27.

elephants were indispensable in the building of monumental temples such as Angkor Wat. Due to their ability to negotiate the most difficult terrain they became known as 'the ship of the forest'.[90] In many mountainous areas, for example in Thailand and the neighbouring Shan country to the north, the elephant was indispensable in the rainy season, as the rivers and streams were without bridges.[91] Together with bullocks, elephants were the beasts of burden in many parts of Hind, and 'owing to the state of the roads, through the jungle, over high mountain ranges, through almost impassable bogs and deep streams, the elephant was almost the only mode of travel for journeys of any distance'.[92] In addition, it performed numberless domestic and agricultural tasks, including plowing land.

Further demonstrating its importance from early times onwards, there was the development of an Indian 'elephant science' (gajashiksha, gajashāstra), a body of lore which fell outside the scope of military manuals. This was, rather, a technical science and, while a minor branch of arthashāstra, entirely pre-occupied with the taming and training of elephants and these animals' anatomy and zoölogical or medical features. It is found in several Sanskrit works which have been preserved, for example in the Mātanga Līlā or 'Elephant Sport' of Nilakantha, which has chapters on 'the origin of elephants', 'favourable marks', 'unfavourable marks', 'marks of longevity', 'the catching of elephants', and so on, but almost nothing on their use in battle.[93] Elephantology was an ancient and, to an extent, irrational science, founded by a mythical sage Pālakāpya, which accounts for the origin of elephants by pointing out how the first of all elephants, Airāvata, was produced from the churning of the milky ocean—a story frequently referred to in Hindu mythology and in the Ramayana.[94] Unlike China, where the acquisition of elephants for war was considered ominous,[95] and, on occasion, early Islam (the aṣḥāb al-fīl attacking

---

[90] Bowie, 'Ethnicity and Elephants', pp. 15-16.
[91] Ibid., pp. 14-15.
[92] Dodd, quoted ibid., p. 14.
[93] F. Edgerton, The Elephant-Lore of the Hindus: The Elephant-Sport (Mātanga-Lilā) of Nilakantha (Delhi, 1985).
[94] Cf. H. Zimmer, Myths and Symbols in Indian Art and Civilization (New York, 1962), pp. 102-9.
[95] MD, I, p. 7.

Mecca!), in India the use of elephants was never considered inauspicious. On the contrary, eulogies of their superior intelligence, their height, light trod, and their sweet and servile nature abound.[96] They were given names and pet-names ('the tusked one', 'the defender'), like the most famous of immortal elephants, Indra's Airāvata. The elephant was raised to godhead: Ganesha, Ganapati, Vināyaka, Gajānana, or Vighneshvara, that is, the elephant-headed god of Good Luck, the remover of all impediments and obstacles, and the grantor of success and prosperity. And of the greatest importance was also that the elephant acquired a ceremonial function. With its elaborate make-up, rings and bells and necklaces, the elephant, above all, looked good. Inevitably, too, the elephant in India became a symbol of power, more particularly of royal power, while the number of elephants in a king's possession was taken as an indication of his potential or real military might, even though the practice of kings fighting from the *haudaj* is a rather late, apparently post-Epic, development. Already in the Veda the elephant symbolizes royal splendour, and Indra is 'as it were an elephant'.[97] Just as Airāvata belonged to Indra, so elephants belonged to kings as a special prerogative.[98] The symbolic and ritual role of elephants was nowhere more in evidence than in royal processions; as the late twelfth-century *Hariharacaturanga* says: 'there is no god like Rudra and no Shruti like the Veda [and] similarly there is no better means of conveyance for a king than an elephant'.[99] Elephants, thus, also play a prominent role in legends of conquest, as well as the founding of kingdoms, the boundaries of which were often established at the site where the royal elephant walked.[100]

In Islamic India, in the long term the elephant retained greater importance in its ceremonial than in its military role. Among the

---

[96] *Mātanga* means 'elephant' but also denotes the low-caste or out-caste Candāla, people which are meant to serve, not to keep servants, and it is therefore said that 'elephants (*mātangāh*) are ill to take service with' (Tawney, *Prabandhacintāmani*, p. 38).

[97] Zimmer, *Myths and Symbols*, p. 103.

[98] *Ibid.*, pp. 103, 109.

[99] *Harihara-caturanga*, Gajaparicheda, 23.

[100] Cf. Bowie, 'Ethnicity and Elephants', p. 11; C. W. Ernst, 'The Khuldabad Burhanpur axis, and the local Sufism in the Deccan', in: A. Dallapiccola and S. Zingel-Avé Lallemant (eds), *Islam and Indian Regions*, 2 vols (Stuttgart, 1993), I,

Turks who invaded India in the eleventh century, the possession
of elephants again became a royal privilege or, at least, remained
a privilege controlled by the ruling king, and as such we
encounter it under all their Indo-Islamic successors.[101] Elephants
which were captured as booty during the Ghaznavid and later
Muslim raids in India automatically fell into the *hiṣṣat as-Salṭān*,
the Sultan's share of one-fifth. The latter could give them away
as a mark of honour or as a special favour accorded in unusual
circumstances to any one of the amirs, but if they were used without permission this formally constituted an act of rebellion. Copper coins show the Ghurid Ghiyath ad-Din mounted on an elephant when, on the reverse, he began to employ the title *as-salṭān
al-aʿāzim*, a superlative designation which meant 'the most exalted sovereign', while earlier coins employing the title *as-sulṭān al-
muʿaẓẓam*, 'the exalted sovereign', or *al-malik al-muʿaẓẓam*, 'the
exalted lord', had merely shown him on horseback.[102] Jujzani illustrates vividly how among the thirteenth-century Slave Kings of Delhi and their *mamlūk* officers it became a carefully regulated mark
of status to have 'an elephant at the entrance of one's own residence'.[103] As a royal prerogative, it belonged to the same category of distinctions as the *naubat* and other instruments sounded
at stated periods at the gate.[104] If specifically granted by the king,
the same distinctions would lift a Turkish *mamlūk* far above his
peers. As Firishta says, 'in those days no-one except the king kept
an elephant at his gate'.[105] In the thirteenth century, we also get
the first evidence of slave officers riding on elephants, a phenomenon which would recur in India until as late as the eighteenth century.[106]

But there can be little doubt that war-elephants were not used
in the same numbers under the Islamic dynasties of India as they

---

pp. 170-1; Modave's account of 1776, in: G. Deleury, *Les Indes Florissantes: Anthologie des Voyageurs Francais (1750-1820)* (Paris, 1991), pp. 135-6; F. Bernier, *Travels
in the Mogul Empire, AD 1656-1668* (Delhi, 1989), pp. 246-7.
  [101] Cf. *TYA*, p. 324.
  [102] Cf. W. F. Spengler, 'Numismatic Evidence of Ghorid Personal Nomenclature and Royal Titulature' (Mimeo); S. Lane-Poole, *Catalogue of Oriental Coins in
the British Museum*, Vol. IX (London, 1889), Nos. 588 d & e.
  [103] *TN*, pp. 192, 198, 236, 269.
  [104] *TN*, p. 76.
  [105] '... *wa dar ān zamān ghayr az pādshāh digar-i fīl na-mi-dāsht*' (*TF*, p. 69).
  [106] *TF*, p. 61. In the eighteenth century, under the Bangash Nawabs of Far-

were in the early medieval period and before. We have seen that the Arabic sources described the most important ninth- and tenth-century Hindu dynasties as equipped with tens of thousands or more elephants of various kinds.[107] Although it is unlikely that these numbers indicated war-elephants in a state of readiness— they probably included the guessed number of untamed and half-tamed ones—, and although some of the figures are contradictory,[108] they are larger than those of later times. Certainly the Arabs of Sind, the Saffarids, and the later Buyids made almost no use of them at all.[109] It became evident in the eleventh century that in the defense against the Muslim Turks, the elephant was not a crucial advantage for Indian rulers—who may in fact have overrelied on them. At an early stage, moreover, the Turkish invaders adopted elephants for the same purposes, and even made strategic improvements in their deployment. In set battles, as had already been experienced by Porus against the Greeks, elephants easily got out of hand and could start to trample their own side, so that their drivers had to be provided with a chisel and mallet to pole-axe and kill them before they could do too much damage.[110] From the Mahabharata we know that elephants, if they became uncontrollable, were killed with the end of a sharp stoke of iron. If the *haudaj* caught fire, or the elephant got wounded, it would escape at the top of its speed, especially when highly intoxicated (as seems to have been a requirement when pitched against the Turks) and throw itself into a river or off a cliff.[111] 'If

---

rukhabad we still find slaves riding on elephants; see W. Irvine, 'The Bangash Nawabs of Farrukhabad', *Journal of the Royal Asiatic Society of Bengal*, 47 (1878), p. 69: '... although many of his slaves had risen to ride in palkis or on elephants, all earthly ambition for him was now over'.

[107] *Al-Hind, I*, pp. 267, 284, 305.

[108] The Gurjara-Pratiharas, for instance, are accredited with 2000 elephants 'dressed up for combat' by Mas'udi, who, furthermore, explains that this is a low number 'in comparison with other kings' (*MD*, I, p. 167). Others, however, say that the same kings possessed more than any other (Cf. *Al-Hind, I*, p. 284).

[109] Cf. *Al-Hind, I*, pp. 129, 187, 201, 375; *MD*, II, p. 12; Bosworth, *Ghaznavids*, p. 115.

[110] In spite of its warlike qualities, the elephant remained the most unpredictable and unreliable unit of war. Porus' experience is memorialized in the Urdu metaphor, *Porus ka hathi*, 'an elephant of Porus', used for someone who betrays a friend (S. Z. Haider, *Islamic Arms and Armour of Muslim India* (Lahore, 1991), p. 276).

[111] Cf. also *Al-Hind, I*, pp. 204-5. For all we know, elephants were given spirits

they are wounded they take to flight at once, and overthrow one another, even those on their own side.'[112] Mahmud of Ghazna, to avert the danger of elephants being repulsed and turn against his own troops, made sure that the elephants were part of his line, placing them in the intervals, so that if they fled they would have room to do so.[113]

The Ghaznavids, as the first of the Turkish Muslim rulers in India, still used elephants in relatively large numbers—several hundreds at a time. They used them in India itself, and occasionally to scare off nomad horsemen of the Qarakhanids or Seljuqs in the western and northern parts of their empire.[114] The Ghaznavids either captured their elephants from their vanquished opponents—who deployed large numbers against them—as especially valuable booty, or received them as tribute. One expedition, that against Thanesar in 1014-15 AD, is said to have been motivated by Mahmūd's ambition to acquire the famous Saylamānī or Sri-Lankese elephants which were prevalent there. They are referred to as 'Muslim elephants' because of their faithfulness, and they turned out to be useful in war.[115] These elephants, prized as they were, 'were brought [to Mahmūd] by God' (*khudā-āwad*). Exactly how many elephants Mahmud and his son Mas'ūd had in their *pīlkhāna* is not known, but the sources mention between 1300 and 2500 war-elephants, probably the highest figure which any Indo-Islamic ruler ever reached.[116] Many of these were kept at Kabul or Ghazna. But lean and weak animals were always sent back to Hindustan to recover.

The Ghurids and their slave commanders were also opposed by war-elephants—as many as 3000 on one occasion. And the Ghurids appear to have had some themselves, as is attested by several authors. But how they used them is not clear.[117] Barani confirms the importance of elephants for the control of Hindustan

---

to make them drunk before an engagement—a most common procedure which is recorded for all periods of Indian history.

[112] Longworth-Dames, *Duarte Barbosa, I*, p. 118.
[113] *TF*, p. 25.
[114] Bosworth, *Ghaznavids*, pp. 115-6; *TF*, p. 31.
[115] *TYA*, pp. 332-4; *TF*, p. 26.
[116] *TN*, p. 9; Bosworth, *Ghaznavids*, pp. 116-7; Digby, *War-horse and Elephant*, pp. 55-56.
[117] *TYA*, pp. 332-4; *TYP*, p. 655; *TF*, pp. 57-58; *ZA*, p. 66; *TN*, pp. 95, 119, 121.

under the thirteenth-century·slave ruler Balban.[118] Still, the Delhi Sultans at no time appear to have possessed more than 750 to 1000 war-elephants.[119] It has been argued, on good grounds, that the control of the supply of elephants—next to that of horses— became one of the important factors in the establishment of the political hegemony of the Delhi Sultanate.[120] Yet the conclusion seems inescapable that, while the numbers of elephants declined but the possession of the *pilkhāna* remained an important asset, after the Ghaznavids, and probably already in the eleventh century, elephant warfare in the Indo-Islamic state receded to the background, until eventually improved musketry rendered it almost obsolete after the sixteenth century.

This decreasing importance of the war-elephant can be explained by two factors: diminished availability on the one hand and the gradual shift to a war-horse economy on the other. The decrease in availability reflects the deforestation and expansion of settlement and agriculture that occurred in much of India throughout this period.[121] The elephant appears to have been abundant still in many parts of *al-Hind* in the early medieval centuries.[122] All kings acquired them, for warfare or defense and other purposes, if not from their own realm then (like for instance the kings of Kashmir) by importing them. There were reserved forests for elephants, where they were captured, preferably at about twenty years of age (if they were not hunted down for their tusks and anklebones). It was always cheaper to catch wild elephants, as they acquired no economic value until they were at least fifteen years of age. Raising elephants in captivity is possible but, for this reason, not practiced. Elephants could be caught, thus, in many of the forests of India, although not in all, and some forests were more important in this respect than others. 'The best forest is that where elephants are born ... it is the primary duty of the king to protect [such] forests in his country'.[123]

---

[118] Cf. p. 99.

[119] Digby, *War-horse and Elephant*, p. 59.

[120] *Ibid.*

[121] See also Digby, *op. cit.*, pp. 56, 65-66; and Chapter VII.

[122] The sources distinguish from the dark elephant (which in Sanskrit is referred to as 'blue elephant') the 'white elephant' as a special object of veneration and royal distinction. The latter was always extremely rare.

[123] Someshvara, quoted in Misra, *Fine Arts and Technical Sciences*, p. 216.

Eastern India, Bengal and Assam, as well as South Bihar and Oris-sa or *Jājnagar*, are most frequently mentioned as particularly important sources of elephants, from the pre-Christian into the Islamic era, and from these areas elephants were exported to all parts of South Asia.[124] The forests of Eastern India were often exposed to invaders who came specifically to raid 'in quest for elephants'—particularly Jājnagar is often mentioned in this con-text in the chronicles of the kings of not only Delhi and Bengal, but also of Malwa and the Deccan. Elephants of an especially tall variety were plentiful in parts of South India, in Ma'bar and Al-Akhwār, the region on the Indian coast opposite to Sri Lanka.[125] The trade in elephants from Sri Lanka (noted for their bravery in war) to the mainland appears to have been important in pre-Islamic times and continues to be referred to by later writers.[126] Sumatra, too, is often mentioned for its many elephants. The old-est cultural artefact concerning the elephant in Sumatra is a four-armed image of the elephant-headed god Ganesha of the eighth-ninth century.[127] From the ninth century, accounts begin to mention war-elephants in Sumatra, especially in the armies of the kings of Shrivijaya. The elephant seems to have abounded in the forests throughout the island, respresenting a species which was different from that of the South-Asian mainland but identical with that of Sri Lanka.[128] Pegu and Thailand, Laos and Cambodia were also full of elephants, of which many were exported to neigh-bouring countries.[129] The country of Champa, known to Arab writ-ers from the ninth century as *Sanf*, corresponding with Cochin-China, the Chinese *Lin-y*, is singled out as having had 'very great

---

[124] *Arthashāstra, II*, Ch. 3; Stein, *Rājatarangini*, IV, 147; Maqbul Ahmad, *Al-Idrisi*, pp. 71, 162; Digby, *War-horse and Elephant*, pp. 22, 62-63, 68, 73; M. Glanius, *A relation of an unfortunate voyage to the kingdom of Bengala* (London, 1682), p. 163.

[125] Digby, *op. cit.*, p. 69; Maqbul Ahmad, *Al-Idrisi*, p. 36.

[126] Digby, *op. cit.*, pp. 62, 69-73; Longworth-Dames, *Duarte Barbosa*, II, pp. 113-4; I, p. 118.

[127] F. M. Schnitger, *Forgotten Kingdoms in Sumatra* (Leiden, 1939), p. 47.

[128] *Ibid.*, p. 49; Takeshi Ito, *The World of the Adat Aceh: A Historical Study of the Sultanate of Aceh* (Unpublished PhD Thesis, Australian National University, 1984), pp. 51-52, 413-27; Yule, *Marco Polo*, II, pp. 285, 289 n.5.

[129] Cf. Longworth-Dames, *Duarte Barbosa*, II, pp. 154-6, 162-3; Bowie,'Ethnicity and Elephants', p. 11; C. Bock, *Temples and Elephants: Travels in Siam in 1881-1882* (London, 1884). For Marco Polo's description of the abundance of elephants in Laos (Laugigu) and Cambodia (of which Lawek was the capital), see Yule, *Marco Polo*, II, pp. 116, 279.

numbers of elephants', the king alone owning 14,000 tame ones in the time of Odoric (c. 1323).[130]

However, with the expansion of agriculture, the possibilities for elephant breeding in large parts of Hind would be substantially reduced over the course of these centuries. Elephants needed a transhumance circuit in a forested area which included elevated as well as lowland, even swamplike, terrain, a *nāgavana* under supervision of an adhyaksha and his subordinate foresters.[131] These reservations were maintained on the frontier of the cultivated realm.[132] Here the bulk of the elephants was kept, half-tamed at best but often wild, or let loose to graze and breed, while elephant hunters had to be kept out, or, as the Arthashāstra prescribes, summarily executed.[133] They must have been extensive areas, at one time, which were excluded from any other use, including irrigated and shifting or *ladang* cultivation. At some stage, with the agricultural population increasing, the keeping of elephants, in this way, must have become uneconomical. And this would be even more the case when the reservations were at some distance—as they increasingly were—from the capital where the king resided. In addition, it would become a more and more difficult task to keep the elephants out of, and at a safe distance from, the cultivation area—which explains why, in our period, the elephant forests were already predominantly restricted to the east of the subcontinent and the hilly forest regions of Burma, Thailand and Cambodia, while they had to be imported in other areas, even, at times, in the south of the subcontinent. It possibly also explains why by the early modern period there was a substantial seaborne traffic in elephants from Achin, Thailand, Pegu and other areas in Southeast Asia, to the South-Asian subcontinent (including the Coromandel, Hindustan, Bengal, Malabar, and Kambaya).[134] We do not know when this began, but the trade between Thailand and Burma and the Indian subcontinent was said to be 'very old'.[135] It can perhaps be speculated that the eco-

[130] Yule, *Marco Polo*, II, pp. 268-71; Komroff, *Contemporaries of Marco Polo*, p. 225.

[131] Cf. *Arthashāstra*, 2. 2. 5, ff.

[132] *Ibid.*, 2. 2. 6.

[133] 2. 2. 8.

[134] Cf. Ito, *World of Adat Aceh*, pp. 51-52, 413-27; Bowie, 'Ethnicity and Elephants', p. 23; Longworth-Dames, *Duarte Barbosa*, II, pp. 154-6.

[135] Bowie, 'Ethnicity and Elephants', pp. 22-24.

logical situation of elephants in many parts of South Asia would have come to resemble more and more that of horses since forests, like grassland, stood in a competitive relationship with agriculture. Horses, however, needed extensive grazing (and breeding) areas but these did not have to be contiguous and especially supervised territories. Moreover, horses were always tame, and hence, in contrast to elephants, controllable; they were also more mobile, or rather more easily movable, and hence could be relocated or concentrated more rapidly. Elephants were expensive to keep in reservations (because of the competitive relationship with agriculture) but to get 50 or 100 elephants from a reservation into a reasonably orderly battle line has been a daunting problem even under the best of circumstances. To keep them in a state of readiness in stables—requiring heavy stone foundations—could, again, become prohibitively expensive and compound the fodder problem (which would in any case reduce their mobility). We can argue, therefore, that from the eleventh to thirteenth centuries and onwards, the disadvantages of the keeping and use of horses relative to the keeping and use of elephants were probably gradually reduced to a point at which it became feasible to concentrate more on horses and exclude the extensive use of elephants.

At the same time, horses were tactically more useful in mobile warfare, while elephants could best be deployed statically, in set battles. This means that a second reason for the decreased use of elephants is probably to be found in the fact that elephant battalions were beginning to be outmanoeuvred by tactical horse movements of the Central-Asian type.

Unfortunately, the positive evidence we have on this subject is extremely fragmentary, and to a considerable extent this second part of our argument can only be rendered plausible by the absence of contrary evidence. We find that the routine use of elephants in military operations among Indian rulers never presented an insurmountable tactical problem for the invading Turkish horsemen and that elephant troops could be dispersed and turned back by concentrated volleys of arrows. Muhammad Ghuri, in his Indian campaigns during the period 1178 to 1191, was twice opposed by elephant forces which successfully withstood him; but in both cases the circumstances were unusual. In the first, the Ghurid army was defeated near Mount Abu by an elephant phalanx in the army of the Caulukyan king of Gujarat, but the sources explain that the Ghurid army was famished and was in a state of exhaustion after crossing the desert.[136] In the second case, Muhammad Ghuri was opposed, near Thanesar, by the Rajas of Ajmer and Delhi, in alliance with other Indian princes, with 200,000 horse and 3,000 elephants.[137] Here the Ghurid leader was wounded and almost wholly deserted by his army. It was one of the events which occurred on the eve of the Second Battle of Tarā'in and proved to be a turning point, since it was only after this that the Ghurid army seriously began to prepare itself for the encounter with Indian war-elephants. Accordingly, some practice was done with mock elephants 'made of mud and wood.'[138] And at Tarā'in in 1192, there was a phalanx of 'steel-clad, ferocious elephants' at the front of the Indian army, but the Turkish cavalry was able to make an assault on the elephant-drivers and easily sent the whole phalanx to flight.[139] Juzjani, describing the same encounter, refers to 10,000 mounted archers who decided the outcome of the battle,[140] and says that the latter were ordered to keep a distance of a horse's course between themselves and the frontline of elephants, and that thus the 'infidel host' was overthrown.[141] According to Firishta, this 'infidel host' consisted of 300,000 horse, more than 3,000 elephants, and a body of infantry.[142]

Examples like this point at some of the practical experiences that are likely to have contributed to the demise of the war-elephant in India.[143] This demise, to be sure, was a gradual one. Not until early modern times did the elephant lose its usefulness on battlefields entirely, except as command vehicles or in siege operations and various other paramilitary functions.[144] The increase in the number of firearms and, more especially, the growing effectiveness of firearms, following upon the spread of mounted archery, caused its final obsolescence.

---

[136] *TF*, p. 56; *TN*, p. 116; *FS*, vs. 1307-14.

[137] *TF*, p. 57.

[138] *FS*, vs. 1413-23.

[139] *Ibid.*, vs. 1424, 1475-81.

[140] Cf. p. 93.

[141] *TN*, p. 119.

[142] *TF*, p. 58.

[143] For another relatively detailed description of how mounted archers could outmanoeuvre elephant battalions, see Yule, *Marco Polo*, II, pp. 98-106.

[144] Cf. Streusand, *Mughal Empire*, p. 55; Haider, *Islamic Arms*, p. 274.

Significantly, in Southeast Asia, where the transition to Turko-Mongol mounted archery was never made, the war-elephant appears to have retained a much more central role down to early modern times. One isolated, but revealing, episode is recorded by Ma Tuan-lin in the twelfth century which shows that the Chams, in their wars against Angkor, successfully introduced mounted archers to combat elephants.[145] According to Ma Tuan-lin, a mandarin from Fukien was shipwrecked on the coast of Champa in 1171, while a war against Angkor was in progress. The mandarin advised that the Cham forces should rely less on elephants and more on cavalry with bows and arbalests. He also instructed the Chams how to shoot arrows from horseback, and arranged for the purchase of some superior horses. These advantages, it was then claimed, decided the war in favour of the Chams. But this appears to have been a highly exceptional situation. Centuries later we still find large elephant battalions being deployed in Southeast-Asian mainland states. According to Joao de Barros, the Thai army at the beginning of the sixteenth century still consisted of '20,000 cavalry, 250,000 infantry, and 10,000 war-elephants'.[146] Fitch states in the latter half of the sixteenth century that 'the King of Pegu was said to have 4,000 fighting animals [elephants]'.[147] In Achin, the development of firearms was not such that it could replace its 900 war-elephants.[148] Like in Thailand, where elephants were trained to endure artillery being fired from their backs (never over their heads), in Achin elephants were being accustomed to the sound of guns by firing weapons in front of them at set times. These facts, again, strongly suggest that the gradual elimination of elephants from warfare in South Asia was due to the here proposed combination of factors, and that next to the development of artillery and firearms, the widespread use of mounted archers as well as a steady supply of superior horses from Iran, Arabia and Central Asia, in combination with the reduced availability of elephants, were essential in it.

---

[145] Ma Touan-lin, *Ethnographie des Peuples Etrangers à la Chine*, Tr. Le Marquis d'Hervey de Saint-Denys (Paris, 1876), pp. 555-8; I. Mabbett and D. Chandler, *The Khmers* (Oxford, 1995), p. 157 and plate 29.

[146] Bowie, 'Ethnicity and Elephants', p. 12.

[147] *Ibid.*, p. 13.

[148] D. Lombard, *Le Sultanat d'Atjeh au temps d'Iskander Muda* (Paris, 1967), pp. 83-100; Ito, *The World of Adat Aceh*, pp. 51-52.

CHAPTER IV

THE OPENING OF THE GATES OF HIND

Indian vernacular sources describe the conquest—at length—as 'the opening of the gates of Hind',[1] while inscriptions in Sanskrit which survived from these centuries frequently mention the violent irruptions of the *Turushkas*, the 'country-conquering Turks', 'beef-eating barbarians (*mlecchas*)', 'Shaka princes', or, at a somewhat later stage, of the 'Mongols' (*Mudgalas*).[2] To piece together a coherent narrative of the conquest, however, from the late tenth to the early thirteenth century, would be impossible on the basis of the Indian materials alone. It is disconcertingly difficult even with the aid of the Arabic and Persian sources. The latter, however, on the most basic level, deal with sequences of events (rather than individual events), and they allow us to distinguish two stages in the conquest: the first, commonly called the Ghaznavid period, from 977 to 1186 AD; and the second, the Ghūrid period, from 1186 to 1206 AD. In addition, the Muslim sources allow us a fairly comprehensive view of the ethnic composition and military divisions of the invading warbands; they present us with a list of the most important military confrontations that occurred, although with numerous inconsistencies and lacunae; they describe some of the effects of the conquest; and we get a broad idea of the itineraries of the conquerors. In this chapter we will synthesize this material for each of the two periods.

---

[1] Cf. Harishcandra, Bhārat-durdashā, Act 3, in: R. S. Mc Gregor, *Hindi Literature from its Beginnings to the Nineteenth Century* (Wiesbaden, 1984), p. 3.

[2] Other terms that are used include *Tājika* and *Yavana* ('Ionians'). On the term *mleccha*, see T. R. Sharma, *Personal and Geographical Names in the Gupta Inscriptions* (Delhi, 1978), pp. 149-52. For the use of *Tājika* or *Tāyi*, see J. Newman, 'Islam in the Buddhist Kālacakra Tantra' (Paper presented to the 1989 Annual Meeting of the American Academy of Religion, Annaheim, CA, 1989), and D. C. Sircar, *Studies in the Geography of Ancient and Medieval India* (Delhi, 1971), pp. 126-7, 131. For 'Shaka princes', see *Epigraphia Indica, Arabic and Persian Supplement*, 1913-14 (Calcutta, 1917; reprint Delhi, 1987), pp. 35-45. For *Mudgalas*, see G. Buhler, *The Jagaducharita of Sarvanada: a Historical Romance from Gujarat* (Vienna, 1892), p. 19. For *Yavanas*, see Sircar, *Studies in Geography*, p. 396; *Epigraphia Indica*, III, pp. 338-9; A. K. Narain, *The Indo-Greeks* (Delhi, 1980), pp. 165-9.

GHAZNAVIDS, 977-1186 AD

In so far as there is any emphasis on the Turkishness of the Ghaznavids and their following, it always comes from the very early
years of the dynasty.[3] Later Ghaznavid chronicles in Arabic and
Persian still corroborate that the dynasty spoke Turkish (*Turkī*) up
to the time of Mas'ūd (1031-41), and that, while *ghulāms* who had
been in Ghaznavid service for a long time acquired some knowledge of Persian, new recruits continued to speak Turkish. But at
Ghazna and Lahore, with the aid of Persian chroniclers, secre-
taries and officials, the transformation of a congeries of pagan
Turkish slaves into a Perso-Islamic ruling elite which could put to
use the administrative nomenclature and political rhetoric of the
eastern caliphate seems to have been effected almost overnight.
Obliterating the pagan Turkish past, the dynasty was provided with
a Persian pedigree harking back to pre-Islamic times. It was cast
in the role of defenders of Sunnī orthodoxy against the Shī'ite
Būyids. And, in the wider Islamic context, it became the historic
mission of the Ghaznavid dynasty to raid and conquer 'the infidels of *al-Hind*'.[4]

If the Turks were the most important ethnic component of the
Ghaznavid armies at all levels, they were not the only one, and
we can see that in actual fact these armies were usually rather
heterogeneous. The Ghaznavid army was said to be 'not of one,
but of ten sorts'.[5] As has been stressed by C. E. Bosworth, such
ethnic heterogeneity was seen as a source of strength by contemporaries, and it was by no means unique to the Ghaznavids.[6]

From the very beginning most of the commanders and high
officers (*amīrs, sarhangs, sipahsālārs*) and a substantial majority of
horsemen of the Ghaznavid armies were Turkish. Around Ghaz-

---

[3] For example, in the *Pandnāma*, Sabuktigin proclaims that his origin is 'in
Turkestān', and that he was bought there by a slave-merchant (M. Nazim (ed.
and transl.), 'The Pand-Nāmah of Subuktigīn', *Journal of the Royal Asiatic Society*
(1933), ff. 226b-227b; see also *TN*, p. 6).
[4] Cf. Bosworth, *Ghaznavids*, pp. 3-66; idem, *The Later Ghaznavids: Splendour
and Decay: The Dynasty in Afghanistan and Northern India, 1040-1186* (Edinburgh,
1977); *TB*, pp. 188, 191, 263; M. R. Waldman, *Toward a Theory of Historical Narrative: A Case Study of Perso-Islamicate Historiography* (Columbus, 1980), pp. 31, 33-
34.
[5] *AH*, f. 64a.
[6] Bosworth, *Ghaznavids*, pp. 107-8; idem, *Later Ghaznavids*, p. 59.

na itself, the four major districts were all granted to Turkish officers and their sons.[7] In what numbers new groups of Turkish military slaves kept arriving from Central Asia is not easy to make
out—not least because these, like the mamlūks of Egypt and Syria, sometimes appear to have adopted non-Turkish names. It is
possible that, over the course of almost two centuries, in India
the higher offices came to be shared more and more with Indians or Indian Muslims and Afghans, especially by the time that
the Ghaznavids lost direct access to Central Asia, but it cannot be
doubted that here too Turks continued to be ascendant at all
times.

As long as Ghazna was the capital, the governorship (*sipahsālārī*)
of Lahore and Hindustan and the high command of the 'army of
al-Hind' (*jaysh al-Hind*) as well as other high offices on the frontier appear not only to have been in Turkish hands but frequently
in the hands of bloodrelatives (brothers or sons) of the Ghaznavid
sultans.[8] These governors commonly employed their own relatives
in various subordinate positions or repartitioned their offices
among numerous sons of their own.[9] Turkish names, like Arslan,
Altūntash, Nāyaltigīn, Nūshtigīn, Tughāntigīn, and so on, continue to be found among the high officers of the Ghaznavids, especially those who conducted raids deep into India, until as late as
the twelfth century.[10] Whether relatives or slaves, these commanders, with their own retinues of Turkish slave troops, and using
the wealth acquired in Hindustan, easily turned against the sultans. Turkish slaves who obtained military command in Ghazna
and in India also lacked, and failed to develop, laws of succession
which would have been able to assure unbroken dynastic continuity. Succession difficulties appeared at the deaths of Sabuktigīn,
Mahmūd and Mas'ūd, and henceforward became a regular pattern. With Sabuktigīn included, only seven of the eighteen Ghaznavid amirs came to the throne uncontested. The presence of
Turkish slaves at court continued to foster an atmosphere of political intrigue and factionalism, and this was further enhanced by

---

[7] *AH*, f. 61b.
[8] *TYA*, pp. 329-34; *TF*, pp. 42, 44, 46; *TB*, p. 538.
[9] E.g. *TF*, p. 50.
[10] *TYA*, pp. 321-4; *TB*, pp. 168, 188, 261, 266, 270-1, 274, 323-9, 495-500, 523-
4; *TF*, pp. 26, 31, 40-42, 44, 46-47, 49-50; J. Sauvaget, 'Noms et Surnoms de
Mamelouks', *Journal Asiatique*, CCXXXVIII (1950), pp. 31-58.

the workings of an unstructured and *ad hoc* cash dispensation through which the treasure obtained in the conquests was redistributed.

Turks were the mainstay of the slave troops (*bandagān, ghilmān, mamālik*), which constituted the core of the Ghaznavid armies— of those stationed in the capitals of Ghazna and Lahore as well as those engaged in frontier warfare.[11] The impression we sometimes get is that all or almost all of the regular or professional Turkish troops were slaves or of slave origin.[12] Turkish slaves originally constituted the bulk of the palace guard. Mahmūd's court 'was guarded by 4000 Turkish slave youths (*ghulām-i-turk-i-wushāq*)', which were to be partly replaced and counterbalanced by Indian slaves only much later.[13] In the early period, the Turkish slaves were often obtained, either by the Ghaznavid sultans or by their governors, from within the Ghaznavid empire, or they were collected by purchase or gift beyond its confines, from among the Qarlugh, Yaghma, Qay, Tukhsi, Chigil, Khotan, and later also from the Tatār and Kirghīz tribes and Kāshgar and the Khitā.[14] In India we occasionally also come across Ghuzz, Saljūqī and Sharkasī (Circassian) Turks as part of the multi-ethnic armies.[15] Direct access to the source of supply of Turkish slaves was cut off after Mas'ūd's reign but this is not likely to have suspended the trade in slaves at any time, although it may have reduced their number.[16] The sources frequently mention these elite troops of Turks (*Turkān-i-tīr*) as especially awe-inspiring archers; stories of their bravery and skills abound.[17] As already indicated (cf. pp. 91-92), among the total number of the regular armies—which could run as high as 54,000 during Mahmūd's reign, excluding the provincial troops and garrisons (while figures for individual expeditions are much lower)—the Turkish slaves were in fact only a nucleus. But it was such a valuable nucleus that slave status virtually determined Turkish ethnic identity.[18]

---

[11] See also Bosworth, 'Ghaznevid Military Organization', pp. 37, 44.
[12] Cf. *TN*, p. 26.
[13] *TN*, p. 9.
[14] Bosworth, *Ghaznavids*, p. 109.
[15] *TYA*, p. 270; *TYP*, p. 184; *TF*, pp. 26, 31-32.
[16] Bosworth, *Ghaznavids*, p. 59.
[17] See e.g. *ZA*, p. 72; *AH*, ff. 53b, 102b; *TF*, pp. 30-31; B. De (transl.), *The Tabaqāt-i-Akbarī of Khwājah Nizāmuddin Ahmad*, Vol. I (Calcutta, 1927), p. 14.
[18] So valuable indeed that very small numbers could make a considerable dif-

Next to the number of slave troops (of which we do not have exact figures) and other regular troops, however, the number of Turks which joined the Ghaznavid armies in India as irregulars or volunteers seems to have been much higher.[19]

In addition to these various categories of Turks, recruited from Transoxania and elsewhere, we find in the Ghaznavid armies which occupied the Panjab and penetrated further into India in the eleventh and twelfth centuries, a number of other ethnic groups. It is at this time that especially the Afghans come into the limelight, when commercial traffic through their territories intensified and they became participants in the Indian campaigns. Who the Afghans were, and where they lived, in the centuries immediately preceding the expansion of Islam is not very clear. Varāhamihira's work of the sixth century AD, the *Bṛhat Samhitā*, mentions the *Avagāna*, but from a mere astrological point of view. Hiuen Tsang, in the early seventh century, does not fail to mention the Afghans—Chinese *A-po-kan*—but their exact location in the area which later became known as Afghanistan is not identified by him with precision.[21] The Arabic accounts, however, from the ninth century on, point at the Zhob district and the *koh sulaymān*, along the road from India to the west, as the original habitat of the *'Abghān'*, who, moreover, at this early stage already appear to have been involved in mercantile enterprise.[22] With the advent of the Muslims, the Afghans expanded further to the border of the Indus valley and the Khyber Hills, and some of them are alleged (by much later writers) to have converted to the faith even before the Arab conquest of Sind and before the Islamicization of large parts of Zābul and Kābul gained momentum under the early Saffārids. In Samanid times, the Afghans held power in Roh, from Swat and Bajaur in the north to Sibi and Bhakkar in Sind, and from Hasan Abdal in the east to Kabul and

---

ference. Baihaqi describes how Ahmad Nayaltigin secretly made special arrangements to send men to Turkestan, via Panjshir, to obtain seventy more military slaves before he rebelled as governor of Hindustan, shortly after his raid on Benares in 1033 AD (*TB*, pp. 323, 495-8, 500-3, 523-6).

[19] Cf. pp. 91-92.

[20] M. Ramakrishna Bhat (ed. and transl.), *Varāhamihira's Bṛhat Samhitā* (Delhi, 1981), p. 143.

[21] Watters, *Yuan Chwang*, II, p. 265.

[22] Cf. *Al-Hind, I*, pp. 95, 167-8.

Qandahār in the west, apparently deflecting Samanid power southward.

While the origins of the Afghans are obscure, there is no direct genealogical link between Afghans and Turks.[23] The Afghans later merged with the 'Khalaj Turks'—who, as we have seen, were probably not ethnic Turks but a Turkicized group.[24] The Khalaj in a later stage adopted the Afghan language and became the largest subgroup of Afghans under the Indian name of *Ghilzai*.[25] Rashid ad-Din, in the fourteenth century, classifies the Afghans with the Mongols (*Mughul*), while 'Abd ar-Razzaq, in the fifteenth century, considers them to be *Hazāras*—a branch of the Mongols—and also Turks (*Atrāk*).[26] Probably the changing political conditions of these later times are responsible for this confusion of ethnonyms. Moreover, when the Afghans began to spread in various directions, especially in the eleventh to thirteenth centuries, a gradual mixing occurred between Afghans, Turks, Mongols, and others like the Khalaj.

Afghan conversion to Islam appears to have accelerated under the Ghaznavids but to have been incomplete by the twelfth century. The evidence for this is inconclusive. All Afghan chronicles of the seventeenth and eighteenth centuries, however, agree about the decisive role of the Afghans in the spread of Islam and the *jihād* campaigns in India under the Ghaznavids, Ghurids, Delhi Sultans, Timurids, and Durranis.[27] 'The Afghans', we read in the *Khulāṣat al-ansāb*, 'dwelt in the area of Ghaznin [Ghazna] and Qandahar until the time of Sultan Mahmud [of Ghazna], who several times invaded Hindustān in order to reduce *Hind* but had to return without success, but then had recourse to the Afghans living here [in Ghazna and Qandahar] and sought their support. Upon which, it is said, 12,000 horse (*sawār*) and 12,000 foot (*payāda*) from among the Afghans joined the king and accompa-

---

[23] *Ibid.*, pp. 95, 167. Early Jewish penetration of the area of Afghanistan led to the spurious claim of *Banī Isrā'īl* descent in the later Afghan chronicles.

[24] Cf. p. 70.

[25] W. Barthold, *An Historical Geography of Iran* (Princeton, 1984), p. 72; Minorsky, 'The Turkish Dialect of the Khalaj'.

[26] B. Dorn (ed. and transl.), *Makhzan-i-Afghānī*, 2 vols (London, 1965), II, p. 40.

[27] Cf. Hāfiz Rahmat Khān, *Khulāṣat al-ansāb* (1184 A. H.), BL: Egerton 1104, ff. 46a-72b.

nied him to Hindustān, constituting the van'.[28] The contemporary Ghaznavid historians, on the other hand, do not confirm such
prominence of the Afghans in the campaigns of the Muslim Turks
of the eleventh and twelfth centuries—which appears to have
been an exaggeration. Ghaznavid historians describe them as both
participants in the *jihād* and 'rebels'. Mahmūd also undertook a
number of campaigns against them. And we know that Afghan
troops served Muslim rulers as well as Hindus, while later they
also sided with the Mongols. Nonetheless, their support role in
the early stages of Turkish expansion was quite significant, and
particularly their role in the Ghaznavid armies. The Afghans who
were placed in the garrisons in Multan and Lamghan by Jayapāl,
the Hindu Raja of Lahore, together probably with a number of
Khalaj, already became military retainers of Sabuktigīn when the
latter first started invading these areas.[29] A multitude of thousands
of Afghans and Khalaj 'of the low-lying desert areas' (*kah sahrā'-
nishīnān i biqā'*) declared their allegiance to Sabuktigīn, while
many enlisted in his army, after the latter's second raid into India,
which resulted in new conquests in the area for Islam.[30] But not
before the accession of Sabuktigīn's son Mahmūd were all
Afghans, as we are informed, 'forced to submit'.[31] And under the
latter we find the 'Afghan demons' (*'afārīt-i-afghāniyān*), generally bracketed with the Khalaj, and always under Turkish command,
serving in India as well as in Central Asia.[32] Turkish and Afghan
prisoners, of both sexes, were made by Mahārāja Mandalika and
Bhīm Deva of Gujarat, when the latter pursued Mahmūd's army
after the destruction of Somnath.[33] Elsewhere, especially about

---

[28] *Ibid.*, ff. 47a-b.
[29] Cf. *Al-Hind, I*, p. 169; *TF*, pp. 17-18; Dorn, *Makhan-i-Afghānī*, II, p. 76.
[30] *TF*, p. 20; *TYP*, p. 39.
[31] *TF*, pp. 17-18.
[32] *TYP*, pp. 184, 211; *TYA*, pp. 270, 333; *TF*, p. 26.
[33] R. A. Diwan, *Tarikh-i-Sorath: A History of the Provinces of Sorath and Halar in
Kathiawad* (Bombay, 1882), p. 112. These prisoners appear to have been Muslims
but subsequently mingled with the local Hindu population of Kathiawar and
Gujarat. 'Turkish, Afghan and Mughal female prisoners were, if they happened
to be virgins, considered pure according to their own belief, and were without
any difficulty taken as wives, the bowels of the others, however, were cleansed by
means of emetics and purgatives, and the captives were after that disposed of
according to the command, "the wicked women to the wicked men, and the good
women to the good men" (*Qur'ān*, XXIV, 26); the low females were joined to
low men. Respectable men were compelled to shave their beards, and were
enrolled among the Shekāvat and the Wādkel tribes of Rājputs; whilst the lower

Lahore, Mahmūd, on returning from Somnath, left the Afghans behind 'for the establishment of Islam'.[34] While before the mid-eleventh century the Afghans again broke away from Turkish control, we still find 'Afghans and Khalaj' among the army of Muhammad Bayhram, the Ghaznavid governor of Lahore in 1118 AD, 'who committed great devastations in the domains of the Indian kings' and aspired to the throne.[35]

A third ethnic group which we find penetrating further into India in the eleventh and twelfth centuries are the Arabs. Unlike the Muslim armies which conquered Makran and Sind in the seventh and eighth centuries, in the Ghaznavid armies the Syrian and Iraqi Arabs were no longer numerically very important, but the semi-nomadic Arab population which had been transferred from Basra to Khurasan—turning it into a 'second Arabia'—in the first century of Islam seems to have continued to provide some of the best cavalry, particularly known for their dashing raids into hostile territory, as early as Alptigīn's time.[36] The '6000 Arabian horse' which were sent against the Indian king Ānandapāla in 1008 AD, near Peshawar, could well have originated from here.[37] At Nardin, in 1013 AD, the advance guard consisted of Arab horsemen, 'sticking to the back of their horses like horsecloth'.[38] As late as 1118 AD, Arabs are still found in the army of the Ghaznavid governor of Lahore, participating in raids further into India.[39] Lahore had acquired a special Arab quarter (muhallat-i-'arab) by this time.[40]

The other ethnic groups which became prominent in Ghaznavid India served in roles which were complementary to the cavalry which was thus made up of Turks, Afghans and Arabs of a nomadic or semi-nomadic background. The Dailamīs, originating from the Caspian mountain areas but already widespread as infantrymen (rajjāla-l-daylam) in the tenth century in many parts

---

kinds were allotted to the castes of Kolīs, Khānts, Bābriās and Mers' (Ibid.).

[34] Hāfiz Rahmat Khan, Khulāsat al-ansāb, ff. 47b-48a. Under Mahmūd, also, an Afghan shahna and kotwāl was appointed at Nardarī, close to the country of Jayapāl (AH, f. 125a).

[35] TF, p. 26.

[36] Bosworth, Ghaznavids, pp. 111-2; Al-Hind, I, p. 111.

[37] TF, p. 26.

[38] TYA, p. 332.

[39] TF, p. 50.

[40] AH, f. 122a.

of the Islamic world, are found in the Ghaznavid armies in India, for instance at Nardin again in 1013 AD,[41] and, more generally, in the foothills of Kashmir. Titled Dailamī Muslim chiefs (a'yān-i-day-lam), which were among the cavalry, occupied prominent positions in the expanding Ghaznavid state in India, at least under Mas'ūd I, but at Ghazna they were an alien element, and they seem to have been encouraged to move on to the Indian frontier as their presence at Ghazna caused considerable tension.[42] Tājik or 'Persian' soldiers were recruited from Khurasan for the jihad in India and the Kabul valley already by Alptigīn, and later levies, particularly those made by Mahmūd, in Khurasan must have included many more.[43] Unlike the Arabs, Afghans and Dailamis, the Tājīks were sometimes recruited as slaves—which may indicate that they were not converted. The presence of 'people from 'Ajam' in the Ghaznavid armies in India is attested as late as 1120 AD, when they were still employed in plundering expeditions in territories of the Indian princes.[44] Their numbers cannot be estimated with any accuracy. Moreover, as Persian names began to be adopted by Turks, Indian Muslims, Afghans, and others, even the pre-eminence of Persians among the elite cannot be gauged. But it is clear that Persians became ascendant among the administrative cadres in the Panjab in the later eleventh and twelfth centuries. Among these administrative cadres, it seems, the Turks did less well.

More generally, the higher administrative functions in India may also have come to be increasingly shared with non-Muslim Indians or Indian Muslims. Indians (hunud, hindū, hindwān), partly recruited as slave soldiers (the bandagān-i-hind), and, as their names indicate, commonly retaining their ancestral religion, were also an important part of the Turkish-led armies and, in later times, the palace guard at Ghazna, providing a great deal of local knowledge, a mediating role, as well as special fighting skills which were put to use even in Central Asia.[45] Indian slaves were obtained by raiding. But often too, Indian forces which capitulated were

---

[41] TYA, p. 333; TYP, p. 211.
[42] TB, pp. 327, 329; TF, p. 40.
[43] TF, p. 29; AH, f. 54a.
[44] TF, p. 50.
[45] Cf. AH, ff. 53b-54a; TYA, p. 270; TYP, p. 184; TB, pp. 271, 523-4, 532; TN, p. 15.

forced to deliver up hostages, which then sometimes entered Ghaznavid service, or capitulating garrisons offered their services en masse.[46] Mas'ūd employed local troops of the Panjab on a wide scale against his rebellious governor Nāyaltigīn. From these was to emerge 'Tūlik al-Hind', the son of a barber, who was made a commander of Indian troops in Balkh, and subsequently became the first Hindu to be elevated to sit among the Turkish chiefs— by which time he began to be referred to as 'the *amīr al-umarāy Hind*'.[47] In the service of the Ghaznavid king Mas'ūd, Tūlik brought the Hindu Kathors and others, such as the Jats, under his rule. In a later period, about 1149 AD, we still hear of Indian troops in the Ghaznavid army during Bahram Shah's struggle with the Ghurids. Another rebel leader, in Bahram Shah's reign, collected an army of 70,000 men, both Muslims and Hindus, including 'a large number of Rānās, Thākurs and leaders of Hindustān (*muqaddamān-i-hindustān*), infidel irregulars, both horse and foot'.[48]

Further evidence pertaining to the first half of the eleventh century clearly indicates that these 'Turkish' armies of the Ghaznavids, mostly of recent nomadic extraction, were not only relatively small as far as their regular components were concerned, but highly mobile and could cover great distances in a short time. In spite of the fact that women could be brought along (but of this we hear very little),[49] in this regard they were wholly unlike the Mughal armies of the seventeenth century. The latter were in practice more like moving cities, equipped with servants, grooms, prostitutes, and bazaars, and unable to move more than sixteen km a day for five days per week. Until the end of Mahmūd's reign, the Ghaznavid armies retained Ghazna as their only permanent base and their only capital in the *dyār-i-islām*, and from here

---

[46] Cf. *ZA*, p. 69. Shortly after the capitulation of Nagarkot in 1009 AD, Jayapāl, 'the king of Hind', offered tribute and seems to have complied with the stipulation that an Indian force of 2000 men would be sent to the Ghaznavid court by turn every year (*TYP*, p. 341).

[47] *TYA*, pp. 303-5; *TYP*, p. 198. *Tūlik bin Ja Sin* could write both in *Hindwi* and *Fārsi*, and we are told that he lived for a long time in Kashmir, 'where he learned dissimulation, amours and witchcraft (*lukht-i-zarq-o-'ishwaq-o-jādu'i*)' (*TF*, p. 42; *TB*, pp. 500-3, 523-4).

[48] *AH*, ff. 148a-b.

[49] The only evidence on this appears to be the *Tarikh-i-Sorath* (Cf. p. 117).

almost annual jihād raids were undertaken into the *dyār-i-hind.*
The sultans, typically, would leave the city immediately after the
monsoon, 'when the Indus and other rivers were still swollen',
and 'returned with booty to Ghazna' after each raid, usually
before the onset of the next monsoon, although it did happen
that Mahmūd had to return during the rains, 'losing many men
and much baggage'. From about 1013-14, garrisons were beginning to be left behind in conquered forts or were stationed on a
more permanent basis in towns (earlier on, residents had sometimes been left behind, who were easily evicted), but this occurred
only infrequently. More commonly Hindu chiefs were co-opted as
tributaries in an extensive system of indirect rule—which however also remained in constant flux. The idea of shifting the capital further into the subcontinent was on occasion put forward,
but failed to materialize. After the expedition to Somnath, in
1025, Mahmūd, according to Firishta, proposed to transfer the
capital from Ghazna to Nahrwala, the main political centre in
Gujarat, 'because of its convenience and alleged gold mines'.[50]
The plan fell apart, and Mahmūd instead returned to Ghazna
again. In 1039, Mas'ūd, in his turn, proposed to abandon Ghazna for Lahore. 'He sent a message to his mother, sisters, daughters, aunts, and freed slaves, to prepare themselves for a journey
to Hindustān, and to leave nothing behind at Ghazna'.[51] But again
the plan was abandoned, and Lahore, while emerging gradually
as a second Ghaznavid city from Mahmūd's time onwards, did not
become the main capital until the reigns of the last two Ghaznavid sultans, in the second half of the twelfth century, after the
Ghurids and Seljuqs had deprived them not only of Ghazna, but
of most of Iran and Turan. Even then there were no permanent
territorial gains beyond the Panjab and what is now part of western U.P., so that the pattern of Turkish invasions in these centuries remained overwhelmingly one of fast-moving small armies
under mamlūk leadership, conducting lightning raids, sometimes
deep into 'infidel' territory, but always using a home base much
further to the west, on the Islamic frontier, be it Ghazna or
Lahore, to which they would return after each expedition.
   The consequences and effects of these 'victories in al-Hind'

---

[50] *TF*, pp. 32-35.
[51] *TB*, p. 828.

(*futūh al-Hind*) in the eleventh and twelfth centuries were, thus, variable. Political dislocations among the Indian ruling groups were severe in those areas which came under more or less permanent Turkish control early in the eleventh century. In the Panjab, the Hindu Shahi 'ruler of Lahore' (*ḥākim-i-lāhūr*) was gradually but inexorably forced out of the domain to which he had taken refuge after losing control of Kabul and Waihind.[52] This ruler, Ānandapāla (Ar. Ānandbāl), variously described as the *ʿaẓim al-hind* and the *pādshāh-i-hind*, fled to Kashmir in 1006 AD after a first encounter with Mahmūd, when the latter sought to penetrate to the Ismāʿīlī Amirate of Multan. Al-ʿUtbī refers to the Hindu Shahi ruler as the 'high mountain and blocking pass' of the entire area, which means he was the linchpin of an alliance system which extended across the Panjab and into Sind.[53] When the Amir of Multan learned about the Hindu Shahi defeat, 'he packed his treasure and belongings on the backs of elephants and repaired to *Sarāndib* [one of the islands in the Indus]'.[54] Multan was given over to Sukhapāla, one of the sons of the Shahi king who had been taken prisoner and who appears to have converted to Islam. But in 1007, Sukhapāla apostasized and rebelled, and was then forced to withdraw 'to the hills of Kashmir' in his turn, probably ending up in the Salt Range (Khewra), where he linked up with Ānandapāla again, and Hindu Shahi power for a while succeeded in reconstituting itself.[55] In 1009, 'the king of Hind' offered submission to Mahmūd, hostilities ceased, and traffic between Khurāsān and Hind resumed.[56] Later Hindu Shahi rulers resumed their struggle against the Ghaznavids, seeking aid from Kashmir again, but were ultimately compelled to leave the Panjab behind entirely and seek refuge at the court of the Kashmir rulers—in the valley which always remained beyond the Ghaznavid reach.[57] With the departure of these rulers, as Al-Biruni noted, the Hindu sciences left the Panjab as well, relocating themselves beyond the mountain ramparts of Kashmir in the same way, or in Benares and other areas where the Turks were not yet in permanent con-

52 Cf. *Al-Hind*, I, pp. 125-6.
53 *TYA*, pp. 261-4; *TYP*, pp. 180-1.
54 *TYA*, p. 263; *TYP*, p. 180.
55 *ZA*, pp. 68-69; *TF*, pp. 24-25; *TYA*, pp. 264-78; *TYP*, pp. 182-6.
56 *TYP*, p. 198; *TYA*, p. 305; *Al-Hind*, I, p. 126.
57 Cf. *Al-Hind*, I, pp. 127, 254.

trol.[58] 'The Hindus became like atoms of dust scattered in all directions', says Al-Biruni, probably referring to an exodus of brahman literati from the Panjab which we cannot trace in any detail.[59] Al-Biruni further testifies that 'not long before our time, Vasukra, a native of Kashmir, a famous brahman, has of his own account undertaken the task of explaining the Veda and committing it to writing. He has taken on himself a task from which everybody else would have recoiled, but he carried it out because he was afraid that the Veda might be forgotten and entirely vanish out of the memories of men, since he observed that the characters of men grew worse and worse, and that they did not care much for virtue, nor even for duty'.[60] In effect, the oldest surviving Veda manuscripts were written in Nepal in 1040 AD, and this may mean that Nepal has been another focus of brahman migration.[61]

It is also in the Panjab and adjacent hill regions that we find the first references to native conversion to Islam. Such conversion occurred as early as 1004-5, possibly even earlier, in Bhātīya, 'the land of the Bhā(t)tīs' which was part of the Hindu Shahi domain; here a part of the population, including perhaps numbers of Jats, turned to Islam.[62] In 1013-14, according to Firishta, 'Mahmūd forced Islam upon the inhabitants' of the hills bordering on the south of Kashmir, and defeated the Kashmir troops sent in support of the Hindu Shahi ruler Trilochanpāla, after which 'many neighbouring rajas pledged loyalty to the conqueror and many inhabitants embraced Islam'.[63] Several years later, some of the rajas (*buzurg-i-hind*) of southwest Kashmir submitted to Mahmud—at least one of which, the raja of Barma, with 10,000 followers, converted to Islam.[64] The ruler of two other hilltracts, referred to as the *darra* of Qīrāt and Nārdīn, which also included Nūr, located 'in the country between Turkestān and Hin-

---

[58] *Ibid.*

[59] E. C. Sachau (transl.), *Alberuni's India* (New Delhi, 1983), I, p. 22; M. Witzel, 'Toward a History of the Brahmans', *Journal of the American Oriental Society*, 113, 2 (1993), pp. 264-8.

[60] Sachau, *Alberuni's India*, I, pp. 126-7.

[61] Cf. Witzel, 'Toward a History of the Brahmans', p. 264, note 7.

[62] *TYA*, pp. 258-61; *TYP*, pp. 178-9; *TF*, p. 24; *ZA*, pp. 66-67; *Al-Hind*, *I*, p. 162.

[63] *ZA*, p. 72; *Rājatarangini*, VII, 53, 56-58.

[64] *TYA*, pp. 395-9; *TYP*, pp. 242-4.

dustān', submitted to Mahmud and accepted Islam in 1022.[65] Prior to this date, the inhabitants of these hilltracts are recorded to have been 'worshippers of lions' (*sherparast*), which probably means that they were Buddhists of some sort.[66]

Beyond the Panjab and the Himalayan foothills of Kashmir, the Turkish conquests had a more limited impact. In the Middle Country, the Ganges-Yamuna Doab, some of the most important sacred sites of Indian culture were destroyed or desecrated, or, again in the rhetoric of several texts, 'the idols of the Hindus were scattered in the dust'. While such destruction could be widespread, it should be distinguished from permanent conquest.[67] Typically, what occurred amounted to a huge transfer of wealth and a relatively more modest demographic shift from these centres to the Islamic frontier, and hence further westwards. Even more than had been the case with the Arab conquests in the Middle East, vast amounts of immobilized treasure were brought back into circulation. The sources repeat ad nauseam that from the destroyed temples and sacred sites, and as booty or tribute obtained from vanquished Indian rulers, the 'army of Islam obtained abundant wealth and unlimited riches'.[68] For whatever they are worth, the figures quoted are astronomical. Precious stones, rubies and pearls, gold and silver in coins and ingots or bullion, as well as gold and silver icons, which together were valued at millions of dirhams and dinars and must have represented the accumulated treasure of centuries, were forcibly collected and carried off to Ghazna. At Kanauj and Mathura, according to Firishta, 'Mahmūd broke down or burned all the idols, and amassed a vast quantity of gold and silver, of which the idols were mostly composed ... Then he went back to Ghazna with twenty million dirhams worth of gold and silver bullion. And the private spoils of the army were no less than that which came into the royal treasury'.[69] After plundering the major centres of Madhyadesha and, finally, Somnath—where he found 'a greater quantity of jewels and gold than it is thought any royal treasury ever con-

---

[65] *TF*, p. 31.
[66] *ZA*, p. 78.
[67] Cf. Chapter IX.
[68] *TYP*, p. 155. For other references, see *ibid.*, pp. 37, 180, 188, 244, 247; *TF*, pp. 24-25, 28-29, 33-34; etc.
[69] *TF*, pp. 28-29.

tained before'—, Mahmud contemplated to settle in Nahrwala, in Gujarat. 'Some historians relate', says Firishta, 'that in that age there were gold mines in Gujarat, which induced Mahmūd to wish to reside at Nahrwala; but there are now no traces of these mines, although in that time there might have been, like in Sistan, which was swallowed up by an earthquake in the following reign. The king, having heard of gold mines on the island of Sri Lanka and in Pegu (jazīra' sarandīp-o-peku), it is [also] said, seriously intended to fit out a fleet for the conquest of these regions, but he was diverted from this scheme ...'[70] At Ghazna, a part of the bullion and precious stones was used for decorative purposes, or dispensed among the far-flung clienteles, but most of the bullion was used for minting purposes, facilitating the newly activated and ever-intensifying trade between the Islamic world and India.[71] When later Ghazna was plundered by the Seljuq armies, a part of the accumulated treasure of the Ghaznavid sultans was, in its turn, carried off by them, and a further drain of the Ghaznavid treasure occurred through tribute payments to the Seljuqs. Thus, a vast expansion of the amount of precious metals in circulation occurred from India to Central Asia, and as far as the Levant and Asia Minor.

Of considerable but less importance, in the Panjab as well as beyond, were also the demographic shifts which occurred as a consequence of the invasions. Looking at the Indian population as a whole, the number of war-casualties as such was minor. The 'slaughter and pillage' perpetrated among the Hindus is sometimes described as 'fearful', and the numbers of people who reportedly were killed reach into the tens of thousands, but this was not systematic and appears to have been avoided in the absence of sustained opposition, while, in any case, it was normally confined to the 'fighting men' (mardān-i-kārzār), as it was among the Muslims—who on occasion suffered heavy casualties too.[72] Nor did collective self-destruction among Hindu warriors or brahmans facing defeat reach such proportions that it would have significant demographic effects.[73] Of much greater impact

---

[70] TF, pp. 32-34.
[71] Cf. Bosworth, Ghaznavids, pp. 78-79.
[72] TYA, pp. 26, 258-61, 398-9; TYP, pp. 38, 178-9; TF, pp. 24-25, 27, 41; ZA, pp. 66-67, 70.
[73] For examples, see TF, p. 30; TYA, p. 245.

than both of these factors combined was probably a famine which occurred in 1033 AD and which may have been an indirect result of, or at least aggravated by, the conditions created by the prolonged campaigning of especially the first three decades of the eleventh century. 'This year of 1033 AD', writes Firishta, 'was remarkable for a great famine (*qaht*) in many parts of the world. The famine was followed by a pestilence which swept many thousands from the face of the earth. In less than one month 40,000 people died in Isfahan alone. Nor did it rage with less violence in Hindustan, where whole countries were entirely depopulated'.[74] In addition, severe demographic effects resulted, according to the emphasis of numerous sources, from the forced transfer of enslaved Indian captives (*ghilmān-o-jawārī, burda, sabāyā*), especially women and children, to areas to the west of the subcontinent. In relative terms this was far less significant than the transfer of wealth. The figures on occasion reach into the hundreds of thousands and are no doubt exaggerated, but even so are significantly higher than those which obtained under the Arabs in the early eighth century.[75] Slave-raiding began in the time of Sabuktigīn, in the densely populated area of Lamghān, as well as in Multan, and continued until at least the year 1079, in the reign of Ibrahim, and probably longer.[76]

---

[74] *TF*, p. 41.

[75] *TYA*, pp. 26, 178-9, 329-36, 395-408; *TYP*, pp. 38, 155-6, 210-12, 245-7, 249, 313; *TF*, pp. 18, 24, 27-28, 30-31, 35, 41, 48; *ZA*, pp. 66, 72, 75-78; *TB*, p. 665; *KT*, X, pp. 72-74; *Al-Hind, I*, pp. 171-2.

[76] According to Al-'Utbī, Mahmūd, during his second expedition to Peshāwar and Waihind, took away 'about 500,000 slaves of the children and girls of that area' ('*qarab pānsad hazār-i-burda az atfāl-o-dharārī-o-jawarī' ān wilāyat*'; *TYP*, pp. 155-6 (*TYA*, pp. 178-9)). *ZA*, p. 66 says: 'a lot of booty in treasure and slaves (burda) and animals'. During Mahmūd's ninth expedition, to Nārdīn in 1013-14 AD, 'the Sultan returned with so many slaves that they became very cheap, and men who were respectable in their own country were degraded by becoming slaves of common shopkeepers' (*TYA*, pp. 329-36; *TYP*, pp. 210-12; *ZA*, p. 72). After the capture of Thanesar in 1014 AD, 'the army of Islam brought to Ghazna about 200,000 captives (*qarīb do sīt hazār banda*), and much wealth, so that the capital appeared like an Indian city, no soldier of the camp being without wealth, or without many slaves' (*TF*, pp. 27-28). After his twelfth expedition, to Kanauj and Mathura in 1018-19, Mahmūd collected so many prisoners that the price of each fell to two to ten dirhams; these were afterwards taken to Ghazna, 'and merchants came from distant cities to purchase them, so that the countries of Mā warā' annahr, 'Irāq and Khurāsān were filled with them, and the fair and the dark, the rich and the poor, mingled in one common slavery' (*TYA*, pp. 395-408; *TYP*, pp. 245-9). In 1079, Ibrahim raided a place called Dara, in the neighbourhood of

It is only with difficulty that we can obtain a broad idea of the itineraries of the Turkish armies beyond the Panjab and Sind, especially in the twelfth century, and we often learn little or almost nothing of the actual battle tactics and military strategies which were followed—except that these usually involved opportunistic alliance building with local groups (across any religious divide) and the intervention in local conflict over tribute payments, succession, and the like.[77]

The main concern of the Ghaznavid Turks, from the beginning, appears to have been to penetrate into the major river valleys, of the Indus first, then the 'five-river land' of the *Panj-āb*, and finally the 'two-river land', the Ganges-Yamuna *Do-āb*. The very earliest expansion eastwards, into *al-Hind*, began under Alptigīn, in the period c. 933-963 AD, when his general Sabuktigīn raided Lamghān and Multān.[78] Here, and in the area immediately

Multan, the inhabitants of which came originally from Khurasan and still constituted a separate and independent community, from which were taken '100,000 persons, whom they carried in bonds to Ghazna' (*TF*, pp. 48-49).

[77] Among contemporaries, Al-'Utbī produced a reliable narrative in Arabic, taking us up to 1021 AD, which agrees with other evidence on major points; but he was ignorant of Indian languages and had a very poor knowledge of Indian topography, with the result that his descriptions are full of mistakes. The Persian translation of Al-'Utbī's *Tārīkh al-Yamīnī* which was made by Jurbādqānī in the early thirteenth century is an independent work of rhetorical art, and allows itself many liberties, adding images of its own, although it does reproduce the basic narrative. For a good source-critical discussion and comparison of these two works, see Th. Nöldeke, 'Das Kitāb Jamīnī des Abū Nasr Muhammad ibn 'Abd al-Gabbār al-'Utbī', *Sitzungsberichte der Kaiserlichen Akademie*, Vol. XXIII (Vienna, 1857), pp. 15-102. Gardīzī's *Zayn al-Akhbār*, written in the reign of the Ghaznavid Sultan 'Abd ar-Rashīd (1049-52), has rightly been called 'a heterogeneous assemblage of historical, geographical and ethnographical data', but is quite terse (Cf. A. P. Martinez, 'Gardīzī's two chapters on the Turks', *Archivum Eurasiae Medii Aevi*, II (1982), pp. 109-217. Ibn al-Athīr (1160-1233) provides important information especially on the later Ghaznavids, but wrote in Iraq and is therefore not only often wrong or uncertain but vague about geographical locations. Baihaqī's voluminous *Ta'rīkh*, begun in 1018-19, while providing an unprecedented wealth of detail, is extant only for the reign of Mas'ūd (1031-41) (Cf. Waldman, *Toward a Theory of Historical Narrative*, pp. 16, 44-45). Later Indo-Persian historians almost always used these earlier ones, with the exception of Firishta, who sometimes advances information not found in the extant contemporary historians.
   There is no lack of secondary accounts: see, for instance, M. Habib, *Sultan Mahmud of Ghazna* (Delhi, 1967); J. Prasad, *History of Medieval India* (Allahabad, 1966); M. Nazim, *The Life and Times of Sultān Mahmūd of Ghazna* (New Delhi, 1971; orig. publ. 1931); Bosworth, *Later Ghaznavids*; A. Alami, *Les conquêtes de Mahmūd al-Ghaznawi d'après le Kitāb al Yamīnī d''Utbī*, 2 vols (Doctorat d'Etat, Paris III, 1989).
   [78] Cf. *Al-Hind*, *I*, p. 126.

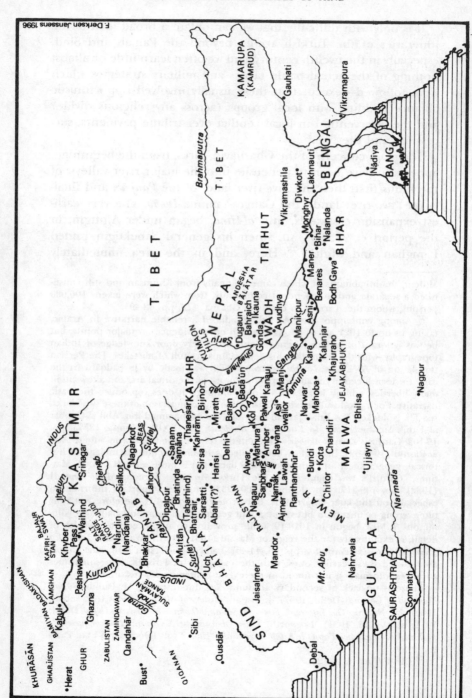

Map 2 Ghaznavid and Ghurid/Mamlūk conquests in Hind

beyond, in the Panjab, numerous conflicts were to follow between
the Ghaznavids and the Hindu Shahi dynasty—successors of the
Zunbils and Kabulshahs—, who had shifted their capital to Waihind. In Alptigīn's time these 'Rais' still held on to Lamghān, in
what is now eastern Afghanistan. Sabuktigīn, however, after his
succession, extended his power into the area by forging an
alliance with the Afghan and Khalaj tribal garrisons which had
been stationed there by the Hindu Shahi king.

In the first year of his reign, in 977-8 AD, Sabuktigīn also conquered Bust, the second most important fortified city in Sijistan
(after Zaranj), on the limits of Zabulistan, and the main *marḥala*
on the route which traversed the region of Garsmīl along the
Khawash river and the desert banks of the Helmand, near its confluence with the Arghandāb. Qusdār, another fortified Muslim
town in Turan (Sind), which gave its name to an entire subre-
gion, fell to the Ghaznavid in the same year, and then the entire
province of Qandahar.[79] Within a decade, Jayapāl, the Hindu
Shahi king, whose 'hereditary kingdom' now stretched from the
Chenab river to Lamghān and from Kashmir to Multan, was
attacked twice.[80] On a third occasion, in 991 AD, the assembled
army of a coalition of Indian kings headed by the Hindu Shahi
was dispersed, after which Ghaznavid power was established in virtually all areas to the west of the Indus.[81]

Sabuktigīn's son and successor Mahmūd (r. 998-1030), obtaining caliphal sanction (*mauqif-i-khilāfat*) for his actions, expanded
the Ghaznavid empire as far as the Caspian Sea, and from Samarqand to Ray, while invading *Hind* about seventeen times and ultimately establishing permanent control over the Panjab.[82] After
renewed campaigning into Lamghān, and to Peshāwar (Ar.,
Parshāwar), Waihind, on the road from Peshāwar to Lahore, was
taken from the Hindu Shahi.[83] In 1004-5 followed the conquest
of Bhatinda or Tabarhind, which, together with Bhatnair, Sirsa
and Abahr, was one of the four important forts which were situ-

[79] *TYA*, pp. 20-21, 23; *TYP*, pp. 33-35; *TF*, pp. 18-19; Alami, *Conquêtes*, pp. 193-9.

[80] *TYA*, pp. 23-26; *TYP*, pp. 35-39; *TF*, p. 19.

[81] *TYA*, p. 26; *TYP*, pp. 38-39, 152; *TF*, pp. 19-20; *Al-Hind, I*, pp. 126, 216.

[82] *TYA*, pp. 161-3; *TYP*, pp. 138-9; *TF*, p. 23; *ZA*, p. 62.

[83] *ZA*, pp. 63, 65; Alami, *Conquêtes, I*, pp. 400-3, 405-16; *TYA*, p. 179; *TYP*, pp. 155-6; *TF*, p. 24; *Al-Hind, I*, p. 126.

ated at the angles of a nearly square figure with a quadrilateral in the path of any invader from the North-West, and had to be reduced in order to gain access to the trans-Gangetic plain. It was the capital of an entire region, called Bhātīya (identified with Bhīra), from where a direct route went to Kabul via the Salt Range or Koh-i-Jūd, across the Suhan river, a small tributary of the Indus.[84] The Fatimid-backed Ismāʿīlīs were attacked in 1006, and again in 1008 and 1010—to break further Hindu Shahi opposition in the area and impose direct rule.[85] Nagarkot (Bhīma Naghara) was taken in 1008, and, again, Waihind.[86] Much further inland (Al-ʿUtbī says 'in the middle of al-Hind'),[87] the capture of Nārāyan (present Narayanpūr, near Alwar, Rajasthan) appears to have been aimed at gaining another route of access to the Ganges-Yamuna Doab. Similarly, Nārdīn (Nandana, Nandūna), on the northern spur of the Salt Range, in the Jud hills, still in the hands of a Hindu Shah subordinate, was taken to gain command over the main route to the Doab: 'the most glorious victory of Islam since the time of the Prophet'.[88] When the Turkish armies, after opening these 'gates', finally broke through to the Middle Country, the temple city of Thānes(w)ar (Ar. *Tānisar, Tānishar*), to the north of Delhi, was destroyed first, probably in 1011 (the city was entered unopposed);[89] then Mathura (*Matrā, Mahura, Mātūra*) (also entered without opposition), on the Yamuna;[90] then the capital city, Kanauj (*Qanauj, Qannauj*), which was still governed by a Pratihara ruler that Al-ʿUtbī refers to as 'the pre-eminent Indian king' (*muqaddam-i-mulūk-i-hind*).[91] The latter king, however, had evacuated the city before Mahmūd's arrival, crossed the Ganges,

[84] *TYA*, pp. 258-61; *TYP*, pp. 178-9; *TF*, p. 24; *ZA*, pp. 66-67; *Al-Hind, I*, p. 126; Alami, *Conquêtes*, II, pp. 417-26.

[85] *TF*, pp. 24-25, 27; *TYA*, pp. 261-4, 316-7; *TYP*, pp. 180-1, 205; *ZA*, pp. 67, 70; *Al-Hind, I*, pp. 185, 188, 216-218; Sachau, *Alberuni's India*, I, pp. 116-7; *KT*, IX, p. 159.

[86] *TF*, pp. 26-27; *TYA*, pp. 278-86; *TYP*, pp. 187-8; *ZA*, p. 69; Alami, *Conquêtes*, II, pp. 454-67.

[87] 'tawassuṭ dyār al-hind', 'wāsiṭa' mamālik-i-hind' (*TYA*, p. 303; *TYP*, p. 198).

[88] *TYA*, pp. 329-36; *TYP*, pp. 210-2; *TF*, p. 28; *ZA*, p. 72; Alami, *Conquêtes*, II, pp. 500-17.

[89] *TYA*, pp. 336-8; *TYP*, pp. 213-4; *TF*, pp. 27-28; Sachau, *Alberuni's India*, p. 117; *ZA*, pp. 71-72; Alami, *Conquêtes*, pp. 484-91.

[90] *TYA*, pp. 395-400; *TYP*, pp. 242-4; *TF*, p. 29; *ZA*, pp. 75-76; Alami, *Conquêtes*, II, pp. 525-8.

[91] *TYP*, pp. 244-5; *TYA*, pp. 400-1; *TF*, p. 29; *Al-Hind, I*, pp. 286, 290; Alami, *Conquêtes*, II, pp. 528-32.

and took refuge in Bārī, a place about four days travelling to the east of Kanauj. Manj, 'the citadel of the brahmans' (*qalāʿa' barāhima*), the old town of Ma(n)jhāwan, the ruins of which are still visible near the Pandu river, about sixteen km south of present-day Kanpur, to all appearances the last refuge of the brahmans of Kanauj, was put under siege.[92] Facing overwhelming force, many of these brahmans, as well as the fighting men, threw themselves from the walls, burned themselves in their houses, with their wives and children, or rushed out against the invader, so that ultimately 'not one of the garrison survived'. Mahmūd, as always, returned to Ghazna after this, but in the fall of the same year 1019 crossed the Yamuna again, and now, possibly for the first time, the Ganges, in an attack on the Candellas—by that time the most powerful rulers of North India in Jejākabhukti (Bundelkhand), Khajuraho, and Gwalior.[93] Gurjara-Pratihāra power was finally put to an end in Bārī. A few years later, after further campaigns in the areas which are now comprised in Swat, Bajaur and parts of Kafiristān, and thereabout, Lahore was taken without opposition.[94] The forts of Gwalior (Gwālīyār) and Kālanjar were taken from the Candella ruler in 1022-3.[95] Somnath, the wealthy harbour and pilgrimage centre in Saurashtra, Gujarat (which had been deemed safe behind the desert and boasted 'the greatest idol of al-Hind'), was destroyed in 1025-6.[96]

With the Panjab coming under permanent control by the end of Mahmūd's reign, Mahmūd's son and successor Masʿūd (r. 1030-41) did not abandon plunder raids and military campaigns deep into India, beyond the confines of the area which was now the formal Ghaznavid dominion under an investiture patent sent from Baghdad in 1030-31. To the west, this area included Qusdār, Sibi or Walishtan, Qiqanan, and Makrān, while Ghūr remained in a state of loose subordination throughout the eleventh century. In 1031, Masʿūd sent an army to Makrān, causing its coinage to be struck in his name, and mediating in a dispute between the local

---

[92] *TYA*, pp. 400-1; *TYP*, p. 245; *TF*, p. 30; Alami, *Conquêtes*, II, pp. 532-3.

[93] *TYA*, p. 415; *TYP*, pp. 251-2; *KT*, VII, p. 301; *TF*, p. 31; *Al-Hind, I*, p. 286; Alami, *Conquêtes*, II, pp. 547-58.

[94] *ZA*, pp. 78-79; *TF*, p. 31; Alami, *Conquêtes*, II, pp. 562-6.

[95] *ZA*, pp. 79-80; *TF*, p. 31; Alami, *Conquêtes*, II, pp. 566-71.

[96] *Al-Hind, I* , pp. 68, 185, 218, 307; *TF*, pp. 32-35; *KT*, IX, pp. 241-2, 345-6; *ZA*, pp. 87-88; Alami, *Conquêtes*, II, pp. 571-85.

Muslim rulers.[97] From later references it appears that this province, as far west as Tīz, remained within the Ghaznavid orbit, separated by an almost inaccessible stretch of terrain from the Seljuq amirate of Kirman.[98]

In 1030-31, a significant new initiative was the first invasion of Awadh under Sayyid Salār Mas'ūd Ghāzī, a nephew of Mahmūd, who had been born in 1015. From a military point of view, it was a complete failure, and hardly any of the invaders returned alive. Nothing indicates, in other words, that Sayyid Salār's conquest was in any way permanent. An account of it is given in an historical romance written by a Sufi, 'Abd ar-Rahmān Chishtī, during the reign of the Mughal emperor Jahangir, entitled *Mir'āt-i-Mas'ūdī*. This work is said by its author to have been mainly based on a book called the *Tawārīkh-i-Mahmūdī*, written by Muhammad Ghaznawī, a servant of Amīr Sabuktigīn and one of the followers of Sayyid Salār who related events of which he had personal knowledge. There are also numerous tombs, scattered all over the northern districts of Awadh, which are said to cover the remains of martyrs of Sayyid Salār's army.[99] In some places, even in recent times, people would point at portions of roads along which they would not pass after dark, saying that at night 'the road is thronged with troops of headless horsemen—the dead of the army of Sayyid Salār—[and that] the vast array moves on with a noiseless tread. The ghostly horses make no sound, and no words of command are shouted to the headless host'.[100] There are various dispersed Muslim communities in the area which date their history from the time of Sayyid Salār's invasion, for example in Nagram and Amethi, of pargana Mohanlalganj, through which he is said to have passed and where muhallas still exist which are said to contain the descendants of his followers who founded them.[101] The Muslims of Awadh however are apt to associate with Sayyid Salār every object or tradition to which they cannot ascribe a certain origin.[102] All the evidence, nonetheless, points at Satrikh, in the

[97] *TF*, p. 40.

[98] Bosworth, *Later Ghaznavids*, pp. 7-8.

[99] *Gazetteer of the Province of Oudh*, 3 vols (Lucknow and Allahabad, 1877-78), III, p. 487.

[100] *Ibid.*, I, p. 457; cf. also II, p. 452.

[101] *Ibid.*, II, pp. 293, 352, 511-12, etc.; and cf. A. H. Sharar, *Lucknow: The Last Phase of an Oriental Culture* (London, 1975), p. 36.

[102] *Gazetteer of Oudh*, II, p. 452.

Bara Banki district, as the place where Sayyid Salār fixed his headquarters, sending out his lieutenants with their parties of soldiers
in every direction.[103] Satrikh is still celebrated for the shrine of
Sayyid Salār's father, locally known as 'Borda Baba', the husband
of the sister of Mahmūd of Ghazna, who is supposed to have died
a natural death in this place.[104] Bahraich was probably reached
in 1033, and Sayyid Salār appears to have been able to repeatedly defeat the local raīs on the banks of the river Kosala (probably the Kauriala), until reinforcements arrived in the Hindu camp
and the 'prince of martyrs' fell with virtually all his followers.[105]
Bahraich is still celebrated for the shrine of Sayyid Salār.[106] When
Sleeman passed through Bahraich in 1849 he thought it 'strange'
that Hindus as well as Muslims made offerings to this shrine.[107]
'All our Hindoo camp followers paid as much reverence to the
shrine as they passed as the mahomedans ....The Hindoos worship any sign of manifested might or power, though exerted
against themselves ..'.[108]

If the first invasion of Awadh was a failure, it may have been
the precursor of another, more successful, attempt, to seize the
wealth of Benares undertaken by a rebellious governor of the Panjab, Ahmad Nayaltigin, a son of Mahmūd, in 1033. Nayaltigin,
joined by the ghazis and the army of Lahore, crossed the Ganges
and, going down the left bank, arrived at Benares, 'where no army
of Islam had ever reached', plundering the markets of the drap-
ers, perfumers and jewellers and returning with great spoil.[109]
This money was diverted into the procurement of more Turkish
slaves and a fruitless attempt to seize power in the Panjab. None
of the conquests this far east was to last.

By 1033, the year of the famine,[110] it was becoming clear that
the great age of Ghaznavid conquests was drawing to a close. The
Seljuqs were rapidly emerging as the dominant power in the east-

---

[103] *Gazetteer of Oudh*, I, p. 112; II, p. 293.

[104] P. D. Reeves (ed.), *Sleeman in Oudh* (Cambridge, 1971), p. 288.

[105] *Gazetteer of Oudh*, I, p. 112.

[106] Cf. T. Mahmood, 'The Dargah of Sayyid Salar Mas'ud Ghazi in Bahraich:
Legend, Tradition and Reality', in: Ch. Troll (ed.), *Muslim Shrines in India* (New
Delhi, 1984).

[107] Reeves, *Sleeman*, p. 69.

[108] *Ibid.*, pp. 288-9.

[109] *TB*, pp. 323-9, 495-8, 500-38.

[110] Cf. p. 126.

ern Islamic world. After the Seljuq victory at Dandanqan in 1040,
Khwarazm, Western Khurasan and Jibal up to Afghanistan, and
the whole area down to Sistan were lost to them. The Ghaznavids
retained their possessions in northern and eastern Afghanistan,
as well as their Indian conquests for over a century more, until
the rise of the Ghurids. But the later raids are especially poorly
documented on both the Islamic and the Indian side. All we can
conclude is that there were no permanent gains from now on—
and not a few losses.[111] Ghazna remained the capital for 120 years
after Dandanqan, Lahore (which was almost lost in 1043-4) for
twenty years thereafter. Treasure from India kept coming in, and
was of ever greater relative importance.[112] Ghaznavid power continued to be contested by governors in combination with native
Indian troops.[113] In the years 1079-80 there are reports of new
campaigns under Ibrahim—but the dates are not sure.[114] Probably Ibrahim started raiding earlier in his career. We do not know
where he went, the geographical references being unclear too. It
is possible, however, that these raids extended into eastern
Rajasthan. Between 1066 and 1070, one of Ibrahim's sons appears
to have led an army of ghazis and 40,000 cavalry into the Doab.
Inscriptions of the Gahadavalas, from 1090 on, mention a tax,
called the *turushkadanda*, 'Turkish punishment', which was possibly a defence tax ('Türkenhilfe') or an amount which was set
apart to be paid as tribute to the Ghaznavids.

Incidental victories are still mentioned by Ghaznavid poets in
the half century from Ibrahim's death until the struggle for eastern Afghanistan with the Ghurids began.[115] These reached as far
as the Ganges-Yamuna Doab, and there was some activity in Central India, possibly in Ujjayn and Nagpur, and against the Candellas again, 'farther than any Muslim conqueror had hitherto
gone, except the emperor Mahmud'.[116] Bahram Shah, up against
the Paramaras, Kalacuris and Gahadavalas, probably penetrated
into many regions that none of his predecessors had reached.
After the death of Mas'ud III in 1118, however, Seljuq suzerainty

---

[111] Cf. *KT*, IX, pp. 354-5; *TF*, p. 44.
[112] See Bosworth, *Later Ghaznavids*, pp. 31-33.
[113] *TF*, pp. 46-47.
[114] Bosworth, *Later Ghaznavids*, pp. 61-68; *TF*, pp. 48-49; *KT*, X, pp. 72-74.
[115] Bosworth, *Later Ghaznavids*, pp. 82-88.
[116] *TF*, p. 49.

was established over Ghazna. This was a fact of great significance
to contemporary chroniclers. But by this time the real menace to
the Ghaznavids came not from the Seljuqs but from the Shansabānīs of Ghur.

GHŪRIDS, 1186-1206 AD

The Shansabānī or 'Ghūrid' sultans who superseded the Ghaznavids in the second half of the twelfth century and finally succeeded in extending Islamic dominion beyond the Panjab were
of an eastern Persian or *Tājīk* origin, as were the inhabitants of
Ghūr, the mountainous heartland of what is now Afghanistan, in
general.[117] They were genealogically separate from the Turks and,
with resident Jewish colonies monopolizing the trade of Ghūr with
the outside world, primarily agriculturists, and not nomads, even
though they were in the possession of herds of cattle and did rear
horses.[118] They were to acquire a Turkish retinue in the twelfth
century, but it was not before the demise of Ghūrid power in the
early thirteenth century that Turkish and Mongol pastoralists penetrated in the area of Ghūr itself.

The *Tājīk* Ghuris are also consistently distinguished from the
Afghans of the Indian frontier by Al-ʿUtbī and all later writers,
while the language they used is recorded to have differed considerably from the Persian which was in use at Ghazna. One way
in which the subsequent Ghūrid expansion into India was legitimized by Juzjani, the chief chronicler of the dynasty, was by trac-
ing the origin of the Shansabānī family to a tyrant of Iranian
mythology, Azhd Zahāk (*sic*; Pahlavī *Azh-i-Dahāk*), popular in
Ghazna and Zabulistan, who became ruler of all nomad Arabs
(ʿarab-i-warāʾ) and allegedly had held 'Hind and Sind' (or 'Hind

---

[117] Cf. L. S. Leshnik, 'Ghur, Firozkoh and the Minat-i-Jam', *Central Asiatic Journal*, 12 (1968-69), p. 37.
[118] C. E. Bosworth, 'The Early Islamic History of Ghur', *Central Asiatic Journal*,
6 (1961), pp. 116, 118; A. Bruno, 'Notes on the Discovery of Hebrew Inscriptions
in the Vicinity of the Minaret of Jam', *East and West*, 14, 3 (1963), pp. 206-8; G.
Gnoli, 'Further Information Concerning the Judaeo-Persian Documents of
Afghanistan', *East and West*, 14, 3 (1963), pp. 209-10; idem, 'Jewish Inscriptions
in Afghanistan', *East and West*, 13 (1962), pp. 311-2; Wink, *Al-Hind, I*, pp. 61, 95-
96, 117, 119, 123.

and Ghūr') through his son Bustam—who is also said to have peopled Ghūr with Arab tribes.[119] But, obviously, all accounts which relate the Ghūrids to Arabs of nomadic origin are apocryphal.

The early Ghaznavid rulers had propped up the Shansabānīs, intervened in their family disputes, and organized expeditions into Ghūr in the period leading up to the mid-twelfth century, when the dynasty was able to consolidate its hegemony over the numerous other mountain chiefs of Ghūr and assumed the title of Sultans. The Shansabānīs maintained their links with Ghazna when the Seljuqs took Khurasan and western Afghanistan, but some of the Ghūrid rulers paid an annual tribute to the Seljuqs as well as to the Ghaznavids.[120] The Sultans of Ghazna held several fortresses in Ghūr, and there was some connubial exchange between the two houses.[121] The Shansabānī subordination to the Ghaznavids, however, came to an end in the mid-twelfth century, when 'Alā' ad-Dīn Jahānsoz destroyed Ghazna, as well as the palaces and other Mahmūdī buildings in Bust. After the sack of Ghazna, 'Alā' ad-Dīn stopped paying tribute to the Seljuqs as well, and supported an anti-Seljuq rebellion in Herat, but was defeated when his troops defected to the Seljuqs. Subsequently he was authorized by the Seljuq Sultan Sanjar to reclaim his dominion in Ghūr.[122] 'Alā' ad-Dīn now assumed the title of *Salṭān al-Mu'aẓẓam* and adopted for his official processions the *chatr* or ceremonial parasol, following Seljuq and Ghaznavid practice, and distinguishing himself from the earlier Shansabani rulers who merely styled themselves *Amīr* or *Malik*, or *Malik al-Jibāl*, 'King of the Mountains'.[123] Under 'Ala' ad-Dīn, Ghūrid dominion was also extended over neighbouring principalities like Tukharistan, Bamiyan, Zamindawar, Bust, and parts of Khurasan. Fīrūzkūh became the capital of this extended dominion and here the main branch of the family—of pure Shansabānī lineage—fixed its seat, while minor branches of the family, the products of concubinage with Turkish slave girls (*kanīzak-i-turkī*), occupied minor seats in Tukharistan, Bamiyan and elsewhere.[124]

---

[119] *TNL*, pp. 375-82.
[120] *TF*, p. 55.
[121] *Ibid.*
[122] *TN*, pp. 59-62.
[123] *KT*, IX, p. 109.
[124] *TN*, pp. 47, 85, 102, 106.

When, in the second half of the twelfth century, the Ghūrid dominion expanded 'from Hindustan and the frontier of Chin and Mahachin to Iraq and from the Jihun river and Khurasan to Hormuz,'[125] the composition of the armies changed entirely, and cavalry was introduced. Until then, the trocps which were recruited from mountainous Ghūr had been predominantly footsoldiers (*piyādagān*) who were equipped with a shield of bullock-hide and cotton cloth, known as *karwa*, which covered them from head to foot and, when closing ranks, could make them appear like an impenetrable wall, able to withstand small bodies of cavalry and perhaps one or two elephants (if these could be completely surrounded), but useless against large cavalry regiments.[126] As a result, by the second half of the twelfth century, the infantry troops had begun to appear inadequate by themselves, and, with the influx of amirs and maliks from Gharchistan and the Jibal, Kirman and Khurasan, from Bamiyan, Sijistan, Timran, Wakhsh (in Badakhshan), Makran, Zamindawar, Wajiri (Wajiristan?), and elsewhere, we find not merely the recruitment base for the soldiery widening but also the cavalry becoming all-important.[127] From this time on, the Ghūrid sultans generally appear to have been mounted, while they are also represented as expert bowmen, capable of intimidating 'even the Turks'.[128]

Most, if not all, of the cavalry, in effect, came from beyond Ghūr. In the late twelfth century, Afghans were of considerable importance in the Ghūrid cavalry operating in India—as they had been in that of the Ghaznavids; they also appear to have settled in Ghūr itself by this time.[129] Among the picked troops which marched into India under the Ghūrid slave commander Aybak were the *Damghānīs*, inhabitants of the region of Damghān, the capital of Qumis and a district in northern Iran.[130] In the armies which marched from Ghazna to India between 1192 and 1206 there were numerous *Tājik* horsemen from Khurasan and *Khalaj* troops from Garmsir in Zamindawar.[131] There were six thousand

---

[125] *Ibid.*, p. 76.

[126] *Ibid.*, p. 56.

[127] *Ibid.*, pp. 65, 68, 73, 84, 89; *TNM*, ff. 238a-b.

[128] *TN*, p. 110; Spengler, 'Numismatic Evidence', p. 5.

[129] Dorn, *Makhzan-i-Afghānī*, I, pp. 37-39; II, p. 74 ff; *TF*, p. 57.

[130] *Gazetteer of Oudh*, II, p. 463; Barthold, *Historical Geography of Iran*, pp. 87, 112, 119-20.

[131] *TF*, pp. 57-58; *TN*, p. 89.

Khalaj and Ghuzz Turks among the Ghurid army at Herat in 1152 who went over to the Seljuqs.[132] And there were also Seljuqs among the maliks of the Shansabānī Sultans of Ghazna,[133] while families of Seljuq Turks originating from 'Rum' were settled in the Juggaur district of Awadh who claim to have arrived in 1184, when they allegedly accepted the governorship of the province on behalf of Shihāb ad-Dīn and colonized numerous villages in this area. The latter claimed to be descendants of the brother of Nūr ad-Dīn Muhammad (1167-85), the Artuqid ruler of Diyārbakr, a chief of the Doger tribe of the Oghuz.[134]

Many more Ghuzz Turks appear to have entered the Ghūrid armies after having overrun large parts of Khurasan at the time of the death of the Seljuq Sultan Sanjar in 1157, and especially after the Ghuzz succeeded in taking Ghazna, Kabul and Zabul out of the hands of the Ghaznavid sultan Khusrau Malik in 1163, forcing the latter to shift his capital to Lahore. These Ghuzz Turks had entered *Mā warā' an-nahr* from the north, possibly as early as the late eighth and the ninth century, subsequently converted to Islam, while remaining engaged in constant hostility with the Qarlughiya Turkmans. After Sanjar ascended the Seljuq throne in 1118 AD, 40,000 Ghuzz families entered Khutlan and Chaghaniyan, paying a tribute of 24,000 sheep to the Seljuq ruler.[135] In 1150 AD they were given lands in Tukharistan. And about eight years later they appear to have taken possession of Sarakhs, Marw and Balkh and some adjacent areas. In 1163 Sayf ad-Dīn Muhammad of Ghūr was killed in a battle against the Ghuzz of Balkh, and it was also at about that time that they moved into Ghazna, retiring before the Qarlughiya Turkmans. Muʿizz ad-Dīn Ghūrī made constant raids upon the Ghuzz from Tiginabad, and was placed on the throne at Ghazna by his brother Ghiyāth ad-Dīn in 1173, defeating the Ghuzz.[136] Subsequently to this, the Ghuzz maliks of Kirman and different parts of Khurasan paid submission to Ghiyāth ad-Dīn as well.[137] Similarly, the Ghūrid sultans could impose their generals on the most important districts along the

---

[132] *TN*, pp. 59-60.
[133] *TNM*, ff. 238a-b.
[134] *Gazetteer of Oudh, II*, p. 101.
[135] *TNR*, p. 374, note 5.
[136] *TN*, pp. 15, 72-73, 105; *TF*, p. 52.
[137] *TN*, p. 73.

lower route from Ghazna to Lahore, in Sanquran and Karmān, and here too, in all probability, many Ghuzz were recruited.[138] These districts contain a number of *daras*, long valleys with rivers running through them, extending from the southern slopes of Spinghar, the White Mountain, and the south-westerly slopes of the Salt Range on the north, to the Gumal in the south, and from the range of hills separating the district of Gardiz on the west, and the Sindsagar or Indus on the east. This was a very populous area, with remains of several towns, watered by the Kurma (or Kurram) river and its tributaries. One of the *daras* is called *Shaluzan* or *Sanquran*, a name which appears to have been derived from that of the Ghuzz tribe which held it before the Ghūrids took the area.[139] This *dara* later became populated by Torī Afghans and some Awankar Jats, the latter of whom were displaced again by other Afghan tribes migrating to the east in later times.[140]

There is sufficient evidence to show that in the Ghūrid state of the later twelfth century, the cavalry came largely under Turkish *mamlūk* leadership.[141] This Turkish elite cavalry was purchased in various parts of Central Asia, while much larger numbers of non-slave Turkish horsemen, next to Afghans and Tājīks, joined in the jihad expeditions into India as well.[142] The shift from a local, clan-based Ghūrid polity to a *mamlūk* state occurred almost surreptitiously. In 1161 AD, when Sultan Sayf ad-Dīn Muhammad succeeded his father to the throne of Fīrūzkūh, he did so 'with the concurrence of the whole of the maliks, chiefs and amirs of Ghūr' —but Turkish slaves are not yet mentioned as a separate interest group.[143] Within a decade after that, however, references to the *bandagān-i-turk* or *ghulamān-i-turk* on horseback become quite frequent.[144] The Ghūrid conquests in *al-Hind* were largely the work of Sultan Mu'izz ad-Dīn ('Muhammad Ghūrī') and his Turkish slaves, the *ghulamān-i-salțān*, Qutb ad-Dīn Aybak, Nāsir ad-Dīn Qabacha, Tāj ad-Dīn Yaldiz, and one non-slave, Ikhtyār ad-Dīn Muhammad bin Bakhtyār Khalajī.[145] Mu'izz ad-Dīn Muhammad

---

[138] *TNR*, pp. 498-9, notes 7 and 8.
[139] *Ibid.*
[140] *Ibid.*
[141] Cf. *TN*, pp. 60, 70, 87; *TF*, pp. 52, 57.
[142] E.g. *TF*, p. 57.
[143] *TN*, p. 64.
[144] *Ibid.*, pp. 69, 81, 88; *TF*, p. 57.
[145] Cf. *TF*, pp. 58-60.

was ruler in Ghazna from 1173 to 1203, and subsequently held the Fīrūzkūh throne for another three years; he had no sons, but, as Juzjani says, 'he took a liking in purchasing Turkish slaves, and he bought a great many of them—who all became famous throughout the East'.[146] Mu'izz ad-Dīn's slave Aybak was already actively 'subduing Hindustān while he was still merely the ruler of Ghazna'.[147] During his lifetime, Mu'izz ad-Dīn had announced that his Turkish slaves would be the heirs to his dominions, while stipulating that his own name would be preserved in the khutba everywhere.[148] When he died in 1206, the Turkish mamlūks appear, in effect, to have become so powerful that they prevailed over the chiefs of Ghūr.[149] Most parts of Ghūr, Gharchistan, Talqan, Guzarwan, and the districts of Faras and Garmsir by that time came under the jurisdiction of the Turkish slaves of the late Mu'izz ad-Dīn, all of whom solicited and obtained letters of man-umission (khuṭūṭ-i-'itq) from his successor Ghiyāth ad-Dīn Mah-mūd.[150] Tāj ad-Dīn Yaldiz was invested with the dominion of Ghaz-na.[151] Qutb ad-Dīn Aybak received the deed of investiture of Hindustān, with a scarlet canopy of state, in 1206 or 1209.[152] As stipulated, coins continued to be struck and the khutba contin-ued to be read in the name of the Ghūrid sultan, in Ghūr, Ghaz-na, and Hindustān.[153] But even so, while Ghiyāth ad-Dīn contin-ued to purchase more and more Turkish slaves, the old Ghūrid elite was completely superseded.[154] In 1212 AD, Bahā' ad-Dīn was raised to the throne of Fīrūzkūh after 'the bandagān-i-turk had slayed the competitors for sovereignty'.[155] Ghūr was then about to be incorporated by the Khwārazm-Shāh, not long before what Juzjani calls 'the irruption (khurūj) of Chingiz Khan the Mughal and the Turks'.[156]

The Ghūrid conquest of Hind was initiated from Ghazna. Hav-ing defeated the Ghuzz at Ghazna in 1173, Ghiyath ad-Dīn had

---

[146] *TN*, p. 132.
[147] *Ibid.*, p. 120.
[148] *Ibid.*, p. 132.
[149] *Ibid.*; *TNR*, p. 431 note, and pp. 432, 492-5.
[150] *TN*, pp. 89-90.
[151] *Ibid.*
[152] *Ibid.*, pp. 90, 140.
[153] *Ibid.*, p. 90.
[154] *Ibid.*, pp. 92-93.
[155] *Ibid.*, p. 94.
[156] *Ibid.*, p. 124.

placed the city in the charge of his younger brother Mu'izz ad-
Dīn, the future 'conqueror of Hind' (khusrau-i-hindgīr), who
'ascended the throne of Ghazna like Mahmūd'.[157] One difference
was that Mu'izz ad-Dīn received Ghazna as a family appanage. In
fact, throughout the reign of Ghiyāth ad-Dīn, the appanaging of
territories to collateral lineages continued.[158] Each kinsman held
supreme power in his own appanage, and until he ascended the
throne of Ghūr itself, Mu'izz ad-Dīn's rights to parts of India were
always seen as an extension of his appanage of Ghazna, and as
such they were jealously guarded from interference by other members of the Ghūrid family.[159] This meant that Mu'izz ad-Dīn would
not allow his kinsmen to participate in any further conquests in
the subcontinent and monopolised its wealth for himself. As a
result there were very few Shansabānī kinsmen serving in the
Ghūrid campaigns in India. Those who did serve on the frontier
all returned after a brief period to areas in Afghanistan, like other members of the upper elite from Ghūr in general.[160] Participation in the conquests in India on a more permanent basis
appears to have appealed to a lower stratum of the free Ghūrid
elite; and it is these only that are seen to shift their major interests away from Ghūr—to bolster their position—, and it is these
too that are seen consolidating their new holdings by moving in
their own kinsmen again.[161] Thus, even after 1203, when Mu'izz
ad-Dīn was the most powerful member of the Shansabānī family
and had assumed the right to dispense appanages to his kinsmen
of choice, he still kept these kinsmen out of his own appanage of
Ghazna and instead relied largely on slaves in order to be able
to keep Hind as his own privileged domain.

The character of these later conquests was also beginning to
change. On the one hand, even though Mu'izz ad-Dīn issued ever-
increasing quantities of gold and silver coins (which increased in
size and quality as well) from Ghazna, jointly in the name of his
brother and himself,[162] the treasure, especially of gold and silver,

---

[157] FS, vs. 1296-1306; TN, pp. 115-6; TF, p. 52.
[158] Cf. S. Kumar, The Emergence of the Delhi Sultanate, 588-685/1192-1286 (Unpublished PhD Dissertation, Duke University, 1992), pp. 9-10.
[159] Ibid., pp. 11-12.
[160] Ibid., pp. 12, 19, 29.
[161] Ibid., pp. 20-29.
[162] Spengler, 'Numismatic Evidence', p. 9; D. Sourdel, Inventaire des monnaies
musulmanes anciennes du musée de Caboul (Damascus, 1953), p. xviii.

that came in from India does not seem to have been as voluminous as it was during Mahmūd's expeditions almost two centuries earlier. Captives were still taken into slavery—from Ghazna, Ajmer, Nahrwala, or Kalanjar—but, although the figures are occasionally still high (in the five-digit range), their numbers appear to have fallen precipitously since Mahmūd's time.[163] On the other hand, it is significant that it is at this stage of the conquests that we obtain the first evidence of the creation of regular supply corps or commissariats which served the seasonal demand for grain of the still ceaselessly moving armies. It can perhaps be argued that in the earliest stages of the Turkish conquests of India, in the early eleventh century above all, most of the destruction in the countryside was actually caused by marauding bands of irregulars in search of food or supplies rather than the highly disciplined military actions of the professional soldiery. But this came to a stop when the roving bands of graindealers with their bullock trains, which became known as *Banjāras* in later times, made their appearance. Whatever we know of this seems to indicate that the involvement of Banjāras or Banjāra-like groups with Muslim invaders can be taken back to the late twelfth century. Some Banjāras, too, date their adoption of Islam from this period.[164] Thus, the sometimes sedentary groups of Banjāras of the long tract of country under the northern hills from Gorakhpur to Hardwar in the nineteenth century claimed that they were converted to Islam by Muhammad Ghūrī. These first Muslim Banjāras had, apparently, all come from Multan.[165] Literary evidence from the fourteenth century does not mention Banjāras yet, but refers to *kārwāniyān*, nomad caravaneers who were dealing in corn and supplied moving armies; and these may be the same people.[166] It is significant too that similar groups, grain-trafficers with bullock trains supplying highly mobile armies of cavalry—the almost indispensable intermediaries between the nomadic frontier and agricultural society—do not seem to have existed in India prior to the Turkish conquest.

---

[163] Cf. *TF*, pp. 58, 62; *TM*, pp. 54a-b.

[164] M. A. Sherring, *Hindu Tribes and Castes*, Vol. III (New Delhi, 1974; or. publ. 1881), p. 90; H. M. Elliot, *Memoirs on the History, Folk-lore, and Distribution of the Races of the North Western Provinces of India*, Vol. I (London, 1869), p. 52.

[165] P. Carnegy, *Notes on the Races, Tribes and Castes, inhabiting the Province of Awadh* (Lucknow, 1868), p. 137.

[166] *TFS*, p. 304.

Multan, allegedly the original homeland of the Banjāras, is, in any case, where Mu'izz ad-Dīn directed his army first. Hoping to bypass the Ghaznavid dominion in the Panjab, he took off, in 1175, through the Gomal passage—not the Khyber—and captured Multan, delivering it once more 'from the hands of the Qarāmita', and then Uch, in Upper Sind.[167] Conferring these cities on a governor, he returned to Ghazna. A year later, he brought to terms the Ghuzz tribe of the Sanqurān (ahl-i-sanqurān, ṭā'ifa' sanqurāniyān).[168] Two years afterwards, in 1178, Mu'izz ad-Dīn returned, again via the Gomal Pass, to Multan and Uch but now, forgetting the experience of Mahmūd and numerous small Turkish raiding parties (which, as Sanskrit inscriptions point out, for some time prior to this date had been attempting unsuccessfully to penetrate through western Rajasthan), continued his route through the sandy desert towards Nahrwala, in Gujarat.[169] Acting against the dictates of geography, the idea behind this expedition was still to outflank the Ghaznavids in the Panjab and to open up an alternative route into Hindustan, through the rich territories of the Caulukyas. 'The Turushkas', states the Pṛthivirāja-vijaya (S. VI), 'came across the desert (marusthalī); by the time they reached the Cāhamāna dominions they were so thirsty that according to Jonarāja they had to drink the blood of their horses'. Exhausted and famished, the Turkish army was defeated with great slaughter by Mularaja II, the Caulukya king of Gujarat, at the foot of Mt. Abu, 'driving his elephant phalanx onto the battlefield in such a manner that all the horses of the army of Ghazna were scattered'.[170] This defeat appears to have induced the Ghurids not to persist with the southern route into Hindustan via the Gomal Pass. Gujarat as a whole remained exempted from any further serious Muslim attack for more than a century, although Nahrwala was occupied twenty years later, and various other raids were undertaken in the intermediate time.

After further campaigning during more than five years, in which he secured Sind as far as Debal and Makran, Peshawar,

---

[167] TF, pp. 52, 56; TN, p. 116; TNM, ff. 238a-b.

[168] TN, p. 116; TNM, ff. 238a-b.

[169] TN, pp. 24, 116; TF, p. 56; FS, vs. 1307-14; Epigraphia Indica, IX, pp. 62-63; XI, pp. 46-51.

[170] Epigraphia Indica, IX, p. 69; XI, p. 72 ; Indian Antiquary (1877), pp. 186, 198; FS, vs. 1307-14.

Sialkot, and finally, through strategem, Lahore, Mu'izz ad-Dīn in 1186 brought Ghaznavid rule to an end, and with his own governor installed at Lahore, he now found himself in possession of the Indus basin and in a strategic position to advance further into the fertile plains of India.[171] 'Shahabuddin was vigorously trying to subjugate the earth', reports Nyacandra Suri in the Hammīra Mahakavya.[172] 'Shahabuddin had arisen for the destruction of kings, and ... he had pillaged and burnt most of their cities, defiled their women, and reduced them altogether to a miserable plight ..'.[173] It seems that, prior to 1191, a number of clashes occurred with the Cāhamānas, whose leader, Prthiviraja, ruled the territory from Ajmer to Delhi and thus guarded the gate into Hindustan. On these occasions the Muslim invaders were repeatedly repulsed.[174] An inscription of Prthiviraja records the fortification of Hansi to check the progress 'of the Hammira [Amīr] who has become the cause of anxiety to the world'.[175] Bhatinda, about 160 km north of Hansi, an important Cāhamāna stronghold by 1191, was taken and then lost again. 'The [king of the] land of the North-West, where horses abound, the beef-eating Mleccha, named Ghuri, who had captured Garjani [Ghazna], hearing that Prthiviraja had vowed to exterminate the Mlecchas, sent an ambassador to Ajmer ... . When these fiends in the shape of men took possession of Nadul [Nadole], the warriors of Prthiviraja took up their bows and the emperor (Bharateshvara, 'lord of Bharat') resolved to lay Ghur's glory to the dust'.[176] Prthiviraja's most celebrated and last victory over the mlecchas took place at Tarā'in (Taraori), near Thanesar, in 1191. 'All of the Ranas of Hind came along with the Rai Kola Pithora [Prthiviraja]', writes Juzjani.[177] According to Firishta, the alliance of Indian princes mobilized 200,000 horse and 3,000 elephants on this occasion.[178] The Sul-

---

[171] *TN*, pp. 116-18; *TF*, pp. 52-57; *FS*, vs. 1315-22; I. H. Siddiqui, *Perso-Arabic Sources of Information on the Life and Conditions in the Sultanate of Delhi* (New Delhi, 1992), p. 57.

[172] N. Janardan Kirtane, 'The Hammira Mahakavya of Nyachandra Suri', *Indian Antiquary*, VIII (1879), p. 60.

[173] *Ibid.*

[174] *Ibid.*; *Indian Antiquary* (1890), pp. 202, 215-17.

[175] *Indian Antiquary (1913)*, p. 17.

[176] H. B. Sarda, 'The Prthviraja Vijaya', *Journal of the Royal Asiatic Society* (1913), pp. 279-80.

[177] *TN*, pp. 118-9.

[178] *TF*, p. 57; cf. also *FS*, vs. 1325-60.

tan was struck and wounded, so that the 'army of Islam' was irretrievably routed and had to retreat to Lahore and then, after appointing governors to the different dominions he possessed in India, returned to Ghur.

In the following year, the Sultan returned with an army said to have been made up of 120,000 or 130,000 horse. What followed was the decisive defeat of the Cāhamānas in the so-called Second Battle of Tarā'in.[179] Pṛthivirāja's cumbrous army—300,000 horse and 3000 elephants as well as a body of infantry in Firishta's account—was broken and scattered by an attack of 10,000 elite mounted archers.[180] Here, many of the opposing Indian princes were killed on the battlefield. Coins of Pṛthivirāja, with the inscription of *Hammīra* in Sanskrit on the obverse, seem to indicate that he himself initially accepted Mu'izz ad-Dīn's suzerainty.[181] But later he too was captured in the neighbourhood of Sarsatti, and put to death.[182] According to the *Prabandhacintāmani*, 'the Turushka king ... who, being eager to behold Pṛthivirāja's valour, took him to his own capital; but when he was about to reinstate him as sovereign in his own palace, he saw there in the picture-gallery Mlecchas represented as being slain by droves of pigs, [and] the sovereign of the Turushkas was exceedingly incensed at this biting insult and he put Pṛthivirāja to death by cutting off his head with an axe'.[183] Mu'izz ad-Dīn was now virtually master of the country. The forts of Sarsatti, Hansi, Samana, and Kahrām surrendered,[184] and 'the country-conquering Turks seized Ajmer [and there] annihilated the abodes of their enemies'.[185] Mu'izz ad-Dīn placed Aybak in the fort of Kahrām, from where attacks could be made in all directions: Mīrath, Baran, Delhi, and Kol were all taken before 1193.[186] Aybak now gained virtually independent power over 'the countries of Hind and Sind', although Mu'izz ad-Dīn continued to be involved in the conquests, and soon received a patent for its government, gradually building up Delhi as his new

[179] *TN*, p. 119; *TF*, p. 57; *FS*, vs. 1441-92.
[180] *TF*, p. 58; *TN*, pp. 119-20.
[181] E. Thomas, *The Chronicles of the Pathan Kings of Delhi* (New Delhi, 1967), pp. 17-18.
[182] *TF*, p. 58; *TN*, p. 120; *FS*, vs. 1490-91.
[183] Tawney, *Prabandhacintāmani*, p. 191.
[184] *FS*, vs. 1497-1500; and cf. *TF*, p. 58.
[185] *FS*, vs. 1497-1500; and cf. *TF*, p. 58.
[186] *TN*, pp. 120, 139; *TF*, p. 58; *FS*, vs. 1600-25.

capital, where he installed the first triumphal arches and a Jāmi'
Masjid.

But the Ghurid advance did not stop here. Jayachandra, the last
of the Rathor dynasty of Kanauj and Benares, was overthrown in
the following year.[187] The fort of Asni and Benares were occupied.[188] In 1195-6, Thangīr (Tahangarh), later known as Bayāna,
the stronghold of the Jadon Bhatti Rajputs, was taken by Mu'izz
ad-Dīn himself.[189] Soon afterwards, Gwalior, 'the pearl of the necklace of the forts of Hind', fell too.[190] And at about the same time,
Ajmer was re-occupied and garrisoned, thwarting an attempt by
the tribal Mhers, in alliance with the dispossessed Cāhamānās and
the Caulukyas, to retake it.[191] In 1197, Aybak plundered Nahrwala,
in Gujarat, although the province was not subdued.[192] Badā'ūn
and Katahr, on the Upper Ganges (northern Doab), were conquered at this time (1197-8), and, in the words of Juzjani, 'other
territories of Hindustan, as far as the frontier of the country of
Ujjayn'.[193] Subsequent operations appear to have been directed
at Kanauj again—which was not taken posssession of before 1198-
9, and Rajasthan, perhaps as far as Malwa, and then, with the conquest of the northern Doab and the surrounding country completed, against the last major dynasty of Rajputs, the Candellas of
Jejakabhukti—to the south-east of the growing Turkish dominion—whose principal forts Kalanjar, Mahoba and Khajuraho were
taken by Aybak in 1202-3 AD.[194]

Badā'ūn appears to have been the starting point for further
conquests, first in Awadh, and then in Bihar and Bengal, undertaken by Muhammad bin Bakhtyār Khalajī, in Aybak's service,
sometime in the last years of the twelfth and the first few years
of the thirteenth centuries.[195] Proceeding into Awadh, then initi-
ating raids into Māner and Bihār, he obtained ample resources
in terms of horses, arms and men, and was joined by numerous
bodies of Khalaj 'from different parts of Hindustān'.[196] The ter-

---

[187] *TN*, p. 120; *TF*, p. 58; *FS*, vs. 1752-53; *TM*, ff. 42b-54a.
[188] Cf. also *TF*, p. 58.
[189] *TN*, pp. 120, 140; *TF*, pp. 59, 62.
[190] *TN*, p. 120; *FS*, vs. 1543-45; *TM*, ff. 53b-54a.
[191] *TF*, pp. 58-59; Kirtane, 'Hammira Mahakavya', p. 62; *TM*, ff. 42b-54a.
[192] *TN*, p. 140; *TF*, p. 59; *TM*, ff. 53b-54a.
[193] *TN*, pp. 120, 140; *TF*, p. 59; *FS*, vs. 1626-30.
[194] *TF*, p. 62; *TM*, ff. 54a-b.
[195] *TN*, pp. 146-57; FS, vs. 1865-90.
[196] *TN*, pp. 146-7.

ritories of Bihār were extensively raided by his forces, culminating in the capture and sacking of a fortified city which Juzjani refers to by the same name (Bihār), but which must have been Uddandapura.[197] Juzjani describes the whole of this fortress and city as a *vihāra*, which, he explains, is 'a madrasa' or 'place of learning in the Hindwī language', inhabited largely by 'shaven-headed brahmans', that is by Buddhist monks.[198] These were all slain, he continues, so that when a great number of books was discovered in this monastery town 'there was no-one left who could explain their content'.[199]

A Tibetan author of the early seventeenth century, Taranatha, in his 'History of Buddhism in India', writes that during the time of the last four Sena rulers the number of Buddhist monastic establishments had gone on increasing in Magadha, but that then many *Stag-gzigs*, 'Turks', of the *mleccha* view, had started to appear.[200] To protect places like Uddandapura and Vikramashilā, the Sena kings converted these partially into fortresses and stationed some soldiers in them.[201] The *Stag-gzigs* 'overran the whole of Magadha and massacred many ordained monks in Uddandapura'.[202] They later built a fort on the ruins of the Uddandapura vihāra, and destroyed Vikramashilā, further to the northeast, as well.[203] Taranatha leaves no doubt about the outcome: 'The Law became almost extinct in Magadha'.[204]

In the account of the Tibetan pilgrim Dharmasvamin, who visited eastern India in the years 1234-36, the *Vihāra* of Uddandapura is mentioned twice as the residence of a Turushka military commander.[205] Of Vikramashilā 'there were then no traces left, the Turushka soldiery having razed it to the ground, and thrown the foundation stones into the Ganges'.[206] In Nalanda, Dharmasvamin observed about eighty small vihāras which were damaged

---

[197] *TN*, pp. 147-8.
[198] *TN*, p. 148.
[199] *Ibid.*
[200] D. Chattopadhyaya (ed.), *Tāranātha's History of Buddhism in India* (Calcutta, 1980), p. 318.
[201] *Ibid.*
[202] *Ibid.*, p. 319.
[203] *Ibid.*
[204] *Ibid.*
[205] G. Roerich (tr.), *Biography of Dharmasvamin* (Patna, 1959), pp. xli-xliv & text, pp. 64, 90.
[206] *Ibid.*, p. 64.

by the Turushkas, 'and there was absolutely no-one to look after them, or to make offerings', although two of them were in a serviceable condition.[207]

Contemporary evidence on the destruction of the Buddhist monasteries in eastern India hardly exists. But it can be shown that Lakshmana Sena engaged himself in several armed conflicts with the Muslim invaders, and two of his court poets, in effect, eulogized him as 'a smiter of Turushka forces'.[208] The *Sekashubhodayā* tells us that Lakshmana Sena 'kills any yavana who goes there' and that there is 'none that can vanquish him'.[209] But there was already a clear apprehension of the impending catastrophe 'throughout the territories of Lakhnautī and Bihār, and the countries of Bang and Kamrud ... [as well as] in Nādīya (Nūdīya), the capital of the Ray Lakhmania [Raja Lakshmana Sena]'.[210] By the time that the Muslims were subjugating Bihar, a number of astrologers began to predict the fall of the Sena kingdom in the near future.[211] Juzjani says that although the Sena king himself could not yet be persuaded to abandon his country and flee eastwards, 'most of the brahmans and inhabitants of that place left, and retired to the province of Sankanāt [probably in east Bang], the cities and towns of Bang, and towards Kamrud'.[212]

Muhammad bin Bakhtyār, having received a robe of honour for his earlier victory from Aybak, again set out for Bihār, and then to Nādīya, a Sena capital, which he took possession of in May 1204, finally driving Lakshmana Sena to Sankanāt and Bang, where the latter's reign soon came to an end.[213] What Juzjani refers to as *Sankanāt* is probably *Sankakot*, a centre of the mercantile or *Banik* community in the twelfth century, not far from Vikramapura, where Lakshmana Sena's descendants are archaeologically recorded to have ruled for the next three generations.[214] Epigraphic evidence shows that only ten months after the sack of

---

[207] *Ibid.*, pp. 90-91.
[208] S. Sen (ed. and transl.), *Sekashubhodayā of Halayudha-Mishra* (Calcutta, 1963), p. iv.
[209] *Ibid.*, Ch. 9, p. 179.
[210] *TN*, p. 148.
[211] *Ibid.*, p. 150.
[212] *TN*, p. 150.
[213] *TN*, pp. 150-1; Eaton, *Rise of Islam*, p. 32, note 10.
[214] N. K. Dutt, 'The Vaishyas in Mediaeval Bengal', *The Indian Historical Quarterly*, XVI (1940), pp. 705-6.

Nādīya a great sacrifice, known as the *Aindrī Mahāshānti*, was performed by the Sena king to propitiate the gods for help in averting the occurrence or repetition of a great calamity.[215] Muhammad bin Bakhtyār left Nādīya in desolation, despatching a large part of its accumulated treasure to Aybak, and transferring the seat of Muslim government to Lakhnautī, a northern Sena capital on the Ganges, near Gaur. A provincial administration was set up, the khutba was read, coins were issued in Mu'izz ad-Dīn's name, and mosques, madrasas and khanaqas were founded all over the area.

Even this was not the end of the conquest. Muhammad bin Bakhtyār subsequently became tormented by the idea of reaching Tibet, from his eastern outpost, and to that effect began to equip an army of about 10,000 horse.[216] Juzjani's description of the final—and ill-fated—attempt to open an eastern gate of Hind is supported by the evidence of Sanskrit inscriptions found at Gauhati, Assam, which recorded that a Turushka force reached the Brahmaputra and there met with destruction in 1206 AD.[217] Following the river for sixteen days, the Muslim army apparently did succeed in reaching 'the open country of Tibbat', where—we are now coming full circle—they ran up against people who 'were Turks, archers, and equipped with long bows'. The Muslims had to withdraw when news arrived of an advancing army of 50,000 'Turkish horsemen'. On the way back, Bakhtyār's army was starved of food and cut to pieces by the mountain tribes of Kamarupa, who planted spiked bamboo walls in the ground and used bamboo spears.[218] Bakhtyār died of disease or was assassinated shortly after this failed expedition. It was an event which occurred shortly before the Ghurids lost their original homeland to the Khwarazm Shah, and then the Mongols. Boundaries were now beginning to be re-drawn in the east as well as in the west: with Ghur gone, and even Ghazna, and with Tibet out of reach, what was left to the Ghurid slave generals was the area they had conquered in *al-Hind*.

[215] N. K. Bhattasali, 'The Rājāvādī (Bhāwāl) Plate of Lakshmana Sena Deva', *Journal of the Royal Asiatic Society of Bengal*, VIII (1942), pp. 19-20.

[216] *TN*, p. 151; and cf. *FS*, vs. 1908-9.

[217] *TN*, pp. 152-6; *Journal of Indian History*, 15 (1936), pp. 175-6.

[218] *TN*, pp. 152-6.

CHAPTER V

THE SLAVE HOUSEHOLD OF DELHI

In the new capital of Delhi, the slave kings ruled for less than a century, from 1206 to 1290 AD. Some authors, like Ibn Battuta, exclude Qutb ad-Dīn Aybak,[1] the Turkish slave of Muhammad Ghuri, from the list of Muslim kings of Delhi because the latter ascended the throne in Lahore and not in Delhi. Technically still a slave (whose formal manumission was not obtained until 1208), Aybak was given the 'title of Sultān' (laqab-i-salṭānī, khiṭāb-i-salṭānī) as well as the 'title of Bādshāh' (khiṭāb-i-bādshāhī) and a 'canopy of state' (chatr) and 'staff' (dūrbāsh) in 1205, when Muhammad Ghuri died and the latter's nephew Ghiyāth ad-Dīn Mahmūd became the Ghurid suzerain at Fīrūzkūh.[2] This occurred at the same time that Aybak's fellow slaves Yaldiz and Qabacha—with whom he had concluded matrimonial alliances—were appointed Sultans of Ghazna and Multan respectively. Accordingly, Aybak now proceeded from Delhi to the Panjab, where in June 1206 he ascended 'the throne of the Sultanate of Lahore' (takht-i-salṭanat-i-lohor).[3] A contemporary author, Fakhr ad-Dīn Mubārakshāh, who witnessed Aybak's succession in 1206, refers to Lahore as 'the centre of Islam in Hind and the second capital of the kingdom of Ghazna'.[4] Clearly, at this point, although Delhi was occupied, there was as yet no Sultanate of Delhi established on an independent footing. Aybak was still appointed ruler of Lahore 'in order to subjugate Hindustān'.[5] He abolished 'unorthodox' measures instituted in the previous reign, but his rule did not imply any decisive break with Ghurid and Ghaznavid precedent.[6] And, even though Juzjani refers to Aybak as, at this time, having

---

[1] Also Aybek, Aybeg; Skt Shuduvadina, Shutubadina (Indian Antiquary, XIX, p.186; Epigraphia Indica: Arabic and Persian Supplement (1913-14), p. 43).
[2] TN, p. 140; TMS, pp. 14, 16; TF, p. 63.
[3] TN, p. 140; TFM, p. 30; TF, p. 63.
[4] TFM, p. 30.
[5] FS, vs. 1963 ff.
[6] TFM, p. 34.

become 'one of the kings of al-Hind',[7] inscriptions still call him simply *Malik* or *Sipāhsālār*.[8] Like Muhammad bin Bakhtyār Khalajī, his fellow Sipāhsālār in Bengal, Aybak seems to have issued no coinage in his own name, but restricted himself to circulating coins as a local governor, in the name of his suzerain.[9] Similar reserve in the issuing of coins in his own name was exercised by Tāj ad-Dīn Yaldiz, who perpetuated his master's name in the currency long after the latter's assassination.[10] Also in accordance with precedent, the Ghazna throne remained superior to that of Lahore, although both Aybak and Yaldiz endeavoured to put an end to the duality of Lahore and Ghazna. Aybak captured Ghazna and 'in this capital sat on the imperial throne' (*dar dār al-mulk-i-ghaznīn bar takht-i-bādshāhī*) for forty days in the year 1208 AD.[11] But he was ousted from Ghazna in his turn by Yaldiz and had to return to Lahore, where he eventually died in 1210-11, about twenty years after the capture of Delhi. The oldest Muslim inscription in Palwal, of that year, refers to Aybak as '*riqāb al-imām saiyid at-turk wa-l-ʿajam*', 'the master of the rulers of the Turks and the Persians'.[12]

Aybak's conquests, apart from Delhi (1191-2),[13] included the fortress of Mīrath (1193);[14] Kol, across the Yamuna, about sixty km north of modern Agra (1193-4);[15] the fortress of Thangīr (modern Bayana) (1195-6);[16] Benares (1194), in combination with Muhammad Ghuri;[17] Ajmer (1194-5);[18] Kanauj (1194 or 1198);[19] Nahrwālā, the capital of Gujarat (1196-7);[20] Badā'ūn, on the

---

[7] *TN*, pp. 137-141.

[8] E. Denison Ross (ed.), *Epigraphia Indo-Moslemica, 1911-12* (Calcutta and Bombay, 1912), p. 2.

[9] Thomas, *Chronicles*, pp. 34, 37; H. Nelson Wright, *The Coinage and Metrology of the Sultans of Dehli* (New Delhi, 1974), p. 69.

[10] Thomas, *Chronicles*, p. 23.

[11] *TMS*, p. 15; *TN*, p. 140; *TF*, p. 63; *FS*, vs. 1947-1996.

[12] *Epigraphia Indo-Moslemica, 1911-12*. p. 2.

[13] Thomas, *Chronicles*, p. 23; *TMS*, p. 11; *TFM*, p. 22; *TF*, p. 60. Defrémery and Sanguinetti, *Ibn Batoutah*, III, p. 161 however has 584/1188—which is also the date on the mihrāb of the great mosque in the city.

[14] *TMS*, pp. 11, 14; *TF*, p. 60.

[15] *TMS*, p. 11; *TF*, p. 60.

[16] *TFM*, p. 23; *TN*, pp. 137-141; *TF*, p. 61.

[17] *TN*, pp. 137-41; *TFM*, p. 23; *TF*, p. 60.

[18] *TFM*, p. 22; *TF*, pp. 61-62.

[19] *TMS*, p. 11.

[20] *TFM*, p. 23; *TN*, pp. 137-41; *TF*, p. 62.

Upper Ganges (1197-8);[21] Ujjayn and other parts of Malwa (1199);[22] Mahoba, the capital of Kālpī, west of the Yamuna and the Ganges (1202);[23] and the fortress of Kālanjar, in Bundelkhand (1202-3).[24] These conquests were not always permanent. But they were all achieved by Aybak while he was Sipāhsālār or 'chief commander' of the army in Hind, and none is recorded in the four years between 1206 and his death in Lahore in 1210-11.

Little is known of Aybak's successor and adopted son, Ārām Shāh, who may or may not have been a Turkish slave, and who ruled in all likelihood for less than a year in 1210-11. He too did not issue any coinage, and similarly is not mentioned by Ibn Battuta in his list of Delhi Sultans.[25] The first mention of Delhi as a separate dominion does not occur until 1211, the year of the accession of Iltutmish, an Ilbari Turk whose former slave status is not in doubt—he was in fact the slave of Aybak, and hence the slave of a slave. As Juzjani writes, at this time the 'dominions of Hindustān' (mamālik-i-hindustān) became divided in four parts: the 'mamlakat-i-dihlī' which went to Iltutmish, the 'mamlakat-i-sind' which was taken by Qabacha, the 'mamlakat-i-lakhnautī' which was brought under subjection by the Khalaj chiefs, and the 'mamlakat-i-lohor' which was seized 'sometimes by Qabacha and sometimes by Iltutmish ..'. [26]

In practical terms the situation which now arose implied that there were three Muslim sovereigns in Hind—Qabacha in Sind and the Panjab, Iltutmish in Delhi, and the Khalaj chiefs in Bengal—who engaged in a contest for primacy which was ultimately won by the Delhi ruler Iltutmish. At first, as could be expected, this was largely a contest between Delhi and Lahore. Lahore had to be incorporated in the Delhi dominion, and the terms of the relationship had to be reversed. If this could be achieved, the subjection of the Khalaj rulers in Bengal would follow suit.

Nāsir ad-Dīn Qabacha,[27] a former Muʿizzi slave and the son-in-

[21] TMS, pp. 11, 24.
[22] TN, pp. 137-41; TFM, p. 24.
[23] TF, pp. 62-63.
[24] TFM, p. 24; TF, p. 62.
[25] TNR, p. 529, note 4; TN, pp. 141-2; TF, p. 64; Nelson Wright, Coinage and Metrology, p. 69; Defrémery and Sanguinetti, Ibn Batoutah, III, p. 164.
[26] TN, pp. 141-2.
[27] Srī Kubācā Suritān in the Sanskrit legend on his coins.

law of Aybak, took advantage of the struggle between Ārām Shāh and Iltutmish to occupy Lahore in 1211. According to Juzjani, 'Qabācha appropriated Sind (as far as the sea-coast) and Multān, Bhakkar and Sīwistān, and, subsequently, the territory of the north-east as far as Sarsattī and Kahrām'.[28] Uch, and possibly many of the other forts and qasbas of these areas he had already possessed de facto when he was still the slave of Muhammad Ghuri and in the period between the latter's death and 1211.[29] But from now on he is mentioned as 'Sultān' on his coins and appears to have assumed the *chatr* as a further symbol of his sovereignty. The territories of Multan, Siwistan and Debal he made over to his son Bahram Shah after Aybak's death. Qabacha himself was subsequently ousted from Lahore, Multān and Uch by the forces of Yaldiz, leaving Ghazna before the Khwarazm Shah.[30] But when Yaldiz was put to death by Iltutmish, Qabacha again got possession of these territories, subject apparently to Iltutmish. There was constant contention between him and Iltutmish, up to the battle between Jalal ad-Din Khwarazm Shah and Chingiz Khan on the banks of the Indus, after which Jalal ad-Din entered Sind and proceeded to Debal and Makran in 1221.[31] The Panjab and Sind entered a period of great turmoil owing to the struggles between Qabacha, the Khwarazm Shah and the Mongols. Iltutmish merely watched the latter erode Qabacha's position in the area. There are many discrepancies in the various sources about the Mongols' investment of Multan—many say that the Mongols subdued and temporarily occupied the city.[32] But whatever their role may have been in this interlude, it is an established fact that in 1228-29 Iltutmish, taking advantage of Qabacha's difficulties, occupied Lahore, and drove Qabacha from Multan and Uch to a death by drowning in the Indus.[33] 'Sind was acquired as far as the ocean'.[34]

---

[28] *TN*, p. 141. The *TMS*, p. 16 says that Qabacha 'marched towards Sind, and took possession of the iqtāʿ of multān-o-uch-o-bhakhar-o-siwistān'.
[29] *TN*, pp. 142-4. See aslo *TNR*, pp. 532-4, note 4.
[30] *TN*, p. 143; *TNR*, pp. 532-4, note 4.
[31] *TN*, p. 143.
[32] *TN*, p. 143; *TNR*, pp. 535-6, note 1; Siddiqui, *Perso-Arabic Sources*, p. 4 and p. 38, note 9.
[33] *TN*, pp. 143-4. Here again there are numerous discrepancies. Cf. *TN*, p. 172; *FS*, vs. 2139-69; *TF*, p. 65; Siddiqui, *Perso-Arabic Sources*, pp. 29-30.
[34] *TN*, p. 172.

Qabacha's son and the remainder of his following presented themselves at Iltutmish's court.

It was thus, in the words of Ibn Battuta, Sultān Shams ad-Dīn Iltutmish who became 'the first who ruled in the city of Dihlī with independent power'.[35] Bought by Aybak at Delhi, he had been advanced from one position to another and ended up as *iqtā`*-holder of, first, Baran, then Badā'ūn, and he had also distinguished himself against the Kokhars.[36] He caught the attention of Muhammad Ghuri, who conferred a special dress of honour on him and directed him to be manumitted.[37] When Aybak was succeeded at Lahore by his adopted son Ārām Shāh, Iltutmish was raised to the throne by the army at Delhi in 1211. Ārām Shāh was slain while marching on Delhi.[38] And the succession was by no means undisputed. Even after his succession, Iltutmish received a *chatr* and a *dūrbāsh* and other emblems of royalty which were sent to him by Yaldiz from Ghazna and Lahore.[39] But Yaldiz ceased to play a role by 1215, when he was captured at Tarā'īn and imprisoned at Badā'ūn. It could perhaps be argued that Iltutmish's primacy in Islamic India as the ruler of Delhi formally started at the latter date.

Iltutmish, like the later Delhi monarchs, in his inscriptions uses the title '*maulā mulūk al-`arab wa-l-`ajam*' ('king of the kings of the Arabs and the Persians'), which had been used already by Mas`ūd, as well as by earlier Muslim kings in view of their conquest of the non-Arab nations which they styled '*ajamī*.[40] He also

---

[35] Defrémery and Sanguinetti, *Ibn Batoutah*, III, p. 164. Battuta actually refers to this king as 'Lalmish'. There is a number of variant spellings of the name, but the proper name appears to have been Iltutmish, 'holder of the realm' (Cf. S. Digby, 'Iletmish or Iltutmish? A reconsideration of the Name of the Delhi Sultan', *Iran*, 8 (1970), pp. 57-64; Thomas, *Chronicles*, pp. 43-44, 71; Nelson Wright, *Coinage and Metrology*, p. 70). In Sanskrit his name was rendered *Lititimisi*, or he was referred to as *Suritan Srī Samasadin* or *Samusdina*, or simply 'the Turushka lord' (*Turushkādhipamadaladan*) (Z. A. Desai, 'Inscriptions of the Mamluk Sultans of Delhi', in: Z. A. Desai (ed.), *Epigraphia Indica: Arabic and Persian Supplement (1966)* (Delhi, 1967), pp. 1-18; 'References to Muhammadans—AD 730-1320', in: *The Journal of Indian History*, 15 (1936), p. 177.)

[36] TN, pp. 165, 168-9; Defrémery and Sanguinetti, *Ibn Batoutah*, III, p. 164; Thomas, *Chronicles*, pp. 41-80.

[37] TN, pp. 169-70. Defrémery and Sanguinetti, *Ibn Batoutah*, III, p. 164 however says that Iltutmish was manumitted only after Aybak had died.

[38] TN, p. 170; FS, vs. 2047-61; TMS, p. 16 ff.

[39] TN, p. 170.

[40] *Epigraphia Indica, Arabic and Persian Supplement, 1913-14*, pp.14-15.

uses the title '*maulā mulūk at-turk wa-l-'ajam*' as well as '*saiyid as-salāṭīn at-turk wa-l-'ajam*', 'master of the kings of the Turks and the Persians' or '*riqāb al-imām maulā mulūk at-turk wa-l-'ajam*', and also '*Hindgīr*', 'Conqueror of Hind', '*Shāh-i-Sharq*', 'King of the East' (at his death in 1236), and '*Salṭān Salāṭīn ash-Sharq*', 'the Sultan of the Sultans of the East'.[41] The latter title occurs with Iltutmish for the first time, as does the title *Shāhanshāh*, 'King of Kings', which had been associated with the emperors of Persia.[42] Iltutmish's court, in effect, has been compared by Barani in the fourteenth century to the courts of Mahmud of Ghazna and the Seljuq king Sanjar, and was described by him as 'equal in splendour' to those of the Sultans of Egypt and the Kings of 'Iraq, Khurasan and Khwarazm.[43] Iltutmish was also the first ruler in India to receive sanction for his rule from the Khalifa in Baghdad, whose emissaries he received in 1228-9.[44] He is credited with the introduction of a new coinage system which remained essentially the same up to 1387: the silver tanka of one tola weight (172 grams) and the copper jital, distinct from Delhiwalas as well as the fractional coins of copper.[45] The silver tanka and billon jital of Iltutmish appear to have served as models in the succeeding period, and in one form or another even survived the Sultanate itself. To Iltutmish's tanka can be traced the modern rupee.[46]

Under Iltutmish, then, the decision to establish an independent Sultanate in Delhi must have been partly determined by the city's position as the source of money for much of northwestern India. But in Delhi, Iltutmish inherited mints which continued to produce the pre-conquest Rajput coinage—and this is what necessitated the reform.[47] It was not until the later thirteenth century,

---

[41] *Ibid.*; *Epigraphia Indo-Moslemica, 1911-12*, pp. 3, 27-30; *FS*, pp. 123-4.

[42] *Ep. Indo-Moslemica*, 1911-12, op. cit., p. 27; Z. A. Desai, 'Inscriptions of the Mamluk Sultans of Delhi', *Ep. Ind: Arabic and Persian supplement* (1966), ed. Z. A. Desai (Delhi, 1967), (pp. 1-18), p. 17.

[43] *TFS*, pp. 25, 27.

[44] There is a rare coin of Iltutmish which contains only the name of the Caliph and which was probably issued to commemorate the arrival of the Caliphal diploma of investiture (Thomas, *Chronicles*, p. 46; Nelson Wright, *Coinage and Metrology*, p. 18; *TN*, p. 174; *TF*, p. 66).

[45] S. Moosvi, 'Numismatic evidence and the economic history of the Delhi Sultanate', *Proceedings of the Indian History Congress* (1989-90), pp. 207-8.

[46] Nelson Wright, *Coinage and Metrology*, pp. 72, 75.

[47] J. S. Deyell, *Living without Silver: The Monetary History of Early Medieval North India* (Delhi, 1990), p. 213.

after the further military expánsion of the Delhi Sultanate, that
the quantity of the new coinage began to expand substantially due
to the release of the hoarded treasure of frontier rulers and temples.[48] As distinct from his Ghurid predecessors, it was Iltutmish's
task to assert the primacy of Delhi among Muslim rivals, and to
regularize its governance, rather than pursue further expansion.

From a strategic point of view, the location of Delhi had the
decisive advantage that it enabled Iltutmish to isolate Bengal from
the Muslim kingdoms to the west, thus allowing him to deal with
his opponents individually, while yet it was well placed for further
raids into the Indian subcontinent at a later stage. In 1211,
Qabacha was still occupying Lahore, and Yaldiz had not yet abandoned his claim to the Ghurid conquests in Hind. But Yaldiz was
defeated in 1215, retiring before the Khwarazmians. In 1228,
when Qabacha was preoccupied with the Mongols, Lahore was
occupied. But by then Iltutmish's effective frontier was drawn back
east of the Beas river and Iltutmish avoided a direct confrontation with the Mongols. Instead, Delhi was beginning to fill up with
refugees from Mongol-ravaged territories in Khurasan and adjacent areas as well as others who sought Iltutmish's largesse.[49] In
1225, Iltutmish led an army to Bihar and Lakhnauti (Gaur), where
he exacted tribute from Muhammad bin Bakhtyār Khalajī and
changed the Bengal currency to his own name, putting the governance of the eastern dominion in the hands of one of his sons,
Nāsir ad-Dīn Mahmūd—by whom Bakhtyār was slain.[50] In
Lakhnauti the khutba was now read in Iltutmish's name. But
another campaign was necessary in 1230 to keep the area from
slipping away.[51] Around the same time, in the period from 1226
up to 1235, the year of his death, we find Iltutmish campaigning
in other parts of Hindustān, capturing, at least temporarily, Ranthanbhūr (1226), Mandor (1227), Gwalior (1231-2), and raiding
and plundering Bhīlsā and Ujjayn (1234-5).[52]

After Iltutmish's death, in the period from 1236 to 1265, three
of his sons, one daughter, and a grandson sat on the throne of

---

[48] *Ibid.*, pp. 218-9; T. Raychaudhuri and I. Habib (eds), *The Cambridge Economic
History of India, Volume I: c. 1200-c.1750* (Cambridge, 1982), p. 96.
[49] Cf. *TN*, p. 166; and below, Chapter VI.
[50] *TF*, p. 66; *TN*, p. 171.
[51] *TN*, p. 174; *FS*, vs. 2362-96.
[52] *TN*, pp. 172-176; *TMS*, pp. 16-21; *TF*, p. 66; *FS*, vs. 2302-18.

Delhi. First his eldest son, Rukun ad-Dīn Fīrūz Shāh,[53] ruled for six months and twenty-six days, during which time he left the affairs of state to his mother, but was then ousted by the maliks and replaced by Iltutmish's daughter Raziyya.[54] Raziyya, 'of warlike talent', had been made heir apparent by Iltutmish, who considered her more worthy than any of his sons, appointing her regent during his absence, but she had lacked, in the first instance, sufficient support to survive the factional struggle (fitna) which ensued after Iltutmish's death.[55] Now, however, with the support of the army, she was put on the throne, and 'ruled with absolute authority for four years'.[56] Coming out of purda, 'mounting a horse like a man', she was suspected of sexual intimacy with one of her favoured Habshi slaves, thereby arousing the jealousy of the Turks.[57] She was deposed in 1240, and imprisoned, while her half-brother Bahrām Shāh was seated on the throne.[58] Mu'izz ad-Dīn Bahrām Shāh[59] was the youngest son of Iltutmish and he ruled for a little over two years, during which he successfully met a renewed challenge to his rule by Raziyya and reinforced the Lahore frontier against the Mongols, but then went under in another factional struggle and was 'martyred'.[60] Now, 'Alā' ad-Dīn Mas'ūd Shāh,[61] one of Iltutmish's grandsons, a son of Rukun ad-Dīn Fīrūz Shāh, was brought forth from the White Castle (Qaṣr-i-Safed)—the state prison where the sons and grandsons of Iltutmish were kept—and he ruled for a little over four years.[62] It was a reign equally undistinguished: an overbearing Wazir acquired

---

[53] Persian coins of this king are rare; on his Hindi currency he is called Suritān Srī Rukunadin, and elsewhere Perujasāhi (Cf. Thomas, Chronicles, p. 103).

[54] Skt Jalāladina (?); TN, pp. 181-5; TF, pp. 67-68; TMS, pp. 21-23; FS, vs. 2454-2572.

[55] TN, pp. 185-7; TF, p. 68; Defrémery and Sanguinetti, Ibn Batoutah, III, p. 167. In fact, Raziyya's rise dates from the capture of the Queen Mother, so that the transfer of power was really from one woman to another. On the sovereignty of women, see Thomas, Chronicles, pp. 104-5.

[56] Defrémery and Sanguinetti, Ibn Batoutah, III, p. 167. However, on one of her rare coins the name of her father is still used to the exclusion of her own (Nelson Wright, Coinage and Metrology, p.76).

[57] FS, vs. 2517-72; TN, p. 187; TF, p. 68; Defrémery and Sanguinetti, Ibn Batoutah, III, p. 167.

[58] Defrémery and Sanguinetti, Ibn Batoutah, III, p. 167; TN, pp. 188-190; TF, pp. 68-69; FS, vs. 2573-93.

[59] Skt Maujadina.

[60] TMS, pp. 28-32; TN, pp. 190-7; FS, vs. 2594-2699; TF, pp. 69-70.

[61] Skt Alāvadina.

[62] TN, pp. 197-201; TF, p. 70; FS, vs. 2713-41; TMS, pp. 33-34.

almost complete control over the kingdom, but was executed in 1242; 'victories' in different parts of the kingdom are reported by Juzjani—who was in Bengal at the time; a Mongol army investing Uch had to be repelled; more Mongol raids occurring; and, in the end, Mas'ūd Shāh was removed too, on account of his 'unworthy acts and habits' and general neglect of state affairs.

Then followed the twenty-year reign, from 1246 to 1265, of another incompetent son of Iltutmish, Nāsir ad-Dīn Mahmūd,[63] who was born in Delhi in 1228, and was also kept in the White Castle until the late king Mas'ūd released him and gave him the government of Bahraich.[64] A reclusive, he left the affairs of the kingdom to his slave and future son-in-law Balban, whom he appointed Wazir and in effect allowed to run the government with only a brief interruption throughout his reign and ultimately to position himself to succeed him. As Wazir under Nāsir ad-Dīn, Balban was actively engaged in the Panjab and Multan, attempting to ward off the Mongols and reduce the power of the Kokhars and other tribes which had facilitated Mongol penetration in the area.[65] It appears that previous to this the Mongols made almost annual raids upon the border tracts of Sind and Multan. In the following years, Balban undertook expeditions in the Doāb, the country between the Ganges and the Yamuna, to subject local rulers, and also to obtain booty to pay for further campaigns against the Mongols (1247);[66] to the Kohpāyah [skirts of the hills of Mewat] and Ranthanbhūr, and to the extreme confines of the Upper Country (*taraf-i-bālā*) and the Beas river (1248);[67] to Awadh (1249);[68] to Nagaur, Gwalior, Chandīrī, Narwār, and Malwa and Kālanjar (1251);[69] to Lahore and the Beas river and Multan (1252);[70] to Uch, Multan and Tabarhind (1253);[71] to the Kohpāyah of Bandār and Bijnor, the Rahab [Ramganga] river, and

---

[63] Skt *Nasaradiṇa.*

[64] *TN*, pp. 201, 289; *TMS*, pp. 35-39; *TF*, pp. 70-71; Defrémery and Sanguinetti, *Ibn Batoutah*, III, pp. 168-9; Thomas, *Chronicles*, p. 124; *FS*, pp. 140-1; Nelson Wright, *Coinage and Metrology*, pp. 78-79.

[65] In 1246-7 (*TN*, pp. 208-10, 290-1; *TF*, p. 71; *FS*, vs. 2771-2844).

[66] *TN*, pp. 210-2, 291; *TF*, pp. 71-72.

[67] *TN*, pp. 212, 292; *TF*, p. 72.

[68] *TN*, pp. 213, 294.

[69] *TN*, pp. 215, 296-7; *TF*, p. 72; *FS*, vs. 2874-2909.

[70] *TN*, p. 297; *TF*, p. 72.

[71] *TN*, p. 217.

Katahr (1254);[72] into Hindustān or Awadh, and later to Santūr and the Kohpāyah, to oust seceding amirs (1256-7);[73] against the Mongols again in 1258 in various parts of the Panjab and west of Delhi;[74] into Awadh (1258);[75] into the Siwalik and to Ranthan-bhūr, where the rajas of Mewat had begun to create disturbances, and the Kohpāyah [the hilltract of Mewāt, near Delhi] (1259);[76] and again to the Kohpāyah of Delhi to put down the Mewāt (1260).[77]

Nāsir ad-Dīn died in 1266, probably childless, but having nom-inated Ghiyāth ad-Dīn Balban[78] as his successor. Balban, having in reality governed (as Wazir, but using many of the insignia of royalty) the kingdom since a long time, was raised to the throne with the support of all the great maliks. This marks the beginning of a new period in the history of the Delhi Sultanate, as the reign of the dynasty founded by Iltutmish now came to an end. Balban had been Iltutmish's slave, of Ilbari Turkish origin (like Iltutmish himself), brought to Delhi in 1232 as a member of the *chihilgānī* or 'forty' who rose to prominence during the weak governments of Iltutmish's successors while creating a kind of loosely cement-ed military oligarchy.[79] In effect, as a former slave, after having been promoted by degrees by Iltutmish and his successors, and already maintaining the de facto independent possession of the Panjab under Rukun ad-Dīn, distinguishing himself in campaigns against the Mewat in the reign of Bahrām Shāh, on becoming king Balban's first goal was to use his new power to eliminate his rival Turkish mamluks.[80] Balban restored the authority (*haiba*) of the throne of Delhi.[81] More than any contemporary Muslim ruler, he attracted followers from outside, including numerous princes from Turkestan, Khurasan, Iraq and Iran, who had been driven out by the Mongols.[82] Balban built up Delhi 'and with the splen-

[72] *TN*, p. 218.
[73] *TN*, pp. 220-2, 305-6; *TF*, p. 73.
[74] *TN*, pp. 225, 310.
[75] *TF*, p. 73; *TN*, pp. 311-2.
[76] *TF*, p. 73; *TN*, pp. 313-5.
[77] *TN*, p. 227.
[78] Skt *Hamīra Gayāsadin*.
[79] *TN*, pp. 281-2; Defrémery and Sanguinetti, *Ibn Batoutah*, III, pp. 171-2, 174; *TF*, p. 74; *TFS*, pp. 25-27.
[80] *TF*, pp. 74-75; *TN*, pp. 284-287.
[81] *TFS*, pp. 25, 28-29.
[82] *TF*, pp. 75-76; *TFS*, p. 25. And see below, Chapter VI.

dour of the Sultans of Persia he adorned in it a court for himself'.[83] His rule is identified with the appearance of a gold
coinage, following the silver models already in circulation, struck
in bold relief, and an extension of the mint system, as is shown
by the existence of coins, both silver and copper, struck at mints
other than the capital.[84] A Sanskrit eulogy describes Balban as 'he,
whose enemies are turned back from afar by the dust of the earth
raised by the trampling of the hoofs of his swift horse galloping
in the front of his army, he, the central jewel in the necklace of
the earth girdled with its seven seas, the illustrious prince Hamīra
Gayāsadīn ..'.[85] Like Iltutmish, Balban used the title of *Shāhanshāh*,[86] in addition to '*malik mulūk al-ʿarab wa-l-ʿajam*'.[87] He maintained the dignity (*waqār*), magnificence (*dāb*) and urbanity
(*adab*) of the throne 'in a manner that could not be surpassed',
while also re-organizing the army, imposing an inflexible system
of justice, and appointing confidential spies. Balban was pre-occupied—or so later writers depict him—throughout his reign (1266-
87) with the defense of the western marches against the Mongols
and, early in his reign, with the suppression of the Mewatis in the
dense jungles of the Doab near Delhi (occupying an extensive
tract about hundred-thirty km south of the capital) and similar
tribes elsewhere (in the Kumaon hills, the Koh-i-Jud, Katahr). The
latter had been obstructing the flow of traffic, of caravans and
merchants, in the previous period, threatening Delhi itself, and
had not been interfered with since the time of Iltutmish.[88] In
these areas new forts were built, to be garrisoned by Afghans, and
the towns with surrounding country were given out to distinguished chiefs, and 'the roads to Hindustān were thus cleared'.[89]
New conquests, or re-conquests of areas like Gujarat and Malwa
that were passing out of control, were put off. Delhi's supremacy
over Bengal was re-established at the very beginning of Balban's
reign. But the governor of Bengal broke away again fifteen years
later, until the province was given over to one of Balban's sons,
Bughra Khan.[90]

[83] *TFS*, p. 25; see also *TF*, p. 75.
[84] Thomas, *Chronicles*, p. 134; Nelson Wright, *Coinage and Metrology*, pp. 80-81.
[85] *Epigraphia Indica, Arabic and Persian Supplement, 1913-14*, pp. 40, 43-44.
[86] Thomas, *Chronicles*, p. 134.
[87] Desai, 'Inscriptions of the Mamluk Sultans of Delhi', p. 13.
[88] *TFS*, pp. 30-45, 50, 55-57, 61, 64-67, 80; *TF*, pp. 77-79.
[89] *TFS*, pp. 55-60; *TMS*, p. 40; *FS*, vs. 3110-23; *TF*, p. 77.
[90] *TF*, pp. 77, 79-82; *TFS*, pp. 81-106; *FS*, vs. 3124-3243; *TMS*, pp. 41-42.

Since Balban's eldest son and designated heir Muhammad was killed in a struggle with the Mongols,[91] and his second son Bughra Khan preferred to stay in Bengal, when Balban died, he was succeeded by his eighteen-year old grandson Mu'izz ad-Dīn Kaiqubād, the son of Bughra Khan, in 1287.[92] The latter, having been brought up under the stern Balban, plunged headlong into a life of dissipation, and, unable to withstand the factional intrigues between Turks and Khalajis, was eventually displaced by his infant son Kayūmarth, a puppet in the hands of the Turks and then the Khalajis, until one of the latter, Jalāl ad-Dīn, assumed the power of the Sultanate for himself in 1290, bringing the rule of the Turkish slaves to an end.[93] As Firishta puts it: 'Jalāl ad-Dīn thus put an end to the dynasty of Ghūrī, and established that of Khalajī'.[94]

---

[91] *TFS*, pp. 109-10; *TMS*, pp. 41-44; *FS*, vs. 3244-3454; *TF*, pp. 82-83.
[92] *TFS*, pp. 120, 122-3; *TMS*, p. 51.
[93] *TFS*, pp. 126-73; *TF*, pp. 83-88; *FS*, vs. 3525-3712, 3756-3808; *TMS*, pp. 52-61.
[94] *TF*, p. 86.

CHAPTER VI

A WORLD ON THE MOVE

The Sultanate of Delhi, which was thus established in the thirteenth century, provided the crucible in which the two types of society—nomadic and sedentary—merged. The Turkish conquerors and their retinues were small in number by comparison with the mass of the Indian population which was conquered. Among the nomads or former nomads expansion was swift and wideranging, albeit often ephemeral, while leadership was rigid, concentrated and brittle, dependent on immediate success. By contrast, in the Indian ecosystem of settled agriculture, movement was restricted, and potentially disruptive, while leadership remained dispersed through networks of primordial ties of kinship, connubium, and sharing arrangements which used formulas of genealogy and companionage to regulate the repartitioning of the proceeds of the soil. In the world of the sedentary peasant, expansion was slow and laborious but durable. Vedic sources already reveal this divide—but also dependency—between nomadic warriors and settled cultivators.[1] And already in ancient times, the cultivators, with their resources immobilized in arable fields, saw the nomadic realm (both inside and outside the subcontinent) as a source of military manpower and mobile wealth.

By the end of the early medieval period, the great alluvial crescent from the delta of the Indus to that of the Ganges, the demographic centre of al-Hind, had become one of Asia's richest agricultural regions.[2] We cannot reconstruct in any detail the history of its settlement. And it is impossible to determine the number of villages and towns of early medieval India. Such figures do not become available before the sixteenth century. By then, it can be ascertained, they are overwhelmingly large. A Mughal author, Khwāja Nizām ad-Dīn Ahmad, wrote of the Mughal territories in

---

[1] Cf. J. C. Heesterman, 'Warrior, Peasant and Brahmin', *Modern Asian Studies*, 29.3 (1995), pp. 637-57.

[2] Cf. S. F. Dale, *Indian merchants and Eurasian trade, 1600-1750* (Cambridge, 1994), p. 15.

the 1580s: '... At present there are three thousand and two hundred towns; and one or two or five hundred or a thousand villages appertain to each of these towns .... Out of these there are one hundred and twenty great cities, which are now well populated and flourishing'.[3] It is fairly generally agreed upon that approximately 85% of the inhabitants of the Mughal territories lived in rural areas, and about 15% in towns and cities.[4] Population estimates of the whole of India in Mughal times vary. Using contemporary statistics, the Mughal population in 1598 has been calculated at between 60 and 98 million. South Asia's total population at that time might well have been something in between 100 and 155 million people.[5] By 1800 it could have been 185 million.[6]

The information we have on the period prior to the sixteenth century is currently extremely sketchy. Before 1500 AD we do not really have systematic data concerning the population of the Indian subcontinent at all, although, obviously, the demographic development of South Asia between the eleventh and fifteenth century should be considered particularly worthy of attention, as this was the India of which the wealth and power had captured the imagination of Europe in a way that Marco Polo's China had not. In fact, India may well have been wealthier than and as populous as China in this period.[7] In the absence of systematic data, the real issue is to somehow determine the rate of population increase over time.[8] Demographers have assumed that, on a general level, the world's population growth between 1650 and 1750 probably did not exceed 0.3% a year, and that before that time average rates were much lower still, as the world's population had probably only doubled from 0 AD to the end of the seventeenth

---

[3] De, *Tabaqat-i-Akbari*, p. 811; Dale, *Indian merchants*, p. 15.

[4] Dale, *Indian Merchants*, p. 15.

[5] Cf. D. Morris, 'Trends and Tendencies in Indian Economic History', *The Indian Economic and Social History Review*, 5, 4 (1968), pp. 345, 361; T. H. Hollingsworth, *Historical Demography* (Ithaca, 1969), p. 228; C.McEvedy and R. Jones, *Atlas of World Population History* (New York, 1978).

[6] The total population of Asia in 1750 has been put at 475 million in a toal world populaion of 728 million (W. D. Borrie, *Population, Environment and Society* (Auckland, 1974), p. 13).

[7] Hollingsworth, *Historical Demography*, p. 318.

[8] I am indebted here to J. Hoover, 'A South Asian Age of Anxiety: Part Two, Demography and Economy' (Termpaper, Department of History, UW-Madison, Spring 1992), p. 2.

A WORLD ON THE MOVE

century.[9] There is evidence that in earlier times the recuperative
powers of countries and regions following catastrophes of war,
famine and disease were remarkable.[10] In general, war was probably the least significant check on population growth. Diseases
arising in ever more populous agglomerations of people appear
to have been the most effective limiting factor in growth in
medieval times.[11] In South Asia there are clear indications that a
dense population was already present in some parts very early on.
Some demographers maintain that by 500 BC it contained a population of about 25 million, of whom some 15 million lived in the
Ganges basin—which remained the demographic heartland of the
subcontinent ever since.[12] If we can assume this to be a figure of
some accuracy, the question is why India's population expanded
so slowly until early modern times. In South Asia, exceptionally
among major world regions, we cannot conclude that a large
ancient and medieval population was dramatically cut back to size
in one generation during the fourteenth-century outbreak of
bubonic plague, as there is no evidence that the epidemic penetrated beyond the ports of Tamil Nadu, if indeed it ever reached
South Asia at all.[13] There are indications that malaria spread in
parts of Sri Lanka and Southeast Asia in the thirteenth and fourteenth centuries. In mainland Southeast Asia—estimated to have
had a total population in about 1000 AD of perhaps 5 million, a
figure which may have doubled by 1500 AD[14]—, in the period from
the 1220s to the 1350s, malaria probably had a destructive effect
on the rural population of Angkorian Cambodia, in combination
with ecological change, possibly related to deforestation and
changes in climate.[15] The lowlands of the eastcoast of Sumatra,
for centuries the home of Malay civilization and the locus of the
capital of Shrivijaya, also became increasingly malarial and
unhealthy from the thirteenth century on, and were overtaken in
cultural and political importance by the Minangkabau high-

Borrie, *Population*, p. 12.
[10] *Ibid.*, p. 15.
[11] *Ibid.*
[12] F. Fenner *et al, Smallpox and Its Eradication* (Geneva, 1988), p. 211; McEvedy
& Jones, *Atlas of World Population History*; D. R. Hopkins, *Princes and Peasants: Smallpox in History* (Chicago, 1983).
[13] Hoover, 'South Asian Age of Anxiety', p. 5.
[14] Fenner, *Smallpox*, p. 219.
[15] Cf. p. 374.

lands.[16] In Sri Lanka, malaria came in the wake of the destructive Cola invasions of the mid-thirteenth century and found ideal breeding places in abandoned tanks and channels, and then spread further to pose an obstacle to re-settlement in many parts of the island; indeed, it proved an obstacle to large-scale re-settlement of the dry zone until the 1930s.[17] Malaria may have spread at about the same time in South India as well. But in the northern plains there is no evidence of devastating epidemics in the thirteenth and fourteenth centuries.

The answer to the question why India's population expanded so slowly probably lies in the peculiar disease conditions which prevailed in the Indian plains over the long term. William McNeill has argued that in particular the population in the Ganges valley increased at a slow pace because the forests which used to cover it were a cauldron of microparasites. The warm climatic conditions in India were obviously more propitious for the survival of infectious microparasites than colder climates, and infections established among cattle and other animal herds could more easily be transmitted here to animal hosts.[18] In the Ganges valley there were dense enough human settlements living in close contact with animal herds in the early centuries for smallpox to be able to transfer to people.[19] Bubonic plague and cholera perhaps also began their careers as human diseases in this part of India. McNeill speculates that Indian diseases were possibly a more effective protection against invaders from the Northwest than military defence, as there must have been a high casualty rate among troops entering the Indian plains for the first time.[20] The outbreak of the epidemic of 1033 AD, spreading to the West as far as Isfahan, Baghdad and beyond, may well be related to such exposure of new population groups to microparasites which were endemic in North India.[21] Smallpox, in particular, has been present in India for at least 2000 years, especially in the densely populated rural settlements of the Ganges plain, and it always

---

[16] Ch. Dobbin, *Islamic Revivalism in a Changing Peasant Economy: Central Sumatra, 1784-1847* (London and Malmö, 1983), p. 7.

[17] K. M. De Silva, *A History of Sri Lanka* (Delhi, 1981), pp. 83-84; R. Murphy, 'The Ruin of Ancient Ceylon', *Journal of Asian Studies*, 16, 2 (1957), pp. 181-200.

[18] W. H. McNeill, *Plagues and Peoples* (New York, 1976), p. 95.

[19] *Ibid.*

[20] *Ibid.*, p. 83.

[21] Cf. p. 126.

remained one of the leading causes of death, an endemic disease
with dry season maxima, punctuated by outbreaks of epidemic
intensity every 5-7 years.[22] Smallpox begins to be mentioned in
South-Asian writings in the seventh or eighth century AD, in conjunction with a number of other diseases. It became especially
lethal at the end of Mughal rule—which was the time when Sita-
la Mata was transformed into a smallpox deity—, but an earlier
manifestation of the smallpox Goddess may have occurred in
South India, on the eastcoast, in the thirteenth century.[23] Al-
Bīrūnī recorded in the eleventh century that 'the Hindus ...
believe that the smallpox is a wind blowing from the island of
[Sri] Lanka towards the continent to carry off souls'.[24] And he
adds that after a procedure which appears to be a form of variolation (a primitive form of inoculation), 'perhaps nine people out
of ten will be proof against this malady'.[25] Variolation in India
may thus be dated from at least the eleventh century AD, and the
practice is thought to have been brought to China from India
during the same century by Buddhist monks via Tibet.[26] From
India the practice of variolation also spread to West Asia and from
there into Central Europe and the Balkans, and, probably with
Arab slave traders, to East and West Africa. But variolation
remained a very precarious method to fight the ravages of smallpox with, causing many accidental deaths by itself in many areas,
particularly in the Indus valley and Afghanistan. In South Asia,
2000 people per million probably contracted smallpox annually,
almost always in childhood, while the death rate was perhaps 200
per million in most places during a non-epidemic year.

If, then, the average annual growth rate of pre-industrial civilizations can be estimated to be 0.3%, a better estimate for the
Indian growth rate prior to 1600 AD is probably 0.1% annually or
10% per century.[27] The reason for this low growth rate lies in the
endemic presence of diseases like smallpox and numerous unspec-
ified 'fevers' which as late as 1877 were found, as a group, to kill
off approximately 2000 to 2400 people per million in major

[22] Fenner, *Smallpox*, pp. 214, 218.
[23] *Ibid.*, p. 219.
[24] Sachau, *Alberuni's India*, I, p. 309.
[25] *Ibid.*
[26] Fenner. *Smallpox*, p. 253 ff.
[27] Hoover, 'South Asian Age of Anxiety', pp. 6-7.

regions of South Asia.[28] It follows that, if we project our estimates
backward from a total South-Asian population of 155 million in
1571, we arrive at a figure of 112 million in 1272 ad, and in 1171
AD there would have been 102 million people in South Asia—
approximately the same number as in China at about the same
time.[29]

Very roughly, we can thus estimate that, in the thirteenth century, the total population of South Asia was at least twenty times
as large as that of either Iran or Turan. Modern scholarship has
proposed that in Iran the numbers of the sedentary and nomadic
population together run from five million to ten million in the
seventeenth century, while it has also been suggested that even
five million is an improbably high number.[30] In the previous centuries it was probably considerably less than that. The ratio of
urban to rural settlements appeared to contemporaries to have
been higher in Iran than in Mughal India, with, reportedly, 90
walled towns and approximately 40,000 villages in 1627.[31] With a
relatively low population density per area unit, a dry climate, and
overall unfavourable ecology, Iran's demography was deeply affected—much more so than that of India—by the repeated invasions
of Turkish and Mongol nomad tribes and armies from the thirteenth century onwards. Following upon the massacre and dispersal of populations—some two million and more—, the Mongols sponsored a great migration into the Middle East.[32] About
170,000 men, accompanied by 680,000 women and children and
perhaps the equivalent of 17 million sheep in accompanying
camps and herds, were detached for the conquest and occupation of the Middle East. One-fifth to one-fourth of these were stationed in Anatolia, and the rest in Iran (with some of these win-
tering in the lowlands of Iraq). The two processes combined
altered the ethnic composition of Iran, with the proportion of
Turkish and Mongol nomads in the population as a whole increasing dramatically, up to a point at which they reproduced in such

[28] *Ibid.*
[29] *Ibid.*, p. 8; for China, see: C. P. Fitzgerald, *China: A Short Cultural History*
(New York, 1961), p. 387; Ping-ti Ho, 'An Estimate of the Total Population in
Sung-Chin China', *Etudes Song I: Histoire et institutions*, ser. 1 (Paris, 1970), p. 52.
[30] Cf. Dale, *Indian Merchants*, p. 18.
[31] *Ibid.*
[32] Cf. Chapter I; Masson Smith, 'Turanian Nomadism', esp. pp. 67-68; idem,
'Mongol Manpower', esp. pp. 282-8.

numbers that they could no longer be accommodated without generating pervasive conflict.

Turan, like Iran, was also a region of continual competition between agriculturists and pastoral nomads. The most important item of external trade for this area was, as we have seen, the war-horse, huge numbers of which came to India. Within *Mā warā' an-nahr*, irrigated and settled agriculture occupied probably less than 10% of the total land area, but it produced most of the revenue for the various rulers in Uzbek Turan.[33] The total population of Uzbek Turan in the early seventeenth century, including Balkh, probably did not exceed five million people.[34] In the seventh century, when Hiuen Tsang passed through the area on his way to India, it was even more thinly populated, and not before the tenth century does competition for grazing land appear to have become intense. The population of Turan probably grew at a faster rate than that of Hind, at about 20% per century, due to a more favourable disease situation and a more secure diet than what was prevalent in India.[35] In the 400 years that passed since Hiuen Tsang's visit, the population of the area, while relatively small, could almost have doubled. Conflict and migration in the eleventh century would thus have become inevitable and provided the drive behind the Ghaznavid and Ghurid invasions of India which may have absorbed as much as one-tenth of the available manpower in the twelfth century. Migration from Turan to Iran and Hind reached a peak in the thirteenth century, after which it persisted however down to the eighteenth century. Around 1260, the total nomadic population of Central and Inner Asia, all of which was included in the Mongol empire at that time, would have been about 4,250,000.[36] Two-fifths of this, or 1.7 million people, would have been found in Outer and Inner Mongolia; one-fifth, or 850,000 people, in the Chaghatay realm of Transoxania, Semerichiye and parts of Jungaria and the Tarim Basin; one-fifth in the Juchids' domains in northern Central Asia and the North Caucasian and South Russian steppe; and the remaining fifth in the Middle East with Hülegü.[37]

---

[33] Dale, *Indian Merchants*, p. 20.
[34] *Ibid.*, p. 21.
[35] Cf. Hoover, 'South Asian Age of Anxiety.', p. 18.
[36] Masson Smith, 'Mongol Manpower', p. 287.
[37] *Ibid.*, pp. 287-8.

For the above figures to become really meaningful, one would have to differentiate the various regions of India in terms of the overall population volume. Sind under the Arabs was much less populated than the Ganges-Yamuna Doab, probably counting no more than several hundreds of thousand people along the lower Indus, and not more than perhaps 50,000 in Baluchistan. Much of Sind was still wilderness, a land of marshes and reeds, and much of the population made up of nomadic tribes, even in the delta around Thatta, which later could easily support an agricultural population of two million. Mansura and Multan were the only important centres of settled cultivation. It is, hence, not surprising that it was in Sind that the largest immigrations occurred. The Baluchis, having begun to move eastwards in the tenth, eleventh and twelfth centuries under the impact of the Buyids, Ghaznavids and Seljuqs, spread throughout Makran and Sistan and probably entered Sind in the turbulence of the thirteenth-century Mongol invasions.[38] It was also in the thirteenth century that the Afghans extended their domains from the Koh-i-Sulaymān to the east, into India, and, to a lesser extent to the north, towards the Khyber Pass and Peshawar and to the south-west, towards Qandahar, as well as into Mastung, northern Baluchistan.[39] Such large-scale tribal movements from frontier areas into al-Hind had a considerable impact in these areas. But in the more settled parts of the northern plains the numbers of immigrants, including the armies, was dwarfed by that of the masses of cultivating peasants and other indigenous groups that they encountered. Again, we do not know the numbers of Muslims which occupied some of the major urban centres in North India in the thirteenth century. Judging from the mosque architecture in Delhi of the time of Iltutmish, one can see a considerable increase in the Muslim population, but not much more. Barani, referring to Iltutmish's time—the time when 'Hindustan was newly conquered (naugīr)'—, says that 'the Hindus were so many that the Muslims among them are like salt (namak) among them ..'.[40]

---

[38] Al-Hind, I, pp. 142-3; R. N. Frye, 'Remarks on Baluchi History', *Central Asiatic Journal*, 6 (1961), pp. 46-47.

[39] I. H. Siddiqui, 'The Afghans and their emergence in India as ruling elite during the Delhi sultanate period', *Central Asiatic Journal*, 26, no. 3-4 (1982), p. 246.

[40] Quoted in K. A. Nizami, *Studies in Medieval Indian History and Culture* (Allahabad, 1966), p. 23.

In Kaiqubād's time, 'there were nearly 5000 nobles in attendance upon him, with an army of 100,000'—and the latter figure included locally recruited men.[41] If we do not know how many Muslims entered India in the thirteenth century, the number probably did not exceed several hundred-thousands and was, in any case, a small fraction of the 100 million or so native inhabitants of Hind. Unlike Iran, it was however not the number of immigrants that was all-important in India, but the new mode of organization that they brought along. This new mode of organization was characteristic of the world of Irano-Turanian frontier nomadism, of mobile elites, of Islam, of raiding and long-distance trade, and it promoted urbanism and the extension of money flows. It was the organizational mode of the frontier that now finally merged with the sedentary world of the Indian peasant.

a. AGRARIAN SOCIETY, NOBILITY AND 'COMPANIONS OF HONOUR'

Thus the first major change that occurred in the new cosmopolitan context of Muslim rule in the thirteenth century amounted to a paradigm shift in the concept of political dominion itself. India, like Europe, by the early medieval period, was developing an agrarian aristocracy of an unmistakably noble character, i.e. an hereditary ruling elite with a legal status of its own which confirmed and made effective the superiority to which it laid claim and which cultivated ideals of chivalry. Prior to the eleventh-thirteenth centuries, without being much affected by nomadic upheavals or external invaders, aristocratic power in much of the subcontinent had become associated with land and with lordship over land. In this circumscribed world, external linkages to the frontier of nomadism and long-distance trade were already quite important—indeed often decisive as a source of mobile wealth—, but it was the control of fortresses, castles and land that bound families to their localities over the generations, and local connection permeated the political world in which this aristocracy exercised its authority. With the family at the heart of aristocratic power, honour and heredity were to become the major preoccupations which determined aristocratic assumptions about

---

[41] H. M. Elliot and J. Dowson, *The History of India as told by its own Historians*, 8 vols (London, 1867-77), III, p. 525.

rank and status. India's early medieval nobility, like that of Europe in the same period, did not have long pedigrees. It arose in the newly expanding agrarian economies of the time, representing a tiny segment of a vast peasant society in the making. And it excluded servile status.

As we have seen, bardic tradition contrived a purification rite, conducted in the eighth century at Mount Abu, in Rajasthan, through which the extinct warrior caste of ancient India was regenerated in the 'fire-born' Rajput clans, whose duty it was to fight off the Muslims.[42] Unlike the ancient *kshatriyas* which we know largely from the Epics, the rise of the medieval North-Indian aristocracy can be followed, in some detail, in the historical record. More specifically, we know that the 'royal' Pratīhāras who established themselves at Kanauj in the early ninth century originated mostly from groups of pastoral Gurjaras—after the invasions of the White Huns (of whom they assimilated minor elements as well)—and it is very probable that the other 'fire-born' Rajput clans like the Caulukyas, Paramāras, Cāhamanas (or Cauhāns), as well as perhaps the Tomaras, and others who in the eighth and ninth centuries were subordinate to the Gurjara-Pratīhāras, were of a similar pastoral origin, that is, that they originally belonged to the mobile, nomadic groups based in the semi-arid interstices and zones.[43] None of the major dynasties of North India can be traced back to a period prior to the seventh century. The author of the Hammīra Mahākavya, relating the exploits of Hammīra Cauhān of Ranasthambhapura against the Ghurids, is in fact unable to come up with any satisfactory genealogy of the Cauhān house at all and seems to have known virtually nothing about the early kings of the dynasty, which does not emerge from obscurity before 685 AD.[44] The pre-eminent Hindu Shāhi dynasty, to which many *kshatriya* lineages continued to trace their descent long after it had been pushed out of the Panjab and into Kashmir in the eleventh century, had been unknown—its origin is disputed and it may have been brahmans—until it succeeded the Zunbils and Kabulshahs in the third quarter of the ninth century.[45] In the valley of Kashmir itself, the Karkota dynasty emerged

---

[42] *Al-Hind*, *I*, p. 281.
[43] *Ibid.*, pp. 279, 281.
[44] Janardan Kirtane, 'Hammīra Mahākavya', pp. 56-57.
[45] *Al-Hind*, *I*, pp. 125-6, 254.

in the early seventh century, superseding the White Huns and Later Guptas; until that time the *Rājataranginī* gives a bare dynastic list and mere summaries of legendary traditions concerning individual kings.[46] Further to the west, the Rāī and Brahman kings of Sind more or less burst upon the scene, apparently coming out of the same obscure conditions.[47] And in Bengal, Gopāla, the founder of the Pala dynasty, was 'elected' in 750 AD without even a mythical pedigree, and he probably represented a shudra or brahman caste turning itself into kshatriyas, and hence was, as an Arabic text explains, 'not of noble origin'.[48]

Projecting themselves as the reincarnates of the ancient Indian kshatriyas, but also adopting elements of the Persian-Sasanid tradition, and constructing genealogies which linked them to Persian emperors or ancestors in Zabulistan or even Central Asia, these new Rajput aristocracies quickly obliterated their obscure, often pastoral, origins in the expanding agricultural society of early medieval North India.[49] While their genealogical links were forged, especially in the eighth to twelfth centuries, the early Rajput tradition was in practice a rather open and flexible one, able to accommodate newcomers from the frontier areas beyond the pale of settled Hindu society. As a rising agricultural gentry and ruling elite, the medieval Rajputs differed widely from the urbanized and highly educated classical *varna* of kshatriyas, at least as they are depicted in the literature. The largely illiterate warrior groups of Rajputs, adopting landholding along with their newly found kshatriya identity and dharmic code, associated themselves with the brahmans and with a brahmanical religion that was hostile to Buddhism.

By the eleventh and twelfth centuries, ideals of chivalry and heroism were widespread in Indian society. And this was the case not merely among the Rajputs, although, unquestionably, Pṛthivīrāja Cauhān, the last 'emperor of India' (Bharateshvara) who defeated the Muslims at Tarā'īn in 1192, remains the very embodiment of these noble ideals, as is celebrated in widely known historical poems which were being composed already during his lifetime.[50] In the literature of the *mahākāvyas* the image is

[46] *Ibid.*, pp. 233, 239-40.
[47] *Ibid.*, p. 240.
[48] *Ibid.*, p. 265.
[49] *Al-Hind, I*, pp. 279, 281-3, 292-3.
[50] Cf. Sarda, 'Prithviraj Vijaya', pp. 259-81.

found of the dead hero welcomed by celestial maidens in heaven. But he had to have died in battle, and natural death at home was despised.[51] Heroic acts on the battlefield were compared with an act of sacrifice, conform to the idea which is found in Manu: 'for one who is killed, without trespassing the code of kshatriyas, with uplifted weapons in battle, a sacrifice is completed at the same time, and the impurity of death is cleansed' (V. 98). Hero-stones (*vīragals, naukals, pāliyas, govardhan-stambhas, kīrtistambhas*) were erected all over India to commemorate those who had sacrificed their life in battle or while defending brahmans and cattle.[52] Another important body of literature was produced in the Kannada language, between the time of Nrpatunga (ninth century) and that of Basava (late twelfth century), which was characterized by *vīra-rasa*, the emotion of heroism.[53] *Vīra* was here identified with dharma, the good of all brave men. And at the root of chivalry, compassion and charity, are found courage and conviction. Chivalry itself was classified in three forms: that of the warrior, that of the compassionate, and that of the munificent. Heroism was an object of universal acclaim in this literature, while Sahagamana, the self-immolation of widows, is also vividly described in the literature of this period. Heroes were more concerned with their honour than with material gain. Chivalry was assiduously fostered by kings, chieftains, parents, and consorts alike. If a warrior failed to put his valour to the test on the appropriate occasions, he was no better than an eunuch. Ranna recognized four such occasions: a cattle raid, an assault on the modesty of women ('the loosening of the girdle of women', which inscriptions compare to the attempted disrobing of Draupadī), an order of the master, and the desecration of one's village.

It was part of the same chivalrous code that kings and sometimes entire garrisons would immolate themselves in fire or deliberately seek death in battle when faced with a particularly humil-

---

[51] Cf. P. Filliozat, 'The After-death destiny of the Hero According to Mahābhārata', in : S. Settar and G. D. Sontheimer (eds), *Memorial Stones: A Study of their Origin, Significance and Variety* (Dharwad, 1982), pp. 3-8.

[52] Settar and Sontheimer, *Memorial Stones, passim*; A. Dandekar, 'Landscapes in Conflict: Flocks, Hero-stones, and Cult in early medieval Maharashtra', *Studies in History*, 7, 2, n. s. (1991), p. 320.

[53] S. Settar and M. M. Kalaburgi, 'The Hero Cult: A Study of Kannada Literature from the 9th to 13th Century', in: Settar and Sontheimer, *Memorial Stones*, pp. 17-36.

iating defeat. This too we find in India in the eleventh century, and it survived in the subcontinent until as late as the seventeenth century, while on the remote islands of Bali and Lombok a variant of this practice was still encountered by the Dutch in the nineteenth and twentieth centuries. It was, of course, a last resort, identical in essential respects to the *jauhar* of the later Rajputs, but in this early period it was known as *sak*. We read, for example, that prior to the fall of Ajmer, Hariraja 'determined to perform the *sak* and gathered together all the members of his family, ascended the funeral pile along with them, and so went to the other world'.[54] Firishta, describing events in the late tenth and early eleventh century, refers to the custom 'of the people of India, and especially the Rajputs (*ahl-i-hind khushūshan-i-ṭā'ifa'i rājpūt*), who, if driven to desperation, kill their wives and children, set fire to their houses, let loose their hair, and rush on to the enemy, heedless of death'.[55] Al-'Utbī, a contemporary observer, calls this 'the code of honour which prevails in al-Hind' (*ḥamīyat al-hind*).[56] How common this practice really was in the eleventh century we do not know, but examples of it, occurring among Rajput 'fighting men' but also among brahmans, are given by contemporary and later Indo-Muslim historians with a certain regularity.[57] The later practice of *jauhar*, which seems to be a continuation of the much older 'custom' in a more systematized and ritualized form, was maintained until as late as 1567, when Akbar besieged Chitor. After that final great *jauhar*, however, this type of collective suicidal action, together with its chivalric philosophy and sensibility, appears to have become an anachronism. In the context of the Indo-Muslim empire of the late sixteenth and seventeenth centuries, Rajput clan cohesion lost much of its strength, and with some of their women in the imperial harem, Rajput rule was routinized within the overarching Mughal system of imperial rule, while 'honour' became a monetized commodity, a question of negotiable title-deeds and revenue rights, no longer demanding great sacrifice.

Still in the eleventh century, another important element of Indian chivalry had become the rule (which Al-'Utbī describes as

---

[54] Janardan Kirtane, 'Hammīra Mahākavya', p. 61.
[55] *TF*, p. 19.
[56] *TYA*, p. 25; *TYP*, p. 37 has *ḥamīyat-i-hind*.
[57] Cf. *TYA*, pp. 258, 348-9, 404; *TYP*, pp. 179, 244; *TF*, pp. 24, 30.

'having been established for a long time') that if any raja fell in the hands of the Muslims (*ahl-i-islām*) he should no longer hold his kingdom and no further allegiance would be due to him.[58] A related maxim appears to have been that such a raja would abdicate all power, resign the throne to his son, shave his head, and throw himself into a fire, with his queens. Among Indian kings mutually, it was common to make defeated opponents, rulers and soldiers alike, adopt various characteristic marks of humiliation, such as having them carry their arms at their back, or having them shave their head, or half their head, but it was not current practice to put them to death. It is mentioned, by Firishta again, that confinement for life of a captive raja in a dark pit under the throne of the victor was 'customary' but deemed too cruel to be practiced routinely.[59]

Ritualized self-destruction in the face of defeat, however frequent or infrequent it may have been in the eleventh to thirteenth centuries, was certainly not restricted to the Rajput-dominated parts of North India. Well-known are also the 'suicide squads', called *Caver*, which originated in Kerala in the Cera period (ninth to twelfth century) and became quite popular afterwards.[60] When in Kerala a king died in battle, these guard corps, which constituted his *akampadi*, set out to avenge him by spreading death and destruction in the enemy camp and courting death as they went along. Duarte Barbosa, the Portuguese traveller who visited Kerala in the sixteenth century, gives an elaborate account of the life, initiation rites, and vows of these royal guards, who lived and died for the king and were selected from the aristocratic Nayar families of dominant landholders, and the system by which they undertook to wreak vengeance on the enemy or to kill themselves.[61] Closely related to it was the widespread phenomenon of the 'companions of honour', groups of men, officers, elite guards, or special servants and sometimes a few selected slaves, which were asso-

---

[58] *TYP*, p.156; *TYA*, pp. 178-9; *KT*, VII, p. 214; *TF*, p. 24 says that a raja had 'to be broken twice by the Muslims' (*kah do naubat az muslimānān shikast*) before he became disqualified to reign.

[59] *TF*, p. 34; and cf. *TYA*, pp. 26-30.

[60] E. B. N. Kunhan Pillai, 'The Suicide Squads of Ancient Kerala', *Proceedings of the Indian History Congress* (Bombay, 1947); M. G. S. Narayana, 'The Institution of "Companions of Honour" with Special Reference to South India', *Proceedings of the Indian History Congress* (Muzaffarpur, 1972), pp. 74-83.

[61] Longworth-Dames, *Duarte Barbosa*, pp. 37-40.

ciated with the persons of Indian monarchs and which followed him in death, often by voluntary self-immolation. Although variants of this institution have been found in Tibet and among the Qipchaq Turks and Mongols, as well as elsewhere, e.g. in Japan and Ethiopia, it is probably best known from India.[62] Abu Zayd, the Arab traveller of the ninth century, speaks of a numerous group of 'companions' (*ashāb*) who attach themselves to the king and 'burn themselves voluntarily on a pyre, to the last man, on the very day when the king ceases to live'.[63] Al-'Umarī, in the fourteenth century, writes that 'in India, every raja maintains a group of his loyal courtiers according to his resources; if the king dies, or is killed or some calamity befalls him, all his courtiers kill themselves, [and] if the king falls ill, they also become ill'.[64] Chau Ju-kua observed a similar custom in eastern Sumatra in the twelfth century, and it appears to have obtained in Java as well.[65]

Actual incidences of these practices are frequently described for all areas of *al-Hind*.[66] Marco Polo, in his account of Ma'bar, calls the companions of honour 'the King's Trusty Lieges', and according to him they had great authority in the kingdom; but when the king died 'these Lieges cast themselves into the fire round about his body, and suffer themselves to be burnt along with him'.[67] A number of inscriptions of the Ganga of Talkad mention officers who committed suicide at the death of kings like Niti-marga and Rajamalla Satyavakya.[68] In the Hoysala and Vijayana-gara kingdoms such officers were known as 'garudas' or 'lenkas', or 'velevālis', and their number ranged from one hundred to

[62] For examples among the Turks, Tibetans and Mongols, see N. De Wailly (ed.), *Jean de Joinville: Histoire de Saint Louis* (Paris, 1868), pp. 177-8; Irwin, *Middle East*, p. 16; Beckwith, 'Central Asian Guard Corps', p. 34; idem, *Tibetan Empire*, p. 15; for other examples from beyond India, see Yule, *Marco Polo*, II, pp. 347-8, note 5.

[63] M. Reinaud, *Relations des voyages faits par les Arabes et les Persans dans l'Inde et à la Chine, antérieurement au XIe siècle de l'ère Chrétienne*, Tome I (Paris, 1895), p. 115; cf. also K. A. Nilakanta Sastri (ed.), *Foreign Notices of South India from Megasthenes to Mahuan* (Madras, 1972), p. 128.

[64] Siddiqui, *Perso-Arabic Sources*, p. 142.

[65] Hirth and Rockhill, *Chau Ju-kua*, p. 61.

[66] Cf. *Al-Hind*, I, p. 245; Stein, *Rājatarangiṇī*, V, vs. 206-7; VII, vs. 1481, 1488, 1490; VIII, vs. 1547; E. B. Cowell and F. W. Thomas (transl.), *The Harshacarita of Bāna*(London, 1897), p. 161; S. H. Hodivala, *Studies in Indo-Muslim History*, I (Bombay, 1939), p. 161.

[67] Yule, *Marco Polo*, II, p. 339.

[68] *Epigraphia Carnatica* (Bangalore, 1886-1919), III, Tri. 91; V. 5, 27, etc.

thousands on occasions.[69] These too believed in the total abnegation to their sovereign, to the point of self-sacrifice, the most remarkable example of which, among the Hoysalas, is that of Kuvāra Lakshma, Vira-Ballala's general, who on his master's death committed suicide with his wife and his thousand companions.[70] In the Kannada country, as well as in Andhra, the velevāli clearly chose this mode of death as a point of honour. *Vele* means time or occasion, and *vāli* means duty or obligation: the idea of the *velevāli* was to do his duty and fulfill his obligation whenever he was called upon—and this is probably the reason that they are sometimes referred to as 'slaves', or are called the 'sons' of the king.[71] But they were not of slave origin, and there was a distinct code of honour involved in their role, and these men, regarding themselves as the sons of their master, or of the master's wife, and ready to sacrifice themselves, are referred to as 'the fierce heroes under the vow of the vele'. Ranna compares their emotions and enthusiasm to the waves of the surging sea at whose roaring approach the stars, i.e. enemy soldiers, fall, like withering stalks. Their rhythmic movement, their lightning turns, and their ability to arrange themselves into a beautiful line, are also vividly described.[72] No instances of the actual immolation of lenkas after the death of their master are actually on record in the Kakatiya state, but such did take place in neighbouring Karnataka.[73] What exactly was the social origin of the lenkas or velevālis is not clear. It is possible, but nowhere stated, that they at times included enslaved war-captives, as may have been the case in the creation of military service groups elsewhere.[74] But most likely they originated from dominant landholding groups in the vicinity of the court, and they were not only not of slave origin, but also technically not slaves and merely slave-like in their devotion to the master.[75] Muslim authors referred to the 'companions of hon-

---

[69] *Epigraphia Carnatica*, VI, Kl. 9, 10.

[70] *Epigraphia Carnatica*, V, Belur, 112; Deloche, *Hoysala Sculpture*, p. 38.

[71] Settar and Kalaburgi, 'The Hero Cult', p. 31; M. Somasekhara Sarma and M. Venkataramanayya, 'The Kakatiyas of Warangal', in: G. Yazdani (ed.), *The Early History of the Deccan*, 2 vols (New Delhi, 1982), II, p. 760.

[72] Settar and Kalaburgi, 'The Hero Cult', p. 33.

[73] Somasekhara Sarma and Venkataramanayya, 'Kakatiyas of Warangal', p. 670.

[74] Cf. V. B. Lieberman, *Burmese Administrative Cycles: Anarchy and Conquest, c. 1580-1760* (Princeton, 1984), p. 48.

[75] Other examples can be quoted from frontier areas of al-Hind where the

our' or 'heroic companions' as *balā' al-jār*, and regarded them as a typically Indian institution and as one of the 'marvels of *al-Hind*' (*'ajā'ib al-hind*), while emphasizing their essentially noble character, which was consecrated through an act of ritual commendation. 'Only men of distinguished family who are themselves comely and valiant and of good understanding are admitted among the *balā' al-jār* .... The king makes them eat rice with him, and gives them betel from his own hand. Each hacks off his little finger, and sets it before the king. And, from that moment on, they follow him about, wherever he goes .... If he dies, they commit suicide; if he burns, they cast themselves into the flames; if he falls ill, they mishandle themselves in order to share his sufferings. When a battle is fought, in the attack they cluster around him and never leave his side'.[76] An early thirteenth-century Byzantine author, Barhebraeus (Ar. Ibn al-'Ibr), describes how an agreement between Mahmud of Ghazna and the Raja of Gwalior was sealed by the demand of the Muslims that 'the king must put on our clothes, tie a sword and belt around his waist, and, to ratify the oath, cut off the tip of his finger, as is Indian custom'.[77] The historian Ibn al-Jawzī (d. 1200 AD), describing the same events, adds that Mahmud carried around with him numerous such fingertips obtained in this way.[78]

The 'companions of honour' of *al-Hind*, then, have to be sharply distinguished from the slave or mamlūk aristocracies typical of so much of the pre-modern Islamic world and found (on a very restricted scale and usually at the centre) in imperial systems elsewhere.[79] Unthinkable within European feudalism, and mostly non-existent in India before they were introduced by the Muslim Turks, the latter were military-political elites which were composed of 'dishonoured' people recruited from the monetized

---

attendants of kings would not be immolated but entombed with the deceased; cf. S. K. Bhuyan (ed.), *Deodhai Asam Buranji* (Gauhati, 1990), p. xvi; Glanius, *Unfortunate Voyage*; Reid, *Southeast Asia*, pp. 139, 165. Such burial practices were not unknown among the Mongols and other steppe nomads, as also the Tibetans.

[76] L. Marcel Devic (transl.), *The Book of the Marvels of India* (New York, 1929), pp. 99-101; Nilakanta Sastri, *Foreign Notices*, pp. 128-9.

[77] E. A. Wallis Budge (transl.), *The Chronography of Gregory Abu'l Faraj Barhebraeus*, Vol.I (London, 1932), pp. 190-1.

[78] Ibn al-Jawzī, *Al-Muntazam fī tārīkh al-mulūk wa-l-'umam*, vols. 5-10 (Hyderabad, 1938-9), VII, 12.

[79] Beckwith, 'Central Asian Guard Corps', however, seems to confuse comitatus-like companionship and slavery.

frontier, through war, raiding or trade over long distances. The companions of honour represented communities of which they were themselves members, and, while occurring elsewhere (even, in a limited way, among nomads), they were paradigmatic of the agrarian-aristocratic order of India, projecting an ideal of nobility and of chivalry, and flourishing in the context of expanding agricultural societies with vast populations. The mamluk slaves were cut loose from their communities and clans, exchanged on the basis of a cash value, and recruited from outside the community—indeed, more often than not from far away. If slaves originated in the context of raiding activity and long-distance trade, historical evidence of elite slaves, wherever it is found, shows that these were natally alienated and dishonoured people who were personal assets of the imperial masters they served and who had no legal personality of their own. Rather than an aberrant type of slaves, they were the 'ultimate slaves' since it was on account of their lack of honour and their 'social death' that they could be closely associated with the person of the emperor in positions of personal subservience that the aristocracy of nobles, with its own notions of what was virtuous and honourable, and disdaining personal subservience, would be unable to adopt.[80]

The most commonly quoted examples of elite slaves from outside the Islamic world include the Familia Caesaris of imperial Rome, the palace eunuchs of Byzantium and imperial China, the larger number of bondservants which served as infantry men and officers in the frontier armies of the late Ming, and the privately owned Muscovite military slaves.[81] It was only in the Islamic world that slave armies and slave aristocracies became a widespread feature of the state. For about a millennium, from the ninth until the nineteenth century, in areas which stretched from Central Africa to Central Asia, and from Spain to Bengal, and even beyond, Muslim rulers used slaves as surrogate aristocracies and administrative cadres, and as soldiers and officers.[82] Egypt, being

---

[80] Cf. O. Patterson, *Slavery and Social Death: A Comparative Study* (Cambridge, Mass., 1982), esp. pp. 299-333.

[81] Cf. Patterson, *ibid.*; M. M. Anderson, *Hidden Power: The Palace Eunuchs of Imperial China* (Loughton, Essex, 1991); J. P. McDermott, 'Bondservants in the T'ai-hu Basin During the Late Ming: A Case of Mistaken Identities', *Journal of Asian Studies*, XL, 4 (August, 1981), pp. 675-701; R. Hellie, *Slavery in Russia, 1450-1725* (Chicago and London, 1982), pp. 460-74.

[82] For a survey of their occurrence, see D. Pipes, *Slave Soldiers and Islam: The*

an unusually well-documented case, has often provided the point of comparison for other work on this ubiquitous institution.[83] The case of India is rather unique, however, and offers no close parallel to Egypt (where mamluk power was largely concerned with the control of Cairo). In India, mamluk slavery occurred in the thirteenth century, on the interface of frontier and settled society. And here, this entire mode of political domination, with its origins on the monetized frontier of fluid resources, was superimposed on the much more structured, more circumscribed, and relatively immobile political and social order of the Indian peasant world. In India, therefore, the Islamic conquest state—characterized by raiding, migration, dethesaurisation of precious metals, long-distance trade, and the garrisoning of towns—was soon superseded by a new situation in which the absorption of local agrarian elites, and the expansion of agrarian settlement, became as important as the recruitment of ethnic outsiders from the frontier.

Mamluk slavery in North India was, above all, short-lived. A transition occurred from a conquest state dominated by Turkish mamlūks to one in which Indians played a large role, especially in the context of agrarian expansion. This transition can be analysed in stages. When raiding predominated, in the eleventh and twelfth and still in the thirteenth century, considerable numbers of Indians, sometimes in the tens of thousands, were removed from their localities simply by force. These included especially rural children and women, which had little value in India itself, as they were unfamiliar with the conveniences of city life and were considered 'dirty'. Many were carried off by the Muslims, as also by Mongol parties, and were then put in 'the chains of bondage', often to be sold as slaves and find employment as concubines or labourers across the Hindu-Kush, with not a few of them dying in these mountains because of the cold and snow.[84] An entire servile

---

Genesis of a Military System (New Haven and London, 1981), pp. 45-53.

[83] See esp. Ayalon's articles in *Mamlūk Military Society*.

[84] For the eleventh and twelfth centuries see Chapter IV. For the late twelfth and thirteenth century, see *TF*, pp. 62, 71-73; *TFM*, p. 21; Defrémery and Sanguinetti, *Ibn Batoutah*, III, pp. 84, 388; *FS*, vs. 2404, 2812-2835; *TFS*, p. 57; *TN*, pp. 195, 212, 214, 216, 289, 292, 295, 299, 315, 323; J. Aubin, 'L'Ethnogenèse des Qaraunas', *Turcica*, I (1969), p. 68; I. H. Siddiqui, 'The Qarlūgh Kingdom in North-Western India during the Thirteenth Century', *Islamic Quarterly*, LIV, 1 (1980), pp. 79-80.

labour force was created in the Iranian marches, and the majority of the Hindus living in Iran in the royal villages (*inju*) at the beginning of the fourteenth century were descendants of the victims of raids carried out in India, especially in Kashmir, by Sali Noyin prior to the 'creation of Hülegü's state. Already in Ghaznavid times we find Indian mamluks in the army and palace guards, and again from Aybak's time onwards numerous Hindus were being recruited in the armies (the *hasham-i-hindustān*), men like the Todar, Chitoy, Khāshgah,` Kokhar, and Bīrāh, 'war-mongers and men-hunters'.[85] Balban, proceeding into Awadh, ordered a general levy of 'two lakhs of men of all classes', and in a big parade in 1286 AD there were 200,000 footmen and 50,000 horse, with many recruited locally.[86] Under Kaiqubad, 'all the swordsmen of the country of Hind, [and] all the spearmen of the province of Sind' were counted among the army of 100,000 men.[87] But in the thirteenth century, especially under Balban, Hindus (still disparagingly decsribed as 'of crow countenance', *zāghchihra*) still rarely achieved positions of real power.[88] Not before the fourteenth century do we find that the 'native inhabitants' or *mutawaṭṭinān* of Hindustan and the Deccan begin to loom large in the Indo-Islamic chronicles, and these can be identified, if not as Rajputs or predecessors of the Rajputs, as Jats, Marathas, and other gentry groups ('tribes') who henceforward were also designated by the generic term *zamīndārs*, lit. 'landholders'. Non-Muslims, thus, already at the turn of the thirteenth century, became participants in the Indo-Islamic empire—and they were recognized as such. By the fourteenth century claims to honourable *kshatriya* status were again assertively made by the leading categories of Rajputs, linking them to a revived ancient heritage that was uniquely Indian in form if not in substance. In the making of the Indo-Islamic world it was, in short, the fourteenth and fifteenth centuries which stood out as the crucial period in which a synthesis of frontier and settled society was worked out, superseding the Islamic conquest state of the Turkish elite slaves. Elite slavery in India was and always remained a frontier phenomenon. While it flourished in the thirteenth century, it subsequently

---

[85] *TFM*, p. 33; *FS*, vs. 2612-69.
[86] *TFS*, p. 86; *TN*, p. 317.
[87] Elliot and Dowson, *History of India*, III, p. 525.
[88] *TN*, pp. 248, 300, 304; *TF*, p. 75; *TM*, f. 68b.

became of marginal importance in North India. In the fifteenth
century it was largely confined to Bengal. By the sixteenth and
seventeenth centuries, it was confined to the Deccan, where
African mamlūks could still rise to the summits of power. In the
North-Indian plains, and even in Bengal, it was by then long gone
or of minor importance.

b. NOMADIC SOCIETY, MIGRATION AND THE FORMATION OF THE INDO-ISLAMIC STATE

It was paradigmatic of the nomadic societies of Central Asia as
well as the post-nomadic polities which arose in the Islamic world
that their leadership was highly concentrated and instable because
they revolved largely around individuals and there was virtually
nothing in the way of self-perpetuating political institutions or corporate structures through which leadership was normally dispersed in settled society. In short, frontier society was the domain
of the individual, of the individual leader and his mobile
resources, of warbands of men attached to him personally, and of
goods with cash value, and it was sustained by a thoroughly commercial and monetized morality of exchange. To the extent that
peasant society was structured but lacked movement, nomadic
society, with little permanent structure, was driven by movement.
The bands of warrior-herdsmen, and even more so the slave
armies, lacking to a large degree the primordial ties of the peasantry, were held together by exclusive allegiance to a chosen
leader. The leadership qualities and personal characteristics,
rather than the legitimacy, of such a leader, were all-important,
and the major qualification for rule was the ability to seize power. As Joseph Fletcher has emphasized, steppe empires came into
existence through the efforts of individual aspirants for the office
of supratribal ruler, and hence, in its classical form, the steppe
empire was so closely tied to the person of the ruler that when
the latter died it stood in real danger of immediate collapse.[89]
This same 'individualism' accounts to a large degree for the perceived shiftless nature of the politics—often seen as 'disorder'—
and the absence of transgenerational loyalties and institutions in

---

[89] Fletcher, 'Mongols', esp. pp. 21, 47.

the Turkish-Muslim state. It explains why it is so difficult to find 'basic units' or 'building blocks' in these polities in general.[90] What mattered here was the intensity of personal, face-to-face bonds which allowed rulers to manipulate, cajole and stay on top of fractious elites. And, in these conditions, neither individuals nor the community were in any way attached to an abstract notion of 'the state' as separate from the persons who constituted its administration. Loyalty went to the master who gave support to someone. And the result was an inherent need for negotiation as a method to assert and maintain personal authority. This discretionary and personal nature of authority, apart from introducing a large measure of instability at the death of a ruler, was also manifest in revenue collection, the frequency with which imposts were added or abstracted, the employment of power to benefit one's relatives, servants and clients, and the way edicts and treaties had to be specifically renewed by the successor of a ruler if they were to continue in force. Much of the attention of the ruler was, at all times, absorbed by the possibility of contested succession or of rebellion and usurpation. In any contest, the richest party would normally win.

It was, then, the elite household and not the state or any other autonomous corporate body that was the focus of political and social power.[91] The history of the formation of the Delhi Sultanate, rather than the study of formal institutions, becomes really the study of the practices of the patriarchal household, of 'economics' in the Aristotelian sense of the word.[92] And these have to be studied in the context of *fitna*, seditious struggle, leading to a continuous reshuffling of power and resources, as rulers did not have the independent power to coordinate the elites on whom they were dependent. In this society—which was much more monetized than Europe—descent and status were uncoupled. Rule was by competing warrior households leading ethnic outsiders which were recruited with cash.

---

[90] Cf. R. P. Mottahedeh, *Loyalty and Leadership in an Early Islamic Society* (Princeton, 1980), esp. pp. 3-5, 27-28; M. Chamberlain, *Knowledge and social practice in medieval Damascus* (Cambridge, 1994); A. Wink, *Land and Sovereignty in India: Agrarian Society and Politics under the Eighteenth-century Maratha Svarājya* (Cambridge, 1986).

[91] Cf. Chamberlain, *Knowledge*, pp. 2, 4, 8-9, 25, 29-30, 44-46.

[92] For this concept, see O. Brunner, *Neue Wege der Sozialgeschichte* (Göttingen, 1956), pp. 7-32.

The Turkish mamlūk state

Institutional indeterminacy or what we may call random patri-
monialism prevailed on all levels of the polity. To begin with, the
thirteenth-century Delhi Sultanate, like many other Turkish states,
had no specific law of succession and, in effect, alternated
between dynastic rule and military oligarchy.[93] At first, Aybak was
succeeded by his adopted son Ārām Shāh.[94] This succession was
however contested and Ārām Shāh was 'martyred', after which
Iltutmish, Aybak's slave, ascended the throne 'in the manner of
kings' (*bar rasm-i-shāhān*), again not without opposition. Iltutmish
initially still sought recognition for his rule in Delhi from Yaldiz
in Ghazna.[95] The latter was considered the adopted son of Mu'izz
ad-Din (Muhammad Ghuri) and thus heir to the Mu'izzi empire
east of the Hindu-Kush; he himself considered the other Turkish
slaves as inferior and assumed the titles *salṭan al-mu'aẓẓam* and
salṭan ash-sharq, striking coins from Karman and Ghazna like his
master. His superior status is reflected in the chatr and dūrbāsh
which Yaldiz sent to Iltutmish from Lahore and Ghazna. But after
Yaldiz had been expelled from Ghazna and, having fled to Lahore,
was taken prisoner, he allegedly addressed Iltutmish as follows:
'You know that I am fitter than you to rule the kingdom of Hindustan .... I am as good as a descendant of the kings of Iran
(*farzand-i-shāh-i-'ajam*). As for you, you are but a slave of the slaves
of the king (*tū khūd banda' bandagān-i-shāhī*) ..'. [96] To which Iltutmish replied: 'You know that today the dominion of the world is
enjoyed by the one who possesses the greatest strength. The principle of hereditary succession is not extinct, [but] long ago destiny abolished this custom. If this were not so, Ghazna would still
be governed by the house of the Turks (*āl-i-turkān*). The
Khwarazmian and Ghurid kings would not have held dominion
over it if they had not seized it by force (*dar taghlīb*) Conquest

---

[93] For Egypt, see A. Levanoni, 'The Mamluk Conception of the Sultanate',
International Journal of Middle East Studies, 26 (1994), pp. 373-392. On the absence
of laws of succession in Turkish and Mongol polities in general, see Fletcher,
'Mongols', pp. 22-23; Woods, *Aqquyunlu*, pp. 12-13; Waldman, *Toward a Theory of
Historical Narrative*, pp. 31-33.
[94] *TN*, pp. 141-2.
[95] Cf. *TNR*, pp. 606, n. 3, 607 n. 5.
[96] *FS*, vs. 2084-2138.

by force has since become the order of the day. ... You cannot take the world by inheritance ..'. [97]

Ironically, it was with Iltutmish that hereditary succession to the throne was re-introduced in practice. Iltutmish was succeeded first by his daughter Raziyya, then by a son, Rukun ad-Din, and both invoked their father's name on their coins, giving him the higher title *al-a'zam* while calling themselves *al-mu'azzam*.[98] Bahram Shah, another son of Iltutmish, was raised to the throne in 1240, and then Mas'ud Shah, a grandson of Iltutmish. Juzjani, in effect, writes that 'the sovereignty of Hind is the heritage of the Shamsi family' (*saltānī' hind ast ars-i-dauda' shamsi*).[99] A curious custom crept in. All sons and grandsons of Iltutmish were kept in confinement in the Qasr-i-Safed (also called Kūshk-i-Saped) or 'White Castle'—a structure made of stone, the site of which is unknown—with the possible exception of the heir apparent.[100] This custom may have been introduced by the Habshis at the court of Delhi (where they achieved some prominence from Mas'ud Shah's reign onwards, maintaining connections in the Middle East, Africa, and various parts of Hind),[101] in an attempt to eliminate conflict among heirs. In Ethiopia it had been an established custom for centuries that the sons—again with the possible exception of the heir apparent—of the reigning king who were eight years old or more, and all male descendants in the male line of former rulers of the ruling dynasty (which claimed descent from Solomon) should be compelled to live on the mountain of Amba Geshen near Maqdala.[102] Persian texts of the early modern period describe the imprisonment of the princes in Asirgarh as an established custom of the Faruqi dynasty of Khandesh, another kingdom where Ethiopian Habshis exercised great power. But whether it was an Ethiopian influence or not, the existence of this practice demonstrates beyond doubt that heredity had become de facto important as a principle of succession among the descendants of the first of the slave kings of Delhi. In the thirteenth century,

---

[97] *Ibid.*, vs. 2101-6.
[98] *TN*, pp. 180-4; Nelson Wright, *Coinage and Metrology*, p. 75.
[99] *TN*, p. 191.
[100] Cf. *TN*, p. 269.
[101] Cf. *TMS*, p. 34; *Epigraphia Indica, Arabic and Persian-Supplement, 1913-14*, pp. 32-33; *TN*, pp. 186-8, 279; *TF*, pp. 68-69; *FS*, vs. 2540 ff.
[102] Cf. C. F. Beckingham, 'Amba Geshen and Asirgarh', *Journal of Semitic Studies*, 2, 3 (1957), pp. 182-8.

the accession of Balban shows that it was not the main or only principle at work. In India, however, unlike Egypt, the Turkish slave elite often passed on their wealth and status to their sons, who followed similar careers.[103] Balban again appointed his son and grandson to high positions.[104] And Mu'izz ad-Din Kaiqubad was king by virtue of three descents: the first from Iltutmish, the grandfather of his grandmother; the second from Nasir ad-Din Mahmud Shah, the father of his grandfather; and the third from Balban, his own grandfather.

Secondly, there was a certain amorphous quality about the Turkish slave elite as a ruling group. Juzjani, the author of the one major historical chronicle of the thirteenth century, the *Ṭabaqāt-i-Nāṣiri*, organized his narrative largely around the political careers of this slave elite. Of all the immigrants to India in the thirteenth century, this small group of the most powerful individuals is therefore by far the best known. Other chronicles, contemporary, near-contemporary or of later times, also devote their attention to them almost exclusively. Juzjani presents lengthy biographical accounts of about twenty-five Turkish slaves which were acquired during the reign of Iltutmish, but he does not reveal much of a social structure or any specific political organization among them.[105] They make their appearances as opportunistically motivated individuals who formed alliances with other Turkish slaves for reasons of personal ambition, and they appear to have closed ranks as an ethnic group only when non-Turkish amirs threatened to gain positions of power equal or superior to theirs. Our sources stress the aristocratic origin of some of the Turkish slaves (especially of those who became Sultans)—which seems to have been preferred—, but the main emphasis, in many of these biographies, is on their leadership qualities and 'manly' virtues, and on such individual characteristics as resolution, impetuosity, valour, energy, boldness, 'lion-heartedness', magnanimity, 'good looks', 'sincere piety', as also on intellectual capabilities, sagacity, and the like.[106]

---

[103] Cf. *TN*, pp. 233-6; *TFS*, pp. 56, 61-62.
[104] *TF*, pp. 75, 78, 81-82; *TFS*, pp. 66, 120, etc.
[105] *TN*, pp. 233-323. See also Ahmad, 'Early Turkish Nucleus', pp. 100-8.
[106] 'Spare no pains to discover men of genius, learning, and courage' says *TF*, p. 80. The *FS*, vs. 2742 has it that 'he who is born to rule has the signs of generosity imprinted on his forehead'. See also: *TFS*, p. 136; *TF*, pp. 60, 63-65, 74;

A WORLD ON THE MOVE

Although we do not know exactly how many Turkish slaves entered Hind in the thirteenth century, nothing indicates that their numbers were large—they were certainly much smaller than in Egypt—and to a large degree this would explain the relatively unsystematic acquisition, training, manumission, and so on, that the sources bear out as well. The Turkish slaves, before they became amirs or commanders of troops, served in various departments, starting in very humble positions and going through a cursus honorum which included 'every degree of employment'.[107] The string of humble positions included those of 'lord of the stables', 'keeper of the hunting leopards', 'personal cupbearer', 'keeper of the wardrobe', and others like these. Aybak, Qabacha, Iltutmish, and Balban all held such posts for many years. Balban, when at Iltutmish's court, was assigned to the stable to remove the dung, night and day, and groom the diseased horses.[108] Promotion would be faster if the slave in question was considered exceptionally able, but too fast a promotion would arouse the jealousy of the others.[109] The idea was that each slave should be in the personal service of the king before he became an amir, a commander of troops with a revenue assignment or iqtāʿ of varying importance. No slave ever became king without first having been an *amir*, and then a *khān* (at least among Iltutmish's successors), of yet superior rank. Symbols of royal authority such as the tāj, takht, dūrbāsh, sword of state, kaukaba, the large kettle drum, kūs, the dais or sofa, and the black, red, green and vermilion umbrellas, elephants, and robes of honour, were widely shared among the Turkish mamluks.[110] The black canopy, or *chatr-i-siyah*, was apparently borrowed as a symbol of royalty from the Abbasid caliphs, and it was among the few that were restricted to Sultans and Princes and hence in the same category as the issuing of coins

---

FS, vs. 2328-38, 2340; TN, pp. 138-9, 142, 166-9, 232-3, 236-7, 239, 242, 247, 250-1, 253-4, 256, 259, 268, 275-6, 279, 247, 250,252, 254, 259, 265, 281, 297-8.

[107] TN, pp. 139, 142, 169, 232-3, 236, 238, 242, 248, 250-1, 256, 258, 262, 273, 279, 293-4; FS, vs. 2342-60; TF, pp. 68, 81; TFS, p. 26.

[108] FS, vs. 2343-4.

[109] The TF warns: 'Raise not a man too hastily to a high station, lest he forget himself, and be an eyesore to men of superior merit' (p. 81).

[110] P. Hardy, 'The Growth of Authority Over a Conquered Political Elite: The early Delhi Sultanate as a Possible Case Study', in: J. F. Richards (ed.), *Kingship and Authority in South Asia* (Madison, 1981), p. 207; Thomas, *Chronicles*, pp. 25-26, 32-37; TN, pp. 133, 142, 147-8, 157-8, 161, 191-2, 198-9; TF, pp. 62-63, 65, 69-70, etc.

and the reading of the khutba. Manumission was not uncommonly treated as a routine matter. We know that the Turkish slaves of the late Mu'izz ad-Din all solicited and obtained letters of manumission (khuṭūṭ-i-'itq) from his successor Ghiyath ad-Din Mahmud before they became Sultans.[111] Aybak's accession, however, took place in 1206, when he was technically still a slave. His formal manumission was not obtained until 1208, and it is perhaps significant that in inscriptions no higher titles are used with his name than 'malik' and 'sipahsalar'. Yaldiz was made king of Ghazna after he was freed.[112] Iltutmish received 'the felicity of the free' (daulat-i-aḥrārish) from Mu'izz ad-Din.[113] But Juzjani, in his biographical sketches of the Turkish slaves of Delhi, almost never talks of manumission. We know only from Barani that 'Balban had been one of the Shamsi slaves and among the forty Turkish slaves freed'.[114] Formal manumission, as is often found elsewhere in the Islamic world (although in Mamluk Egypt there was a communal ceremony, during which official certificates were given out), appears to have been more or less automatic once a slave had been promoted to the rank of amir.[115]

Similarly, there were in India, again unlike Egypt,[116] no military schools in which slaves were trained in the military arts. Even the Ghaznavids did not have them. The account of Sabuktigin's early training, as given in the Pandnāma, is of a general one in handling weapons and in the equestrian arts, and not of a specific course. The training of the Ghaznavid military slaves must have come primarily from experience in the field. Of Aybak we read that 'he was brought from Turkestan, came to Nishapur, [where] the governor .... bought him. And in attendance on and along with his sons, he read kalām-i-allāh and learned horsemanship and bowshooting (sawari-o-tīr-i-andāzī)', so that in a short

---

[111] Cf. p. 140.

[112] FS, vs. 1963 ff.

[113] TN, p. 169; Defrémery and Sanguinetti, Ibn Batoutah, III, p. 164 says that Iltutmish (Lalmish) showed a letter of manumission to the fuqahā' after Aybak's death; and that the latter then pledged allegiance to him.

[114] TFS, p. 25.

[115] See also G. Hambly, 'Who were the chihilgāni, the forty slaves of Sultān Shams al-Dīn Iltutmish of Delhi?', Iran, 10 (1972), p. 60.

[116] For Egypt, see H. Rabie, 'The training of the Mamlūk Fāris', in : Parry and Yapp, War, Technology and Society; D. Ayalon, 'Notes on the Furūsiyya Exercises and Games in the Mamlūk Sultanate', in: Mamluk Military Society.

time he became commended and favourably spoken of 'for his manly bearing'.[117] Then, the account goes on, when he attained adolescence, certain merchants brought him to the court of Ghazna. Another slave of Mu'izz ad-Din was at first bought by the Amir-i-Shikar of Ghazna, 'whom he accompanied in all circumstances and situations and from whom he learnt martial accomplishments and the modes of warfare and thus became a perfect master in the art'.[118] We read about a slave of Balban that he 'received his training among military men (*lashkarān*)'.[119] Another slave was purchased by Iltutmish, who 'gave him to his eldest son, ... and in the hall of felicity, along with him, he was nurtured and brought up'.[120] The emperor Mu'izz ad-Din Kaiqubād 'from infancy up to the day he succeeded to the throne had been trained under the eye of his grandfather Balban, and so many rigorous guardians were appointed to look after him that he had no chance of enjoyment. ... They instructed him in writing, and science, and *adab*, and there were others who taught him to shoot ...'[121]

Thirdly, Turkish slaves in thirteenth-century Hind would never have the monopoly of political authority that they enjoyed in Mamluk Egypt. While in Egypt, in campaigns against the Mongols, free-born Arabs and the *wāfidiyya* or 'immigrant' bodies of Turkish, Kurdish and Mongol cavalry bodies could swell the armies to 100,000 men or more, the main pre-occupation was always the control of Cairo.[122] The number of royal mamluks, largely of Qipchaq-Turkish origin, stationed in Cairo during the early Sultanate (1250-1382), rose from over 4000 in Baybars' reign (1260-1277) to between 6000 and 12,000 at the end of Qalawun's reign (1279-1290). To these numbers must be added the mamluks in the service of the amirs, both in Egypt and Syria. In the thirteenth-century Delhi Sultanate, the number of Turkish slaves that can be identified is not only much smaller, but these were spearheading the first Islamic expansion in densely populated 'infidel' territory, an area of wide expanse, while Egypt, controlled from a single centre, had been ruled by Muslim dynasties for cen-

---

[117] *TN*, p. 138.
[118] *TN*, p. 234.
[119] *TFS*, p. 83.
[120] *TN*, p. 232.
[121] *TFS*, p. 128.
[122] Cf. Irwin, *Middle East*, pp. 9, 33, 50, 55, 69.

turies. Juzjani, as mentioned before, describes in detail a mere twenty-five Turkish slaves, and he mentions a few other bandagān up to the reign of Nasir ad-Din.[123] A number of these had their own slaves, but we do not hear of large numbers here either. Of the Slave Kings of Delhi, down to 1290, only Aybak, Iltutmish and Balban were actually of slave origin. The others who ruled between 1236 and 1266 were all descendants of Iltutmish.

Iltutmish, moreover, was not merely the founder of a 'slave dynasty' but actively promoted the immigration to Delhi of innumerable Muslims 'from various parts of the world', especially from Mongol-occupied Iran, 'men of all sorts and degrees'. Similarly, the Turkish amirs of the household were joined by numerous free-born Muslims—military people, bureaucrats, merchants—from Ghur, Khurasan and other parts of Iran, and from as far away as 'Rūm', while Bihar and Bengal, with their new capital at Lakhnauti, became the focus of Khalaj migration from all over Hindustan and the Northwest.[124] As J. Ross Sweeney has noted, the displacement of vast numbers of people was one of the most visible by-products of the expansion of the Mongol empire in the thirteenth century.[125] There is as yet no systematic study of these medieval *fugitivi*. But the accounts of the Mongol conquest of Khwarazm in 1220 offer abundant illustrative detail on refugee rulers and soldiers, and we know that the invasion of Kievan Russia, beginning in 1223, created a host of refugees, as did the Mongol conquest of China in the second half of the thirteenth century, and the conquest of Europe and Hungary.[126] Great numbers of the elites of Iran and Khurasan—especially those areas longest exposed to invasion—from the early thirteenth century onwards migrated to India, while a smaller number of these moved to the west.[127] Immigrants to Cairo from Iran appear to have originated especially from clusters of sites along the main routes of access

---

[123] *TN*, pp. 137-164, ff., p. 229 ff.

[124] See also P. Jackson, 'The Mamlūk Institution in Early Muslim India', *Journal of the Royal Asiatic Society* (1990).

[125] J. Ross Sweeney, '"Spurred on by the Fear of Death": Refugees and Displaced Populations during the Mongol Invasion of Hungary', in: M. Gervers and W. Schlepp (eds), *Nomadic Diplomacy, Destruction and Religion from the Pacific to the Adriatic* (Toronto, 1994), p. 35.

[126] *Ibid.*, pp. 34-37.

[127] For the westward migration, see C. F. Petry, *The Civilian Elite of Cairo in the Later Middle Ages* (Princeton, 1981), esp. pp. 61-64.

to the Iranian plateau from the northeast and from the plateau into Syria and Anatolia, routes which were followed by the Mongols in the thirteenth century and again by Timur in the fourteenth century.[128] In their eastward migration towards al-Hind, many of the fugitivi also appear to have followed the trade routes, while making use of pre-existing connections. Among the earliest refugees arriving in India were the Lachin Hazaras, 'of Turkish origin', whose home had been near Balkh or Qarshi and Pyrmurgh, and who fled to India during Chingiz Khan's time.[129] A number of the Lachin Hazaras, among which the ancestors of Amir Khusrau, had accompanied the Khwarazm Shah in his flight before the Mongol armies.[130] But it seems that these Hazaras of Lachin had already settled in Northwest India before the Khwarazm Shah crossed the Indus. This is, in any case, where many of them settled in the Mongol period, with some of them moving on to Delhi.[131]

The court of Iltutmish, in particular, became a haven for refugees from 'the toils of the calamities sustained by the provinces and cities of 'Ajam and the misfortunes caused by the irruption of the infidel Mongols'.[132] These refugees included renowned maliks and amirs, wazirs, traders, artists, craftsmen, and learned elites, poets and Islamic devotees, and many others.[133] 'Delhi became the ka'ba of the seven climates (haft iqlīm) and the whole region became the home of Islam'.[134] Thus, while in the early years of the Sultanate, Baghdad, Bukhara and Samarqand had been looked upon as the centres of Muslim learning and culture, after the Mongol irruption it was Delhi which became preeminent as the Muslim city of the east.[135] Iltutmish and his wazir Nizam al-Mulk Junaidi patronized the translation of Arabic into Persian. The first important Arabic work to be translated at Del-

---

[128] Ibid., p. 64.

[129] M. Wahid Mirza, The Life and Works of Amir Khusrau (Lahore, 1962), pp. 6, 8.

[130] Ibid., p. 12.

[131] Ibid.

[132] TN, p. 166.

[133] See esp. TFS, pp. 26-27; FS, vs. 2180-7; Siddiqui, Perso-Arabic Sources, pp. 28, 33.

[134] Ibid.

[135] Cf. Nizami, Studies, pp. 1, 7-8, 20, 25; TF, p. 66; Siddiqui, Perso-Arabic Sources, pp. 54, 46.

hi, with much new material being added and with the use of Hindi equivalents along with Persian terms, was al-Biruni's book on *ṭibb*, the Greek system of medicine, the *Kitab al-Ṣaydana fī-l-ṭibb*.[136] This was probably no coincidence, given the previously mentioned health hazards involved in the movement of large numbers of people from the frontier areas to Hind. The translator, we are told, came from Kasan, in Central Asia, at the beginning of Iltutmish's reign, and was driven from his ancestral place 'by the hot wind of calamity'.

Later in the thirteenth century refugees continued to arrive at Delhi. By 1258, the year that Baghdad was taken, there were at Delhi 'twenty-five Shāhzādas of 'Irāq, Khurāsān and Mā warā' annahr, with their retinues', who had sought protection from the disturbances of the Mongols.[137] It was said that it was one of the greatest sources of pride of Balban's reign that 'upwards of fifteen of the unfortunate sovereigns from Turkestan, Mā warā' annahr, Khurāsān, 'Irāq, Ajarbayjan, Irān amd Rūm', who had been driven from their countries by the Mongol armies, were enabled to find an honourable asylum at his court at Delhi.[138] Princely allowances and palaces were assigned to each, and on public occasions they arranged themselves before the throne according to their rank, all standing on the right and left, except two princes of the family of the Caliphs, who were permitted to sit on either side of the masnad.[139] The parts of the city in which the royal emigrants resided took their names from the princes who occupied them and were denominated their muḥallas.

Not only Delhi, but also Multan, which in the early part of the century, under Qabacha, was on the route of the Mongol invaders, gathered a large number of refugees from the Mongol onslaught. '... During the calamities of the *kuffār-i-chin*, the great of Khurasan, Ghur and Ghaznin, many of them, came into Qabacha's service'.[140] Awfi's translation of Tanukhi's *Kitāb al-Farj ba'z ash-Shidda* mentions in its preface that Qabacha's court had become 'the cynosure for the oppressed of the world'.[141] Many of these

---

[136] Siddiqui, *Perso-Arabic Sources*, p. 46.
[137] *TF*, p. 73.
[138] *TF*, pp. 74-75.
[139] *Ibid.*
[140] *TN*, p. 143.
[141] Siddiqui, *Perso-Arabic Sources*, p. 3.

refugees, like Awfi himself, and also a number of saints who may
have been instrumental in the earliest conversion of local population groups, arrived by sea, via Kambaya, where they were helped
along by rich merchants from a variety of places in Iran.

At any particular time, then, a large number of the great amirs
of the state were not Turkish slaves at all, but Ghuris, Tajiks or
Khalaj, or Arabs, Armenians, Damghanis, Dailamis, and so forth,
as we can deduce from separate lists in Juzjani's work and stray
references in other chronicles.[142] This meant in practical terms
that the Turkish slave elite—which may have been no more than
several hundred, possibly less—had to share power with numerous other groups, including people of slave origin (e.g. Habshis
and sometimes Hindus), but largely free-born immigrants from
Iran, Turan (free-born Turks, also numerous among the soldiery),
or 'Khurasan', as well as 'neo-Muslim' Mongol immigrants (especially after 1260), next to Indian converts to Islam, unconverted
Indians, Afghans, and the Khalaj tribesmen who ultimately supplanted the Turkish slave kings by establishing their own dynasty
(1290-1320).[143] The Afghans, notorious for their uncouth manners (Amir Khusrau still refers to them as 'man-catching
demons'), took a long time to attain positions of rank in the army
and administration.[144] We first hear of the Afghans in the thirteenth-century Sultanate of Hind in 1259-60, when Balban
brought an area known as the Kohpayah-Bharatpur, Dholpur and
parts of what became Jaipur and Lawar, under the sword with the
help of a body of Afghans, who penetrated everywhere in defiles
and ravines, a total cf 3000 horse and foot, in a locality of Hind
where Muslim troops had not been before.[145] From about the
same time fortresses on the Mongol frontier had begun to be garrisoned by Afghans—where they were still found in Amir Khusrau's time.[146] Balban garrisoned other forts in Mewati territory

---

[142] TN, passim; TF, pp. 64, 66, 73, 75; FS, vs. 2180, 2411-40, 3230-43, 3569-81;
Gazetteer of Oudh, II, pp. 81-82.

[143] Cf. also Jackson, 'Mamlūk Institution'; Aubin, 'Ethnogenèse des Qaraunas',
p. 68; TN, pp. 143, 146-7, 161, 278-81; TF, p. 65; FS, vs. 3582-90; TFS, pp. 138-9,
171-3. Khalaji influence at Delhi and in Bengal was largely reduced in Iltutmish's
reign, but revived in Balban's time.

[144] Cf. Siddiqui, 'Afghāns', p. 252; Wahid Mirza, Amir Khusrau, pp. 51-52. For
another description of the Afghans, see TN, p. 315.

[145] TN, p. 315.

[146] Cf. Wahid Mirza, Amir Khusrau, pp. 51-52.

with Afghans, who kept the road between Delhi and Bengal open, and they were employed later again in Awadh.[147] By the time the Khalaji dynasty came to power, a new generation of Afghans, brought up in Hind, had come to the fore which had attained a certain level of urban culture in the context of the Turkish mamluk state.[148]

Without a monopoly of power, the Turkish slave elite existed as a separate but amorphous and random collection of individuals with special qualifications. The core of this elite consisted of the *chihilgānī* or 'Forty', a group which included the twenty-five or so names that Juzjani gives us in his biographies. These Forty slaves of Iltutmish assumed a dominant role in the three decades between the death of Iltutmish in 1236 and Balban's seizure of power in 1266, throughout which period they appear to have controlled the succession of weak rulers, who in effect were mostly puppets in their hands. The Forty were certainly not a cohesive group of slave commanders within a larger ruling elite bent upon the exclusion of outsiders.[149] It has been suggested that the term may well have been a popular nickname, or an expression of opprobrium which became used in later times, especially by Barani who was allegedly outraged by the rise of the 'low-born' (while Juzjani does not mention the term *chihilgānī*).[150] Or it is speculated that the Forty were possibly all manumitted at the same time, at the death of Iltutmish, and that it was this that set them apart, a parallel to the *khushdāshiya* in Mamluk Egypt. In the latter case, the *khushdāshiya* were a group which was held together not only by service to the same master, but even after their manumission by loyalty to their former companions in servitude. In Egypt, a mamluk's *khushdāsh* was one who had been acquired, trained and manumitted by the same master. And, according to some analysts, this type of group solidarity could play a role in politics at times. In India, however, while there is some indication that such·ties between former slaves of the same master were not unknown, they appear to have been too weak to have had any real impact.[151] Barani says about the band of *chihilgānī* that they

---

[147] *TFS*, pp. 57-58; *TF*, p. 77; Elliot and Dowson, *History of India*, III, p. 525.
[148] Cf. Siddiqui, 'Afghans', p. 252.
[149] Cf. Hambly, 'Who were the *chihilgānī*?', pp. 57-62.
[150] *Ibid.*
[151] Cf. *TFS*, pp. 27-28; *TN*, pp. 271, 278, 307.

obtained power after Iltutmish's death, and that they had been fellow slaves but when they became all great and powerful they became jealous of each other.[152] Firishta describes this development as follows: 'In the reign of Shams ad-Din Iltutmish, forty of his Turkish slaves (*chihil ghulām-i-turk*) who were called the *chihilgānī*, and who were in great favour, entered into a solemn covenant with each other, and agreed to have the empire divided among themselves after the King's death. Jealousies and dissensions arose among them and prevented this project from being carried out. Balban was of this number, and as several of them had succeeded to great power in the kingdom, the first act of his reign was to rid himself of all who remained'.[153] In fact, rather than a solidarity group, it seems more likely that the name Forty refers to the number in which these slaves were originally sold at the Delhi court. The earliest reference to the Forty—which bears this out—is not in Barani, who wrote in 1351-57, but in 'Isāmi, a few years earlier, in the *Futūh as-Salāṭīn*, which was composed in 1349-50. 'Isāmi simply says: 'I am told that one day some Chinese merchants (*tujjār-i-chīn*) arrived at the court of His Majesty [Iltutmish] and displayed before him all kinds of commodities from their country. ... I am told there was also a group of forty Turkish slaves (*chihil banda' turk*) who were put in a line and presented to the king'.[154]

Fourthly, since most of the Turkish mamluks were taken to India as children, they were not much aware of their tribal identity (although this was known), and they related to themselves mostly through the names of their places of origin. In general, the Turkish slave elite—essentially the powerbase of the thirteenth-century Delhi Sultanate—could be distinguished by its lighter complexion and entertained pretensions of superiority not merely on grounds of religion but of their ethnicity as well. Without esprit de corps, they were therefore still a closed elite group, which restricted intermarriage to descendants of other Turkish slaves as much as possible, although wives and concubines were also taken from the native Indian population.[155] Sultan Rukun ad-

---

[152] *TFS*, pp. 25-28, 50, 64-65.
[153] *TF*, p. 75.
[154] *FS*, vs. 2328-31.
[155] *TN*, pp. 141-2, 185, 188, 190, 192, 213, 219, 249, 252, 265, 293; *TF*, pp. 65,

Din, for example, was born of a Hindu mother and a Turkish father (*hindavī zād wa turkī nasab*).[156] Pure Turkish lineage was considered important, however, and the mothers of the slave kings are identified as Turkish, or as Turkish slaves (*kanīz-i-turkīya, kanīzak-i-turk*) in every other case we know of.[157] The Turks are always mentioned separately from Ghuris, Khurasanis, Khalajis, Hindustanis, and so on, in the chronicles, and great emphasis is given to the distinctiveness of the 'Turkish race' (*dāsil-i-turkān*) or 'Turkish descent' (*aṣl-i-turkān*) of the slave kings.[158] Turkish names and titles are found among the slave elite of the thirteenth century, as under the Ghaznavids, even though they have a tendency to disappear quickly in favour of Arabic appellations.[159] There is but scanty evidence of Turkish being a spoken language in the Delhi Sultanate. Amir Khusrau, however, in the late thirteenth and early fourteenth century, refers to the speaking of Turkish by immigrants to the Sultanate—by his time mostly free Turks, no longer slaves—, and he also refers to the many Tajiks 'who have learnt Turkish with industry and erudition in India'.[160]

Small in number, the Turkish slaves of Delhi were therefore a very exclusive elite, with a highly developed elite consciousness, in which ethnicity played a large role. But this should not obscure the essential fact that the Sultanate was an ethnically inclusive state, in other words that it depended on the inclusion of people of a great variety of ethnic origins, and increasingly so over time. According to Juzjani, under Balban, 'the maliks and bandagān [slaves] of the Sultanate's court were all Turks of pure lineage (*turkān-i-pāk-aṣl*) and Tājīks of noble birth (*wa tāzīkān-i-guzīda waṣl*)'.[161] If the Forty were destroyed by Balban, a Turkish slave elite, next to free Turks and the numerous Turkish horsemen which made up the armies, continued to be found up to the end

---

69, 72, 75; *TFS*, p. 65. None of this material describes marriages of Turks with Tajiks, Afghans or other ethnic groups.

[156] *FS*, vs. 2472.

[157] *TF*, pp. 64, 67-68; *TN*, p. 181.

[158] *TN*, p. 196; *TFM*, p. 33; *FS*, vs. 2848; *TFS*, p. 171.

[159] There is, for instance, the use of the term *khaqan* for 'king' or 'emperor' but applied to the great nobles without their being sovereign princes (*TN*, p. 230); see also A. Von Le Coq, 'Türkische Namen und Titel in Indien', in: *Aus Indiens Kultur: Festgabe Richard Von Garbe* (Erlangen, 1927), pp. 1-7.

[160] Digby, 'Iletmish', p. 57 note 1.

[161] *TN*, p. 300.

of Balban's dynasty. Under Kaiqubād the non-Turkish elements
increased significantly in power, and the Khalajis, as we have seen,
brought Turkish slave rule to an end. Barani, describing this transition, says that 'the popular feeling was averse to the Khalajis,'
but from the day of Mu'izz ad-Dīn Kaiqubād's death the sovereignty fell to that race and passed away forever from the family
of the Turks'.[162] The same author laments the disappearance from
the Delhi market of Turkish royal slaves.[163]

Most of the Turkish slaves of which we know the origin appear
to have come from the Qipchak Steppe, like the mamluks of Egypt
during the first part of the Mamluk Sultanate, although less exclusively so, and there were nuclei of Ilbari Turks (to which both
Iltutmish and Balban belonged) and Qara Khitay and others. The
nomadic Qipchaqs had been the northern steppe neighbours of
the Khwarazmians from the middle of the eleventh century
onwards, and their arrival in Khwarazm dates mainly from the
reign of the Khwarazm Shah Tekesh, who, from 1182 AD onwards,
began to invite them to serve in the Khwarazmian army as mer-
cenary tribal units.[164] Khwarazm became a stronghold of Qipchaqs
with the marriage of Tekesh and Turkan Khatun, a daughter of
the Qipchaq leader. In the West, the Dast-i-Qipchāq or 'Qipchaq
Steppe', north of the Black Sea and the Caucasus to as far west
as the Dnestr River, became known as the steppe of the Golden
Horde in the Mongol period.[165] In the pre-Chingizid period,
Qipchaq culture displayed the usual 'shamanic' features, including divination practices which harked back to the wolf-myth of
Ashina origins, but they were already assimilating Islam. Qipchaqs
and other Turks which were to be sold as slaves, however, were
not supposed to be Muslims.[166] They were obtained from their
lands of origin as young children through merchants, known as

---

[162] '... wa az roz-i-naql-i-salṭān mu'izz ad-dīn mulk az khāndān-i-turkān bi-raft wa dar
aṣl-i-khaljīyān uftād' (TFS, p. 173).

[163] TFS, p. 314.

[164] Cf. Y. Bregel, 'Turko-Mongol influences in Central Asia', in: R. L. Canfield
(ed.), Turko-Persia in Historical Perspective (Cambridge, 1991), pp. 59-60; H. H.
Howarth, History of the Mongols, Part II (London, 1880), p. 1 ff; U. Schamiloglu,
The Golden Horde (13th-14th Centuries) (forthcoming), pp. 62-63; Golden, History of
the Turkic Peoples, p. 281.

[165] After which the Qipchaks are no longer mentioned.

[166] Cf. TN, p. 256, where the suspicion is voiced that one of them may have
been a Muslim.

'khwājas', who operated far-flung trading networks extending from Delhi to Khwarazm, and to Aden and Egypt, holding licences and 'letters of protection' from the Mongol overlords. These khwājas could be Iranians, or Iraqis, or even Habshis, and they achieved very considerable influence in Delhi.[167]

One Khwāja Shams ad-Dīn 'Ajamī is referred to as 'the chief of the merchants (malik at-tujjār) of the countries of 'Ajam, 'Iraq, Khwarazm, and Ghaznin' and a slave purchased by Iltutmish was named 'after that great man'.[168] Malik-i-Kashli Khan Sayf ad-Din Aybak, an Ilbari Turk, fell into the hands of the Mongols, was then bought by a khwāja who brought him 'to the cities of Islam', as far as Aden and Cairo, and sold him to another khwāja, Abu Bakr Habshi, who had proceeded from the court of Delhi on a mission to Egypt and Baghdad and purchased the future malik on the way.[169] The latter episode was probably connected with the arrival of emissaries from Baghdad with a robe of honour from the Khalifa at the court of Iltutmish—who ultimately ended up buying this slave.[170] Since the khwājas played such an essential role in the early careers of the slaves, the latter were often bound to them with very strong ties of affection and veneration, especially if they had been the ones who severed them from their country of origin. One khwaja, Jamal ad-Din of Basra, 'noted for his piety, honesty, resolution of purpose, and conscientiousness', having purchased Balban, 'used to foster him in the hall of his kindness like a son' until the latter was presented to Iltutmish for sale at Delhi.[171] We know from the Egyptian case that factors which led to the sale of slaves by the inhabitants of the Qipchaq Steppe included the general destitution which forced the population in certain years to sell its children; the need to sell children in lieu of taxes; and the ruler's capturing and selling the children and women of his subjects. The Mongol attacks on the Qipchaq Steppe filled the slave markets with Turks from this area. Even then, cooperation by local elements was generally required to safeguard the supply of slaves.[172] From the biographies of the

---

[167] TN, pp. 198, 232, 248, 253, 256, 265, 274-5, 278, 281-2; TF, p. 74.
[168] TN, pp. 274-5.
[169] TN, pp. 265, 278.
[170] Ibid.
[171] TN, pp. 281-2; TF, p. 74.
[172] See also A. N. Poliak, 'Le Caractère Colonial de l'Etat Mamelouk dans ses

Turkish slaves who came to India we also know that the cooperation of kindred groups was frequently obtained by the slave merchants who then often took them on long journeys, across Iran, to Baghdad, back and forth into Turkestan, and to Syria and Egypt, and that some of them passed hands several times before ending up in Delhi.[173]

In spite of continued hostilities with the Mongols and in spite of Mongol encroachment on the Panjab, the trade in slaves was effected with the active cooperation of Mongol intermediaries. We see this on various levels. On one level, the merchants would receive Mongol protection. This happened in Lahore, a city which, next to Multan, was one of the most important entrepots for trade with the west, including the trade in slaves. When Lahore was taken by the 'infidel Mongols' in 1241, we read that many of the principal inhabitants of the city at that time were merchants who had travelled into Upper Khwarazm and Turkestan with their merchandise and who had provided themselves with letters of protection from the Mongol rulers and did not seem to oppose the Mongol occupation of the city.[174] On another level, we see that a little further to the west of Lahore a small Turkish kingdom was founded in 1235 by the Qarlugh chief Malik Sayf ad-Din Hasan which became an intermediary between the Mongol empire and the Delhi Sultanate until 1266 AD.[175] Both the Qarlughs and the Mongols, as we will see in the remainder of this chapter, played important roles in the formation of the Indo-Islamic state in the thirteenth century. While both created their own states, these should not be seen as separate from but rather as overlapping with that of the Turkish mamlūks and their retinues. Just as there were no ethnically exclusive states in the eleventh-thirteenth centuries, there were also no territorially exclusive dominions. The Indo-Islamic world was a world which was constantly on the move. It was characterized by openness and fluidity, and it knew no hard and fast boundaries anywhere.

Rapports avec la Horde d'Or', *Revue des Etudes Islamiques*, III (1953), pp. 231-48.
[173] Cf. *TN*, pp. 165-8, 232, 265, 275, 278.
[174] *TN*, p. 195.
[175] Cf. Siddiqui, 'Qarlūgh Kingdom'.

Qarlughs

The Qarlughs (or *Kharlukh* of the Arab geographers) were of Turkish origin and are recorded to have attained a certain early political importance in the second half of the eighth century, with one of their chiefs adopting Islam in 799 AD (even though the conversion of the entire tribe took a long time). In the thirteenth century Hasan Qarlugh was among the retinue of Sultan Jalal ad-Din Khwarazm Shah (Mangbarni), entering India in 1221, while another Qarlugh chief, Arslan Khan, joined Chingiz Khan.[176] Hasan Qarlugh was among the nobles left behind in India by the Khwarazm Shah to govern the territories that he had conquered from Sultan Nasir ad-Din Qabacha.

The Qarlugh kingdom in India comprised the areas of Bīnbān and Koh-i-Jūd. Bīnbān (with Kurramān) was the link between Ghazna and Hind, a link which acquired further importance when the Mongols occupied Turan: in addition to the merchant caravans, the Mongol armies passed through it.[177] From 1229, the year when Iltutmish destroyed Qabacha, until 1235, Hasan Qarlugh entered the service of the Delhi Sultan, whose domains were thus extended up to Nagrahar, Kurramān and Ghazna. But in 1235 Qarlugh again pledged allegiance to the Mongols, assuming a royal title and issuing coins in his own name. Iltutmish intended to take action against him, but died in 1236. After Iltutmish's death, Qarlugh began to have designs on the Panjab and Sind. Prolonged conflict followed with the Delhi Sultan's *iqtāʿ*-holders in the Panjab and Sind, and the Hindu rajas of the Salt Range and the Kohpāyah (the foothills of the eastern Panjab Himalayas) started paying allegiance to him. In 1238 however he was attacked by the Mongols again and possibly forced to accept a Mongol shahna or 'superintendent' at his court. Thereafter, from 1241 onwards, Qarlugh joined the Mongols in raiding the border regions of India. In 1244 the Qarlugh chief conquered Multan, but had to evacuate it in 1245 on the approach of a Mongol army under Manguta. He invaded Multan in 1249 a second time, but again did not retain it for long. Hasan Qarlugh was by then succeeded by his son, Sultan Nasir ad-Din Muhammad, who, during his twenty year rule, maintained diplomatic ties with the Mongols and followed

---

[176] *Ibid.*, pp. 75-76.
[177] *Ibid.*, pp. 76-77.

Map 3. The Qarlugh kingdom

a policy of pragmatic compromise with the Delhi court, avoiding armed conflict with both, while promoting agriculture and trade, as an abundance of coins found in the Salt Range shows. Muhammad Qarlugh's coins do not mention the Mongol overlord. But in practice he was a subordinate of the Mongol Khan. In that capacity he also allied himself with Sultan Jalal ad-Din Mas'ud Shah, the son of Iltutmish, in Lahore, and 'Izz ad-Din Balban Kashlu Khan, a governor of Multan and Sind who had become independent of the Delhi Sultan and had begun to acknowledge the overlordship of the Mongol emperor Möngke in 1254. The Qarlugh ruler in Bīnbān, for long a mediator between the Mongols and Delhi, fell sometime after 1266 AD, when Balban re-occupied the bilads of Sind and Multan and Lahore and the destruction of the Mongol vassal Sultans caused estrangement between Hülegü and Qarlugh as the latter was suspected of complicity. Balban did not come to the aid of Qarlugh when the latter's rule was supplanted by that of the Mongols and Bīnbān and the Koh-i-Jūd became part of the Chaghatay Khanate.

Mongols

India escaped the type of wholesale Mongol onslaught that
occurred in China, Central Asia, Iran, and Russia in the thirteenth
century. Nonetheless, between 1221, when Chingiz Khan first
appeared on the Indus river in pursuit of the Khwarazm Shah,
and 1398, when Delhi was sacked by Timur, there were numerous incursions, principally in the Northwest Frontier regions and
the Panjab, but also in Kashmir, and the threat posed by the 'infidels of Chīn' was at times considerable.[178] But most Mongol incursions into India were small by comparison, led by second-rate commanders, and ill-timed.

Protracted hostilities on the frontier were accompanied by
diplomatic exchanges. And, on the diplomatic level, the Delhi Sultanate always remained a direct challenge to the world supremacy of the Mongol Khans, especially after it had become recognized
by the Caliph of Baghdad in Iltutmish's time, and, even more,
after it had begun minting coins in the name of the dead Caliph
after 1258.[179]

Nothing suggests that the Mongols, who had defeated the
Jürchen Chin empire (which would have been their strongest
opponent), regarded the Delhi Sultanate, or the Mamluks of
Egypt, or any of the European powers, as too strong to overcome.
The politics of succession, after 1241 and again in 1260, probably played an important role in thwarting Mongol expansion in
these areas.[180] In the case of India, it has also been claimed that
the Mongols withdrew in 1221, after having reached Multan,
because of the heat; and that when Chingiz Khan entered it again
in 1224 he withdrew because he considered the sighting of a rhinoceros a bad omen.[181] There was also the additional factor of
insufficient pasture land. A recently discovered letter which was
sent by Hülegü, the Mongol Khan of Iran, to Louis IX of France,
suggests that the Mongols found it difficult to campaign in Syria
for any long period of time because of the lack of pasturage
there.[182] In Western Europe, and even in Hungary, there were not

---

[178] There were some Mongol campaigns into mainland Southeast Asia and to
Java as well; these are dealt with separately in Chs I and XI.
[179] Cf. C. W. Ernst, *Eternal Garden* (Albany, 1992), p. 56.
[180] Fletcher, 'Mongols', pp. 45-46.
[181] *Ibid.*, p. 46.
[182] Cf. D. Morgan, *The Mongols* (Oxford, 1986), p. 157.

enough pastures for the Mongol cavalry and stock.[183] India, too, was unsuited climatically and geographically for Mongol-style nomadism.[184]

Chingiz Khan, in any case, first appeared north of the Indus in 1221, in pursuit of the Khwarazm Shah. The Khwarazm Shahs had incorporated the entire Ghurid domain as far as the Indus, perhaps even as far as the Jhelum. The mountain fortifications of Ghur and Gharchistan put up a stiff resistance against the Mongol armies, but were conquered, and after the completion of the conquest Mongol detachments were left in the country.

Most of the later Mongol invaders attempted the Multan route to Hindustan. This was a route which, while the Gaggar and Sutlej rivers still held their ancient courses, was much easier to follow than in later centuries, and it was also easier than the Khyber route most of the time. In 1224, Nandana was taken by the Mongols, and Multan was invested and possibly temporarily taken.[185] Soon afterwards there appears to have been a second Mongol invasion of Qabacha's dominions. Measures were taken to defend Multan during its siege by the Mongols, who had arrived with great preparation and a large army and with siege equipment, but took to flight after three months.[186] In general, during Iltutmish's reign, the Mongol presence on the Hindu-Kush and the Indus served to weaken his rivals Yaldiz and Qabacha. Mongol troops under Chaghatay and Ogedai also ravaged the southern Panjab, and Chaghatay spent a winter in Kalanjar. At about the same time, an embassy arrived of Barka of the Golden Horde, which had newly converted to Islam.

After Iltutmish's death in 1236, his son Jalal ad-Din attempted to gain the Delhi throne with the aid of an expeditionary force sent by Möngke, but unsuccessfully, and Jalal ad-Din merely had a frontier principality bestowed upon him by the Mongols. It was

[183] Cf. R. P. Lindner, 'Nomadism, Horses and Huns', *Past and Present*, 92, 3 (1981), pp. 3-19; A. M. Khazanov, 'The Spread of World Religions in Medieval Nomadic Societies of the Eurasian Steppes', in: M. Gervers and W. Schlepp (eds), *Nomadic Diplomacy, Destruction and Religion from the Pacific to the Adriatic* (Toronto, 1994), p. 27.
[184] Cf. R. Amitai-Preiss, *Mongols and Mamluks: The Mamluk-Ilkhānid War, 1260-1281* (Cambridge, 1995), p. 232; S. Ratnagar, 'Pastoralism as an Issue in Historical Research', *Studies in History*, n.s., 7, 2 (1991), pp. 181-2.
[185] *TN*, p. 143; *TNR*, pp. 535-6, note 1.
[186] Siddiqui, *Perso-Arabic Sources*, p. 4.

at this time also that Mongol rulers began to acquire political influence in the Panjab and Sind, and it was in 1236 that Hasan Qarlugh, the Wali of Binban and the Koh-i-Jud, repudiated his allegiance to the Sultan of Delhi in favour of the Mongol Khan Ogedai (1229-1241). Lahore, Jullundar, Multan and Upper Sind were also turned into Mongol vassal states, and the river Sutlej became the boundary between the Delhi Sultanate and the Mongol empire—a situation which prevailed until the succession struggle which followed Möngke's death in 1259. Lahore was taken in 1241, during Bahram Shah's reign, by Mongols appearing from Khurasan and Ghazna.[187]

In 1245-6, 'Manguta the accursed' led a Mongol army from the borders of Tālqān and Qunduz into Sind, and invested Uch and the country of Mansura. The Kokhar chief in the Koh-i-Jūd or Salt Range appears to have cooperated by acting as a guide to the invaders on this occasion.[188] Already by 1221 the rivalry between this chief and Qabacha had been of long standing. Balban went to the provinces of the Indus in 1247, and to the Jud hills, to wreak vengeance on the Kokhar rajas of these hills who in the previous year had acted as guides for the Mongols.[189] The investment of Uch was also raised.[190] 'Fear of Balban spread as far as Turkestan'.[191] It seems that prior to this the Mongols made almost annual raids upon the border tracts of Sind and Multan. But because of Balban, in 1247 no Mongol army came to Sind from the west.[192]

A new governor, Sher Khan, was now appointed to the Panjab, Multan, Bhatnair, and Sirhind, to watch the movements of the Mongols, and the forts of Bhatnair and Sirhind were rebuilt. In 1250, Sher Khan raised troops and drove the Mongols out of Ghazna, striking coins there in the name of Nasir ad-Din.[193] But the Mongols continued to encroach upon the Panjab and gradually located themselves permanently on the banks of the Beas.[194]

---

[187] TN, p. 195.
[188] Cf. P. Jackson, The Mongols and India, 1221-1351 (Unpublished PhD Dissertation, Cambridge, 1976), p. 70.
[189] TN, pp. 209, 290; TF, p. 71.
[190] TN, pp. 287, 200; TF, p. 70.
[191] TN, p. 290.
[192] TN, p. 291; TNR, p. 816.
[193] TF, pp. 71-72.
[194] TNR, p. 689, note 4.

In the period 1252-53, Delhi troops were sent to the Beas river to keep these in check, and to secure Uch and Multan.[195] But Kishlu Khan, another governor of western Sind, in 1257 transferred his allegiance to the Mongols which had come from Khurasan to Uch and Multan.[196] In 1258, 'there came an army of infidels who raided Uch and Multan fiercely. The troops fortified themselves in every fortress and cried for help against the violent raids of those accursed invaders. The whole area, including the countryside was overrun and the peasants' holdings were ruined'.[197] A shahna was imposed on Sind and Multan, and the Mongols dismantled the defences of the citadel of Multan.[198] Kishlu Khan conspired with some other amirs to overthrow the Delhi kingdom, but this project was discouraged by Hülegü, who merely wanted the fortifications of Multan razed and not a fullscale invasion.[199] When Balban heard about the dismantling of Multan, in 1259, he assembled large troops in the neighbourhood of Delhi, which made the Mongols recoil beyond the frontier again.[200]

In 1259, the year of the death of Möngke Khan, a succession struggle broke out among the Mongols. Taking advantage of these developments, Balban, the regent of Delhi, recaptured the territories of Lahore, Jullundar, Multan and Upper Sind, after entering into a secret alliance with the Qarlugh ruler of Bīnbān and Koh-i-Jūd in 1258 and concluding a no-war pact with the latter's help with Hülegü. Balban's defence line became the Dipālpūr-Bāyāna tract. Here an elaborate system of frontier defences checked Mongol raiding into India. An impressive reception was given to envoys of Hülegü in the same year, to arrange a marriage alliance between Malik Hasan Qarlugh and the son of Balban.[201]

Here we become aware that, after the sack of Baghdad, and with the resistance of the Mamluks of Egypt still unsubdued, and in the face of growing hostility of the newly converted Golden Horde, Hülegü's policy in India was one of caution. The initia-

[195] TN, pp. 216-7.
[196] TN, p. 255.
[197] FS, vs. 2771 ff.
[198] TN, pp. 271-3, 277, 310.
[199] A. Ahmad, 'Mongol Pressure in an Alien Land', Central Asiatic Journal, VI (1961), p. 184.
[200] TN, pp. 225, 310-1.
[201] TF, p. 73; TN, pp. 317-320.

tive of attacking India passed to the Chaghatays even before the Ilkhanids themselves converted to Islam. Surrounded by their more powerful cousins, the Chaghatays had remained unresponsive to the urban Muslim culture of Transoxania, and, unlike the other Mongols, they were still nomads. Having consolidated their position in Afghanistan and having seized Bīnbān and the Koh-i-Jūd territories, they had only one way to go and started making organized attempts to penetrate deep into India—attempts that were sustained and took on dangerous forms into the fourteenth century. Muslim records of both Iran and India refer to Mongol inroads during the latter half of the thirteenth century which brought large bands of freebooters under a leader called Nogodar, the nephew of Chaghatay, to the borderlands of Iran and India, and even as far as Lahore. These inroads appear to have begun from about 1260 AD, and continued right through the reign of Sultan Ghiyath ad-Din Balban (1265-86).

With the accession of Balban in 1265, however, a new phase began in the relations with the Mongol empire. The latter by now had broken into several distinct parts which were controlled by the grandsons of Chingiz Khan and were hostile to one another. Balban took effective measures, including putting Lahore in a proper state of defence, against both the Ilkhans and then the Chaghatays of Central Asia. The 'Mughal Tartars' had become so powerful in the north, talking even about the conquest of Delhi, that Balban abandoned plans to undertake expeditions to reduce Gujarat and Malwa.[202] Sher Khan, a cousin of Balban, was again given charge of the districts that were exposed to the Mongol inroads—Sanam, Lahore, Dipalpur, and others—and utterly routed the Mongol troops several times.[203] Balban's younger son, Kurra Khan, was appointed to Samana and Sanam to watch over the movements of the Mongols.[204] And the Sultan also seems to have employed the trained soldiers and officers of the fallen Qarlugh ruler of Bīnbān, who had come over to him.[205]

Balban was thus able to defend the frontier areas of the Sultanate, although the strategic territories of Bīnbān and the Koh-i-Jūd continued to be ruled by the Chaghatay Khan. In the latter

---

[202] *TF*, p. 77; *TFS*, pp. 50-51, 61.
[203] *TF*, p. 65.
[204] *TF*, p. 78.
[205] Siddiqui, 'Qarlūgh Kingdom', p. 292.

areas, the Mongol occupation appears to have led to the devastation of agricultural land on a large scale, with vast tracts of agricultural land being turned into pasture to sustain the Mongol cavalry.[206] Both of these areas were converted into a military base where Mongol hazāra contingents of 1000 were stationed and from where raids could be carried out into the Indian plains. Muslims had been present in large numbers in Bīnbān ever since Afghans and other immigrants, Muslim Shaykhs and Saiyids, had settled here during the later Ghaznavid period.[207] The number of Muslims in the towns of the Koh-i-Jūd was also considerable since Nandana and Merekala had emerged as centres of Muslim culture during the thirteenth century.[208] With both regions deprived of their local Muslim elites, the Delhi Sultans could not re-establish their control over the region north-west of the Ravi river until the beginning of the fourteenth century.[209] Even Balban could not establish control further than the Ravi.

In 1285 Muhammad Khan, the Khan of Multan, the eldest son and heir apparent of the Sultan, proceeded to Lahore, Multan and Dipalpur but was 'martyred' in a battle against the Mongols.[210] This was the time, a period of five years in which there were a number of encounters with the Mongols, when Amir Khusrau was staying in Multan. 'Although each year the Mongols come from Khurasan in serred ranks like storks, with owlish wings and ominous faces', the poet wrote, '... fondly do the enemies yield up their ghosts wherever the Turks send the showers of their fatal arrows. Each time when an army of the enemies surging like the sea arrives, a new splendour is imparted to the dust of Multan'.[211]

Further to the north, the Mongols also penetrated into Kashmir—a fact which is often overlooked, since Jonaraja, the continuer of Kalhana's Rājataranginī, chronicling the events of the

---

[206] *Ibid.*, p. 293.

[207] *Ibid.*, p. 303.

[208] *Ibid.*

[209] *Ibid.*, pp. 293-4.

[210] *TFS*, p. 80; *TF*, p. 81; *FS*, vs. 3244-83.

[211] Wahid Mirza, *Amir Khusrau*, p. 55. Khusrau describes the Mongols as clad in cotton, wearing caps of sheepskin on their shaven heads, with steel-like bodies, faces like fire with narrow piercing eyes, flat noses, broad nostrils, long mouths, sullen cheeks, overgrown moustaches and scanty beards; their bodies as covered with lice, their skin rough as leather, and 'they devoured dogs and pigs with their nasty teeth'.

period between 1150 and 1420 AD, and all the other Indian or Kashmirian historiographers, make no mention of Mongols or Mongol influence in Kashmir at any time. In Rashīd ad-Dīn's *History* (compiled about 1303-6), however, we read that the Mongols repeatedly invaded Kashmir, temporarily subjugated the country and for some time appointed its kings.[212] The first great invasion of Kashmir by the Mongols, resulting in a transitory supremacy, occurred in the reign of King Rāmadeva (1212/13-1235). The Mongol army, under the orders of Ogedai but led by Ukutu Noyin, besieged the capital of Kashmir, conquered it, plundered the town, and appointed a governor, who was expelled seven years later. In Möngke's time, another Mongol army invaded the country under the leadership of Sali Noyin and Takudar. Kashmir was again plundered, the chief inhabitants of the capital killed, and the rest carried away into slavery with their wives and children, after which the country remained subject to Mongol rule for many years.[213] From Hülegü's time onwards, Kashmir was politically and culturally probably more closely bound to the Mongols of Iran than to those of China.[214] Marco Polo refers to a third inroad of Mongols in Kashmir by Nogodar, the nephew of Chaghatay, in 1272-3.[215] This time the route led across the Mandal Pass into the Kafir of Bashgal and then down to Arnawai on the Kunar. From 'Pashai-Dir' the route went down to the Panjkora valley and through the open tracts of Lower Sawt and Buner to the Indus about Amb. From there it led through the open northern part of the present Hazara district, to the valley of the Jhelum river at its bend near Muzaffarabad. The gorges through which the Jhelum River cuts its way from below the 'Gate' of Baramula and the precipitous rugged spurs rising above were the most serious obstacles for entering Kashmir with a large body of horse from the west.

---

[212] K. Jahn, *Rashīd Al-Dīn's History of India* (The Hague, 1965), pp. xiii, lxxxvii-xci.

[213] Rashīd ad-Dīn, in a story attributed to his Indian informant. Kāmalashrī, a hermit of Kashmir, traced the genealogy of the Mongol dynasty directly from the ancient legendary dynasties of India (Jahn, *ibid.*, pp. lxxviii-lxxxvi).

[214] *Ibid.*, pp. xc-xci; K. Jahn, 'Zum Problem der Mongolischen Eroberungen in Indien (13.-14. Jahrhundert)', in: *Akten des 24. Internationalen Orientalisten-Kongresses* (München, 1957), pp. 617-9.

[215] A. Stein, 'Marco Polo's Account of a Mongol Inroad into Kashmir', *The Geographical Journal*, LIV (July-Dec. 1919), pp. 92-103.

Mongol immigration, as distinct from military raiding, into Hind, and into the borderlands to the west, also occurred in the thirteenth century, although it was on a small scale by comparison with Iran. Some Mongol groups found niches for themselves in the mountainous areas of Central Afghanistan. Here the *Hazāras* were to represent, to later observers, a mixed population made up of an Iranian substratum with a heavy Mongolian overlay. Amir Khusrau's parents are described as 'Hazāras'—which probably suggests a nomadic origin. The term is merely Persian or Tajik for 'Ming', 'a thousand' unit of Chingiz Khan's army.[216] Spoken by a mixed population, Hazāragī contains a considerable number of Mongolian words. How many of these 'Hazāras' migrated further to the east, however, cannot be made out.

It is also impossible to determine how large were the numbers, in the thirteenth-century Delhi Sultanate, of the so-called 'Qarā'ūna Turks'. *Qarauna/Qaraun* in Turkish indicates blackness or darkness in colour and it has been suggested, first by Marco Polo, that the Qarā'ūnas were the product of unions of Mongol or 'Tartar' fathers and Indian mothers which occurred on the frontier marches of Northwest India that were often invaded or occupied by the Mongols.[217] They appear to have been a group separate from those Mongols which were called 'New Muslims' and which settled down in India during the reign of Balban and intermarried with the Muslim amirs.[218] Ibn Battuta refers to the Tughluqs (1320-1399), the dynasty which succeeded the Khalajis and the Turkish Slave Kings of Delhi, as 'Qarā'ūna Turks'.[219] Later traditions, reflected in Muslim authors, refer to the founder of the Tughluq dynasty as the son of a Turkish slave of Balban and a Jat mother from the Panjab.[220] The origins of the Qarā'ūnas are in fact quite obscure. Marco Polo encountered the Qarā'ūnas at

---

[216] H. F. Schurmann, *The Mongols of Afghanistan: An Ethnography of the Moghols and related peoples of Afghanistan* ('s-Gravenhage, 1962), esp. pp. 7, 14-17; E. E. Bacon, 'An Inquiry into the History of the Hazara Mongols of Afghanistan', *Southwest Journal of Anthropology*, 7 (1951), pp. 230-47.

[217] Cf. Ahmad, 'Early Turkish Nucleus', pp. 106-7; G. Doerfer, *Türkische und Mongolische Elemente im Neupersischen*, I (Wiesbaden, 1963), pp. 403-4; Yule, *Marco Polo*, I, pp. 98-106.

[218] For which see below.

[219] Defrémery and Sanguinetti, *Ibn Batoutah*, III, p. 201.

[220] I. Prasad, *A History of the Qaraunah Turks in India in India, Vol. I* (Allahabad, 1936), p. 1.

Kirman and other places in Iran and describes them as a predatory and marauding tribe. Muslim historians of the Ilkhanid period do not identify them as a mixed group but merely dwell upon their warlike qualities and their peculiar physiognomy, while describing them as a subtribe of Mongols who entered Khurasan and Iran, forming a tuman (division of 10,000), under Hülegü or some time after his invasion, and afterwards scouring the eastern frontiers of Iran. They appear to have been in the margins of other groups of Mongol and Turko-Mongol origin. Contemporaries mention their cruelty, rapidity of movement, predatory instincts, and lack of discipline. Yule thought that Polo's account was misguided and that the latter in fact confounded the Qarā'ūnas with the Baluchis 'whose Turanian aspect shows a strong infusion of Turki blood and who might be rudely described as a cross between Tartars and Indians'.[221] Recent research has suggested again that the Qarā'ūnas were a mixture of Turks of Transoxania, Mongols, Khalaj, Afghans, and Indians (especially Indian slaves) but that the Qarā'ūna noyins of the Mongol forces were composed of different tribes.[222] Rather numerous already in the last third of the thirteenth century, they were active on the Indian frontier, but also in Transoxania, Iran and what is now Afghanistan. Like the Nogodarīs, Jurmā'īs, and other similar groups with whom they are often mentioned together, the Qarā'ūnas arose in the middle of the thirteenth century as a dissident, i.e. anti-Ilkhanid, Mongol nomadic element, and they probably all played important roles in the politics of the period.[223]

There are strong indications that Balban, after destroying the Forty, created a new group of supporters among yet other groups of Mongols who were immigrants to Delhi. Firishta writes that in Kaiqubād's time 'the Mongol amirs which in the reign of Sultan Balban came into Hindustan and became [his] servants constituted about one-fifth and had a large retinue ..'. [224] Some of the sons of the slaves of Balban who were great maliks had established

---

[221] Prasad, *History of the Qaraunah Turks*, p. 3; Yule, *Marco Polo*, I, p. 94, note 4.

[222] Aubin, 'Ethnogenèse des Qaraunas', pp. 65-94.

[223] Cf. Schurmann, *Mongols*, pp. 20-22.

[224] '... *kah umarāy mughal kah dar zamān-i-salṭanat-i-salṭān balban bi hindūstān āmad naukar shudand ham [himmat?] ek-khams and wa hasham-i-basyār dārand* ...' (*TF*, p. 85).

connections with these amirs through connubial arrangements and alliances.[225] Under Balban a special neighbourhood was created in Delhi which became known as the *muhalla' changīzī*, after certain Mongol princes who occupied it.[226] These Mongols in the service of the Delhi Sultans, of whom we first hear in the reign of Balban, were referred to as 'New Muslims' (*nau muslimān*). They were converts, a part of them possibly warcaptives. But they are also described as 'traitors of infidel stock (*ghaddār-i-kāfir*)'.[227] Under Mu'izz ad-Dīn Kaiqubād these Mongols were largely eliminated in their turn. By then the New Muslims 'of the old regime' (*i-mulk-i-kuhan*) had become so dominant that Mu'izz ad-Dīn was perturbed, as they 'had become masters of the situation to such an extent that without their knowledge it was not possible for the king to take water by day or night'.[228] According to Barani, they were 'of one mind' and 'of one stock' and they were suspected of treachery and intentions to overthrow the government, while heading a numerous clientele.[229] It was anticipated that in case of a Mongol invasion they would join the invaders as they had reached a secret understanding with them.[230] The majority of their chiefs were put to death under Kaiqubād, and those among the rest of the ruling elite which were associated with them, uprooted or dispersed.[231] A Mongol invasion was staved off.

---

[225] *TFS*, p. 134.
[226] *TF*, p. 75.
[227] *FS*, vs. 3536.
[228] *FS*, vs. 3525-33.
[229] '... *yakdil* ... *yekjins and wa hasham-i-basyār dārand* ..'. (*TFS*, p. 133).
[230] *TF*, p. 85.
[231] *TFS*, pp. 133-4; see also, for this episode: *TMS*, pp. 53-54; *TF*, p. 85; *FS*, vs. 3525-59.

CHAPTER VII

GARRISON, PLAIN AND MARCH

This chapter will focus on the rise of garrison towns—and the evolution into cities of some of these—in the thirteenth-century Mamlūk Sultanate, while exploring the rise of a new cash nexus in the context of this new urbanization and the creation of the *iqṭāʿ* system of revenue assignment. Garrison towns and cities, as will be shown, became the fulcrum of both the sedentary world and of nomadic, mobile wealth and expansion. In the chronicles these towns and cities, the nodal points of the money economy and the system of surplus mobilization, appear as an embattled arena rather than the frontier itself. In other words, it is here that the fusion of settled society and frontier ultimately took place.

The Delhi Sultanate, in effect, was the sum of its *iqṭāʿs*—defined not as local territorial units, but as garrisoned urban centres (*khiṭṭa*) with dependent areas (*muẓāfāt*)—and some *khāliṣa* or 'crown' holdings of minor proportions. In principle the *iqṭāʿ* provided a temporary right to collect revenue. To assess accurately the period of turnover of most of the *iqṭāʿs* at this time is not possible. Juzjani typically says that a particular amir held such or such an *iqṭāʿ* 'for some time'. Periods of two, three or four years are mentioned. And changes in their distribution commonly occurred with the accession of a new ruler to the throne. The length of tenure probably varied a great deal. Even more variable was their size, ranging from rights over large provinces like Awadh or Bengal to a small number of villages. And, typically also, these rights could be assigned over newly conquered and well-controlled areas. Royal farmans relating to the posting of governors or *iqṭāʿdārs* in their provincial units demonstrate that the Sultans attached the greatest importance to the expansion of agriculture and internal and external trade from the very beginning.[1] These documents, drawn up according to a standard blueprint, indicate sizable bureaucratic establishments. And they show that the

---

[1] Cf. Siddiqui, *Perso-Arabic Sources*, pp. 167-189.

assignees, amirs of the slave household, commanded troops which
were stationed in a garrison in the *iqṭāʿ*. In a formal sense these
troops were in the service of the Delhi Sultans, but they and their
commanders were often in open opposition against the centre
and not uncommonly joined forces with other assignees without
authorization from Delhi.[2] Revenue had to be submitted, too, on
an annual basis but often was not. The amount of supervisory control in practice also varied a great deal. It was tightest under Balban, who appears to have appointed confidential spies everywhere.[3] Control was difficult to maintain because the *iqṭāʿdārs*
generally lived in the provinces assigned, and only some, largely
those near the capital, were absentee governors who ruled
through deputies.[4]

Before proceeding, let us first take a look at the monetary situation that prevailed in North India in the thirteenth century. If
the new urbanization of this period (following upon the Muslim
urbanization of Sind which occurred under the Arabs and their
Ghaznavid and Ghurid successors)[5] and revenue assignment system was the product of an expanding money economy, where, we
may ask, did the money come from which made this possible?

A growing body of evidence suggests that ancient India was not
devoid of gold and silver mines.[6] Gold mining shafts have been
difficult to uncover as they were out of use for many centuries
and are often covered with thick layers of black cotton soil. Silver was sometimes associated with gold or found in argentiferous
galena mines, as in Bihar, Orissa, Karnataka, or Rajasthan, or—
to a very limited degree—obtained from lead ore. There were two
major silver mines in Afghanistan, one at Panjshir and the other

[2] Cf. *TN*, p. 305.
[3] *TFS*, p. 45; *TF*, pp. 76-77.
[4] Cf. *TN*, p. 223.
[5] Cf. *Al-Hind, I*, pp. 174-189.
[6] Cf. R. Nanda, *The Early History of Gold in India* (New Delhi, 1992); F. R.
Allchin, 'Upon the Antiquity and Methods of Gold Mining in Ancient India', *Journal of the Economic and Social History of the Orient*, 5 (1962); H. C. Bhardwaj, *Aspects
of Ancient Indian Technology* (New Delhi, 1979); M. Wheeler, *The Indus Civilization*
(Cambridge, 1968); Deyell, *Living without Silver*; I. G. Khan, 'Metallurgy in Medieval India: 16th-18th Centuries', in: A. Roy and S. K. Bagchi (eds), *Technology in
Ancient and Medieval India* (Delhi, 1986); G. Kuppuram, *Ancient Indian Mining,
Metallurgy and Metal Industries*, 2 vols (New Delhi, 1989); L. Ferrin, 'Gold and Sil-
ver in the Indian Subcontinent: A Review of Some Problems and Prospects'
(Termpaper, UW-Madison, Dep. of History, Spring 1991).

at Wakkhan, which were worked under the Samanid and Ghaznavid dynasties and probably produced limited amounts of silver for the Delhi Sultanate. But by 1222 these mines were under Mongol control and their silver was used primarily for the minting of Chingiz Khan's Ghazna dirhams. The mines at Zawar in Rajasthan were not exploited until the fifteenth century.

In the medieval period as a whole, domestic mining of precious metals in India was insignificant or absent. Firishta, as already mentioned, writes that in the eleventh century there were still gold mines in Gujarat, but that in his time there were no traces left of these mines, and we simply do not know when they were shut down.[7] Rather than through mining, gold continued to be made available through panning outwashes, from the sands of many of the great rivers of India, as in Afghanistan. Gold was thus panned from the Indus from the earliest times, and Assam was famous for its gold-washing industry, while gold was found in numerous rivers in the Himalayas.[8] But the Indian subcontinent as a whole did not produce significant alluvial gold in either the ancient or medieval periods. Instead, by the thirteenth century, Tibet, Sumatra and various places in mainland Southeast Asia are often mentioned as important sources of gold.[9] Sumatra is said to have abounded in gold and silver, while the Bawdingyi or 'great silver mines' in Burma were among the richest in Southeast Asia.[10] Gold mines are supposed to have existed in Sri Lanka in the eleventh century, and in Pegu.[11]

It seems clear, therefore, that already by the eleventh and twelfth centuries, the most important source of new precious metals in South Asia was external trade with these and other areas that produced them. To be sure, there had been a persistent flow of precious metals towards the Indian subcontinent from antiquity onwards. This flow was only temporarily reversed during the Ghaznavid and Ghurid raids, when vast amounts of gold and silver were dethesaurized and reminted, thus providing coinage which stimulated trade within eastern Islam. The Ghurid rulers Mu'izz ad-

---

[7] Cf. p. 125.

[8] Cf. Watters, *Yuan Chwang*, *passim*.

[9] For Tibet, see Komroff, *Contemporaries of Marco Polo*, p. 118; Roerich, *Biography of Dharmasvamin*, pp. 98, 106.

[10] For Sumatra, see e.g. Odoric's account in Komroff, *Contemporaries of Marco Polo*, p. 222; for the Bawdingyi mines, see *Al-Hind*, *I*, p. 274 ...

[11] *TF*, pp. 33-34.

Dīn and Ghiyāth ad-Dīn were still issuing ever-increasing quantities of gold and silver coins from Ghazna, based on the immense amounts of bullion seized in India.[12] But Indian trade with the outside world was much enlarged by the thirteenth century and now generated correspondingly much larger inflows of gold and silver by sea (through Kambaya, Quilon, or Sri Lanka) and by land, from both east and west: Indian products like spices and textiles, and numberless others, were exchanged for the precious metals from as far away as Hungary and the Balkan; for sub-Saharan gold which came in via the Middle East (Cairo and Alexandria); for Ethiopian gold (via Cairo); for Tibetan gold via Nepal and Kashmir; for silver from Pegu and Yunnan via Bengal; and for silver from Canton and the other South China ports.[13] The increased presence of many merchants and traders in North India from Khurasan, Iran and China is especially well-attested from Iltutmish's time.[14]

Trade, in effect, was massively promoted by all thirteenth-century rulers of Hind. In Kambaya there was a flourishing community of Muslim traders engaged in trade between India, China and the Middle East. Many of the principal inhabitants of Lahore, by the first half of the thirteenth century, were merchants, who had travelled to Khurasan and Turkestan and had provided themselves with letters of protection from the Mongol rulers.[15] The great abundance of coins found in the Salt-Range districts points to intensive trade carried on by merchant caravans between India, Iran and Central Asia through this region.[16] Multan was a prosperous trading centre and the 'Multanis' by the thirteenth century had become a very important and powerful community of Hindu and possibly Muslim merchants, Sāhs or Sāhūs, operating in Delhi itself, and advancing loans to Balban's amirs.[17] Other Hindu merchants are mentioned at the Delhi court who had acquired vast fortunes by usury and monopolies in the bazaar.[18] Writing of

---

[12] Cf. Spengler, 'Numismatic Evidence', pp. 6-14.

[13] Cf. Chapter I; and J. F. Richards, 'Precious Metals and India's Role in the Medieval World Economy' (Paper submitted to the 16th International Congress of Historical Studies, Stuttgart, August 26, 1985).

[14] *TN*, pp. 144-6, 159, 166; *FS*, vs 2181, 2331-8.

[15] *TN*, p. 195.

[16] Siddiqui, 'Qarlugh Kingdom', p. 81.

[17] P. Prasad, *Sanskrit Inscriptions of Delhi Sultanate, 1191-1526* (Delhi, 1990), p. 7; Raychaudhuri and Habib, *Cambridge Economic History of India*, I, p. 85.

[18] Cf. *TF*, p. 75.

Balban's time, Barani says: 'The Multanis and Sāhs of Delhi have acquired abundant wealth and have derived it from the resources (*daulat*) of the old maliks and amirs of Delhi. The latter took loans from the Multanis and Sāhs beyond limit, and repaid the advances with largesses (by drafts) upon their *iqtā's* ..'.[19] Hindu merchants at Delhi not only gained immense wealth by advancing loans to Balban's governors and commanders of garrisons but also by long-distance trade.[20] Under Iltutmish and Balban, special efforts were made to render the roads safe for commercial traffic (*kārawāniyān-o-saudāgarān*) by the suppression of 'predators'.[21] In fact, the whole purpose of the *iqtā'* system and the garrison towns was to safeguard the flow of traffic, revenue and precious metals throughout the conquered realm. Above all, this meant that local 'predatory' groups, which could deflect these flows, had to be integrated into a system of protection racketeering. In a sense, this was perhaps the most difficult part of the conquest.

The successes achieved in these attempts, however, became conspicuously visible in the coinage and revenue reforms which were implemented from the early thirteenth century onwards. Already Iltutmish introduced a great coinage reform, as part of the restructuring of the Ghurid administration, based on the pure silver tanka of one tola weight. This coin appears to have been first struck in Bengal in 1208-10 AD and was adopted at Delhi in the 1220s.[22] For some time, agricultural revenue continued to be collected in the pre-conquest *Dihlīwalas* but these were gradually withdrawn from circulation around Delhi about 1210, and the old Dihlīwāla had disappeared a decade or so after Iltutmish's death. Iltutmish did not yet convert to a heavy pure silver coin; his various billon and copper coinages abound. But in the later thirteenth century enough treasure was obtained to maintain a precious metal circulating coinage. From the time of Nāsir ad-Dīn (acc. 1246) silver coinage began to increase, although the average annual output of silver money remained much less than that of billon and copper. From Balban onwards the annual silver currency output surpassed the billon and copper minting.[23] Under

---

[19] *TFS*, p. 120; Raychaudhuri and Habib, *Cambridge Economic History of India*, I, p. 85.
[20] *TFS*, pp. 113, 120, 164, 298, 353; Prasad, *Sanskrit Inscriptions*, p. 48.
[21] *TFS*, pp. 56-59.
[22] Deyell, *Living without Silver*, pp. 212-9; and see above, p. 208.
[23] Moosvi, 'Numismatic Evidence', p. 214.

'Alā' ad-Din Khalajī, coinage again increased in all metals, including gold, due to the influx of treasure from the Deccan.

The list of garrison towns, with subordinate iqtā's, in the thirteenth-century Delhi Sultanate includes twenty to thirty names.[24] As the following analysis will show, the importance of these towns varied in political terms, and they varied greatly in size.

DELHI

Delhi or Ar.-Persian *Dihlī* was a city in a category by itself, as it was the capital or '*dār al-mulk*' of *Hindūstān*.[25] It was referred to as the capital of 'the whole kingdom of Hindūstān' (*hama mulk-i-hindūstān*) or 'the domains of Hindūstān' (*mamālik-i-hindūstān*) or 'the parts and tracts of the country of Hindūstān' (*aknāf-o-atrāf-i-mamlikat-i-hindūstān*), and so forth, but also as the capital of 'the entire kingdom of Hind' (*hama mulk-i-hind*).[26] *Hindūstān*, as distinct from *Hind*, was sometimes an appellation reserved for the regions of Delhi and Awadh, in short for the provinces immediately east of the Panjab.[27] In some texts, the '*mamālik-i-hindūstān*' are said to be divided in four parts: the '*mamlakat-i-sind*', the '*mamlakat-i-dihlī*', the '*mamlakat-i-lakhnautī*', and the '*mamlakat-i-lohor*'.[28] But of these four parts, Delhi achieved pre-eminence in Iltutmish's reign.

The name *Dihlī* derived from *Dhillī* or *Dhilī* (we also find *Dhillikā*, the Sanskritized form of the vernacular *Dhillī*), the name of 'the old town which was constructed by the idol-worshipers' ('*dihlī wa hiya-l-qadīma min banā'-l-kuffār*'),[29] also known as Yoginīpura or 'fairy town' in Jain texts (which refer to it as a place of pilgrim-

---

[24] This list is not complete. There were some small iqtā's which are mentioned no more than once or twice and which could not be located on the map: *Kashmandī* and *Mand Mandīyāna* (*TNR*, p. 549; defective in almost all copies; *TN*, p. 260); *Nārnūl* (*TN*, p. 237); *Janjāna* (*TN*, p. 260); *Barīhūn* and *Darangawān* (*TN*, p. 250); *Barhamūn* (*TN*, p. 268). It is also impossible to locate the iqtā's of the Doab that were revoked by Balban, as mentioned by Barani: '2000 horsemen of the army of Shams ad-Dīn [Iltutmish]' had received villages in the Doab as iqtā's; but after 30 or 40 years and more these assignees did not perform service anymore, and their sons took them by inheritance (*TFS*, pp. 61-62).

[25] *TN*, p. 166.

[26] *TN*, pp. 37, 142, 166; *FS*, vs. 2353, 2357.

[27] *TN*, p. 220; Wahid Mirza, *Amir Khusrau*, p. 7.

[28] E.g. *TN*, p. 142.

[29] Defrémery and Sanguinetti, *Ibn Batoutah*, III, p. 145.

age),[30] and Indraprastha.[31] It is often mentioned in conjunction with Tilpat, which was a village to the south of Delhi, in the thirteenth century the place where troops marching out of Delhi usually assembled.

The Muslims conquered Delhi in 1188 or 1191.[32] But in Aybak's time, Lahore is still described as the '*markaz-i-Islām-i-Hind*', 'the centre of Islam in Hind'.[33] And Aybak sat 'on the throne of Lahore and Ghazna'.[34] When, after Aybak's death, Iltutmish moved from Badā'ūn to Delhi, it was because 'of all parts of Hind' it was the place which appealed to him most.[35] Here he ascended the throne in 1211. And, although Iltutmish still sought to be recognized by Yaldiz from Lahore and Ghazna,[36] it was at this time that Delhi not only became the '*dār al-mulk-i-hindūstān*', 'the capital of Hindūstān', but also that the honorific prefix '*hazrat*' was added to its name.[37] It became 'the centre of the circle of Islam' (*markaz-i-dā'irat-i-Islām*) when it started filling up with immigrants from various parts of the Islamic world.[38] Nāsir ad-Dīn was the first king to be born in Delhi and continued to maintain it as a capital—which he often left, during numerous expeditions (especially against the Mongols), for a moving camp or a camp near Delhi.[39]

Situated in a transitional zone between the arid regions of Rajasthan and the more humid regions to its east, Delhi strikingly exemplifies the new type of city of this period in which frontier and agriculture came together. Through a large part of the thirteenth century, Delhi remained exposed to predatory incursions from the marches which began in its immediate vicinity. As late as the beginning of Balban's reign the Mewatis or *Mīwān* 'used to come prowling into the city ... and plundered the country houses in its neighbourhood'.[40] 'The daring of the *Mīwān* in the neigh-

---

[30] *FS*, vs. 2051 ff refers to Delhi in the early thirteenth century (when Iltutmish had himself installed there) as 'one of the *parganāt-i-dyār* ... in which lived devotees ('*ubbād*)'.

[31] *Epigraphia Indica, Arabic and Persian Supplement, 1913-14*, pp. 37-38; Prasad, *Sanskrit Inscriptions*, pp. xxi, 6.

[32] *TFM*, p. 2; Defrémery and Sanguinetti, *Ibn Batoutah*, III, p. 145.

[33] *TFM*, p. 30.

[34] Cf. pp. 150-1; *FS*, vs. 1947-96; *TN*, p. 140; *TF*, p. 63; *TMS*, p. 15.

[35] *FS*, vs. 2055 ff.

[36] *TN*, p. 170.

[37] Cf. *TN*, p. 166.

[38] *TN*, p. 166; *FS*, vs. 2179-87.

[39] *TN*, pp. 201, 222, 225.

[40] *TFS*, p. 55.

bourhood of Delhi was carried to such an extent that the western gates of the city were shut at afternoon prayer ..'.[41] These
Mewatis lived in the large and dense jungles in the Delhi area
where they cut off the roads and took to robbery.[42] At that time,
it was said, no-one had interfered with them since Iltutmish, and
Balban needed a whole year to put an end to their predations.[43]
He kept them in check by placing several garrisons of Afghans in
the area.[44]

With the city thus protected by Afghan garrisons, Delhi quickly gained further in size and magnificence. As we have seen,
princes from the Mongol-occupied territories were assigned their
own palaces and had special *muhallas* named after them.[45] The
mamluks and other amirs of the household followed their examples so that Delhi became a city full of palaces.[46] Sultan Mu'izz
ad-Dīn ceased to reside in the red fort of the city and left for
Kīlokharī, a locality in the neighbourhood which acquired the
name of 'Shahr-i-Nau' or New City, in which another magnificent
palace and park were laid out.[47] A Sanskrit inscription of Balban's
time says: 'Under this king (Hamīra-Gayāsadīn) and lord of many
a hundred of great towns, prospers the heart-ravishing great town
of the name of Dhillī—a deadly arrow to his foes. Like the earth,
she is a receptacle of sundry jewels; like heaven, full of joy; like
the town of the lower worlds, an abode of Demons [-] and like
illusion, full of fascination'.[48] Amir Khusrau says of Delhi that 'its
lofty palaces raise their heads to the skies and overshadow the sun
itself, while its streets are so thronged with men that the eye roving on them is filled with images that leave no place, even for the
pupil of the eye'.[49] Less than half a century later Ibn Battuta wrote
of Delhi as 'the greatest city of *al-Hind*, and even of all the Islamic lands in the East'.[50]

---

[41] *TFS*, p. 55.
[42] *Ibid.*
[43] *Ibid.*, p. 57.
[44] See also *FS*, vs. 3110-23.
[45] Cf. pp. 191-2.
[46] *TF*, p. 75.
[47] *FS*, vs. 3806; *TFS*, p. 130.
[48] *Epigraphia Indica, Arabic and Persian Supplement, 1913-14*, vs. 12 (pp. 41, 44).
[49] Wahid Mirza, *Amir Khusrau*, p. 51.
[50] Defrémery and Sanguinetti, *Ibn Batoutah*, III, p. 145.

BADĀ'ŪN

The *Tāj al-Ma'āthir* refers to Badā'ūn as 'one of the mothers of cities, and one of the most important of the country of Hind'.[51] Little is known for certain about the town before the advent of the Muslims towards the end of the twelfth century. Beyond question, however, Badā'ūn can be identified with the pre-Islamic city of the Sanskrit name *Vodamayutā*, which is described as 'the ornament of the land of Pāñcāla' and praised copiously.[52] A local tradition has it that Badā'ūn owes its origin to an Ahar prince Buddh who founded the city in the tenth century.[53] At the time of the Muslim conquest it was held by the Rathor Lakhanapāla [Lakshmanapāla], the eleventh successor of Chandra, the founder of the dynasty, a branch of the Rashtrakutas.[54] While tradition ascribes its fall in 1030 AD to Mas'ūd Sālār, the alleged nephew of Mahmūd of Ghazna, Badā'ūn was in fact conquered around 1197 AD by Aybak, and again occupied in 1203-4 AD, after which it was held continuously by the Muslims.[55]

In the thirteenth century, and especially in the first half of it, the *iqṭā'* of Badā'ūn was among the most important assignments of governors, and as such it is frequently mentioned in the chronicles, from the Mu'izzi Sultans onwards. Troops could move from Badā'ūn to Delhi in a week.[56] Under Balban, the governor of Badā'ūn maintained 4000 horsemen.[57] We can trace in the historical record three instances, all of the earlier half of the thirteenth century, in which troops from Badā'ūn were deployed in the service of the Delhi Sultan, or supported a rebellion of its governor.[58] The *iqṭā'* appears to have had a sizable establishment of administrative staff (including spies, the *barīd-i-badā'ūn*, at least under Balban), a slave market, and a fort which was used for prison—Yaldiz died here in 1230.[59] Both Iltutmish and Rukun ad-

---

[51] *TM*, ff. 54a-b.

[52] Prasad, *Sanskrit Inscriptions*, p. 87, note 106; *Epigraphia Indica*, I, p. 61.

[53] M. A. Ahmad, *Political History & Institutions of the Early Turkish Empire of Delhi, 1206-1290* (Lahore, 1972), p. 143, note 3.

[54] Ahmad, *Political History*, ibid.; *Epigraphia Indica*, I, pp. 63-64.

[55] Cf. *TF*, pp. 59, 62.

[56] *FS*, vs 2050.

[57] *TF*, p. 76; *TFS*, p. 40.

[58] *TN*, p. 182; *TF*, p. 67.

[59] Cf. *TN*, pp. 147, 170, 181, 198, 212, 215, 254-6, 258, 260, 271, 302; *TF*, pp. 67, 69, 70, 72, 76; *TMS*, p. 17; *TFS*, p. 40.

Dīn came to the throne of Delhi while they were governors or *iqṭāʿ*-holders of Badāʾūn.[60] Especially Iltutmish was closely associated with Badāʾūn in the early part of his career, and at least two of his inscriptions are found here.[61] Badāʾūn was one of the earliest centres of Muslim culture in North India. Hundreds of Muslim martyrs lie buried there. Some of the earliest Muslim architecture in the area dates back to its first governors. Iltutmish built the Shamsī ʿIdgāh during his governorship at Badāʾūn, a massive brick wall 100 meters in length with ornamental lines at the top.[62] Another building that adorns the city is the Jāmiʿ Masjid Shamsī built by Rukun ad-Dīn, one of the largest buildings in India, dated 1223.[63] Of the same period are the dargah of Miranjī, which has an Arabic inscription of Iltutmish; the masjid of Ahmad Khandān, built by Rukun ad-Dīn; the house of Būndīwāllā in Muhalla Sotah with an Arabic inscription of Iltutmish; the Saltani Dargah with an inscription of Nāsir ad-Dīn Mahmūd (1229); the tomb of Alham Shahīd with an Arabic inscription of Iltutmish; and the masjid of Dādā Hamīd built by Nasir ad-Din Mahmud in 648/1250.[64] The city had its own mint under Nāsir ad-Dīn.[65]

In the thirteenth century, Badāʾūn as an *iqṭāʿ* was identified either by itself,[66] or as 'the city (*shahr*) of Badāʿūn with dependencies',[67] or, as in the later Firishta, as the '*pargana*' badāʾūn',[68] the '*ṣūba*' *badāʾūn*', or the '*wilāyat-i-badāʾūn*'.[69] It is virtually certain that in this *iqṭāʿ* of Badāʾun were included the *mawās* or 'rebellious' march area of Katahr, east of the Ramganga, and what later became the Mughal districts of Sambhal and Badaʾun, the entire region between the Himalayas and the Ganges which became known as Rohilkhand from about 1740 onwards, when groups of Indo-Afghans known as Rohilas or Rohillas made their main settlement in India in the area thus denoted. In the reign

[60] *TN*, pp. 141-2, 169-170; *TMS*, p. 16.
[61] Desai, 'Inscriptions of Mamluk Sultans', p. 14.
[62] A. Fuhrer, *The Monumental Antiquities and Inscriptions in the North-western Provinces and Oudh* (Allahabad, 1891), p. 20.
[63] *Ibid.*
[64] *Ibid.*, pp. 21-22.
[65] *TNR*, p. 690, n. 8; Nelson Wright, *Coinage and Metrology*, p. 79, silver tanka no. 225.
[66] E.g. *TN*, p. 147, 169, 174, 247, 247, 254-6, 181; *TFS*, p. 40.
[67] *TN*, p. 271.
[68] *TF*, pp. 67, 70.
[69] *TF*, pp. 67, 72, 76.

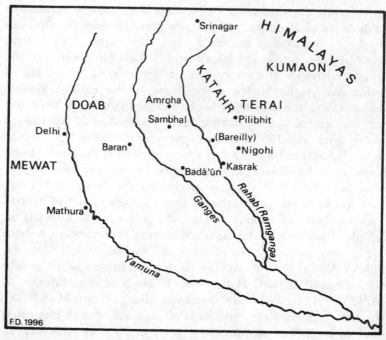

Map 4. Iqtā' of Badā'ūn

of Akbar the Sarkār of Badā'ūn formed part of the Ṣūba of Delhi. The importance of Badā'ūn decreased and Bareilly became
the regional capital under Shah Jahan, while Aurangzeb included the district of Sambhal (Western Rohilkhand of later times) in
the territory ruled by the governor of Katahr. Firishta, still, speaks
of 'Badā'ūn and Katāhr' as the site of an insurrection early in Balban's reign, and in the same context refers to 'Badā'ūn, Amroha
and Sambhal'.[70] Barani, writing in the fourteenth century about
the same events, speaks of disturbances breaking out in 'Katahr
... and the wilāyat of Badā'ūn and Amroha', but indicates that at
that time Badā'ūn and Amroha made up *two* iqtā's.[71] And another garrison appears to have been stationed at Kasrak, a place close
to Badā'ūn, now a village in pargana Miranpur Katra in the Tilhar

---

[70] *TF*, p. 77.
[71] *Ibid.*

tahsil of Shahjahanpur district.[72] The latter town is also mentioned together with Nigohi, in an inscription of 1282 AD, while on its own it occurs in Juzjani, who says of a slave officer of Iltutmish that 'Kasrak with the office of Chief Justiciary' was given to him in iqtā'.[73] Nigohi, as mentioned in the inscription, is a pargana in the northeast of Tilhar tahsil in the same district, and thus in Katahr, but it was probably an administrative centre under the Sultan's government.[74]

From the early thirteenth century onwards, Badā'ūn thus held its position as principal Muslim garrison town, among several others, in an area which included Katahr, the site of recurrent uprisings of what are called the *Katahrīya mawāsāt* ('brigands of Katahr'). While two major disturbances are recorded around the middle of the thirteenth century, the last Katahriya outbreak is said to have taken place in 1555-6. The area was always turbulent. After Balban's campaign (soon after 1266), writes Barani, 'the wilāyat of Badā'ūn and Amroha and Sambhal and Kanwarī was safe from the violence and turbulence (*sharr-o-fasād*) of the people of Kātahr'.[75] Balban 'sent forth 5000 archers, and gave them orders to burn down Katahr and to destroy it, to slay every man, and to spare only women and children .... The whole district was ravaged and so much plunder was obtained that the royal army was enriched, and even the people of Badā'ūn were satisfied ..'.[76]

The origin and meaning of the name *Katahr* is disputed. It is connected with the name of the dominant Katahrīya Rajput clan of the area, and traditions current in Bada'un derive this from Kathiawar, allegedly the original home of the clan.[77] Other traditions point at the coming of the Katahriyas to this area, from Benares or Tirhut, in the twelfth and fourteenth centuries.[78] The Katahriyas are said to have first occupied the country between the Rāmgangā and the Ganges and to have spread east of the former river afterwards, ousting the Bachhil rajas in about 1174 AD.[79] The

[72] Prasad, *Sanskrit Inscriptions*, pp. 81-82.
[73] Raverty in *TNR*, p. 791, n. 1 is unable to find this place; see also Prasad, *Sanskrit Inscriptions*, p. 81.
[74] *Ibid.*
[75] *TFS*, p. 58. See also *TN*, p. 218 for Nāsir's campaign in 1254.
[76] *TFS*, p. 58.
[77] *Imperial Gazetteer of India*, new ed., Vol. XXI (Oxford, 1908), p. 305.
[78] *Ibid.*
[79] *Gazetteer of Oudh*, I , p. 241.

Bachhils thus may have retired before the Katahriyas until they had lost all their land to the west of the Deoha or Pilibhit river. Here they held on to some territory between the Deoha river and the forests of Pilibhit, while frequently confronted by the Muslim powers, but also remaining involved in the management of the iqtāʿ as moneyed magnates who, in repayment of debts, held villages in mortgage.[80] Most likely, however, the name of *Katahr* is derived from the type of soil that predominated in this area, called *Kathar* or *Katahr*, a soft well-areated loam highly suitable for cultivation, quite unlike the moist *Terai* jungles along the Himalayan foothills.[81] The reason that this area of Katahr was so important in the context of the emerging Delhi Sultanate was that it offered excellent pasture land along the strips of swampy soil (khādar) and loose sand (bhūr) which ran parallel to the numerous rivers. On the alluvial pastures along the rivers from the northern hills grew the nutritious *dūb* grass which could be stored during the dry season.[82] *Dūb* grass could grow for over eight months, from the beginning of the monsoon until the spring.[83] In addition, the chaff of other winter crops produced in the area, such as gram (*ʿanā*), lentils (*masūr*) and grains like wheat and barley served as additional sources of fodder.[84] It is probably a safe conclusion that in the thirteenth century these grazing lands were highly valued and that the horse breeding in the region which we know best from Rohilla times was already prevalent in what was, back then, the *iqtāʿ of Badāʾūn*.

BARAN

Baran was another town which was subjected to Muslim rule at the very beginning of the thirteenth century, having been taken by Aybak. Its present name, *Bulandshahr* (headquarters of the district with the same name in U.P.), is locally believed to be a Persianized version of *Unchānagar*—elevated city—on account of its elevated position on the right bank of the Kālī Nadī river.[85] Tra-

---

[80] Cf. *TFS*, p. 107; Prasad, *Sanskrit Inscriptions*, pp. 82-84.
[81] Cf. Gommans, *Rise of the Indo-Afghan Empire*, pp. 113-5.
[82] *Ibid.*, p. 93.
[83] *Ibid.*, p. 94.
[84] *Ibid.*, p. 94.
[85] Desai, 'Inscriptions of the Mamluk Sultans of Delhi', pp. 1-3.

dition associates a mosque in the Kot Muhalla of the city with the name of Shihāb ad-Dīn Ghūrī.[86] But there is no epigraph of the Ghurid ruler on the mosque. It does contain, however, a fragmentary tablet with an epigraph of Raziyya, consisting of a single line, recording part of the titles of the queen and part of the date. And there is a second fragmentary inscription which can probably be assigned to the early part of Iltutmish's reign.[87]

Close to Delhi, Baran was, to all appearances, one of the very important *iqtāʿs*, sometimes assigned to amirs who would immediately afterwards be appointed to Badāʾūn. In Aybak's reign it was assigned to Iltutmish.[88] We can trace various governors—almost all Turkish slaves—of 'the iqtāʿ of the qasba of Baran and its dependencies' or 'the wilāyat of Baran' from Aybak's to Nāsir's reign and then again in Kaiqubād's reign.[89]

KAHRĀM

Kahrām is about 110 km from Delhi. Aybak, when still a slave, in 1192 received the *iqtāʿ-i-kahrām* from Muʿizz ad-Dīn Muhammad Ghūrī as his first assignment. The latter, we read, placed him in 'the fortress of kahrām' (*hisār-i-kahrām*) with 'a strong detachment of troops' (*ʿasākir-i-qāhir*), while himself returning to Ghazna.[90] The *Futūh as-Salātīn* says that 'His Majesty [Muʿizz ad-Dīn] posted him at Kahram whence an assault could be made upon every district,'[91] and that Aybak brought the iqtāʿ 'under his control'.[92] We can trace this iqtāʿ further into Iltutmish's reign,[93] and we know that it was combined with *Sāmāna* in one iqtāʿ under Masʿūd Shāh,[94] and with *Khatayl* under Nāsir ad-Dīn.[95]

---

[86] *Ibid.* On the architectural remains of Baran see also Fuhrer, *Monumental Antiquities*, pp. 4-5; H. R. Nevill, *District Gazetteers of the United Provinces of Agra and Oudh, Vol. V, Bulandshahr* (Lucknow, 1922), pp. 203-10; *Annual Report on Indian Epigraphy II (1962-3)*, pp. 250-63.
[87] Desai, 'Inscriptions of the Mamluk Sultans of Delhi', pp. 15-16.
[88] *TN*, p. 248.
[89] *TN*, pp. 169, 237, 251, 256, 259, 260, 268, 276; *TFS*, p. 134.
[90] *TN*, pp. 139-40; *TMS*, p. 10.
[91] *FS*, vs. 1604.
[92] *Ibid.*, vs. 1600-25.
[93] *TN*, p. 232.
[94] *TN*, pp. 259, 307.
[95] *TF*, p. 72.

KOL, BAYĀNA, BALĀRĀM AND GWALIOR

These four towns, with their dependencies, constituted an *iqṭāʿ* which we do not hear of as a single assignment until 1259. Until that time or somewhat earlier, Kol, Bayana, Balārām [?], and Gwalior were separate *iqṭāʿs*.

The conquest of *Kol* [modern Aligarh] in or before 1193 had opened the gates of the Upper Gangetic Valley and hence the entire East to the Turks. *Kol* was first assigned in *iqṭāʿ* to a Turkish mamlūk, Hisham ad-Din Aghulbak, by the Ghurid Sultan. The extent of this iqṭāʿ is, however, unclear. Under Iltutmish the *iyālat* or 'governorship' of Kol became the *iqṭāʿ* of the chief minister Nizam al-Mulk Junaidī.[96] It appears that from this time, until at least Masʿūd Shah's reign, Kol was often assigned to the chief ministers of the Delhi Sultanate.[97]

Bayāna, with the fortress of *Thangīr*, after it was taken, was assigned to Malik Bahāʾ ad-Dīn Tughril al-Muʿizzī, a high-ranking former slave of Muhammad Ghuri. Juzjani writes that 'this territory and adjacent parts were, in the beginning of Islamic rule (*dar auwal-i-ʿahd-i-islām*) made flourishing and cultivated by him'.[98] The same author elaborates: 'He made this part flourishing and prosperous (*maʿmūr*). From different parts of Hindūstān and Khurāsān merchants and men of repute (*tujjār-o-muʿārif*) joined him [there]. He gave them houses and goods which became their property so that they would reside near him. In *Bayāna* he founded the town of *Salṭānkot* (*shahr-i-salṭānkot*), where he took up residence and from where he continually sent horsemen to Gwālīyūr'.[99] In the Bayāna area, Bahāʾ ad-Dīn erected a number of monuments—which possibly include the Caurāsī Kambhā mosque at Kāmān (near Bharatpur), the mosque of Ukha Mandir (identified with the Jāmiʿ Masjid at Sultankot, built in 1204) and the ʿīdgāh in Bayāna—which resemble the Qutb mosque in Delhi in size and grandeur and also rely on disassembled temple materials, while displaying trabeate arches and rectangular courtyards flanked with colonnade bays and aisles.[100] An inscription of 1206

---

[96] Desai, 'Inscriptions of the Mamluk Sultans of Delhi', pp. 4-18.
[97] *TN*, pp. 198, 273.
[98] *TN*, p. 265.
[99] *TN*, pp. 144-6.
[100] M. and N. H. Shokoohy, 'The Architecture of Baha al-Din Tughrul in the

or thereafter, from the Caurasi mosque at Kaman, refers to Bahā' ad-Din Tughril as 'Salṭān'.[101] His family's political control over Bayāna continued until the 1250's, even though in the final years of Iltutmish's reign, two years after the fortress of Gwālīor was taken, the *iqṭāʿ of Bayāna* (Bhayān) and Sultānkot, together with the *shahnagī* (military command) of the *wilāyat-i-G[w]ālīyūr* was assigned to another Muʿizzī slave, Malik Nusrat ad-Dīn Tā-yasī.[102] Juzjani writes that Iltutmish conferred a daughter of Bahā' ad-Dīn Tughril on one of his slaves, Malik Tāj ad-Dīn Arsālān Khān Sanjar Khwārazmī, and that 'by this connection, in the reign of Nāsir ad-Dīn, Bayāna was made Arsālān Khān's *iqṭāʿ*'.[103] There are many discrepancies among various authors regarding the conquest of Gwalior. Ultimately the fortress was given up to Aybak, who contended for it with Tughril. According to Firishta, Muhammad Ghuri had assured Tughril that if he conquered the place he would receive its government.[104] But its raja, distressed by the lack of supplies, after a year surrendered it to Aybak.[105] Thus Aybak's seizure of Gwalior in 1200 thwarted Tughril's rise to further power in Bayāna. Aybak, in his turn, made Iltutmish the first 'Amīr of Gwālīyūr'.[106]

Gwalior's importance was that it stood at the gate into northern Rajasthan and Bundelkhand. After Aybak's death, the fortress was soon recovered by the Hindus, to be taken again by Iltutmish in 1227. When, two years later, Malik Nusrat ad-Dīn Tā-yasī received the *iqṭāʿ* of Bayāna and Sultankot together with the Gwalior command, the armies of Kanauj (for which see below) and Mahir and Mahāūn were also placed under his control in order that he might make inroads into Kālanjar and Jandīr.[107] In Raziyya's and Masʿūd Shāh's reigns, Bayāna was given out as *iqṭāʿ* twice to Malik Ikhtyār ad-Dīn Qarāqīsh Khān.[108] In Nāsir's reign,

---

region of Bayana, Rajasthan', *Muqarnas*, 4 (1987), pp. 114-32; Kumar, *Emergence of the Delhi Sultanate*, pp. 56-57; M. W. Meister, 'Indian Islam's lotus throne: Kaman and Khatu Kalan', in: A. L. Dallapiccola and S. Zingel-Avé Lallemant (eds), *Islam and Indian regions* (Stuttgart, 1993), pp. 445-6.

[101] Shokoohy, 'Baha al-Din Tughrul', p. 115.
[102] *TN*, p. 239; Kumar, *Emergence of the Delhi Sultanate*, p. 64.
[103] *TN*, p. 265.
[104] *TF*, p. 64.
[105] *Ibid.*; and see *TN*, pp. 144-6; *TNR*, p. 545, notes 5 & 7.
[106] *TN*, p. 169.
[107] *TN*, p. 239.
[108] *TN*, p. 250.

Malik Nusrat Khān Badr ad-Din Sunqar-i-Sūfī Rūmī held Bayāna in iqṭāʿ and 'stayed there for some time and punished the seditious'.[109] By 1259, Kol and Bayāna and Balārām—the latter is still mentioned as a separate iqṭāʿ under Raziyya[110]—and Jalīsar, Mahir, Mahīwar, and the fortress of Gwalior were joined into one governorship or iqṭāʿ.[111] From here Ranthanbhūr was attacked. Balban, in his early reign, assigned 'Kol and some districts dependent on it' (kol-o-chand-wilāyat-i-hawālī' kol) in iqṭāʿ to his eldest son.[112]

KANAUJ

Kanauj, the Hindu capital of Madhyadesha, separated from Delhi by a distance of a ten-day march, was first sacked by Mahmūd of Ghazna in 1018-9 and then taken by Muhammad Ghūrī in 1198-9.[113] We do not hear of Kanauj as an iqṭāʿ until Raziyya's reign, although it probably existed as such much earlier.[114] Masʿūd Shāh assigned it to one of his uncles 'who carried on holy war (ghazwāt) and attended to the prosperity of the peasants ('umārat-i-raʿīyat)'.[115] In Nāsir's reign, the king's brother held the iqṭāʿ of Kanauj.[116] Under Kaiqubād there was a 'garrison of Kanauj' (lashkar-i-qanauj) commanded by its governor.[117]

HĀNSĪ

The Ghaznavid sultan Masʿūd had first reduced Hānsī, the ancient capital of Siwālikh, in 1036, and appointed an officer to it. It was reconquered from Maudūd's governor by a coalition of Indian rulers, together with Thanesar, Nagarkot and other places, in 1043-4, when Lahore was also besieged for seven months.[118]

---

[109] TN, p. 274.

[110] TN, p. 265.

[111] TN, pp. 226, 278, 312-313; TF, p. 73.

[112] TFS, p. 66; see also 'Inscription of Sultan Balban from Bayana, Bharatpur State', Epigraphia Indo-Moslemica (Calcutta, 1937-38), pp. 5-6.

[113] On the revival of the city after 1018-9, see Al-Hind, I, p. 286; for the distance from Delhi, Defrémery and Sanguinetti, Ibn Batoutah, III, p. 144.

[114] TN, p. 247.

[115] TN, pp. 199, 262; TF, p. 70.

[116] TN, p. 212; TF, p. 72.

[117] TMS, p. 57.

[118] KT, IX, pp. 354-5; TF, p. 44; Bosworth, Later Ghaznavids, pp. 32-33.

In 1192 Hānsī surrendered to Muhammad Ghūrī.[119] It was assigned, soon afterwards, as an *iqṭāʿ*, in combination with *Jīnd* and *Barwāna* [Barwāla].[120] Several inscriptions of Íltutmish's reign exist in Hānsī, including one on the Johāhon-ki-Masjid, and we know that the *khiṭṭaʾ hānsī* was the first *iqṭāʿ* of Iltutmish's eldest son, who appears to have held it up to 1226.[121] After that date it changed hands at regular intervals as the *iqṭāʿ of Hānsī* under Rukun ad-Dīn Fīrūz Shāh and Masʿūd Shāh.[122] Under Bahrām Shāh the *parganaʾ hānsī-o-rawārī* became the *iqṭāʿ* of Balban, from which position he undertook actions against the Mewatis (*kuffār-i-miwāt*).[123] Balban, Juzjani writes, greatly improved the *iqṭāʿ-i-hānsī*, increasing its prosperity.[124] With its dependencies, it came to be known as 'the territory of Siwālik and Hānsī'.[125] The town itself by the mid-thirteenth century is already described in inscriptions on saints' tombs as 'the cynosure of piety and learning'.[126] Ibn Battuta, arriving at the *madīna hānsī* from Ṣarsatti, writes that it is 'among the most beautiful cities, the best constructed and the most populated; it is surrounded with a strong wall, and its founder is said to be one of the great infidel kings, called Tara'.[127]

NĀGAUR

Towards the southwest of Hānsī, beginning in the southern Siwā-likh, we find in the thirteenth century another cluster of *iqṭāʿs*, running into Rajasthan, with Nāgaur as their main garrison town. The military and political subjugation of parts of Rajas-than by the Muslims is attested in inscriptions which date from Iltutmish's to Balban's time and are found at Bari Khatu (or Khatu Kalan) in the Jael tahsil of the Nagaur district. Here the most outstanding mosque is the Masjid-i-Aqsāʾ, located on the hill, and attributed to Iltutmish on account of its architectural

---

[119] Cf. p. 145.
[120] *TN*, p. 239.
[121] *Epigraphia Indica, Arabic and Persian Supplement, 1913-14*, pp. 14-16; *TN*, p. 180.
[122] *TN*, pp. 182, 199.
[123] *TF*, p. 74; *TN*, p. 285.
[124] *TN*, pp. 217, 285, 298.
[125] *TN*, p. 217.
[126] *Epigraphia Indica, Arabic and Persian Supplement, 1913-14*, pp. 14-16, 34-35.
[127] Defrémery and Sanguinetti, *Ibn Batoutah*, III, p. 143.

style which resembles that of the Arhāi-Din-kā Jhonprā mosque at Ajmer.[128]

In 1227, Iltutmish assigned what was then called 'the wilāyat of Siwālik and Ajmer and Lawjah [Lawah] and Kābalih and Sanbhar Namak' to the charge of one of his Turkish slaves.[129] The main garrison town at that time was probably *Sanbhar Namak*, which is on the great salt lake, north of Ajmer. Its commander proceeded to Ajmer and 'undertook expeditions and holy war against infidel Hindus, devastating their country and performing great deeds'.[130] Nāgaur appears to have become the administrative-military centre of this iqṭāʿ by Masʿūd Shāh's reign (1242-6). At that time, we read, 'the country of Nāgaur, Mandor and Ajmer' was made over to ʿIzz ad-Dīn Balban.[131] In another version, Masʿūd Shāh assigned 'the wilāyat of Nāgaur and one elephant' to ʿIzz ad-Dīn Balban.[132] And in yet another it is said that 'Nāgaur and Sind and Ajmer' were put in the charge of ʿIzz ad-Dīn Balban.[133] When, after Nāsir's accession, in 1251, the latter was assigned to Uch and Multan, 'he only relinquished Nāgaur after an army was sent to force him'.[134] Nāgaur was then assigned to Ulugh Khān Balban, the future Sultan who was then still a Malik.[135] It was from here that, repeatedly between 1251 and 1258, Balban led troops to Ranthanbhūr (Ratanpūr, Rantabhūr), Bundī (Bhundi) and Chitor (Chitror).[136] The Raja of Ranthanbhūr at that time is still described as 'the greatest of the kings of Hind'. Ranthanbhūr had already been occupied by Iltutmish, but the fort was attacked by the dispossessed Cauhāns after his death. Raziyya had to send reinforcements to its garrison.[137] Subsequently, the fortifications

---

[128] Desai, 'Inscriptions of the Mamluk Sultans of Delhi', pp. 4-18; M. A. Chaghtai, 'An unpublished inscription of the time of Iltutmish, showing the construction of a reservoir at Khatu (Marwar)', *Proceedings of the All India Oriental Conference, 8th Session, 1935* (Bangalore, 1937), pp. 632-4; idem, 'Muslim inscriptions from Khatu (Marwar)', *Proceedings of the Indian History Congress, 8th Session, 1945* (Allahabad, 1947), pp. 286-8.

[129] *TN*, p. 236.

[130] *TN*, p. 236.

[131] *TN*, p. 198.

[132] *TN*, p. 269.

[133] *TF*, p. 70.

[134] *TN*, pp. 215, 270; *TF*, p. 72.

[135] *TN*, pp. 298-9.

[136] *Ibid.*, p. 299.

[137] Cf. A. B. M. Habibullah, *The Foundation of Muslim Rule in India* (Allahabad, 1961), pp. 127-8.

were dismantled and the garrison withdrawn, providing an opportunity for the Cauhāns to found a successor dynasty in Ranthanbhūr. The Mewatis probably acknowledged this newly revived Cauhān rule, as probably did Bundi—which was founded a few years earlier—and the Kota state. There may have been links here with the Guhilots of Mewar as well. The latter, between 1213 and 1252, also enjoyed considerable power and claim to have defeated the Turushkas. Lawah, Kasili and Sanbhar are in any case no longer mentioned in the *iqṭā's* of the area—as they had been in Iltutmish's time. But Balban put the Cauhāns of Ranthanbhūr to rout. With great booty, and numerous horses and slaves, he returned to Nāgaur, 'which, because of his presence, became a large city'.[138]

Other clans that the Turks came up against in this area were those of the *Bhattīs*. In the twelfth century the Bhattī Rajputs still held a large part of Sind, although not as far as Uch probably, as some later writers state.[139] *Bhaṭṭīya*, or *Bhatiyā*, with its capital Bhatinda (also known as Tabarhind), had been part of their dominion when Mahmūd in the beginning of the eleventh century had penetrated it to gain access to the trans-Gangetic plain.[140] Twelfth-century Sanskrit inscriptions show that the Bhattīs by this time were considered to be of the Yadava (colloquially Jādon) Rajput clan, and of the lunar dynasty, descendants of one Bhattīya or Bhattika—who may have flourished in 623-4 AD, the epoch year of the Bhattika era.[141] There was a close connection between the Bhattīs or Bhātīs of Māda (modern Jaisalmer district) and the Caulukyas of Gujarat in the mid-twelfth century.[142] Epigraphic evidence also reveals that Muhammad Ghūrī marched through Jaisalmer in 1178 AD on his way south and that on this occasion, the Bhatti prince Jaisal enlisted the help of the 'Pātasāha of Gajni' to slay his nephew and seize the throne.[143] But another branch of the Jadon Bhatti Rajputs was established in the 'Kohpāyah of Mewat', in northern Alwar, which they appear to have held

---

[138] *Ibid.*
[139] *TNR*, p. 449; Habibullah, *Foundations*, p. 28.
[140] Cf. p. 123.
[141] A. O'Brien, 'The Bhuttos and the Bhattīs of the Twelfth Century AD', *South Asian Studies*, 4 (1988), pp. 32, 36.
[142] *Ibid.*
[143] *Ibid.*

throughout the thirteenth century, when they continue to be referred to as 'infidels' (they seem not to have converted to Islam until the reign of Fīrūz Shāh Tughluq). Thus, while Ranthanbhūr is frequently mentioned in connection with the operations in Mewat, this probably points at the existence of an alliance of the Bhatti-Mewatis with the Cauhāns and other dynasties in eastern Rajasthan. In 1256 the Mewatis raided Hānsī and carried off cattle which they distributed as far as Ranthanbhūr. If Balban clamped down on the Mewatis, he did not eliminate their power, and the Ranthanbhūr dynasty continued to assert supremacy in Malwa, Amber and 'Kerkaralagiri', Chitor, Mewar, Abu, Ajmer, Sanbhar and elsewhere.[144] The ruler of Mewar is described as having 'lifted the deeply sunk Gujara land high out of the Turushka sea'.[145] In Jaisalmer, the Bhattis effectively prevented the governor of Nāgaur from getting a foothold in that area.[146]

CHANDIRĪ

Sultan Nāsir ad-Dīn marched to Chandirī, in Malwa, in 1250 and 'subdued these countries', appointing 'governors-iqṭāʿdārs' (*umarāy ṣāḥib-i-iqṭāʿdār*).[147] There was still a governor (*iqlīmdār*) of Malwa under Sultan Balban, but there is no further information on Chandirī from this period.[148]

MĪRATH

Aybak conquered the fortress of *Mīrath* (*Mīrāt*) in 1192, starting out from Kahrām. It took one week to bring the surrounding countryside under control.[149] We hear nothing about it until it was assigned as '*the iqṭāʿ of Mīrāt*' to a Shamsi slave in 1255 AD.[150] This *iqṭāʿ* included the town and fortress of Mīrath and dependencies 'up to the skirt (*dāman*) of the Koh-i-Bandīārān [=the

---

[144] *Epigraphia Indica*, XIX, pp. 45-47; *Indian Antiquary* (1879), p. 65.

[145] *Indian Antiquary* (1887), p. 347.

[146] Cf. J. Tod, *Annals and Antiquities of Rajasthan*, 2 vols (New Delhi, 1983), I, p. 247.

[147] *TF*, p. 72.

[148] *TFS*, p. 93.

[149] *FS*, vs. 1622-5; *TMS*, p. 10.

[150] *TN*, pp. 220, 279.

Kumaon mountains]'. After 1255, it took some years to make the whole area 'zabt', i.e. to 'subject' it. Possession was now also taken of the country within the mountain territory (kohistān) of Bandīārān, and Darkī and Mīyāpūr, by 'extorting tribute, overthrowing rāyagān and mawāsāt'.[151] A Jāmiʿ Masjid at Mīrath, assigned by local tradition to a minister of Mahmud of Ghazna, Hasan Mahdī, carries an inscription in Persian which dates it to Sultan Nāsir ad-Dīn, 1249-50.[152]

TABARHIND

Early references to Tabarhind—including a poem in praise of Ibrahīm, the Ghaznavid ruler of the later eleventh century, who appears to have organized an expedition against it—are vague.[153] Very early in the thirteenth century Tabarhind is referred to as a 'preserved city' (mahrasaʾ tabarhinda), with its own slave governor, amir oi shahna, and which was khālisa, i.e. produced revenue for the king himself.[154] By 1240, Tabarhind is referred to as an iqtaʿ.[155] Its governor rebelled against Raziyya—which led to her imprisonment in the fort and a failed attempt to seize the throne.[156] When Masʿūd Shāh ascended the throne, he assigned the iqtāʿ of Tabarhind to a Shamsi slave.[157] Up to 1261 'the preserved city of Tabarhind and Sanām and Jajhar, and Lakhwāl and all the territories up to the Beas river' changed hands several times.[158] This appears to have been the same place as Bhatinda, the capital of Bhatiya.[159]

SĀMĀNA AND SANĀM

Together with Lahore, Multan, Bhakkar, Tabarhind, and Dipalpur, these were among the districts which were exposed to Mongol

[151] TN, p. 279.
[152] Desai, 'Inscriptions of the Mamluk Sultans of Delhi', p. 5.
[153] Bosworth, Later Ghaznavids, p. 65.
[154] TN, pp. 168, 232, 250.
[155] TN, p. 188.
[156] TN, pp. 188, 190, 251.
[157] TN, p. 262.
[158] TN, pp. 218, 266, 271, 274, 277-8.
[159] Cf. p. 144.

incursions.[160] There was a separate '*iqṭāʿ of Sanām*' (also referred to as '*ḥawālī* Sanām') under Iltutmish and Rukun ad-Dīn Fīrūz Shāh.[161] It was, as we have seen, combined with Kahrām under Masʿūd Shāh.[162] In 1261, Sanām was made over to a slave governor in one assignment with Tabarhind, Jajhar, and Lakhwāl and the areas up to the Beas river.[163] Balban, in the fourth year of his reign, assigned Sanām and Sāmāna together to another amir, after which they became the *iqṭāʿ* of his younger son Kurra Khan, entitled Nāsir ad-Dīn, who was enjoined to recruit and discipline an army to watch the movements of the Mongols from there.[164] Balban observed that 'the iqṭāʿ of Sāmāna was an important one' (*kah iqṭāʿ-i-sāmāna iqṭāʿ-i-buzurg ast*), and its garrison of crucial importance, and he sent spies (*barīdān*) to supervise Kurra Khan.[165] In 1279 Sanām and Sāmāna were still the province of Balban's younger son.[166] Its forces were deployed not only against the Mongols, but also in the Doab and Lakhnauti.[167] Sāmāna was still an *iqṭāʿ* under Sultan Kaiqubād.[168] And Jalāl ad-Dīn Khalaji held the position of *nāʾib-i-sāmāna* shortly before he achieved the throne of Delhi.[169]

PALWAL

This was an *iqṭāʿ* which is first mentioned under Iltutmish, and later appears for some time to have become associated with the position of *Amīr-i-Dād* (Justiciary) of Delhi.[170] It can be identified with the iqṭāʿ of 'Palwal and Kāma', in Bharatpur country, on the route from Mathura to Firuzpur.[171]

---

[160] *TF*, p. 78.
[161] *TN*, pp. 234, 237.
[162] Cf. p. 225.
[163] *TN*, p. 274.
[164] *Ibid.*; *TFS*, p. 80.
[165] *TFS*, p. 81.
[166] *TF*, p. 80.
[167] *TFS*, pp. 81, 84-85.
[168] *TMS*, p. 54.
[169] *TFS*, p. 170.
[170] *TN*, pp. 234, 276.
[171] *TN*, p. 276; M. Muhammad Shuaʿib, 'Inscriptions from Palwal', *Epigraphia Indo-Moslemica, 1911-12*, pp. 1-3.

LAHORE

As this was the Muslim capital of the Panjab already in Ghaznavid and Ghurid times, we are bettter informed about Lahore than about any other of the cities and towns which are here described. The origins of Lahore, nonetheless, remain obscure. Tradition attributes the founding of the city or *Lahāwaranā* to Lāvā, the son of Rām. Two of the earliest records, dated to 1043 and between 1210 and 1236, credit Haj or Chach, son of Bhandra, and Parichhit, a descendant of the Pandavas, both of unknown date, with the founding of the city of Lahore.[172] Excavations conducted in Lahore Fort and the haveli of Dhayan Singh in the Saif Mittha Bazaar allow us to extend the history of Lahore City no further back than the sixth century AD.[173] And it is the consensus among historians, supported by some medieval Persian materials, that Lahore had existed several centuries before the conquest of the region by Mahmūd of Ghazna in the early eleventh century. In the anonymous *Ḥudūd al-ʿālam* of 982 AD, Lahore is mentioned as a *shahr* or 'town' inhabited by infidels, with numerous districts, markets, temples, and orchards; it was then a dependency of Multān.[174] Biruni, Gardizi and Baihaqi, in the earlier part of the eleventh century, write about Lahore as the name of a province or district, the capital of which was Mandahukur or Mandakkakor. Lahore appears as the capital of the Panjab for the first time under Ānandapāla, the Hindu Shahi king—who is referred to as the 'ruler of Lahore' (*ḥākim-i-lāhūr*)[175]—, after leaving behind the earlier capital of Waihind.

Under the Ghaznavids, in the eleventh century, while Ghazna remained the permanent capital, Lahore became known as 'Little Ghazna'. Mahmūd, after conquering Lahore in 1014, left it in the hands of viceroys. The name 'Mahmūdpur' appears on silver tankas in 1027 and 1028, and some scholars, like Cunningham, have attempted to show that Mandahukur is a corruption of Mahmudpur and that both can be identified with Lahore.[176] There is

[172] M. A. Khan, *The Walled City of Lahore* (Lahore, 1993), p. 10.

[173] *Ibid.*, p. 9; M. Wali Ullah Khan, *Lahore and its Important Monuments* (Karachi, 1964), pp. 40-41; S. M. Latif, *Lahore: Its History, Architectural Remains and Antiquities* (Lahore, 1892); K. K. Mumtaz, *Architecture in Pakistan* (Singapore, 1985).

[174] Minorsky, *Ḥudūd al-ʿālam*, pp. 89-90, 246-7.

[175] Cf. p. 122.

[176] Khan, *Lahore*, p. 10.

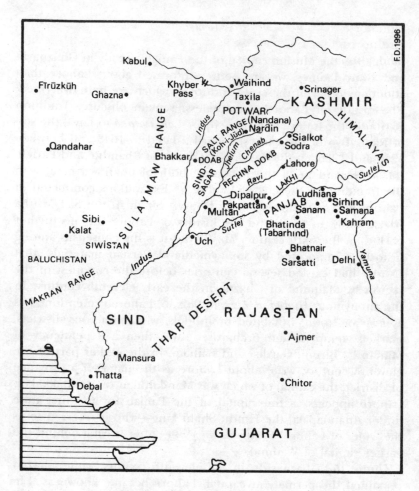

Map 5 Iqṭāʻs of Lahore, Multān and Uch

uncertainty about where exactly Mandahukur was located, except
that it was on the east bank of the Ravi river.[177] Most historians
now think that the city that Mahmūd (or his slave general Malik
Ayyaz) founded was on the site of the present-day Walled City.[178]
The Lahore of the Ghaznavid period was probably confined to
the area lying east-west between the Shah Alami and Bhati gates

---

[177] *Ibid.*
[178] *Ibid.*, p. 11.

and north-south between the two circular roads.[179] Although there
are no contemporary accounts of the city's layout in this period,
and although there are no vestiges of the buildings that were
erected then, we know this because Muslims bury their saints and
rulers outside the inhabited area of the city.[180] A commercial centre also came into existence, probably on the site of the present-
day Lahori Mandi in the Walled City; some scholars attribute the
development of that area already to the vice-regency of Malik
Ayyaz (1036-42 or 1057).[181] Mahmūd of Ghazna built a palace,
probably in the fort, and two mosques in 1022 and 1026—of which
there is not a trace today.[182] All that is left from this period is an
unadorned grave which is believed to be that of the Ghaznavid
slave general Malik Ayyaz in the Rang Mahal area, outside the
eastern limits of Ghaznavid Lahore.

Lahore, gradually emerging as a second Ghaznavid city from
Mahmūd's time onwards, did not become the main capital until
the reigns of the last two Ghaznavid sultans, after they had been
deprived of not only Ghazna, but of most of Iran and Turan in
the second half of the twelfth century, by the Ghurids and Seljuqs.
For most of the Ghaznavid period, therefore, Lahore retained the
status of a provincial capital, in effect serving as a springboard for
raids further to the east. But in this period, between 1014 and
1186, Lahore rose to very considerable prominence. In the later
eleventh century it was already a flourishing town, the residence
of what later became its patron saint.[183] And by the middle of the
twelfth century, al-Idrisi mentions Lahore as one of the important
cities of Hind.

From Lahore attempts were made to bring the entire Panjab
under control. Ghaznavid expansion in the northern Panjab in
the twelfth century had succeeded as far as the mountains, with
the cooperation of the local tribes of the Kokhars (P. *Khokharān*)
who lived at the foot of the hills, around Manglān [Makhīālā],
and who, with Ghaznavid support, aspired to stop paying tribute
and taxes to the Jamun Raja of Sialkot.[184] Sultan Muhammad

[179] *Ibid.*, p. 13.
[180] *Ibid.*
[181] *Ibid.*
[182] *Ibid.*
[183] *Ibid.*, p. 10.
[184] Not to be confused with the Ghakkars (cf. *Al-Hind, I*, pp. 168-9).

Ghuri, in his turn, was incited by the Jamun Raja to invade the Panjab, and, after repairing the fort of Sialkot, with his aid to take Lahore. The Ghurid capture of Lahore was thus also a setback for the Kokhars. But the Kokhars, who 'inhabited the country along the banks of the Nilab, up to the mountains of the Siwa- lik', continued to be a threat, cutting off the roads between Peshawar and Multan, laying waste the country between the Jhelum and Sodra, forcing links with 'other rebels of the hills of Lahore and the Jud hills' and even prepared, perhaps, to take Lahore.[185] The area of Lahore was not fully recovered until the Kokhars were engaged and dispersed simultaneously by Aybak from the east and Muhammad Ghuri from the west.

Even now, the Kokhars continued to make incursions on the Muslims, until finally some of their chiefs fell captive to Muham- mad Ghuri and began to be converted. Firishta writes that 'a great part of these mountain people, having very little notion of reli- gion, was easily persuaded to adopt the tenets of the true faith, while at the same time most of the infidels who inhabited the mountains between Ghazna and the Indus were also converted ..'. [186] In early modern times, the majority of the inhabitants of these areas thoroughly obliterated their pagan past. Many professed to be descendants of Arabs. The Kokhars said that they were descen- dants of the Sasanid king Nushirvan (531-579 AD), or of the pre- decessors of the Sasanids.[187] They also gave out that they had lived in Kashmir for sixteen generations, until the reign of their king Kabul Shah, who took service with Sabuktigin, and that Kokhar Shah, the son of Kabul Shah, came to India with Mahmud of Ghazna, who conferred upon him the dominion of the Sind-Sagar Doab.[188] In the thirteenth century, however, the Kokhars are still often referred to as a hostile tribe. The same people were deployed against Qabacha in 1220. Awfi refers to an expedition by Qabacha against the Kokhar chief in the Salt Range, which probably occurred after the departure of the Khwarazm Shah from Sind to Iran in 1224, whose aides the Kokhars had been.[189]

---

[185] *TN*, pp. 123-4; *TF*, pp. 59-60.
[186] *TF*, p. 60.
[187] Cf. J. G. Delmerick, 'A History of the Gakk'hars', *Journal of the Asiatic Soci- ety of Bengal*, XL, 1 (1871), pp. 67-69.
[188] *Ibid.*, p. 69.
[189] Cf. Siddiqui, *Perso-Arabic Sources*, pp. 27-28.

According to Awfi, Qabacha's statesmanship produced for him the goodwill of the Kokhars, and afterwards 50,000 Kokhar swordsmen turned into the Sultan's servants.[190] But the Kokhars continued to aid the Mongols in invading India. And they were always involved in factional struggles for the Delhi throne.

By 1228, Lahore had become a special 'governorship', the *iyālat-i-lāhūr*, and an *iqtā'* which was defined loosely as 'the province of Lahore, with the whole of the dependencies and districts belonging to that territory' (*lohor bā tamāmat muzāfat-o-atrāf-i-ān mamlakat*), and as such it was often assigned to the sons and grandsons of the rulers.[191] In 1241, its governor evacuated the city when it was invested by the Mongols. The latter sacked the city without meeting much resistance from the remaining inhabitants—largely merchants enjoying immunity from Mongol attack.[192] After the sack of Lahore by the Mongols in 1241 we do not find it mentioned again as a separate *iqtā'* until 1254.[193] With the Mongols departed, the Kokhars and others seized the city, killing numerous people or carrying them off as slaves.[194] Nāsir ad-Dīn again had the Kokhars severely castigated, crossing the Ravi or 'Lahore' river in 1246 and ravaging the Jūd hills and the area around Nandana.[195] Some measure of control was re-established in the Panjab and Multan, but we do not know much about the situation in Lahore at this time.[196] By 1249 we again encounter a 'governor of Multān and Lahore' (*hākim-i-multān-o-lāhūr*), commanding 20,000 chosen horse against the Mongols in Ghazna.[197] This governor, it is specified, was appointed to 'Lahore, Multan, Bha[t]nair, Sirhind, Dīpālpūr, and the other *iqtā's* which were exposed to the incursions of the Mongols'.[198] He not only dealt with the Mongols, but also brought under his control the Jats, Kokhars, Bhattis, Mīnas, Mandāhars, and other similar tribes (*tawā'if*)'.[199] In 1266 the greatly damaged city of Lahore was

---

[190] *Ibid.*, p. 28.
[191] Cf. *TF*, pp. 67-68, 78, 81-82; *TN*, pp. 181, 235-6; *TFS*, pp. 65, 109-10; etc.
[192] *TF*, p. 69; *TN*, p. 195.
[193] *TNR*, p. 684, n. 9.
[194] *TN*, p. 195.
[195] *TN*, pp. 208-10; *TF*, p. 71.
[196] *FS*, vs. 2772-2844; *TN*, p. 290; *TF*, p. 71.
[197] *TF*, p. 72.
[198] *TF*, p. 78.
[199] *TFS*, p. 65.

ordered to be restored, including the fort that had been pulled down by the Mongols.[200] Many of the inhabitants of Lahore, who had been scattered about in the countryside, were now brought back to the city and were re-settled.[201] 'Lahore and the qasbas and villages of Lahore (*lohor-o-qasbāt-o-dihhāy lahor*) which the Mongols had devastated and laid waste were repeopled and restored'.[202]

Changes that occurred in the thirteenth-century *iqtā' of Lahore* appear to have affected the whole of the Panjab. Apart from the restoration of towns and of the city of Lahore itself, and the re-settling of their populations, these changes included a general expansion of agriculture in most areas which were not turned into pasture land by the Mongols. In some of the latter areas, agriculture did not revive until the fifteenth century and later.[203] But elsewhere we observe a vast expansion of the Jat population in conjunction with agricultural settlement.[204] This was affecting an area broadly co-extensive with the British-Indian province of the Panjab, the land of *five rivers* (Indus, Jhelum, Chenab, Ravi, Sutlej) but without the areas which now belong to Haryana and Himachal Pradesh, and extending from the foothills of the Himalayas to where the five rivers join near Multan, near the desert of Rajasthan; in the west it was bordered by the Sulayman mountains, and in the east by the river Yamuna.

Thus delineated, the Panjab as a whole can be divided in two parts of unequal size: the largest, the alluvial plains which run towards and drain into the Indus; and the other, the Potwār plateau, with the site of Taxilā and the fort of Rohtās, bordered in the south and southeast by the Salt Range, in the West by the Indus, and in the North by the foothills of the Himalayas. The plains of the Panjab are vast alluvial plains, at between 400 and 80 meters above sea level.[205] Since the Panjab rivers, when leav-

---

[200] *TF*, p. 77; *TFS*, p. 61.

[201] *TMS*, p. 40.

[202] *TFS*, p. 61.

[203] I. Habib, *The Agrarian System of Mughal India* (Bombay, 1963), p. 17; idem, 'Jatts of Punjāb and Sind', in: H. Singh and N. G. Barrier (eds), *Punjab Past and Present: Essays in Honour of Dr Garda Singh* (Patiala, 1976), p. 97.

[204] Cf. *Al-Hind, I*, p. 163.

[205] See O. H. K. Spate and A. T. A. Learmonth, *India and Pakistan: A General and Regional Geography* (London, 1967), p. 513 ff; Habib, 'Jatts of Punjāb and Sind', pp. 92-93.

ing the Himalayas, flowed in deep channels, often reaching as deep as 30 meters below groundsurface, irrigation was largely confined to the sub-montane plains which were served by tributary streams of the major rivers, and to the banks of the main, seasonably active, abandoned channels of these rivers. The result was that two distinct areas of cultivation developed in the alluvium: one, above the 200 meter level, from the Jhelum to Ludhiana, which included the towns of Sialkot and Lahore; the other, in the southeast, created by the numerous channels of the major rivers as they come together, and containing the cities of Multan, Uch and Pakpattan. These were to constitute the two blocks of cultivated land in the Panjab, and they were connected at several points by the narrow margins of cultivation along the main rivers, while elsewhere they were separated by the Sindsagar Doab desert, the steppes of the Rechna Doab, and the Lakhī jungle.[206] The Lakhī jungle had been created by the Beas-Sutlej river channels in the region of Dīpalpur. It became a horse-breeding and extensive grazing area at an early date. Here, according to Moorcroft, the Bhattis became Muslims and horse-breeders after they had settled in the jungle and wastes during the reign of Mahmud of Ghazna.[207] The Panjabi Jangla horse was bred in the Lakhi jungle, a breed improved by regular injections of Vilayati horses. And in Mughal times, Central-Asian import horses were kept grazing in these wastes before being distributed to the markets of the Panjab, Rohilkhand, Awadh, Benares, and Bihar. Bhatinda was then the great entrepot of the Lakhi jungle.

But the *barr* country between the five rivers, of thinly populated land, with its scanty rainfall, accommodated a type of pastoral nomadism which was based primarily on the herding of goats and camels.[208] These pastoralists of the western Panjab moved across distances of about a hundred or hundred-fifty kilometers, down to the riverain in the hot dry months and back to the *barr* and *thāl* after the rains, never leaving the Panjab plains (unlike the nomads of Baluchistan and Afghanistan).[209] They appear to have been primarily Jat groups that had been moving up from Sind

---

[206] Habib, 'Jatts of Punjāb and Sind', p. 93.
[207] Cf. Gommans, *Rise of the Indo-Afghan Empire*, p. 95, note 77, and pp. 76, 80, 94-95, 83, 109.
[208] Eaton, 'Shrine of Baba Farid', pp. 341-2.
[209] *Ibid.*, p. 342.

into and beyond the Multan area between the seventh and eleventh centuries.[210] It is with the settlement of these groups that the governors of Lahore appear to have been primarily preoccupied. The Jats, between the eleventh and sixteenth centuries, became an essentially peasant population, taking advantage of the extension of cultivation. As we have seen, it was also in the Panjab and adjacent hill-regions that we find evidence of incipient conversion to Islam among the native population, already in the eleventh century. This occurred among the Bhattis, among the hill peoples, and then among the Kokhars in the thirteenth century.[211] And in the Panjab as well, many of the Jats now, in the later thirteenth century, while being turned into peasants, began to convert to Islam on a more extended scale.[212] The vast majority of the Jat and Rajput groups of the Panjab that became Muslim in medieval times claims to have been converted either by Shaykh Farid ad-Din Ganj-i-Shakar (d. 1265 AD), 'Baba Farīd' of Pakpattan (the ancient town of Ajudhan) or by his contemporary Bahā' al-Haqq Zakariya (d. 1263), whose tomb is in the city of Multan.[213] Probably, it was not Baba Farid himself but his shrine which served as the agent of these clans' conversion, giving them access to Islam and making them participants in the Sultanate without being directly subservient to Delhi.[214]

MULTĀN AND UCH

Next to Lahore, the capital of the Panjab and the Potwar plateau, a second administrative division developed in and around Multan, which became the capital of the southern Panjab, including northern Sind and the Sibi territory. In the thirteenth century the provinces of Multan and Uch were often grouped together in one governorship or iqṭāʿ, and the two territories combined were at times referred to as 'Sind', although some authors continued to refer to the entire area as far north as the Salt Range by this name.

---

[210] Al-Hind, I, p. 163.
[211] Cf. pp. 123-4, 238.
[212] Eaton, 'Shrine of Baba Farid', p. 345.
[213] Ibid., p. 345.
[214] Ibid., p. 347.

It was in the area of Multan, the capital of Arab Sind for three centuries, and in the part of the Salt Range nearest Multan, that the Ghaznavids first came up against the *Jats* in 1026-7.[215] The latter also lived along the banks of the Indus between Multan and Mansura, the districts further to the northwest, and in the Sindsagar Doab. In some of the same regions, the Ghaznavids also encountered another indigenous group known as the *Ghakkar*, in 1008-9. And it was here too that were found the *Sūmras*, a tribal group of which we first become aware in the eighth and ninth centuries. The *Sūmras* became the rulers throughout the Multan region after the death of Mahmud of Ghazna and succeeded in retaining a great deal of regional power down to the thirteenth century, when the area became a separate *iqtāʿ*.

The first time we hear of 'the iqtāʿ of Uch and Multān' is still in Muhammad Ghuri's time, just before Qabacha acquired this area under the same title.[216] We have no details about the early development of this iqtāʿ. But Qabacha, we read, 'proceeded ... to Uch, possessed himself of the city of Multān and Sindustān (i.e. Siwistān), and Debal ... brought these under his sway, and subjected the fortresses and qasbas and towns of the territory of Sind, while assuming the chatr and annexing the country up to Tabarhind and Kahrām and Sarsattī'.[217] In another version it is said that 'Qabacha appropriated Sind and Multan, Bhakkar and Sīwīstān, and, subsequently, the territory to the northeast, as far as Sarsattī and Kahrām'.[218] In yet another version, that 'Qabacha took possession of the *iqtāʿ* of Multan and Uch and Bhakkar and Siwīstān'.[219] Losing it briefly to Yaldiz, the same *iqtāʿ* came to be held by Qabacha when he was subject to Iltutmish.[220]

Already then, the area and the city of Multān itself was beginning to be invaded by the Mongols, but this did not prevent its governor from turning Multan into an important cultural centre for the Muslims. The city also became a very significant trading entrepot, situated as it was at the crossroads of the overland and riverine routes that connected India with the lands to the west,

---

215 Cf. *Al-Hind, I*, p. 162.
216 *TN*, p. 142.
217 *TN*, pp. 142-3; and above, p. 153.
218 *TN*, pp. 141-2.
219 *TN*, p. 161.
220 *TN*, p. 143.

Iran and the Arabian sea.[221] Multanis were already prominent in India's long-distance trade—dealing in horses, slaves, and indigo. And in the decades after Qabacha, 'the city and fortress of Multān, with all its qasbas, districts and dependencies', in combination with Uch or sometimes separate from it, remained an important *iqṭā* under a series of governors, 'who caused these territories to flourish'.

The successive governors of Multān were pre-occupied with invading groups of Qarlughs and Mongols. They sometimes broke away from Delhi, in temporary alliances with Mongol commanders, or operating under a Mongol *shaḥna*.[222] Internally, the main pre-occupation of the governors of Multan and Uch appears to have been the pacification and incorporation of the *Sūmras*. Since the eleventh century, these people had ruled, under Muslim overlordship, from several capitals in succession. A number of other tribal groups in the area, such as the Baluchis, Sodhas, Kurejahs, and Sammas, had been paying homage to them. They revolted against Masʿud of Ghazna but were reinstated in Multan, after agreeing to pay an annual tribute. Soon after a kind of Sūmra kingdom was established which was not broken until the invasions of Muhammad Ghuri and his successors. We know that Muhammad Ghuri captured both Uch and Multan in 1175, but the history of the former city is less clear. Some Muslim authors, beginning with Ibn al-Athir, state that Uch was held by the Bhatti Rajputs, but the Bhatti annals do not record their ever having held Uch.[223] It was probably in Sūmra hands as well or part of a wider Sūmra dominion which was still Ismāʿīlī in orientation and propped up by the Fatimids, even though Ismaʿili Multan and Mansura as such had already been destroyed by Mahmud of Ghazna. In origin, the Sūmras were a local Hindu people, some of whom may have been converted already after the Arab conquest— although this probably did not amount to much—and intermarried with the Arab settlers. Their leader was approached, while in Thatta, by the Ismāʿīlī Druze leader Muqtana in 1033. Afterwards, the Sūmras seem to have maintained an Ismāʿīlism of their own, which set them apart from the Turkish Sunnī Islam of the con-

---

[221] Siddiqui, *Perso-Arabic Sources*, p. 4; *TN*, p. 143; *TNR*, pp. 535-6, note 1; and see above, p. 192.

[222] *TN*, pp. 182, 233-5, 237-8, 249-50, 259, 269, 271-3, 277.

[223] *KT*, IX, pp. 77-79; Tod, *Annals*, s. v.

querors, as well as from their Hindu environment.[224] Juzjani
writes, in effect, that Sultan Muhammad Ghuri 'delivered Multan
from the hands of the Qarmatians'. It is quite likely that one of
the Sūmra brothers Khafīf or Unar was in possession of Multan
at that time.[225] When the Sūmras were being defeated at Multan,
Uch and elsewhere, by Muhammad Ghuri, the ruling Sūmra clan
gathered at Debal, which became their temporary capital. But
Muhammad Ghuri, sweeping through Sind, occupied Debal sev-
en years later, and after that date the Sūmra rulers appear to have
lingered somewhere else in Sind until Sūmra rule revived in Thatta.[226]

From 1210 onwards, Qabacha weakened the Sūmras, 'of which
some were Muslim and others infidel', so that 'they retained only
Thatta as their capital and some frontier places and resigned to
agriculture and tending herds'.[227] When the Sūmras gradually
regained power after Qabacha's death, it was within the context
of the emerging Delhi Sultanate. Thus, when Multan and Uch
were taken over by Iltutmish, and Sind was acquired 'as far as the
ocean', the Sūmra ruler at Thatta and Dehal presented himself
at the Shamsi court.[228] After the Khwarazm Shah, fleeing from
Chingiz Khan, was repulsed from Lahore, he rushed to Sind and
occupied Thatta, and the Sūmras were again forced to move on.
Under their next leader Muhammad Tor they retreated into the
desert and arrived at a place by the Indus river where they settled down and which they named 'Muhammad Tor', after their
leader. It was situated in the Drik district which is now called
Chachgām. Here Muhammad Tor saved the remnants of the
Sūmra tribe and their Ismāʿīlī tradition, making a stance against
repeated invasions by the Delhi Sultan's governors and the Mongols.[229] The eldest son of Sultan Balban, Muhammad Khan, when
governor of Multān, is still reported to have marched against the
Sūmras (Sumragān).[230] And what this and the previously pre-

---

[224] A. Hamdani, 'The Fātimid-ʿAbbāsid Conflict in India', *Islamic Culture*, XLI,
3 (July, 1967), p. 187.
[225] Cf. A. Hamdani, *The beginnings of the Ismāʿili Daʿwa in Northern India* (Cairo,
1956), p. 12.
[226] *Ibid.*
[227] *Al-Hind, I*, p. 167; *Taʾrikh-i-Tāhiri: BM, Add. 23,888*, Tab. 1.
[228] *TN*, p. 172.
[229] Cf. Hamdani, *Ismāʿili Daʿwa*, pp. 12-13.
[230] *FS*, vs. 3244-83, 3331-3433.

sented fragmentary evidence probably means is that these groups of indigenous rulers in Sind were gradually forced to submit to the Muslim power located in Multan.

KARA-MANIKPUR

We now turn eastward, to the conquests across the Ganges—a river which had ceased to be an obstacle to Ghurid ambition by the close of the twelfth century, when North Bihar and parts of Awadh were already taken. Kara and Manikpur were the two strongholds, on opposite sides of the river, which commanded its passage. To secure these was a measure of the greatest importance, and subsequently we find that the government of the iqtā' of the area was almost always assigned to princes of the blood or eminent household slaves. The limits of the *iqtā' of Kara-Manikpur*, at least in the beginning, seem to have been those of the previous dominion of the Gharwar chieftain Manik Chand.[231] Later the *iqtā' of Kara* is sometimes mentioned separately from that of *Manikpur*. More commonly, however, throughout the thirteenth century they seem to have been combined.[232] From here, 'many expeditions were undertaken against the infidels'.[233] We know that the garrisons stationed here were deployed as far away as Lakhnauti and Malwa.[234]

Among the first Shaykhs of the Manikpur pargana there are those who are said to have come with Sayyid Salar of Bahraich.[235] Around 1194 AD, Manikpur was definitely one of the earliest, if not the earliest, Muslim settlement of what later became the province of Awadh. After the capture of Kara and Manikpur, Aybak left it in the hands of his Damghanī troops. Although their power subsequently declined they maintained an important presence in Manikpur until the mid-fourteenth century. The part of Manikpur which was formerly occupied by them is now known as Chaukaparpur, the site of which covers an extensive area with numerous ruins of masonry buildings and tombs.

---

[231] *Gazetteer of Oudh*, II, p. 464.
[232] *TN*, pp. 221, 247, 250, 267, 276, 279, 312,; *TF*, p. 73; *TFS*, p. 172.
[233] *TN*, p. 247.
[234] *TN*, pp. 250, 267.
[235] *Gazetteer of Oudh*, II, p. 462.

Bharā'ij

Bharā'ij, Bharaych or *Bahraich* was another *iqṭāʿ* which was distinct from Awadh and which we can trace under various governors from about 1241 onwards.[236] From here too, we learn repeatedly, 'holy war expeditions were undertaken against the infidels and the prosperity of the peasants was promoted'.[237] In the trans-Ghaghara part of the district a Muslim government was not established, probably, until the middle of the thirteenth century. The jungle then must have run as far south and west as the edge of the belt of high ground which ran through the district in a southeasterly direction, and only the plain of the Sarju and the Ghaghara yielded any revenue.[238]

About seven km west of the present town of Nanpara, on the edge of the same tableland and on the bank of the Sarju, there are the remains of a very large town, the houses of which were (at least partly) built of burnt bricks, and which was locally known as Dugaun.[239] In Mughal times this appears to have been an important commercial centre still (it was deserted by the end of Shah Jahan's reign), with considerable trade with the hill people, and with a mint for copper coin.[240] Since Nāsir ad-Dīn is mentioned as having made his power felt even in the hills and having made Bahraich extremely prosperous, it is quite possible that this town was established during his governorship.[241]

The first Muslim colonies in Bahraich were, in the meantime, probably already established in about 1226 AD, when Malik Nāsir ad-Dīn Muhammad, the elder son of Iltutmish, was appointed to Awadh.[242] These were the Ansaris, who settled in the south of the Bahraich district, in Pachambar, Hisampur, and Tawakkulpur, occupying and bringing under cultivation about twenty-five villages and building a fortress with fifty-two towers.[243] It was the

---

[236] *TN*, pp. 199, 208-9, 221, 303, 304; *TF*, pp. 70, 72; Siddiqui, *Perso-Arabic Sources*, p. 8.
[237] *TN*, p. 199; *TF*, p. 70.
[238] *Gazetteer of Oudh*, I, pp. 114-5.
[239] *Ibid.*
[240] *Ibid.*
[241] *Ibid.*
[242] *Ibid.*, p. 113.
[243] *Ibid.*, pp. 114-5.

Ansaris who appear to have given the name of Hisampur to the town of Pureni, the capital of the Bhar chief Puran Mal, who is said to have been overthrown by one of the companions and co-martyrs of Sayyid Salar, named Hisam al-Haq.[244] There is also the tomb of Sayyid Salar in the town of Bahraich. Sayyid Salar Mas'ud, staying in Bahraich for three years, allegedly penetrated the area as far as Ikauna.[245] The name of Bahraich is sometimes derived from that of a local people called the 'Bhars'.[246] There is a nine-teenth-century local tradition which gives an account of a 'Bhar' dynasty, founded about 918 AD by Tilok Chand, who fixed his cap-ital at Bahraich, and from there defeated Raja Bikrampal of Del-hi.[247] According to the same tradition he held all the country up to Delhi, and all of Awadh up to the mountains, and his dynasty lasted for nine generations, up to 1093 AD. Tilok Chand was said to have been a worshiper of the sun, and near Bahraich there is a sun-temple called *Bala-ark*. The founder of the Bhar dynasty wished to give a new and better name to his people, in imitation of the Surajbans, and he accordingly called them the *Arkbans*, and to his own immediate family he gave the title of *Arkrajbansi*.[248] The historical status of the 'Bhars' however is in doubt, and their role in the district under Muslim rule cannot be determined.

AWADH

If the first invasions of Awadh took place under Sayyid Salār Mas'ūd Ghāzī, in 1030-1, and in 1033 under Ahmad Nayaltigin, and if there are certain Muslim communities in the area which date their history from this time, permanent conquests in the area were not yet effected in this period.

'Az dihlī tā āwadh masāfat-i-basyār ast', 'it is a great distance from Delhi to Awadh', writes Barani.[249] *Āwadh* or *'Aywaz*—a name which is usually derived from the Sanskrit *Ayudhya*, 'not conquerable', the name of the old Hindu city—became the garrison town of an *iqṭā'* in the early thirteenth century. This capital, the place where

---

[244] *Ibid.*, p. 114; II, p. 81.
[245] *Gazetteer of Oudh*, II, p. 87; I, pp. xxxiv-xxxv.
[246] *Gazetteer of Oudh*, I, p. 110.
[247] *Gazetteer of Oudh*, II, p. 353.
[248] *Ibid.*
[249] *TFS*, p. 140.

the imperial pavilion was pitched on visits, is described as being located on 'the river Sarju' (Āb Sarū).[250] Muhammad bin Bakhtyār Khalajī was the first Muslim ruler to organise the administration of Awadh and to establish it as a base for military operations. Later again, we read, Iltutmish brought Awadh and Benares under control.[251] When an hereditary governorship was established in Bengal, Awadh was wrested from the Bengal dynasty and maintained as an iqṭāʿ of Delhi, between Bahraich and Manikpur. Iltutmish's eldest son Nāsir ad-Dīn overthrew the local ruler Bartūh and 'reduced the infidels and rebels of different parts of Awadh'.[252] He ruled the area like a 'monarch' (farmānrawā), and had a son who was brought up in Awadh 'in princely luxury and delicacy'.[253] After Nāsir ad-Dīn, a son and a younger brother of successive later kings of Delhi governed the province, declaring themselves independent or turning hostile after intercepting the revenues from Bengal on their way to the capital.[254] And various governors are mentioned who took possession of Awadh as well as the area of Andesha Bālātar, now included in Nepal, and Tirhut, while plundering Bhatī-Ghorā, east of Benares, and organizing expeditions against the mawās in various parts, in the Doab, between Kalanjar and Kara, and as far as Bihar.[255] Amir Khusrau stayed here for some time, in the later thirteenth century, when Hātim Khan was its governor. 'In the rainy season', Khusrau wrote, 'I had to travel back to the darkness of Hindustān. ... Weeping I started at every stage with the royal army on the journey, till after a long march of two months when the king arrived at Awadh, he was pleased to bestow on our Khan the governorship of that province. The city of Awadh [Ajodhya] was entrusted to the Khan, and a slow poison was henceforth my food. Though I had no patience I was forced to stay there. The city of Awadh is, no doubt, charming. ... It is a city, nay, a garden, where one can easily live happily and contented. Its ground is the ornament of the earth, and its surroundings abound in pleasures. The river Sar[j]ū flows by it, and the mere sight of it quenches one's thirst. All essentials

[250] Ibid., p. 141.
[251] TN, p. 171.
[252] TN, pp. 163, 180; Siddiqui, Perso-Arabic Sources, p. 59.
[253] FS, vs. 2362-86.
[254] TN, p. 183; TF, p. 67.
[255] TN, pp. 185, 211, 219-20, 242-3, 249, 258, 260, 262-3, 266-7, 291-2, 303, 305-6; TF, pp. 68, 70, 76, 79.

of happiness are plentiful; flowers and wine are numerous and abundant. The branches of the trees in its orchards bow down to the ground with their load of fruit. There are grapes, limes, pomegranades and oranges, and a hundred other fruits with Indian names, sweet and luscious, like bananas and mangoes that refresh the brain ... Then there are all sorts of perfumes and spices. ... The inhabitants are hospitable and courteous, good-tempered and well-mannered, faithful and generous. Rich and poor are content and happy, busy with their worth, art or trade ..'.[256]

We have no information on the various population groups that inhabited Awadh at the time except what was passed on as tradition. The local tradition of Awadh, as recorded in the later nineteenth century, says that it was the Tharus who first came down from the hills and cleared the jungles as far as Ayudhya in the eighth and ninth centuries.[257] Sharar wrote that Awadh was a wilderness and deserted by the seventh century, but that then, subsequently, in the eighth century, 'the Tharus tribe, from the foot of the Himalayan mountains, descended upon this area'; and that afterwards, by the ninth century, the whole region became part of the kingdom of Kanauj.[258] Nineteenth-century British writers, observing the 'Chinese', 'Tartar' or 'Turanian' features of the Tharus of their day, sometimes speculated that the Tharus irrupted into India with the assistance of the Tibetan king, about the middle of the seventh century AD.[259] By the ninth or tenth century, in any case, the Tharus are alleged to have been subjected by a clan of Somavamshi or 'Lunar' lineage, which had adopted the rules of purity, and which ruled at Sravasti when Sayyid Salar occupied Bahraich; the latter was one of the last dynasties of North India to profess Jainism, and the memories of Jain rule still cling to the deserted remains of their city.[260] In its turn, this small northern kingdom was allegedly subverted by the Rathor king of Kanauj, in the last quarter of the eleventh century. Other Tharus were ousted by Domkatar military brahmans; still others, it is said, by the Bhars, who were beginning to prevail in most places—also driving out the Domkatars—until they were themselves expelled

---

[256] Wahid Mirza, *Amir Khusrau*, pp. 71-72.
[257] *Gazetteer of Oudh*, I, p. xxxiv.
[258] Sharar, *Lucknow*, p. 233, note 1.
[259] Cf. M. Martin, *Eastern India*, Vol. II (London, 1838), p. 342; *Gazetteer of Oudh*, III, p. 502.
[260] *Gazetteer of Oudh*, I, pp. xxxiv-xxxv.

by Rajputs.[261] Tradition again presents the Bhars to have been the dominant group throughout much of Awadh from about the end of the eleventh century—though not without a Tharu dynasty at Gonda putting up claims to supremacy in the tenth and eleventh centuries as well. The Tharu raja of Gonda is also, in some legends, presented as a Jain, and tradition connects him with Sayyid Salar as well.[262] The latter-day Tharus had themselves all retained the tradition that they were driven from Chitor by ʻAlāʼ ad-Dīn Ghūrī [i.e. Khalajī], and fled to the jungles of Khairagarh (to the south of the later city of Agra), where they stayed for a while, then moved on to Dholpur, where there exists an old city called 'Tharu'.[263] These later Tharus were not Hindus, did not have caste, buried their dead, maintained a village system that was prevalent among all the hill people, and refused all service while never leaving their forests.[264]

While these are local traditions, it has to be emphasized that in the epigraphic record of the political history of the four or five centuries preceding the Delhi Sultanate there is not a trace of this Tharu gentry in any of the areas where these traditions located them and it seems that that a part of this history is quite possibly invented.[265] Much the same can be said about the Bhars.[266] Nothing is known really about these people which tradition designated as 'Bhars'.[267] The Bhars which were found in fairly large numbers in the nineteenth century, living on the verge of cultivation, were seen as 'ethnical brothers' of the Tharus, Doms, and the numerous other 'aboriginal tribes whose despised remains yet linger unabsorbed by the conquering Indian stock'.[268] Such Bhars were still very numerous in the later nineteenth century in parts of the low country subject to Nepal.[269] Elsewhere they were 'reduced to a few miserable families, who live in the skirts of the

---

[261] Martin, *Eastern India*, II, p. 343.
[262] *Gazetteer of Oudh*, I, p. 111.
[263] *Gazetteer of Oudh*, II, pp. 126, 208; III, p. 502.
[264] *Gazetteer of Oudh*, II, p. 216.
[265] Cf. S. Guha, 'Introductory Chapter: Older Races, Lower Strata' (Mimeo, 1995), esp. p. 12.
[266] *Ibid.*
[267] Cf. Reeves, *Sleeman in Oudh*, pp. 276-7 (Gonda-Bahraetch 'district', 11-14 December 1849).
[268] *Gazetteer of Oudh*, I, p. xxxv.
[269] F. Buchanan Hamilton, *An Account of the Kingdom of Nepal (1819)* (New Delhi, 1971), I, p. 129.

forests by collecting the natural production of these wilds'.[270]
Some of them were still found on the lowest levels of society as
cultivators, policemen, and so on, in Awadh and other districts
north of the Ganges,[271] while in some parts of the Bengal Delta,
Bhars were living in scattered clumps of houses on the brink of
marshes and swamps.[272] Not a trace of them could be found in
Bahraich, which had allegedly been the centre of their rule.[273]
But the idea was put forward, specifically by H. Elliot, that the
Bhars overran most of Awadh in a time when it had apparently
relapsed into primeval wilderness.[274] Aboriginals, like the tribes
of Kols, Bhils, Kirats, or Tharus, they came from the Tarai.[275]

What is certain is that a far greater portion of the country was
then covered with jungle. In Kheri district, we are told that in the
reign of Firuz Shah III (1351-88 AD), a chain of forts was established along the north bank of the river Sarju to repel maraud-
ers from the mountains of Dhoti and Garhwal. As is recorded in
the 'Ain-i-Akbari, the Sultan ascended the tallest tower of the
Khairigarh fort, and cast his eyes over a boundless sea of trees, in
which no house-roof, no tempel-spire, no smoke, or any other
sign of human habitation appeared, and was so appalled by the
solitude of the place that he immediately abandoned it, and the
fort too was abandoned, it is believed, for centuries.[276] The whole
of North Hardoi was a jungle at this time.[277] The district of Kheri,
in the extreme north-west of the province of Awadh, with the sites
of Shahabad, Muhandi, and Aurangabad, was then covered with
forest.[278] Whether any Bhars came from the south of Nepal is historically uncertain.[279] The tradition of Awadh, with British colonial authors in its wake, however, cast the Bhars in the role of the

---

[270] Martin, *Eastern India*, II, p. 345.

[271] Reeves, *Sleeman in Oudh*, p. 77.

[272] Asim Roy, 'The interface of Islamization, regionalization and syncretization:
the Bengal paradigm', in: A. L. Dallapiccola and S. Zingel-Avé Lallemant (eds),
Islam and Indian Regions, 2 vols (Stuttgart, 1993), I, p. 101.

[273] *Gazetteer of Oudh*, I, p. 110.

[274] *Gazetteer of Oudh*, II, p. 353.

[275] *Ibid.*, pp. 353-4.

[276] *Gazetteer of Oudh*, II, pp. 128-9.

[277] *Ibid.*, II, p. 56.

[278] *Ibid.*, II, p. 243.

[279] Cf. Ch. Lassen, *Indische Altertumskunde*, 5 vols (Leipzig, 1847-62), I, p. 448;
Buchanan Hamilton, *Account of Nepal (1819)*, I, p. 128; Martin, *Eastern India*, II,
pp. 342, 345, 386.

last great powers which ruled in Awadh prior to the Muslims.[280] They are alleged to have ruled in the eleventh century throughout southern Awadh, the Doab, and the country between the Ganges and Malwa.[281] Sultanpur, under another name, was made out to have been one of their capitals until the early fourteenth century.[282] So was Bahraich.[283] They dominated the Lucknow district up to the end of the twelfth century. The Bhars are alleged to have been still powerful in the fourteenth century, in Bareli and Dalman in the Rai Bareli district.[284] It is also speculated that the Bhar supremacy languished as Muslim power gradually became consolidated (and as early as Sayyid Salar), and even that 'they seem to have been systematically extirpated by the Mahommeddan conquerors in the early part of the fourteenth century'.[285] Some are alleged to have converted to Islam.[286] The overthrow of the Bhars was supposed to have been followed by the establishment of a variety of 'Rajput' chieftaincies, recruited from leading clans in the north or from the south-west.[287] These provided the elements of modern Awadh society.

In any case, popular tradition ascribed numerous remains of walled towns and forts in Awadh to the Bhars.[288] These 'Bhar towns' all seem to have been built of burnt brick, unlike later towns. There are also numerous wells still in use which were built of the finest burnt brick and cement. Brick ruins of forts, houses and wells are the only remains found of the Bhars—no temples. No arms, coins or utensils are ascribed to them, and they have not left a name, date, or legend inscribed on any monument.[289] Everything is based on popular tradition: the Ahir women of the Rai Bareli district mourned for their Bhar kings, giving up the practice of wearing anklets, and this gave rise to a theory that

[280] Cf. *Gazetteers of Oudh*, passim.

[281] Cf. *Gazetteer of Oudh*, I, p. xxxv.

[282] Reeves, *Sleeman in Oudh*, p. 276.

[283] *Gazetteer of Oudh*, I, p. 110; II, p. 353.

[284] *Ibid.*, III, pp. 219-20.

[285] Reeves, *Sleeman in Oudh*, pp. 276-7; *Gazetteer of Oudh*, I, p. 24; II, pp. 90-95, 99, 100-101, 353.

[286] *Gazetteer of Oudh*, II, p. 428, etc.

[287] *Ibid.*, I, pp. xxxvi-xxxvii, p. 110; II, pp. 421, 428; Martin, *Eastern India*, II, p. 386.

[288] *Gazetteer of Oudh*, I, pp. xxxiv, 23, 110, 333, etc; Reeves, *Sleeman in Oudh*, pp. 276-7.

[289] Reeves, *Sleeman in Oudh*, p. 277; Guha, 'Older Races, Lower Strata', p. 12.

the Bhars were connected with the Ahirs;[290] of the Bhars, as of other aboriginal groups, it is said that by them no conquest of any fort was effected except by plying the occupants with wine;[291] traces of a buffalo sacrifice are ascribed to the Bhars in Rai Bare-li.[292]

Attempts to identify the Bhars with certain of the rulers of Awadh that are mentioned in the Muslim chronicles remain of very doubtful value at best. *Bartūh*, the ruler of Awadh which was overthrown in 1226 and which is mentioned in Juzjani's chronicle, has been identified as a Bhar ruler on purely etymological grounds.[293] Al-'Utbī refers to the fortress of Ajaigarh as Āsī, on the left bank of the Yamuna, 10 km west of Etawah, whose ruler was *Chandāl Būr* (or *Bhūr*), 'one of the chief men and generals of the Hindus'.[294] We learn from the same author that there was a great jungle around this fort, and that this ruler had been at war with the Raja of Kanauj, but that five of his forts were demolished by Mahmud of Ghazna.[295] From two inscriptions from Ajaigarh and Kalanjar in Bundelkhand we learn that there was a line of rulers in Ajaigarh which ended with Malika.[296] Dalki, the brother of Malika or 'Malki', on the overthrow of the Kanauj king, conquered the whole of the Doab, and Firishta has recorded the utter defeat and destruction of Dalki and Malki by Nasir ad-Din Mahmūd, the Sultan of Delhi, in 1246-7. The tradition of southern Awadh preserved the memory of these rajas and wants them to be Bhars.[297] Amir Khusrau and Barani refer to the military class in Awadh merely as 'the nāyakas of Awadh', 'the lords of Awadh', without providing any clue to their identity.[298]

What seems certain is merely that the first colonization of the area around Ayudhya by Rajputs arriving from the west occurred in the thirteenth century. Characteristically, since the time of the

---

[290] *Gazetteer of Oudh*, I, p. 110; II, p. 353; III, p. 220.
[291] *Ibid.*, II, p. 353.
[292] *Ibid.*, III, p. 221.
[293] See supra, p. 249.
[294] *TYA*, p. 401.
[295] *Ibid.*, pp. 401-2; *TYP*, pp. 245-6.
[296] Cf. Ray, *Dynastic History*, II, pp. 665-735.
[297] *Gazetteer of Oudh*, I, p. xxxvi; Cf. Lassen, *Indische Altertumskunde*, III, pp. 795-800.
[298] M. Habib, *The Campaigns of Alauddin Khalji* (Madras, 1931), p. 29; *TFS*, p. 541; Prasad, *Sanskrit Inscriptions of Delhi Sultanate*, p. xxiii.

Rajput colonization and Muslim invasions, from about the end of the twelfth century, all villages terminate in *pur* or *nagar* or *khera*, or in the Muslim *abad*; other names than those are difficult to trace, and seem to belong to another order of things.[299] It can also be established with a fair degree of certainty that the first Muslim settlers in Awadh came from about 1184 onwards, and in greater numbers from about the middle of the thirteenth century.[300]

BIHĀR

The name of this province, a separate iqṭāʿ in the thirteenth century, derived from *Vihāra*, 'monastery', which at first denoted a town, later the entire South Gangetic plain.[301] Prior to the Islamic conquest, Bihar was divided in at least four divisions: Magadha or South Bihar, Anga or East Bihar, Kajangala or the latter day Santal parganas, portions of Bhagalpur beyond the Ghagha and the Purnea district, and Mithila or Tirhut, which was North Bihar (ancient Tirabhukti).[302] Persian chroniclers consistently use the term 'Tirhut' when referring to any of the invasions of North Bihar, while reserving at times the term 'Bihar' for ancient Magadha.

Bihar as a whole, containing extensive lands with rich fertile soil, large navigable rivers, forests, and wealthy cities, had no natural barrier against invading armies from the West—a factor which explains why it was so often subordinate to Lakhnauti, the Muslim seat of government in Bengal. In ancient times, under the Mauryas and the Guptas, the important cities of Pataliputra (Patna), Rajgir, Bodh Gaya, and Nalanda, had all been located in the northern part of the South Bihar plain and were clearly dependent on agricultural hinterlands. These agricultural hinterlands did not yet extend very far: Dharmasvamin, in 1234, observed forests beginning only a few kilometers south of Gaya city.[303] But

---

[299] *Gazetteer of Oudh*, II, p. 312.

[300] *Ibid.*, I, pp. 224, 255; II, pp. 56, 101, 293, 352-3, 428-9; III, pp. 16, 219, 446, 567.

[301] Cf. A. N. Ansari, 'Historical Geography of Bihar on the Eve of the Turkish Invasions', *Journal of the Bihar Research Society*, 49 (1963), pp. 253-60.

[302] *Bihar District Gazetteer, Vol. 16: Shahabad* (Patna, 1966), p. 59.

[303] Cf. Roerich, *Dharmasvamin*, p. 73.

by the thirteenth century the system of irrigation channels in the northern part of the plain was extensive by comparison with the southern parts, where agricultural settlement was quite sparse. The southern Bihar plain was the area where Hindu people encountered the non-Hindus of the Chota Nagpur plateau. The most important change we note in the thirteenth century, after the arrival of the Ghurids, is that a new wave of immigrants, of Rajputs, Afghans, and Muslims, to South Bihar occurred which led to an increase of cultivation here—a process that was to continue in later centuries. As the 'Ain shows, a large part of the southern region had been cleared for agriculture by the end of the sixteenth century.[304] Even then large parts of the southern area remained under forest. Muslim rulers never penetrated into the hills of the Santal parganas; as late as Sher Shah's rule in the sixteenth century, Afghan iqtā'dārs, while occupying the fringes of the highlands of South Bihar and West Bengal around Orissa, did not control the interior of the hills and plateaus which were still entirely occupied by their original inhabitants. And, thus, the 'Jhārkhand' or 'jungle divison', as this hill country was known, is rarely mentioned in the Muslim chronicles.[305] Muslim arms also did not penetrate the Rohtas valley, nor Palamau, nor any part of the Chota Nagpur division, nor the submountainous region of Monghyr. In general, in the south, independent princes held sway which the Tibetan chronicler of the fifteenth century assigned the insignia of *pithipatis*.

Bardic annals also recount Rajput attempts in the thirteenth century to free Gaya and other places from the Turks. But the latter probably held on to the fertile crescent of Shahabad, Patna, Gaya, Bhagalpur up to Sakrigali, and perhaps parts of Mithila. It had been Muhammad bin Bakhtyar Khalaji who, with Chunar as his base of operations, had begun making incursions into Maner and Bihār, bringing Vedagarbhapura (Buxar), Mahasara (Masarh), and other towns under his control, then attacking the 'fort of Bihār' itself, and erecting a fortress on the site of Uddandapura

[304] Cf. G. Prakash, *Bonded Histories: Genealogies of Labor Servitude in Colonial India* (Cambridge, 1990), p. 13 ff.; C. E. A. W. Oldham (ed.), *Journal of Francis Buchanan kept during the survey of the district of Bhagalpur, in 1810-1811* (Patna, 1930), pp. vii-viii; F. Buchanan, *An Account of the District of Bihar and Patna in 1811-1812* (Patna, 1936), 2 vols, I, pp. 192-3.

[305] Oldham, *Journal of Francis Buchanan*, p. vii.

(Adwand Bihar or modern Biharsharif), before moving into Bengal and making Lakhnauti his capital in 1193.[306] What happened to Bakhtyar's dominion in Bihar after his death is not clear; but it was probably absorbed in Aybak's sphere. Iltutmish in 1225 and 1230, and Balban in 1280-1; led expeditions against Lakhnauti and made Bihar into a separate iqtā'—such arrangements as made by them however did not last long.[307] During this period some Turkish slaves came to the throne of Lakhnauti via Bihar, which was then relegated to a subordinate position.[308]

LAKHNAUTĪ

This was the garrison town and administrative capital of what was undoubtedly the largest *iqtā'* of the thirteenth century, 'half the kingdom of Delhi' (*nīm-i-mulk-i-dihlī*),[309] the '*iqtā'* of Bengal', covering all of eastern India, with extensions into Assam and Orissa, and frequently turning into a separate dominion with its own throne, the *takht-i-lakhnautī*. A city with walls (at least by the mid-thirteenth century),[310] and surrounded by mountains and marshes, Lakhnauti was the premier centre of the Muslims almost from the beginning of their rule. There were however two other towns of major importance in Bengal: *Laknūr* and *Sunārgāw* [Sunārgaon]. The administrative division of the *iqlīm-i-bangāla* or 'region of Bengal'[311] was thus often named after one or more of these urban centres: it was called the *iqlīm-i-lakhnautī-o-bangāla*,[312] the *bilād-i-lakhnautī*,[313] *lakhnautī-o-sunārgāw*,[314] or the *iqtā'-i-lakhnautī-laknūr*.[315]

The city of Lakhnautī itself also acquired the nickname '*Bulghākpur*', 'city of rebellion'. As Barani explains: 'Shrewd and knowing people had given to Lakhnautī the name of Bulghākpur, for

---

[306] *TN*, pp. 147-8, 150-1.
[307] Cf. Q. Ahmad (ed.), *Corpus of Arabic & Persian Inscriptions of Bihar* (Patna, 1973), pp. 3-19.
[308] Cf. also *TN*, pp. 163, 242, 239, 259.
[309] *TFS*, p. 88.
[310] *TN*, p. 267.
[311] *TFS*, p. 90.
[312] *TFS*, p. 81.
[313] *TN*, p. 242.
[314] *TFS*, p. 93.
[315] *TN*, p. 243.

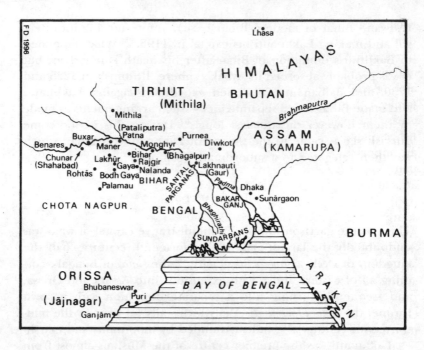

Map 6. Iqṭāʿs of Bihār and Lakhnautī

since the time when Sultan Muʿizz ad-Din Muhammad Sām conquered Delhi, every governor that had been sent from there to
Lakhnautī took advantage of the distance, and of the difficulties
of the road, to rebel. If they did not rebel themselves, others
rebelled against them, killed them and seized the country'.[316]
Even when formally assigned as a mere *iqṭāʿ*, Lakhnautī enjoyed
a degree of autonomy like no other assignment. Entrance to the
Bengal delta from the west was difficult, as it was obtained via a
bottleneck at Monghyr, with steep hillslopes to the south and
numerous tributaries of the Ganges to the north. It was this bottleneck which turned the *iqṭāʿ of Lakhnautī* into a separate political arena within the Delhi Sultanate. Beyond Monghyr, the delta
was surrounded by natural boundaries on all sides—hills in the
direction of Kamarupa (Assam) to the northeast and towards Burma as well as the rest of India towards the west.

Lakhnautī (former Gaur) was taken by Muhammad bin Bakh-

---

[316] *TFS*, p. 81.

tyār in 1204. From about 1204 to 1227, it was a pseudo-independent principality under the Khalaj kings and sultans (who sometimes issued their own coins, and read the khutba for themselves), and we find the area divided up in a number of smaller *iqtā's* among the lesser Khalaj amirs, while tribute was enforced from Jājnagar, Bang, Kamarupa (Kamrud), Tirhut, and other outlying areas.[317] Khalaj rule in Bengal came to an end when the Mamluk Kings of Delhi took it over.[318] Even then, the Khalaj maintained an important presence in Bengal until much later.[319] And Lakhnautī not only always remained an *iqtā'* with special privileges attached to it, but its revenue, if it was not used to support a rebellion of a governor-proclaiming-himself-king in Lakhnautī itself, a source of real danger in so far as it could be intercepted in Awadh.[320] Large as it was, the territory of Bengal was commonly divided up in two parts, *Laknūr* and *Lakhnautī*, 'the one part of which they style Rāl [Rārh] which is towards Lakūr [Laknūr], and the other is Barind [Barinda] on the side of Basankot', and these were at times separate iqtā's, one on each side of the Ganges, with Lakhnautī retaining some kind of precedence over the other.

The economy of this whole area was to a very large extent determined by the two great river systems of the Brahmaputra and the Ganges. These rivers, combine in the plains, created an alluvial delta which made Bengal one of the most fertile regions—with potentially the greatest revenue-producing capacity—in al-Hind. The general trend in Bengal was an eastward shifting of the rivers. River shifts occurred in the entire delta constantly, and were very drastic. Western rivers like the Sarasvati and Bhaghirathi were losing prominence by the twelfth and thirteenth centuries, while eastern rivers like the Brahmaputra were gaining in importance, thus extending the area of cultivation eastwards at the very same time that Muslim control was imposed over this area.[321] Numberless small rivers empty out into the Bay of Bengal between the

---

[317] *TN*, pp. 142, 157-63.
[318] *TN*, pp. 163-4, 171, 174, 180; *TMS*, pp. 18-19; *FS*, vs. 2362-96.
[319] Cf. Siddiqui, *Perso-Arabic Sources*, pp. 33-34.
[320] *TN*, pp. 225, 243, 249, 263-5, 267-8; *TNR*, pp. 737, n. 7, 770-79, n. 9; *TF*, pp. 73, 77-79, 81; *FS*, vs. 3124-52, 3198-3243, 3560-81, 3591-3712; *TMS*, pp. 40-41; *TFS*, pp. 81-91.
[321] M. K. Mukherjee, *The Changing Face of Bengal: a Study in Riverine Economy* (Calcutta, 1938), p. 7.

mouths of the Bhaghirathi and Padma. There, in the southernmost portion of the delta, known as the Sundarbans, we find primarily marshland and jungle with patches of rice paddy. Bākar-
ganj was probably only inhabited in its extreme northern parts,
part of a Hindu kingdom south of the Buriganga which was ruled
from Rāmpāl (Dhaka district). This kingdom appears to have been
outside of Muslim control for nearly a century after Muhammad
bin Bakhtyar Khalajī conquered the rest of Bengal.[322]

The delta, with its frequently shifting rivers, in combination
with the exceptionally heavy rainfall (monsoon rains in the delta
lasting four to five months of the year), prolonged floods, and
dense forest growths, was unlike any other area the Turks had
subjected in northern India or further west, and it was an area of
which they had little or no previous knowledge. The deltaic terrain of Bengal turned to mud in the monsoon and was not a
horse-breeding region, 'a land of footsoldiers' (zamīn-i-rijāla).[323]
Cavalry was ineffective in many parts of the region. The north-
west delta was most conducive to Turkish military strategy; this
was the single sizeable highland plateau where the Ganges splits
into the Bhaghirathi and Padma—and this was, consequently, the
first centre of Muslim control. But further on the Turks had to
co-opt the naval capabilities of the indigenous elites to a higher
degree than was the case anywehere else, quickly leading to the
'Bengalification' of Turkish rule in the delta.[324] Unlike the Muslims of Northern and Western India who confined themselves normally to one fixed residential capital, the iqṭāʿ-holders and kings
of Bengal made use of unprecedented river communications and
set up various capitals, always accessible by water, within easy reach
of each other, and linked at any season with the seaboard cities
of the Ganges and the towns on the narrow channels of the western streams.[325] These shifting residences of the Muslim rulers of
Bengal were designated ḥazrat on coins issued during the rulers'

---

[322] Bengal District Gazetteers, Vol. XXXVI: Bakarganj (Calcutta, 1918), pp. 16-17.
[323] Even in early modern times, zamindars in Bengal developed no significant
cavalry forces and customarily recruited men from outside the region (T. R.
McLane, Land and Local Kingship in Eighteenth-century Bengal (Cambridge, 1993),
p. 44).
[324] Cf. K. R. Downey, 'Changing Modes of Consolidation: A Comparison
between the Turks in Delhi and Lakhnauti in the Thirteenth through Sixteenth
Centuries' (MA Thesis, University of Chicago, 1993), pp. 50-51.
[325] Thomas, Chronicles, p. 150.

visitations, even though Lakhnautī remained the main political centre from where control was asserted within the delta.[326] To facilitate the political control of the delta and enhance its agricultural potential, the early Khalaj rulers undertook the construction of an extensive embankment, of a type that had been pioneered on a massive scale by the ancient rulers of Bang.[327] 'From Lakhnautī to the gate of the city of Laknūr, on the one side, and as far as Dīwkot on the other side, Sultan Ghiyāth ad-Dīn 'Iwāz caused an embankment (pul) to be constructed, extending about ten days' journey, for the reason that in the rainy season the whole of that tract becomes inundated, and that route is filled with mud-swamps and morass; and, if it were not for these dykes, it would be impossible [for people] to carry out their intentions, or reach various structures and inhabited places except by means of boats. From this time, through the construction of those embankments (in pulhā), the route was opened up to the people at large'.[328]

Lakhnautī, slightly later, also became the centre of the production of a silver currency. Silver coinage we now find penetrating the formerly overwhelmingly kaurī-based Bengal economy of the interior. The trade—in eunuchs, cotton, spikenard, galingale, ginger, sugar, 'and many other precious spices', still concentrated on the southeastern seaboard, although the silting of the Meghna appear to have reduced access to these regions in the eleventh to thirteenth centuries and there was increasing competition from the Coromandel, especially in the direction of Java.[329] But with the growth of Bengal's agrarian economy from the thirteenth century onwards, we find traces of considerable immigration to the delta, not only of Muslims and Sufis who began the construction of mosques, khanaqahs, dargahs, madrasas, and so on, but also of brahmans, leaving Kanauj, and other Hindus who appear to have participated in the agricultural transformation of the delta.[330]

---

[326] Ibid.
[327] Cf. TNR, p. 586, n. 9.
[328] TN, p. 162.
[329] TN, p. 149; Thomas, Chronicles, pp. 109-10; Defrémery and Sanguinetti, Ibn Batoutah, IV, p. 121; G. Hambly, 'A note on the trade in eunuchs in Mughal Bengal', Journal of the American Oriental Society, 94.1 (1974), pp. 125-30; Al-Hind, I, pp. 275-7.
[330] Cf. McLane, Land and Local Kingship, p. 145.

Further to the south, it is noticeable that *Jājnagar* or Orissa was also incorporated in the expanding economy of Bengal. An area prized for its elephants, which had often been raided (by the Colas for instance), its ruler was deemed, in the early thirteenth century, to be 'the most powerful of the rais of Hindustan'.[331] By the end of the eleventh century it had come under the rule of the Eastern Gangas of Kaliganagara (the modern Mukhalvigam in the Ganjām district), and their rule lasted until 1434-5. The greatest king of this dynasty was Chodaganga, who extended his rule from the Godāvari to the Ganges and built the temple of Jagannāth at Purī in the first half of the twelfth century. Narasimha I, another Ganga king (r. 1238-64), became known as the builder of the temple of Konārak, dedicated to the sungod Arka at Konā. The temple of Megheswar at Bhubaneswar was erected by a general of one of his predecessors, Ananga-bhīma, around 1200 AD, just before Orissa became exposed to Muslim conquerors. Inscriptions of Bhubaneswar say of Ananga-bhīma that 'he destroyed in battle the Yavana ..'.[332] There was, in effect, no lasting permanent Muslim conquest of Orissa, but raids back and forth between Lakhnautī and Jājnagar occurred throughout the thirteenth century.[333] As far as the Muslims were concerned, the purpose of these raids was, as always, to obtain the elephants for which Jajnagar was known.

Similarly, the northeastern realm of Kāmarūpa ('Kamrud'), the Para Lauhitya of Hindu texts, was invaded on several occasions, but not permanently occupied by any Muslim garrisons, although at some point the reading of the khutba and the Friday religious ceremony were instituted briefly, while 'signs of the people of Islam appeared here'.[334] The Muslim invasions in fact resulted in the temporary imposition of tribute, but in the end there was always a precipitous retreat. This area was later to become known as 'Assam', after the 'Ahoms' who arrived here from Burma perhaps as early as the thirteenth century, as their own legends have it, but possibly later.

In any case, Assam did not exist as a territorial concept in medieval times. Juzjani mentions neither Ahoms nor Assam, but

---

[331] Siddiqui, *Perso-Arabic Sources*, p. 7.
[332] 'References to Muhammadans—AD 730-1320', p. 179.
[333] *TN*, pp. 199-200, 244-6; *TF*, p. 79.
[334] *TN*, pp. 263-5.

he does refer to three tribal groups of people, the *Kūch* (or
Kūnch), the *Meg* (or *Mech*), and the *Thārū*, in the mountains
between Tibbat and Lakhnauti, 'with Turk countenances'.[335]
About the agricultural development of this region in the thirteenth century we know little or nothing. Legend, as recorded in
the Assamese Buranji literature, has it that the Tai-Ahoms penetrated to the area under the command of one Chao-Ka-Pha in
1228 AD, and that they occupied the banks of the Dikhon river
after ousting the 'Kachari' settlers. However, Chao-Ka-Pha, while
a celebrated pioneer of the Ahoms, remains a hazy and question-
able figure. Even before the Ahoms settled in Assam, wet-rice cultivation was practiced.[336] The Kacharis had devised a way to build
embankments to divert water into canals, thereby creating areas
where paddy cultivation was possible. Fragmentary evidence suggests that the Ahoms familiarized themselves with this agricultural technique.[337] There were other groups of indigenous peoples,
such as the Morans and the Barahis, who were mostly forest gath-
erers and small traders. But there is no doubt that the Ahom settlement pattern further encouraged large-scale deforestation and
resulted in more land being brought under the plough, while a
regular waterworks system appears to have been developed as well.

We cannot be sure however when this began. In the earliest
period the Ahom *muang* was confined to the region between the
rivers Tipam and Dikhon, and the Kacharis contested their claim.
To the northwest of the Ahoms was the Chutia kingdom, which,
according to the Dheodhai Buranji, was carved out in the late
twelfth century. The Chutia king was really a 'big merchant'. He
controlled the trading posts to the country of 'Dharma Raja',
which was called Bhūt or Bhūtān, and through which ran, since
early medieval times, the famed trade route between Tibet and
Bengal or Gaur, the later Lakhnautī. Along this route came *Tan-
gan* horses, gold, musk, silks, rhinoceros horns, and even Buddhism. The Ahoms from the very beginning desired to secure the
ready-made economy of the Chutias. And although it was not until
the fifteenth century that the Ahoms completely achieved their

---

[335] *TN*, p. 152.
[336] F. Bray, *The Rice Economies. Technology and Development in Asian Societies*
(Oxford, 1986), p. 8 ff ; S. K. Bhuyan (ed.), *Satsari Buranji* (Gauhati, 1969), 13:5.
[337] Bhuyan, *Deodhai Asam Buranji*, 153: 100.

goal, it is possible that the first Ahom penetration of this economy occurred in the thirteenth century and that their attempts in
this direction were linked to the expansion of the Bengal economy beyond their frontiers in the same period.

The Ahoms, without doubt, opened up the critical overland
route bridging mainland South and Southeast Asia. The information which we have on what appears to have been a form of
continued interaction between the Ahoms and the Nora kingdom
to the east, in what later became Burma, is quite explicit about
this and available in the voluminous Buranji literature in old Tai-
Ahom as well as Assamese. A trading pattern between these areas
was established, in which the Ahoms sent elephants, cotton, textiles and a variety of silver and earthen jars from Assam, and in
return received from the Noras horses and war implements, primarily long-range bows.[338] When the Ahoms annexed the Chutia
domain and seized its flourishing trading economy, the Noras still
demanded a share in the acquisition.[339]

<h3 style="text-align:center">CONCLUSION</h3>

In drawing together the material of this chapter we observe that
in the entire conquest area—from Lahore to Lakhnauti—similar
patterns emerged in the ways that frontier and settled society
merged together in the thirteenth century. The new horse-troop
garrison towns established by the Turkish conquerors became centres of *iqtāʿ* management, aiming at the safeguarding of trade
routes, markets, the subjugation of the marches, as well as at agrarian expansion, monetization, and the regulation and rationaliza-
tion of landrevenue collection. The span of Turkish control varied to some degree from region to region, but there can be no
doubt that everywhere in the conquest state—and affecting areas
far beyond it—a more effective mobilization of goods, precious
metals, and people was achieved at this time in an agricultural
economy that appears to be expanding everywhere. The case of
Bengal already shows that such expansion was not only beginning
to be felt in an eastern direction, beyond the orbit of Turkish control, but was also beginning to seek more maritime outlets.

---

[338] Bhuyan, *Deodhai Asam Buranji*, 12: 9; Bhuyan, *Satsari Buranji*, 117: 48.

[339] Komroff, *Contemporaries of Marco Polo*, p. 118; Bhuyan, *Deodhai Asam Buranji*, 12:9; Bhuyan, *Satsari Buranji*, 117: 48.

CHAPTER VIII

'TWIXT LAND AND SEA

The garrison towns and urban centres which were now established throughout the conquest state became islands of Islamic culture and Islamization. But it should not be thought that in the thirteenth century any sustained attempts were made by the Turkish rulers and their retinues at conversion of the native population, in the way that, for instance, the Spanish conquistadores went about in Nueva España. Although there are traditions which attribute the conversion of large numbers of Hindus to the activities of Muslim mystics at this time, contemporary historical chronicles say very little or nothing about it.[1] What the historical record bears out is that there was something like an Islamic 'sanctification' of North India. This included the appropriation of non-Muslim buildings or building materials to create mosques,[2] the introduction of Islamic prayer and of cadres of religious clergy and jurists, and the introduction of the Sufi tradition.[3]

To be sure, Arab Sind had already produced, by the eleventh century, a substantial amount of Muslim scholars and traditionists, and Lahore became an important centre of Islamic learning under the Ghaznavids. The first Sufi to reach Lahore, Hujwiri, arriving from Ghazna in 1071, came to be regarded as the patron saint of the city under the name of Data Ganj Bakhsh. Later, in the succeeding centuries, when the Sufi tradition was introduced from the Islamic lands to the west, it provided a local Muslim identity to the newly formed community in Hind.[4] The Sufi Shaykh who became thought of as the guardian of the Muslims throughout Hind was Mu'in ad-Dīn Chishtī. He became

---

[1] Cf. K. A. Nizami, *Some Aspects of Religion and Politics in India during the Thirteenth Century* (Delhi, 1974), pp. 320-1.

[2] For more on this subject, see Chapter IX.

[3] Cf. S. Digby, 'The Sufi Shaikh as a Source of Authority in Mediaeval India', in: M. Gaborieau (ed.), *Islam et Société en Asie du Sud* (Paris, 1986), pp. 57-77.

[4] Cf. Digby, 'Sufi Shaikh', p. 59.

known as the 'Deputy of the Prophet in India' or 'the Prophet of India' (nabī al-Hind).[5] Prior to Mu'in ad-Dīn's arrival in India, in 1192, it was said that 'the whole of Hindūstān was submerged by unbelief and idol-worship'.[6] As Allah's appointed evangelist, Mu'in ad-Dīn is regarded to have been instrumental in the victory of the Muslim armies in the final invasion of India. But historical information on his shrine in Ajmer is sketchy for the thirteenth century, and there is no mention of conversion here either.[7]

The same must be said about another important shrine of the thirteenth century, that of Shaykh Farīd Ganj-i-Shakar or 'Bābā Farīd', in the ancient town of Ajudhan, the later Pakpattan.[8] Bābā Farīd reached Ajudhan early in the thirteenth century, when there was already a Jāmi' mosque and a qadi, while the town itself was subordinate to a governor at Dipalpur. Apart from serving an elite group of initiates, Bābā Farīd also handed out ta'wīdh to the common people. When the saint died, a vast shrine complex arose around his tomb, and in the period from 1281 to 1334, under patronage of the Delhi court, devotionalism was extended to the countryside.[9] But, again, the earliest primary sources on Bābā Farīd do not mention his having converted any non-Muslims, and, as we have seen, conversion of the Jats, while it probably began during his lifetime, was a gradual process and remained remarkably slow.[10]

In the capital of Delhi itself, the religious clergy or 'ulamā' and certain 'Sharia-minded' Sufis (the latter especially after Iltutmish) commanded considerable influence among the Muslims and in various ways assisted the Delhi Sultans in consolidating their authority in the newly conquered domain.[11] Rules and regulations for religious offices were promulgated, and scholarly activities aimed to preserve the Islamic heritage in a foreign environment.[12] Here the khanaqah of Shaykh Nizām ad-Dīn Aulīya (1244-1325) became a rendezvous for people from a variety of backgrounds.[13]

---

[5] Ibid., p. 59; P. M. Currie, The Shrine and Cult of Mu'in al-din Chishti of Ajmer (Delhi, 1989), p. 96.

[6] Currie, Mu'in al-din Chishti, pp. 22, 30.

[7] Ibid., pp. 96, 185.

[8] Eaton, 'Shrine of Bābā Farīd', pp. 333-56.

[9] Ibid., pp. 337-8.

[10] Cf. p. 242.

[11] Cf. Kumar, Emergence of the Delhi Sultanate, pp. 232-5.

[12] A. Schimmel, Islam in the Indian Subcontinent (Leiden, 1980), p. 14.

[13] K. A. Nizami, The Life and Times of Shaikh Nizamuddin Auliya (Delhi, 1991).

Nizām ad-Dīn was entrusted with the spiritual heritage (*khilāfat*) of Bābā Farīd; he was appointed as the latter's chief successor and directed to settle at Delhi in order to further the expansion of the Chishti silsila. People flocked to his khanaqah, especially under the threat of Mongol invasions, and his *jamāʿat khāna* became an important welfare centre. According to some sources it was through his efforts that many parts of Hind became studded with the khanaqahs of the order. Allegedly he sent 700 senior disciples (khalīfas) to different parts of the country. Effective centres of the silsila sprang up in Haryana, Malwa, Gujarat, the Deccan, and Bengal.[14] But nowhere does this appear to have led to a substantial conversion movement.

In order to find evidence of native conversion in thirteenth-century India we have to turn to the coastal regions of Gujarat, the Konkan, Malabar, the Coromandel, Bengal, Sumatra, and the numerous Indian Ocean islands to the west. In its own particular way the littoral of al-Hind constituted a frontier zone between land and sea which was characterized by permeability and supported a type of trading activity that was not unlike the overland caravan trade in its essential characteristics.[15] As a frontier zone it did not exist to separate and enclose, but to facilitate exchange, and in the case of India this meant especially the exchange of precious metals. Coastal regimes were primarily geared to facilitate this. By comparison with the inland cities, with their military garrisons (often extending previously existing networks of control), the port towns were therefore not normally favoured with a great deal of investment in works of infrastructure. They were rather left to themselves, and this was a difference which also expressed itself in a lack of scope and diversification of the harbours, which were primarily relay stations, in other words transmission points. In social terms, the situation in the port towns was one of indeterminacy and openness, of an absence of rigid boundaries. And in the thirteenth century, it appears, conversion to Islam was largely confined to the maritime ports of this coastal zone.

---

[14] For Bengal, see also Eaton, *Rise of Islam*, pp. 71-94; for the Deccan, see Ernst, 'Khuldabad-Burhanpur Axis', p. 177; R. M. Eaton, *Sufis of Bijapur, 1300-1700: Social Roles of Sufis in Medieval India* (Princeton, 1978), pp. 14, 32.

[15] Cf. J. C. Heesterman, 'Littoral et Intérieur de l'Inde', in: L. Blussé, H. L. Wesseling and G. D. Winius (eds), *History and Underdevelopment: Essays on Underdevelopment and European Expansion in Asia and Africa* (Leiden, 1980), pp. 87-92.

Even then, in many of these areas the record is spotty and difficult to interpret. As has already been seen in the preceding volume, there are problems in dating the penetration of Muslims in the coastal regions of *al-Hind* and the introduction of Islam among local peoples precisely because of the nature of this penetration. Instead of conquest memorials, as in the North, we have fragmented testimony of a slow and peaceful infiltration by Arabian and Persian merchants occurring over centuries.[16] These merchants usually left nothing but their graves as evidence of their former presence, although there are some allusions to them in literature and in oral traditions. Not until the mid-fourteenth century, in the travel account of Ibn Battuta, do we obtain a total view of this far-flung Muslim culture that arose on the littoral from the eighth and ninth centuries onwards. From Ibn Battuta and later sources we learn that in the ports and towns of the Indian littoral Muslim merchants and preachers were kept at a distance by the high-caste, landowning Hindu population which did not eat with them and refused them access to their houses, but that they married or temporarily married (through the institution of *mutʿa*) women of low-caste fishermen and seafarers who did accept to prepare food for them. It seems to have taken several centuries before these coastal Muslims, the Mappillas of Malabar, Navayat of the Canara coast, Ilappai of the Coromandel, and other groups elsewhere which were constituted by migrant residents ('Creoles') as well as, more and more, by people of mixed origin ('Mestizos'), emerged from their obscure conditions and superseded the Jewish and Christian groups which in some areas, like Malabar, had played comparable roles in overseas trade.

Since the littoral was a frontier zone, here too trading and raiding went together. Therefore, in order to acquire a foothold on the Indian coast—which was entirely dominated by Hindu rajas—the Muslims often sought employment as mercenaries in the indigenous armies as well. From the beginning of the thirteenth century, Giovanni di Montecorvino noticed such groups in the armies of the rajas of Malabar, and Marco Polo observed the same in Sri Lanka slightly later.[17] It seems quite likely that these Mus-

---

[16] Cf. *Al-Hind*, I, Chapter III; and G. Bouchon, 'Quelques Aspects de l'Islamisation des Régions Maritimes de l'Inde à l'Époque Médiévale (XIIe-XVIe s.)', *Puruṣārtha*, 9 (1986), pp. 29-36.

[17] Bouchon, 'Islamisation', p. 30.

lim mercenaries of South India attained greater visibility in the
context of Cola expansion in the tenth to thirteenth centuries.
But, as we will see in this chapter, the world of the Indian Ocean
littoral went through a general transformation in the eleventh to
thirteenth centuries which was no less significant than that which
occurred in the agrarian interior. It is no coincidence that the
expansion of the Turkish-Muslim empire in North India and the
increase of control of an expanding agricultural production went
hand in hand with the development of commercial operations on
the seaboard. In effect, we will argue that these developments—
of the interior and the littoral—were closely linked and part of
the wider process which characteriezd these centuries, the fusion
of the world of sedentary agriculture with the frontier world of
nomads, overland and maritime long-distance traders, of movable
goods and precious metals.

GUJARAT

We will begin our survey of the developments in the coastal world
of the Indian Ocean in the eleventh to thirteenth centuries with
Gujarat. This region of western India, which includes modern
Gujarat, Cutch, Saurashtra, south Rajasthan, and parts of Malwa
and the northern Konkan, is bounded in the north by the desert
of Marwar, in the north-west by the Great Rann of Cutch, in the
west by the Indian Ocean, in the south by the Deccan plateau, in
the east by the gorges of the Narmada and Tapti rivers with the
Satpura range in between, and in the north-east by the Mewar
and Malwa plateaux. With its alluvial plains in the centre and
along the coast and its orientation towards the sea in the west and
with links to the North-Indian plains through routes running
through the northern and eastern ranges, it was ideally situated
for the development of trade.[18] Trade, in effect, flourished here
from early times, and in the early medieval period had been intimately linked to the vicissitudes of the Abbasid caliphate with its
capital in Baghdad. The Caulukyas of Anahilvāda (941-1297 AD)
gave a political and geographical unity to this area for the first
time. With the Caulukya kingdom expanding from its base at

---

[18] Cf. V. K. Jain, *Trade and Traders in Western India (AD 1000-1300)* (New Delhi, 1990), p. 11.

Anahilvāda in the Sārasvata mandala in north Gujarat, the region came to be called *Gurjara Mandala* or *Gurjara Bhūmi*. In the thirteenth century this Gurjara dominion did not yet include Lāta and Saurashtra, which maintained separate political identities until the Muslims, by the fourteenth century, conquered northern and southern Gujarat along with Saurashtra and governed it from their headquarters at Anahilvāda, and it was not until then that the term Gujarat came to be applied to the whole region.

The Caulukyas appear to have stimulated agricultural expansion and internal as well as external trade simultaneously. Central and northern Gujarat contains settlements of great antiquity, but in these areas agricultural tillage expanded considerably in the post-tenth centuries, when numerous stepwells and water reservoirs were excavated.[19] Although it is not known how much of the cotton area of Gujarat was exploited in the eleventh to thirteenth centuries, it is clear that cotton was the leading agricultural product of Gujarat, although the region was also famous for indigo and oilseeds, and cereals were among its staple products as well, as were sugarcane and hemp.[20] Due to improved irrigational facilities, the cultivation of these crops in northern Gujarat, Saurashtra, Cutch, and south Rajasthan increased.[21] But coastal Gujarat was really the prized possession of the Caulukyas. Here commercial contacts were promoted which reached across the Indian Ocean, leading to a considerable growth of mercantile activity in the region and intensified contact between Cutch and Canara.[22] Kambaya or Stambhatīrtha was the main port of the Caulukyas, and at the time of the Muslim conquest in 1298 it was referred to as 'one of the richest towns in India'.[23] A 'military road' was constructed, connecting Junagadh with Wadhwan, and hence with the capital town of Anahilvāda and with the coastal ports of western Saurashtra. Wadhwan, on a raised plateau, representing a narrow bridge to the Gujarat plain, thus became the gateway to Saurashtra.[24] In Cutch, a region of transition between western India and the Thar desert, the town of Bhadreshwar appears to

---

[19] *Ibid.*, p. 12.
[20] *Ibid.*, pp. 20-21.
[21] *Ibid.*, pp. 25-34.
[22] *Ibid.*, pp. 19-20.
[23] *Ibid.*, p. 12.
[24] *Ibid.*, p. 14.

have become the most important trade centre in these centuries.[25] But the coastal belt of Gujarat includes the gulfs of Cutch and Kambaya, and the coasts of Saurashtra and north Konkan, and here every creek which could provide safe anchorage had a port of some significance.[26] The Gulf of Kambaya had better navigational facilities than that of Cutch, and the economic prosperity of Gujarat, in effect, depended principally on the ports of Kambaya, Broach (Bhrgukaccha) and their satellites which lay in this gulf. The southwest coast of Saurashtra also had many harbours, the most important of which were Somanātha (Veraval) and Mangrol. And the list of important ports in the region further included Ghogha on the Saurashtra coast, and Kavi, Gandhara, Rander, Sopara, Sindan (Sanjana), Saymur (Chaul), and Thana on the coasts of south Gujarat and north Konkan.[27]

Since Gujarat served as a gateway to the north and an entrepot for the goods shipped to Sind and western Asia, most of the goods which were brought here seem to have formed part of a transit trade.[28] Imports to western India included precious and base metals, silk, gems, ivory, fine spices, wine, frankincense, and horses.[29] A large number of spices which is noted in contemporary inscriptions seems to have come into Gujarat from South India and Southeast Asia.[30] The main exports from western India were textiles, manufactured goods and leather, sugar, timber, certain dyes, spices and aromatics, precious and semi-precious stones and slaves.[31] A shift occurred in these centuries towards a more comprehensive range of goods, and bulk goods, away from mere spices and luxury goods.[32] Much of the foreign trade continued

---

[25] *Ibid.*, p. 16.
[26] *Ibid.*, pp. 18-19.
[27] *Ibid.*, p. 129.
[28] *Ibid.*, p. 91.
[29] *Ibid.*
[30] *Ibid.*, p. 94.
[31] *Ibid.*, p. 98. Among the products that were traded in Gujarat, Marco Polo mentions pepper, ginger and indigo, and especially the cotton which was produced locally, and the great quantities of leather goods (locally produced were also tanned hides of goat and buffalo, wild ox and unicorn, and other animals) (Latham, *Travels of Marco Polo*, pp. 277-8, 293). Among the imports Polo mentions gold, silver and brass (*Ibid.*, p. 293). Chau Ju-kua mentions among the native products of Hu-ch'a-la (Gujarat) 'great quantities of indigo, red kino, myrobalans and foreign cotton stuffs of every color' (Hirth and Rockhill, *Chau Ju-kua*, p. 92).
[32] Jain, *Western India*, pp. 105-6.

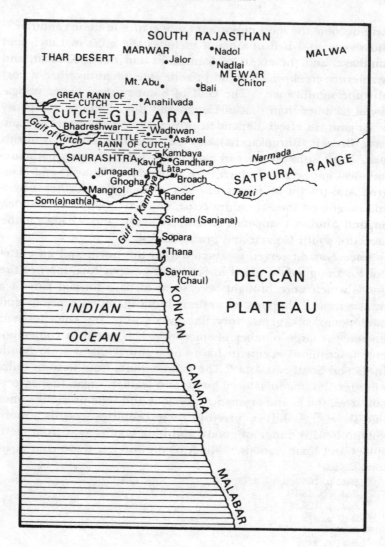

Map 7. Gujarat

to be conducted through barter, but there was also an increase in the use of money as, above all, the numerous hoards of gadahiyā or gadhaiyā coins indicate.[33] Unlike Sind, the Panjab,

---

[33] *Ibid.*, pp. 108, 145-67.

Kashmir and Bengal, the internal trade of Gujarat was conducted by means of carts and pack animals, as rivers were not navigable except for a few kilometers from their mouths.[34] Along the northern route, the increase in traffic resulted in the commercial and agricultural development of south Rajasthan, where new towns emerged such as Nadlai, Nadul, Bali, and Jalor, while already existing settlements increased in prosperity.[35]

As the commercial hinge between North India and the Indian Ocean, the Caulukya kingdom of Gujarat was a Hindu kingdom—with 4000 temples and '20,000 dancing girls' according to the Chinese account—but the literature of the period was largely produced by Jain authors and this was a literature which normally focused on merchants and mercantile activity.[36] Jains constituted the bulk of the trading community of eleventh-thirteenth century Gujarat, but they were also the cornerstone of the Caulukya polity, and members of their community were often appointed to the administrative, military and financial offices of the state.[37] Because of their opulence, these Jain merchants dominated the political, social and economic life (trade, credit and banking) of the region, becoming great patrons of learning and literature, builders of temples and works of public utility, and they also derived power from their guilds and autonomous corporations.[38] Their business conduct generally received high acclaim from foreign travellers, although there are many references in contemporary texts to their dishonesty and unscrupulousness as well.[39] Marco Polo refers to the banians of Gujarat as 'among the best traders in the world and the most reliable... They eat no meat and drink no wine...'.[40] The *Prabandhacintāmani* of Merutunga Acarya takes great interest in Jayasimha or Siddharaja, in whose reign the great Jain teacher Hemacandra first comes into prominence.[41] King Kumārapala was practically converted to Jainism and aspired to make Gujarat a model Jain state.[42] Under the guid-

---

[34] *Ibid.*, p. 53.
[35] *Ibid.*, pp. 119-23.
[36] Hirth and Rockhill, *Chau Ju-kua*, p. 92; Jain, *Western India*, p.4
[37] Jain, *Western India*, pp. 133, 240
[38] *Ibid.*, pp. 191, 197, 209, 227, 233, 242 ff, 245
[39] *Ibid.*, pp. 224-6.
[40] Latham, *Travels of Marco Polo*, pp. 277-8.
[41] Tawney, *Prabandhacintāmani*, p. xi.
[42] *Ibid.*, p. xiii.

ance of Hemacandra, the latter promulgated an edict which enjoined abstention from the taking of animal life, prohibited animal sacrifices by brahmans, the chase, butchers, spiritous drinks, dice-playing, animal combat and betting.[43] Whether such legislation had much, or any, effect may be doubted, and it is well known that Kumarapala also adhered to Shaivism, the family denomination of the Caulukyas.

If the Jains were predominant within Gujarat, their trade seems to have been confined largely to local coastal and inland trade, with the Muslims monopolizing more and more the external, overseas trade across long distances.[44] This division of labour was not absolute, but there is no indication that Arabs and Persians directly controlled the internal trade of Gujarat to the same degree as the Jains. Some foreign authors—Benjamin of Tudela, Marco Polo, and, in the fourteenth century, Ibn Battuta—also refer to Indian participation in foreign trade as far as Qays, Aden, Hormuz, and even China, but it is not clear whether these refer to Jains, Hindus, or perhaps Indian-based Muslims or Indian converts to Islam.[45]

Beyond doubt, it was the Arabs who, in the eleventh-thirteenth centuries, dominated the maritime trade of the area. There was a flourishing Muslim mercantile culture on the Gujarat-Konkan coast already by the tenth century, with roots going back to the ninth and eighth centuries and perhaps even earlier.[46] In the twelfth and thirteenth centuries, prior to the conquest of Gujarat in 1298, the entire coast of western India became studded with Arab and Persian trading settlements, and these, with the increase of maritime trade in these centuries, came to include more and more local people, both through conversion and intermarriage.[47] Ultimately, these Muslim communities were to contain not merely wealthy traders, and shippers and seafarers, but also indigenous groups like oil-men, masons and others, in quite sizeable numbers. Siddharaja's reign (1094-1143) became a landmark in the development of the coastal Muslims of Gujarat, when they were afforded exceptionally generous treatment.[48] In the popular imag-

[43] Ibid., pp. xi, xiii.
[44] Jain, Western India, pp. 70, 79, 81-82.
[45] Jain, Western India, pp. 81-82.
[46] Cf. Al-Hind, I, pp. 68-69.
[47] Jain, Western India, p. 72.
[48] S. C. Misra, Muslim Communities in Gujarat (Baroda, 1964), pp. 7-9.

ination of later times, Siddharaja became the founder of all the
important Muslim communities in Gujarat, and three Muslim pirs
are reported to have converted this king to their own particular
sects, those of the Bohras, the Khojas and the Sunnis (the latter
arriving largely from the Northern Turkish-dominated areas).[49]
The Ismāʿīlī communities of Bohras and Khojas became larger in
Gujarat than anywhere else in India, but in an almost impercep-
tible way, through peaceful accretion.[50] Conversion and the inclusion of indigenous people allowed them to strengthen their ties
with Indian traders and to some degree a gradual penetration of
the inland towns and markets of western India.[51] Al-Idrisi includes
in his list of 'countries' of western India, Māmuhal, Khābīrūn,
Asāwal (modern Ahmadabad), along with Kambāya, Sūbāra
(Sopara), Sindan and Saymūr, and he points out that 'at the present time the Muslims have reached most of these countries, and
have subjugated the regions surrounding them'.[52] Nahrwāla or
Anahilvāda, the Caulukyan capital, was also 'frequented by a large
number of Muslim merchants'.[53] Inscriptions in Arabic, found on
mosques and Muslim graves in towns like Kambaya and Somanātha but also in more inland towns like Junagadh and Anahilvāda
and dating from 1218 to 1291, confirm the presence of Arab and
Persian traders, who were almost all shipowners.[54] The normal situation was that the Muslim merchants of Gujarat, with their varied origins, benefited from the support of the rulers, who also
endowed their mosques, and from the financial support of or association with Jain or Hindu merchants.[55]

KONKAN AND MALABAR

The origins of the coastal Muslims in these areas are also obscure.
In the Konkan, there were the Nāvayats, elite Shāfiʿī Muslims who
are thought to have migrated from West Asia, perhaps the area

[49] *Ibid.*, pp. 9-13.
[50] *Ibid.*, pp. 15-19, 55-57.
[51] Jain, *Western India*, pp. 72, 74-75.
[52] Maqbul Ahmad, *Al-Idrisi*, p. 57, no. 110.
[53] *Ibid.*, p. 60, no. 16.
[54] Jain, *Western India*, pp. 75-76; Z. A. Desai (ed.), *Epigraphia Indica: Arabic and Persian Supplement 1961* (Calcutta, 1962), pp. 2-24.
[55] Jain, *Western India*, p. 5; M. Shokoohy, *Bhadreshvar: The Oldest Islamic Monuments in India* (Leiden, 1988), pp. 3-11; Ernst, *Eternal Garden*, p. 33.

of Basra, and settled here in the thirteenth century but did not
rise to prominence as merchants and state officials until the rise
of the Adil Shahis of Bijapur.[56]

Further south, we have already looked briefly at the Muslim
communities of Malabar.[57] Unlike Sind, Gujarat and the Konkan,
Malabar was never exposed to northern conquest, and its Muslim
culture retained its Arab-Shafi'ite orientation through the centuries. The Malabar coastal Muslims consisted of a Creole element
which was known as 'Pardeshīs' or 'foreigners' and a—larger—
Mestizo category of 'Mappillas', i.e. Muslims who had become
mixed with Malabari low castes in earlier centuries through marriage and conversion. Both Pardeshīs and Mappillas became much
more visible in the thirteenth century. On the one hand, the rise
of the great medieval trading city of Calicut brought the 'Samv-
dri Raja' or 'Ocean King' (otherwise known as the 'Zamorin') to
the fore. This meant the decline of Quilon and the victory of the
Cairo merchants or Karimis over their rivals from southern China.[58] Calicut, while first emerging in the eleventh century, benefited in particular from the great upsurge of Asian trade which
occurred in the mid-thirteenth century, when, after the collapse
of Baghdad, the Karimis began to sail to the city directly from a
revived Aden. The Arabs appear to have assisted the Samudri Raja
in his territorial expansion, and legends (confirmed by medieval
travel writing) preserved the memory of a great political transformation occurring in Malabar just prior to the turning of the
trade. On the other hand, although it is likely that Yamani and
Hadrami emigrants had been settling on the Malabar coast from
the beginnings of Islam, it is from about 1200 AD that the number of emigrants from Southern Arabia to many parts of the Indian Ocean littoral, especially South India, but also, slightly later,
East Africa and Southeast Asia, becomes large.[59] This increased
flow of emigrants was in all likelihood caused by a shortage of
good arable land in both Yaman and the Hadramaut, in other

---

[56] Cf. S. Bayly, *Saints, Goddesses and Kings: Muslims and Christians in South Asian
Society, 1700-1900* (Cambridge, 1989), p. 97.

[57] Cf. *Al-Hind, I*, pp. 69-78.

[58] Cf. A. Das Gupta, *Malabar in Asian Trade, 1740-1800* (Cambridge, 1967), pp.
4-5.

[59] A. D. W. Forbes, 'Southern Arabia and the Islamicisation of the Central Indian Ocean Archipelagoes', *Archipel*, 21 (1981), p. 80.

words by demographic pressure.[60] The resulting emigration movements carried Hadramis to South India after 1200, to East Africa
after 1250, and to Southeast Asia after 1300 AD.[61] Many of the
emigrants, who bore no arms , and generally paid no taxes, were
local Saiyids and Sharifs, learned in Shafi'i jurisprudence and *tafsir*
or, on occasion, members of Sufi tā'ifas, and many of them
claimed descent from the Prophet Muhammad through his son-
in-law 'Alī.[62] The result of their widespread influence around the
Indian Ocean littoral was that their ancestral home, the Wādī
Hadramaut, gained a reputation which attracted students of Islam
from the Arab colonies and Arabicised regions of South India,
Southeast Asia and East Africa. From observations made in later
times we know that the main difference betwèen the Arabs on the
Indian coasts and their compatriots in Hadramaut was the fact
that there were no women in India who were born in Arabia and
even no women of mixed blood which received their education
in the Hadramaut.[63] It was probably also the case earlier that the
members of the overseas communities of Arabs were either married to indigenous women or to the daughters of their compatriots, who had never left the country and were entirely like
indigenous women in terms of language, culture and manners.
The consequence of this was that all Samudri Arabs were more
or less of mixed blood.[64] Arab families, therefore, had a tendency to assimilate themselves in several generations to the indigenous populations, in Malabar as much as in the Indonesian Archipelago. What disappeared first was the Arab language, then dress,
and finally the family name.[65] But their assimilation rarely went
so far that they were admitted in the agrarian village communities, or became laborers, and they remained repulsed by the idea
of corvée, focusing instead on trade, retail or small industries.[66]
In Malabar, the agrarian economy always remained dominated by
the Nambūtiri brahmans and the Nāyars.

---

[60] *Ibid.*, p. 84.

[61] *Ibid.*, p. 84.

[62] *Ibid.*, pp. 84-85.

[63] L. W. C. Van Den Berg, *Le Hadramout et les Colonies Arabes dans l'Archipel Indi-
en* (Batavia, 1886), pp. 97, 184.

[64] *Ibid.*, p. 213.

[65] *Ibid.*, p. 215.

[66] *Ibid.*, pp. 215-16.

By the beginning of the early modern era, Portuguese texts tell us that all merchants of the sea in Malabar were Muslims and that 'the Gentiles do not travel by sea'.[67] In Calicut, the premier market of the Indian Ocean since the thirteenth century, the Muslims were then dominated by the Pardeshīs, who controlled the exterior trade and who were either seasonal or permanent residents and came from all parts of the Muslim world. The Portuguese referred to these foreign Muslims as the 'Mouros da Meca', although most of them did not come from Mecca but from the various parts of Arabia, and from Persia, Syria, Egypt, Tunis, the Ottoman realm, and even from Ethiopia, Sumatra and Pegu.[68] These 'Mouros de Meca' enjoyed a very privileged status among the Muslims in Malabar, acquiring the protection and services of the Nāyar military caste and provisions from the Chetti merchants right from their arrival.[69]

Because of the dominance of the Pardeshis, and also because of the presence of Gujarati merchants, the Mappillas at Calicut occupied a somewhat subaltern position. The latter were referred to by the Portuguese as 'Mouros da terra'. Recognizable by their long beards and their round caps, they served as stock-jobbers, commercial intermediaries, or transporters, and, while dominating the other cities on the coast, specialised in the 'country trade' in India itself—in spices, but also in rice, which they imported from Tamil Nadu and the Canara coast—and served in the navies which protected mercantile ships.[70] Among the earliest Mappilla communities there was that of Kolāthunād.[71] Its traditions are mixed with those of Ceruman Perumal and accredit their chiefs with extended authority in the three principal ports of Kolāttiri, Cananore and Dharmapatam. The notables of Cananore, in their turn, extended their dominion over the archipel of the Maldives, and we know that in the fifteenth and sixteenth centuries they obtained their wealth above all in the horse trade from Hormuz to South India, as well as in the distribution of Canara rice—a situation which may already have existed in the thirteenth centu-

---

[67] G. Bourhon, 'Les Musulmans du Kerala à l'Époque de la Découverte Portugaise', *Mare Luso-Indicum*, 2 (1973), p. 50.
[68] *Ibid.*
[69] *Ibid.*, p. 51.
[70] *Ibid.*, pp. 40-41, 51, 54.
[71] *Ibid.*, p. 51.

ry.[72] In Cochin, the Chinese described the Mappilla Muslims as second in the social hierarchy to the Nāyars.[73] Here there was a powerful family of Mappillas, the members of which bore the title of *Marakkars* (which was given to them by the king) and were allowed to wear silk turbans, and who controlled mercantile affairs.[74] In other, inferior, harbours—Pantalāniyi-Kullam, Ponnani, Cranganore, Kayam Kullam—there were also substantial groups of Mappillas, but in the latter two they were less important than the Christians.[75]

The association between the kings of Malabar and the Muslim merchants, while founded on an economic basis, was also manifest in the protection and patronage of cults and local institutions of Hindus and Muslims.[76] A fifteenth-century Chinese observer says that the two communities had agreed to abstain from the consumption of beef and pork, and that respect for the cow was a condition for settlement of the Muslims. The latter were not only guaranteed, in return, the free exercise of their own religion, but also exemption from landtaxes, while their residences were protected from unauthorized entry. The Muslims relied on their own system of justice, except in capital cases. Muslim notables maintained close relations with the dominant landholding caste of the Nāyars and also took part in the royal councils.[77] Banians and Chettis, and Nāyars of the lower ranks, all worked for the Muslims, providing them with a variety of services.[78] But the Muslims found their closest collaborators at the extreme low end of the social scale, among the Moger and the Mukkuvan who, like them, were people of the sea, mariners and fishermen, providing escort services for the kings while travelling, and performing multiple tasks of ship maintenance, and so on.[79] It was among such people that conversion to Islam principally occurred (the converts obtaining exemption for themselves from the royal confiscation of their goods), while high-caste women were, at all times, pre-

---

[72] *Ibid.*, pp. 51-52.
[73] *Ibid.*
[74] *Ibid.*, p. 52.
[75] *Ibid.*, p. 53.
[76] *Ibid.*, p. 55.
[77] *Ibid.*, p. 56.
[78] *Ibid.*, p. 57.
[79] *Ibid.*

vented from association with the Muslims by rules of endogamy.[80] In Malabar, Islam took root by conversion and matrimonial alliance, and Indianized itself in the process, as we can observe in the adoption of matrilineal succession among the first generation of Mappillas. Succeeding generations, while polygamous, tended to practice endogamy themselves. And some ancient Mappilla families, like that of Ali Raja of Cananore, claimed to have Nāyar and even kshatriya origins.[81]

COROMANDEL

Moving further south and east, we come to the parts of western and eastern Sri Lanka and the Coromandel coast, which together consituted a region in its own right. We know that in some of the ports of Sri Lanka there were important Muslim entrepots in the eleventh-thirteenth centuries, and we encounter Muslims serving as mercenaries in Sri Lanka at the same time, providing officials at the Sinhalese courts as well, but we do not know any solid facts about conversion on the island.[82] We can only speculate that the situation here was not very different from that in Malabar, in that conversion occurred largely among groups at the lower end of the social scale, but that the numbers involved were much smaller.

On the Coromandel coast, Muslim settlement, while antedating the eleventh century, accelerated at this time, and we begin to encounter famous religious missionaries in the area.[83] The connection of these coastal Muslims with the Karnataka, the Deccan and with North India was and always remained thin. The Ilappai, who were later called Maraikkāyar or Kayalar, retaining their Arab-Shafi'ite identity—so typical of the Indian Ocean littoral— through the centuries and later asserting a distinct Islamic port orthodoxy, distinguished themselves from the rural Tamil Muslims whom they stigmatized as mere converts of a much later date. On the Coromandel coast itself not much conversion appears to have occurred by the thirteenth century. There were probably Muslims

---

[80] *Ibid.*
[81] *Ibid.*
[82] Cf. *Al-Hind, I*, pp. 80-81.
[83] *Ibid.*; pp. 78-80.

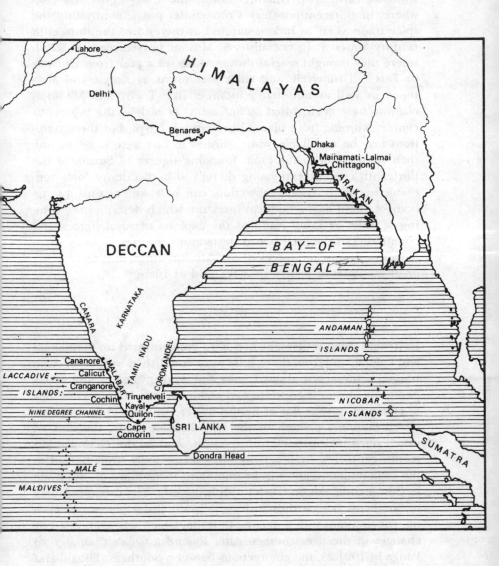

Map 8. Malabar, Coromandel, Sri Lanka, Indian Ocean archipelagoes

from Bahrayn, Iraq, Oman, Qazwin, and from Egypt and elsewhere, in thirteenth-century Coromandel ports, controlling the
spice trade as far as Indonesia. And at the end of the thirteenth
century Marco Polo encountered Muslim horsedealers at Kāyal,
where they brought several thousand horses a year from Hormuz
or Fars.[84] Tirunelveli, and such port towns as Kottar and Mut-
tupet, as well as hinterland localities like Trichy and Madurai,
claim to have been visited by Sufi saints as early as the thirteenth
century, coming from places like Mamluk Egypt, but these traditions may be unreliable. Many shrines in fact were eager to link
their foundation to the great founding figures of Sufism of the
thirteenth century, expressing thereby at best a desire for a ven-
erable lineage.[85] Similar objections can be raised against a large
body of Tamil hagiographical literature which describes the coming of Sufis to Tamil Nadu as the exploits of royal heroes and
conquerors in the twelfth and thirteenth centuries, fighting titan-
ic battles against the forces of non-Muslim kings, and conducting
great numbers of people into the fold of Islam.[86]

BENGAL

In Bengal, Arab settlement had been concentrated on Mainamati
and Lalmai, and from there links were established with other Arab
trading settlements, about Dhaka and Arakan and on the Malay
peninsula and in the Indonesian archipelago.[87] Here, in the 'Sea
of Harkand' (as the Bay of Bengal was known), the Arabs monopolized merely a portion of the long-distance trade, the bulk of
which remained in non-Muslim hands. And by the eleventh-thirteenth centuries, Arab activity was shifting away from Bengal to
the Cola domains, and was beginning to focus more on the trade
in Coromandel cotton fabrics with Indonesia. The urban complex
of Southeast Bengal thus suffered a gradual decline in our period, concomitant with a decline in trade, which was aggravated by
changes in the river courses. After Rajendra Cola's campaign to
Vanga in 1021-25, the connections between Southeast Bengal and

---

[84] Cf. pp. 86-87.
[85] Bayly, *Saints, Goddesses and Kings*, pp. 110-11, 155.
[86] *Ibid.*, pp. 183-4.
[87] Cf. *Al-Hind, I*, pp. 82-83, 274-5.

Shrivijaya appear to have been largely severed, although some urban centres of Mainamati survived into the thirteenth century.

As a result of the shifts in the course of the Ganges and other rivers which sometimes resulted in the flooding of entire cities, the role of Muslims in Bengal at this stage is less well known. Conversion was probably very limited at this time. How far the Arabs penetrated inland, into Bengal, from the coast, is also not clear. Stories about Māhīsawār and other Muslim saints coming by the sea route are widespread in parts of Bengal, but it is difficult to attach any definite chronology to them.[88] The evidence of the preponderance of Arabic words in the dialect of Chittagong and the facial resemblance of the people of Chittagong with the Arabs has been adduced to demonstrate early Arab colonisation and conversion, but these influences could well have come about in later centuries, when Muslims became predominant in Bengal and carried on trade with the Arab world through the port of Chittagong.[89] Coins indicate that contacts with the Abbasid caliphate existed in and prior to the thirteenth century, but the size of the Muslim community on the Bengal coast and the importance of native conversion to Islam are unknown. The 'numerous islands' in the Bay of Bengal which later became known as the Andaman and Nicobar islands, and whose wealth was constituted by cauris, appear to have been visited by the Arabs but were not permanently inhabited by them, and here too there appears to have been no conversion.[90]

MALDIVE AND LACCADIVE ISLANDS

By contrast, the Maldives and Laccadives had probably already entirely converted to Sunni Islam and had adopted the Shāfiʿī madhhab by the thirteenth century. South-Arabian links with these two island groups appear to have been important in the period between the establishment of the Mappilla community in Malabar and Ibn Battuta's visits in 1343-4 and 1346.[91] The use of Malé as

---

[88] Cf. A. Karim, *Social History of the Muslims in Bengal (Down to AD 1538)* (Dacca, 1959), p. 18.

[89] *Ibid.*, p. 17.

[90] Cf. *Al-Hind, I*, p. 81-83.

[91] Forbes, 'Central Indian Ocean Archipelagoes', p. 72.

a mid-Indian Ocean stopover predated the conversion of the islanders to Islam.[92] Ibn Battuta only visited the Maldives, leaving the Laccadives out of his account. He recounts the story of their conversion, which is more or less consistent with that of the Maldivian Ta'rikh, except that Battuta credits it to a fellow Maghribian and the Ta'rikh to a Tabrizi.[93]

From at least the mid-tenth century, the Maldive islanders conducted a regular trade in dried fish ('Maldives fish'), coir and cauris, with Arabia and the Yaman (probably at Aden), Persia, and the South-Asian subcontinent.[94] Coir was exported to Yaman to be used in the well-known 'sewn boats' of the South-Arabian coast, while Yamani trading vessels which visited the Maldives carried away large quantities of cauris which they used as ballast in place of sand.[95] The patterns of Arab-Muslim trade appear to have differed but little from those which the South- Arabians are thought to have followed in the pre-Islamic era. From the major Arab navigational texts it can be inferred that ships leaving the South-Arabian ports of Aden, Mukalla and Shihr for Malabar and Southeast Asia normally sailed north-eastwards across the Arabian sea towards localities at the later sites of Diu and Goa, and then sailed down the Malabar coast to Cape Comorin.[96] From there they sailed around Dondra Head (on the southernmost tip of Sri Lanka), across the southern Bay of Bengal to North Sumatra. And by taking this route, the Arabs could avoid the direct crossing of the Southern Arabian sea and using the violent and unpredictable Southwest monsoon of the summer. On the return voyage, however, the Arabs rounded Dondra Head and then took advantage of the gentler Northeastern monsoon of the winter in order to sail directly across the Southern Arabian sea from east to west.[97] And then ships bound for South Arabia or the Red Sea would either call at one of the ports of Malabar before heading towards the Gulf of Aden via the Nine Degree Channel, or pass by the Malabar coast and sail through the northern atolls of the Maldives before turning north-west towards Suqatra. In addition,

---

[92] Ibid., p 80.
[93] Ibid., p. 70.
[94] Ibid., p. 70.
[95] Ibid.
[96] Ibid., p. 72; G. R. Tibbetts, Arab Navigation in the Indian Ocean Before the Coming of the Portuguese (London, 1971).
[97] Forbes, 'Central Indian Ocean Archipelagoes', pp. 72-75.

there was a subsidiary route which linked Malabar directly with the northern Maldives, and the route linking Malabar with the Kilwa sultanate on the Swahili coast of East Africa also passed through the Nine degree Channel.[98] It was only after the initial conversion in the twelfth century of the Central Indian Ocean Archipelagoes to Islam that the influence of South Arabia in many port towns of the seaboard became paramount.

SUMATRA

The island of Sumatra participated in the trading world of the Indian Ocean throughout its coastline, reaching out from its northern shores to the Coromandel coast, and from there connecting with the trade routes towards the Middle East, while reaching out to the South China Sea and beyond from its eastern shorelines which guarded the Strait of Malacca and, further south, terminated in the Sunda Strait which separates Sumatra from Java.[99] In the eleventh-thirteenth centuries, the competitive and open world of coastal trade was becoming more closely linked with the Sumatran highlands, where agriculture was predominant, a chain of mountains which ran parallel to the shore on its western side and which was known as the Bukit Barisan or 'Line of Hills'.[100] Certain areas of a trough-like groove which runs from one end of the chain to the other, and form saucer-like upland valleys in places, were well-suited for intensive agriculture.[101] Conversion to Islam began on the north-east coast in the thirteenth century.

Urban life and international trade had, of course, been present in Sumatra and the Archipelago many centuries prior to the beginnings of the conversion to Islam, while Malay traders and ships had been present in the Indian Ocean from ancient times, venturing as far as East Africa at times.[102] The eastcoast lowland

---

[98] Ibid., p. 75.

[99] Cf. Dobbin, Islamic Revivalism, p. 1.

[100] Ibid., pp. 1-2.

[101] Ibid., p. 2.

[102] For the following sketch, see: O. J. A. Collet, Terres et peuples de Sumatra (Amsterdam, 1925); E. M. Loeb, Sumatra: Its History and People (Singapore, 1989); W. Marsden, The History of Sumatra (London, 1811); F. M. Schnitger, The Archaeology of Hindoo Sumatra (Leiden, 1938); Schnitger, Forgotten Kingdoms.

Map 9. Sumatra

(much of it swamp and unsuited for human habitation) had been the original home of Malay civilization, and until the later thirteenth century had outstripped the Minangkabau highlands in importance. It held the capital of the trading empire of Shrivijaya, located near Palembang, which was dominated by an elite which practiced an esoteric form of Buddhism and which controlled the two great sea passages between the Indian Ocean and the South China Sea, possibly as far as western Kalimantan. Shrivijaya, with its maritime orientation, is poor in antiquities, and, apart from a few stone inscriptions found around Palembang and elsewhere (as far north as southern Thailand), almost everything that is known of it comes from foreign visitors. Its own records, which would have been written on strips of *lontar* palm leaves, have not survived.

Chinese obervers tell us that in the late twelfth century 'the southern sea trade' was entirely 'in the hands of the Arabs', i.e. Muslim traders.[103] This explains why the realm of the Malay Maharaja in the west of the archipelago and the sea route to China were known to the Arab geographers, while Java and eastern Indonesia, which Muslim traders visited more rarely or not at all, were still, in the words of B. Schrieke, 'veiled in the mists of parageography'.[104] Shrivijaya's capital does not appear to have been a densely populated city, but merely a single row of houses which stretched for several kilometers along the Musi river. A Chinese chronicle of 1225 relates that 'in order to protect the capital from attacks, there was formerly an iron chain stretched over the Musi. This chain could be raised or lowered by an ingenious device. Later, after many years of peace, when the chain was no longer necessary, it was deposited on the bank where for a long time it was an object of veneration among the natives'.[105]

If Shrivijaya retained hegemony in the Indonesian Archipelago until the eleventh century, its decline as an independent power began with the Cola invasion of 1015 AD, and its final demise can perhaps be dated to the final quarter of the twelfth century, after which the lowlands became increasingly infested with malaria. With Chinese involvement in the Nanyang expanding rapidly

---

[103] B. Schrieke, *Indonesian Sociological Studies*, 2 vols (The Hague and Bandung, 1955-7), II, p. 232.
[104] *Ibid.*, p. 232.
[105] Quoted in Schnitger, *Forgotten Kingdoms*, p. 8.

under the Sung, the commercial stakes in the area went up and the Shrivijayan alliance system disintegrated. Other harbours, under the new hegemony of the Colas, rose to prominence, and Java became an increasingly important rival as well, perhaps already surpassing Shrivijaya in wealth by 1178 AD. More and more merchants from Malabar and the Coromandel, and Muslims and Jews from Cairo, were attracted by the prospects of this expanding trade. The Colas subjected to their control no less than thirteen ports in Southeast Asia, and in 1067 they invaded the Malay peninsula. Tamil trading guilds left their mark in Sumatra during this time, for instance at Barus, on the westcoast, a port famous for its camphor, where an inscription dates their presence to 1088 AD. Other Sumatran ports which began to attract trade included Malayu, on the Batang Hari River, in the province of Jambi, which from 1080 appears to have been able to reduce Shrivijaya to subordinance. Malayu is usually associated with the site of Batang Hari, where important discoveries have been made during the restoration of temples which began in 1976; among the new finds there is a *Prajñāpāramitā* statue of the thirteenth or fourteenth century and a bronze gong with a Chinese inscription dated 1231 AD. The archaeological remains at Muara Jambi point at Malayu's political and economic domination of Sumatra during the twelfth and thirteenth centuries. And there were still other new centres coming up in Sumatra at this time in the context of the expanding trade with the Tamils and the Chinese. At Muara Takus, on the right bank of the Kampar Kanan, there is a number of ruins from the eleventh and twelfth centuries which appear to have been part of a town, with temples that are probably the graves of royal personages. They contain the Maligai stupa, and a terrace to the west, which is called Candi Bungsu.[106] It formerly supported a twenty-sided foundation, with a stupa in a wreath of smaller stupas, and recalls the upper terrace of the Borobudur. In the Padang Lawas ('Great Plain') region, in the upper reaches of the Barumun, lie the remains of the kingdom of Panai, which were first explored and made famous by F. M. Schnitger in the 1930s. These remains date largely from the twelfth and thirteenth centuries, although there are some which are older and some which are later.[107] The Panai kingdom is mentioned for the first time in

---

[106] Schnitger, *Forgotten Kingdoms*, pp. 27-35.
[107] Schnitger, *Forgotten Kingdoms*, pp. 66-83.

the Chinese annals of the sixth century, under the name of *Puni* or *Poli*, and by the eleventh century it ranked as the principal state in this part of Sumatra. It was an important crossroads, with access to valuable forest resins ·in the Bukit Barisan and to alluvial gold deposits in the south. Here too there is evidence of external trade with South Asia and China. It was conquered by the Cola king Rajendracoladeva in 1018 AD. Its temples, which date from after the Cola intervention up to the thirteenth century, include three brick candi · or biaro ('viharas') located at Bahal near Portibi, east of Gunung Tua, and these have strong Eastern-Indian and Buddhist-Tantric associations.

Further to the south, the Minangkabau highlands remained in many respects 'a world apart' until the late thirteenth century, but the Tanah Datar region of Minangkabau produced gold and it was through the gold trade that external influence penetrated the, area by the twelfth and thirteenth centuries, even before the highlands finally superseded the eastcoast in importance and the Minangkabau built a powerful state and commercial system based upon its gold resources in the fourteenth century.[108] Archaeological evidence and oral tradition show that in the twelfth and thirteenth centuries South-Indian Chettis entered Tanah Datar and took up residence in the Pariangan area, on the southern slopes of Mount Merapi.[109] The leader of these Indians was entitled *Mahārājādhirāja* and the community is known to have survived here up to at least the mid-fourteenth century, and it had considerable influence on Minangkabau life; many Dravidian and Sanskrit words arc commonly used for the most basic Minangkabau family, village and legal institutions. It also seems possible that Malabar traders either introduced or reinforced matrilineal institutions in the Minangkabau rice-growing areas.

To the north, finally, in the volcanic basins at the northern end of the Bukit Barisan, around Lake Toba, with the island of Samosir in its middle, lived the Batak people.[110] The first historical reference to the Toba Batak comes from the thirteenth-century Chi-

---

[108] Dobbin, *Islamic Revivalism*, pp. 7, 60-61.
[109] N. J. Krom, *Hindoe-Javaansche Geschiedenis* (The Hague, 1931), pp. 83, 303; idem, *Inleiding tot de Hindoe-Javaansche Kunst*, 2 vols (The Hague, 1923), II, pp. 422-3; Dobbin, *Islamic Revivalism*, p. 61.
[110] The coastal Muslims used the designation 'Batak' for the upland, pagan peoples in many parts of the Archipelago at later times.

nese geographer Zhau Rugua, who speaks of the *Ba'ta* in the northeast of Sumatra. William Marsden in 1783 referred to them as cannibals who possessed a system of writing. In spite of their relative isolation, the Batak had regular trade connections with the outside world, exchanging gold, rice and cassia (a kind of cinnamon), and tree resins like camphor and benzoin for salt, cloth and iron. They also exported horses. The latter trade was on a large scale, at least in the eighteenth century. According to Marsden, 100,000 bamboo measures of salt were imported annually into the Tapanuli region. Indian influence is found among the Batak too. Their language contains about 175 words of Sanskrit origin, and Batak writing, chess, spinning, religious ideas, and clan names are of Indian origin. Indian artefacts and sherds of Sung, Yuan and Ming stoneware have been found in the Karo villages. And Karo folktales refer to armed Indian traders of past centuries. The Sinyombak Karo have family names—Berahmana, Culia, Depari, Keling, Meliyala, Pandya, Tekang and Mukham—which derive from South-Indian dynasties or castes and probably indicate an early association with the South-Indian trading guild of the Ayyavole which appeared in northern Sumatra in the eleventh century AD. More South-Indian influence is found in Karo place names like Lingga, Cingkem and Kubuculia. And at Medan's port of Belawan, at the confluence of the Belawan and Deli rivers, there is the archaeological site of Kota Cina, where remains (Vaishnavite and Buddhist images and other artefacts) have been found of eleventh- to fourteenth-century South-Indian and Chinese trading settlements.

Muslim traders had been visiting harbours and establishing colonies in the archipelago, even beyond the area dominated by Shrivijaya, for centuries before substantial conversion began to occur in about the second half of the thirteenth century and a number of small Islamic kingdoms arose on the northeastern littoral of Sumatra. If, until the mid-thirteenth century, the political centres of the island had been located near Palembang, or in Jambi, and the entire island had been called 'Jawa' or 'Jawa Minor' by travelers and traders, it now took the name of one of its flourishing ports in the northeast, known as *Samudra*, meaning 'ocean' in Sanskrit, and from this the name *Sumatra* was derived. In Marco Polo's time, Samudra was still a small kingdom ruled by people who, he claims, were as pagan as those of the interior, while he reported that the neighbouring kingdom of 'Ferlec' or Perlak (near modern Langsa) had already turned to Islam owing to their contacts with Muslim merchants.[111] When Ibn Battuta visited the town of Samudra in 1323, it had become a Muslim Sultanate with trading contacts extending to South Asia and China. By then many South-Indian Muslim traders had settled in the city and, under its Muslim name of *Pasai*, its rulers issued gold coins and developed a system of writing Malay in the Arabic script, while it was becoming the first centre of Islamic scholarship in the Archipelago.[112] The *Hikayat Raja-Raja Pasai* also advances the claim that Samudra-Pasai was the first state in the Archipelago to enter Islam.[113] But, while it is generally accepted that Islam was its major religion for about three decades before its first Muslim ruler died in 1297, in fact Samudra-Pasai was probably not the first state in North Sumatra to adopt Islam. All sources agree that at least Perlak and Aru preceded it by a few years.[114]

On the northeastern coast of Sumatra, the site of the earliest Islamic kingdoms, there is a number of short, fast-flowing rivers which descend from the Bukit Barisan to the shore, providing sheltered anchorages, water and provisions for ocean-going ships.[115] It is certain that, whatever the precise timing, ports which developed here, like Samudra-Pasai, Langsa, Perlak, Aru, Samalanga, and Pidie (Sigli) all converted to Islam in the thirteenth and fourteenth centuries. Samudra-Pasai, while fading from historiography in later times, did not disappear and always retained a certain distinction among the Muslim kingdoms of Sumatra. According to Tomé Pires, Samudra-Pasai counted 20,000 inhabitants in the early sixteenth century, by which time it was heavily involved

---

[111] Cf. p. 42.

[112] In Pelliot's view, the name *Pasai* was older than the thirteenth century, and he suggested that in the eleventh and twelfth centuries the name *Po-se*, while generally indicating Persia in Chinese, may sometimes have been employed to indicate a Malay state and that this was the origin of the name *Pasai* (Cf. G. W. J. Drewes, 'New Light on the Coming of Islam to Indonesia', *Bijdragen tot de Taal, Land- en Volkenkunde*, 124 (1968), pp. 436-7, note 6; *Al-Hind, I*, pp. 48-49).

[113] G. E. Marrison, 'The Coming of Islam to the East Indies', *Journal of the Malayan Branch of the Royal Asiatic Society*, XXIV, Pt 1 (1951), p. 29.

[114] A. H. Johns, 'Islam in Southeast Asia: Reflections and New Directions', *Indonesia*, 19 (April 1975), p. 25.

[115] Cf. J. Anderson, *Acheen and the Ports on the North and East Coasts of Sumatra; with incidental notices of the trade in the eastern seas and the aggressions of the Dutch* (London, 1840).

in the pepper trade and was soon to be incorporated in the Sultanate of Achin. Even then the city retained its high status as 'in former times here was the seat of kings; from here the religion of Islam took its rise'.[116] Under Achinese government, Pasai was a royal domain administered by a 'bentara blang kubur' or 'superintendent of the distinguished tombs'. These tombstones of Pasai, including those of the first Islamic rulers of the Archipelago, and dating back to the late thirteenth century, became the object of a royal Achinese pilgrimage in 1638-9. Their presence legitimized the sovereignty of Islamic Achin over Sumatra and the Straits area.[117]

It is thus clear that the growth of trade and trading cities provided the initial spur to the Islamicization of the Archipelago. After the rise of Samudra-Pasai and other cities on the northeast coast of Sumatra, especially during the 'spice orgy' which began in the late fourteenth century and coincided with increased Ming-Chinese activity in Southeast Asia, there were other Islamic cities developing, on the Malay peninsula, the north coast of Java, Kalimantan, and Sulawesi, occupying a power vacuum or challenging existing rivals. The actual conversion of these cities is not documented in any detail, nor do we know much about how Islam spread to the hinterland.[118] Most sixteenth-century Portuguese sources, following Marco Polo, assume that contact with Muslim merchants from the West was a sufficient explanation for conversion.[119] The gulf between the interconnected urban centres on

---

[116] G. W. J. Drewes (ed.), *Hikajat Potjut Muhamat, An Acehnese Epic* (The Hague, 1979), s. 1538-39.

[117] Cf. T. J. Veltman, 'Nota over de geschiedenis van het landschap Pidie (Pedir)', *Tijdschrift voor Indische Taal-, Land- en Volkenkunde*, 58 (1919), pp. 15-19; Lombard, *Sultanat d'Atjeh*, pp. 32-33; Schrieke, *Indonesian Sociological Studies*, II, pp. 254, 256.

[118] Legendary Malay literature, the *Hikayat Raja-Raja Pasai* and the *Sejarah Melayu*, preserved the memory of the early spread of Islam but these sources are no longer regarded as very authoritative guides to the events in Pasai during the thirteenth and fourteenth centuries (Cf. Johns, 'Islam in Southeast Asia', p. 40; A. Teeuw, 'Hikayat Raja-Raja Pasai and Sejarah Melayu', in: J. Bastin and R. Roolvink (eds), *Malayan and Indonesian Studies* (Oxford, 1964), pp. 222-34; Drewes, 'New Light', p. 436; *Malay Annals: translated from the Malay language by J. Leyden* (London, 1821), pp. 66-68.

[119] Cf. Johns, 'Islam in Southeast Asia', pp 37-39; A. Reid, 'The Islamization of Southeast Asia', in: M. A. Bakar, A. Kaur and A. Z. Ghazali (eds), *Historia: Essays in Commemoration of the 25th Anniversary of the Department of History, University of Malaya* (Kuala Lumpur, 1984), p. 14.

the Indian Ocean littoral and their hinterlands has generally been assumed to have been immense.[120] Melaka is an extreme example, but prior to the rise of Achin the commercial cities of northern Sumatra are always described as enclaves surrounded by tattooed cannibals.[121] That such a gulf existed cannot be denied because of the large foreign element in the cities. Yet, all of these cities shared a culture which was Malayo-Muslim and a distinctively Southeast-Asian urban settlement pattern.[122] In other words, they too were products of the successful fusion of the maritime frontier and settled society. Islam was brought to them by traders, and associated itself with the sophisticated lifestyle of the cities, and the latter were becoming more and more closely linked to extensive hinterlands which had been opened up from pre-Islamic times. And if these cities were not ruled by Muslims, a situation developed which was not unlike that of Malabar, in which 'the king is a pagan; the merchants are Moors'.[123] The latter must still have been the situation in Samudra in 1282, when a non Muslim king sent Muslim envoys to China. But it also applies to Patani in the fourteenth century, Melaka in the early fifteenth, Banjarmasin in the early and Makassar in the late sixteenth century.

---

[120] Reid, 'Islamization of Southeast Asia', p. 21.
[121] Ibid.
[122] Ibid.
[123] Ibid., p. 24.

CHAPTER IX

THE IDOLS OF HIND

We have seen in the preceding two chapters that the establishment of Islamic rule in North India did not entail any systematic attempts at conversion of the native Indian population, and that whatever conversion occurred in the eleventh to thirteenth centuries mostly fell outside the scope of the conquest state. Islamic conquest resulted in the formation of new urban centres under the aegis of Muslim immigrants, and an expansion of the money economy, but no great demographic shifts or widespread Islamicization. Unlike the Middle East, which converted to Islam almost entirely, in the settled societies of *al-Hind* a non-Islamic substructure survived.

But without the independent Hindu king, the intimate connection of kingship, temple building and Hindu religious worship was lost in the areas which were conquered. If the temples were not destroyed, patronage dried up, and few great temples were built in North India after the thirteenth century. Even without conversion, India's sacred geography was uprooted by the Islamic conquest, and the newly evolving Indo-Islamic polity transcended it in the name of the new universal religion. Thus, the fusion of frontier and settled society became engraved in the architectural landscape as well. Most importantly perhaps, Islamic iconoclasm—a religious phenomenon of the frontier—undermined the potential power of the icons as communal symbols, as expressions of the communal life of the peasantry. For the veneration of icons and relics was a collective experience of a mass of believers, exciting powerful emotions, while the power exhibited by icons, through miracles, like that of relics, was overwhelmingly public.[1] The present chapter aims to explore how Islamic iconoclasm in India reflects the structural urge for social atomization and the attempt to integrate the authority of the Muslim emperor among local polities and elevate it above them.

---

[1] Cf. A. P. Kazhdan and Ann Wharton Epstein, *Change in Byzantine Culture in the Eleventh and Twelfth Centuries* (Berkeley, Los Angeles and London, 1985), pp. 12-13.

a. KINGS AND TEMPLES: INDIAN RELIGION AND ARCHITECTURE ON THE EVE OF THE TURKISH CONQUEST

Let us first look again into the relationship of kingship and religion as it existed in pre-Islamic India. It has been shown in the previous volume that, by the time that the Turks arrived, the building of monumental temples in stone for congregational worship and theistic cults had become a characteristic feature of kingdoms throughout al-Hind.[2] Such temples arose from the Gupta period onward, expressing new vertical patterns of social and political organization which brought the brahman priesthood to ascendancy and which superseded the loose, 'imperial' organization of Buddhism as supported by itinerant traders and monks. The building in stone reflected a pattern of increased sedentarization and agricultural expansion. Permanent materials were used in the new building style—not without betraying its origin in wood and bamboo architecture—and many of the earliest stone buildings, in effect, survived to the present day, wholly or partially intact, with the detail of their surface decoration still showing. The building of temples marks the early medieval period as an especially creative one. From the beginnings of this period we also have texts on temple building: the Bṛhat-Samhitā of Varāhamihira,[3] and the Vishnudharmottara Purāna.[4]

Henceforward, temples continued to be built in stone. Or, when suitable stone was not easily available, in brick, with mortar, as in central and eastern India, the Himalayas, and parts of mainland Southeast Asia and the Indonesian Archipelago. Many of the great brick temples, of Bengal for instance, have not survived.[5] Others did: the small, isolated brick temples of the Majapahit period in eastern Java are still standing; while those of Bali, with carved stone lintels and cornices and with wooden superstructures, dating from perhaps as early as the eleventh century, were levelled by earthquakes. Many of the most famous buildings in North India at the time of the Turkish invasions must have been built entirely of brick, and were decorated with terracotta ornaments and

---

[2] Al-Hind, I, pp. 226–30

[3] A. Tripathi (ed.), The Bṛhat-Samhitā of Varāhamihira (Varanasi, 1968).

[4] P. Shah (ed.), Vishnudharmottara Purana, Khanda III, 2 vols (Baroda, 1958-61).

[5] Cf. Al-Hind, I, p. 264.

alto-relievos.[6] This was the case with the great sun-temple at Multan, with the shrine of Jagsoma at Thanesar, with the great Buddhist buildings at Sankisa, Kosambi, and Sravasti, and with all the
brahmanical temples of the Gupta period at Bilsar, Bitargaon,
Garhwa, and Bhitari.[7] In Bihar and Bengal the absence and cost-
liness of stone led to the creation of the great brick temples of
Bodh Gaya and Nalanda. In Champa we find towers which were
constructed of dried brick mortared with resin from the cau day
tree; when completed, these structures were enveloped in fire for
several weeks, fusing the resin and bricks together and creating
an edifice which could withstand anything but modern warfare.
It was in stone, however, that Hindu architecture found its most
durable, as well as typical, expression. Both stone and brick came
to be reserved almost exclusively for religious architecture and
were rarely employed in secular buildings (except in fortification
walls), even though wood would continue to play an important
role in tempels.[8] The building pattern of all known styles was tra-

---

[6] Cf. A. Cunningham, *Report of Tours in the Gangetic Provinces from Badaon and
Bihar in 1875-6 and 1877-8 (Archaeological Survey of India, Vol. XI)* (Varanasi, 1968),
p. 42.

[7] *Ibid.*

[8] Cf. *KT*, IX, p. 241. In the Indus valley, many major buildings, and individual portions thereof, were constructed in brick. By Hiuen Tsang's time however:
'... most of the city-walls are built of bricks, while walls of houses and enclosures
are wattled bamboo or wood. Their halls and terraced belvederes have wooden
flat-roofed rooms, and are coated with chunam, and covered with tiles burnt or
unburnt'(Watters, *Yuan Chwang*, I, p. 147). At an early date, Buddhist monasteries ceased to be constructed only of perishable substances, and stupas ceased
to be only mounds of mud or earth, both types of structure beginning to be erected in stone and brick, or carved out of living stone (J. Heitzman, *The origin and
spread of Buddhist monastic institutions in South Asia, 500 BC-300 AD* (Philadelphia,
1980), p. 6). In Vijayanagara, 'royal residences are indicated by stone basements,
steps, balustrades, plastered concrete floors, and internal walls of earth and rubble'(J. M. Fritz and G. Michell, *City of Victory: Vijayanagara, the Medieval Hindu
Capital of Southern India* (New York, 1991), p. 100). An exception are alleged to
have been the Bhars of Awadh, who appear to have built all their towns in brick,
but no temples (Cf. Reeves, *Sleeman in Oudh*, pp. 276-7: 'All their [the Bhars']
towns seem to have been built of burnt brick while none of the towns of the present day are so .... I am not aware of any temples having been found to indicate
their creed'). In Angkor, all domestic buildings, as well as some superstructures,
were made of wood and similar perishable materials; according to Chinese
sources, sheet metal was also much used, but that was probably taken by later
conquerors, just as all the iron and bronze fittings of the buildings have been
removed. Generally, in India, it was meritorious for a king to convert a wooden
temple into a stone structure (E.g. Tawney, *Prabandhacintāmani*, pp. 217-8). Thus
the situation described by Moldave in 1776 seems to have prevailed throughout

beate, with horizontal and vertical components only, and in the total absence of true arches, vaults and domes could always easily be distinguished from Islamic architecture. If we can speak of a Hindu arch, it was one in which the voussoirs were placed end to end, instead of face to face, as in a true arch.[9] This type of arch, although strong enough for small domes, was defective, as each ring of bricks formed a distinct and separate arch, which had no bond with its neighbours, and the outer ring was therefore always liable to peel away or fall from the face of an arch.

The monumental temples with their image shrines—which, needless to say, existed side by side with numerous smaller structures of merely local significance—provided the setting for elaborate royal cults, especially of Shiva and Vishnu. The buildings themselves came about mainly as a result of royal patronage. Temple styles and art, therefore, closely follow dynastic developments rather than variations of cult.[10] Royal patrons fostered the rise of regional styles, which often acquired dynastic appellations In competition with rivals, kings sought to erect the most splendid structures, the dimensions of which would reflect their political ambitions.

It is all the more remarkable, with this in mind, that we have very little information from inscriptions about the builders of most temples in India. The information which the Muslim conquerors of the eleventh century were able to gather concerning the antiquity of icons and temples is mostly useless: 'an inscription declared the great stone idol (budda) at Nārdīn to be 40,000 years old';[11] 'at Kanauj there were about 10,000 temples, which the infidels believed had been in existence for 200,000 to 300,000 years';[12] and so on. There is historical evidence about the dynasties which patronized particular temples, and it is also clear that the resources needed to start and successfully complete these grandiose projects could only be found by kings with extensive dominions. An unique manuscript from Orissa, written in an anti-

---

historical times: '... dans les villes des Indes ... la plupart des maisons ne sont que de terre' (Deleury, *Indes Florissantes*, p. 135).

[9] Cunningham, *Report of Tours*, p. 43.

[10] Cf. G. Michell, *The Hindu Temple: An Introduction to its Meaning and Forms* (Chicago and London, 1988), pp. 18, 50, 53, 89, 92; S. Kramrisch, *The Hindu Temple* (Delhi, 1980).

[11] *TYA*, pp. 335-6.

[12] *Ibid.*, p. 403; *TYP*, p. 245.

quated Oriyā script of the thirteenth century, lists the day-to-day expenses which were incurred in the construction of the gigantic Sun temple at Konārka.[13] This account shows how the building was completed, thanks to skillful organization and adherence to a strict time schedule, in less than thirteen years. And that, while the work progressed, many spontaneous donations came in from wealthy people throughout the region, but that the main patrons always remained the royal family. It is striking that everywhere in South Asia representations or portraits of these royal patrons in the temples were rather rare. What we have are depictions of scenes of enthronement, warfare, and so on, in the form of temple decoration, providing evidence of the close association of the lives of the rulers with the activity of temple building. Everyone, too, was free to see the Candella kings appear in the erotic scenes of Khajuraho. We read that in Gujarat, Siddharāja built a temple in Siddhapura, where 'the king caused to be made figures of distinguished kings, lords of horses, lords of elephants, and lords of men, and so on, and caused to be placed in front of them his own statue (svām mūrttim), with its hands joined in an attitude of supplication ...'[14] Images of kings represented as worshipers in Hindu or Jain temples were not uncommon in Gujarat, as were those of their ancestors, and of merchants and ministers.[15] Hiuen Tsang observed representations of kings and queens in mansions and shrines, probably pictures of them painted on the walls opposite the entrance, of a type that was familiarly observed in small temples by all travellers in India.[16] But the religious identification of these kings with the temples they built normally went no further than that.

It is only in Cambodia and Java that we find a more direct identification of king and temple, in so far as here the king was at times seen as a divine incarnation or as a part (amsha) of Shiva.[17] The concept of communion between kings and gods, on a sacred (terraced) 'temple mountain', may, in the case of Angkor, be relat-

---

[13] A. Boner, 'Economic and Organizational Aspects of the Building Operations of the Sun Temple at Konārka', *Journal of the Economic and Social History of the Orient*, XIII (1970), pp. 257-72.

[14] Tawney, *Prabandhacintāmani*, pp. 149-50.

[15] J. Burgess and H. Cousens, *The Architectural Antiquities of Northern Gujarat (1902)* (Varanasi, 1975), pp. 5, 17.

[16] Watters, *Yuan Chwang*, II, pp. 2-3.

[17] H. Kulke, *The Devarāja Cult* (Ithaca, 1978).

ed to an indigenous Southeast-Asian mountain cult which goes back to the days of Funan. Thus, as a deviation from the normal Indian pattern, under the Shailendra and Khmer dynasties of Java and Cambodia, the temple was dedicated to the god and the king simultaneously, while the architectural forms generally were more closely linked to cosmological and mythological belief systems. The association of religious architecture with the royal capital induced an emphasis on axial planning and a strict orientation to the cardinal dimensions. Hence we find here the combined idea of the temple as a religious site and a memorial to the king. The same can be said about the Buddhist monuments of these areas. At the Bayon in the walled city of Angkor Thom, for instance, the carved giant faces on the towers represent the Buddha, but also, it is commonly thought, the king or god-king himself. The four separate heads, of four different persons, at the south gate of Angkor Thom, of the twelfth-thirteenth century, are the four *Mahārājikka*, the guardian kings of the four Orients. We know that at Prah Khan, Yayavarman VII had erected a statue of his father, represented as Lokeshvara, the compassionate Boddhisattva Avalokiteshvara and 'world lord', the Universal Buddha. The great Buddhist edifices of Java are all connected with the names of the Shailendra kings. And the statues of Brahma, Shiva, Vishnu, and other Hindu gods that were installed in the many stone temples or *candi* of medieval Indonesia, especially Java, were also representations, perhaps even portraits, of the rulers. In some cases, the historical identity of the ruler can be identified from an inscription. Chau Ju-kua writes about Shrivijaya: 'There is in San-fo-ts'i [Palembang, eastern Sumatra] a (kind of) Buddha (i.e. image) called "hill of Gold and Silver", and it is cast in gold. Each succeeding king before ascending the throne has cast a golden image to represent his person, and they are most particular to make offerings of golden vessels to these images, and the golden images and golden vessels all bear inscriptions to caution future generations not to melt them down'.[18] Marco Polo writes about a king of Sri Lanka that 'he had an image made in his likeness, all of gold and precious stones, and caused it to be honoured by all people of the country and worshipped as a god. ... And he is deemed by the idolaters to be the best and greatest god they have.

---

[18] Hirth and Rockhill, *Chau Ju-kua*, p. 61.

And you must know that this was the first idol ever made by the idolaters and hence come all the idols in the world'.[19] In South Asia itself, the closest we get to this are the commemorative stone columns in the temples of Nepal, on which sometimes an image of the ruler and patron-builder of the temple is placed, facing the main entrance of the building.

Yet, either way, whether he was merely the patron-builder of the temple or whether the temple was actually dedicated to god *and* king, the vital constituent of these religious complexes was the Hindu or Buddhist king. What this means is that, before the conquests of Islam, the temples were an integral part of the regional polity because of their embeddedness in the authority structure. Kings, great and small, shared their sovereignty with the deities installed in the temple, the community of worshipers overlapping with the political community.[20] In the most important temples, kings would devote their daughters to service in prostitution.[21] The temples were not only associated with kingship, but they were the locus where kingship was contested and revitalized. With their sovereign status, temples became, like courts, centres of intellectual and artistic life, accumulated treasure and landed wealth, acted like wealthy patrons or employers, enjoyed tax exemptions, and, not infrequently, independent jurisdiction, and inviolability or immunity from military attack, while in South India they also served as fortresses.[22] If temples came to control increasing amounts of revenue, they also accumulated fixed assets such as jewels, bullion, and a variety of paraphernalia, like image frames, thrones, parasols, crowns, and vestiments of the deity.[23] The *devapūjā* or devotional cult of the image or symbol of the deity installed in the 'womb-chamber' of the temple also encompassed the temple itself, the components of which evoked the presence of the divine. Images were carved in relief in niches on the outer side of the temple walls. And as much as the images and sym-

---

[19] Latham, *Travels of Marco Polo*, p. 283. Elsewhere Polo writes: 'The people of Kashmir are also idolaters ... they are the past masters of idolatry and it is from them that idols are derived' (*ibid.* p. 78).

[20] Cf. B. Stein (ed.), *South Indian Temples: An Analytical Reconsideration* (New Delhi, 1978).

[21] As, for example, in Somnath (*TF*, p. 33).

[22] Cf. Michell, *Hindu Temple*, p. 58.

[23] Cf. M. D. Willis, 'Religious and Royal Patronage in North India', in: V. N. Desai and D. Mason (eds), *Gods, Guardians, and Lovers: Temple Sculptures from North India, AD 700-1200* (New York, 1993), p. 51.

bols of Hindu religious art were temporary receptacles for gods and goddesses, the temple itself—often built at a sacred site where the gods might easily reveal themselves—became a temporary abode of the gods on earth: the deity would take up residence, if the appropriate rituals were performed, as a royal guest in the temple.[24] The act of *pranāma*, prostration or bowing, was made to images of gods and great persons alike. It was a way in which the association of royalty with the divine was expressed in worship. And it was in the ritual, meant to persuade the deity to accommodate itself in the image of the temple as a king, that the role of the brahman temple-priests became essential.

If in the Hindu icon we find the expression of the shared sovereignty of king and deity, or of the (semi-) divinity of the king, and if the temple, constituted by the king, could become the temporary accommodation of the deity on earth, Islamic iconoclasm in India could not fail to have a political dimension. Students of iconoclasm in the Judeo-Christian context are quite familiar with this. In ancient Israel, where images were symbols of a hated ruling elite, prophetic iconoclasm was politically motivated as well. And in Byzantium, during the Controversy, victorious military campaigns were inextricably entwined with iconoclastic theology. Islamic iconoclasm in the Middle East appears to have been typically associated with successful political and military expansionism. This was also the case in *al-Hind*. It accompanied the Islamic conquest, but once the conquest was becoming consolidated, iconoclasm became relatively rare. What Islamic iconoclasm in India achieved was a new fusion of universalism and particularism, transcendent authority and local power, of mobility and sedentariness, nomadic space and cultivated realm.

b. THE POWER OF IMAGES

From early times, the religion of *Hind* or *Hinduism* developed as an 'image-making' tradition, the fundamental tenet of which was that divinity could express itself in a multiplicity of transient forms in the visible world.[25] The divine world could become manifest in images, but also in people and sacred places. Hinduism is embed-

---

[24] *Ibid.*, pp. 62-68.
[25] Michell, *Hindu Temple*, p. 36; D. L. Eck, *Darshan: Seeing the Divine Image in India* (Chambersburg, 1985), p. 10.

ded in a sacred iconography, a sacred prosopography and a sacred geography, all of which are bound up with pilgrimage and mythology. Mountain ranges are the abodes of gods; there are sacred rivers, foremost the Ganges, and sacred springs and lakes; and sacred caves, providing the idea of the sanctuary in the temple. The temple itself was regarded as a mountain, an idea which was especially developed in the northern building style. In the Indianized states of Southeast Asia, the temple represented the sacred mountain of Meru, which had a universal significance, associated with Shiva, the 'lord of the mountain'.[26] While the Hindu religion is the product of a 'polytheistic imagination'[27] which is polycentric and pluralistic, the actual fabrication of images, like the building of temples, became a carefully regulated art form and was not left to the imagination of individual artists. The general principles of Hindu iconography and iconometry, the techniques of iconoplastic art, developed along with architecture and town-planning in the so-called *shilpashāstra* literature, the texts of artists who made icons and who were called *shilpins*.[28] This body of literature took form in the course of centuries, and even though only a portion of what was composed survived, became so vast that no single scholar could ever treat it exhaustively. The oldest texts of an iconographic or iconometric character, of the sixth-century *Brhat-samhitā*, incorporate orally transmitted material of a much earlier period. In the earliest period of Hindu art, and in the Gupta period, there was still considerable variation and latitude permitted in image-making. But in the early medieval period the images became more and more stylized, with general principles being applied by the brahman theologians to the choice of image, execution, dress, posture, proportions of the body (the face-length mostly determining the size of the figure), gestures of the hands (*mudrās*), emblems and weapons, and the appropriate animal mount of each particular deity. The more naturalistic images of the earlier period were now left behind, and, while the temples became larger, the increasing number of images in stone and precious or non-precious metal became, like the temples themselves, subject to strict mathematical control and canons of

---

[26] *Al-Hind, I,* p. 338.

[27] Eck, *Darshan,* pp. 22-24.

[28] Cf. *Al-Hind, I,* p. 297; J. N. Banerjea, *The Development of Hindu Iconography* (Calcutta, 1956).

prescribed rules, the neglect of which would render worship fruit-less. Hindu iconography in its broadest sense became the inter-pretative knowledge of the religious, largely figural, art of Hin-duism, the religious tradition of Hind, in which Buddhism too became absorbed, primarily an art of sacred icons of gods, god-desses, demons, and semi-divine beings. Buddhism did not pro-duce the first images of its founder until about the first century AD. The earliest Buddhist bas-reliefs represented the Buddha ani-conically, through symbols like footprints, trees, wheels, stupas, and empty thrones. But these symbols were already objects of ven-eration. It is a much-debated question whether the origin of the Buddha image is to be found in depictions of indigenous Indian divinities or derived from Hellenistic influence in north-western India. But whatever the answer may be, once the Buddha image was established, it contributed to the development of a whole pan-theon of enlightened beings. The worship of celestial Buddhas became a typical feature of Mahāyāna Buddhism. Buddha images, in fact, became a great stimulus to the development of iconic tra-ditions in East Asia and China, concomitant with the spread of the Buddhist religion.

In the Indian tradition in its widest sense, major deities thus take a whole range of images and forms, each of which commu-nicates different aspects of the divine. The most significant ele-ment in Hindu worship is 'seeing' the divine image, *darshan*, and what is most characteristic about this worship is not merely the multitude of images that meets the eye but the sensuousness of it, the way it relates to the senses: seeing, but also touching, smelling, tasting and hearing.[29] The Greek *eikoon* (Latin *icon*), meaning 'figure', 'representation', 'likeness', 'image', especially of deities meant for worship, has a close parellel in the Sanskrit *arcā*, *bera*, *vigraha*, and other terms; these, in effect, denote sen-sible representations of gods and saints which are worshiped.[30] And these icons are described as the body or form (*tanu, rūpa*) of the gods or saints. Such 'representations', 'forms', or 'images' were and are mainly anthropomorphic or theriomorphic, or a composite thereof, with arms and heads multiplied to communi-cate their superhuman character. In addition, side by side with

[29] Cf. Eck, *Darshan*, esp. pp. 2, 11, 17.
[30] Banerjea, *Hindu Iconography*, p. 1.

the icons, existed, from a very early period, the aniconic symbols which are not 'forms' or 'images' and do not aim to be a representational likeness. Early Vedic religion, like early Buddhism, was entirely aniconic, just as it had no permanent temples or sanctuaries. Image worship in India dates from before the first century AD, and phallicism, the worship of the *lingam* (which is the most prevalent of aniconic Hindu symbols), is attested as a part of Shiva worship at the time of the Kushanas by the ithyphallic feature of the god on a goldcoin.[31] Its counterpart, the display of the female *yoni*, in combination with depictions of ritual copulation, is also attested for early times, while eroticism in general came to be perceived as auspicious in ritual and temple art, generating an uniquely Indian eroto-religious context for all forms of worship, which came to include (as already indicated) temple prostitution.

The importance of the visibility of the image is confirmed even in those cases where it is restricted by limited access to the temple. Often, a god or goddess would be secluded from the gaze of particular impure sections of the population. Even then, however, the visibility of the god would be restored during processions, on specific occasions, with the aid of portable god-images or 'moving images' (*calantī pratimā*), replicas, usually smaller, of original cult images (*mūla bera*) which remained fixed in the temple.[32] During major temple festivals, the image itself or the portable replica with which it was temporarily identified could be brought out from the sanctuary on a chariot in which it was carried around as in a mobile temple, for the duration of the festival. At certain times of the year, images were carried around in procession to tanks, where they were placed in floating shrines.[33] Such enhanced visibility could have an electrifying impact on the assembled worshipers, as can still be observed in India. It is probable that in Angkor the *devarāja* was such a portable image of Shiva and was worshiped as a substitute for the original *lingam* which was established in 802 AD at the foundation of the state by Jayavarman II.[34]

---

[31] *Ibid.*; p. 152.

[32] Shah, *Vishnudharmottara Purāna, Khanda III* , II, pp. 190-1; Kulke, *Devarāja Cult*, esp. pp. xvi, 24-29; Michell, *Hindu Temple*, p. 65; R. Inden, 'The Temple and the Hindu Chain of Being', in: J.-C. Galey (ed.), *L'Espace du Temple*, Vol.I (Paris, 1985), p. 65.

[33] Cf. Michell, *City of Victory*, p. 67.

[34] Kulke, *Devarāja Cult*.

c. IDOLATRY

Just as it would be an impossible task to survey everything that has been written on iconography in the polytheistic tradition of India, so it would be an equally impossible task to survey everything that was written against images in the monotheistic tradition. The word *idolatry* is formed from the Greek *eidoolon*, 'image', and *latreia*, 'adoration'. Hence, from a strictly etymological point of view, *idolatry* would mean nothing more than 'adoration of images'. However, the concept of idolatry originated in the context of the monotheism of Israel, i.e. in the application of the Second Commandment, forbidding the making of representations of the divinity.[35] Idolatry is what was to be censured of the pagan cults by the prophets of Israel. As such the concept passed into the New Testament and early Christianity, and, ultimately, into Islam, with the result that all three great monotheisms censured idolatry. In other words, it was through Greek translators of the Bible that *eidoolon* acquired the meaning of 'false god': nothing but vanity, molded metal and carved wood.

For Judeo-Christianity, to worship as God things which are not God is, hence, idolatry. But there was, next to the infinite variations in the interpretation of the Second Commandment, also a theology of images which defended an iconodule position.[36] Thus the common *apologia* of Byzantine authors was essentially the pagan argument that images or statues are men's teachers and can direct men's minds towards the divinity, or that they were 'copybooks through which man engraves on his memory the lineaments of the divinity'.[37] This pragmatic point of view closely connected the icons with their prototypes: they would direct the mind from the visible to the invisible, they were the books of the illiterate. This was the educationalist point of view which found easy acceptance in the theologically less sophisticated Christianity of early Europe, and it was the view which triumphed in Byzantium in 843 AD, after intense theological debate and the Icono-

---

[35] J. Ries, 'Idolatry', *The Encyclopaedia of Religion*, Vol. 7 (New York, 1987), pp. 72-82.

[36] L. Barnard, 'The Theology of Images', in: A. Bryer and J. Herrin (eds), *Iconoclasm: Papers given at the Ninth Symposium of Byzantine Studies* (Birmingham, 1975), pp. 7-13.

[37] *Ibid.*, p. 13.

clast Controversy, providing continuity not only with the pagan
worship of statues but also with earlier anti-Jewish apologetics.[38]
All of the arguments used among the Byzantines in the debates
about whether Christian images were or were not different from
pagan idols, re-appear among the Reformation critics of images,
when again theological arguments had a direct bearing on iconoclastic practice.[39] When the first European traders and travelers
came to India in the sixteenth century, they were frequently
appalled by the overwhelming multitude of images, which they
saw, indeed, as mere 'idols'. In this vein, Ralph Fitch wrote about
Benares: 'The town is a vast museum of idols—and all of them
crude, misshapen, and ugly. They flash through one's dreams at
night, a wild mob of nightmares'.[40]

However, it might be pointed out that the Hindu position on
images was that they were not intrinsically sacred, and likewise
that there is a Hindu theological view which was perhaps in
essence not very different from the Christian iconodule position
which regarded the images as useful because they led from the
visible to the invisible, because they were 'aids' in contemplating
the divine. If in India the icons were more than statues and were
connected with a divine prototype while becoming the abode of
deities, it would be with the implicit understanding that the divine
lay behind appearances. Gods and goddesses would assume the
outer form of images in order to aid the defective imagination of
the worshipers. The image had the function of an *yantra*, an
'instrument' which allowed the worshiper to glimpse a reflection
of the deity whose effulgence transcends what the physical eye
can see.[41] The *Vishnudharmottara Purāna* defends image worship
with the argument that 'in the former three ages, Kṛta, Tretā, and
Dvāpara, men were able to see a god directly but in the Kali age
men have lost that faculty; therefore they have to worship them
(the gods) in an image'.[42] Elsewhere the same text explains: 'Vishnu's ... image is made not for his satisfaction because he is always

---

[38] *Ibid.*; *Al-Hind, I*, p. 40.
[39] D. Freedberg, 'The Structure of Byzantine and European Iconoclasm', in :
Bryer and Herrin, *Iconoclasm*, pp. 166-77.
[40] Quoted in Eck, *Darshan*, p. 17.
[41] S. Kramrisch, 'Hindu Iconography', *The Encyclopaedia of Religion, Vol.* 7 (New
York, 1987), p. 40.
[42] Shah, *Vishnudharmottara Purāna, Khanda III*, I, adhyāya 93; II, pp. 1-2.

satisfied, but for the satisfaction of his devotee. He does not want his image but he concedes his image to his devotees only to satisfy their devotion (*bhakti*). It is for favouring (*anugraha*) the devotees that he has allowed his images to be made. He who has no body comes to assume a body in order that his devotee can meditate upon him (*bhaktalakshana bandārtham*) because it is very difficult to concentrate on what is formless, while it is easy to do so on what has forms. So Mārkandeya has instructed as to how his form is to be made and how he is to be inducted. After meditating on god through a particular form (*sākāra*), a man becomes capable of meditating on him without the aid of any form (*anākāra*)'.[43] Almost a millennium later, in the early seventeenth century, an Indo-Persian text, the *Dabistān al-Madhāhib*, dismissed the charge of idolatry in the same way: 'Strangers to their [the Hindus'] faith supposed them to look upon the idol as God, which is by no means the case, their belief being as follows: "The idol is merely a *qibla*, and they adore under that particular form the Being who has neither accident nor form"'.[44]

Put in another way, it could be said that in Hinduism we find all possible forms of image worship, from the didactic notion to the notion that an image or statue could possess divine powers, dispense life and death, pleasure and pain, reward and punish, cure disease, and so on. Especially the latter were, however, characteristic only, as al-Biruni writes, of 'the uneducated', 'the common peole' (*al-ʿāmmi, al-ʿawāmm*), since the popular mind leans towards the concrete (*maḥsūs*) only, and is incapable of abstraction, which is the domain of the highly educated few. For this reason, al-Biruni continues, the leaders of many religious communities, including the Hindus, have introduced pictorial representations which then began to be venerated. Uneducated Mus-

---

[43] *Ibid.*, I, adhyāya 103-108; II, p. 189.

[44] D. Shea and A. Troyer (transl.), *Dabistān al-Madhāhib* (Lahore, 1973), p. 199. See for a comparable view: Law de Lauriston, 'Les Indiens ne sont pas idolatres', in Deleury, *Indes Florissantes*, pp. 706-9: '... il n'êst pas moins vrai que la religion des Indiens originaires est pure dans son principe, sans mélange de ce que nous nommes idolatrie. ... Elle ne reconnait qu'un être supreme avec ses attributs qui sont adorés sous diverses emblemes ou figures. ... c'est que la religion des Gentils dans l'Inde n'est pas une idolatrie ..'. See also: K. Narayan, *Storytellers, Saints, and Scoundrels: Folk Narrative in Hindu Religious Teaching* (Philadelphia, 1989), p. 33: 'If you want to reach the formless, you can only go from what has form [sākār] to what has no form. First form, then the formless'.

lims would be prone to do the same thing if they would be offered a picture of the Prophet, for example, or of Mecca and the Ka'ba. Whatever absurd views on image worship among the Hindus he is about to recount, al-Biruni adds, they are merely the notions of the ignorant crowd. Philosophers and theologians, those who seek liberation, worship nothing but God alone and would not dream of worshiping an image made to represent Him (*'an sūrati-hi al-ma'mūla*). To illustrate this, al-Biruni offers some quotations from the Bhagavad Gita.[45]

For all that, it seems safe to conclude that Hinduism never produced a theology of iconoclasm. Of course, just as in Christian Europe, and in Byzantium and the Islamic world, in India people can be seen to have engaged in acts of destruction, of buildings and statues, for purely utilitarian reasons, especially in times of economic hardship, or to enable themselves to erect new buildings, or when conquering the dominions of rivals, or in attempts to obliterate the architectural heritage of a previous dynasty, or in acts of aggression (thus Hindus destroying mosques).[46] Marble works of art from Amarāvatī, for instance, appear to have been brought down by the local people to supply them with lime.[47] But these remained incidental or random acts which were not backed up by any iconoclastic motivation as such. The same can be said about the incidental confiscations of temple treasure or lands by Hindu kings, or the periodic 'purifications' of the Buddhist sangha, which primarily served financial or political purposes and should be distinguished from iconoclasm. The well-known 'looting' of images which was pervasive in early medieval India and the Buddhist mainland of Southeast Asia should be seen in the same light. Thai chronicles refer to certain Buddha images which were regarded as the palladia of principalities, acting as their protectors and guardians of prosperity. When a ruler was dethroned,

---

[45] *Kitāb al-Hind*, pp. 84-95.

[46] For an example of the latter: M. Nizam ad-Din (ed.), *Jawāmi' al-Ḥikāyat*, (Hyderabad, Deccan, 1966), vol. I, pt. II, pp. 255-8. For an example of a Hindu king destroying temples of his father, see Tawney, *Prabandhacintāmani*, p. 245: 'Ajayadeva was set on the throne [in Gujarat] ... When he began to destroy the temples set up by his predecessor .... Hearing that his younger son had quickly destroyed them, he said: "Why even His Majesty Ajayadeva did not destroy his father's religious edifices, until his father had gone to the next world, but you are the lowest of the low, for you destroy mine while I am still alive"'

[47] Banerjea, *Hindu Iconography*, p. 33.

he would surrender his palladium and send it to the conqueror's capital. Here however it would be held as a hostage and treated with respect. It also happened within the context of Buddhist polities that rulers demolished each other's temples before carrying off famous Buddha images and relics. In the destruction of Ayuthaya, in the years following 1767, monasteries were looted, images and texts were destroyed or lost, and monks were forced to flee. And many similar incidents are recorded in South Asia in the early medieval period. As Richard Davis reminds us, 'We would certainly be wrong to picture Islamic iconoclasm or European commoditization, however profound their impact, as impinging on a previously static Hindu domain, where all such [sacred] objects occupied and remained in their own fixed places, recognized and respected by all'.[48] The appropriations of sculpted images by medieval Indian rulers can be seen as political acts. These rulers often proudly and repeatedly proclaimed their expropriation of objects from other kings. Such 'looting' was a normal an public aspect of war, directed towards symbolic objects, a matter of 'victory' not theft.[49] Commodities such as gold and silver and all regalia and images were reserved for the king, the centre of a redistributive network involving expropriated objects. Here too, 'the appropriation of Indian images recasts their significance without altering what they are and fundamentally represent'.[50] Intentional defilement or public mutilation of divine images is rarely mentioned in Hindu texts as a politically meaningful act.[51]

Apologists for Islam, as well as some Marxist scholars in India, have sometimes attempted to reduce Islamic iconoclasm in India to a gratuitous 'lust for plunder' on the part of the Muslims, unrelated in any direct way to the religion itself, while depicting Hindu temples as centres of political resistance which had to be suppressed.[52] Concomitantly, instances have been described in the

---

[48] R. H. Davis, 'Indian Art Objects as Loot', *Journal of Asian Studies*, 52, 1 (1993), p. 22.

[49] *Ibid.*, p. 27.

[50] *Ibid.*, p. 28.

[51] *Ibid.*, pp. 28-29, 42.

[52] For an example of this Marxist view, see K. A. Nizami (ed.),' Politics and Society during the Early Medieval Period: Collected Works of Professor Mohammad Habib, 2 vols (New Delhi, 1974-81). Nizami writes: '... His [M. Habib's] study of Mahmud of Ghazni led him to the conclusion that the Sultan's Indian campaigns were not

popular press of Hindu destruction of Buddhist and Jain places
of worship, and the idea was promoted that archaeological evidence shows this to have happened on a large scale, and hence
that Hindu kings could be placed on a par with the Muslim
invaders. The fact is that evidence for such 'Hindu iconoclasm'
is incidental, relating to mere destruction, and too vague to be
convincing. Shashānka, for instance, the wicked king of Karna-
suvarna in eastern India in the early seventh century, a precursor
of the Palas, is described by Hiuen Tsang as a persecutor of Buddhism.[53] Among other things, Shashānka is said to have attempted to remove the Buddha's footprints from a stone located near
Pātaliputra, but he failed to do so and then had the stone thrown
into the Ganges, from where however it miraculously returned to
its original place. Shashānka also cut down the Bodhi Tree at
Bodh Gaya, destroyed its roots down to the water, and burned the
remainder; but the tree was resuscitated by Pūrnavarman, 'the last
descendant of Ashoka', and in one night the tree became above
three meters high again. Shashānka also attempted to replace the
image of Buddha in the Mahābodhi temple—but only to replace
it by one of Shiva. Another incidence is the one described by
Taranatha of the reign of Dharmapala in the mid-ninth century:
the Hindu sect of Saindhava Shrāvakas, joined by Hinayana Buddhists, breaking the silver image of Heruka at Bodh Gaya.[54] An
inscription mentions the destruction of a Buddhist image in
Dakshināpatha by king Varmashiva in the first half of the 12th
century, by the efficacy of his *mantras*.[55] In Kashmir, the kings
Shankaravarman (883-902) and Harsha (1089-1101) acquired iconoclastic reputations. But Shankaravarman merely confiscated
treasure and lands of temples; the temples themselves he left
intact, with their icons.[56] In Harsha's case, statues of gods were
defiled by 'naked mendicants whose noses, feet and hands had
rotted away', and these were dragged along the streets 'with ropes

---

inspired by any religious objective but were motivated by a desire for economic
exploitation'. (p. xi; see also p. xiii).

[53] *Al-Hind*, I, p. 264; Watters, *Yuan Chwang*, I, p. 343; II, pp. 43, 92, 115-6.
[54] D. Chattopadhyaya, *Tāranātha's History of Buddhism in India* (Calcutta, 1980),
p. 279.
[55] *Epigraphia Indica*, I (1892), pp. 61-66.
[56] Cf. *Al-Hind, I*, p. 249; Stein, *Rājatarangini*, V. 166-70.

around their ankles, with spittings instead of flowers'.[57] There was hardly a temple in Kashmir whose images were not despoiled by this king, and reconverted into treasure. But in all likelihood, Harsha—who employed Turkish officers in his army—had followed the Muslim example, as the epithet applied to him, *Harsharājaturushka*, seems to indicate. In the same way, when the Kashmiri poetess Lalla criticized the worship of idols ('the temple is but stone; from top to bottom all is stone') she appears to be influenced by Islamic notions of iconoclasm.[58] And, to take a final example, when the Jain sect of the Lonkagachcha (or its later offshoots) claimed that there was no mention of image-worship in the canonical scriptures, this was the result of Islamic influence on its founder in the fifteenth century; and the same holds for Kabir and Nanak when they tried to establish the main principle of their religion as devotion to an attributeless god, or what is known in Hindi as *niruna upasana*.[59]

Similarly, it can be made out that the earlier Central-Asian invasions of the Hephthalites or 'White Huns' and the Kushanas lacked any specific iconoclastic motivation. The former, in the late fifth century, as reflected in the *Rājatarangini*, caused considerable disturbances in Kashmir, the Panjab, and wide areas of Sind, Afghanistan, and Rajasthan, leading to or furthering the erosion of Buddhism, but they do not appear to have been directed against icons as such.[60] Hiuen Tsang's testimony shows that in many parts of North-West India Buddhist vihāras, chaityas and stūpas, next to the 'heretical' deva temples, survived the White Hun onslaught in excellent condition. Whether Buddhist monasteries in eastern Afghanistan or elsewhere on the North-West Frontier were damaged or destroyed by the White Huns cannot be made out. Areas like Kusinagar and Kapilavastu which were not visited by the White Huns also had dilapidated buildings in Hiuen Tsang's time. The persecution of Buddhists by Mihirakula is probably a fact. But these earlier Central-Asian conquerors— predecessors of the Turks—enhanced rather than discontinued

---

[57] Stein, *Rājatarangini*, VII. 1092-95.

[58] Cf. M. Ishaq Khan, 'The impact of Islam on Kashmir in the Sultanate period (1320-1586)', *The Indian Economic and Social History Review*, XXIII, 2 (April-June 1986), pp. 197-9.

[59] A. K. Roy, *A History of the Jainas* (New Delhi, 1984), pp. 4, 144-5.

[60] Cf. *Al-Hind, I*, esp. pp. 149, 240.

the iconographic developments which had been started by the
Shakas and which became incorporated in the Indian tradition.[61]
Pious endowments had been made in Kashmir by Turkish rulers
from the neighbouring regions in the early eighth century, before
they turned to Islam: these included the famous stupa at Pari-
hasapura, attributed to Cankuna, who also equipped two vihāras
with gold statues. Under the Kushanas, the relations between
Gandhara and Mathura became very close. The Hellenistic and
Parthian elements which had been incorporated in the art and
architecture of Gandhara around the beginning of the Christian
era as a result of the Shaka invasions, were passed on to Mathura, which rapidly developed into the Kushana capital of mainland
India.[62] While the newcomers converted to Buddhism, they also
brought about a revival of Sūrya worship. New elements of iconography which were closely connected with the Kushanas in India
were the halo, the appearance of the Sun and Moon on either
side of royal or divine figures and the representation of flames
coming from the shoulders.[63] All of these elements had been related to the Shaka concept of divine kingship. In addition, the post-
nomadic invaders influenced Indian iconography by dressing up
such deities as Pancika and Hārītī—who were partly Iranian in
origin—in 'Scythian' clothes and making them sit in the 'European' posture. The same influence can be detected in the iconography of Sūrya, the adoption of boots for the Sun-god, the revival
of the Solar cult generally, and the establishment of numerous
Sūrya temples in northern and especially western India, from
Kashmir to Rajasthan.[64] The promotion of the Sun-god by the
Kushanas fitted in well with the concept of divine kingship, and
had considerable success apparently, even though these tribes
were non-vegetarian and the Sanskrit authors do not hide their
contempt for them and their descendants who settled in Sind and
the Panjab, pointing out their predilection for garlic, onions and
wheat.[65]

---

[61] D. M. Srinivasan (ed.), *Mathurā: the Cultural Heritage* (New Delhi, 1989), p.
79.
[62] *Ibid.*, pp. 46, 74-75.
[63] *Ibid.*, p. 78.
[64] *Ibid.*
[65] *Ibid.*, p. 79.

d. THE ISLAMIC THEOLOGY OF ICONOCLASM

In spite of attempts to link Islamic iconoclasm and iconomachy to a Zoroastrian influence which made itself felt from the ninth century,[66] the evidence seems overwhelming that Muhammad's view of idolatry, like the concept of idolatry in its very origin, as well as the later Islamic opposition to images, developed from a Judeo-Christian inheritance. Here the monotheistic tradition can be opposed to the Indo-Iranian tradition in its entirety—even though in practice religious labels like Muslim or Hindu have historically not been markers of exclusive groups or understandings of cultural symbols.

The Second Commandment forbids the making of representations of the divinity (Ex. 20: 4-6; Dt. 4: 15-19 & 5: 6-9; Lv. 26:1). The Biblical God Yahveh simultaneously forbids the worship of false gods and the worship of images that are claimed to represent Him, on the ground that it is impossible to represent the God of Israel. The repeated condemnation of idol-worship by various Old Testament prophets has been taken, quite plausibly, as evidence of the ongoing popularity of iconolatry. When considering the uncompromising Muslim attitude to images, however, it is important to note that Islam evolved from the Judaism of the Christian period, when the earlier permissive attitudes of Hellenistic Judaism had been shed in the confrontation with the Christians.[67] Uncompromisingly, the Qur'ān denies validity to any form of image worship, including the didactic form, which, it says, is favoured by those who say they worship images 'only that they may bring us near to Allāh' (*illā li-yaqribūnā ilā allāh*).[68]

The Qur'ān makes Abraham the progenitor of the monotheistic faith which Muhammad espouses and which sees idols as the enemies of God and His worshipers, condemning these along with

---

[66] E.g. M. Boyce, 'Iconoclasm among the Zoroastrians', in : J. Neusner (ed.), *Christianity, Judaism and other Greco-Roman Cults: Studies presented to Morton Smith*, Vol. 4 (Leiden, 1975), pp. 93-111, suggests that an iconoclastic movement in Zoroastrianism 'may well have played a part' in inspiring Christian and Islamic iconoclasm and iconomachy. This however remains purely hypothetical, and moreover would lead us to suppose that the formation of Islamic iconoclast theology did not begin before the ninth century—which seems too late.

[67] P. Crone, 'Islam, Judeo-Christianity and Byzantine Iconoclasm', *Jerusalem Studies in Arabic and Islam*, II (Jerusalem, 1980), p. 66, note 30.

[68] *Qur'ān*, 39:4.

the whole Semitic ancestral tradition which is at the origin of their worship and which is radically opposed to the worship of the one true God (26: 69-83). The Qur'ān also tells how Abraham smashed the idols which were being worshiped by his countrymen (21:52/53-70). These idols were without substance and could not create anything (25:3-4/5). Moses had to interfere against the sons of Israel as they had begun to worship idols after their flight from Egypt (7:134/138). Even the turning away from Jerusalem was justified by an appeal to the 'religion of Abraham'.[69] About one-and-a-half year after the Hijra, when the good relations with the Jews had begun to fail, the *Ka'ba* and the *Hajj* are mentioned in the revelations. In the Qibla edict, the faithful are exhorted no longer to turn towards Jerusalem in the salāt but to the *Ka'ba*. It is argued that the religion of Abraham, the prototype of Judaism and Islam, was obscured by the Jews but brought back to light by Muhammad: thus the Ka'ba was presented as the first sanctuary founded on earth (3:90), the sanctuary of the Meccan cult, the sanctuary of which Ibrāhīm and Ismā'īl had laid the foundations (2:121), 'the Holy House' (5:98), 'the Ancient House' (22:30, 34). From now on, the eyes of the Muslims were turned to Mecca, while an ancient pagan cult was given a foundation in religious history—not without making the Muslims vulnerable to the charge of idolatry by non-Muslims. Such a charge was, in effect, repeatedly made. Germanus, the Patriarch, pronounced the Arab worship of the Black Stone (*al-ḥajar al-aswad*)—which was made of lava or basalt—inside the Ka'ba as idolatrous, after which 'Umar is said to have had qualms about kissing it.[70] Similarly, Hindus are reported to have made the point that Muslims should not reproach the 'adorers of idols' as they themselves worship the Ka'ba.[71]

The Qur'ān opposes idols, idolatry and idolaters throughout, and most forcefully. Ibn Ishaq, the first Arabic biographer of the Prophet, devotes many pages to a description of Arab polytheism before the rise of Islam. In Mecca there was an idol in every house. Ibn al-Kalbī, in his *Kitāb al-asnām*[72], describes the prevalent cult-objects in the *Jāhilīyā*: *ansāb*, raised stones; *jaris*, stones upon which

---

[69] *Qur'ān*, 2: 129; 3:89, etc.
[70] A. A. Vasiliev, 'The Iconoclastic Edict of the Caliph Yazid II, AD 721', *Dumbarton Oaks Papers*, 9 (1955), p. 27.
[71] E.g. Shea and Troyer, *Dabistān al-Madhāhib*, p. 199.
[72] Cairo, 1914.

sacrificial blood was poured; sacred trees; small statues, 'which were bought and sold at markets'. For 'idol' these texts use the word *sanam* (pl. *asnām*), which is also found in the Qur'ān (6:74, 7:134, 14:36, 21: 58, 26:1) and in Qur'ānic commentary, 'an object venerated next to God'. In the Qur'ān we also find the word *shirk* in the Madina verses, describing Muhammad's attacks on the 'associators', *mushrikūn* (6:94, 10:19, 30:12, 39:4). *Shirk* designates the act of associating a person with divinity, or 'polytheism'. In the Qur'ān and hadīth, *shirk* is the opposite of Islam, 'worship of God'.

In addition to this, the Qur'ān demands from the Muslims that they fight against idolaters (9:36), or turn away from them (15:94), as they are nothing but liars (16:86/88-88/90), who will be treated like their idols (10:28/29), and so on. Idolaters are distinguished from Jews and Christians, however, who are 'unbelievers' (*kāfirs*) but possessors of scripture. Idolatry is an insult to God as it confers on creatures the honour and worship reserved for the Creator. The Qur'ān however nowhere speaks out against representation of living beings as such. It is silent on images (*ṣūra*), except as idols. The latter prohibition is only found in the hadīth, the traditions attributed to the Prophet and his followers, the oral law of Islam, which were recorded in the eighth and ninth centuries. The Islamic prohibition, moreover, may have been concerned, at first, primarily with sculpture—which could lead mankind back into idolatry.[73] In the hadīth, representations of living beings, those that have a *rūḥ*, are forbidden on the ground that the making of them is *ḥarām*, because it is an imitation of Allah's creative activity.[74]

Iconoclasm, then, became an integral part of the theology of Islam. But with regard to secular art the situation is ambiguous and complex. Manuscripts of the Qur'ān and hadīth were never illustrated, but their calligraphy sometimes assumed an almost iconic quality.[75] Until recently, objections were often made to photography. Hardly any sculptural art developed in Islam, but ara-

[73] A. Schimmel, 'Islamic Iconography', *The Encyclopaedia of Religion*, Vol. 7 (New York, 1987), p. 65.

[74] R. Paret, 'Textbelege zum islamischen Bilderverbot', in : *Das Werk des Künstlers. Studien zur Ikonographie und Formgeschichte H. Schrade dargebracht* (Stuttgart, 1960).

[75] Schimmel, 'Islamic Iconography', pp. 64-67.

besques and calligraphy may be regarded as a substitute for it. In secular buildings there was an abundance of representations of kings, musicians, or dancers, and so on. Illustrative painting developed, predominantly in Iran, especially after the Mongol occupation in the thirteenth century, when the influence of the 'picture house' of China grew. Islamic painting reached its peak in Iran and India in the sixteenth and seventeenth centuries. Human faces are shown, portraits of Sufis are frequent, and even the Prophet is depicted with his face uncovered; sometimes however these are found mutilated by later critics. Maps to guide Indian Muslims around places of pilgrimage exist in abundance, as they do for Jains or Hindus.[76] Islamic hostility to images was, it appears, limited to artistic expressions which were directly and exclusively related to religion and the religious legitimation of the polity. Thus, mosques in Kerala, for example, while in most respects virtually identical to neighbouring temples, lack decoration of any kind of human or animal representation in sculpture, frieze or painting.[77] In Bengal, the similarities between the brick mosques of the early Islamic period and the Hindu brick temples are striking; but the mosques were equipped with multiple mihrabs--as many as their are entrances in the mosque—which aimed to dilute the resemblance of the single mihrab with the image niche of a temple.[78] The central tradition of Islamic art always downplayed respresentations of living beings.[79] Islamic culture did develop a visual symbolic system and an argument about representation which was a form of 'aniconism' rather than 'iconoclasm': images were irrelevant because the truth or reality of anything alive did not lie in its shape or physical character, but in its inner worthiness which is hidden by its accidental shape.[80]

---

[76] J. B. Harley and D. Woodward (eds), *The History of Cartography, Volume Two, Book One: Cartography in the Traditional Islamic and South Asian Societies* (Chicago and London, 1992), p. 303.

[77] S. F. Dale, 'Islamic architecture in Kerala', in: A. L. Dallapiccola and S. Zingel-Avé Lallemant (eds), *Islam and Indian Regions*, 2 vols (Stuttgart, 1993), I, pp. 491-5.

[78] P. Hasan, 'Temple niches and mihrābs in Bengal', in: A. L. Dallapiccola and S. Zingel-Avé Lallemant (eds), *Islam and Indian Regions*, 2 vols (Stuttgart, 1993), I, pp. 87-94.

[79] O. Grabar, 'Islam and Iconoclasm', in : A. Bryer and J. Herrin (eds), *Iconoclasm: Papers given at the Ninth Symposium of Byzantine Studies* (Birmingham, 1975), p 49.

[80] *Ibid.*, p. 51.

e. ISLAMIC ICONOCLASM IN INDIA

The universalism of Islam—itself born in the desert, the locus of revelation and religious vision—soon acquired its operational and high-profile iconoclastic dimension on the frontier of conquest. Iconoclastic activity can, in effect, be dated from the very beginning of the religion of Islam. The Prophet himself, according to Ibn Ishaq, ordered all idols around the Kaʿba to be destroyed. We have sporadic evidence of the removal and destruction of idolatrous objects, e.g. the Christian cross, or images, from the early conquests on.[81] In 721 AD, Yazid II issued an iconoclastic decree, alleged in the non-Muslim sources to have led to a systematic destruction of Christian crosses and images, even in churches and private homes.[82] Iconoclasm was, however, as the archaeological evidence shows, more characteristic of the Abbasids than the Umayyads. Unlike Christian iconoclasm, Islamic iconoclasm was virtually always directed against non-Muslim objects, with the exception of the late defacing of miniatures in manuscripts by pious librarians.[83]

The archaeological and literary evidence of Islamic iconoclastic activity does not become substantial until the eleventh century, when the Ghaznavids penetrate into India. It probably reached its highest pitch then, but remained a recurrent phenomenon until much later—Nadir Shah is still seen directing his artillery against the Buddhas at Bamiyan—, and into modern times. 'Skilled image-makers', writes Taranatha, 'abounded in every place wherever the Law of the Buddha flourished. In the regions that came under the influence of the mlecchas the art of image making declined'.[84] As the following will show, it seems highly probable that al-Hind was more affected by Islamic iconoclastic activity, at least in the eleventh to thirteenth centuries, than any other metropolitan area which was conquered by Muslims.

Byzantium went through an Iconoclast Controversy in the period of 726 to 824 AD, i.e. several decades before the Abbasids rose to power; and here an important Islamic influence has been postulated, or it has been seen as a response to Islam, by both con-

---

[81] Crone, 'Islam', p. 68.

[82] Vasiliev, 'Iconoclastic Edict'; Crone, 'Islam', p. 69. Grabar, 'Islam and Iconoclasm', p. 46 denies the historical validity of Yazid's document.

[83] Grabar, 'Islam and Iconoclasm', p. 45.

[84] Chattopadhyaya, *Tāranātha's History*, p. 348.

temporary and modern historians.[85] Others have seen it as 'a Near Eastern movement' or 'a Semitic movement' rather than as a strictly Byzantine one which originated within the Church or with the Emperor Leo III.[86] There was, in any case, a coincidence in time between Byzantine iconoclasm and the rise and expansion of Islam. And in the arguments used by the Byzantine iconoclasts the same Judaic condemnation of idolatry turned up. In the Controversy, religious, economic, military, and political factors were inextricably entwined.[87] The iconodules ultimately prevailed in 843 AD. The pagan legacy was, once again, linked to the Christian tradition, and Byzantium was to be the bridge between the Greco-Roman world and medieval Europe. Later, during the Turkish conquests of the eleventh and twelfth centuries, there is some evidence in the sporadic chronicles that considerable damage was done to ecclesiastical foundations throughout Anatolia.[88] Even before the battle of Manzikert, the Turkish raids had resulted in the pillaging of the churches of St. Basil at Caesareia and of the Archangel Michael at Chonae.[89] In the decade after 1071 the destruction of churches and the flight of clergy became widespread.[90] When Antioch was taken by Sulayman in 1085, many of the churches were desecrated, the priests driven out, and the churches were used as stables. William of Tyre presents one of the earliest descriptions of the destruction and defacing of religious pictures.[91] In Antioch, he writes, the Turks removed or covered the pictures of the saints on the walls, gouging out the eyes and mutilating the noses; occasionally churches were converted into mosques.[92]

What we see in Persia in the wake of the Muslim conquest is the gradual evanescence of the Zoroastrian fire cult in most places. To all appearances, iconoclastic activity by the early Muslims was directed against some major targets, but far from sys-

---

[85] *Al-Hind*, I, p. 40; Crone, 'Islam'.

[86] J. Herrin, 'The Context of Iconoclast Reform' in: A. Bryer and J Herrin (eds), *Iconoclasm: Papers given at the Ninth Symposium of Byzantine Studies* (Birmingham, 1975), p. 20.

[87] *Ibid.*

[88] S. Vryonis, Jr., *The Decline of Medieval Hellenism in Asia Minor and the Process of Islamization from the Eleventh through the Fifteenth Century* (Berkeley, 1971), p. 195

[89] *Ibid.*

[90] *Ibid.*

[91] *Ibid.*, p. 196.

[92] *Ibid.*, pp. 196-7.

tematic. Its impact, as far as we can tell, was patchwise. Fire temples in Khurasan and Transoxania, for instance those of Nishapur
and Bukhara, were demolished by the Arabs.[93] Ubaidallah b. Abi
Bakra, the later general of al-Hajjaj, had been assigned to Fars
and Sistan specifically to take charge of the suppression of the
sacred fires and the confiscation of temple treasure—tasks which
he performed with great diligence.[94] In Sistan, however, mosques
remained scarce until the tenth century, and during the first four
centuries of Muslim rule Zoroastrian religious centres remained
present in large number, falling into disuse before the tenth century only in the cities. In many areas, urban and rural, of eastern
Iran the Zoroastrian institutions declined between the tenth and
twelfth centuries due to conversion. In Sistan, Muslims did not
become the numerically dominant community before the mid-
thirteenth century. Above all, iconoclastic activity in Persia appears
to have been tempered by the Muslim belief that Zoroastrians
were People of the Book.[95]

This was not the case in Hind. Or, rather, the idea of treating
Hindus as protected subjects, while it was advanced during the
conquest, could not claim Qur'ānic authority, nor could it be
found in classical Qur'ānic interpretation or in hadīth.[96] The
account of the conquest of Sind points at a practical compromise
with idolatry, but in general there is nothing more striking in the
Arabic literature on *Sind* and *Hind* than its constant obsession with
the idol worship and the polytheism of the Indians.[97] Islamic tradition almost equates Indian culture with idolatry.[98] One hadīth
holds that India was the first country in which idolatry was prac-

---

[93] J. K. Choksy, 'Conflict, Coexistence, and Cooperation: Muslims and Zoroastrians in Eastern Iran during the Medieval period', *The Muslim World*, LXXX, 3-
4(1990), pp. 213-33; idem, 'Zoroastrians in Muslim Iran: Selected Problems of
Coexistence and Interaction during the Early Medieval Period', *Iranian Studies*,
XX, 1 (1987), pp. 17-30.
[94] *Al-Hind*, I, pp. 121-2.
[95] *Al-Hind*, I, p. 143.
[96] *Al-Hind*, I, p. 193.
[97] *Al-Hind*, I, p. 5.
[98] Y. Friedmann, 'Medieval Muslim Views of Indian Religions', *Journal of the
American Oriental Society*, 95, 2 (1975), pp. 214-5. For a Chinese perception which
runs somewhat parellel, see R. B. Mather, 'Chinese and Indian Perceptions of
Each Other between the first and seventh centuries', *Journal of the American Oriental Society*, 112, 1 (1992), p. 4: '... The Hu-barbarians have no humanity ... When
Lao-tzu entered the Pass [into Central Asia and India] he intentionally created
a doctrine of images and idols to convert them (perhaps on the assumption that
they could not handle abstract concepts?)..'

tised, and that the ancient Arabian idols were of Indian origin. Another has it that the brahmans of India in pre-Islamic times used to travel to Mecca to do worship at the Ka'ba, which was the best place for worship. After the rise of Islam, Mu'āwiya is said to have sent golden idols which he had obtained in Sicily for sale in India.[99]

Iconoclastic activity is already in evidence in Sind and Afghanistan under the Arabs. Unfortunately, for a long time it has been all too common among Sindi archaeologists to explain almost every ruin as the result of Arab iconoclasm.[100] The evidence, dating from this early period, is in fact still quite limited. At Debal, the *budd* temple was destroyed, and in the construction of a mosque, the earliest inscription of which goes back to 727-8 AD, Shaivite lingams were used as a step in front of the threshold.[101] In other cities of Sind we know that mosques were built to replace 'idolhouses'.[102] In the shrine of Zun, an Arab general broke off a hand from the idol and plucked out the rubies which were its eyes.[103] Muhammad al-Qasim is reported to have hung a piece of cow's flesh on the neck of the great *budd* statue at the Sun-temple of Multan, while he confiscated its wealth and made captives of its custodians.[104] Later Muslim governors always threatened to break the idol or mutilate it when they were confronting the hostility of neighbouring Hindu powers; until in the late tenth century the Ismā'īlīs finally did break it and killed its priests, erecting a mosque on its site.[105] The Arab chiefs who ruled Sind in the ninth and tenth century, rather than transmitting revenue, on occasion sent cartloads of idols to Baghdad.[106] This is about all we know. And it is in contrast to the general practice of the Arabs in Sind which allowed for old temples to be re-built, new ones erected, and Hindu/Buddhist practices to be continued.

Such piecemeal evidence which we have, then, on Arab iconoclasm in Sind, can be set off against what we know of the wholesale and far more systematic onslaught launched by the Muslim

---

[99] Friedmann, 'Medieval Muslim Views', pp. 214-5.
[100] D. N. Maclean, *Religion and Society in Arab Sind* (Leiden, 1989), p. 24.
[101] F. A. Khan, *Banbhore* (Karachi, 1969), pp. 24-30.
[102] *Al-Hind, I*, p. 203.
[103] *Ibid.*, p. 120.
[104] *Ibid.*, pp. 186-7.
[105] *Ibid.*, pp. 187-8.
[106] *Al-Hind, I*, p. 212.

Turks against the major religious sites of North India. As already indicated, iconoclastic motives can be distinguished from economic and political motives only with the greatest difficulty, if at all. Iconoclasm escalated, no doubt, because the Indian temple cities still contained vast amounts of immobilized treasure. But the Ghaznavid reputation throughout the Islamic world was based on two interrelated accomplishments: the 'breaking of the idols' and the de-hoarding of the temple treasure of *al-Hind*.

Iconoclastic motives are already interwoven in the early life stories of both Sabuktigin and Mahmud. On the first we read in the *Pandnāma*: 'I was taken to the tribe of the Bakhtiyans. They were idol-worshipers and had, in the plain, carved out a stone in human form which they said had grown of itself on the spot. They used to prostrate themselves before this stone at all times, and it was a place of pilgrimage for them. They had sent me to tend their sheep, and I used to remain in the plain where I passed that idol every day. God put it into my heart that those Bakhtiyans were a miserable people who prostrated themselves every day before a stone. One day I said to myself that I should offend against that idol in order to see if I was punished. I looked about me and finding nearby filth and droppings of animals which were sacrificed to that idol, I placed them on a piece of wood and daubed them on the face and body of that image. I came to no harm on the following day, and in fact what harm could come from inert stone? I did this every day, and my belief in the existence of God increased'.[107] Concerning Mahmud, we read that in the same night that he was born, 'an idolhouse in Hind' (*butkhānā bi-hind*), which was situated on the confines of Barshābūr, on the bank of the Sind [Indus] river, split asunder spontaneously.[108] Mahmud replaced, it is also recorded, many thousands of idol-houses with mosques.[109] Alone among his contemporaries and successors, Mahmud described himself (on his coins, issued at Lahore in the seventh year of his reign) and was described by others as *Mahmūd butshikan*, 'Mahmud the breaker of idols'.[110]

What is often not easy to make out is to what extent temples

---

[107] Nazim, 'Pand-Nāmah', pp. 611-2 (tr. p. 622).

[108] *TN*, p. 9.

[109] *Ibid.*

[110] E.g. *TF*, p. 33.

were demolished and then replaced with mosques, or whether they were sometimes just converted into mosques. Or to what extent already ruined temples were disassembled and used for the construction of new buildings. Obviously, the Muslims had no qualms about re-using materials from destroyed temples, although many Muslims refer to the Qur'an as the source for a prohibition against this.[111] In many of the early Islamic monuments in India, plunder from Hindu or Jain temples appears to have been a common source of building material. In one case, that of the early thirteenth-century Caurāsī (or Causat) Kambhā Masjid at Kāmān, Rajasthan, one of the earliest Indian monuments of the Ghurids, dating from before the establishment of the Slave Kingdom by Aybak in 1206, we find elements in use which were taken not from recent Hindu structures, but rather from monuments which were built four or five centuries earlier.[112] This appears to have been done with calculated consistency; and, possibly, the practice may have been much more widespread. Building materials for the Kāmān mosque were removed from pavilions (*mandapīkas*) and monasteries (*mathas*) and a variety of other structures, including temples, which were built during the rule of the Shūrasena dynasty in the seventh and eighth centuries and the Pratiharas in the ninth century. The resulting mosque still substantially expresses a Hindu sensibility, and, built by Hindu craftsmen (at least in part) under Muslim patronage, integrates Hindu architectural design with Islamic ornament and use.[113]

Most of the mosques which were built from the materials of, and on the sites of, demolished Hindu temples, are known to the Archaeological Survey of India, and their histories are related in local traditions. What replaced the images which were effaced, destroyed or removed was God's Word, in calligraphic Arabic—in the way that the Decalogue came to rule in the churches of the West in the later sixteenth and seventeenth centuries. Inscriptions

---

[111] It is explicitly forbidden in the Hindu shastras. The materials used for a Hindu temple could only function effectively in their original context; for a new building all materials had to be made or collected expressly—a rule which was however frequently violated.

[112] M. W. Meister, 'Indian Islam's lotus throne: Kaman and Khatu Kalan', in: A. L. Dallapiccola and S. Zingel-Avé Lallemant (eds), *Islam and Indian regions*, 2 vols (Stuttgart, 1993), I, pp. 445-52.

[113] *Ibid.*

in Arabic, quoting the Qur'ān, state the date and founder of the mosque as well.[114] The seventh to eighteenth centuries have also generated an enormous mass of literary evidence of Islamic iconoclasm in the area from Transoxania and Afghanistan to Tamil Nadu and Assam, the whole of which is littered with ruins of temples and monasteries.[115] These texts speak of the destruction of 'places of worship' (*ma'ābid, biya'*), 'idol-houses' (*buyūt al-asnām, butkhānahā*), 'fire-temples' (*kunishthā, ātashkhānahā*), and their *budda* stone idols, 'deaf and dumb idols', and so on.[116] Or, at some more length, we are told, for example, that 'Aybak built the jāmi' masjid at Delhi, and adorned it with stones and gold obtained from the temples which had been demolished by elephants, and covered it with inscriptions in Toghra, containing the divine commandments'.[117] Such texts survived from all periods of Indo-Islamic history, indicating that, while iconoclasm was at its peak in the eleventh to thirteenth centuries, there are many instances which occurred in a context which was otherwise characterized by all kinds of accommodation between Hindus and Muslims (which often included patronage of each others' shrines and religious complexes). What happened in historical times in areas like Sinkiang, Transoxania, Sistan, and Afghanistan—which converted almost entirely to Islam and eradicated all vestiges of Hinduism and Buddhism—, happened still recently in Pakistan and Bangla Desh, where many temples were destroyed by Muslims as recently as 1989, and, still continuing, in Kashmir.

In the thirteenth century and afterwards, large temples continued to be built, but not with the same frequency. The Islamic conquest put temples at risk, and the power of Indian ruling elites to patronize temple construction became increasingly circumscribed.[118] In the temples that were built after 1200 AD, as for example at Rānakpur in Rajasthan, the emphasis shifted from carving to the articulation of grand spaces. In North India this resulted, after 1200, in a significant dearth of well-carved sculp-

---

[114] Most of these texts are collected in the *Epigraphia Indica—Arabic and Persian Supplement* and *Epigraphia Indo-Moslemica*.

[115] On this, see also (with caution): S. R. Goel, *Hindu Temples: What happened to them, pt. II: The Islamic Evidence* (New Delhi, 1991).

[116] *TYA*, pp. 402-4; *TYP*, pp. 31, 38, 187, 244; *ZA*, p. 75.

[117] *TM*, p. 222.

[118] Willis, 'Religious and Royal Patronage in North India', pp. 49-65.

tures. The temples that survived the thirteenth and fourteenth centuries are now abandoned and stand as hollow shells in secluded spots, but some of the greatest temple complexes of the North obviously survived the Muslim invasions intact. This was the case with about twenty-five of the approximately eighty temples of Khajuraho, built by the Candellas. These, however, appear to have occupied a site which had already been abandoned before the Muslims penetrated the area.

After the thirteenth century, then, the building of monumental Hindu temples became more and more a feature of the South of India, the area which for many centuries longer remained beyond the frontier of Islamic expansion.[119] In mainland Southeast Asia it was the spread of Buddhism which brought the age of monumental temple building to an end. Java and other parts of the Indonesian Archipelago converted to Islam under indigenous rulers, starting from the coast, but gradually in the interior as well. Islamic conversion stories from Indonesia show little evidence of iconoclasm and there is a general absence of stories of temple destruction or desecration.[120] Hindu-Buddhist temples were eventually destroyed or built over in Malaya and Sumatra (e.g. the site at Indrapuri in Achin Besar), but not in Java. Nowhere is there much evidence that their destruction was part of the initial conversion. The tombs of the Pasai royalty are made of reworked marble pieces from Hindu temples—but these are from Gujarat and were imported. There is the conversion story of Kedah which has the newly converted ruler produce 'his idols of gold and silver, porcelain, wood and clay, human figures' for the missionary to destroy.[121]

It was only in South India that the building of large temple complexes remained embedded in a Hindu polity and continued to be organically linked to the other institutions of kingship and social organization in a variety of complex ways. Hindu temples in South India show a relatively unbroken, linear development,

---

[119] Cf. Stein, *South Indian Temples*, pp. 1-31; Michell, *Hindu Temple*, pp. 18, 131, 149-51, 183. For the effects of the early Muslim raids on a major temple complex in Shrīrangam, South India, see G. W. Spencer, 'Crisis of Authority in a Hindu Temple under the Impact of Islam', in: B. L. Smith (ed.), *Religion and the Legitimation of Power in South Asia* (Leiden, 1978), pp. 14-27.

[120] Cf. Reid, *Southeast Asia*, p. 142.

[121] Quoted *ibid.*, p. 142.

from the earliest rock-cut temples of the Pallavas in the seventh century to the great Cola structures of the eleventh century, and then to the sprawling urban temple ensembles, with their gopurams or 'gates', of the sixteenth- and seventeenth-century Vijayanagara and Nayaka dynasties. This tradition did not decline before the seventeenth century, under the impact of Muslims and Europeans. And even modern temples of the South are still done in a style that continues the earlier tradition. In North India, by contrast, the Muslim invasions, apart from destroying many temples, interrupted the evolution of Hindu temple architecture. If temples continued to be built in the Northern style (as developed by the Candellas or the Solankis), it was on a much reduced scale. Parallel to developments in Gwalior and Khajuraho, we find that temples continued to be built in a related style in the West of India and in Kathiawar. Here the Jain temple cities stand out. These were built, with elaborate ornamentation, from the tenth century on, and they are built in the same style to this day. The city of Satruñjaya, Palitana, is the most sacred of the Jain temple cities: most of its nearly 900 temples date from the sixteenth century; but the original temples, built in the eleventh century, were completely destroyed by the Muslims. Similarly, the town of Ajmer, founded by Ajaipal, one of the Cauhan kings, was sacked in 1024 AD by Mahmud of Ghazna, and again by Muhammad Ghuri in 1193; it had a Jain college, built in 1153, which was turned into a mosque by putting a massive screen of seven arches in front of the pillared hall which was left standing: 'the hut of two-and-a-half days', built supernaturally, according to Muslim tradition, in two-and-a-half days. Other great Jain temples, like the one at Rānakpur, in Rajasthan, built around 1439, were equipped with holes in the ground leading to cellars where the images could be hidden from the Muslim iconoclasts. We know of underground Jain temples which were built for the protection of images in Mughal times, and it is quite likely that these existed in our period as well, or that underground portions were beginning to be added to temples, with narrow passages as their entrance.[122] Of the great Buddhist establishments, Vikramashila had been completely destroyed before 1206, its foundation stones hurled into

---

[122] Cf. K. C. Jain, *Jainism in Rajasthan* (Sholapur, 1963), p. 128.

the Ganges. Nalanda was severely damaged by 1234 (when visited by Dharmasvamin) and abandoned. In Bodh Gaya at that time—deserted by all except four monks—an ancient image had been walled up by a brick wall and a new one had been put up in the ante-chamber. The old image had already been despoiled of its emerald eyes earlier. With the departure of the Muslim force, people returned to the site, removed the wall, and again made the old image accessible to devotees.[123] In a Jain poem we hear of another image, which was fashioned in the city of Kannanaya in the Cola country in 1176; when in 1192 AD Pṛthiviraja, the Cauhan leader, was killed, Ramadeva sent a letter to the Jains, stating: 'the kingdom of the Turks has begun; keep the image of Mahavira hidden away'.[124] This image, accordingly, was kept concealed in the sand at Kayamvasatthala and remained there for about sixty years.

Some of the oldest temples, e.g. at Pushkar, eleven km to the west of Ajmer, on the bank of the most sacred lake of India (described as such in the fifth century by Fa Hsien), were not destroyed before the time of Aurangzeb. Mathurā, the birthplace of Krishna, was destroyed again and again. Aurangzeb ultimately raised a great red sandstone mosque on the ruins of its Kesava Deo temple. Chitorgarh, the most famous of Rajput fortresses, founded about 728 AD, was taken by Muslim armies three times: the first by ʿAlāʾ ad-Dīn Khalajī in 1303, the second by Bahādur Shāh in 1535, and the third by Akbar in 1567. Here again we find many temples dating back to the fifteenth century, when a revival of Jain architecture took place. But often, like in the case of the Temple of Mirabai, erected in 1449 AD by Rana Kumbha of the Mewar dynasty, they were built on an eighth- or ninth-century substructure which was demolished centuries earlier. Another example is the sun-temple in Chitorgarh, probably dating to the eighth century, where Sūrya is de-faced by the Muslim iconoclasts on one side of the temple, while left intact on the other side; the temple itself was re-dedicated to Kali, after having been destroyed by the Khalajīs and again by later Muslims. Nowhere in the North did the Hindu temple building tradition perpetuate itself without hin-

---

[123] Roerich, *Dharmasvamin*, pp. xix, xxxii, 64.
[124] K. Mitra, 'Historical references in Jain poems', *Proceedings of the Indian History Congress*, 5 (1941), p. 299.

drance. Even in the East, in Orissa, the climax of the Hindu architectural tradition was clearly reached with the thirteenth-century
Sūrya temple at Konarkā, after which stylistic decline set in, imi-
tative of earlier forms, but less flamboyant and without the same
quality of surface decoration as for instance can be seen in the
Jagannath temple at Puri.

The temples, with their incumbent images, rather than being
turned into mosques directly, most often appear to have been
destroyed, after their portable wealth was taken, and then replaced with mosques or Muslim shrines built from the rubble.[125]
Icon pieces were sent to Ghazna to be trodden under foot by the
believers, or to be fastened into doors and walls of the Jāmi'
Masjid; fragments of religious statues were also sent to Mecca,
Madina, and Baghdad for propaganda purposes.[126] On first discovery, temples and icons would immediately be stripped of their
valuable parts, gold or red gold, silver, precious stones, the eyes
made of jewels being picked out first.[127] Temples were destroyed
with 'nafta and fire' (*nafta wa-l-dirām*), and with the aid of elephants. The greatest statues, like the one at Somnath, which was
almost five meters in height, were first mutilated by the Sultan
himself with a mace, and then destroyed—like any temple—by
lighting fire around it so that it would burst into pieces.[128]

Comprehensive destruction, clearly, was not always the aim. It
was essential to render the images powerless, to remove them from
their consecrated contexts. Selective delapidation could be sufficient to that purpose. It is hard to gauge the depth of religious
convictions here. Did fear play a role in the iconoclastic destruction of the early Muslim conquerors in India? Were the images
destroyed, desecrated or mutilated because they were potent or
impotent? Mathurā is described in the contemporary Muslim
sources as 'the work of demons (*jinn*)', while the images themselves as well as the image-worshipers are referred to as 'devils'
(*shayāṭīn*), indicating the association of idolatry with evil. Hand
in hand with iconoclasm and the destruction of temples went the
hounding of temple priests, brahmans, as also Buddhist monks,

---

[125] *TYP*, pp. 38, 179; *TF*, pp. 26-27.
[126] *TYP*, p. 250; *TF*, pp. 27, 32-33.
[127] *TF*, p. 27; *TYA*, p. 402; *TYP*, p. 244; *ZA*, pp. 75-76.
[128] *TF*, pp. 32-33.

who were seen as proponents of images and the ritual specialists which made image worship possible. This is also what happened in Sind, where many of the custodians of the budd temples were either made captives or killed by the Arab conquerors.[129] In the late tenth century the Ismāʿīlīs who occupied Multan and smashed the image of the Sun-god also killed its officiant priests.[130] The Ghaznavids too 'struck at the idol-worshipers (butparastān)', especially at Somnath, where the casualties are reported to have been as high as 50,000. Whether other objects which were associated with image worship were destroyed is not easy to determine; but the destruction of books, so familiar in European history and known from pre-Islamic India as well,[131] probably occurred during attacks on the Buddhist viharas in the early thirteenth century, and elsewhere.

It seems beyond doubt that, in India too, Islamic iconoclasm was almost always directed against non-Islamic objects. When Mahmud attacked the Ismāʿīlīs of Multan he did not destroy their mosque, but just left it to decay. The Ghaznavid expeditions, from the time of Sabuktigin onwards, are described in the sources as a jihād against the inhabitants of Hind who are all 'worshipers of images and idols' (muʿabbid-i-ausān-o-asnām).[132] Rhetorically, the texts describe the aim of the Ghaznavid operations as 'to extinguish the sparks of idolatry', 'to humiliate the sinners, Hindu unbelievers, the idol-worshipers', 'to destroy the deaf and dumb idols of al-Hind', and to replace the idolatrous belief by Islam, 'to spread the carpet of Islam', 'to cleanse the country of the odiousness of the idolatrous', and so on.[133]

The Turkish invaders were certainly familiar with Hindu sacred geography. The main religious sites were easily identified and taken out serially in the first quarter of the eleventh century. An unknown number of temples was destroyed by Sabuktigin, while nothing has survived of the mosques which he erected, largely in Lamghān and adjacent areas, as appears from the literary material. As Mahmud's first great triumph against the idolatrous reli-

---

[129] Cf. p. 426; Al-Hind, I, pp. 203, 205.
[130] Al-Hind, I, p. 188.
[131] E.g. Tantra treatises, which were burnt in the reign of Dharmapala because of their content (Chattopadhyaya, Tāranātha's History, p. 279)
[132] TYP, pp. 31-39; TYA, pp. 258-61.
[133] See especially TYA and TYP, passim.

gion is recorded the expedition of 1008 AD against *Bhīm-naghar*, 'the storehouse of a great idol', which was full of precious goods and metals and jewels donated by neighbouring kings, and which was situated in the foothills of the fort of *Nagarkot*.[134] *Thāneswar* or *Tānesar*, a city about 48 km west of Delhi, called *Tāneshar* by Biruni, came next, in 1011 AD. This was a city which 'was held in the same veneration by idolaters as Mecca by the faithful'.[135] Without doubt it was an important place of worship, but it was left undefended, and plundered by the Muslims with ease, while many of the icons were broken, and the chief icon *Yugasoma* or *Cakrasvāmin*, made of bronze and nearly the size of a man, was despatched to Ghazna—where it was put in the hippodrome.[136] It was only after Tānesar, however, that the major religious sites were reached. There were three of these, and it is in their destruction that the systematic nature of Islamic iconoclastic activity in India is most apparent.

Mathura

This city, *Mathura* or *Mathurā*, Biruni's *Māhurā*,[137] present-day *Muttra*, was already an important religious site in ancient times—Ptolemy's 'Madoura of the Gods'—, due to its location on the Yamuna, at the very centre of the Ganges-Yamuna Doab. 'Utbī calls it *Mahrah al-Hind*.[138] No Ashokan inscriptions have been found in the area, although archaeology suggests that the first transition to urbanism was made in the area in the Mauryan period. According to Hiuen Tsang there existed in his time three stupas of Ashoka at Mathura. We merely know from inscriptions that there were Buddhists in Mathura by the first century BC, but also that there were probably more Jains than Buddhists in these early times. The city appears to have retained its Buddhist-Jaina imprint up to 300 AD, with a great increase of Buddhist relics being noticeable under Kanishka. Unprecedented urban growth occurred when it became the principal capital of the Kushanas in India. With close relations developing between Gandhara and

---

[134] *TYA*, pp. 278-82; *TYP*, p. 187; *TF*, pp. 26-27.
[135] *TF*, p. 27.
[136] *Ibid.*; *TYA*, pp. 336-8; al-Bīrūnī, *Kitāb al-Hind*, p. 89.
[137] Cf. *Al-Hind, I*, p. 299.
[138] *TYA*, pp. 395, 401.

Mathura, Hellenistic and Parthian elements, were passed on and many new elements of iconography were incorporated. In later times, Mathura became a centre of the Krishna cult, a transformation to which Ābhīra and Gūjar pastoralists, following the transhumance route from Saurashtra, probably contributed a great deal.[139]

Mathura was the first city in India to be destroyed by the Muslims. This happened in 1018 AD. 'Utbī, again, describes the extraordinary 'buildings' (mabānī) and 'mansions' (mughānī) which Mahmud saw there, and the one thousand 'idolhouses' (but-khānahā), built in compounds with stone walls (az sang-i-banyād), raised on high ground to protect them from the water of the Yamuna.[140] The main temple of Mathura, according to 'Utbī, represented a total cost of 100,000,000 dinars and could not have been built in less than 200 years. In it were five idols (asnām, sanamhā), in red gold (adh-dhahab al-ahmar, zar-i-sarkh), five meters high, one of which had eyes of rubies worth 50,000 dinars; another contained a blue sapphire which weighed 450 mishqāl. There were 'many thousands' of smaller idols in the city. We are told that the Sultan ordered all the temples to be devastated with fire and laid waste, after collecting vast amounts of gold and silver as well as jewels.

Kanauj

Kanauj was the most important of the religious centres of early medieval India, the brahmanical capital of Madhyadesha, a very large city, consisting of seven fortresses (qilāʿ, qalʿajāt), with a total of 10,000 'idolhouses' (buyūt al-asnām, butkhānahā), 'in which enormous treasure was collected', on the west bank of the Ganges, where 'kings and brahmans' (rāyān-o-barāhima) from far away came to seek religious liberation and do worship 'in the tradition of their ancestors' (bi-taqlīd-i-aslāf).[141] 'Utbī refers to the Kanauj ruler as 'the chief (muqaddam) of the kings of Hind'. It was, in effect, the capital of the Gurjara-Pratiharas from 815 to 1019 AD,

---

[139] Cf. *Al-Hind*, *I*, p. 280; Srinivasan, *Mathurā*; Van Lohuizen-De Leeuw, *The "Scythian" Period*.
[140] *TYP*, pp. 242-4; *TYA*, pp. 401-3; and cf. *ZA*, pp. 74-78.
[141] *TYA*, pp. 403-7; *TYP*, pp. 244-5; *ZA*, p. 76.

when it was sacked by Mahmud. By then the dynasty was already powerless. But Kanauj may well have been the wealthiest of Indian cities still.

When the Muslim army approached, most of the inhabitants had taken refuge 'with the gods', i.e. in the temples. The city was taken possession of in one day, and emptied of its treasure. The 'idols' were destroyed; the 'infidels', 'worshipers of the sun and fire' ('*ubbād ash-shams wa-l-nār*), fleeing, were pursued by the Muslims, and great numbers of them were killed. Kanauj probably never recovered its status as sacred capital of the brahmans. In Biruni's time, Kanauj was still in ruins, and the reigning king had removed himself to the town of Bari, east of the Ganges. Later in the eleventh and twelfth century the city revived under a northern branch of the Rashtrakutas and then the Gahadavalas; it ceased to be of any real importance by 1193 AD, when the last of the Gahadavala kings was defeated.

Somnāth

The temple and town of *Somnāth*, Biruni's *Somnāt*, differs from Mathura and Kanauj in that it was not located on either of the sacred rivers of the Yamuna and Ganges. Away from the land-routes, on the peninsula of Kathiawar, it was thought to be relatively safe from Muslim interference. Not being on a sacred river, fresh Ganges water was brought daily for the god's bath.[142] On a narrow strip of land, it was fortified on one side, and washed on three sides by the sea, while the tide was looked upon as the worship paid to the god by the sea.[143] *Somnāth* (Skt *Soma-nātha*, 'lord of the moon') owed its name to the ebb and flow of the sea.[144] During lunar eclipses, the crowd of pilgrims visiting the temple could swell to 200,000 or 300,000.[145] The nearby town of the same name had become famous because of its maritime connections;[146] it was a station (*manzil*) for 'those who travelled back and forth between Sufāla al-Zanj and aṣ-Ṣīn'.[147] Due to its mar-

---

[142] *TF*, p. 32; al-Bīrūnī, *Kitāb al-Hind*, p. 430.
[143] *TF*, p. 32; *KT*, IX, p. 241; al-Bīrūnī, *Kitāb al-Hind*, p. 431.
[144] al-Bīrūnī, *Kitāb al-Hind*, p. 431.
[145] *TF*, p. 32; *KT*, IX, p. 241.
[146] Cf. *Al-Hind, I*, pp. 185, 218, 199, 307; and *supra*, pp. 271, 275.
[147] al-Bīrūnī, *Kitāb al-Hind*, pp. 430-1.

itime connections, the temple of Somnath could be built on
columns of teakwood imported from Africa.[148] For the same reason, we find Muslims living in Somnath before Mahmud's expedition of 1025 AD.

Somnāth was 'the greatest of the idols of al-Hind'.[149] Thousands
of villages had been donated to its upkeep, 1000 or 2000 brahmans served as its priests, hundreds of sacred prostitutes and musicians belonged to it, and it owned more jewels and gold 'than
any royal treasury had ever contained'.[150] The great idol was a
phallic representation of Mahādeva—next to which there were
thousands of smaller images, wrought in gold or silver—and was
brought, according to some, from Mecca in the time before the
Prophet (but this was denied by the brahmans, according to whom
it had stood near the harbour of Dew since the time of Krishna).[151]

Ibn al-Athīr writes that when the other icons failed to fulfill
their apotropaic functions the Hindus alleged that this was
because Somnāth was displeased with them.[152] Now, however, Somnath had drawn the Muslims to it in order to have them destroyed
and to avenge the destruction of the gods of India.[153] But Mahmud destroyed this idol too, scattering its parts to Ghazna, Mecca and Madina, and taking booty to the amount of two million
dinars.[154] Its destruction was publicised, by both contemporary
and later authors, as the crowning glory of Islam over idolatry,
elevating Mahmud to the status of a hero. It is not possible any
longer to identify the exact site of the icon which was thus
destroyed, as the whole coastline of this area is littered with ruins.
Moreover, there has been a succession of later Muslim invaders
who tried to raze the temple to the ground. Time and again the
Hindus started rebuilding the monument. This went on for 400
years, until the shrine was finally abandoned. In 1842, the British,
after attacking the Afghans at Ghazna, decided to bring back 'the
gates of Somnāth' to India. Lord Allenborough proclaimed, on
that occasion, that he had restored to the princes of India their

---

[148] *KT*, IX, p. 241.
[149] *KT*, IX, p. 241.
[150] *TF*, pp. 31-33; *KT*, IX, p. 241; *ZA*, p. 86.
[151] *TF*, p. 32.
[152] *KT*, IX, p. 241.
[153] *TF*, p. 32.
[154] *KT*, IX, p. 241; al-Bīrūnī, *Kitāb al-Hind*, p. 429.

honour by presenting them with these gates. The gesture, however, merely angered the Muslim princes, while the Maharajas did not want the 'polluted' portal.[155]

The destruction of Somnāth was clearly regarded as the climax of Muslim iconoclastic activity in Hind, and iconoclastic events after 1025-6 receive less attention in our sources. This is true even of the raids on Benares. We do not know much about the first Muslim raid on Benares, by Ahmad Nāyaltigīn in 1033 AD, which appears merely to have been a plundering expedition.[156] When Muhammad Ghuri marched on the city, we are merely told that 'after breaking the idols in above 1000 temples, he purified and consecrated the latter to the worship of the true God'.[157] Numerous other iconoclastic incidents are recounted throughout the eleventh-thirteenth centuries, indicating that in some cases new icons were introduced by the Hindus where the earlier ones were destroyed, and also that sometimes Hindu kings were allowed to retain their dominion on the condition that they demolished their own temples themselves.[158] Most significant, by the late twelfth and in the thirteenth century, was doubtlessly the destruction by the Turks of the Buddhist monasteries of Uddandapura, Vikramashila and Nalanda, all in Eastern India.[159] The Turkish invasions proved fatal to the existence of Buddhism as an organized religion in the country of its origin. Here again, conversion played no role. The Buddhist religion disappeared from North India because it had been almost exclusively concentrated in a few major monastic centres and these centres were destroyed by the Muslims. In so far as Buddhism survived the thirteenth century, outside the orbit of Islamic conquest, in Sri Lanka, Tibet, and in mainland Southeast Asia, it was as a religion with roots in the peasant societies of these areas. It is this problem which the two final chapters will address.

---

[155] On Somnath, see also R. H. Davis, 'Unmiraculous Images: Early Muslim Encounters with the Idols of India' (Unpublished paper read at the meeting of the Association for Asian Studies, April 1991).

[156] *TB*, p. 497.

[157] *TF*, p. 58.

[158] E.g. *TF*, pp. 44-45, 65; *FS*, vs. 1546-99; Siddiqui, *Perso-Arabic Sources*, p. 170; *TMS*, p. 20.

[159] Cf. *TN*, pp. 147, 151; Chattopadhyaya, *Tāranātha's History*, pp. 318-9; Roerich, *Dharmasvamin*, intro, pp. xli-xliv; text, pp. 64, 90.

CHAPTER X

THE WELL OF BUDDHISM DEFILED

It cannot be said that the Buddhists of India had not been anx-
iously anticipating the demise of their religion. According to tradition, the Buddha himself had prophesied that the death of his
doctrine would follow 1500 years after his own death. And as early as the seventh century AD we find the Chinese pilgrim Hiuen
Tsang expressing distress at the signs of the approaching fulfill-
ment of this prophecy. There were other prophecies current in
India in Hiuen Tsang's time about the imminent catastrophe,
some of which tended to suggest a 1000-year lifespan for the doctrine of the Buddha.[1]

When the end finally came, Indian Buddhism had become an
almost exclusively monastic religion, found in a small number of
religious establishments in the 'Eastern Tract', in Magadha, the
region of its origin which in the literature is often referred to as
the 'well of Buddhism'. These Buddhist viharas were—more than
ever before in their history—vulnerable to outside interference,
as they were not only few in number but also large in size.

In view of the long history of these monastic establishments and
their great fame throughout Asia, it is remarkable that we know
so little about the events of the late twelfth and thirteenth centuries which led to their destruction. Leaving aside some brief references in Muslim chronicles, there is barely one eyewitness
account— that of the Tibetan Buddhist scholar Dharmasvamin.
Even that account gives no more than a melancholy glimpse of
sacked and all but abandoned viharas, turned into camps by roving bands of *Turushka* soldiers on horseback.[2] Later Tibetan historical traditions are again mixed with legendary materials, and
these can be summarized by Taranatha's statement that 'the
Turushka army conquered the whole of Magadha and destroyed
many monasteries; at Nalanda they did much damage and the

---

[1] Cf. Watters, *Yuan Chwang*, I, p. 372.
[2] Roerich, *Dharmasvamin*, intro, pp. xli-xliv; text, pp. 64, 90.

monks fled abroad'.[3] For all we know, the Turks put an end to
Buddhism in eastern India almost overnight—in a matter of
decades—by obliterating these great monasteries. Attempts to for-
tify the viharas had, to all appearances, been faint and ineffectu-
al.

Although in India material support for the Buddhist Sangha
had never been lacking and continued to be provided by certain.
rulers, by the twelfth century a Buddhist lay population hardly
existed. In so far as it did, it was not a cohesive and clearly defin-
able community. Buddhism had not penetrated the lives of the
vast mass of the Indian peasant population in a way that could
have guaranteed the religion's survival outside the monastic institutions. The religion survived, after the thirteenth century, in Sri
Lanka and the emerging states of mainland Southeast Asia, but
here it was almost completely transformed. In the latter areas, it
arrived as the first scriptural high tradition to take root outside
courtly circles, expanding its scope in the context of emerging
rice-cultivating peasantries. Here, trade and city life were monopolized by non-Buddhist diaspora groups, mostly Chinese and Muslim, and Buddhism became associated with the expansion of agriculture.

a. INDIAN BUDDHISM

Many historians of Buddhism have rightly emphasized that the
long-anticipated demise and final obliteration of Buddhism in the
Indian subcontinent were in large part due to its lack of interest
in the laity and the lack of organisation among the laity. Max
Weber was among the first to argue this forcefully. According to
Weber, the original Buddhism was a 'quite specific soteriology of
cultivated intellectuals' and 'a specifically apolitical and antipo-
litical status religion, more precisely, a religious "technology" of
wandering and of intellectually-schooled mendicant monks'.[4] If
rural surroundings, cattle and pasture, were characteristic of the
ancient brahmanical teachers and schools, at least in the period
of the Upanishads, the city and the urban palace with its elephant-

---

[3] A. Schiefner (transl.), *Tāranātha's Geschichte des Buddhismus in Indien* (St.
Petersburg, 1869), p. 94.
[4] M. Weber, *The Religion of India* (New York and London, 1967), pp. 205-6.

riding kings were characteristic of the Buddha's teachings, while the culture of the city was also reflected in the dialogue form in which Buddhist doctrines were often expounded.[5] Weber also concluded that there was no 'bridge' from the ideal of salvation to 'the world of rational action' and 'to any actively conceptualized "social" conduct' because 'salvation is an absolutely personal performance of the self-reliant individual'.[6] It is true that the Buddhist layman was promised wealth and other benefits for his faithful observance of Buddhist lay morality, but lay morality was merely a kind of 'insufficiency ethic of the weak who will not seek complete salvation'.[7] Weber thus denied that the Buddha had any social-political aims. Since for the Buddha the cause of suffering, which had to be overcome, was in the nature of worldly existence, such aims could not have had any relevance. This was both the strength and weakness of 'the most ruthlessly consistent of all Hinduistic cultured intellectuals' soteriologies'. And if the Buddha did, in effect, found the Sangha, the order of Buddhist monks and nuns, this order had a very loose structure; Weber even speaks of an 'absence of structure' (Strukturlosigkeit).[8] The only really important structural element in the organization of the oldest community were precedence according to seniority (counted from entrance into the order) and certain special rules which determined the relationship between teacher and pupil. Early Buddhism, therefore, did not have a political dimension, even though, as others have argued, the Sangha's relationship with the laity was vital because of the material support the latter gave, and even though the Sangha had a missionary motivation from the start and directed itself at a newly rising urban stratum for which it represented an emancipatory ideology.[9] The dependence of the

---

[5] *Ibid.*, pp. 204-5.

[6] *Ibid.*, p. 213.

[7] *Ibid.*, p. 215.

[8] Weber's views on these matters are confirmed by H. Bechert, 'Max Webers Darstellung der Geschichte des Buddhismus in Süd- und Ostasien', in: W. Schluchter (ed.), *Max Webers Studie über Hinduismus und Buddhismus: Interpretation und Kritik* (Frankfurt am Main, 1984), p. 276; idem, *Buddhismus, Staat und Gesellschaft in den Ländern des Theravada-Buddhismus*, Bd. 1 (Frankfurt am Main, 1966), pp. 3-15; E. Lamotte, 'The Buddha, His Teachings and His Sangha', in H. Bechert and R. Gombrich (eds), *The World of Buddhism* (London, 1984), pp. 41-58.

[9] For the latter see S. J. Tambiah, 'Max Webers Untersuchung des frühen Buddhismus: Eine Kritik', in Schluchter, *op. cit.*, pp. 202-246; idem, *World Conqueror*

Sangha on the laity's support was actually enhanced by its secular aloofness, as it was by the predicament of Buddhist monks who, unlike their Benedictine counterparts, did not engage in physical labour.

Moreover, since Buddhism was not attached to any particular community or locality, it was readily transportable.[10] Like mercantile wealth, Buddhism was not ascribed but achieved; and it appealed to new men. It suited people who were travelling, and hence spread along the trade routes. Ancient Indian Buddhism has been called an 'ethic for the socially mobile' and 'an ideological parallel to monetization' as it represented a great universalistic ideology in a world in which cash was the common denominator.[11] In all this it betrayed its origin in the newly emerging context of cities, states, money-use, organized trade, surplus production made possible by the spread of population, and the concomitant rise of new urban-based professions (traders, state-officials) which were not catered for by brahman orthodoxy[12] The social appeal of Buddhism was thus akin to that of the Protestant reform movements, but the difference was that in Buddhism those seriously interested in salvation were expected to enter the monastic order.

Outside the monastic order, Indian Buddhism always remained amorphous.[13] The Buddhist laity appears at all times to have been a very fluid social category. The soteriological doctrine of the Buddha, which emphasized the individual, could not but have had very limited relevance, at least in its pure form, for the day-to-day workings of lay society.[14] The Buddha preached nothing but a soteriology and showed little interest in communal religion, in the religion of man in society which prescribes primarily a pattern of action relating to life crises, ritual, or etiquette, and so on, and the custodians of which were the hereditary priesthood. Such communal religion he regarded as something to be left behind in the quest for salvation. Some forms of Mahayana Buddhism did

---

and World Renouncer: A Study of Buddhism and Polity in Thailand against a Historical Background (Cambridge, 1976).

[10] R. Gombrich, Theravada Buddhism: A Social History from Ancient Benares to Modern Colombo (London and New York, 1991), pp. 77-78, 80-81.

[11] Ibid., pp. 78, 80-81.

[12] Ibid., pp. 51-56, 73-74.

[13] Ibid., pp. 24-31, 74-77.

[14] Ibid.

evolve a communal religion from within themselves (e.g. Newar Buddhism in Nepal), but the attitude of Theravada Buddhism to communal religion remained negative in so far as the latter was considered irrelevant to salvation.[15] Only the professional monks and nuns, those who joined the Sangha monastic order, were required to renounce the norms of the wider society, while Buddhist laymen continued to subscribe to their communal religion. From the doctrinal point of view, a Buddhist layman was someone who had taken the Three Refuges, i.e. had professed his or her reverence for the Buddha, the Dhamma and the Sangha. But in India this did not preclude a simultaneous allegiance to the norms of communal religion. And since in ancient India it was the scripturally ordained duty of laymen to respect and materially support all holy men, of whatever soteriology, the boundary between a Buddhist and a non-Buddhist layman was difficult to draw. In Sri Lanka and, later, the Buddhist countries of mainland Southeast Asia, on the other hand, Buddhism entered societies without a systematized and well-articulated communal religion, made up at best of composite elements of a watered-down Hindu provincial culture and 'spirit cults', and here Buddhism was the only available soteriology. In the latter context, therefore, the question of multiple allegiances did not arise in the same way. And the result was that, here, Buddhism ended up effectively monopolizing education and subsuming virtually all cultural and spiritual life.

Nowhere did 'Buddhist' and 'Hindu' become mutually exclusive identities at any time. Among the laity, Buddhism was always complementary to communal religion. Buddhists are said to worship 'Hindu' gods in Sri Lanka. And beyond India, for example in Japan, Buddhists are also Shintoists, while in China Buddhists were also Confucianists or Taoists, and so on. The term 'layman' can thus cover a range of possibilities in Buddhism. In contemporary Theravada societies the term 'layman' or upāsaka is not applied to just any Buddhist but rather to people who spend a great deal of time and energy on Buddhist activities, whether privately or in supporting the Sangha, or who may be donors. In ancient India, a Buddhist layman was, at the very least, encouraged to take certain moral vows. But he would at the same time

---

[15] *Ibid.*, p. 28.

continue to practice the local, communal religion. The lay followers of Buddhism, in any case, did not constitute a separate group of the population.[16] While for them it was sufficient to 'take refuge in the Buddha, the Dhamma and the Sangha' in the presence of a monk or even another layman, in practice their ties to the Sangha were loose. There was no special rite analogous to baptism in Christianity or circumcision like in Islam. There was also no demand for an explicit repudiation of previous doctrinal errors, nor was it necessary to repudiate religious practices that were current in the layman's society. The upāsaka merely made a personal vow to observe the five rules of Buddhist morality (not to kill, steal, commit adultery, lie, or become drunk). This vow was not registered by the community, nor was the layman registered as a new Buddhist among the existing number of believers. Moreover, Buddhist monks begged food from everyone, not just Buddhist laymen. What the Sangha expected from a Buddhist layman were, above all, gifts (of food, clothes, or land) and deference, but one could become a Buddhist layman without changing anything in one's lifestyle. And to a degree this remains the case today. Even now, in Buddhist countries no formality exists by which one becomes a Buddhist layman.[17]

This is not to say that that there was no accommodation between ancient Indian Buddhist soteriology and society at all.[18] There was to emerge, mostly after the Buddha's lifetime, a certain number of practices and attitudes that became characteristic of Buddhist lay religiosity. An example is the Buddha's becoming an object of faith and devotion himself. We also find it in the creation of stupa burial mounds, which became objects of pilgrimage; and in the cult of relics in general. And, in Theravada practice, the rather simplistic treatment of 'merit' as a form of spiritual currency was typically an accommodation to the needs of peasant society (what Weber was apt to call 'emotional mass religiosity'), even though the original conception evolved against a commercial background.

It should also be pointed out that, although laymen were an open and fluid social category, and one with no specifically Bud-

---

[16] Cf. R. Lingat, *Royautés Bouddhiques* (Paris, 1989), pp. 21-22.
[17] *Ibid.*
[18] Gombrich, *Theravada Buddhism*, pp. 118-36.

dhist internal social structure, they were nonetheless crucial not only in materially supporting the Sangha (which monopolized the soteriology) but also in furthering the expansion of monastic Buddhism in early as well as in later times. This was especially true for kings. Ashoka, on account of his role in promoting the religion, has been named the most important Buddhist layman in history.[19] The first ruler who openly professed the Buddhist faith, he became a *cakkavattin* or 'world ruler', a kind of lay counterpart of the Buddha who denied himself the ultimate salvation.[20] Many authors have spoken of Ashoka's conversion, referring to the fact that he became an upāsaka, but again we have to be clear about what this means. For Ashoka the profession of the Buddhist faith was not merely a private matter, nor was Buddhism for him merely an instrument for effective rule or 'mass domestication' as has sometimes been claimed. Ashoka was sincere in his religious convictions and, putting these convictions on billboards throughout South Asia, it was his ambition to inaugurate a new style of politics. This does not imply that Ashoka effectively brought the subcontinent under his control as a ruler (his edicts do not deal with administrative measures at all), but rather that he brought forward a radical change in the conception of his own role as king, which he conceived of as a specifically Buddhist one.[21] If this were not the case it would have been difficult to understand why Ashoka became, and always remained, a model for Buddhist kings in later times. In actual fact, Ashoka displays in his edicts a constant obsession with morality and, adopting a paternalistic tone, propagated—to the whole of humanity— a set of virtues which have perhaps little to do with Buddhism in the strict sense, but are not inconsistent with it, or rather aim to bring out the universal truths of all existing religions of his time and preach concord between the sects to the ultimate benefit of the Buddhist religion.[22]

Nothing certain can be concluded about the number of lay adherents of Buddhism in Ashoka's time, or about any possible increase of this number. It is remarkable that the Sangha itself

---

[19] Cf. *Ibid.*, pp. 127-36.
[20] The following sketch of Ashoka's position in Buddhism is based on Lingat, *Royautés Bouddhiques*, pp. 15-60.
[21] Lingat, *op. cit.*
[22] Lingat, *op. cit.*

does not appear to play any role in the instruction of the Dhamma; this, according to Ashoka, was the mission of the king, and of his officials, who were also laymen. The Sangha was entirely passive and, in its turn, does not appear to have had any control over the king. Remarkably, Ashoka's inscriptions are addressed at all his subjects, but virtually leave the Sangha unmentioned. There are no Buddhist religious advisers. There is no proof that Ashoka appointed any specific ecclesiastical dignitaries or that he took in hand the administration of the Sangha. From the inscriptions it appears that the Sangha existed aside from politics, and was stripped of all means to involve itself in the government of the state. The Sangha also does not appear to have played any role in the conversion of people to Buddhism. The starting point of formal relations between king and Sangha is found in one of the rare inscriptions in which Ashoka addresses himself directly to the Sangha; the so-called 'schism-edict'. This edict does not refer to points of doctrine, and it was certainly not an attempt to sponsor a Buddhist orthodoxy to resist the brahmans.[29] It merely alludes to measures taken by Ashoka to forbid members of religious sects which were not ordained in the regular manner, or who had violated the rules, to reside in the same localities as the regularly ordained monks and nuns who did live according to the vinaya. Once this purification was given effect, each of the monastic communities was referred to as 'united'. What had happened here is that the growth in size of the Sangha had led to internal disorder and division, and finally to a schism, a 'splitting of the communities' and this had to be addressed by the king—who thereby set an example for all later Buddhist kings.

There is no doubt, therefore, that Ashoka's politics has been favourable to the expansion of Buddhism and an increase in the size of the Buddhist Sangha. From a religious sect Buddhism became a universal religion. But even under Ashoka, Buddhism remained essentially a monastic religion. While lay Buddhists did exist, among the urban mercantile groups and itinerant traders, and while the king himself was a lay Buddhist, we do not know their numbers. There is no evidence to show that the population of South Asia was affected by Buddhist ideals in a more general

---

[29] H. Bechert, 'Ashokas Schismenedikt und der Begriff Samghabheda', *Wiener Zeitschrift für die Kunde Süd- und Ostasiens*, 5 (1961), pp. 18-52.

sense; everything indicates that the vast majority of people continued to practice one or another form of communal religion, while leaving the Buddhist soteriological ideals to the monastic community. One Ashokan edict says that Buddhist monks went to 600 places, from the Indo-Greek kingdoms in the Northwest to South India and Sri Lanka. The later Sri Lankan chronicle known as the *Dīpavaṃsa* also mentions missionaries, and the *Mahāvaṃsa*, in a chapter called 'The Conversion of Different Countries', describes how the missionaries of the earlier chronicle converted people to Buddhism by the thousands. But this is part of the legend, and there is no trace of these missionaries and no later record of their achievements except of those who went to Sri Lanka. It is also part of the legend that Ashoka built 84,000 monasteries and as many stupas. In later times almost every old stupa was attributed to him. All that can be plausibly asserted is that the propagation of Buddhism in Ashoka's reign prepared the ground for the rise of the Sangha in areas which later fell within the Satavahana empire—whose historic mission it was to integrate North and South. But if it was Ashoka's aim to use Buddhism for the consolidation of the Maurya empire we can only conclude that he failed.

From archaeological evidence we know that the locational tie between Buddhism, trade and empire continued to exist into the Christian era, when the number of monastic sites increased again, and new regions entered the picture.[24] Buddhist monastic sites typically existed in nodes of permanent settlement which constituted the centres of imperial power and long-distance trade, and they appear to have served as symbolic structures mediating social hierarchy within an urban complex.[25] The first network of long-distance trade routes becomes discernible at the same time that we begin to obtain archaeological evidence of the first Buddhist monastic sites. The tie was especially strong in Gandhara in the early Christian era. But archaeological evidence does not suggest that these Buddhist sites had themselves any specifically political or economic role.[26] They were always located in the proximity of

---

[24] Cf. J. Heitzman, 'Early Buddhism, Trade and Empire', in: K. A. R. Kennedy and G. L. Possehl (eds), *Studies in the Archaeology and Palaeoanthropology of South Asia* (New Delhi, 1984), pp. 121-37; idem, *Buddhist Monastic Institutions*.
[25] Heitzman, 'Early Buddhism', p. 121.
[26] *Ibid.*, p. 132.

non-monastic sites or along routes connecting urban locations.[27] At Taxila, almost all of the Buddhist remains are found outside the walled towns, and the same was the case at Nagarjunakonda and elsewhere. The evidence also does not point at military, storage, or industrial functions of monasteries and appears to indicate that the monasteries were not directly involved in the major governmental and commercial organization of the times. They merely benefited from royal and mercantile largesse.[28]

In addition, archaeological study of the development and spread of Buddhist monasteries throughout the subcontinent reveals a number of significant transformations of these establishments occurring over time, culminating in the rise of the great monastic universities of the Eastern Tract, such as Nalanda, Vikramashila, Uddandapura, and Jagaddala.[29] Unfortunately, reliable figures of the numbers of religious establishments of the various successive types and their inmates are lacking, thus making it difficult or impossible to unambiguously identify any particular period as the beginning of a general decline of Buddhism in South Asia generally.[30] The growth of the academic Buddhist centres, which appears to supersede the merely conventual character of some of them, extends at least through the seventh to twelfth centuries. While it is in this period that in many parts of South Asia a decline appears to have occurred in the number of smaller monasteries, it could be argued that we should perhaps also interpret this as a process of concentration and expansion of scope. In other words, that if the monasteries acquired more and more the character of centres of learning, and a library tradition developed, it is possible that the economics of scale dictated the concentration of resources in a relatively small number of large academic centres or Mahāvihāras, and that the latter simply drove the smaller ones out of business. This may have been the reason that Buddhism became geographically restricted again to its original domain in the Eastern Tract.

Already in the Gupta age, in the fourth to sixth centuries, we see that monasteries grew bigger and richer in decorations. Larg-

---

[27] Ibid., p. 124.
[28] Ibid., p. 133.
[29] Cf. S. Dutt, Buddhist Monks and Monasteries of India: Their History and their Contribution to Indian Culture (New Delhi, 1962).
[30] Ibid., p. 28.

er and larger manuscript collections were beginning to be accumulated in the monasteries—a tradition which was later inherited by Tibet (where most of the great monasteries were storehouses of manuscripts). From now on it became the object of many Chinese and Tibetan pilgrims to collect manuscripts in India. The White Hun incursions reduced to ruins viharas in Gandhara, Kashmir, and elsewhere, but there were revivalist efforts in many parts of North India until as late as the twelfth century, and even after the Muslims had overrun Magadha.[31] Nalanda, perhaps the longest lived of the Mahāvihāras of India, began its career under the Guptas. In I-Tsing's time it contained more than 3000 monks and perhaps 10,000 residents. By the Pala period there were five major monastic universities in eastern India, and a small number of less well-known ones. Uddandapura was founded about 10 km from Nalanda. As Mahāvihāras, these centres acquired a more general educational function, on which account they appear to have drawn resident lay students, focusing on Logic, Grammar, Philology, Medicine, Magic, Philosophy, and other subjects, as well as Tantric Buddhism. Nalanda, the preeminent educational monastic establishment, fenced around by a wood, brick or stone wall, and with provisions for months, was not only a storehouse of old manuscripts, but also an emporium which supplied medicine to the sick, alms to beggars, garments, shelter, and so on.[32] Nalanda was also the most truly international of the Buddhist universities, with streams of pilgrim-students coming from China, Tibet and Korea, distant provinces of India, and Sri Lanka, up to the thirteenth century. It also sent out scholars to these same places. A great number of Chinese pilgrims came to it between 950 and 1033 AD, and according to Chinese chronicles there were never so many Indian monks at the Chinese court as at the close of the tenth and the beginning of the eleventh century.[33] The archaeological evidence, again, shows that Nalanda was destroyed more than once.[34] And we know that a total of perhaps 200 villages, some at a distance of 50 km, was bestowed on it. Throughout its career, it had many royal patrons, most of

---

[31] *Ibid.*, p. 169, ff., 202-9.
[32] H. D. Sankalia, *The University of Nalanda* (New Delhi, 1972), p. 32.
[33] *Ibid.*, p. 233.
[34] *Ibid.*, p. 47.

whom were not Buddhists, and some of whom lived as far away as Suvarnadvipa and Yavadvipa.[35]

The fairly voluminous travel literature produced by the Chinese and Tibetan Buddhist pilgrims strongly reinforces the impression that Buddhism in ancient and early medieval India remained confined to the monasteries and, within that setting, became ever more academic in orientation up to the time that the last Mahāvihāras were destroyed by the Muslim conquerors.[36] Fa-hsien (399-414 AD), the first Chinese traveller in India whose writings are known to us, and his fellow pilgrims grieved that they had been born 'among the outer barbarians' rather than in the land of the Buddha.[37] But Fa-hsien nowhere demonstrates the existence of any widely accepted popular form of Buddhism in India. Moreover, his account seems to indicate that he only went to places where he knew Buddhist pilgrims from China could count on local support.[38] Fa-hsien, everywhere he went, stayed in the monasteries, and in his account focused almost exclusive attention on Buddhist 'fakelore' and memorabilia: places where the Buddha was supposed to have left his shadow on a rock; places where the Buddha stuck a piece of his willow chewingstick (for cleansing his teeth) in the ground; footprints of the Buddha; the Buddha's birthplace; tooth and skull-bone relics of the Buddha; the prevalence of vegetarianism and teetotalism; and so on.[39] Fa-hsien also recalled memories of Ashoka, and of other kings who were Buddhists. And he mentions days on which monks and laymen came together, such as the festival in the middle of the third moon.[40] But nothing indicates widespread acceptance of Buddhism outside the monastic order.

Later Buddhist pilgrims, like Sung Yun and Hwei Sang, who came to India to obtain Buddhist books in 518 AD, basically provide a very similar picture, and have an equally narrow focus. They write at length about places where the Buddha was supposed to

---

[35] *Ibid.*, pp. 46-67.
[36] See H. A. Giles (transl.), *The Travels of Fa-hsien (399-414 AD), or record of the Buddhistic Kingdoms* (London, 1956); S. Beal (transl.), *Si-Yu-Ki, Buddhist Records of the Western World*, 4 vols (Calcutta, 1957-8); Watters, *Yuan Chwang*; K. L. Hazra, *Buddhism in India as Described by the Chinese Pilgrims, A.D. 399-689* (New Delhi, 1983); Roerich, *Dharmasvamin*.
[37] Giles, *Fa-hsien*, pp. 32, 65.
[38] *Ibid.*, pp. 19-20.
[39] *Ibid.*, pp. 15, 17, 20, 29.
[40] *Ibid.*, pp. 38-39, 69-71, 73, etc.

have dried his clothes, about Buddhist relics, places where Ashoka
raised a pagoda, memories of Kanishka, but not much more.[41]
Hiuen Tsang, in the seventh century, came to India with the
twofold aim to see the holy land and shrines of his religion and
to procure Buddhist books in the original and study with Indian
teachers.[42] He brought back 657 books on Buddhism, images of
the Buddha and his saints, and relics, on the backs of twenty horses. But Hiuen Tsang was not a good observer of Indian society,
and, with his easy belief in miracles, merely comments on the
same rarefied religious phenomena as his predecessors, while presenting his readers with endless statistics about the distances
between monasteries, the numbers of monasteries and inmates of
the various schools, and information about kings who were considered adherents of Buddhism.[43] All along he displays his anxiety about the general state of decline of Buddhism in India,
recording information about the White Hun destruction of
monasteries and their killing of numerous believers, as also about
Shasanka's alleged attempts to exterminate Buddhism.[44] There is
almost nothing in his lengthy and often tedious account about
lay Buddhism. Only once, in Sind, Hiuen Tsang refers to the
inhabitants as formerly 'thorough believers in Buddhism'.[45] As
Hiuen Tsang writes:'Among the low marshes near the Sintu
(Indus) for above 1000 li were settled some myriads of families
of ferocious disposition, who made the taking of life their occupation, and supported themselves by rearing cattle; they had no
social distinctions and no government; they shaved off their hair
and wore bhikshu garb, looking like bhikshus yet living in the
world; they were bigoted in their narrow views and reviled the
"Great Vehicle". According to local accounts the ancestors of this
people were originally cruel and wicked and were converted by a
compassionate arhat who received them into the Buddhist communion; they thereupon ceased to take life, shaved their heads
and assumed the dress of Buddhist mendicants; in the course of
time, however, the descendants of these men had gone to their
old ways, but they still remained outwardly bhikshus'.[46] This pas-

---

[41] Beal, *Si-Yu-Ki*, I, pp. 55-73
[42] Watters, *Yuan Chwang*, I, pp. 10-11.
[43] *Ibid.*, p. 15.
[44] *Ibid.*, p. 289; II, p. 43.
[45] *Ibid.*, II, p. 252.
[46] *Ibid.*, pp. 252-3.

sage illustrates, once again, the difficulties involved in identifying lay Buddhism.

Dharmasvamin, in the 1230s, must have been one of the last of many Tibetan monks to travel to India. He goes to pay homage to the Buddha temple at Bodh Gaya. But most of the Buddhist manuscript libraries had already been destroyed in India itself, and Dharmasvamin has to obtain his copies in monasteries in Nepal.[47] And after him, although India continued to enjoy a reputation for higher studies in Buddhism, Tibetan scholars would always go to Nepal.[48] More generally, Dharmasvamin observed that in India the non-Buddhists were numerous, the Shravakas [Hinayanists] were fewer, and the followers of Mahayana even fewer;[49] that Hindus gave alms to Buddhist monks; that the Buddha had long been transformed into an incarnation of Vishnu; and that the main differences between Hinduism and Buddhism revolved around animal slaughter, and the absence of a salvation method among Hindus and the wrong belief of the latter in a soul.[50]

Still worse, among the Muslim chroniclers of the eleventh to thirteenth centuries we find very little interest in Buddhism in any form; these often fail to distinguish it from the other religions of *al-Hind*. Gardizi, in the eleventh century, while not failing to mention, erroneously, Shrāvasti as the birthplace of the Buddha, and Kushinagara, which is said to be the place where the Buddha died, describes a bewildering variety of sects and religious beliefs prevalent in India in his time.[51]

The upsurge of brahmanical Hinduism which had taken place in North India in the early medieval period is perhaps best illustrated in the influential Sanskrit drama *Prabodhacandrodaya*, an allegory of the defeat of Buddhist and Jain heterodoxy and of devotion to Vishnu which was composed at the Candella court in the later eleventh century.[52] The population of North India, it shows, was now generally Vaishnava, Shaiva or Shakta. But the

---

[47] Roerich, *Dharmasvamin*, p. ii.

[48] *Ibid.*, pp. ii-iii.

[49] *Ibid.*, p. 87.

[50] *Ibid.*, pp. 82-3, 96.

[51] V. Minorsky, 'Gardizi on India', *Bulletin of the Schoool of Oriental and African Studies*, 12 (1948), pp. 629-30.

[52] Cf. McGregor, *Hindi Literature*, p. 4.

absorption of Buddhist elements by Hindu culture had been going on for centuries.[53] And anti-Buddhist propaganda was also widespread, reaching a peak already in the eighth century under Shankara, who organised his own monastic order on the model of the Buddhist Sangha. There is a general lack of evidence for literary activities in languages other than Sanskrit and dramatic Prakrit in the central parts of North India in the eleventh and twelfth centuries, which can probably also be explained by the growth of brahmanical orthodoxy and the decline of Buddhism and Jainism in these areas.[54] Beyond such literary evidence, materials for the reconstruction of the history of the decline of Buddhism in North India are as unsatisfactory as they are for the South.[55] After the Guptas, the Maitraka kingdom in Saurashtra appears to have inherited the Gupta tradition of royal patronage to monasteries, with Buddhism flourishing in its capital Valabhi, but the dynasty itself was Shaivite. I-Tsing, in 690 AD, speaks of Valabhi and Nalanda as the two most distinguished centres of Buddhism in his time.[56] Valabhi shows that the old connection of cities and Buddhist Sangha continued to exist in early medieval India.[57] Similarly, Buddhism may still have prospered under Turkish rule in Gandhara and Udyana in the eighth century, and there was possibly something of a revival in twelfth-century Kashmir. In Sind we only get glimpses of Buddhism up to the Arab conquest. There is no evidence here that the provincial government of Sind was in the hands of a Buddhist priesthood, as has sometimes been maintained,[58] although there may have been governors who were lay adherents of Buddhism of some sort. The whole idea of a 'Buddhist theocracy', as it was known from Tibet in later times, is inapplicable to South Asia throughout its entire history. Nor can it be shown that Buddhists anywhere in India 'converted' to Islam.[59]

---

[53] Cf. L. Joshi, *Studies in the Buddhistic Culture of India (During the 7th and 8th Centuries AD)* (Delhi, 1964), Ch. XII; and R. C. Mitra, 'The Decline of Buddhism in India', *Visva-Bharati Annals*, Vol. VI (Santiniketan, 1954), pp. 1-164.

[54] Mitra, 'Decline of Buddhism', p. 6.

[55] *Ibid.*, p. 36.

[56] Dutt, *Buddhist Monks*, pp. 224-31.

[57] Cf. M. Njammasch, 'Buddhistische Klöster der Maitrakas von Valabhī', *The Journal of the Economic and Social History of the Orient* (forthcoming).

[58] Cf. W. Ball, 'The Buddhists of Sind', *South Asian Studies*, 5 (1989), pp. 119-31.

[59] As is hypothesized in Maclean, *Religion and Society in Arab Sind*.

While Buddhist institutions in Sind were already declining in importance several centuries prior to the arrival of Islam, we can still see, on the eve of the conquest, that the parts of Sind which show most traces of Buddhism were those, like Makran, Turan and Budha, which had particularly strong trading connections and were served by searoutes.

The seventh-thirteenth centuries were also the period in which Islam arrived in South Asia and replaced Buddhism as the great cosmopolitan trading religion in many parts, while agrarian expansion in the subcontinent itself was accompanied by a further consolidation of the communal peasant religions of Hinduism. Buddhism, it should be emphasized, arose and went through its major expansion at a time when the Indian subcontinent was sparsely inhabited, urbanisation was but incipient, and trade relatively small in volume by comparison with early medieval times. If it was the ideological mediator between the urban-nomadic-trading world and the world of peasant settlement, it fitted the ancient situation in which the agricultural potential of the subcontinent was merely beginning to be tapped by organized polities. From early medieval times this entire relationship—between Indian agriculture and long-distance trade, nomadism, and urbanisation—was beginning to be redefined in he context of Islam and the creation of a new intermediary economy in the Middle East. By then, trade had greatly increased in volume and scope, raiding and conquest movements had become bolder, and agricultural states had arisen which generated far greater surpluses. With the stakes going up, the relationship between the frontier of nomadism and trade and Indian agriculture changed. It became more confrontational. But, at the same time, interdependence between the two increased as well. Both of these tendencies occurred on an almost global scale. India, however, was at the centre of this realignment of trade and production because of the sheer size of its agricultural economy and the vastness of its human resources. In this new situation, in which the nomadic element gradually fused with the settled realm, Buddhism lost its relevance as a mediator between the two worlds. It then perpetuated itself ever more exclusively as an academic tradition of high learning.

It seems noteworthy, with this in mind, that Buddhism survived longer in Iran than it did in the South-Asian subcontinent, al-

though we know little about the form of Buddhism that was professed for about fifty years by the Mongols of Iran until the time
of Arghun (1284-91) and his son Ghazan (1295-1304).[60] Iran sheltered a large number of Buddhist 'Bakhshīs' and was strewn with
Buddhist establishments.[61] When Ghazan converted to Islam in
1295, this was accompanied by the destruction of the Buddhist
places of worship and the migration of many Buddhists to Kashmir, India, China, Tibet, and Uyghuristan. But it can be shown
that Buddhism lingered in Iran for some time longer, until the
fourteenth century.[62] And it appears from Kamalashri's account
that the Buddhism of Iran was more like that of Kashmir and the
rest of South Asia than that of the eastern Mongols which soon
became akin to the Tibetan-Lamaist variety. In Tibet, the lamas
or 'spiritual preceptors' were not necessarily fully ordained
monks, and hence monks did not monopolize the Dhamma to
the degree that they did in India; here there was a host of qua-
si- or semi-monastic priestly types with overlapping aims. The
Tibetan Sangha was also extremely inclusive, and at the lower end
included a vast population of menial monks which embraced the
belief that all human activity could be directed to achieving
Enlightenment on an interim level. In Tibet too, from early times,
monks belonging to noble clans were appointed as ministers and
accorded a higher rank than their lay colleagues.[63] In 1244 the
power of the Sa-skya-pa school reached its apex when the Mongol Khan Kodan summoned the head lama of Sa-skya to his court.
The Mongol Khan demanded and received the submission of
Tibet from the Sa-skya lama, who was then appointed regent of
Tibet.[64] The succeeding head of the Sa-skya monastery, 'Phags-pa
(1235-80), succeeded in winning the confidence of Kublai Khan.
Thus Tibet, for the first time since the ninth century, became subject again to a single political leadership, at the same time avoiding direct Mongol conquest. This leadership was that of a religious hierarchy. Here, and not in India, do we find the origin of

---

[60] Jahn, *Rashīd al-Dīn's History of India*, pp. xxxi-lxxvii.
[61] *Ibid.*, p. xxxiii; B. Spuler, *Die Mongolen in Iran* (Leipzig, 1939), p. 180.
[62] Jahn, *Rashīd ad-Dīn's History of India*, p. xxxiii.
[63] P. Kvaerne, 'Tibet: the Rise and Fall of a Monastic Tradition', in: H. Bechert
and R. Gombrich (eds), *The World of Buddhism* (London, 1984), pp. 253-70.
[64] *Ibid.*, p. 261.

that 'theocratic' or 'hierocratic' rule which was to become so characteristic of Tibet throughout its later history.[65]

b. JAINISM

If the survival of Buddhism in the Indian subcontinent depended on the strength of its monasteries rather than its diffusion
among a widespread non-monastic population, Jainism—a religion which in its origins was remarkably close to Buddhism—
imposed a much tighter control on its lay adherents. And this is
perhaps the essential difference in its organizational infrastructure which explains why, while Buddhism virtually ceased to exist
in India after the Islamic conquest, there are still several million
adherents of Jainism, predominantly in the northwest and south
of the subcontinent.

With its origins going back further than those of Buddhism,
Jainism had a similar social constituency, and it arose in the same
part of the subcontinent. Likewise, it denied the claims of the
priestly brahmans, attaching little value to birth and ascribed status, and instead focused on moral superiority. It also denied the
authority of the Veda, opposing animal sacrifice and the killing
of animals generally (although neither the Buddha nor Mahavira
were strict vegetarians). And both Buddhism and Jainism were
missionary and polemical religions, making use of the vernacular
language rather than Sanskrit.[66] In comparison with Buddhism,
however, Jainism provided a much more complete worldview and
systematic and authoritative instruction in an entire metaphysical
system that was better atuned to ordinary believers. The Buddha's
teaching, while more in-depth, did not cover a lot of ground, and
shied away from metaphysics. Buddhism did not conceive of
Nirvana as a 'place' or a positive condition, but merely as cessation. Soteriologically, the Jainas held to a conception that had
a more immediate appeal, and was more in line with the Indian
tradition in general: liberation from matter. Jain ascetisim, in
extreme cases leading to religious suicide, also gave the religion
a more conventional aspect, closer to the mainstream of Hindu

---

[65] *Ibid.*, p. 262.
[66] See esp. F. R. Hamm, 'Buddhismus und Jinismus: Zwei Typen indischer Religiosität und ihr Weg in der Geschichte', *Saeculum*, XV (1964).

soteriology, while Buddhism, with its Middle Way, shunning ascetism (considering it useless for salvation) was in fact unconventional.

Both Buddhism and Jainism were typically monkish religions— their ultimate aims could only be reached by monks and nuns— and both were, unlike the Christian monastic orders, entirely dependent on the laity for material support. But the difference is that in Jainism, throughout its history, laymen were supposed to emulate the monks as much as possible.[67] They were constantly instructed by monks, and were subject to numerous rules concerning food, conduct, professional orientation, and so on, and these rules reached very deeply into their daily life. In reverse, the laity watched very closely over the conduct of the monks, as the religious effectiveness of its donations was dependent on the purity and correct performance of the monkhood.

The Jains also concentrated their religious resources far less in monasteries or permanent religious establishments.[68] The rule that the Jain monk still often follows is that outside the rainy season he should lead a wandering life. This meant that the monk had to prove himself again and again in the eyes of strangers. In addition, in Jainism it was he laity which took the leading role in cultic practice; in particular, the daily worship of images was undertaken not by the monks but by the laity. Paradoxically, while the Jains always stayed more within the mainstream of Indian tradition (adopting caste, which they had initially ignored), they at the same time remained rigidly attached to their own dogmatism and succeeded in remaining separate in areas of communal practice where Buddhism adapted itself to the theistic tendencies of Hinduism. Jainism, at the same time, did not spread where it did not find a Hinduised context. Hence we do not find it in Sri Lanka or Southeast Asia.

Jainism typically remained associated with trade throughout its history, even though, in the South, material support for Jainism at times also came from the rural areas and in more recent times a fair number of Jains in Tamil Nadu became farmers.[69] People engaged in commerce and trade were drawn to Jainism from at

---

[67] *Ibid.*

[68] *Ibid.*

[69] Roy, *History of the Jainas*, pp. 2-3, 110; Weber, *Religion of India*, p. 193; *Al-Hind, I*, p. 312.

least the early centuries of the Christian era, and probably from the time of Mahavira. It was the practice of *ahimsa* ('non-violence'; lit. 'absence of a desire to kill') which led the Jains to exclude themselves from all occupations endangering life. Only the trader could truly practice *ahimsa*; but it had to be resident trade, or banking and moneylending. As much as monks were enjoined to wander, there was a rule against travel for the laity, since travel would put it in danger of falling into sin.[70]

As was the case with Buddhism, the rise and expansion of Jainism was to a considerable extent determined by the favour and patronage of kings. According to Hemacandra, the historian of the Jain religion, Jainism, in the early stages, was spread principally due to the missionary efforts of Ashoka's grandson Samprati, 'who caused Jina temples to be erected over the whole of Jambudvipa'.[71] The period of great flowering of Jainism varied from region to region, but by the thirteenth century monumental Jain temples had been built all over the subcontinent. After the thirteenth century, Jainism survived and retained a significant presence in some outlying parts of the subcontinent.

The history of the Jains is most difficult to reconstruct in North India, while in Eastern India, its place of origin, it may have almost disappeared already by the ninth century (for reasons that are not clear).[72] We know that there was a flourishing Jain community in Mathura, in the years between 250 and 350 AD, which continued its existence into the early medieval period. Jainism was firmly established in North India by 600 AD, as it was elsewhere in the subcontinent. Khajuraho still had important Jain temples. And Jains are occasionally mentioned in the service of the Delhi Sultans.[73] But in the North, already by 1000 AD, Shaivism and Vaishnavism had become the dominant religious systems, and Jainism was of relatively minor importance.[74] In the *Prabodhacandrodaya*,

---

[70] Weber, *Religion of India*, p. 197.

[71] *Ibid.*, p. 59.

[72] For Jainism in Eastern India, see: S. L. Huntington and J. C. Huntington, *Leaves from the Bodhi Tree* (Seattle and London, 1990), p. 110; Roy, *History of the Jainas*, pp. 68-69; P. Josh, *Some Aspects of Jainism in Eastern India* (New Delhi, 1989), pp. 70-71, 75-76, 78-80, 83, 85, 90-91; *Al-Hind, I*, pp. 261, 269.

[73] K. L. Srivastava, *The Position of Hindus under the Delhi Sultanate, 1206-1526* (Delhi, 1980), pp. 146-7; Mitra, 'Historical References in Jain poems', p. 301.

[74] Cf. A. K. Chatterjee, *A Comprehensive History of Jainism*, 2 vols (Calcutta, 1978-84), I, p. 150.

354   THE WELL OF BUDDHISM DEFILED

a Jain called Digambara speaks Magadhi Prakrit, indicative of what
the author considers his low class status. He is dirty to look at,
the hair of his head has been plucked out and he wears no clothes;
in his hand he carries a peacock feather; and he has no manliness about him (*nirvirya*). Almost nothing is said in the play about
the Jain doctrines, and the Jain on the stage is merely there to
depict an abject heresy, detestable and comical at the same time.[75]
Like Buddhism, the Jain religion is described as *tāmasika*, the outcome of darkness. And according to the same work, Jainism,
together with other 'heretical' sects, had secretly retired to countries which were 'rich in vulgar people'—by which appear to have
been meant Rajasthan and Malwa and especially the 'places on
the seashore' of Southeast Gujarat and Saurashtra.[76]

    In Rajasthan, Jainism had become a great cultural force from
the eighth century onwards, and even more in the eleventh to
thirteenth centuries, under the patronage of Rajput rulers who
themselves adhered to Shaivism and Vaishnavism.[77] Rajasthan, and
especially Chitorgarh, abounds in Jain antiquities from the latter
period. But, in the long run, Jainism could not escape Islamic
iconoclasm in this region. The Muslims razed many of the Jain
temples to the ground, destroyed Jain libraries, and allegedly
killed unknown numbers of followers. Later Jain temples of the
area are copies of the earlier ones of Abu and Sanganer, but of
inferior quality, and showing influence of Muslim architecture.
Jainism, nonetheless, remained quite significant in Rajasthan; and
almost every state in this area, and every principality or jagir in
the early modern period was served by more than one Jain minister or manager.[78] And most of the castes and gotras among the
Jains in North India claim to have their origin in Rajasthan.[79]

    It was Gujarat, however, that has always remained the Jain coun-
try par excellence. Here kings are reported to have been 'seized
by a desire for asceticism' and committed religious suicide in the
Jain style by starving themselves.[80] Here, in Valabhi, Saurashtra,
the canonical Jain works were put to writing in the fifth century

---
[75] S. K. Nambiar (ed. and transl.), *Prabodhacandrodaya* (Delhi, 1971), p. 45.
[76] *Ibid.*, pp. 49, 127.
[77] Jain, *Jainism in Rajasthan*.
[78] *Ibid.*, p. 213.
[79] *Ibid.*, p. 93.
[80] Tawney, *Prabandhacintāmani*, pp. 48, 59.

AD.[81] Jain temples are found in Gujarat as early as the sixth and seventh centuries AD.[82] The religion was patronized by the Chavadas, Solankis and Vaghelas of Anahilvada, by the Maitrakas of Valabhi, while the Caulukyas, in particular the Shaivist king Kumarapala (1144-74), under the guidance of Hemacandra, set out to make Gujarat a Jain state.[83] Edicts were promulgated against the taking of animal life, and Kumarapala is said to have erected another 14,140 Jain temples.[84] Many Jain temples in Gujarat, especially in Anahilvada, in effect, date from the middle of the twelfth century.[85] Jain architecture, always chaste and elegant, was basically Hindu, but because of their wealth the Jains were much more given to temple-building, becoming the greatest patrons of architecture in Western India, and patronizing mosques at times.[86]

After Kumarapala's reign, Jainism went into decline even in Gujarat. His successor Ajayapala (1173-76) began to destroy many of the temples built in the previous reign and in general did not favour Jainism much.[87] Jain temples were beginning to be swept to destruction by the Muslims in Anahilvāda as early as 1298 AD.[88] From the end of the thirteenth century until Akbar's reign, at the close of the sixteenth century, no Jain or Hindu temple of any pretensions was raised in Gujarat, but destroyed temples, like at Satruñjaya, Palitana, and at other places, were sometimes rebuilt.[89] Early Portuguese writers still testify to the strength of Jainism in Gujarat in the sixteenth century but opine that the Gujaratis were deprived of their kingdom by the Muslims because of their kindheartedness.[90] Varthema describes the Gujaratis as 'a certain race which eats nothing that has blood, and never kills any living thing

---

[81] C. B. Seth, *Jainism in Gujarat (AD 1100 to 1600)* (Bombay, 1953), p. xi.

[82] *Ibid.*, p. xi.

[83] Cf. pp. 273-4; Tawney, *Prabandhacintāmani*, p. xiii, ff.

[84] G. C. Choudhary, *Political History of Northern India from Jain Sources* (Amritsar, 1954), p. 281; Tawney, *Prabandhacintāmani*, p. xiii ff.

[85] Burgess and Cousens, *Architectural Antiquities of Northern Gujarat*, p. 34 ff.

[86] Shokoohy, *Bhadreshvar*, pp. 3, 7-14; Burgess and Cousens, *Architectural Antiquities of Northern Gujarat*, pp. 11-16.

[87] Choudhary, *Political History*, p. 285.

[88] Burgess and Cousens, *Architectural Antiquities of Northern Gujarat*, pp. 5, 18-19.

[89] Cf. p. 325; A. K. Forbes, *Rās Māla: Hindoo Annals of the Province of Goozerat in Western India*, 2 vols (London, 1924), I, p. 6.

[90] Longworth-Dames, *Duarte Barbosa*, I, pp. 109-14; J. Winter Jones (transl.), *The Travels of Ludovico di Varthema* (London, 1863), p. 109.

... and these people are neither Moors nor heathens; ... if they were baptized, they would all be saved by virtue of their works, for they never do to others what they would not do unto them ...'.[91]

In South India, Jainism had spread by the fourth century AD.[92] Here Jains came to be found in most places, but it was in south-west Karnataka, and especially the Tulu-speaking areas, that Jainism remained an important force and received patronage from many dynasties, dominating political and cultural life between the fifth and twelfth centuries, accumulating vast resources, making itself felt in the administration and the army, and with Jain monks emerging as a landowning class.[93] From references in Tamil literature it has been inferred that Jainism was important in Tamil Nadu in the fifth-eleventh centuries, and especially in the Madurai-Tirunelveli area in the eighth and ninth centuries.[94] From the late tenth century, South India's increased involvement in long-distance trade resulted in closer connections between the Tamil area and Karnataka, and in the establishment of Cola control of the routes which were used by the Ayyavale and Nanadeshi merchant associations and a considerable increase in the number of benefactions by the mercantile class to Jain establishments.[95] In the Tamil area, up to the twelfth century, there is evidence of Jain participation in the Ayyavale association itself.[96] And in the Kannada-speaking area, Jain influence is recorded in many epigraphs of the Ayyavale traders in or near Jain temples, in the twelfth and first half of the thirteenth century; until about that time Jains virtually monopolised Kannada literature. A prosperous Jain community continued to exist in some places in Tamil Nadu until as late as the eighteenth century.

In Karnataka, Jainism remained a prominent religion, and Jains, still in the thirteenth century but also in the centuries afterwards, continued to control a considerable amount of the commerce in

[91] Winter Jones, *Ludovico di Varthema*, pp. 107-9.

[92] Roy, *History of the Jainas*, p. 3.

[93] *Ibid.*; R. B. P. Singh, *Jainism in Early Medieval Karnataka (c. AD 500-1200)* (Delhi, 1975).

[94] Roy, *History of the Jainas*, pp. 108-9.

[95] Singh, *Jainism*, p. 114; *Al-Hind, I,* p. 323.

[96] M. Abraham, *Two Medieval Merchant Guilds of South India* (New Delhi, 1988), pp. 97-98.

the region.[97] Under the Hoysalas, who themselves were Shaivite and Vaishnavite, there were ministers and merchant princes who built Jain temples.[98] Great building activity is also in evidence under the Vijayanagara kings, when apparently certain sections of the rural population still adhered to and materially supported Jainism as well.[99] Two factors, however, reduced the influence of Jainism in Karnataka and much of South India from the twelfth and thirteenth centuries onwards, with the result that by the sixteenth century its stronghold was largely the Tuluva country.[100] The first of these was the rise of the Virashaiva or Lingayat sect under Basava's leadership in the twelfth century; and the second, perhaps even more decisive, the conversion of the main mercantile class of the Vira Banajigas from Jainism to Virashaivism.[101] The Basava Purāna, a long hagiographical poem (probably of the thirteenth century) presenting the legendary biography of Basava, the most important saint-poet of the Vīrashaiva sect, displays a strong religious antinomianism and sanctifies violence resulting in hecatombs of slain Jains and brahmans.[102] It abounds in stories in which the followers of Shiva are victorious over Jains and brahmans, putting 'the sharp spear on the skulls of Jains', impaling Jains on spears, and the like.[103] Although much of this is mere literary metaphor, it does appear that Virashaivism, not Islam, greatly reduced the prevalence of Jainism in South India.

---

[97] Roy, *History of the Jainas*, p. 111.

[98] *Ibid.*, pp. 114-5.

[99] *Ibid.*, pp. 116-7; B. A. Saletore, *Mediaeval Jainism. With Special Reference to the Vijayanagara Empire* (Bombay, 1938), p. 180; *Al-Hind, I*, p. 312.

[100] Roy, *History of the Jainas*, pp. 118-9.

[101] *Ibid.*, p. 119.

[102] V. Narayana Rao and G. H. Roghair (transl.), *Siva's Warriors: The Basava Purāna of Pālkuriki Somanātha* (Princeton, 1990).

[103] *Ibid.*, p. 5.

CHAPTER XI

MONKS AND PEASANTS

In this final chapter it will be our task to analyse the emergence of a second Buddhist tradition—largely Theravada—in the context of the expanding agrarian societies of Sri Lanka and mainland Southeast Asia. The latter were based on irrigated rice cultivation and typically they had little or no direct contact with the nomadic world of Central Asia. These societies, as we will see, developed their own internal dynamic, beyond the frontier of Islamic conquest.

a. SRI LANKA

In contrast with most of the Indian subcontinent, we have a continuous narrative history of the dynasties which ruled Sri Lanka, 'the isle of the [Buddhist] doctrine' or *dhammadīpa*, in a series of Pali chronicles of Buddhist inspiration, the *Dīpavamsa*, *Mahāvamsa* and *Cūlavamsa*, beginning with the origins of Sinhalese kingship around the fifth century BC and running up to the British conquest of Kandy in 1815.[1] This historical narrative, which has later parallels in the Theravada countries of Southeast Asia, in Burma, Arakan, Thailand, and Cambodia, evolved out of the practice of recording the meritorious deeds of the kings in 'account books' (*puññapotthaka*). It adds up to a continuous record of a sometimes precariously surviving but ultimately unbroken Buddhist tradition on the island. The 'account books' contained long lists of tanks, temples and hospitals constructed by the kings, of

---

[1] For the following sketch of Buddhism in Sri Lanka I relied mostly on Lingat, *Royautés Bouddhiques*, pp. 61-239. Among recent works see also: R. A. L. H. Gunawardana, *Robe and Plough: Monasticism and Economic Interest in Early Medieval Sri Lanka* (Tucson, 1979); K. M. De Silva, *A History of Sri Lanka* (London, 1981); W. M. Sirisena, *Sri Lanka and South-East Asia (AD 1000-1500)* (Leiden, 1978); T. P. C. Gabriel, *Lakshadweep: History, Religion and Society* (New Delhi, 1989); B. L. Smith (ed.), *Religion & Legitimation of Power in Sri Lanka* (Chambersburg, 1978); H. B. M. Ilangasinha, *Buddhism in Medieval Sri Lanka* (Delhi, 1992); Gombrich, *Theravada Buddhism*, Chapter 6.

monasteries patronized and endowed and of religious festivals sponsored by them, of donations given'to the Sangha, and so on. In Sri Lanka, the great importance which was attached to these meritorious deeds was linked to a particular conception of royal power and to the theory that 'bad' deeds could be compensated for by 'good' ones. This was the doctrine of *ahosikamma*, 'the act which does not exist', which was fully developed by Buddhaghosa in the fifth century AD, but which represented a belief which had been widespread in Sri Lanka from earlier times. Compensation could only be obtained for voluntary acts, that is 'sins' in the proper sense of the word, acts that knowingly violated Buddhist morality, and the proper mechanism for such compensation were meritorious deeds—of which there was an entire hierarchy, and which varied in their effectiveness.

The Buddhist chroniclers of Sri Lanka pursued primarily moralistic aims when they produced their works, passing over many historical events which are mentioned in foreign accounts, while attaching overriding importance to the 'meritorious' acts of kings and everything they did for Buddhism and the Sangha. With these chronicles as our starting point, and in combination with other records, we can divide the social history of Buddhism in Sri Lanka in three periods, each of very different length, with the most decisive transition occurring around 1235 AD.

First, the period in which Anurādhapura was the capital, from 247-207 BC to 981-1017 AD, beginning with the visit of Mahinda, the son of Ashoka (to whom the complete conversion of the island is attributed), and ending with the Cola raids in the late tenth and early-eleventh century, when Sri Lanka became incorporated in the Cola empire and the capital was transferred to Polonnaruva, further to the southeast.

Second, the period in which Polonnaruva was the capital, from 1017 to 1235 AD. Even though Sri Lanka was subject to Cola rule up to 1070 AD, the 'Anurādhapura' and 'Polonnaruva' periods together are considered to have been the most glorious period in the history of the island, while it remained entirely under the authority of a single Buddhist sovereign. Both capitals were situated in the centre-north, the rich zone which receives rain only during the northeast monsoon but which was artificially irrigated through vast reservoirs of water or tanks, the construction of which was among the most meritorious acts of the early Buddhist

kings. In effect, the spread of Buddhism in these first two periods of the island's history is associated not with trade or an indigenous merchant caste—in particular foreign trade was always in
the hands of non-Sinhalese—but with the construction of these
huge waterworks and the expansion of wet-rice cultivation which
came in its wake. Buddhism in these two periods penetrated everywhere and had a profound impact on the population at large,
while at the same time, due to Tamil invasions and constant contact with South India, the island also participated in the religious
developments of the subcontinent, with the influence of Hinduism becoming strong under the Cola occupation.

Third, from 1235 AD to the British conquest—the period which
saw the decline of Sinhalese kingship, the decline of the irrigation works, the abandonment of Polonnaruva, and the relocation
of the capital further to the south, to a chain of fortified towns
in succession, and the establishment of Portuguese power on the
coast in 1505, then the establishment of Kandy as the new capital in the mountainous centre of the island in the middle of the
sixteenth century, and, finally, Dutch dominance on the coasts
from 1658 to 1796, and the British conquest. From the point of
view of the history of Buddhism as presented in the chronicles,
the Kandy kings pale into insignificance next to the Anuradha-
pura and Polonnaruva kings, and even next to some of the later
thirteenth-century kings. Nevertheless, some of the Kandy kings
played a crucial role in the history of Sinhalese Buddhism as they
solicited the intervention of representatives of the Theravada traditions of Southeast Asia to restore the Buddhist religion. Without these efforts, Buddhism would possibly have disappeared from
Sri Lanka as well.

One cannot follow the chronicles further in their assertion that
Sri Lanka has known and practised some form of a caste system
from the earliest times, even prior to the conversion of the island
to Buddhism. The resemblance of the divisions of ancient Sinhalese society to the theoretical varna scheme of four was purely
formal, and it was not until the Polonnaruva period that, probably under the influence of the Tamils, the 'caste system' of Sri
Lanka was taking definitive shape. Caste lost much of the character which it had had in the subcontinent; its rules were always
to remain much less rigid, and the distance which separated the
different castes was much less marked. It became a kind of cus-

tomary law, the secular code of the laity, which was tied up with
the system of government which the king and even the Sangha
sought to maintain. And if there was the notion of a 'warrior
caste', the fact is that from the seventh century or earlier the kings
of Sri Lanka often used mercenaries, especially Tamils, while most
of the 'warrior caste' or *khattiyas* became big landowners. The
essential distinction of the Sri Lankan caste system was, thus, not
founded on the brahmanical varna theory but on the opposition
of agricultural and non-agricultural population. Its organizing
principle was the relationship to the dominant caste, and the legitimation of the system, by the Polonnaruva period, came from the
monarchy. The entire political economy of the island, as reflected in the caste system, was founded on an intricate tenurial system and the repartition of landrevenue and services or *rājakāriya*.
It was a system which was also extended to the landed property
of the monasteries, which played the role of landlords as well, and
which were entitled to *rājakāriya* just the same, as these services
were attached to the land. And the result was that the Sangha
modeled its organization on the political regime.[2]

If the character of caste was attenuated, notions of purity and
pollution had no sense for Buddhists at all, and untouchability
did not arise in Sri Lanka. Brahmans lost their moral and religious guardianship over society and this role, together with the
role of educator, was passed on to the Sangha. The continued
presence of brahmans in Sinhalese society served purely social
needs, those of ritual agents playing a role in the coronation,
birth, marriage or expiatory ceremonies of a communal type that
Buddhism did not provide for. Such communal religion also came
to include the worship of gods of the Hindu pantheon, in particular Vishnu. Yet, while Sinhalese magic and exorcism (and folk
religion in general) derived largely from South India, and the
higher gods are mostly pan-Hindu, the Buddhist values of compassion and non-violence dictated that no god could receive a
blood-sacrifice.[3] Where brahmanism relativized and particular-
ized, Buddhism universalized, so that in Sri Lanka monks and laymen, although they had complementary responsibilities, acknowledged the same ideals.[4] In this sense, Buddhism became a peasant

---

[2] Lingat, *Royautés Bouddhiques*, pp. 89-107.
[3] Gombrich, *Theravada Buddhism*, pp. 144-5.
[4] *Ibid.*, p. 145.

religion in Sri Lanka, obtaining a pervasive character that it never had in the Indian subcontinent itself.

In Sri Lanka, the Buddhist doctrine was also territorialised in a way that was alien to the ancient form of Indian Buddhism.[5] Sri Lanka became in the true sense of the word a Buddhist land. The Sinhalese consider their island as the chosen territory of Buddhism, as the *dhammadīpa*, an island which is consecrated to the religion of the Buddha and which is itself a Buddhist relic—as it was visited by the Buddha himself no less than three times during his lifetime. The most important consequence of this conception of Sri Lanka as the chosen land of Buddhism was that the sovereignty of the island could only legitimately belong to a Buddhist king. The first duty of such a king was not merely to protect the religion of the Buddha but to eliminate all non-Buddhist powers which intruded upon the island. This view is already expressed in the Mahāvaṁsa's account of king Dutthagamani in the first century BC, who, as the legitimate Buddhist king, expelled the Tamils from the island. It was a situation which was to recur throughout Sri Lanka's history: that of an outside conqueror who persecuted Buddhism, destroyed monasteries and forced bhikkhus into exile or hiding. Buddhist doctrine, although pacifist in origin, responded to this situation by allowing recourse to war in the interest of the protection of the community and reserving condemnation only for wars of conquest. It became the sacred duty of every king of Sri Lanka to take up arms against an invader; and Dutthagamani later came to be seen by some as the creator of a kind of religious proto-nationalism or patriotism. At the same time it is indisputable that actual allegiance here was more to the person of the king or to the Buddha than to an abstract national identity.[6] It was a type of religious identification that is also found in the Buddhist countries of Southeast Asia. The principle behind it, however, was always that these countries were countries of the Buddha.

It was the duty of all Sinhalese, thus, to assure that the sovereignty over the island was in the hands of a Sinhalese Buddhist king. Against intruders all means were justified. Non-Buddhists were lumped together with animals—which meant that they

---

[5] Lingat, *Royautés Bouddhiques*, pp. 109-21.
[6] *Ibid.*, p. 114.

counted for nothing. Such an enemy was not worthy of compassion, and the resulting defensive wars could easily become more ruthless than wars of conquest. At least in conception, the Buddhist *cakkavattin* could not become a menace for neighbouring countries, and, in actual fact, the Buddhist kings of Sri Lanka have rarely carried their wars to their neighbours. Once implanted in Sri Lanka, Buddhism seems to have lost the propagandistic zeal which had characterized it in India and which is so much in evidence in the inscriptions of Ashoka and, of course, in the missions themselves. There is another paradox, therefore, in the fact that Sri Lankan Buddhism had such a great impact abroad, in Southeast Asia. But the chronicles never mention bhikkhus being sent abroad to disseminate the doctrine. If several religious ambassadors were sent to Pegu and Thailand, it was not for propaganda—on the contrary their task was to reintroduce the religion in Sri Lanka itself. Proselytism stopped at the boundaries of the island.

It was in Sri Lanka, too, that kingship was not merely put in the service of the Buddhist religion, but that the piety of the king became, in effect, a form of Buddhist piety which was seen as superior to world renunciation.[7] According to the doctrine of the 'king-bodhisattva', which arose from the ninth-tenth century under the influence of Mahayana Buddhism, it was better to renounce nirvana than to obtain it because it benefited all subjects of the king. From then on popular belief had it that every king of Sri Lanka was a future Buddha. This was another major reason why Buddhism became one of the politically most effective ethical systems.

The chronicles extol this boddhisattva ideal. But yet such kings were not seen as the really great kings of Sri Lanka—because they were still more interested in their personal salvation than in the kingdom. The highest esteem was given to kings like Dutthagamini or Parakkamabahu who made the grandeur of the kingdom their highest priority and displayed an 'ethics of responsibility' rather than an 'ethics of conviction'. Here again we return to the brahmanical conception of the *kshatriya vidyā* as a royal virtue, with a morality of its own, and pacifism recedes behind heroism and ruthlessness.

---

[7] *Ibid.*, pp. 123-50.

The Buddhist kings of Sri Lanka, at the same time, acquired substantial authority in spiritual matters, and could enforce compliance with the rules of monastic discipline or Vinaya.[8] Up to the great reforms undertaken by Parakkamabahu in the twelfth century, the Sinhalese kings have been guarded in intervening in the internal disputes of the Sangha. But they made themselves felt in the domain of administration. This is perhaps the most important aspect of royal politics in Sri Lanka with regard to the Sangha—as it was to be in the Theravada states of Southeast Asia. It meant in practice that the lives of the members of the order were usually regulated in the most minute detail. The chronicles refer to purges effected in the monasteries by orders of the kings. The first such purge is recorded to have occurred in the fifth-sixth century, and later ones are recorded and justified as necessary because the order drew numerous individuals with a doubtful religious calling. The king had to guard against abuse, and a purge often took the form of expulsion from the order. Over time, the consequence was that the temporal power gradually established more and more control over the Sangha. And, reversely, that the Sangha became more and more involved in politics, as kingmaker, ally and councillor. From the thirteenth century onwards the educational function of the Sangha was also expanded, and came to include the dissemination of secular knowledge, a development which ended up in the establishment of universities. It would be an error, however, to think of the king as the benefactor of the Sangha, although he put lands at the disposal of the monastic communities, with all kinds of immunities, and the Sangha ultimately became the richest landowner on the island. The Sangha was a 'field of merit', and it was the king who gained merit by his gifts, while the Sangha owed him nothing in return. The monks were not even obliged to teach.

In interior politics in general, the Sinhalese kings, although Buddhists, reverted to Indian traditions even more and in practice did not distinguish themselves from Hindu monarchs. The chronicles enjoin the king to observe old customs and traditions. Not a single work was produced in Sri Lanka which was specifically devoted to politics, and the kings appear to have been familiar only with brahmanical works. We do not have much informa-

---

[8] *Ibid.*, pp. 175-230.

tion on fiscal practices in the various periods. What Sri Lankan kings appear to have been most involved in was the building and maintenance of a network of canals and irrigation works to facilitate rice cultivation, the major productive enterprise of most Sinhalese. These irrigation works extended over the entire island, and they became one of the distinguishing characteristics of ancient and medieval Sinhalese culture which is without parallel in the Indian subcontinent. But if the chronicles attached great religious value to these waterworks, it is probably because many of them were destined for lands which belonged to the Buddhist monasteries. In other words, they too have little direct connection with Buddhism as such. After the death of Parakkamabahu there is no mention of new works of importance. In the following century the system of tank irrigation fell to ruins, after further Tamil invasions had caused it to fall in disrepair, bringing malaria in its wake.[9]

b. ANGKOR, PAGAN, SUKHOTHAI

As in Sri Lanka, but again quite unlike the situation in ancient India, Buddhism on the mainland of Southeast Asia, the area now occupied by Myanmar (Burma), Thailand, Cambodia and Laos, did not make itself felt as an urban-oriented culture supported by a mercantile elite, but primarily as a peasant religion. The results of this can still be observed in the twentieth century. In Cambodia, for instance, prior to 1945, there was hardly a Buddhist-Khmer urban population at all, and commerce was almost entirely in the hands of non-Khmers; Phnom Penh, with a population of 111,000 in 1948, and the provincial towns were primarily Chinese commercial centres, with smaller groups of Vietnamese or Muslim-Cham trading and artisan groups.[10] The dichotomy of Cambodian society in a Khmer population of peasants, ruled over by officials and royalty, and a mercantile element that was mainly composed of non-Khmers, Chinese above all, probably goes back to the Angkor period.[11] But the spread of Theravada Buddhism as a mass-oriented peasant religion in Cambodia, as in most

---

[9] Cf. p. 165.
[10] M. Vickery, *Cambodia: 1975-1982* (Boston, 1984), p. 18.
[11] *Ibid.*, p. 12.

of Southeast Asia, was merely beginning in the thirteenth century. This was late by comparison with Sri Lanka. Yet, even at that late date, the mainland states of Southeast Asia were much less monetized than the Indian subcontinent in the ancient period.[12] Angkor and Pagan produced no coins at all. At the height of Angkor's power, the Khmers were bartering or offering textiles and ingots of gold and silver in the market. Revenue was usually paid in kind, in grain, or in honey and wax.

In mainland Southeast Asia, the task is therefore, once again, to explain the structure of Theravada Buddhism as a mass religion that rests on an elite-oriented doctrine. On the one hand, in order to maintain the Sangha as a valid 'field of merit', its otherworldliness had to be maintained: On the other, the orthodox doctrines of Theravada Buddhism had by themselves insufficient appeal for the majority of Thais, Burmans, and Khmers, whose main concern always remained to improve their position in this world, rather than to transcend the cycle of rebirths, and who were hence interested above all in merit-making acts rather than religious self-discipline and who also remained firm believers in spirits. If, in this social milieu, Theravada Buddhism had remained merely salvation-oriented and had displayed no concern for the everyday life of laymen, it would without a doubt not have enjoyed the wide popular support that it has until today. In fact, it did answer the popular demand for magic, scriptural spells, amulets, and ritual, while generally adopting a wide range of secular functions, particularly educational, which had to do with the preservation and transmission of culture.[13] Unlike Sri Lanka, in the Theravada countries of Southeast Asia we find the practice of temporary entry in he monastic community. Monks and former monks, in a very broad sense, represented the intellectual elites of these societies. The character of the Sangha was also altered by far-reaching adaptation to the capabilities of the average monk, and the recasting of the monasteries as centres of religious missionary activity and culture, concomitant with the concentration of religious activity on the needs of the laity.[14] Monasteries served

---

[12] Reid, *Southeast Asia*, II, p. 95; Wicks, *Money, Markets, and Trade*; Mabbett and Chandler, *The Khmers*, pp. 65, 166, 176.

[13] Y. Ishii, *Sangha, State, and Society: Thai Buddhism in History* (Honolulu, 1986), pp. 20-26.

[14] Cf. Bechert, 'Max Webers Darstellung'.

as hospitals, schools, welfare institutions for the poor, travelers' lodges, social centres, recreational and ceremonial centres, courts, art centres, or stores for jointly owned property, and they were part of the administrative system. And here too, the most powerful supporter of the Sangha was always the king. From the Sukhothai era in the thirteenth and fourteenth centuries, the Sangha was strongly influenced and shaped by the monarchy. Monastic landlordism did not become a major phenomenon anywhere in Southeast Asia except in Pagan Burma—the Sangha continuing in most parts to rely more on the daily offerings of the laity[15]— but the relations between the Sangha and the state became closely regulated, creating mutual dependence and giving rise to an ordered spiritual hierarchy. The idea was also widespread that the power of the world monarch or *cakkavattin* necessarily had to complement the spiritual power of the Buddha, hence the legitimation of the king as the world ruler of Buddhist mythology.

Popular religion, a mixture of Buddhist principles, old Hindu rites and folk beliefs, among the Khmer, or Burmans or Thai, primarily served the needs of a rice-growing peasantry, representing 'a concretion of certain admirable philosophical and moral principles with beliefs and practices which date from pre-Buddhist times, prejudices peculiar to the society, special relationships with ruling classes, and the ability to rationalize the pursuit of material gain, as well as a good many other actions which are contrary to its principles'.[16] Ebihara says about village Buddhism in Cambodia: 'the villager himself rarely conceives of observing separate religious traditions [Buddhist, Hindu, folk]. Rather, for the ordinary Khmer, Buddha and ghosts, prayers at the temple and invocations to spirits, monks and mediums are all part of what is essentially a single religious system'.[17] The Buddhist order often stood for a social stability secure merely from excessive interference by the spirits and their magic powers but not devoid of them.[18] Buddhist monks were in attendance even at rites of the agricultural cycle.[19] If a Cambodian peasant held to the Buddhist idea that

[15] Ishii, *Sangha, State, and Society*, pp. xv-xvi.
[16] Vickery, *Cambodia*, p. 9.
[17] Quoted by Vickery, *ibid.*, p. 9.
[18] Mabbett and Chandler, *The Khmers*, pp. 113-4.
[19] S. Thierry, *Etude d'un corpus de contes cambodgiens* (Paris and Lille, 1978), p. 76.

the individual soul had no existence, he also knew that he had nineteen souls or 'vital spirits' which made up his individuality, and that he would fall ill if one or another of them were lost. Like in Sri Lanka, even violence could be linked to the practice of Buddhism if it was to uphold the official religion; it was one of Lon Nol's favourite themes that 'religious war' could be launched against the Vietnamese and Khmer communists—which were identified as the '*Thmil*', i.e. Tamils, the traditional enemies of the Buddhist faith in Sri Lanka.[20]

Historically, we have to distinguish several stages in the expansion of Buddhism in Southeast Asia.[21] In Shrivijaya we still find it as a trading religion, prior to the development of the 'classical' mainland states of Angkor, Pagan and Sukhothai. But on the mainland, before the development of the latter states in the eleventh to thirteenth centuries, Buddhism defies classification.[22] In this early period, Buddhism in mainland Southeast Asia was infused with elements of Hindu Dharmashastra and brahmanic theology, Mahayana as well as Pali Theravada elements, Tantric practices, Sanskrit Sarvastivadin texts, and a lot more. Buddhism here, in other words, from its earliest beginnings up to the period of the development of monarchical states, was highly eclectic and diverse, and, characterized by miraculous relics and charismatic monks, should be seen as an almost indistinguishable part of the general process of Indianization in these areas.[23] Providing symbols of translocal value, and articulating a worldview in which diverse communities could participate and reformulate their identity, it was merely a first stage in the development of a more organized and systematic religious life.[24] There was already a strong Pali-Theravada presence in Mon-Dvāravatī in Thailand and lower Burma, even though it lacked the homogeneity which is attributed to it by later chroniclers.[25] Among the people of the Pagan-Irrawaddy River basin, in the tenth and early eleventh century, whatever Buddhism there was appears to have been dominated

---

[20] Vickery, *Cambodia*, p. 11.
[21] See also *Al-Hind*, I, pp. 336-58.
[22] Cf. D. K. Swearer, 'Buddhism in Southeast Asia', in: J. M. Kitagawa and M. D. Cummings (eds), *Buddhism and Asian History* (London, 1989), p. 107.
[23] *Ibid.*, pp. 107-8.
[24] *Ibid.*, p. 108.
[25] *Ibid.*, p. 109.

by an eclectic form of Mahayana which was similar to that found in esoteric Shaivism and in animistic naga cults.[26] In other parts of Southeast Asia too, mainland and island, Mahayana, Tantric and Hinayana forms of Buddhism established themselves as part of the general Indian cultural expansion which occurred from about the fifth century onwards. Rulers of the earliest Indianized states, in Champa, Java, or Cambodia, thus supported a variety of priests, monks and religious institutions, while worshiping a variety of gods and spirits.

If diversity and eclectisism characterized the early centuries, during the formation of the classical Southeast-Asian monarchical states in the eleventh-thirteenth centuries, homogeneity of form and institutional orthodoxy began to emerge.[27] Still then, both Buddhist and Hindu elements went into the making of these monarchies. But gradually, a symbiotic relationship developed between the monarchies and the Sangha which tended to support a loose religious orthodoxy which followed the Theravada tradition.[28] In the thirteenth century, which witnessed the conquests of the Thai, Theravada Buddhism began to emerge as the dominant form of religion on the mainland. This type of Buddhism originated from Sri Lanka and is not directly connected, except in very remote ways, with the earlier forms of Buddhism which came to Southeast Asia during the first centuries of Indianization. The shift to Sinhalese Theravada orthodoxy in mainland Southeast Asia took place from the late eleventh to the early thirteenth centuries and afterwards. It was a development which indirectly reflected the decline and diappearance of Buddhism in South Asia itself, as also the rising influence of Sri Lanka under Vijayabāhu I (1055-1110) and Parākkamabahu I, the consolidation of power by the Burmans and Thai, and the closer relationship between Sri Lanka, Burma and Thailand in general. It resulted in the spread of popular Theravada practice among the expanding peasant societies of the mainland which thus far had not assimilated any other literary high tradition (Indianization having been confined to the courts). And it was made possible by the presence of Pali Theravada Buddhism among the Mon who strongly influenced the Bur-

---

[26] *Ibid.*, p. 110.
[27] Cf. Swearer, 'Buddhism in Southeast Asia', p. 111.
[28] *Ibid.*, pp. 111-2.

mans and the Thai (Mon Theravada mediating Sinhala Theravada).[29] In the new monarchies, Buddhism emerged as the legitimating ideology and metaphysical rationale as well as the new moral basis of kingship. The new religion contributed in particular to the classical conception of Southeast-Asian kingship by its emphasis on Dhamma and the role of the king as the moral exemplar and hence to a symbiotic relationship between political and religious leadership.[30] Southeast-Asian chronicles also held to the notion that the Buddha had sacralized these regions by his visits and, frequently, by his having converted the indigenous populations through his own teaching. Architecturally the symbiosis of royalty and Buddhism became manifest in the great chaitiya or stupa monuments of Angkor, Pagan, Sukhothai, and other capitals. And even here, the mythic ideal of the *cakkavattin* remained embodied in Ashoka Maurya. In an inscription of 1292, Rama Khamhaeng of Sukhothai advanced the paternalistic model of a dhammically righteous king which was indebted to Ashoka, and in later times purges of the Sangha were reputedly inspired by Ashoka as well.

Angkor. It is generally agreed that the basis of the Khmer state was rice agriculture. Beyond that, few generalizations can be made about the place of rice in the economy of Angkor or, for that matter, in that of other states of Southeast Asia.[31] In very early times, rice was just one of many crops grown. In the second century BC in northern Indochina, and several centuries later in the southern portions and in the Peninsula and Archipelago, a major transition occurred to a more sophisticated agriculture and the beginnings of large-scale colonization of deltas.[32] Whether the 'conquest of the mud' by Funanese rice growers or the development of Khmer irrigation systems owed anything to Indian influence is unknown.[33] Funan was supported by lowland rice cultivation, but there is evidence only of either a one-year-in-three rain-fed system of rice cultivation with what may be called 'self-

---

[29] Cf. *Ibid.*, pp. 114-5.

[30] *Ibid.*, pp. 112-3.

[31] R. D. Hill, *Rice in Malaya: A Study in Historical Geography* (Kuala Lumpur, 1977), p. 1.

[32] *Ibid.*, p. 14.

[33] *Ibid.*, p. 15.

fallow' and collection of ratoon crops or of three years' cropping of clearings.[34] The agricultural basis of the state's authority had hardly begun to resemble that of classical Khmer times. The sources do not allow us the reconstruction of a picture of agriculture in Champa, on the north of coastal Funan, but here the small extent of lowland suggests a limited role for wet rice.[35] To the northwest of Champa, rice agriculture in Cambodia was already significant by the sixth century, but it cannot be made out whether rice was cultivated by shifting cultivation, by entrapped rainfall and natural rise of the water-table or by controlled irrigation, or by all of these methods.[36] The two-storeyed structure of the forests in the region of Angkor suggests long-continued shifting cultivation, possibly combined with cattle-rearing.[37]

Much of what is now Cambodia has historically been occupied by scattered groups of hunters, forest-produce collectors and slash-and-burn cultivators; such people are still found in the hilly areas, the Cardamom Hills to the south and the Dangrek Mountains to the north, between the Lakes area and the Mun River.[38] The Khmers found their ecological niche between these two zones, and southward to the Vietnamese border, occupying about a third of the total area only but representing the overwhelming majority of its inhabitants.[39] Outside the cities, this is where at present most people are connected with rice cultivation, as have their ancestors. Angkor's success as an imperial centre can be attributed to its position in this relatively fertile zone with good access to resources elsewhere.[40] The region of Siemreap was not only suitable for agriculture but also had access to fish stocks in the lake, and had a good strategic location. The Tonle Sap connects the Mekong with the Great Lake to the north-west, and this route was historically the main artery of communication.[41] As a third of the cultivable lowland area of Cambodia was flooded, this made it possible to supplement the basic rainwater-fed main crop by 'floating rice' and growing a dry-season crop in water tempora-

[34] Ibid., pp. 15-17.
[35] Ibid., p. 17.
[36] Ibid., p. 18.
[37] Ibid., p. 18.
[38] Mabbett and Chandler, The Khmers, p. 30.
[39] Ibid., pp. 30-31.
[40] Ibid., p. 34.
[41] Ibid., p. 35.

rily trapped from the retreating floods by small-scale earthworks.[42] It is possible that the abundance of the Tonle Sap's resources in Angkorian times could sustain a larger population than today.[43]

The exact nature of Angkor's agricultural basis is, however, debated. In the village environment today, elaborately irrigated rice fields are not a basic feature, nor was it in the early centuries of Chenla.[44] The chief known forms of rice-cultivation have always been the wet-season paddy grown in rain-watered fields, and wild rice, or rice in dry fields, as well as 'floating rice' (up to a height of five meters).[45] One can argue that Angkor was in a position to intervene in labour organization, but it is a moot point whether this actually happened.[46] The urban population of Angkor could have been supported by a simple rain-field agricultural system.[47] While in the tenth and eleventh centuries bigger and bigger reservoirs were being built, some of 7x2 or 8x2 km in extent, holding vast amounts of water, the assumption that these were used to irrigate fields has been challenged.[48] Critics have argued that these reservoirs were part of the ritual apparatus of kingship. This has not convinced all historians; and the extent to which Angkor was qualitatively different from earlier states is therefore controversial. Rice agriculture was indisputably essential in the rise of Khmer civilization, as was the upsurge of trade in the late tenth and eleventh century, and it is evident that by the eleventh century the Khmer state had become more populous and its economy more complex, with the rise of an integrated, government-supervised system of temples acquiring a vital function in the economy, controlling vast manpower, and becoming repositories of considerable wealth.[49] From the eleventh century, Angkor was a major power, reaching its peak under Suryavarman II (r. 1113-1145/50), the builder of Angkor Wat.

Although the origins of the Khmer principalities that succeeded Funan are obscure, we know that in the early Khmer state of Chenla the cult of Shiva was practised by the rulers. The seventh-

---

[42] *Ibid.*, p. 36.
[43] *Ibid.*, p. 38.
[44] *Ibid.*, p. 140.
[45] *Ibid.*, pp. 141-2.
[46] *Ibid.*, p. 143.
[47] *Ibid.*, p. 147.
[48] *Ibid.*, pp. 149-54.
[49] Cf. *Al-Hind, I*, pp. 344-6; Mabbett and Chandler, *The Khmers*, p. 102.

century traveller I-tsing wrote that here 'the way of the Buddha prospered and spread, but nowadays a wicked king had expelled and exterminated all the monks'.[50] It was not before the ninth century that a durable Khmer polity was established, near the northern shore of the Great Lake floodwaters, which repudiated the claims to overlordship of Java by setting up its own *devarāja* cult.[51] Ecclesiastical colonization is in evidence from the eleventh century onwards. And we have evidence that the history of Angkor's temples was bound up with the rise, at about the same time, of great landed families with hereditary and independent power bases with which the kings had to compete.[52] Monks and priests were often recruited from the great families and most likely were the chief providers of education and influential government councillors at all levels.[53] These richly endowed religious structures were normally resembling Hindu temples in heir general plan, but they were also partly Buddhist in inspiration. The most famous of them was the Bayon, in Angkor Thom, built by Jayavarman VII (c. 1181-1218). In general they show us a Khmer religion which was still an amalgam of the worship of the Buddha (especially Lokeshvara), Shiva, Brahma, and Vishnu. But it appears that Buddhism, particularly through the mediation of Lokeshvara, was the most popular aspect when Angkor Thom was built. In later centuries all temples reverted to Buddhism, and even Angkor Wat, which was purely Shaivite, becam an object of Buddhist pilgrimage. Already in the thirteenth century, triads of towers and triads of Buddha images were built by both the Khmer and the Mon as focal points of Theravada Buddhist temples.[54] It is most striking that architectural and sculptural achievements came to an end at the same time—in the thirteenth century—, when Theravada Buddhism, which later came to replace everything else, was beginning to be enhanced by an influx of Mon Buddhists from the Lopburi region in the face of Thai pressure. Theravada Buddhism, which in general did not encourage the building of grand stone temples or elaborate works of art, is attested late in the thirteenth century, in the account of Chou Ta-kuan,

---

[50] Mabbett and Chandler, *The Khmers*, pp. 79-82.
[51] *Ibid.*, pp. 85, 87.
[52] *Ibid.*, pp. 167, 171.
[53] *Ibid.*, p. 102.
[54] B. Gosling, *Sukhothai: Its History, Culture, and Art* (Singapore, 1991), p. 12.

which mentions Theravada monks in the Khmer capital. Earlier, in the eleventh and twelfth centuries, Theravada may have existed alongside Mahayana forms, but in the heyday of Angkor, the brahmanical cults of Hinduism were most lavishly patronized. In its political and social manifestations, Theravada Buddhism differed almost as much from the Mahayana Buddhism of Jayavarman VII as it did from Angkor's Hindu cults.[55] Theravada motifs are found in thirteenth-century Angkorean temple iconography. By the end of the thirteenth century all Cambodian towns and villages had their own Theravada Buddhist temple.[56] During Angkor's decline—for which a variety of factors has been adduced, including deforestation, climatic shifts, Thai and Chams incursions, malaria, drugs (opium), as well as a re-orientation towards coastal trade related to developments in China in the thirteenth to fifteenth centuries—the great rituals and cults retreated into their original folk matrix.[57]

Pagan. Like Angkor, Pagan at its height, from the eleventh to thirteenth centuries, was primarily dependent on irrigated rice agriculture, and here too we observe a shift to Theravada Buddhism in this period and the rise of a novel monastic order around which the Pagan monarchy reorganized itself.[58] Although Pagan was located in the dry zone of Burma, with no more than about 115 cm of rain per year, its dynasty exploited a system of rivers by using dams, weirs, sluices, and channels, thereby allowing the cultivation of almost three crops annually.[59] Whether the tenth-century evidence already shows irrigation in Pagan, or whether it shows that rice was a special crop and perhaps still rare, with millet the main cereal, can only be guessed.[60] Under Aniruddha (1044-77), however, there is evidence of major irrigation works

---

[55] *Ibid.*

[56] Gosling, *Sukhothai*, p. 27.

[57] For opium, deforestation and climate change, see G. Gorer, *Bali and Angkor: A 1930s Pleasure Trip Looking at Life and Death* (Singapore, 1986), pp. 170-95; Mabbett and Chandler, *The Khmers*, pp. 38, 105, 175-9, 181, 204, 212-5; for the role of trade: M. Vickery, *Cambodia after Angkor: the chronicular evidence for the fourteenth to sixteenth centuries* (University of Michigan Microfilms, 1977).

[58] Cf. *Al-Hind*, *I*, pp. 346-51.

[59] M. Aung-Thwin, *Pagan: The Origins of Modern Burma* (Honolulu, 1985), p. 97.

[60] Hill, *Rice in Malaya*, p. 18.

being created or repaired in the rich, perennially watered plain of Kyaukse.[61] Pagan's nucleus came to consist of three critically important agricultural plains, which all acquired extensive irrigation networks, surrounding the capital.[62] Many crops were grown here, but paddy rice became the mainstay which allowed Pagan to evolve from a fort on the Irrawaddy river into the centre of a far-flung inland state, controlling a network of economic and diplomatic-political ties which extended as far as the eastern and central South-Asian subcontinent, Sri Lanka, the Malay Peninsula, and the Indonesian Archipelago, and beyond.[63] In the period of c. 1100 to 1250 the state of Pagan controlled the entire Irrawaddy basin. The consolidation of the state's infrastructure, accompanying agricultural growth, appears to have occurred in the reign of Narapatisithu (1173-1210).[64] It was at the same time that most of the monumental construction took place. Trade was of secondary importance here, although the kingdom of Pagan did control most of the coastal cities and towns.[65] Inscriptions point at the presence of colonies of Indian merchants in Pagan Burma, indicating that trade was possibly largely in foreign hands, while in general they give little attention to commercial operations and almost always focus on land and labour as the crucial factors in Pagan's economy.[66]

From its beginnings in the ninth century, the Burmans who founded Pagan had drawn heavily on the Mons' civilization, while also assimilating Tantric Mahayana Buddhism via Manipur. When Buddhism began to disappear from most parts of the South-Asian subcontinent, the Mons maintained contact with the Theravada tradition of Sri Lanka. The conversion of Pagan to Theravada Buddhism and the decline of Tantric Mahayana can effectively be dated from the campaign against Thaton in 1057. According to Burma's Glass Palace Chronicle, the country's political and religious history was changed dramatically by the conversion of the Pagan ruler Aniruddha by Shin Arahan, a Mon Theravada monk from Thaton.[67] Shin Arahan advised the king to secure relics, bhikkhus

[61] Aung-Thwin, *Pagan*, p. 22.
[62] *Ibid.*, p. 101.
[63] *Ibid.*, p. 114; *Al-Hind, I*, p. 350.
[64] Aung-Thwin, *Pagan*, p. 103.
[65] *Ibid.*, p. 98.
[66] *Ibid.*, pp. 113-5.
[67] Swearer, 'Buddhism in Southeast Asia', p. 110.

(monks), and Pali texts from Manuha (Manohari), the king of
Thaton. Manuha's refusal became the excuse for Aniruddha's
invasion of Thaton and the eventual subjugation of the Mons in
lower Burma. Aniruddha then sent a group of monks and Pali
scriptures to Sri Lanka to restore valid ordination in the period
of Cola disruption, in return for which he received a replica of
the Buddha's tooth relic and a copy of the Tipitaka with which
to check the copies of the Pali scriptures at Thaton. This tooth
relic was enshrined as Pagan's palladium in the Schwezigon Pagoda. And subsequently, although Hindu and brahmanic elements
remain in evidence, as well as Mahayana beliefs and Tantric Buddhism, especially as part of Pagan's elite culture, we find Theravada becoming the dominant sect under Kyansittha (fl. 1084-
1113), while Alaungsittha (1113-69) began the institutionalization
of what was to become the Burmese Theravada Buddhist tradition.[68] The alliance between the king and the Sinhala Buddhist
Sangha legitimated his authority over the Mon religio-cultural tradition. Sinhala Buddhism, and in particular the Mahavihara tradition, maintained its superior legitimacy and influence partly
through repeated visits of distinguished Burmese monks to Sri
Lanka. A further shift away from Mon influence thus occurred in
the reign of Narapatisittha (1173-1210). This shift is also reflected in the architectural style and the use of Burmese in inscriptions.[69]

Over 2000 temples, in which Mon as well as ancient Pyu influences have been detected, are still standing at Pagan, spreading
out from the eastern bank of the Irrawaddy over an area of about
40 square km; these are brick-built and usually square in plan with
projecting porticos and superstructures above the main halls
which consist of receding terraces surmounted by spires and stupas.[70] The population that made up Pagan at the peak of its power, supporting these temples, has been estimated at one-and-a-half
to two million.[71]

By the thirteenth century we find evidence of the devolution
of vast wealth in the form of taxable land and corvee labour to

---

[68] Swearer, 'Buddhism in Southeast Asia', p. 110; Aung-Thwin, *Pagan*, pp. 24,
34-36.
[69] Swearer, 'Buddhism in Southeast Asia', pp. 115-6.
[70] Cf. P. Strachan, *Pagan: Art and Architecture of Old Burma* (Whiting Bay, 1989).
[71] Aung-Thwin, *Pagan*, p. 71.

the religious sector.[72] Pagan's decline can partly be attribued to this devolution—which appears to have gone unremedied.[73] In 1271 the Mongols sent their first envoys to the city. Mongol attacks followed in the 1280s, and these put and end to an already internally weakened Pagan, after which new autonomous centres arose in the central plains, the Mons re-emerged in lower Burma, and the newly emerging power of the Thai enters the picture.[74]

Sukhothai. It is not clear where the Thai, or rather their ancestors the *Tai*, came from. But there is evidence to suggest that until the end of the first millennium AD the Tai inhabited the area around what is now the city of Dien Bien Phu, near the border between China and northern Vietnam.[75] For unknown reasons, the Tai began to disperse in the centuries after 1000 AD as far west as Assam and as far south as the Thai peninsula. Once they were separated by mountain ranges, isolated Tai groups created new identities: the Chuang and Lue in China; the Red Tai, Black Tai, and White Tai in Vietnam; the Shan in Burma; and the Kachin in Thailand, are some of these.[76] There were also Tai who, moving towards the southwest, passed through the outer areas of the Khmer empire, and these were exposed to Hinduism and Buddhism, while settling in the lowland river valleys that would later constitute the heartlands of Laos and Thailand.[77] The descendants of those groups came to be known as 'Lao' in Laos and as 'Siamese' or 'Thai' in Thailand.[78] The Thai absorbed much from the Khmer and Mon people.[79] This became even more the case after Kublai Khan's conquest of Nanchao in 1254 caused ever greater numbers of Tai to push south and they began to establish domination over the the latter peoples. As with Burma, Mon Buddhism in particular became a major influence on the Thai as they extended their sway. The Tai also do not seem to have practised

---

[72] *Ibid.*, p. 26.
[73] *Ibid.*, pp. 192-3.
[74] Aung Thwin, *Pagan*, pp. 196-7.
[75] Gosling, *Sukhothai*, p. 20.
[76] *Ibid.*, p. 21.
[77] *Ibid.*
[78] *Ibid.*
[79] Cf. *Ibid.*; C. Stratton and M. McNair Scott, *The Art of Sukhothai* (Kuala Lumpur, 1981).

irrigation whereas the Mon had skills in this field. But the great
Thai achievement, the colonization of the Chạo Phraya valley and
delta, does not seem to have been accompanied by any corresponding development of agricultural technique.[80] Two major
Thai states were established in the later thirteenth and fourteenth
centuries, Sukhothai and Chiangmai, evolving into powerful centres under Rama Khamhaeng (r. c. 1279-99) and Mengrai respectively. During the reign of Rama Khamhaeng, the Thai asserted
their sway over an area extending from Hamsavatī (Pegu) to the
west, Phrae to the north, Luang Prabang to the east, and Nakorn Sri Dhammaraja (Ligor or Tambralinga) to the south. Nakorn
Sri Dhammaraja had been an important centre of Theravada Buddhism by the eleventh century, even when dominated by Shrivijaya, and had sent a mission to Sri Lanka prior to Rama
Khamhaeng's accession to power in Sukhothai.[81] Sukhothai itself
had been a Khmer outpost from at least the time of Jayavarman
VII. It is reported in Sukhothai Inscription II, sometime around
the middle of the thirteenth century, that two Thai chieftains
marched with their troops on Sukhothai and conquered the
Khmer.[82]

The earliest Buddhist temple that the Thai built at Sukhothai
is currently known as Wat Aranyik and was part of a Theravada
monastery of forest-dwelling monks.[83] But there was also a larger
building that the Thai constructed in the early post-Khmer period which was probably a shrine dedicated to the *phi muang*, the
most powerful spirit in the land, protector of all of Sukhothai's
territory.[84] *Phi muang* rites are still widespread in Southeast Asia.
Villagers traditionally worshiped their *phi muang* at small, square
earthen altars in wooded areas outside their settlements.[85] From
Assam to Thailand, on special days dedicated to the *phi muang*,
the Tai-speaking Khamyang built step pyramids of sand outside
their villages.[86] If, as seems very likely, such ceremonies were performed in thirteenth-century Sukhothai, the inscriptional refer-

[80] Hill, *Rice in Malaya*, p. 19.
[81] Swearer, 'Buddhism in Southeast Asia', pp. 116-7.
[82] Gosling, *Sukhothai*, p. 20.
[83] *Ibid.*, p. 22.
[84] *Ibid.*, p. 25.
[85] *Ibid.*
[86] *Ibid.*

ence to them is vague, and the *phi muang* is also referred to by a Buddhist equivalent, *phi devata*. The Buddhists condoned neither the killing of animals nor the drinking of blood and alcohol associated with the rites, which explains why they are not mentioned in Sukhothai Inscription I. The transformation of the spirit cult was already under way.[87]

Although Rama Khamhaeng's stela of 1292 refers to various Buddhist sanctuaries in Sukhothai, Sinhala Buddhism does not appear to have become normative until the reigns of his successors. The latter brought Buddha relics and images and imprinted Buddha footprints throughout the realm in an effort to disseminate Buddhist practice. In the final decade of the thirteenth century, Sukhothai was no longer an isolated settlement, but exterted control over neighbouring Thai *muang* as far as eastern Laos. The network of villages was identified by the central walled city or *muang* which gave its name to the entire area, *Muang Sukhothai* thus referring to both the walled city and to the smaller subsidiary settlements in its domain. Theravada Buddhism was actively supported throughout this area.[88] A reciprocal relationship between the king and the monkhood or Sangha proved advantageous to both. It was the king's prerogative to appoint the head monk, or Sangha-raja. Rama Khamhaeng in the early 1290s, at Si Satchanalai, 55 km north of Sukhothai, completed a wall of huge granite boulders to surround a Buddhist stupa that he had built a few years earlier. The stupa was built over a relic of the Buddha, which he had found nearby, displayed to his subjects for validation, and then buried again. This relic was irrefutably linked to the land; it linked Rama Khamhaeng to his territory.[89] Like in Sri Lanka, the expansion of Buddhism occurred here in the context of peasant settlement. The new state organized itself around the central institutions of the Buddhist Sangha and kingship, and, remaining outside the range of Islam and nomadic conquest, successfully consolidated itself in the succeeding centuries. In mainland Southeast Asia generally, the dynamics of local history from the fourteenth to the eighteenth century show much more continuity than in the South-Asian subcontinent. Here there was no

---

[87] *Ibid.*, pp. 25-26.
[88] *Ibid.*, p. 29.
[89] *Ibid.*, p. 33.

merger with the frontier world of Central Asia, no Islamic conquest, but a Buddhist conquest of an emerging peasant society under the aegis of local rulers.[90]

---

[90] Cf. V. Lieberman, 'Local Integration and Eurasian Analogies: Structuring Southeast Asian History, c. 1350-c. 1830', *Modern Asian Studies*, 27, 3 (1993), pp. 475-572.

CONCLUSION

The first conclusion to be drawn from the foregoing analysis is that ecology was a major factor determining the progress and character of the Islamic conquest of *al-Hind*. For one thing, the subcontinent was unsuitable for Mongol-style nomadism on account of the absence of sufficient good pasture land. With the Mongols failing to penetrate beyond its western periphery, the Indian subcontinent cannot really be said to have experienced a 'nomadic conquest' at all. In this respect the thirteenth-century situation in the north was unlike the Iranian plateau, where Mongol conquest was followed by extensive nomadization and destruction of agriculture.

The Indian situation was also unlike that in much of China. The Mongol conquest of north China wreaked destruction on settled populations on the same scale as it had done in Iran and limited areas on the north-western periphery of the Indian subcontinent.[1] Here too, cities were destroyed and populations massacred; the idea was even contemplated to turn north China into pasture land for Mongol herds. For a quarter of a century after the conquest, north China suffered from endemic warfare and a huge population decrease. The northwest of China became moribund, while the northeast became a relative backwater except for the region around the capital of Peking. South China survived the Mongol conquest with its productive basis largely intact; it was invaded and conquered by a Yüan regime that was already firmly rooted in China itself. But here, too, the population declined seriously in the thirteenth century, although not as much as in the former Chin territories. Overall, China's registered population of between 110 and 120 million people around 1207—at the end of the Chin regime—is thought to have fallen to less than 60 million by 1290. At the same time, it must be pointed out that the Mongols did deploy the vast economic, technical and military potential of China in the service of an expansionist ambition which far exceeded the aims of previous, purely Chinese states.

---

[1] Cf. H. Franke and D. Twitchett (eds), *The Cambridge History of China, Volume 6: Alien regimes and border states, 907-1368* (Cambridge, 1994), pp. 36-37.

In the latter respect the Yüan regime in south China can to some degree be seen to have resembled the thirteenth-century Muslim regime of India. One of the results of this circumstance was, as we have seen, the important increase of overseas trade of the Yüan regime. But when the Yüan state in China collapsed, the Mongols simply retreated to the steppe and there continued to be a major power for centuries. There was, therefore, no real merger of nomadic society and sedentary agriculture in China, let alone a successful one.

We have argued that, in contrast to Iran and China, in *al-Hind* such a merger of the frontier world of nomadic mobility and long-distance trade on the one hand and settled agriculture on the other did occur in the eleventh to thirteenth centuries. Secondly, that this merger brought about a new productive and mercantile dynamism (without any serious deleterious impact on population density), the effects of which deepened and broadened in the subsequent centuries. This is not to deny that the Muslim-Turkish conquest of Hind was quite violent at times, and could be disruptive in some areas as well. It has not been our intention to 'sanitize' the narrative of Hindu-Muslim encounter in these centuries of invasion and extensive raiding. Nor has it been our intention to deny that in many respects the Muslim conquest was a major challenge to the integrity of Indian culture. But the Turkish-led Muslim armies that conquered North India in the eleventh to thirteenth centuries were generally small compared to those of the Mongols operating elsewhere in Eurasia; nor did a vast influx of nomads follow in their wake, unlike in Iran or parts of China. Instead, what we observed in thirteenth-century India was a far more elitist and sustained immigration from Mongol-occupied areas and of Muslims establishing new centres of control in the subcontinent's expanding economy. In purely numerical terms, this population shift pales before those of Iran and China, which did suffer nomadic conquests in the strict sense of the word.

In the same way, noting the successful fusion of frontier and settled society in the North-Indian plains does not necessarily imply a justification of the conquest in moral terms. Nor do we imply that Muslim rule was established, in these centuries, on a previously immobile Hindu domain. As has been argued in the previous volume of this book, the expansion of agriculture and trade had preceded the Islamic conquest and occurred throughout the early medieval period, as well as before. But, in so far as we have been at pains to show the most important social and economic forces at work in these centuries, it has been our intention to move away from an ahistorical paradigm that focused above all on a 'clash of civilizations', on the incompatibility of fundamentally opposed cultural categories, of mutually hostile societies, and of antagonistic modes of life. In effect, we have proposed here that Islamic conquest and trade, the mobilization of people, goods and precious metals (which elaborated previously existing networks and contacts), laid the foundation for a new type of Indo-Islamic society in which the organizational forms of the frontier and of sedentary agriculture merged in a way that was uniquely successful in the late medieval world at large. If anything, this is what set the Indo-Islamic world apart from the Middle East and China in the same centuries, as well as from Europe. Largely, this basic difference derives from the fact that the Turks who conquered North India (like most Central-Asian peoples who, on a smaller scale, entered the subcontinent in earlier centuries) were already at one remove from nomadism by the time the conquest had begun. Just as they had already converted to Islam, most of these invaders—and certainly their Mamluk leaders—were no longer nomads when they undertook their campaigns into India. But their military advantage of mounted archery and enhanced mobility, characteristic of steppe peoples, continued to play a key role. And thus, the areas of the subcontinent that fell under Turkish-Muslim rule were all controlled by a Central-Asian type of cavalry that could still claim a nomadic ancestry even if it was not strictly nomadic anymore. In due course, such conquest movements would extend deeper and deeper into the south of the subcontinent. Here again, the ecological situation was such that it allowed cavalry to be deployed in an agriculturally productive context and in areas of relatively high population density, although in this respect the Deccan plateau differed from the North-Indian plains.

Land-revenue, followed by trade, remained the foundation of Indo-Islamic states everywhere in the subcontinent. But Turkish cavalries never penetrated those parts of *al-Hind* now included in the states of Sri Lanka and Southeast Asia, which developed economies of irrigated rice agriculture in the ancient and medieval periods. The ecological situation simply did not allow the permanent use of such cavalries here on an extensive scale. And it is for the same reason that the Mongol invasions of the Southeast-Asian mainland were, in the broader context of events, mere incidents. Hence, a fusion of frontier and agriculture of the subcontinental type was out of the question here. In these societies, agriculture spread in conjunction with Buddhism, under indigenous rulers, while the mobilization of goods and people over longer distances largely took a maritime turn or focused on the river estuaries and the coastlines—as was particularly the case in Indonesia.

It will be the aim of the subsequent volume to explore in more detail and depth the consequences of the fusion of these two different types of social, economic and political organization in the Indo-Islamic world. In Volume III the previous argument will be taken further into the fourteenth and fifteenth centuries. Especially at the end of this subsequent period, new types of source materials are beginning to make their appearance, including Portuguese and other European sources, which will allow us to give more substance to what has so far remained a fairly abstract scheme of analysis. We can then construct a more detailed picture of a vast range of grassroots phenomena that illustrate broad processes of development relating to agricultural and urban development, overland and maritime trade, population expansion, religious and social change, and transformations in the modes of political domination. The present volume should primarily be seen as setting the stage for this further and more detailed analysis. It is hoped that, together, the first three volumes will also serve to obtain a better perspective on the early modern period, that of the sixteenth to eighteenth centuries. Too often, in our view, the early modern period has been seen as an abrupt new beginning in this region, if not because of the European arrival then because of the almost simultaneous rise and expansion of the great Muslim empires of the Mughals, Safawids and Ottomans. As the present volume has argued, it seems likely that the most important and most fundamental change in the Indo-Islamic world occurred in and prior to the thirteenth century, and that the subsequent centuries were more than anything an era of the elaboration of patterns that were created in this earlier period.

BIBLIOGRAPHY

Abraham, M., *Two Medieval Merchant Guilds of South India* (New Delhi, 1988).

Abu-Lughod, J. L., *Before European Hegemony: The World System AD 1250-1350* (Oxford, 1989).

Ahmad, A., 'Mongol Pressure in an Alien Land', *Central Asiatic Journal*, VI (1961).

Ahmad, A., 'The Early Turkish Nucleus in India', *Turcica*, IX (1977).

Ahmad, M. A., *Political History & Institutions of the Early Turkish Empire of Delhi, 1206-1290* (Lahore, 1972).

Ahmad, Q. (ed.), *Corpus of Arabic & Persian Inscriptions of Bihar* (Patna, 1973).

Ahmad Khan, S. (ed.), *Ta'rikh-i-Firoz Shāhi of Ziā' ad-Din Barani* (Calcutta, 1862).

Alami, A., *Les conquêtes de Mahmūd al-Ghaznawi d'après le Kitāb al Yamini d"Utbi*, 2 vols (Doctorat d'Etat, Paris, III, 1989).

Allchin, F. R., 'Upon the Antiquity and Methods of Gold Mining in Ancient India', *Journal of the Economic and Social History of the Orient*, 5 (1962).

Allsen, T. T., 'Guard and Government in the Reign of the Grand Qan Möngke, 1251-59', *Harvard Journal of Asiatic Studies*, 46, 2 (1986).

Amitai-Preiss, R., *Mongols and Mamluks: The Mamluk-Ilkhānid War, 1260-1281* (Cambridge, 1995).

Anderson, J., *Acheen and the Ports on the North and East Coasts of Sumatra; with incidental notices of the trade in the eastern seas and the aggressions of the Dutch* (London, 1840).

Anderson, M. M., *Hidden Power: The Palace Eunuchs of Imperial China* (Loughton, Essex, 1991).

Annual Report on Indian Epigraphy, II (1962-3).

Ansari, A. N., 'Historical geography of Bihar on the Eve of the Turkish Invasions', *Journal of the Bihar Research Society*, 49 (1963).

Ashtor, E., *A Social and Economic History of the Near East in the Middle Ages* (Berkeley, Los Angeles and London, 1976).

Ashvashāstra of Nakula (Tanjore, 1952).

Aubin, J., 'Y a-t-il eu interruption du commerce par mer entre le Golf Persique et l'Inde du XIe au XIVe siècle?', in: Mollat, M. (ed.), *Océan Indien et Méditerranée* (Paris, 1964).

Aubin, J., 'L'ethnogenèse des Qaraunas', *Turcica*, I (1969).

Aung-Thwin, M., *Pagan: The Origins of Modern Burma* (Honolulu, 1985).

Ayalon, D., 'The European-Asiatic Steppe: A Major Reservoir of Power for the Islamic World', in: *The Mamlūk Military Society* (London, 1979).

Ayalon, D., 'Aspects of the Mamlūk Phenomenon', *ibid*.

Ayalon, D., 'Preliminary Remarks on the Mamlūk Military Insitution in Islam', *ibid*.

Ayalon, D., 'Notes on the Furūsiyya Exercises and Games in the Mamlūk Sultanate', *ibid*.

Bacon, E. E., 'An Inquiry into the History of the Hazara Mongols of Afghanistan', *Southwest Journal of Anthropology*, 7 (1951).

Ball, W., 'The Buddhists of Sind', *South Asian Studies*, 5 (1989).

Baluchistan District Gazetteer, VIII, Las Bela (Allahabad, 1907).

Banerjea, J. N., *The Development of Hindu Iconography* (Calcutta, 1956).

Barnard, L., 'The Theology of Images', in: Bryer, A. and Herrin, J. (eds), *Iconoclasm: Papers given at the Ninth Symposium of Byzantine Studies* (Birmingham, 1975).

Barthold, V. V., *Zwölf Vorlesungen über die Geschichte der Turken Mittelasiens* (Berlin, 1935).

Barthold, W., *An Historical Geography of Iran* (Princeton, 1984).

Bartlett, R., *The Making of Europe: Conquest, Colonization and Cultural Change, 950-1350* (Princeton, 1993).

Bayly, S., *Saints, Goddesses and Kings: Muslims and Christians in South Asian Society, 1700-1900* (Cambridge, 1989).

Beal, S. (transl.), *Si-Yu-Ki, Buddhist Records of the Western World*, 4 vols (Calcutta, 1957-58).

Bechert, H., 'Ashokas Schismenedikt und der Begriff Samghabheda', *Wiener Zeitschrift für die Kunde Süd- und Ostasiens*, 5 (1961).

Bechert, H., *Buddhismus, Staat und Gesellschaft in den Ländern des Theravada-Buddhismus, Bd. I* (Frankfurt am Main, 1966).

Bechert, H., 'Max Webers Darstellung der Geschichte des Buddhismus in Süd- und Ostasien', in: Schluchter, W. (ed.), *Max Webers Studie über Hinduismus und Buddhismus: Interpretation und Kritik* (Frankfurt am Main, 1984).

Beckingham, C. F., 'Amba Geshen and Asirgarh', *Journal of Semitic Studies*, 2, 3 (1957).

Beckwith, C. I., 'Aspects of the Early History of the Central Asian Guard Corps in Islam', *Archivum Eurasiae Medii Aevi*, IV (1984).

Beckwith, C. I., *The Tibetan Empire in Central Asia: A History of the Struggle for Great Power among Tibetans, Turks, Arabs, and Chinese during the Early Middle Ages* (Princeton, 1987).

Bengal District Gazetteer, Vol. XXXVI: Bakarganj (Calcutta, 1918).

Bernier, F., *Travels in the Mogul Empire, AD 1656-1668* (Delhi, 1989).

Bhardwaj, H. C., *Aspects of Ancient Indian Technology* (New Delhi, 1979).

Bhattasali, N. K., 'The Rājāvādī (Bhāwāl) Plate of Lakshmana Sena Deva', *Journal of the Royal Asiatic Society of Bengal*, VIII (1942).

Bhuyan, S. K. (ed.), *Satsari Buranji* (Gauhati, 1969).

Bhuyan, S. K. (ed.), *Deodhai Asam Buranji* (Gauhati, 1990).

Bihar District Gazetteer, Vol. 16: Shahabad (Patna, 1966).

al-Bīrūnī, *Kitāb fī Tahqīqi mā li-l-Hind* (Hyderabad, India, 1958).

Bishop, C. W., 'The Elephant and its Ivory in Ancient China', *Journal of the American Oriental Society*, 41 (1921).

Bloch, M., 'Le problème de l'or au Moyen Age', *Annales d'histoire économique et sociale*, V (1933).

Bock, C., *Temples and Elephants: Travels in Siam in 1881-1882* (London, 1884).

Boner, A., 'Economic and Organizational Aspects of the Building Operations of the Sun Temple at Konārka', *Journal of the Economic and Social History of the Orient*, XIII (1970).

Borrie, W. D., *Population, Environment and Society* (Auckland, 1974).

Bosworth, C. E., 'Ghaznevid Military Organisation', *Der Islam* (1960).

Bosworth, C. E., 'The Early Islamic History of Ghur', *Central Asiatic Journal*, 6 (1961).

Bosworth, C. E., *The Ghaznavids: Their Empire in Afghanistan and Eastern Iran, 994-1040* (Edinburgh, 1963).

Bosworth, C. E., *The Later Ghaznavids: Splendour and Decay: The Dynasty in Afghanistan and Northern India, 1040-1186* (Edinburgh, 1977).

Bosworth, C. E. and Clauson, G., 'Al-Xwārazmi on the peoples of Central Asia', in: Bosworth, C. E., *The Medieval History of Iran, Afghanistan and Central Asia* (London, 1977).

Bosworth, C. E., 'Barbarian Incursions: The Coming of the Turks into the Islamic World', in: *The Medieval History of Iran, Afghanistan and Central Asia* (London, 1977).

Bouchon, G., 'Les Musulmans du Kerala à l'Époque de la Découverte Portugaise', *Mare Luso-Indicum*, 2 (1973).

Bouchon, G., 'Quelques Aspects de l'Islamisation des Régions Maritimes de l'Inde à l'Époque Médiévale (XIIe-XVIe s.)', *Puruṣārtha*, 9 (1986).

Bowie, K. A., 'Ethnicity and Elephants: A Consideration of Society and the State in the Nineteenth Century Lannathai Kingdoms' (Mimeo, 1993).

Boyce, M., 'Iconoclasm among the Zoroastrians', in: Neusner, J. (ed.), *Christianity, Judaism and other Greco-Roman Cults: Studies presented to Morton Smith*, Vol. 4 (Leiden, 1975).

Brady, Jr., T. A., 'The Rise of Merchant Empires, 1400-1700: a European Counterpoint', in: Tracy, J. D., *The Political Economy of Merchant Empires: State Power and World Trade, 1350-1750* (Cambridge, 1991).

Bray, F., *The Rice Economies. Technology and Development in Asian Societies* (Oxford, 1986).

Bregel, Y., 'Turko-Mongol influences in Central Asia', in: Canfield, R. L. (ed.), *Turko-Persia in Historical Perspective* (Cambridge, 1991).

Brunner, O., *Neue Wege der Sozialgeschichte* (Göttingen, 1956)

Bruno, A., 'Notes on the Discovery of Hebrew Inscriptions in the Vicinity of the Minaret of Jam', *East and West*, 14, 3 (1963).

Buchanan Hamilton, F., *An Account of the District of Bihar and Patna in 1811-1812*, 2 vols (Patna, 1936).

Buchanan Hamilton, F., *An Account of the Kingdom of Nepal (1819)* (New Delhi, 1971).

Buhler, G., *The Jagaducharita of Sarvanada: a Historical Romance from Gujarat* (Vienna, 1892).

Burgess, J. and Cousens, H., *The Architectural Antiquities of Northern Gujarat (1902)* (Varanasi, 1975).

Cahen, C., 'Les changements techniques militaires dans le Proche Orient médiéval et leur importance historique', in: Parry, V. J. and Yapp, M. E. (eds), *War, Technology and Society in the Middle East* (London, 1975).

Carnegy, P., *Notes on the Races, Tribes and Castes, inhabiting the Province of Awadh* (Lucknow, 1868).

Casson, L. (ed. and transl.), *The Periplus Maris Erythraei* (Princeton, 1989).

Chaghtai, M. A., 'An unpublished inscription of the time of Iltutmish, showing the construction of a reservoir at Khatu (Marwar)', *Proceedings of the All India Oriental Conference, 8th Session, 1935* (Bangalore, 1937).

Chaghtai, M. A., 'Muslim inscriptions from Khatu (Marwar)', *Proceedings of the Indian History Congress, 8th Session, 1945* (Allahabad, 1947).

Chakravarti, P. C., *The Art of War in Ancient India* (Dacca, 1941).

Chakravarti, R., 'Horse Trade and Piracy at Tana (Thana, Maharashtra, India): Gleanings from Marco Polo', *Journal of the Economic and Social History of the Orient*, XXXIV (1991).

Chamberlain, M., *Knowledge and social practice in medieval Damascus, 1190-1350* (Cambridge, 1994).

Chatterjee, A. K., *A Comprehensive History of Jainism*, 2 vols (Calcutta, 1978-84).

Chattopadhyaya, D. (ed.), *Tāranātha's History of Buddhism in India* (Calcutta, 1980).

Chernenko, E. V., *Skifskii dospekh* (Kiev, 1968).

Choksy, J. K., 'Zoroastrians in Muslim Iran: Selected Problems of Coexistence and Interaction during the Early Medieval Period', *Iranian Studies*, XX, 1 (1987).

Choksy, J. K., 'Conflict, Coexistence, and Cooperation: Muslims and Zoroastrians in Eastern Iran during the Medieval Period', *The Muslim World*, vol. LXXX, 3-4 (1990).

Choudhary, G. C., *Political History of Northern India from Jain Sources* (Amritsar, 1954).

Clauson, G., *Turkish and Mongolian Studies* (London, 1962).

Codrington, K. de B., 'A geographical introduction to the history of Central Asia', *The Geographical Journal*, CIV (1944).

Collet, O. J. A., *Terres et peuples de Sumatra* (Amsterdam, 1925).

Commager, H. S. and Giordanetti, E., *Was America a Mistake? An Eighteenth-Century Controversy* (New York, Evanston and London, 1967).

Cowell, E. B. and Thomas, F. W. (transl.), *The Harshacarita of Bāna* (London, 1897).

Crone, P., 'Islam, Judeo-Christianity and Byzantine Iconoclasm', *Jerusalem Studies in Arabic and Islam*, II (Jerusalem, 1980).

Crone, P., *Slaves on Horses: The Evolution of the Islamic Polity* (Cambridge, 1981).

Crone, P., 'The Tribe and the State', in: Hall, J. A. (ed.), *States in History* (Oxford and Cambridge, Mass., 1986).

Cunningham, A., *Report of Tours in the Gangetic Provinces from Badaon and Bihar in 1875-6 and 1877-8 (Archaeological Survey of India, Vol. XI)* (Varanasi, 1968).

Currie. P. M., *The Shrine and Cult of Mu'in al-din Chishti of Ajmer* (Delhi, 1989).

Daji, B., 'The inroads of the Scythians into India, and the story of the Kālakāchārya', *Journal of the Bombay Branch of the Royal Asiatic Society*, IX (1873).

Dale, S. F., 'Islamic architecture in Kerala', in: Dallapiccola, A. L. and Zingel-Avé Lallemant, S. (eds), *Islam and Indian Regions* (Stuttgart, 1993), 2 vols.

Dale, S. F., *Indian merchants and Eurasian trade, 1600-1750* (Cambridge, 1994).

Dandamaev, M. A. and Lukonin, U. G., *The Culture and Social Institutions of Ancient Iran* (Cambridge, 1988).

Dandekar, A., 'Landscapes in Conflict: Flocks, Hero-stones, and Cult in early medieval Maharashtra', *Studies in History*, 7, 2, n. s. (1991).

Das Gupta, A., *Malabar in Asian Trade, 1740-1800* (Cambridge, 1967).

Dasheng, Chen and Lombard, D., 'Le role des étrangers dans le commerce de Quanzhou("Zaitun") aux 13e et 14e siècles', in: Lombard, D. and Aubin, J. (eds), *Marchands et hommes d'affaires asiatiques dans l'Océan Indien et la Mer de Chine, 13e-20e siècles* (Paris, 1988).

Davis, R. H., 'Unmiraculous Images: Early Muslim Encounters with the Idols of India' (Unpublished paper read at the meeting of the Association for Asian Studies, April 1991).

Davis, R. H., 'Indian Art Objects as Loot', *Journal of Asian Studies*, 52, 1 (1993).

Davy, W. (transl.), *Political and Military Institutes of Tamerlane* (Delhi, 1972).

De, B. (transl.), *The Tabaqāt-i-Akbari of Khwajah Nizāmuddin Ahmad, Vol. I* (Calcutta, 1927).

Defrémery, C. & Sanguinetti, B. R. (eds and transl.), *Voyages d'Ibn Batoutah*, 4 vols (Paris, 1853-58).

Delmerick, J. G., 'A History of the Gakk'hars', *Journal of the Asiatic Society of Bengal*, XL, 1 (1871).

Deloche, J., *Military Technology in Hoysala Sculpture (Twelfth and Thirteenth Century)* (New Delhi, 1989).

Deleury, G., *Les Indes Florissantes: Anthologie des Voyageurs Francais (1750-1820)* (Paris, 1991).

Denison Ross, E. (ed.), *Epigraphia Indo-Moslemica, 1911-12* (Calcutta and Bombay, 1912).

Denison Ross, E. (ed.), *Ta'rīkh-i-Fakhr ad-Din Mubārakshāh* (London, 1927).

Desai, Z. A. (ed.), *Epigraphia Indica: Arabic and Persian Supplement 1961* (Calcutta, 1962).
Desai, Z. A., 'Inscriptions of the Mamluk Sultans of Delhi', in: Desai, Z. A. (ed.), *Epigraphia Indica: Arabic and Persian Supplement (1966)* (Delhi, 1967).
De Silva, K. M., *A History of Sri Lanka* (Delhi, 1981).
De Wailly, N. (ed.), *Jean de Joinville: Histoire de Saint Louis* (Paris, 1868).
Deyell, J. S., *Living without Silver: The Monetary History of early Medieval North India* (Delhi, 1990).
Digby, S., 'Iletmish or Iltutmish? A Reconsideration of the Name of the Delhi Sultan', *Iran*, 8 (1970).
Digby, S., *War-horse and Elephant in the Delhi Sultanate* (Oxford, 1971).
Digby, S., 'The Sufi Shaikh as a Source of Authority in Medieval India', in: Gaborieau, M. (ed.), *Islam et Société en Asie du Sud* (Paris, 1986).
Diwan, R. A., *Tarikh-i-Sorath: A History of the Provinces of Sorath and Halar in Kathiawad* (Bombay, 1882).
Dobbin, Ch., *Islamic Revivalism in a Changing Peasant Economy: Central Sumatra, 1784-1847* (London and Malmö, 1983).
Doerfer, G., *Türkische und Mongolische Elemente im Neupersischen*, I (Wiesbaden, 1963).
Dorn, B. (ed. and transl.), *Makhzan-i-Afghānī*, 2 vols (London, 1965).
Downey, K. R., 'Changing Modes of Consolidation: A Comparison between the Turks in Delhi and Lakhnauti in the Thirteenth through Sixteenth Centuries' (MA Thesis, University of Chicago, 1993).
Drewes, G. W. J., 'New Light on the Coming of Islam to Indonesia', *Bijdragen tot de Taal-, Land- en Volkenkunde*, 124 (1968).
Drewes, G. W. J. (ed.), *Hikajat Potjut Muhamat, An Acehnese Epic* (The Hague, 1979).
Dutt, N. K., 'The Vaishyas in Mediaeval Bengal', *The Indian Historical Quarterly*, XVI (1940).
Dutt, S., *Buddhist Monks and Monasteries of India: Their History and their Contribution to Indian Culture* (New Delhi, 1962).
Eaton, R. M., *Sufis of Bijapur, 1300-1700: Social Roles of Sufis in Medieval India* (Princeton, 1978).
Eaton, R. M., 'The Political and Religious Authority of the Shrine of Bābā Farīd', in: Metcalf, B. D. (ed.), *Moral Conduct and Authority: the Place of Adab in South Asian Islam* (Berkeley, Los Angeles and London, 1984).
Eaton, R. M., *The Rise of Islam and the Bengal Frontier, 1204-1760* (Berkeley, Los Angeles and London, 1993).
Eck, D. L., *Darshan: Seeing the Divine Image in India* (Chambersburg, 1985).
Ecsedy, H., 'Tribe and Tribal Society in the 6th Century', *Acta Orientalia Hungarica*, 25 (1972).
Edgerton, F., *The Elephant-Lore of the Hindus: The Elephant-Sport (Mātanga-Līlā) of Nīlakantha* (Delhi, 1985).
Elliot, H. M. and Dowson, J., *The History of India as told by its own Historians*, 8 vols (London, 1867-77).
Elliot, M., *Memoirs on the History, Folk-lore, and Distribution of the races of the North Western Provinces of India*, Vol. I (London, 1869).
Enzyklopaedia des Islams, IV (Leiden and Leipzig, 1934).
Epigraphia Carnatica (Bangalore, 1886-1919).
Epigraphia Indica (Delhi/Calcutta, 1892-).
Epigraphia Indica, Arabic and Persian Supplement, 1913-14 (Calcutta, 1917; reprint Delhi, 1987).
Epigraphia Indo-Moslemica (Calcutta, 1937-38).

Erdosy, G., 'Ethnicity in the Rigveda and its Bearing on the Question of Indo-European Origins', *South Asian Studies*, 5 (1989).

Ernst, C. W., *Eternal Garden* (Albany, 1992).

Ernst, C. W., 'The Khuldabad-Burhanpur axis and the local Sufism in the Deccan', in: Dallapiccola, A. L. and Zingel-Avé Lallemant, S. (eds), *Islam and Indian Regions*, 2 vols (Stuttgart, 1993).

Fenner, F., *et al, Smallpox and Its Eradication* (Geneva, 1988).

Ferrin, L., 'Gold and Silver in the Indian Subcontinent: A Review of Some Problems and Prospects' (Termpaper, UW-Madison, Dep. of History, Spring 1991).

Filliozat, P., 'The After-death destiny of the Hero According to Mahābhārata', in: Settar, S. and Sontheimer, G. D. (eds), *Memorial Stones: A Study of their Origin, Significance and Variety* (Dharwad, 1982).

Fitzgerald, C. P., *China: A Short Cultural History* (New York, 1961).

Fletcher, J., 'The Mongols: Ecological and Social Perspectives', *Harvard Journal of Asiatic Studies*, 46, 1 (1986).

Forbes, A.D.W., 'Southern Arabia and the Islamicisation of the Central Indian Ocean Archipelagoes', *Archipel*, 21 (1981).

Forbes, A. K., *Rās Māla: Hindoo Annals of the Province of Goozerat in Western India*, 2 vols (London, 1924).

Fragner, B. G., 'State Structures in the Safavid Empire: Towards a Comparative Investigation' (Paper presented at the workshop on The Political Economies of the Ottoman, Safavid and Mughal Empires, Harvard University, March 1991).

Freedberg, D., 'The Structure of Byzantine and European Iconoclasm', in: Bryer, A. and Herrin J. (eds), *Iconoclasm: Papers given at the Ninth Symposium of Byzantine Studies* (Birmingham, 1975).

Friedmann, Y., 'Medieval Muslim Views of Indian Religions', *Journal of the American Oriental Society*, 95, 2 (1975).

Fritz, J. M. and Michell, G., *City of Victory: Vijayanagara, the Medieval Hindu Capital of Southern India* (New York, 1991).

Frye, R. N., 'Remarks on Baluchi History', *Central Asiatic Journal*, 6 (1961).

Frye, R. N. and Sayali, A. M., 'Turks in the Middle East before the Saljuqs', *Journal of the American Oriental Society*, LXIII (1943).

Fuhrer, A., *The Monumental Antiquities and Inscriptions in the North-western Provinces and Oudh* (Allahabad, 1891).

Gabriel, P. C., *Lakshadweep: History, Religion and Society* (New Delhi, 1989).

Gazetteer of the Province of Oudh, 3 vols (Lucknow and Allahabad, 1877-78).

Giles, H. A. (transl.), *The Travels of Fa-hsien (399-414 AD), or record of the Buddhistic Kingdoms* (London, 1956).

Glanius, M., *A relation of an unfortunate voyage to the kingdom of Bengala* (London, 1682).

Gnoli, G., 'Jewish Inscriptions in Afghanistan', *East and West*, 13 (1962).

Gnoli, G., 'Further Information Concerning the Judaeo-Persian Documents of Afghanistan', *East and West*, 14, 3 (1963).

Gnoli, G., '\r-mazdēsn—zum Begriff "Iran" und seiner Entstehung im dritten Jahrhundert', in: *Transition Periods in Iranian History. Actes du symposium de Fribourg-en-Brisgau*, 22-24 May 1985 (=Studia Iranica, Cahier 5) (Paris, 1987).

Gnoli, G., *The Idea of Iran: An Essay on its Origin* (Rome, 1989).

Goel, S. R., *Hindu Temples: What happened to them, pt. II: The Islamic Evidence* (New Delhi, 1991).

Golden, P. B., 'Imperial Ideology and the Sources of Political Unity amongst the Pre-Činggisid Nomads of Western Eurasia', *Archivum Eurasiae Medii Aevi*, II (1982).

Golden, P. B., *An Introduction to the History of the Turkic Peoples: Ethnogenesis and State-formation in Medieval and Early Modern Eurasia and the Middle East* (Wiesbaden, 1992).

Goldziher, I., *Muhammedanische Studien*, 2 vols (Halle, 1897).

Gombrich, R., *Theravada Buddhism: A Social History from Ancient Benares to Modern Colombo* (London and New York, 1991).

Gommans, J. J. L., *The Rise of the Indo-Afghan Empire, c. 1710-1780* (Leiden, 1995).

Gopal, L., 'The Textile Industry in Early Medieval India, c. AD 700-1200', *Journal of the Bombay Branch of the Royal Asiatic Society*, n. s. 39-40 (1964-65).

Gorer, G., *Bali and Angkor: A 1930s Pleasure Trip Looking at Life and Death* (Singapore, 1986).

Gosling, B., *Sukhothai: Its History, Culture, and Art* (Singapore, 1991).

Grabar, O., 'Islam and Iconoclasm', in: Bryer, A. and Herrin, J. (eds), *Iconoclasm: Papers given at the Ninth Symposium of Byzantine Studies* (Birmingham, 1975).

Guha, S., 'Introductory Chapter: Older Races, Lower Strata' (Mimeo, 1995).

Guillot, L., *The Sultanate of Banten* (Jakarta, 1990).

Gumilev, L. N., *Searches for an Imaginary Kingdom* (Cambridge, 1987).

Gunawardana, R. A. L. H., *Robe and Plough: Monasticism and Economic Interest in Early Medieval Sri Lanka* (Tucson, 1979).

Habib, I., *The Agrarian System of Mughal India* (Bombay, 1963).

Habib, I., 'Jatts of Punjab and Sind', in: Singh, H. and Barrier, N. G. (eds), *Punjab Past and Present: Essays in Honour of Dr Garda Singh* (Patiala, 1976).

Habib, I., 'Barani's Theory of the History of the Delhi Sultanate', *The Indian Historical Review*, VII, 1-2 (July 1980-January 1981).

Habib, M., *The Campaigns of Alauddin Khalji* (Madras, 1931).

Habib, M., *Sultan·Mahmud of Ghazna* (Delhi, 1967).

Habibullah, A. B. M., *The Foundation of Muslim Rule in India* (Allahabad, 1961).

Hāfiz Rahmat Khān, *Khulāṣat al-ansāb* (1184 A. H.), BL: Egerton 1104.

Haider, S. Z., *Islamic Arms and Armour of Muslim India* (Lahore, 1991).

Hambly, G., *Central Asia* (New York and London, 1969).

Hambly, G., 'Who were the chihilgānī, the forty slaves of Sultān Shams al-Dīn Iltutmish of Delhi?', *Iran*, 10 (1972).

Hambly, G., 'A note on the trade in eunuchs in Mughal Bengal', *Journal of the American Oriental Society*, 94.1 (1974).

Hamdani, A., *The beginnings of the Ismāili Daʿwa in Northern India* (Cairo, 1956).

Hamdani, A., 'The Fātimid-ʿAbbasid Conflict in India', *Islamic Culture*, XLI, 3 (July, 1967).

Hamm, F. R., 'Buddhismus und Jinismus: Zwei Typen indischer Religiosität und ihr Weg in der Geschichte', *Saeculum*, XV (1964).

Hardy, P., 'The Growth of Authority Over a Conquered Political Elite: The Early Delhi Sultanate as a Possible Case Study', in: Richards, J. F. (ed.), *Kingship and Authority in South Asia* (Madison, 1981).

Harihara-caturanga of Godavara Mishra (Madras, 1950).

Harley, J. B. and Woodward, D. (eds), *The History of Cartography, Volume Two, Book One: Cartography in the Traditional Islamic and South Asian Societies* (Chicago and London, 1992).

Harley Walker, C. T., 'Jahiz of Basra to Al-Fath ibn Khaqan on the "Exploits of the Turks and the army of the Khalifate in general"', *Journal of the Royal Asiatic Society* (1915).

Hasan, P., 'Temple niches and mihrābs in Bengal', in: Dallapiccola, A. L. and Zingel-Avé Lallemant, S. (eds), *Islam and Indian Regions*, 2 vols (Stuttgart, 1993).

Hastyāyurveda of Pālakāpyamuni (Pune, 1894).

Hazra, K. L., *Buddhism in India as described by the Chinese Pilgrims, AD 399-689* (New Delhi, 1983).

Heesterman, J. C., 'Littoral et Intérieur de l'Inde', in: Blussé, L., Wesseling, H. L. and Winius, G. D. (eds), *History and Underdevelopment: Essays on Underdevelopment and European Expansion in Asia and Africa* (Leiden, 1980).

Heesterman, J. C., 'Warrior, Peasant and Brahmin', *Modern Asian Studies*, 29.3 (1995).

Heitzman, J., *The origin and spread of Buddhist monastic institutions in South Asia, 500 BC-300 AD* (Philadelphia, 1980).

Heitzman, J., 'Early Buddhism, Trade and Empire', in: Kennedy, K. A. R. and Possehl, G. L. (eds), *Studies in the Archaeology and Palaeoanthropology of South Asia* (New Delhi, 1984).

Hellie, R., *Slavery in Russia, 1450-1725* (Chicago and London; 1982).

Herrin, J., 'The Context of Iconoclast Reform', in: Bryer, A. and Herrin, J. (eds), *Iconoclasm: papers given at the Ninth Symposium of Byzantine Studies* (Birmingham, 1975).

Hess, A. C., *The Forgotten Frontier: A History of the Sixteenth-century Ibiro-African Frontier* (Chicago and London, 1978).

Hidayat Hosaini, M. (ed.), *Ta'rīkh-i-Mubārakshāhi of Yahya bin Ahmad bin 'Abdullāh as-Sirhindi* (Calcutta, 1931).

Hill, D. R., 'The role of the camel and the horse in the Early Arab Conquests', in: Parry, V. J. and Yapp, M. E. (eds), *War, Technology and Society in the Middle East* (London, 1975).

Hill, R. D., *Rice in Malaya: A Study in Historical Geography* (Kuala Lumpur, 1977).

Hirth, F. and Rockhill, W. W. (transl. and annot.), *Chau Ju-kua: His Work on the Chinese and Arab trade in the twelfth and thirteenth Centuries, entitled Chu-fan-chi* (New York, 1966).

Ho, Ping-ti, 'An Estimate of the Total Population in Sung-Chin China', *Etudes Song I: Histoire et institutions*, ser.1 (Paris, 1970).

Hodgson, M. G. S., *The Venture of Islam: Conscience and History in a World Civilization*, 3 vols (Chicago, 1974).

Hodivala, S. H., *Studies in Indo-Muslim History*, I (Bombay, 1939).

Hoffmann, H., 'Die Qarluq in der Tibetaischen Literatur', *Oriens*, III, 2 (1950).

Hollingsworth, T. H., *Historical Demography* (Ithaca, 1969).

Holt, P. M., *The Age of the Crusades: The Near East from the Eleventh Century to 1517* (London and New York, 1986).

Hoover, J., 'A South Asian Age of Anxiety: Part Two, Demography and Economy' (Termpaper, Department of History, UW-Madison, Spring 1992).

Hopkins, D. R., *Princes and Peasants: Smallpox in History* (Chicago, 1983).

Hopkins, E. W., 'The Social and Military Positions of the Ruling Caste in Ancient India', *Journal of the American Oriental Society*, VII (1888).

Howarth, H. H., *History of the Mongols, Part II* (London, 1880).

Humphreys, R. S., *From Saladin to the Mongols: The Ayyubids of Damascus, 1193-1260* (Albany, 1970).

Humphreys, R. S., *Islamic History: A Framework for Inquiry* (Princeton, 1991).

Huntington, S. L. and Huntington, J. C., *Leaves from the Bodhi Tree* (Seattle and London, 1990).

Husain, A. M. (ed.), *Futūḥ as-Salāṭīn of 'Iṣāmī* (Agra, 1938).

Ibn al-Jawzī, *Al-Muntazam fī tārīkh al-mulūk wa-l-'umam*, Vols. 5-10 (Hyderabad, 1938-9).

Ibn al-Kalbī, *Kitāb al-asnām* (Cairo, 1914).

Ibn Khaldūn, *Kitāb al-'Ibar* (Cairo, 1284 H.).

Ibn Zāfir, *Kitāb al-Duwal al-Munqaṭiʿa*, BM: Or. MSS 3685.

Ilangasinha, H. B. M., *Buddhism in Medieval Sri Lanka* (Delhi, 1993).

Imperial Gazetteer of India, new ed., Vol. XXI (Oxford, 1908).

Inden, R., 'The Temple and the Hindu Chain of Being', in: Galey, J.-C. (ed.), *L'Espace du Temple, Vol. I* (Paris, 1985).

Indian Antiquary (Bombay, 1872-1923).

Irvine, W., 'The Bangash Nawabs of Farrukhabad', *Journal of the Royal Asiatic Society of Bengal*, 47 (1878).

Irwin, R., *The Middle East in the Middle Ages: The Early Mamluk Sultanate, 1250-1382* (Carbondale and Edwardsville, 1986).

Ishaq Khan, M., 'The impact of Islaṃ on Kashmir in the Sultanate period (1320-1586)', *The Indian Economic and Social History Review*, XXIII, 2 (April-June 1986).

Ishii, Y., *Sangha, State, and Society: Thai Buddhism in History* (Honolulu, 1986).

Ito, Takeshi, *The World of Adat Aceh: A Historical Study of the Sultanate of Aceh* (Unpublished PhD Thesis, Australian National University, 1984).

Jackson, P., *The Mongols and India, 1221-1351* (Unpublished PhD Dissertation, Cambridge, 1976).

Jackson, P., 'The Mamlūk Institution in Early Islamic India', *Journal of the Royal Asiatic Society* (1990).

Jacobi, H., 'Das Kālakācārya-Kathānakan', *Zeitschrift D. M. G.*, 36 (1880).

Jahn, K., 'Zum Problem der Mongolischen Eroberungen in Indien (13.-14. Jahrhundert)', in: *Akten des 24. Internationalen Orientalisten-Kongresses* (München, 1957).

Jahn, K., *Rashīd Al-Dīn's History of India* (The Hague, 1965).

Jain, K. C., *Jainism in Rajasthan* (Sholapur, 1963).

Jain, V. K., *Trade and Traders in Western India (AD 1000-1300)* (New Delhi, 1990).

Janardan Kirtane, N., 'The Hammira Mahakavya of Nyachandra Suri', *Indian Antiquary*, VIII (1879).

Johns, A. H., 'Islam in Southeast Asia: Reflections and New Directions', *Indonesia*, 19 (April 1975).

Josh, P., *Some Aspects of Jainism in Eastern India* (New Delhi, 1989).

Joshi, L., *Studies in the Buddhistic Culture of India (During the 7th and 8th Centuries AD)* (Delhi, 1964).

Kaegi, Jr., W. E., 'The Contribution of Archery to the Turkish Conquest of Anatolia', *Speculum*, XXXIX, 1 (1964).

Karim, A., *Social History of the Muslims in Bengal (Down to AD 1538)* (Dacca, 1959).

Kazhdan, A. P. and Wharton Epstein, A., *Change in Byzantine Culture in the Eleventh and Twelfth Centuries* (Berkeley, Los Angeles and London, 1985).

Khan, F. A., *Banbhore* (Karachi, 1969).

Khan, I. G., 'Metallurgy in Medieval India: 16th-18th Centuries', in: Roy, A. and Bagchi, S. K. (eds), *Technology in Ancient and Medieval India* (Delhi, 1986).

Khan, M. A., *The Walled City of Lahore* (Lahore, 1993).

Khazanov, A. M., 'Cataphractarii and their role in the history of military arts' (Katafraktarii i ikh rol' v istorii voennogo iskusstva), *Vestnik drevnei istorii* (Moscow, 1968).

Khazanov, A. M., 'Characteristic features of the Sarmatian military art' (Kharakternye cherty sarmatskogo voennogo iskusstva), *Sovetskaia Arkheologiia*, 2 (1970).

Khazanov, A. M., *Otscherki wojennogo dela sarmatow (Grundriss des Sarmatischen Kriegswesens)* (Moscow, 1971).

Khazanov, A. M., 'Myths and Paradoxes of Nomadism', *Archives Européennes de Sociologie*, XXII,1 (1981).

Khazanov, A. M., 'Les Scythes et la Civilisation Antique: Problèmes des Contacts', *Dialogues d'histoire ancienne*, 8 (Paris, 1982).

Khazanov, A. M., *Nomads and the Outside World* (Cambridge, 1984).

Khazanov, A. M., 'Ecological limitations of nomadism in the Eurasian steppes and their social and cultural implications', *Asian and African Studies*, 24 (1990).

Khazanov, A. M., 'Nomads and oases in Central Asia', in: Hall, J. A. and Jarvie, I. C. (eds), *Transition to Modernity: Essays on Power, Wealth and Belief* (Cambridge, 1992).

Khazanov, A. M., 'The Spread of World Religions in Medieval Nomadic Societies of the Eurasian Steppes', in: Gervers, M. and Schlepp, W. (eds), *Nomadic Diplomacy, Destruction and Religion from the Pacific to the Adriatic* (Toronto, 1994), p. 27.

Klimkeit, H.-J., 'Buddhism in Turkish Central Asia', *Numen*, XXXVII, 1 (1990).

Komroff, M. (ed.), *Contemporaries of Marco Polo* (New York, 1937).

Kowalski, T., 'Les Turcs dans le Šāh-nāme', *Rocznik Orientalistyczny* (Cracow, 1939-49), XV.

Krader, L., 'Principles and Structures in the Organization of the Asiatic Steppe-pastoralists', *Southwestern Journal of Anthropology*, 11, 2 (1955).

Krader, L., *Peoples of Central Asia* (Bloomington, 1966).

Kramrisch, S., *The Hindu Temple* (Delhi, 1980).

Kramrisch, S., 'Hindu Iconography', *The Encyclopaedia of Religion*, Vol. 7 (New York, 1987).

Krawulsky, D., *Iran-Das Reich der Īlkhāne. Eine topographisch-historische Studie* (Wiesbaden, 1978).

Krom, N. J., *Inleiding tot de Hindoe-Javaansche Kunst*, 2 vols (The Hague, 1923).

Krom, N. J., *Hindoe-Javaansche Geschiedenis* (The Hague, 1931).

Kulke, H., *The Devarāja Cult* (Ithaca, 1978).

Kumar, S., *The Emergence of the Delhi Sultanate, 588-685/1192-1286* (Unpublished PhD Dissertation, Duke University, 1992).

Kunhan Pillai, E. B. N., 'The Suicide Squads of Ancient Kerala', *Proceedings of the Indian History Congress* (Bombay, 1947).

Kuppuram, G., *Ancient Indian Mining, Metallurgy and Metal Industries*, 2 vols (New Delhi, 1989).

Kvaerne, P., 'Tibet: the Rise and Fall of a Monastic Tradition', in: Bechert, H. and Gombrich, R. (eds), *The World of Buddhism* (London, 1984).

Kwanten, L., *Imperial Nomads: A History of Central Asia, 500-1500* (Philadelphia, 1979).

Lambton, A. K. S., 'Aspects of Seljūq-Ghuzz settlement in Persia', in: *Theory and Practice in Medieval Persian Government* (London, 1980).

Lambton, A. K. S., *Continuity and Change in Medieval Persia: Aspects of Administrative, Economic and Social History, 11th-14th Century* (New York, 1988).

Lamotte, E., 'The Buddha, His Teachings and His Sangha', in: Bechert, H. and Gombrich, R. (eds), *The World of Buddhism* (London, 1984).

Lane, F. C., *Venice: A Maritime Republic* (Baltimore and London, 1973).

Lane-Poole, S., *Catalogue of Oriental Coins in the British Museum*, Vol. IX (London, 1889).

Lassen, Ch., *Indische Altertumskunde*, 5 vols (Leipzig, 1847-62)

Latham, J. D., 'The Archers of the Middle East: The Turco-Iranian Background', *Iran*, VIII (1970).

Latham, R. (transl.), *The Travels of Marco Polo* (New York, 1987).

Latif, S. M., *Lahore: Its History, Architectural Remains and Antiquities* (Lahore, 1892).

Leach, E., 'Aryan Invasions over Four Millennia', in: Ohnuki-Tierney, E. (ed.), *Culture Through Time: Anthropological Approaches* (Stanford, 1990).

Lees, N. et al (eds),*Tabaqāt-i-Nāṣiri of Ābū 'Umar al-Jūzjāni* (Calcutta, 1894).

Leshnik, L. S., 'Ghur, Firozkoh and the Minat-i-Jam', *Central Asiatic Journal*, 12 (1968-69).

Levanoni, A., 'The Mamluk Conception of the Sultanate', *International Journal of Middle East Studies*, 26 (1994).

Lévi, S. and Chavannes, E., 'L'Itineraire d'Ou-k'ong (751-790)', *Journal Asiatique*, 9e séries, VI (1895).

Lieberman, V. B., *Burmese Administrative Cycles: Anarchy and Conquest, c. 1580-1760* (Princeton, 1984).

Lieberman, V., 'Local Integration and Eurasian Analogies: Structuring Southeast Asian History, c. 1350-c. 1830', *Modern Asian Studies*, 27, 3 (1993).

Lindner, R. P., 'Nomadism, Horses and Hūns', *Past and Present*, 92, 3 (1981).

Lingat, R., *Royautés Bouddhiques* (Paris, 1989).

Loeb, E. M., *Sumatra: Its History and People* (Singapore, 1989).

Lombard, D., *Le Sultanat d'Atjeh au temps d'Iskander Muda* (Paris, 1967).

Lopez, R. S., 'European Merchants in the Medieval Indies: The Evidence of Commercial Documents', *The Journal of Economic History*, 3 (1943).

Lombard, M., 'L'or musulman du VII au XI siècle', *Annales*, II (1947).

Longworth-Dames, M., *The Baloch Race* (London, 1904).

Longworth-Dames, M. (transl.), *The Book of Duarte Barbosa, vol. I* (Nendeln/Liechtenstein, 1967).

Mabbett, I. and Chandler, D., *The Khmers* (Oxford, 1995).

Maclean, D. N., *Religion and Society in Arab Sind* (Leiden, 1989).

Mahmood, T., 'The Dargah of Sayyid Salar Mas'ud Ghazi in Bahraich: Legend, Tradition and Reality', in: Troll, Ch. (ed.), *Muslim Shrines in India* (New Delhi, 1984).

Mainz, E., 'Die Türken in der klassischen arabischen Literatur', *Der Islam*, XXI (1933).

Malay Annals: translated from the Malay language by J. Leyden (London, 1821).

Mānasollāsa, 2 vols (Baroda, 1925-39).

Manguin, P.-Y., 'Relationship and Cross-Influences between Southeast Asian and Chinese Shipbuilding Traditions', in: *Final Report, SPAFA Consultative Workshop on Maritime Shipping and Trade Networks in Southeast Asia* (Bangkok, 1984).

Mann, M., 'European Development: Approaching a Historical Explanation', in: Baechler, J., Hall, J. A. & Mann, M. (eds), *Europe and the Rise of Capitalism* (Oxford and Cambridge, Mass., 1989).

Maqbul Ahmad, S., *India and the Neighbouring Territories in the Kitāb Nuzhat al-Mushtāq fī 'khtirāq al-'Āfāq of al-Sharif al-Idrīsi* (Leiden, 1960).

Marcel Devic, L. (transl.), *The Book of the Marvels of India* (New York, 1929).

Marrison, G. E., 'The Coming of Islam to the East Indies', *Journal of the Malayan Branch of the Royal Asiatic Society*, XXIV, Pt 1 (1951).

Marsden, W., *The History of Sumatra* (London, 1811).

Martin, M., *Eastern India*, Vol. II (London, 1838)

Martinez, 'Gardīzī's two chapters on the Turks', *Archivum Eurasiae Medii Aevi*, II (1982).

Masson Smith, J., 'Turanian Nomadism and Iranian Politics', *Iranian Studies*, 11 (1978).

Masson Smith, J., 'Mongol Manpower and Persian Population', *The Journal of the Economic and Social History of the Orient*, 18 (1975).

al-Mas'ūdī, *Murūj adh-Dhahab*, 2 vols (Cairo, 1948).

al-Mas'ūdī, *Murūj adh-Dhahab*, 4 vols (Paris, 1964).

Mather, R. B., 'Chinese and Indian Perceptions of Each Other between the first and seventh centuries', *Journal of the American Oriental Society*, 112, 1 (1992).

Ma Touan-lin, *Ethnographie des Peuples Etrangers à la Chine*, Tr. Le Marquis d'Hervey de Saint-Denys (Paris, 1876).

McDermott, J. P., 'Bondservants in the T'ai-hu Basin During the Late Ming: A Case of Mistaken Identities', *Journal of Asian Studies*, XL, 4 (August, 1981).

McEvedy, C. and Jones, R., *Atlas of World Population History* (New York, 1978).

McEwen, E., 'Persian Archery Texts: Chapter Eleven of Fakhr-i-Mudabbir's Ādāb Al-Harb (Early Thirteenth Century)', *The Islamic Quarterly*, XVIII, 3 & 4 (1974).

Mc Gregor, R. S., *Hindi Literature from its Beginnings to the Nineteenth Century* (Wiesbaden, 1984).

McLane, T. R., *Land and Local Kingship in Eighteenth-century Bengal* (Cambridge, 1993).

McNeill, W. H., *Plagues and Peoples* (New York, 1976).

Meister, M. W., 'Indian Islam's lotus throne: Kaman and Khatu Kalan', in: Dallapiccola, A. L. and Zingel-Avé Lallemant, S. (eds), *Islam and Indian regions*, 2 vols (Stuttgart, 1993).

Michell, G., *The Hindu Temple: An Introduction to its Meaning and Forms* (Chicago and London, 1988).

Minorsky, V. (transl.), *Ḥudūd al-ʿālam* (London, 1937).

Minorsky, V., 'The Turkish dialect of the Khalaj', *Bulletin of the School of African and Oriental Studies*, X, 2 (1940).

Minorsky, V., 'Gardizi on India', *Bulletin of the School of Oriental and African Studies*, 12 (1948).

Misra, S. C., *Muslim Communities in Gujarat* (Baroda, 1964).

Misra, S. S., *Fine Arts and Technical Sciences in Ancient India with Special Reference to Someshvara's Mānasollāsa* (Varanasi, 1982).

Mitra, K., 'Historical references in Jain poems', *Proceedings of the Indian History Congress*, 5 (1941).

Mitra, R. C., 'The Decline of Buddhism in India', *Visva-Bharati Annals*, Vol. VI (Santiniketan, 1954).

Moosvi, S., 'Numismatic evidence and the economic history of the Delhi Sultanate', *Proceedings of the Indian History Congress* (1989-90).

Morgan, D., *The Mongols* (Oxford, 1986).

Morgan, D., *Medieval Persia, 1040-1747* (London and New York, 1988).

Morley, W. H. (ed.), *Taʾrikh-i-Baihaqi* (Calcutta, 1862).

Morris, D., 'Trends and Tendencies in Indian Economic History', *The Indian Economic and Social History Review*, 5, 4 (1968).

Mottahedeh, R. P., *Loyalty and Leadership in an Early Islamic Society* (Princeton, 1980).

Mukherjee, M. K., *The Changing Face of Bengal: a Study in Riverine Economy* (Calcutta, 1938).

Mumtaz, K. K., *Architecture in Pakistan* (Singapore, 1985).

Murphy, D., *Where the Indus is Young. A Winter in Baltistan* (London, 1977).

Murphy, R., 'The Ruin of Ancient Ceylon', *Journal of Asian Studies*, 16, 2 (1957).

Nambiar, S. K. (ed. and transl.), *Prabodhacandrodaya* (Delhi, 1971).

Nanda, R., *The Early History of Gold in India* (New Delhi, 1992).

Narain, A. K., 'The Greeks of Bactria and India', *The Cambridge Ancient History*, Vol. VIII (Cambridge, 1978).

Narain, A. K., *The Indo-Greeks* (Delhi, 1980).

Narayan, K., *Storytellers, Saints, and Scoundrels: Folk Narrative in Hindu Religious Teaching* (Philadelphia, 1989).

Narayana, M. G. S., 'The Institution of "Companions of Honour" with Special

Reference to South India', *Proceedings of the Indian History Congress* (Muzaffarpur, 1972).

Narayana Rao, V. and Roghair, G. H. (transl.), *Siva's Warriors: The Basava Purāna of Pālkuriki Somanātha* (Princeton, 1990).

Nazim, M. (ed.), *Zayn al-Akhbār of Gardīzī* (Berlin, 1928).

Nazim, M. (ed. and transl.), 'The Pand-Nāmah of Sabuktigīn', *Journal of the Royal Asiatic Society* (1933).

Nazim, M., *The Life and Times of Sultān Mahmūd of Ghazna* (New Delhi, 1971; orig. publ. 1931).

Nelson Wright, H., *The Coinage and Metrology of the Sultans of Dehlī* (New Delhi, 1974).

Nevill, H. R., *District Gazetteers of the United Provinces of Agra and Oudh, Vol. V., Bulandshahr* (Lucknow, 1922).

Newman, J., 'Islam in the Buddhist Kālacakra Tantra' (Paper presented to the 1989 Annual Meeting of the American Academy of Religion, Annaheim, CA, 1989).

Nilakanta Sastri, K. A. (ed.), *Foreign Notices of South India from Megasthenes to Mahuan* (Madras, 1972).

Nizam ad-Din, M. (ed.), *Jawāmiʿ al-Ḥikāyat* (Hyderabad, Deccan, 1966).

Nizām al-Mulk, *Siyāsatnāma* (Teheran, 1284 H.).

Nizami, K. A., *Studies in Medieval Indian History and Culture* (Allahabād, 1966).

Nizami, K. A., *Some Aspects of Religion and Politics in India during the Thirteenth Century* (Delhi, 1974).

Nizami, K. A. (ed.), *Politics and Society during the Early Medieval Period: Collected Works of Professor Mohammad Habib*, 2 vols (New Delhi, 1974-81).

Nizami, K. A., *The Life and Times of Shaikh Nizamuddin Auliya* (Delhi, 1991).

Njammasch, M., 'Buddhistische Klöster der Maitrakas von Valabhī', *The Journal of the Economic and Social History of the Orient* (forthcoming).

Nöldeke, Th., 'Das Kitāb Jamīnī des Abū Nasr Muhammad ibn ʿAbd al-Gabbār al-ʿUtbī', *Sitzungsberichte der Kaiserlichen Akademie*, Vol. XXIII (Vienna, 1857).

O' Brien, A., 'The Bhuttos and the Bhattīs of the Twelfth Century AD', *South Asian Studies*, 4 (1988).

Oldham, C. E. A. W. (ed.), *Journal of Francis Buchanan kept during the survey of the district of Bhagalpur in 1810-1811* (Patna, 1930).

Oppert, G., *On the Weapons, Army Organisation & Political Maxims of the Ancient Hindus* (London, 1880).

Paret, R., 'Textbelege zum islamischen Bilderverbot', in: *Das Werk des Kunstlers. Studien zur Ikonographie und Formgeschichte H. Schrade dargebracht* (Stuttgart, 1960).

Parpola, A., 'The coming of the Aryans to Iran and India and the cultural and ethnic identity of the Dāsas', *Studia Orientalia*, 64 (1988).

Patai, R., 'Nomadism: Middle Eastern and Central Asian', *Southwestern Journal of Anthropology*, 7 (1951).

Patañjali Vyākarana Mahābhāshya, 3 vols (Bombay, 1892).

Patterson, O., *Slavery and Social Death: A Comparative Study* (Cambridge, Mass., 1982).

Petry, C. F., *The Civilian Elite of Cairo in the Later Middle Ages* (Princeton, 1981).

Phillips, J. R. S., *The Medieval Expansion of Europe* (Oxford, 1988).

Pipes, D., *Slave Soldiers and Islam: The Genesis of a Military System* (New Haven and London, 1981).

Poliak, A. N., 'Le Caractère Colonial de l'Etat Mamelouk dans ses Rapports avec la Horde d'Or', *Revue des Etudes Islamiques*, III (1953).

Prakash, G., *Bonded Histories: Genealogies of Labor Servitude in Colonial India* (Cambridge, 1990).

Prasad, I., *A History of the Qaraunah Turks in India, Vol. I* (Allahabad, 1936).
Prasad, J., *History of Medieval India* (Allahabad, 1966).
Prasad, P., *Sanskrit Inscriptions of the Delhi Sultanate, 1191-1526* (Delhi, 1990).
Pritsak, O., *The Origin of Rus', I* (Cambridge, Mass., 1981).
Procopius, *History of the Wars, Books I and II* (London and New York, 1914).
al-Qalqashandī, *Ṣubḥ al-A'shā fī Ṣinā'at al-Inshā'*, 14 vols (Cairo, 1964).
Rabie, H., 'The training of the Mamlūk Fāris', in: Parry, V. J. and Yapp, M. E., *War, Technology and Society in the Middle East* (London, 1975).
Ramakrishna Bhat, M. (ed. and transl.), *Varāhamihira's Bṛhat Samhitā* (Delhi, 1981).
Ratnagar, S., 'Pastoralism as an Issue in Historical Research', *Studies in History*, n. s., 7, 2 (1991).
Raverty, H. G. (transl.), *Ṭabaḳāt-i-Nāṣirī: a general History of the Muhammadan Dynasties of Asia*, 2 vols (London, 1872-80).
Ray, H. C., *The Dynastic History of Northern India*, 2 vols (New Delhi, 1973).
Raychaudhuri, T. and Habib, I. (eds), *The Cambridge Economic History of India, Volume I: c. 1200-c.1750* (Cambridge, 1982).
Reeves, P. D. (ed.), *Sleeman in Oudh* (Cambridge, 1971).
'References to Muhammadans—AD 730-1320', *The Journal of Indian History*, 15 (1936).
Reid, A., 'The Islamization of Southeast Asia', in: Bakar, M. A., Kaur, A. and Ghazali, A. Z. (eds), *Historia: Essays in Commemoration of the 25th Anniversary of the Department of History, University of Malaya* (Kuala Lumpur, 1984)
Reid, A., 'The Rise and Fall of Sino-Javanese Shipping', in: Houben, V. J. H., Maier, H. M. J. & Van der Molen, W. (eds), *Looking in Odd Mirrors: The Java Sea* (Leiden, 1992).
Reid, A., *Southeast Asia in the Age of Commerce, 1450-1680, Volume II: Expansion and Crisis* (New Haven and London, 1993).
Reinaud, M., *Relations des voyages faits par les Arabes et les Persans dans l'Inde et à la Chine dans la IXe siècle de l'ère Chrétienne*, Tome I (Paris, 1895).
Renfrew, C., 'The Origin of Indo-European Languages', *Scientific American* (October, 1989).
Renfrew, C., 'Review of "Parpola, The coming of the Aryans"', *Journal of the Royal Asiatic Society* (April, 1991).
Richards, J. F., 'Precious Metals and India's Role in the Medieval World Economy' (Paper submitted to the 16th International Congress of Historical Studies, Stuttgart, August 26, 1985).
Ridding, C. M. (transl.), *The Kādambarī of Bāna* (London, 1896).
Ries, J., 'Idolatry', *The Encyclopaedia of Religion, Vol. 7* (New York, 1987).
Rockhill, W. W., 'Notes on the relations and trade of China with the Eastern Archipelago and the coast of the Indian Ocean during the fourteenth century, Part I', *T'oung Pao*, XV (1914).
Roerich, G. (tr.), *Biography of Dharmasvamin* (Patna, 1959).
Rolle, R., *The World of the Scythians* (Berkeley, Los Angeles and London, 1989).
Rossabi, *Khubilai Khan: His Life and Times* (Berkeley, Los Angeles and London, 1987).
Ross Sweeney, J., '"Spurred on by the Fear of Death": Refugees and Displaced Populations during the Mongol Invasion of Hungary', in: Gervers, M. and Schlepp, W. (eds), *Nomadic Diplomacy, Destruction and Religion from the Pacific to the Adriatic* (Toronto, 1994).
Roy, Asim, 'The interface of Islamization, regionalization and syncretization: the Bengal paradigm', in : Dallapiccola, A. L. and Zingel-Avé Lallemant, S. (eds), *Islam and Indian Regions*, 2 vols (Stuttgart, 1993).

Roy, A. K., *A History of the Jainas* (New Delhi, 1984).

Sachau, E. C. (transl.), *Alberuni's India* (New Delhi, 1983).

Savory, R. M., 'The History of the Persian Gulf, AD 600-1800', in: Cottrell, A. J. (ed.), *The Persian Gulf States: A General Survey* (Baltimore and London, 1980).

Sahni, D. R., 'Pre-Muhammadan Monuments of Kashmir', *Archaeological Survey of India: Annual Report 1915-16*.

Saletore, B. A., *Mediaeval Jainism. With Special reference to the Vijayanagara Empire* (Bombay, 1938).

Sankalia, H. D., *The University of Nalanda* (Delhi, 1972).

Sarda, H. B., 'The Prthviraja Vijaya', *Journal of the Royal Asiatic Society* (1913).

Sauvaget, J., 'Noms et Surnoms de Mamelouks', *Journal Asiatique*, CCXXXVIII (1950).

Schacht, J. and Meyerhof, E., *The Theologus Autodidactus of Ibn-an-Nafis* (Oxford, 1968).

Schamiloglu, U., *The Golden Horde (13th-14th Centuries)* (forthcoming).

Schiefner, A. (transl.), *Tāranātha's Geschichte des Buddhismus in Indien* (St. Petersburg, 1869).

Schimmel, A., 'Turk and Hindu: A Poetical Image and its Application to Historical Fact', in: Vryonis, Jr., S. (ed.), *Islam and Cultural Change in the Middle Ages* (Wiesbaden, 1973).

Schimmel, A., *Islam in the Indian Subcontinent* (Leiden, 1980).

Schimmel, A., 'Islamic Iconography', *The Encyclopaedia of Religion*, Vol. 7 (New York, 1987).

Schnitger, F. M., *The Archaeology of Hindoo Sumatra* (Leiden, 1938).

Schnitger, F. M., *Forgotten Kingdoms in Sumatra* (Leiden, 1939).

Schrieke, B., *Indonesian Sociological Studies*, 2 vols (The Hague and Bandung, 1955-7).

Schurmann, H. F., *The Mongols of Afghanistan: An Ethnography of the Moghols and related peoples of Afghanistan* ('s-Gravenhage, 1962).

Sen, S. (ed. and transl.), *Sekashubhodayā of Halayudha-Mishra* (Calcutta, 1963).

Seth, C. B., *Jainism in Gujarat (AD 100 to 1600)* (Bombay, 1953).

Settar, S. and Kalaburgi, M. M., 'The Hero Cult: A Study of Kannada Literature from the 9th to 13th Century', in: Settar, S. and Sontheimer, G. D. (eds), *Memorial Stones: A Study of their Origin, Significance and Variety* (Dharwad, 1982).

Settar, S. and Sontheimer, G. D. (eds), *Memorial Stones: A Study of their Origin, Significance and Variety* (Dharwad, 1982).

Shaffer, J. G., 'The Indo-Aryan Invasions: Cultural Myth and Archaeological Reality', in: Lukacs, J. R.(ed.), *The People of South Asia* (New York and London, 1984).

Shah, P. (ed.), *Vishnudharmottara Purāna, Khanda III*, 2 vols (Baroda, 1958-61).

Sharar, A. H., *Lucknow: The Last Phase of an Oriental Culture* (London, 1975).

Sharma, T. R., *Personal and Geographical Names in the Gupta Inscriptions* (Delhi, 1978).

Shea, D. and Troyer, A. (transl.), *Dabistān al-Madhāhib* (Lahore, 1973).

Sherring, M. A., *Hindu Tribes and Castes*, Vol. III (New Delhi, 1974; orig. publ.1881).

Shokoohy, M., *Bhadreshvar: The Oldest Islamic Monuments in India* (Leiden, 1988)

Shokoohy, M. and N. H., 'The Architecture of Baha al-Din Tughrul in the region of Bayana, Rajasthan', *Muqarnas*, 4 (1987).

Shua'ib, M. M., 'Inscriptions from Palwal', *Epigraphia Indo-Moslemica, 1911-12*.

Siddiqui, I. H., 'The Qarlūgh Kingdom in North-Western India during the Thirteenth Century', *Islamic Quarterly*, LIV, 1 (1980).

Siddiqui, I. H., 'The Afghans and their emergence in India as ruling elite during the Delhi Sultanate period', *Central Asiatic Journal*, 26, no. 3-4 (1982).

Siddiqui, I. H., *Perso-Arabic Sources of Information on Life and Conditions in the Sultanate of Delhi* (New Delhi, 1992).

Singh, R. B. P., *Jainism in Early Medieval Karnataka (c. AD 500-1200)* (Delhi, 1975).

Singh, S. D., *Ancient Indian Warfare* (Leiden, 1965).

Singh, S. D., 'The Elephant and the Aryans', *Journal of the Royal Asiatic Society* (1963), Pts 1 & 2.

Sinor, D. (ed.), *The Cambridge History of Early Inner Asia* (Cambridge, 1990).

Sircar, D. C., *Studies in the Geography of Ancient and Medieval India* (Delhi, 1971).

Sirisena, W. M., *Sri Lanka and South-East Asia (AD 1000-1500)* (Leiden, 1978).

Smith, A. D., *The Ethnic Origins of Nations* (Oxford, 1986).

Smith, B. L. (ed.), *Religion & Legitimation of Power in Sri Lanka* (Chambersburg, 1978).

Somasekhara, M. and Venkataramanayya, 'The Kakatiyas of Warangal', in: Yazdani, G. (ed.), *The Early History of the Deccan*, 2 vols (New Delhi, 1982).

Sourdel, D., *Inventaire des monnaies musulmanes anciennes du musée de Caboul* (Damascus, 1953).

Southern, R. W., *The Making of the Middle Ages* (New Haven and London, 1953).

Spate, O. H. K. and Learmonth, A. T. A., *India and Pakistan: A General and Regional Survey* (London, 1967).

Spencer, G. W., 'Crisis of Authority in a Hindu Temple under the Impact of Islam', in: Smith, B. L. (ed.), *Religion and the Legitimation of Power in South Asia* (Leiden, 1978).

Spengler, W. F., 'Numismatic Evidence of Ghorid Personal Nomenclature and Royal Titulature' (Mimeo).

Spufford, P., *Money and its use in medieval Europe* (Cambridge, 1989).

Spuler, B., *Die Mongolen in Iran* (Leipzig, 1939).

Srinivasan, D. M. (ed), *Mathurā: The Cultural Heritage* (New Delhi, 1989).

Srivastava, K. L., *The Position of Hindus under the Delhi Sultanate, 1206-1526* (Delhi, 1980).

Stein, B. (ed.), *South Indian Temples: An Analytical Reconsideration* (New Delhi, 1978).

Stein, M. A. (ed.), *Kalhaṇa's Rājataraṅginī* (Delhi, 1960).

Stein, M. A., 'Marco Polo's Account of a Mongol Inroad into Kashmir', *The Geographical Journal*, LIV (July-Dec. 1919).

Strachan, P., *Pagan: Art and Architecture of Old Burma* (Whiting Bay, 1989).

Stratton, C. and McNair Scott, M., *The Art of Sukhothai* (Kuala Lumpur, 1981).

Strayer, J. R., *On the Medieval Origins of the Modern State* (Princeton, 1970).

Streusand, D. E., *The Formation of the Mughal Empire* (Delhi, 1989).

Swearer, D. K., 'Buddhism in Southeast Asia', in: Kitagawa, J. M. and Cummings, M. D. (eds), *Buddhism and Asian History* (London, 1989).

Ṭabaqāt-i-Nāṣirī of Abū 'Umar al-Jūzjānī: IOL: MSS no. 2553.

Ṭabaqāt-i-Nāṣirī of Abū 'Umar al-Jūzjānī (Lahore, 1954).

Tāj al-Ma'āthir: BM: Add. 7623.

Tambiah, S. J., *World Conqueror and World Renouncer: A Study of Buddhism and Polity in Thailand against a Historical Background* (Cambridge, 1976).

Tambiah, S. J., 'Max Webers Untersuchung des frühen Buddhismus: Eine Kritik', in: Schluchter, W. (ed.), *Max Webers Studie über Hinduismus und Buddhismus: Interpretation und Kritik* (Frankfurt am Main, 1984).

Ta'rikh-i-Firishta (Lucknow, 1864).

Ta'rikh-i-Tāhirī: BM, Add. 23,888.

Tawney, C. H. (ed. and transl.), *The Prabandhacintāmani of Merutunga Ācārya* (Calcutta. 1901).

Teeuw, A., 'Hikayat Raja-Raja Pasai and Sejarah Melayu', in: Bastin, J. and Roolvink, R. (eds), *Malayan and Indonesian Studies* (Oxford, 1964).

Temporini, H. (ed.), *Aufstieg und Niedergang der römischen Welt* (Berlin and New York, 1972).

Thierry, S., *Etude d'un corpus de contes cambodgiens* (Paris and Lille, 1978).

Thomas, E., *The Chronicles of the Pathan Kings of Delhi* (New Delhi, 1967).

Thomas, F. W., 'Sakastana. Where dwelt the Sakas named by Darius and Herodotus?', *Journal of the Royal Asiatic Society* (1906).

Tibbetts, G. R., *Arab Navigation in the Indian Ocean Before the Coming of the Portuguese* (London, 1971).

Tod, J., *Annals and Antiquities of Rajasthan*, 2 vols (New Delhi, 1983).

Tornberg, C. J. (ed.), *Ibn al-'Athīr, Al-Kāmil fi-l-Tārīkh*, 12 vols (Leiden, 1853-69).

Tripathi, A. (ed.), *The Bṛhat-Samhitā of Varāhamihira* (Varanasi, 1968).

Turan, O., 'The Ideal of World Domination among the Medieval Turks', *Studia Islamica*, IV (1957).

Uray-Kűhalmi, C., 'La Périodisation de l'Histoire des Armements des Nomades des Steppes', *Etudes Mongoles*, 5 (1974).

al-'Utbī, *Tārīkh al-Yamīnī* (Delhi, 1847).

al-'Utbī, *Ta'rīkh-i-Yamīnī: Persian translation by Jurbādqānī (1206 AD)* (Teheran, 1334 H.).

Van Den Berg, L. W. C., *Le Hadramout et les Colonies Arabes dans l'Archipel Indien* (Batavia, 1886).

Van Lohuizen-De Leeuw, J. E., *The "Scythian" Period: An Approach to the History, Art, Epigraphy and Palaeography of Northern India from the 1st Century BC to the 3d Century AD* (Leiden, 1949).

Van Lohuizen-De Leeuw, J. E., 'The Contribution of Foreign Nomads to the Culture of the Indian Subcontinent', in: Leshnik, L. S. and Sontheimer, G.-D. (eds), *Pastoralists and Nomads in South Asia* (Wiesbaden, 1975).

Vasiliev, A. A., 'The Iconoclast Edict of the Caliph Yazid II, AD 721', *Dumbarton Oaks Papers*, 9 (1955).

Veltman, T. J., 'Nota over de geschiedenis van het landschap Pidie (Pedir)', *Tijdschrift voor Indische Taal-, Land- en Volkenkunde*, 58 (1919).

Vickery, M., *Cambodia after Angkor: the chronicular evidence for the fourteenth to sixteenth centuries* (University of Michigan Microfilms, 1977).

Vickery, M., *Cambodia: 1975-1982* (Boston, 1984).

Von Le Coq, A., 'Türkische Namen und Titel in Indien', in: *Aus Indiens Kultur: Festgabe Richard Von Garbe* (Erlangen, 1927).

Vryonis, S., Jr., *The Decline of Medieval Hellenism in Asia Minor and the process of Islamization from the Eleventh through the Fifteenth Century* (Berkeley, 1971).

Wahid Mirza, M., *The Life and Works of Amir Khusrau* (Lahore, 1962).

Waldman, M. R., *Toward a Theory of Historical Narrative: A Case Study of Perso-Islamicate Historiography* (Columbus, 1980).

Waley, A. (transl.), *The Travels of an Alchemist* (London, 1931).

Wali Ullah Khan, M., *Lahore and its Important Monuments* (Karachi, 1964).

Wallis Budge, E. A. (transl.), *The Chronography of Gregory Abu'l Faraj Barhebraeus*, Vol. I (London, 1932).

Watson, A. M., 'Back to gold—and silver', *The Economic History Review*, 2nd series, XX (1967).

Watters, T., *On Yuan Chwang's Travels in India, 629-645 AD*, 2 vols (London, 1904-5).

Weber, M., *The Religion of India* (New York and London, 1967).

Wheeler, M., *The Indus Civilization* (Cambridge, 1968).

White, Jr., L., 'Tibet, India, and Malaya as Sources of Western Medieval Technology', *American Historical Review*, LXV, 3 (1960).

White, Jr., L., *Medieval Technology and Social Change* (Oxford, 1963).

White, Jr., L., 'What accelerated technological progress in the Western Middle Ages', in: Crombie, A. C. (ed.), *Scientific Change* (New York, 1963).

White, Jr., L., 'Cultural Climates and Technological Advance in the Middle Ages', *Viator*, II (1971).

White, Jr., L., 'The Crusades and the technological thrust of the West', in Parry, V. J. and Yapp, M. E. (eds), *War, Technology and Society in the Middle East* (London, 1975).

Wicks, R. S., *Money, Markets, and Trade in Early Southeast Asia: The Development of Indigenous Monetary Systems to AD 1400* (Ithaca, 1992).

Wiet, G., 'Les marchands d'épices sous les sultans mamlouks', *Cahiers d'histoire Egyptienne*, Séries VII, Fasc. 2 (May 1955).

Wiet, G., *Baghdad: Metropolis of the Abbasid Caliphate* (Norman, 1971).

Willis, M. D., 'Religious and Royal Patronage in North India', in: Desai, V. N. and Mason, D. (eds), *Gods, Guardians, and Lovers: Temple Sculptures from North India, AD 700-1200* (New York, 1993).

Winter Jones, J. (transl.), *The Travels of Ludovico di Varthema* (London, 1863).

Wink, A., *Land and Sovereignty in India: Agrarian Society and Politics under the Eighteenth-century Maratha Svarājya* (Cambridge, 1986).

Wink, A., *Al-Hind: The Making of the Indo-Islamic World, Volume I: Early Medieval India and the Expansion of Islam, 7th-11th Centuries* (Leiden, 1990).

Witzel, M., 'Toward a History of the Brahmans', *Journal of the American Oriental Society*, 113, 2 (1993).

Woods, J. E., *The Aqquyunlu: Clan, Confederation, Empire* (Minneapolis, 1976).

Yule, H. (ed. and transl.), *The Book of Ser Marco Polo*, 2 vols (New York, 1903).

Zajaczkowski (ed.), *Le Traité Iranien de l'Art Militaire: Ādāb al-Harb wa-sh-Shaghāʿa du XIIIe Siècle* (Warszawa, 1969).

Zimmer, H., *Myths and Symbols in Indian Art and Civilization* (New York, 1962).

INDEX

Abahr, 129
Abyssinia, 97. *See also* Ethiopia
Achin, 107, 110, 292-3
    Besar, 324
Acre, 20
Aden, 21-23, 40, 83, 85-87, 198, 274, 276, 284
Adriatic, 32
Afghan,
    tribal garrisons, 129
    iqtā'dārs, 256
Afghanistan, 10, 12, 52, 59, 62, 67, 70, 72, 85, 115, 116 n. 23, 129, 134-6, 141, 166, 206, 209-10, 213-4, 241, 311, 320, 323
Afghans, 84, 113, 115-9, 135, 137, 139, 160, 169, 193-4, 207, 210, 219, 256, 332
    Torī, 139
    Indo-, 221
Africa, 1, 8, 20, 23, 30, 71, 97 (& n. 75), 98, 166, 185, 332
    East, 19, 276-7, 285
    North, 32
    Central, 179
African,
    East- coast, 17
    coast, 30
    elephants, 97-98
    mamlūks, 182
Agra, 151
Ahoms, 262-4
    Tai-, 263
ahosikamma,
    doctrine of, 359
'ajā'ib al-hind, 178
Ajanta,
    frescoes, 55, 98
Ajarbayjan, 9, 11, 192
Ajmer, 109, 142, 144-6, 151, 174, 230, 232, 266, 325-6
al-Akhwār, 106
Alborz,
    mountains, 8, 13, 46, 84
Aleppo, 13
Alexander, 52-53, 95
Alexandria, 21-22, 32-33, 39, 215
Aloe wood, 42

Altai, 46, 53, 62, 65
Altaic,
    linguistic family, 47
    origins, 64
    world, 64
Altin Tagh, 46
Alwar, 231
Amalfi, 32
Amba Geshen, 185
Amber, 36, 232
American,
    climate, 45
    Indians, 45
Amir Khusrau, 191, 193, 196, 207, 209, 219, 249, 254
Amroha, 222-3
Amu Darya, 46, 67
Anahilvāda, 269-70, 275, 355. *See also* Nahrwāla
Anatolia, 9-11, 14, 16, 44, 45 n. 2, 71-72, 167, 191, 318
Andaman,
    islands, 283
Angkor, 36, 110, 296 n. 8, 298, 304, 366, 368, 370-4
    Wat, 100, 372-3
    Thom, 299, 373
    period, 365
Angkorian,
    Cambodia, 164
Annam, 38
Antioch, 18-19, 30, 32, 318
Anurādhapura, 359-60
Aqaba,
    Gulf of, 33
Aqquyunlu, 16
Arab,
    immigrant groups, 6
    conquest of Sind, 17, 88, 115, 348
    population of Qays, 18
    trading centre of Calicut, 22
    period, 16-17
    amirs of the Banu Qaisar, 18
    geographers, 45, 70, 97 n. 75, 287
    conquest(s), 69, 124, 244
    governors of Khurasan, 70
    conquest literature, 75
    chargers, 83

Errata

p. 189, line thirteen from below: 'bodies'... to be deleted.

p. 369, line ten from below: 'diappearance' should read 'disappearance'.

p. 390, line nine from below: '\r-masdesn' should read 'Er-Masdesn'.